Achieving Sustainable Urban Form

Achieving Sustainable Urban Form

Edited by
Katie Williams, Elizabeth Burton and
Mike Jenks

London and New York

First published 2000
by E & FN Spon
11 New Fetter Lane, London EC4P 4EE

Simultaneously published in the USA and Canada
by E & FN Spon, an imprint of Routledge
29 West 35th Street, New York, NY 10001

E & FN Spon is an imprint of the Taylor & Francis Group

Printed and bound in Great Britain by
St Edmundsbury Press, Bury St Edmunds, Suffolk

British Library Cataloguing in Publication Data
A catalogue record for this book is available from the British Library

Library of Congress Cataloging in Publication Data
A catalogue record for this book has been requested

ISBN 0–419–24450–6

Contents

Part 2   Urban Form and Transport: New Dimensions

Part 3   Approaches and Strategies for Achieving Sustainable Urban Form

Part 4   Built Form and Design Solutions

Contributors

Marina Alberti
Assistant Professor of Urban and Environmental Planning, Department of Urban Design and Planning, University of Washington, USA

Michael Ambrose
Construction Systems Scientist, CSIRO (Commonwealth Scientific and Industrial Research Organisation) Building, Construction and Engineering, Melbourne, Australia

Professor David Banister
Professor of Transport Planning and Director of Research, The Bartlett School of Planning, University College London, London, UK

Dr Elizabeth Burton
Senior Lecturer in Cities and Social Sustainability, Oxford Centre for Sustainable Development, School of Architecture, Oxford Brookes University, Oxford, UK

Dr Michael Buxton
Associate Professor, Environment and Planning, School of Social Science and Planning, RMIT University, Melbourne, Australia

Denvil Coombe
Deputy Managing Director, MVA Ltd, Woking, UK

Michael Crilly
Urban Designer, Newcastle City Council, Planning and Transportation Department, Newcastle upon Tyne, UK

Dr Heidi Dumreicher
Member of the architectural, scientific and social scientific research team for the Westbahnhof SCI project, Oikodrom, Forum Nachhaltige Stadt, Vienna, Austria

Peter G. Fauset
Reader in Architectural Design, University of Northumbria at Newcastle, Newcastle upon Tyne, UK

Torben Gade
Director, Gruppen for By-og Landskabsplanlaegning Aps, Kolding, Denmark

Simon Guy
Lecturer in the Built Environment, Centre for Urban Technology, Department of Architecture, University of Newcastle, Newcastle upon Tyne, UK

Simon Hall
Research Fellow, The Bartlett School of Planning, University College London, London, UK

Tigran Hasic
Architect, Urban Designer and Lecturer,
Royal Institute of Technology,
Department of Infrastructure and
Planning, Division of Regional
Planning, Sweden

Peter Headicar
Reader in Transport Planning, School of
Planning, Oxford Brookes University,
Oxford, UK

Tim Heath
Lecturer, School of the Built
Environment, University of Nottingham,
Nottingham, UK

Hugh Howes
Principal Strategic Planner,
Environment Agency, Reading, UK

Professor Mike Jenks
Head of Research and Director of the
Oxford Centre for Sustainable
Development, School of Architecture,
Oxford Brookes University, Oxford, UK

Alexander E. Kalamaros
Doctoral Candidate, School of Policy,
Planning and Development, University
of California, Los Angeles, USA

Dr Jeffrey R. Kenworthy
Senior Lecturer in Urban Environments,
Institute for Science and Technology
Policy, Murdoch University, Murdoch,
Australia

Professor Richard S. Levine
Director, College of Architecture,
University of Kentucky, Kentucky, USA

Adam Mannis
Researcher, Centre for Sustainable
Technologies, School of the Built
Environment, University of Ulster,
Newtownabbey, Northern Ireland

Teresa Marat-Mendes
Doctoral Research Student, School of
the Built Environment, University of
Nottingham, Nottingham, UK

Professor Simon Marvin
Professor of Regional Development and
Sustainability, Research and Graduate
College, The University of Salford,
Salford, UK

Dr Mohammad-Reza Masnavi
Post-Doctoral Researcher, Department
of Architecture, University of Glasgow,
Glasgow, UK

James Morgan
Research Associate/Lecturer, School of
Planning and Housing, Edinburgh
College of Art/Heriot Watt University,
Edinburgh, UK

Professor Peter Newman
Director of the Institute for Science and
Technology Policy, Murdoch University,
Murdoch, Australia

Dr Peter Newton
Chief Research Scientist, CSIRO
(Commonwealth Scientific and
Industrial Research Organisation)
Building, Construction and Engineering,
Melbourne, Australia

Taghi Radmard
Member of the architectural, scientific
and social scientific research team for
the Westbahnhof SCI project, Centre for
Sustainable Cities, University of
Kentucky, USA

Joe Ravetz
Research Fellow, Department of
Planning and Landscape, Manchester
University, Manchester, UK

Abigail Raymond
Team Leader, Regeneration and Design,
Strategic Planning, Kent County
Council, Maidstone, UK

Dr Mats Reneland
Associate Professor and Researcher,
Department of Urban Transport
Planning, School of Architecture,
Chalmers University of Technology,
Sweden

Dr Gert de Roo
Senior Lecturer, Planning Department,
Faculty of Spatial Sciences, University
of Groningen, Groningen, Netherlands

Ernie Scoffham
Reader in Urban Architecture and
Director of the Centre for Postgraduate
Studies, School of the Built
Environment, University of Nottingham,
Nottingham, UK

Martyn Senior
Senior Lecturer, Department of City and
Regional Planning, Cardiff University,
Cardiff, UK

David Simmonds
Principal, David Simmonds
Consultancy, Cambridge, UK

Dominic Stead
Research Fellow, The Bartlett School of
Planning, University College London,
London, UK

Dr Roger Talbot
Senior Lecturer and Director of the
Edinburgh Sustainable Architecture
Unit, University of Edinburgh,
Edinburgh, UK

Dr Michelle Thompson-Fawcett
Lecturer, Department of Geography,
University of Otago, Dunedin, New
Zealand

Helena Titheridge
Research Fellow, The Bartlett School of
Planning, University College London,
London, UK

Dr Selwyn Tucker
Senior Principal Research Scientist,
CSIRO (Commonwealth Scientific and
Industrial Research Organisation)
Building, Construction and Engineering,
Melbourne, Australia

Uyen-Phan Van
Diploma Student, Department of City
and Regional Planning, Cardiff
University, Cardiff, UK

Professor David van Vliet
Professor (MCIP), Department of City
Planning, Faculty of Architecture,
University of Manitoba, Winnipeg,
Canada

Jo Williams
Research Fellow, The Bartlett school of
Planning, University College London,
London, UK

Dr Katie Williams
Senior Lecturer in Cities and Sustainable
Development, Oxford Centre for
Sustainable Development, School of
Architecture, Oxford Brookes
University, Oxford, UK

Professor Ernest J. Yanarella
Associate Director, Department of
Political Science, University of
Kentucky, Kentucky, USA

Giuseppe Zanré
Principal Planning Officer/Team Leader,
Planning Policy Unit, Planning,
Transport and Development
Directorate, Wycombe District Council,
High Wycombe, UK

Acknowledgements

Our thanks go to all involved in producing this book. In particular, we express our gratitude to: all of the contributors for producing their chapters and showing such enthusiasm for the project; Dr Haroula Balodimou for painstakingly desk top publishing the book and for designing the cover; Asif Din for desk top publishing; Kwamina Monney for preparing and redrawing many of the illustrations; and Jonathan Kemp, Bart Sheehan and Margaret Jenks for their continued support.

Katie Williams, Elizabeth Burton and Mike Jenks

Achieving Sustainable Urban Form:
An Introduction

> The search for the ultimate sustainable urban form perhaps now needs to be reoriented to the search for a number of sustainable urban *forms* which respond to [a] variety of existing settlement patterns and contexts ... (Jenks *et al.*, 1996, p.345)

The central premise of this book is that the form of a town or city can affect its sustainability. It is now widely accepted that a relationship exists between the shape, size, density and uses of a city and its sustainability. However, consensus is lacking about the exact nature of this relationship. The relative sustainability of, for example, high and low urban densities, or centralised and decentralised settlements is still disputed. Certain urban forms appear to be more sustainable in some respects, for example in reducing travel, or enabling fuel efficient technologies, but detrimental in others, perhaps in harming environmental quality or producing social inequalities. Some forms may be sustainable locally, but not be beneficial city wide or regionally.

Consequently, if any advances in urban sustainability are to be made, then connections between urban form and a range of elements of towns and cities, at all geographical scales, need to be established. If an understanding of these connections can be gained, then steps can be taken towards achieving urban forms that are more sustainable than at present. In order to advance this understanding, this book attempts to answer two key questions. First, what is sustainable urban form? and second, how can it be achieved?

The problem of unsustainable cities

That the physical form of urban areas has contributed to the massive problems of cities worldwide is not disputed. Zoning of different land uses has meant that people have had to travel longer distances to work, shopping centres and leisure activities. Developed countries have witnessed a 'mobility explosion' (Potter, 1997). In the UK, passenger kilometres travelled by car have doubled since 1981 (DETR, 1997). In the USA, Australia and Europe not only are people making more trips, but they are travelling further on each excursion. Urban sprawl has enabled urban populations to move out into land-rich suburban developments, whilst central areas have become derelict. Since 1945, in the UK, counter-urbanisation has occurred on an extensive scale. Migration has been predominantly from larger metropolitan areas to smaller, more rural areas. A loss of employment in cities has also been witnessed (Rudlin and Falk, 1999). In the USA, sprawl is now largely recognised as costly in economic, environmental and social terms. Other trends such as increases in poor quality mass housing and car-dominant residential estates, and a reduction of urban greenspace have all contributed to unsustainability.

The price of these types of development patterns is paid in unsustainable levels of resource use and inequitable lifestyles. These effects are not only felt in the developed world, but are 'exported' in terms of unfair shares of global resources, and growing inequity between rich

1

and poor nations. Such inequalities are graphically illustrated using ecological footprints – that is, measures of the amount of land necessary to enable everyday life in a city; for example, London has been estimated to have a footprint of 50 million acres, or 125 times its actual surface area (Sustainable London Trust, 1996). This is the area needed to meet the UK capital's food and timber requirements, and contain the vegetation required to absorb the carbon dioxide it produces. In reality, much of this space is far from London, for example in developing countries, where wood is produced. Similarly, 'environmental space' measures how much of the world's share of resources a country is consuming (FOTE Europe, 1995). Using this measure, current European Union emissions of carbon dioxide are calculated at over four times higher than global environmental space calculations allow (Smith *et al.*, 1998), and most of this output comes from cities. It is clear that cities in developed countries are not functioning in a sustainable way. They are using more than their share of resources and producing too much pollution. It is crucial, therefore, that the performance of these cities is improved to allow greater autonomy and equity.

Clearly, urban sustainability is not dependent on form alone. Huge shifts in behaviour and attitudes are also required. Nevertheless, expectations about the magnitude of urban form's influence on sustainability are high. It has been estimated that as much as 70% of delivered energy is subject to the influence of land use planning (Barton, 1990). Attitudes vary about potential reductions in emissions from transport, but a conservative estimate is that they could be reduced by 16% through a combination of land use planning policies and other supportive measures (ECOTEC, 1993). By implication, manipulating land uses and forms is seen as a valuable method of achieving sustainability in cities. However, it is not yet clear exactly which forms are preferable. A brief review of the sustainable urban form debate to date is useful to set the context for the chapters that follow.

Emerging solutions – the focus of the book

The previous volume to this book, *The Compact City: A Sustainable Urban Form?* (Jenks *et al.*, 1996), investigated the sustainability of the dominant model for urban sustainability at the time: the compact city. This model, which is akin to traditional high-density European cities such as Paris and Barcelona, was seen as a sustainable solution for urban form in most countries of the developed world, and was quickly introduced into policy. In Europe and Australia it was seen to offer a sustainable use of land – because it restricted growth beyond the urban fringe – enable reduced travel demand and create a vibrant, culturally-rich place to live. Economic benefits, in terms of concentrations of businesses and savings in infrastructure, were also associated with compactness.

However, conclusions emanating from *The Compact City* and elsewhere were far from supportive of the model's merits. Research emerged which challenged the fundamentals of the compact city concept. The book concluded that although the compact city did offer some benefits, such as opportunities for public transport and land savings, these were not as straightforward as had previously been thought. Furthermore, there were considerable costs involved which had not been foreseen by the advocates of the model. These were mainly associated with environmental quality and acceptability. Many of the contributors to the book were also at pains to point out the relative merits of other urban forms, and to broaden the portfolio of options for future growth. Hence, the conclusion to the book was that instead of searching for one definitive sustainable form, the emphasis should be on how to determine which forms are suitable in any given locality. This idea was beginning to emerge elsewhere. Breheny and Rookwood (1993, p.156) advocated a 'MultipliCity' approach to sustainability which they reasoned could only be achieved by considering development at the scale of the

'Social City Region'. They proposed that '... a variety of approaches be considered to suit particular settlement types ...'.

The approach taken in this book leads directly from the conclusions from *The Compact City* and other work, such as Breheny and Rookwood's, which puts the emphasis on finding solutions appropriate for different scales and locations of development. A key aim is to reveal what various forms, in addition to the compact city, have to offer, and to begin to develop a more sophisticated understanding of the implications for sustainability of a range of elements. This means addressing not only compaction – although this is given considerable attention by several authors – but also size, mix of uses, block structure and so on. Another goal is to broaden the range of issues which are encompassed by the sustainable urban form debate. Until now the weight of research has been on the implications for travel and fuel consumption, but the effects of urban forms on ecology, wildlife, natural resources, social conditions, behaviour and economic well-being are equally important to sustainability, and hence included in this book. Similarly, concentrating solely on urban scale solutions only offers a partial understanding. So different scales, from the house, through to the block, the neighbourhood, the district, city and region are all considered. By taking this inclusive approach, the danger of developing sustainable 'islands' within 'seas' of unsustainability is avoided.

However, concentrating only on theoretical models of the most sustainable forms is of little practical use. One of the key conclusions from *The Compact City* was that 'If ... urban form ... has any role to play in a sustainable future, then it has to be not only theoretically valid, but achievable in real terms' (Jenks *et al.*, 1996, p.343). The importance of the practicality of various solutions should not be underestimated. The scope for wholesale change in the built environment in developed nations is constrained by many factors, not least space, cost and acceptability. Likewise, the scope for completely new settlements is finite. Hence, much attention is paid in this book to the sustainability of alternative growth scenarios which offer opportunities for incremental change.

Some definitions

It is perhaps useful at this point to clarify how the term 'sustainable urban form' is used throughout the book. Some of the authors develop their own definitions, but these are usually refinements of the definitions given below.

As anyone familiar with research in this field will know, 'sustainable' is an over-used, but convenient, term. To help understand what 'sustainable urban form' might be, it is first helpful to understand the concept of sustainable development, and then relate this to a specifically urban context. The most widely cited definition of sustainable development is that of the WCED (1987), which describes it as development which is capable of meeting today's needs without compromising the ability of future generations to meet their needs. This definition contains concepts of inter-generational equity and social justice, as well as environmental awareness (Haughton and Hunter, 1994). It also implies that a global perspective is necessary and that cross-boundary impacts should be considered. Although there is some agreement about these principles, there is less consensus on how they can be translated into development 'on the ground'.

Several commentators have come close to operationalising such definitions by developing characterisations of 'sustainable cities' or 'sustainable urban development' (Leff, 1990; Elkin *et al.*, 1991; WHO, 1992). Such descriptions usually include principles that sustainable urban form should adhere to. For example, Elkin *et al.* (1991, p.12) state that, '... sustainable urban development must aim to produce a city that is "user-friendly" and resourceful, in terms not only of its form and energy-efficiency, but also its function, as a place for living'. Breheny

(1992, p.1) suggests that sustainable urban development requires the achievement of urban development aspirations, subject to conditions concerning inter- and intra-generational equity, and that the 'stock of natural resources should not be depleted beyond its regenerative capacity'. Smith *et al.* (1998) draw up a list of principles for a sustainable built environment which include: living off environmental 'interest' rather than 'capital'; not breaching critical environmental thresholds; developing a sense of equity and social justice; and forming inclusive procedures for decision making. Based on these descriptions, it appears possible to define sustainable urban form through certain basic characteristics that it should possess. In this book, a form is taken to be sustainable if it: enables the city to function within its natural and man-made carrying capacities; is 'user-friendly' for its occupants; and promotes social equity. The criteria that it should come about through inclusive decision making processes is also included.

Even this definition is difficult to conceptualise: it does not immediately suggest one particular form, or even a preference for high or low densities, dispersed or centralised development or small or large settlements. This is because policy makers and researchers are still undecided about the implications of different development strategies. Nevertheless, the definition can be used as a benchmark for assessing the qualities which sustainable urban form should have, and is a useful reference point when reading the proceeding chapters.

A checklist of the components or 'building blocks' of sustainable urban form is also worth establishing. These are the morphological attributes of an urban area at all scales above the architectural detail of the individual building (sustainable architecture is dealt with comprehensively elsewhere, see Farmer, 1996 and Papanek, 1995). Thus, issues of urban size, shape, density and compactness, urban block layout and size, housing type, greenspace distribution and various growth options such as intensification, extensification, decentralisation and new towns, are explored. In addition, a key element which may or may not be related to physical conditions, but does appear to affect sustainability, is mix of uses, so this too is investigated. A table containing all the elements of urban form studied in this book, and their impacts, can be found in the conclusions.

The structure of the book

The book has four parts which respond to the two key questions outlined at the beginning of this introduction: what is sustainable urban form?, and how can it be achieved? Parts 1 and 2 address the first question, parts 3 and 4 the second. Part 1, *Defining Sustainable Urban Form*, presents research which tests different urban forms or future development scenarios against various aspects of sustainability. The chapters offer insights into which forms may be more sustainable for issues such as urban ecology, social equity, land conservation, greenhouse gas emissions and environmental quality. In so doing urban villages, the compact city, mixed-use and single-use neighbourhoods, and edge, corridor and fringe city models are explored.

Part 2, *Urban Form and Transport: New Dimensions*, continues to question the sustainability of various forms, but from the perspective of travel patterns and behaviour. Since this issue has been dominant in policy and research it seemed appropriate to consider it in some depth here. The chapters compare different urban forms for their effects on travel behaviour, but begin to refine previous research findings and assumptions. For example, the relationship between urban density and travel behaviour is addressed, but is superimposed with detailed information about how socio-economic characteristics affect travel patterns, how people make their travel mode choices, and which types of densification help reduce car travel. Similarly, simplistic assumptions about the impact of various housing location strategies are unravelled, and research is presented which shows how important the regional context is in making such strategies work. Taken together, the chapters offer some evidence of the benefits of different urban forms, but they also show how some assumptions made in the past have oversimplified causal relationships.

In Part 3, *Approaches and Strategies for Achieving Sustainable Urban Form*, the authors present research and theory on how to move towards more sustainable urban forms. Some chapters offer broad strategic thinking about the ways in which future forms can be conceptualised and then developed. The values of advances such as 'sustainable urban management systems' and demonstration projects are reviewed. Other authors concern themselves with overcoming problems such as the acceptability of certain urban forms to local residents, and conflicts related to environmental pollution. Some worked examples of specific strategies created by local authorities and government agencies to move policy and practice towards more sustainable forms are then presented.

Part 4 gives examples of built or planned sustainable urban forms. As the part's title, *Built Form and Design Solutions*, suggests, the chapters outline schemes and projects which have been worked through to the detailed design stage. The projects vary from the scale of completely new settlements to individual buildings. Hence, solutions as varied as the urban village, a 'sustainable city implantation' and a large infill project are presented alongside chapters concentrating on sustainable urban blocks, social housing and non-residential buildings re-used for housing. This part demonstrates that change is happening on the ground, and that some of the theory is being translated into action. Finally, some conclusions are drawn about how far the findings have helped develop an understanding of what sustainable urban form is, and whether it can be achieved.

Part 1
Defining Sustainable Urban Form
Introduction

A prerequisite to achieving sustainable urban form is knowing what it is. To realise the 'sustainable city' there has to be a clear and common-held concept of what it will look like, how it will function, and how it will change over time. Until fairly recently, there was some consensus – although there was also considerable scepticism – that compact urban forms offered the most sustainable future. Subsequently, much research has focused on compact versus dispersed settlement patterns. However, this latter research gave rise to questions about the complexities and impacts of a whole range of urban forms. In presenting their findings, researchers argued that relationships previously assumed to exist between urban form and a number of sustainability benefits were either unsubstantiated by fact, or dependent on a range of intervening variables – some of which were far more significant than urban form.

The chapters in Part 1 are examples of this 'second wave' of research. Many of them refer to previous research and use the invaluable knowledge it provides as the basis of new studies. The chapters advance the debate by offering more sophisticated analyses and testing of the key elements of urban form: density, compactness, concentration, dispersal, mix of uses, housing type and so on. They offer either new evidence which sheds light on aspects of urban sustainability, or they offer alternative views of what sustainable urban form might be.

The first chapter, by Guy and Marvin, questions whether there is such a thing as 'sustainable urban form'. The authors take as their starting point the conclusions of the previous volume, *The Compact City: A Sustainable Urban Form?*, which stated that 'The search for the ultimate sustainable urban form perhaps now needs to be reoriented to the search for a number of sustainable urban forms which respond to the variety of existing settlement patterns and contexts that have been identified'. The argument that such multiple outcomes could, and should, be pursued is developed. Instead of concentrating on finding one solution, those involved in defining and managing sustainable cities should recognise that a diversity of urban futures are likely to co-exist within a single city. To reach these futures, a number of different and competing pathways could be followed. The authors conclude that identifying these pathways is a challenge to policy makers and researchers alike.

The next two chapters, by Burton and Williams, explore one such pathway: urban compaction. They test, through empirical research, the effects of the compact city in key policy areas. Burton investigates perhaps the least explored aspect of sustainability, social equity, and finds that it is affected by urban form, but that the merits of the compact city remain unproved: urban compactness appears to promote social equity in some respects, but not in others. Also, certain aspects of compactness seem to be more beneficial to social equity than others, and some benefits are emerging in response to re-urbanisation and development of previously derelict land. Overall, cities with a greater mix of uses tend to be the most egalitarian, in that the effects of compactness benefit the advantaged and disadvantaged equally. Williams takes a holistic look at the aims and outcomes of urban intensification policies in England. Her research investigates urban intensification in three London boroughs over a ten-year period, to assess whether the benefits stated in planning policies have happened 'on the ground'. It finds that policies have been effective for some purposes, such as using land in a sustainable way, but not for others – there were no noticeable effects on travel patterns or social conditions. Marked differences in impact between residential suburbs and mixed-use centres were also found. Although these findings support many of the key aims of intensification policies, there are also worrying policy failures. Both Burton's and Williams' research sheds new light on the relationship between urban form and some of its claimed impacts. They also reveal the dangerous simplicity of previous definitions of compactness.

The relative sustainability of different urban forms is addressed in the next four chapters. They present comparative research which tests different aspects of urban form against a range of sustainability variables. This research covers spatial scales from the city, to the neighbourhood and to the individual house. Newton reports on the environmental sustainability of alternative urban forms in Australia. He looks beyond the traditional distinction between dispersed and compact city, and adds 'edge city', 'corridor city' and 'fringe city'. The research, based on modelling techniques, supports the merits of the compact city and its close variants over a 'business as usual' scenario. Buxton also reviews the current debate in Australia on preferred urban form in terms of transport and energy use. In this instance, 'urban self-containment' is introduced as an alternative to the dispersed or compact forms, in a model allied to New Urbanism's idea of urban villages. The sustainability of different neighbourhoods in Scotland is investigated by Masnavi – with density and mix of uses as variables. The study reports on behaviour and attitudes of residents in terms of travel patterns, social interaction and perceptions of quality of the environment. Newton *et al.* take the investigation down to the scale of the individual building. They question the sustainability of the preferred Australian housing type – the detached house on its own parcel of land – and review the difference between mid-density and low-density detached forms in terms of energy and greenhouse gases.

In the above chapters the issue of urban ecosystems is hardly mentioned. Yet it is a key component of urban sustainability. This omission is redressed by Alberti, who offers a thorough review of possible effects of urban form on ecosystems. She states that 'Land use is one of the most important factors influencing ecological processes and biodiversity, but there is little understanding of how urban form affects ecosystem dynamics'. She goes on to clarify some of the mechanisms behind the relationships between spatial patterns and ecological processes and suggests key directions for future research.

Finally, Scofham and Marat-Mendes present research on an aspect of urban form that is rarely discussed in the sustainability debate: that of the ability of different urban forms to adapt over time. The authors look to historical precedent to identify physical qualities or 'ground rules' of urban form that allow adaptability to be achieved. They conclude that space is the asset that permits change to occur progressively and gradually, and that there is a consistency in historical precedents in the shape and size of the urban grid that adapts well to change. Their research adds to the debate by providing recommendations in terms of specific dimensions and shapes. In combination, these chapters provide valuable insights into a range of elements of sustainable urban form. When taken together, they do not enable the formation of a 'blueprint' for city form in the future, but they do challenge existing wisdom, and show how simplistic assumptions made in the past have been misleading. They also show how important it is to address the complexity of urban areas before drawing conclusions about their sustainability. Most of all though, they reveal the breadth of urban elements that either impact upon the sustainability of urban form, or are affected by it. Attempting to reconcile conflicts and trade-offs between these elements is the major challenge for those involved in managing the urban environment.

Simon Guy and Simon Marvin

Models and Pathways: *The Diversity of Sustainable Urban Futures*

Introduction

How do policy makers achieve the objective of building a sustainable urban future? This is the critical question that lies at the core of this book. We are not going to approach this question in a straight forward way. Instead, we want to tackle a number of assumptions that, we argue, hinder thinking about how sustainable cities can be achieved. In particular, we want to enlarge the concept of a sustainable city by building a more complex and multi-layered understanding of what the city might become. While we cannot offer policy makers a simple model or pathway towards a sustainable city, we do begin to build a conceptual framework that acknowledges the multiplicity of pathways towards different sustainable futures that often co-exist within a single city. There are three stages to our argument.

First is the shift from the concept of a singular model towards multiple models of what the sustainable city might become. We question the emphasis that is placed on the achievement of sustainability through one model – compact urban form. It is not that we necessarily reject the notion that the physical re-ordering of the city can achieve environmental benefits, though even compact city advocates recognise that the evidence to support sustainability claims are complex and often contradictory. Rather, our concern is that the continued search for a simple and universal model of sustainable urban form can blind researchers and policy makers to the multiplicity of innovations that could each make a quite distinctive contribution towards the development of more sustainable urban futures. Instead, we argue that the compact city debate is perhaps best understood as one amongst a number of different models of what might actually constitute a sustainable city.

Second is the rejection of the simplistic use of models, and the development of competing pathways to sustainable cities. We are concerned that the notion of models is often used in an over deterministic way. Models are often used as straight forward blueprints to be translated into reality through physical planning and design policies in a series of linear stages. Instead, we argue that models should be used in a much softer, more flexible fashion. Rather than viewing models as specifications for a city, we argue that they are better employed as conceptual devices to sensitise us to different visions of what the sustainable city might become. We can, for instance, examine the extent to which the viewpoints and strategies of different urban actors, with often competing social, political and commercial interests, resonate or dissonate with the visions inscribed in particular models of development. In this sense, we can then build an understanding of how the changing social organisation of urban development may promote particular pathways towards distinct urban futures.

Third is the recognition that a wide diversity of sustainable urban futures are likely to co-exist within a single city. In this context, we need to think differently about how the sustainable city could be achieved. Abandoning the search for a singular model, policy makers would

9

chart the multiplicity of pathways towards what might be different sustainable futures. The challenge here is to examine the tensions and similarities between these pathways; in particular, focusing on the different social assumptions and biases built into them. We explore these competing strategies by reference to our own research into the management and development of electricity and water networks in the Newcastle Metropolitan region.

From singular to multiple models
Single model – the compact city discourse
We begin by highlighting a number of contradictions in the claims made for the compact city. A useful starting point here is the discussion and analysis set out in the preceding volume to this book which focuses the debate by asking whether the compact city can be considered a sustainable urban form (Jenks *et al.*, 1996). We do not need to rehearse the arguments made in support of the environmental benefits of the compact city. Instead, we briefly develop an understanding of how the book's editors and contributors grapple with the contradictions of the sustainability claims made for the compact city.

Over the last decade, a phenomenal effort has been expended on the challenge represented by the shift towards more sustainable cities, through UK research council programmes, international research and policy initiatives and a high degree of activity and innovation at both national and local level. The editors note that urban environmental problems 'are the most intractable and difficult to solve' (*ibid.* p.2). At the core of much of this research effort and policy development is the concept of the compact city. Reshaping the environmental profile of resource use in cities through the re-ordering of land uses, the layout of neighbourhoods and the design of buildings is perhaps the dominant discourse in urban sustainability debates. Consequently, the compact city is 'today's visionary solution', hurriedly adopted by academics and politicians as an 'all-embracing panacea of urban ills' (Fulford, 1996, p.122). The compact city is often presented as 'the big idea' with 'nothing less than the future of western lifestyles at stake' (Breheny 1996, p.13). The concept is so dominant that it 'seems inconceivable that anyone would oppose the current tide of opinion towards promoting greater sustainable development and the compact city in particular' (Smyth, 1996, p.103). In this context, it is not surprising that the 'move towards the compact city is now entrenched in policy throughout Europe' (Jenks *et al.*, 1996, p.275).

The compact city discourse is extremely seductive, as suggested by its popular support in the research community, and its rapid translation into the policy arena. However, even its proponents, and certainly the researchers cited above, recognise to differing degrees that there are considerable difficulties in assessing the validity of the environmental claims made for the compact city. For example, the editors argue that 'research has yet to find conclusively either in favour of, or against, the compact city' (*ibid.* p.12), and consequently 'the battle between those in favour of the compact city and those against still rages' (*ibid.* p.240). Detailed empirical analysis illustrates that the environmental benefits from urban compaction policies are likely to be small and the social and economic costs could be significant (Breheny, 1996). Critically, there has been a tendency to focus on the lead role of planning in developing a blueprint of the compact city and rather less attention has been paid to the social, economic and technical processes involved in shaping the feasibility of the concept.

Recognising the complexity of much of the debate, the search for the 'ideal' land use pattern which is able to satisfy specific social, economic, and environmental criteria is at risk of simplifying a complex and continually unfolding topic. Therefore, discussions which focus on the compact city alone can represent just one facet of the debate as it stands today (Thomas and Cousins, 1996). We would certainly agree with the editors that 'an approach which addresses urban form alone is not enough' (Jenks *et al.*, 1996, p.170).

How can the sustainable city debate move forward? Well, there are a number of pointers. The research and policy community need to stop seeing the compact city as a singular model, a standardised pattern or a blanket solution that can be unproblematically implemented within an existing city. Instead, we need to recognise that there may be a range of urban futures that may be called sustainable. The challenge for policy is to develop the most appropriate for a particular local context. Within this context, the 'search for the ultimate sustainable urban form perhaps needs to be re-oriented to the search for a number of sustainable urban forms that respond to a range of different settlement patterns and contexts' (*ibid.* p.345).

Multiple models of sustainable cities

In our own work, we have attempted to link an analysis of new styles of infrastructure provision with their implications for the management of relations between users, buildings and territory in cities (Guy and Marvin, 1996a). We have found that utilities can actively shape resource flows of energy and water through the city using a range of economic, social and technological approaches to facilitate resource saving action (Guy and Marvin, 1996b). These demand-oriented styles of network management do not necessarily rely on the construction of new buildings or the manipulation of land uses. Utilities can have powerful commercial and economic reasons for reshaping resource use within existing buildings on stressed parts of their networks (Marvin and Guy, 1997). While we recognise that the design and layout of buildings can have important implications for shaping infrastructure resource use (Guy, 1998), the very small level of new build means that we have to look at a much wider range of resource saving strategies to reshape resource use in the existing stock, rather than simply examine new configurations of urban form. Consequently, we need to develop an enlarged conception of the styles of sustainable urban management that can shape resource flows along existing infrastructure networks without solely relying on the re-ordering of the physical fabric of the city (Guy and Marvin, 1998).

In our work, we have found Haughton's (1997) work on models of sustainable urban development very useful in helping to think through the connections between competing visions of the type of sustainable city that would support different styles of infrastructure management. Each model represents a competing strategy through which urban form and functions are reconstituted to avoid environmental implications of resource use in the city. Figures 1 to 3 characterise the main elements of each model in diagrammatic form in relation to the water and sewage network (see note 1). Each model attempts to link resource use in the city to its wider zone or 'sphere of influence'. Each model then examines how the extent and scope of the zone of influence could be reshaped through different styles of sustainability.

The Re-Designing Cities (RDC) model is based on the objective of 'planning for compact and energy efficient city regions' (*ibid.* p.191) (Fig. 1). Policies are designed to develop a city with a 'lowered urban metabolism' by reducing excessive resource flows and waste generation. The focus is within the city itself with little attempt to define or reduce the regional boundaries from which the city derives resources. The prime focus is on the development of a plan to redesign urban form and structure to reshape resource flows and human behaviour. These shifts link strongly to the strategic shift to higher densities in order to facilitate lower use of energy and other resources. In this sense, the model clearly echoes many of the central assumptions embodied within the compact city debate. Haughton, however, develops other models of the sustainable city not simply based on the manipulation of urban form and densities.

A second model is the Externally Dependent City (EDC), based on the 'excessive externalisation of environmental costs, open systems, linear metabolism, and buying in additional "carrying capacity"' (*ibid.* p.192) (Fig. 2). This model conceives the city as a node, extracting resources from an increasing hinterland for urban consumption with little attention to the level or quality of wastes produced by the city. The metaphor for the city is of a 'linear urban metabolism' with a very open urban system that is resource profligate and ignores the benefits of more effective resource management. Instead, resource managers invest in infrastructure supply tapping resources in hinterlands, drawing them into the city, consuming resources and depositing wastes in the hinterland. In this context, sustainable resource management would focus on more efficient market pricing mechanisms that would internalise the costs of environmental damage. Rather than attempting to reduce the urban sphere of influence, the objective would be to reshape it through market signals and cost compensation.

Redesign of overall structure and internal
structures of the city through a variety of incentives and regulatory controls

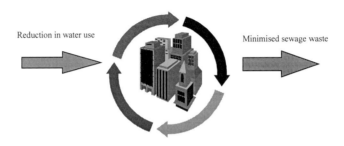

Fig. 1. Re-Designing Cities model.

Reduction of sphere of influence but lacks a distinct regional dimension

The solution to environmental impacts of water use is a combination of
market reform and improved regulatory control

Lacks any explicit regional dimension to water resource management

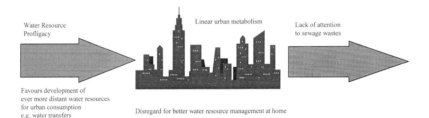

Fig. 2. Externally Dependent City model.

A third model is the Self-Reliant City (SRC), based on 'intensive internalisation of economic and environmental activities, circular metabolism, bio-regionalism and urban autarky' (*ibid.* p.190) (Fig. 3). This model takes as its starting point the objective of reducing the pattern of external dependence on resource use to restrict the urban sphere of influence. Central to this is the development of a 'circular urban metabolism' whereby the inputs of resources and outputs of waste are more closely linked. The sphere of influence is reduced to an appropriate bio-region within which resource flows, consumption and waste flows can be minimised and managed. This would place particular emphasis on the use of small-scale technologies, recycling, and demand management. Linked to this is a different type of social organisation which shifts from economic or technocratic styles of decision making towards more localised and community based styles: the assumption being that users would need to be closely involved in a transition from centralised to decentralised technologies.

This shift from singular to multiple models of the sustainable city is useful in a number of key respects. It helps shift the debate away from a relatively limited one about the effectiveness of a policy based on physically reshaping the form of the city to achieve compactness, to a much enlarged range of policy options. We can start to develop an understanding that there may be alternative policy options not simply based on urban redesign that could also contribute to the creation of sustainable cities. Acknowledging that there are multiple models, and there are likely to be more than those listed above, starts to present a more subtle and complex understanding of what the sustainable city might become. However, we need to be extremely careful to say precisely what 'work' these models can and cannot do.

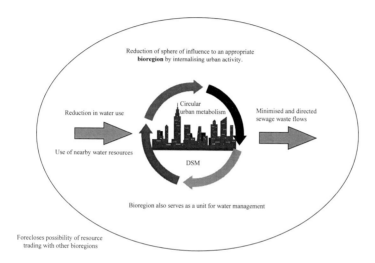

Fig. 3. Self-Reliant City model.

From models to competing pathways
Transcending the constraints of models

At this stage it is important that we are clear about how the above models should be used. First, it would be a mistake to employ them as blueprints to implement within the context of the existing city. It is difficult to justify the claim that one model is any more or less sustainable than another. At the same time, it would clearly be a mistake to view the models as representing sequential stages of development leading to a more sustainable city. Haughton is similarly drawn to the view that 'each model has its own value' and that 'the models lose value only when they inadvertently set in place professional and political blinkers that prevent consideration of a wider range of policy approaches' (*ibid.* p.194). Second, the models are not clearly connected to social processes and interests. Simply using them as end points does not adequately reflect the social, economic and technical complexity involved in re-ordering the city along the pathways implied within each model. Third, although one model – RDC – is the most clearly based on physical changes, this does not mean that other models exclude design policies. For instance, research could examine how pricing, regulatory and technological shifts envisaged in the other models could translate into different types of design and layout. Although the models are not explicitly attempting to define the precise form of the city, each model does provide a different social, economic and technological context within which land use and buildings would be planned and managed.

Haughton's response to these issues is to construct a fourth model, entitled the 'Fair Share City' (FSC) model which, because it 'integrates the better aspects of the other three models, [and is] allied with greater concern for social justice and geographical equity concerns, provides

13

one possible amalgam of approaches' (*ibid.* p.194). We, however, want to suggest a slightly different way of using the models that escapes seeing them as blueprints and therefore avoids the need for searching for the definitive model of sustainable urban development.

The emergence of pathways: towards sustainable urban futures

Rather than search for an ideal model, we argue for the need to recognise that competing models represent multiple pathways towards a sustainable city. In this sense, the achievement of sustainable cities is a process and not the result of implementing a particular model. We argue that pathways do not exist as ideal types but are contested in particular local contexts, as competing social actors grapple with the concept of sustainable development and its relation to wider practices of urban development. Here we are asking the models to do a bit more work than perhaps was originally intended in their formulation. We suggest the models are used as heuristic devices, or conceptual windows through which we can map the contrasting visions of the sustainable city. We are not suggesting that the models should be applied in practice, that they represent the range of sustainable cities that might exist, or that they are mutually exclusive. Instead, we argue their real analytical power is to act as a filter or lens through which we can start to see what the sustainable city might look like (see note 2).

In our own work on infrastructure provision, we have attempted to develop an understanding of the emergence of new styles of sustainable infrastructure provision (Guy and Marvin, 1998). Within the context of comparative work on the shifts in infrastructure provision across energy, water and waste networks in Newcastle, Copenhagen, Berlin and the Greek island of Kos, we developed a research methodology that allowed us to understand the changing social organisation of infrastructure provision, the complex signals sent to infrastructure providers, the story lines and coalitions around sustainability, and the viewpoints that social actors developed (see note 3). This process allowed us to link an understanding of what the sustainable city might become with particular pathways of development.

Figures 4 and 5 provide a diagrammatic representation of the application of this research methodology in the energy and water sectors of Newcastle. First, we focused on two key issues that have been closely linked to the sustainability agenda – energy efficiency and the issue of water transfers, in this case between Yorkshire and the North East. These were two of the most significant sustainability issues being debated in the infrastructure sector when the fieldwork was undertaken. Second, we mapped the organisation of the social interests involved in each infrastructure sector – infrastructure managers, regulators and local government. In particular, we paid special attention to the interactions between these interests and how they attempted to shape each other using a range of modes of interaction. Third, we traced the competing viewpoints emerging in debates around sustainability issues. In particular, we explored the interpretative flexibility of each issue in terms of the contrasting conceptualisations of both the problem and different types of response. Finally, we linked actors' viewpoints on different models of the sustainable city. Here we were particularly interested in how the models resonate and collide with actors' viewpoints, in order to build a better understanding of the competing pathways towards a sustainable city. The short case studies below provide vignettes of the application of this research methodology.

Energy efficiency in Newcastle

The key environmental issue in the energy sector in Newcastle has been improving the efficiency of energy use within the city. However, a number of competing pathways to sustainable energy efficiency and conservation can be identified. Figure 4 shows that a coalition of interests from the economic regulators and the energy providers argue that a competitive market in electricity supply will provide economic signals for energy conservation and efficiency measures. This pathway resonates strongly with the Externally Dependent City model, with its focus on open markets and regulatory reform to improve the efficiency of local energy use. In contrast, locally based actors are demanding more effective regulatory signals and financial support from central government and regulators to stimulate programmes of energy savings at the local level. The local authority, local environmental and fuel poverty groups all stress the longer term environmental and social benefits of energy efficiency. Within these viewpoints there are strong resonances with the Self-Reliant City model as they seek to reduce the sphere of influence of the city, not only through energy conservation measures but also through local energy production from photovoltaics and combined heat and power. However, within these local interests there are differences between viewpoints, with environmental groups arguing most strongly for Self-Reliance, and fuel poverty groups arguing for physical measures (building design and refurbishment) to reduce heat loss of low-income households – strongly echoing the Re-Designing Cities model. An analysis of policy documents produced by the local authority produces a vision of an urban future that combines elements from all three models.

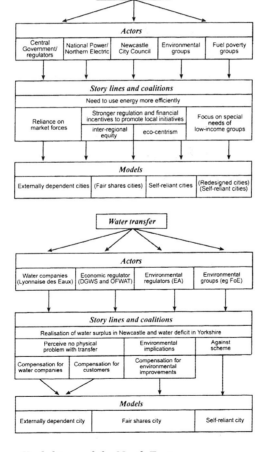

Fig. 4. Views of energy efficiency in the North East region.

Fig. 5. Water transfer between the North East and Yorkshire regions: competing views.

Water transfer between Yorkshire and the North East

This case study focuses on competing views of the solution to the water shortage in Yorkshire between 1996 and 1997. All actors agreed that there was a problem with water shortage in

Yorkshire but each had very different views about how the problem should be solved. The debate revolved around the evaluation of a water transfer scheme involving the construction of a pipe system for moving water between the North East, which had a surplus of water, and 'dry' Yorkshire, to ensure security of supply. First, there was a high degree of overlap between the positions of the water companies and regulators who argued that the scheme should be constructed, providing the water company and users in the North East were adequately compensated for the transfer. This position resonated strongly with the Externally Dependent City model, with both actors viewing water as a commodity which can be traded between regions. Second, the Environment Agency (EA) was concerned to reduce the urban and regional sphere of influence through demand management options. Before considering supply augmentation, the EA was concerned that water suppliers should exhaust demand management options – a position resonating strongly with the Self-Reliant City and Re-Designing Cities models. However, the EA recognised that in some circumstances water trading may be necessary, and indeed desirable for consumers in Yorkshire but they argued that it must take place in the least ecologically disruptive way. Therefore, the EA argued for financial compensation from the scheme to speed environmental improvements within the water and sewerage networks of the North East. In this sense, the EA model appears to lean more closely towards the Fair Share City with a form of autarky within limits, rather than total autonomy. Finally, environmental groups were much more critical of the water transfer scheme and promoted options based on greater autonomy for the Yorkshire region. They proposed a range of social and technical options more closely linked to the Self Reliant City and Re-Designed Cities to lower demand for water and reduce the urban sphere of influence without the need for water transfers.

Reaching closure?

Both case studies illustrate the wide diversity and contested understanding of what the sustainable city might become. There are a number of important points to make here. First, for a particular sustainability issue there are likely to be different strategies that co-exist, supported by particular coalitions of actors. The pathways resonate quite strongly with the different elements of the models proposed by Haughton. In this sense, the models provide us with an understanding of what different types of sustainable city might look like, particularly in terms of their connections with technologies, users and management of place. They are not necessarily options or choices that can be selected from a menu – instead, they provide a way of orienting our thinking about the potential for different types of sustainable city in particular local contexts. We need to develop an understanding of how the different notions of the sustainable city collide or resonate with one another. Second, the debate about the type of sustainable city that might be created can vary across different issues. In the case of energy efficiency, closure has not been reached around one particular option as a number of different pathways continue to co-exist with relatively little interaction between them. But in the case of water transfer, closure has been reached around the construction of the water transfer model. Yet even in this context, with the Externally Dependent City as the dominant model, other models still co-exist because the EA has also strengthened Yorkshire Water's demand management requirements – simultaneously creating the potential for a more Self-Reliant Yorkshire. While multiple pathways towards sustainability can evidently co-exist, we still need a better understanding of how some pathways become more dominant than others. Finally, we need to problematise the notion of the Fair Share model. Again, this does not exist as an independent construct of what a city might become – instead, we should see it as relational, constructed out of a number of intersecting pathways towards sustainability. What is 'fair share' in one context might not be in another. We need comparative research focusing on how pathways are constructed, how they can become dominant and/or marginalised, what interactions take place between them and how closure can be reached on a particular solution.

Conclusions

This chapter questions the use of a singular model to guide the achievement of sustainable cities. Instead, our research suggests that models should be used as heuristic windows through which we can identify how policy and regulatory and commercial strategies mesh or clash with the rather more messy world of urban development practices. We have not developed an argument for the rejection, acceptance, or promotion of a particular model but argue that researchers and policy makers employ them as conceptual devices for developing a more sensitive and richer understanding of the possible pathways towards the sustainable city. As ideal types they provide a lens through which we can begin to examine how different social interests involved in infrastructure provision envision the social, technical, institutional and spatial re-ordering of the city.

Critically, in our own research we did not start with the models. Instead, we reviewed how different sets of social interests created quite different visions of how infrastructure can be restructured socially and technically. As we have seen, these different forms of configuration tend to echo, in varying degrees, the types of cities expressed in Haughton's models. In this sense, the models' power is not in their prescriptive vision, but in the ways in which we can link different social interests to views of future sustainable cities. This said, relatively little work has been undertaken that connects models of sustainability to the complexity of the social world within which infrastructure managers and other urban managers operate. In particular, we have shown how changing strategies of infrastructure management are quite clearly shaped by different ways of seeing the problem and the solution, and by competing visions of the future city. Models therefore need to be more closely related to the specific social organisation of infrastructure in a city and, more particularly, to highlight how opportunities for environmental innovation link to the changing contexts of urban development. In this way, models could help research and policy to trace more carefully the social interests linked to particular visions of urban futures, and the connections between competing viewpoints.

Used in this way, the models can help us to understand the contested nature of shifts towards a sustainable urban future. Critical here is the recognition that there is not a singular future, vision or model, but many different futures that may co-exist, supported by different sets of social interests. Here our approach differs slightly from Haughton's. Rather than attempt to combine the best elements of different models into an alternative vision or model based on a particular type of assessment of the optimum combination of strategies such as the 'Fair Share City', we argue for the need to identify how different social interests may connect to particular visions of the sustainable city. For instance, our empirical findings have shown that particular social coalitions can emerge around a single vision. In other cases, different sets of actors have quite different ideas about the type of city they are trying to create.

The central challenge for researchers is to use more sensitively models of sustainable cities as ideal types through which we can start to map the social and technical possibilities for different types of urban futures in specific cities. Rather than searching for a static notion of sustainable urban form, we need to start to identify the complex pathways towards quite different urban futures that may all claim to be sustainable. We need to examine the social assumptions and biases built into different pathways, the resonances and dissonances between different pathways, to review the relative dominance and weakness of different pathways, and to develop the potential for forging new coalitions of interest around particular development pathways. This agenda represents a significant challenge to a research and policy agenda that still seems to be searching for a singular definition of the sustainable city.

Notes
1. We have had to simplify some of the complexity Haughton makes in developing the models and it is important that his original paper is referred to.
2. While the models were originally intended to help develop an understanding of water flows through the city, the later write-up widened the remit to cover other resource flows. We are particularly interested in the models' applications to infrastructure flows, such as energy and waste.
3. See Moss *et al.* (1998) for project details.

Acknowledgements
We would like to thank Suzie Osborn for undertaking the interviews on which the case studies in this chapter are based and the European Commission 4th Framework Programme for funding the research.

Elizabeth Burton

The Potential of the Compact City for Promoting Social Equity

Introduction

It is now widely accepted, particularly in land use planning policy (for example, DoE and DoT, 1994), that the most effective solution to achieving sustainable urban form is implementation of the compact city idea, that is, advocacy of high-density, mixed-use urban form. The claimed advantages of the compact city have been well documented – they include: conservation of the countryside; less need to travel by car, thus reduced fuel emissions; support for public transport and walking and cycling; better access to services and facilities; more efficient utility and infrastructure provision; and revitalisation and regeneration of inner urban areas. However, to date, there is little evidence to support such claims, and the sustainability of the compact city continues to be contended (Breheny, 1992; Jenks *et al.*, 1996).

Of all the arguments, perhaps the least explored and most ambiguous is the claim that the compact city is a socially equitable city. A significant body of sustainable development rhetoric stresses the importance of social equity (e.g. CEC, 1990; CIDA, 1991; Blowers, 1992; Yiftachel and Hedgcock, 1993). According to Elkin *et al.* (1991):

> sustainable development involves more than environmental conservation; it embraces the need for equity. Both intra-generational equity providing for the needs of the least advantaged in society, and inter-generational equity, ensuring a fair treatment of future generations, need to be considered. (p.203)

This chapter summarises the results of a large-scale study of the relationship between urban compactness and social equity. The objectives of this research were:

- to examine the validity of claims that the higher-density city promotes social equity; and
- to identify the dimensions of urban compactness that offer the greatest potential for facilitating social equity.

The findings advance the debate about sustainable urban form through the provision of empirical data on the social sustainability implications of the compact city (see end note).

Methodology

In essence, the study represents a quantitative investigation, comparing, through statistical tests, a number of social equity criteria in a large sample of UK towns and cities of varying compactness. In order to carry out this investigation, it was first necessary to identify from literature all the claimed effects of urban compactness on social equity, and then to develop means of measuring both these and levels of urban compactness in a range of towns and cities.

For the purposes of the research, the compact city was interpreted as a free-standing urban settlement and defined as embracing one or all of three categories: a high density city, a mixed use city, and an intensified city. The first two categories refer to static conditions or outcomes while the third refers to the compact city as a process. Each of the categories embraces a variety of dimensions. For example, high densities can be measured in terms of either overall or net densities, and can vary according to housing form. As the research objectives stem from sustainable development arguments, the definition of social equity was derived primarily from interpretations of the concept within this context. In summary, it is argued that the compact city is deemed to be equitable (or just) if it is associated with benefits for the life chances of the disadvantaged, thereby reducing the gap between rich and poor. Disadvantage is seen to be most accurately represented in terms of low income; improved life chances stem from increased earning capacity, reduced expenditure on living costs and improvements in quality of life.

The claimed social equity impacts of urban compactness identified in literature and existing research are listed in Table 1.

Claimed effect (balance of evidence/opinion)	Conflicting claims exist	Nature of evidence
1. Better access to facilities (Rees, 1988; Bromley and Thomas, 1993; DoE, 1992)		sparse
2. Poorer access to green space (Breheny, 1992; Knight, 1996; Stretton, 1994)	✓	sparse
3. Better job accessibility (Beer, 1994; Laws, 1994; Elkin *et al.*, 1991)	✓	sparse
4. Better public transport (ECOTEC, 1993; Goodchild, 1994)	✓	contentious
5. Greater opportunities for walking and cycling (Bourne, 1992; Newman, 1992; Bozeat *et al.*, 1992)		contentious
6. Reduced domestic living space (Brotchie, 1992; Forster, 1994; Stretton, 1996)		sparse
7. Poorer health – general, mental and respiratory (Freeman, 1992; McLaren, 1992; Schwartz, 1994)	✓	contentious
8. Reduced crime (Jacobs, 1961; Elkin *et al.*, 1991; Petherick, 1991)	✓	contentious
9. Lower levels of social segregation (CEC, 1990; Hamnett, 1991; Fox, 1993; Van Kempen, 1994)		sparse
10. Increased job opportunities for the less skilled (Porter, 1991; Des Rossiers, 1992; Castells and Hall, 1994)	✓	sparse
11. Less affordable housing (Town and Country Planning Association, 1994)	✓	sparse
12. Increased wealth (Minnery, 1992)	✓	sparse

Table 1. Summary of claimed effects of compactness on social equity.

A large number of indicators was devised to measure each of the three aspects of urban compactness and the 12 different social equity effects (in all, 94 indicators were used – 41 for urban compactness and 53 for social equity). In addition, as each aspect of social equity is subject to many influences, a further range of indicators was developed to measure possible intervening variables, such as the socio-economic status of the town or city and the level of unemployment. Indicators were also devised to measure composite values, for example, overall social equity measures. The nature of these indicators is summarised in Tables 2–4 (for sources, see Burton, 1997).

Dimension of compactness	Nature of indicators	No. of indicators
1. Density		
gross	Persons and households per hectare (within administrative district)	2
net	Persons and households per hectare within built-up area and residential area of district	4
population-weighted	Average ward density, in persons per hectare	1
sub-centres	Extremes and variations in ward densities	3
housing form	Percentage of low- and high-density housing, and small and large dwellings	4
2. Mix of uses		
balance of uses	Quantity of 'key' facilities, and ratio of residential to non-residential land	3
horizontal mix/spread of facilities	Variation in number of key facilities per postcode sector	5
vertical mix	Incidence of mixed retail/residential and commercial/residential development	2
overall provision and spread of facilities	Mix and number of facilities within postcode sectors	1
3. Intensification		
increase in population	Rate of in-migration 1981–91	2
increase in development	Rate of new house building, derelict land reclamation and planning approvals 1981–91	9
increase in density	Changes in conventional and population-weighted densities 1981–91 and 1971–91	4
increase in density of sub-centres	Change in density of most dense ward 1981–91	1

Table 2. Summary of compactness indicators.

Social equity issue	Nature of indicators	No. of indicators
access to superstores	Average distance to nearest superstore, from all wards, most deprived ward, and difference for most and least deprived wards	2
access to green space	Average distance to nearest green space, from all wards, most deprived ward, and difference for most and least deprived wards	3
job accessibility	Percentage of low-income employees working outside the district, in absolute and relative terms (compared with high-income groups), and change 1981–91	4
public transport use	Percentage of low-income employees who travel to work by public transport, and change 1981–91	2
non-motorised travel	Percentage of low-income employees who travel to work on foot or by bicycle, in absolute terms and relative to high-income employees, and change 1981–91	4
amount of living space	Rooms per household (average, and for three-person, low-income households); extent of overcrowding; inequality in housing size	7
health	Percentage of residents with limiting long-term illness; death rate from mental illness and respiratory disease	5
crime	Cost of home contents insurance – all postcode sectors, worst sector, and difference between best and worst	3
segregation	Segregation, by ward, of ethnic households, owner-occupiers, local authority tenants, car-less households and single parent households, average across all groups, and change 1981-91	11
job opportunities	Number of low-income jobs per relevantly qualified economically active resident, in absolute terms and relative to high-income jobs, and change 1981–91	4
affordable housing	Average price of lower-cost dwelling relative to average income of manual workers, and change 1983–91; average local authority rent; level of homelessness	5
wealth	Increase in price of lower-cost dwelling 1983–91, and increase relative to higher cost dwellings	2

Table 3. Summary of social equity indicators.

External influences	Nature of indicators	No. of indicators
level of car ownership	Percentage of car-less households	1
socio-economic characterisics	Deprivation (Townsend score); housing need; inequality in income; average income; percentage of middle class residents; percentage of wealthy households	6
social characteristics	Average household size; percentage of residents over pension age	1
size of manufacturing sector	Percentage of employees working in sector and change 1981–91	2
unemployment	The young unemployed: all 16- and 17- year olds unnemployed as a percentage of those employed	1
tenure	Percentage of households in local authority accommodation, and change 1981–91	2
region	Standard region of England (categorical indicator)	1
type	Standard types of district (categorical indicator)	2
size	Total residents; total built-up area	2

Table 4. Summary of intervening variables.

The following 25 towns and cities were selected for investigation:

Large non-metropolitan cities	Small non metropolitan cities	Industrial	Districts with new towns	Resort and retirement
Derby Southampton	Bath Cambridge Cheltenham Exeter Gloucester Lincoln Worthing Oxford Worcester York	Great Grimsby Luton Ipswich Scunthorpe Slough	Crawley Harlow Northampton Stevenage	Blackpool Eastbourne Hastings Southend-on- Sea

N.B. Cities divided into Craig's (1985) categories

Table 5. Sample of towns and cities.

These towns and cities represent all free-standing English districts (that is, administrative districts with less than approximately 10% of their perimeters bordering on neighbouring towns/cities) with urban populations of 80,000 to 220,000, where the district boundary is close to the edge of the built-up area.

Values for the indicators were obtained by collecting a vast quantity of data on the sample of towns and cities. These data were derived primarily from secondary sources such as the 1991 and 1981 Censuses of Population, *Local Housing Statistics, England and Wales* (e.g. DoE and Welsh Office, 1992), *Mortality Statistics* (e.g. OPCS, 1993) and *Property Market Reports* (Valuation Office, 1991), and a variety of methods and calculations were employed to obtain final values.

These values were then analysed using statistical tests. More specifically, levels of compactness were compared with corresponding levels of social equity across all the towns and cities, using Pearson product-moment correlation coefficients. The purpose of this was to identify any significant relationships between the two sets of indicators. Examination of the correlation coefficients revealed those aspects of compactness most strongly related to positive equity effects, and those aspects of social equity most likely to be influenced by compactness. In addition, because compactness is not the only influence on social equity, step-wise multiple linear regression analysis was employed to establish the most important predictors of greater social equity from the whole range of compactness and intervening variables.

Findings

The findings are discussed in terms of the two main objectives of the research, stated in the introduction.

How valid are the claims that the compact city promotes social equity?

Does the evidence support the claimed social equity effects of compactness?
The findings supported some of the claims made about the compact city, and contradicted others, as shown in Table 6.

Compact city claim	Evidence
better access to facilities	✓
poorer access to green space	✓
better accessibility to jobs	?
better public transport	✓
greater opportunities for walking and cycling	✓ ✗
reduced domestic living space	✓
poorer health	✓ ✗
reduced crime	✗
reduced social segregation	✓
increased job opportunities	✓?
lack of affordable housing	✓
increased wealth	✗

Table 6. Evidence for compact city claims related to social equity.

✓ = supports claim; ✗ = contradicts claim; ✓ ✗ = claim supported in some respects but not others; ? = evidence is ambiguous; ✓? = evidence is weak but tends to support claim.

Does the compact city promote social equity?

The statistical analyses revealed a large number of significant relationships between compactness and social equity indicators. On further investigation, some of these appeared to be meaningless but, in general, each claimed equity effect was found to be related to compactness in some form or other. Table 7 summarises these meaningful associations.

How does compactness affect social equity?

From the analysis, a complex picture emerges of the ways in which elements of urban compactness influence social equity. When social equity is examined in terms of the different issues identified for the purposes of the research, it appears that some aspects of social equity are more strongly influenced by compactness than others. Nearly all of the 14 social equity effects (health split into three separate issues) are related in some way to urban compactness: job accessibility and wealth being the exceptions. Of these, the following – nine in all – were shown to be more strongly related to compactness than to any of the intervening variables, suggesting that urban compactness may be a highly significant influence on social equity:

- access to superstores
- access to green space
- public transport use
- extent of walking and cycling
- amount of domestic living space
- death rate from mental illness
- death rate from respiratory disease
- crime
- social segregation

Social equity effect (on relative or absolute position of poor)	Significant relationships with compactness			More strongly related to intervening variables
	density	mix of uses	intensification	
1. Access to superstores (relative)	+ (households)			
2. Access to green space (relative)	− (households)			
3. Job accessibility				✓
4. Public transport use (absolute)	− (pop./extremes)			
5. Walking and cycling	− (housing form)	+ (spread/no. facilities)		
6. Domestic living space (absolute)	− (net/pop./hshlds/ form)			
7. General health	− (extremes)	+(horizontal mix) − (vertical mix)		✓
8. Mental health	+ (housing form)			
9. Respiratory health		− (spread/no.facilities)		
10. Crime (relative)	− (net/pop./ extremes)			only relative position of poor
11. Social segregation (esp. by tenure)	+ (housing form)		+ (in-migration)	
12. Job opportunities		+ (vertical/no.facs) − (spread facs)	+ (non-res./derelict land)	✓ (for overall measure)
13. Affordable housing (homeowners)	− (housing form)		+(higher densities)	✓
14. Wealth (absolute)	−? (housing form)			✓
Overall measure of social equity	+ (housing form)			
Overall measure of social equality	− (variation)	+ (spread/no. facilities)		

+ = positive relationship; − = negative relationship; ? = unclear.

Table 7. Summary of significant relationships between compactness and social equity (only apparently meaningful relationships included).

It is important to note that the intervening variables used for the research do not constitute an exhaustive list. Although they are likely to represent the most likely external influences on these aspects of social equity, there may be other interpretations that would be found to be more significant.

The key issue for the research relates to where the potential of the compact city concept may lie, in terms of individual social equity effects. The findings indicate that it is likely to be negative for five aspects (in descending order of importance):

- less domestic living space
- lack of affordable housing
- poor access to green space
- increased crime levels
- higher death rate from respiratory disease

But may offer the following benefits (in descending order of importance):

- improved public transport use
- lower death rate from mental illness
- reduced social segregation; and, with remedial measures, possibly
- greater scope for walking and cycling
- better job opportunities for the lower skilled
- better access to facilities

How significant, overall, is compactness for social equity?
When looked at in its entirety, that is, as a combination of all the different indicators, social equity has a limited relationship with compactness; the concept has to be broken down into its constituent elements for meaningful relationships to be apparent. For some composite measures of social equity, there are stronger correlations with compactness indicators than with intervening variables. For example, social *equality* is related to two compactness indicators – the mix of uses and variation in density – but is unrelated to any external factors. In the multiple regression analyses, social equity indicators affecting expenditure were found to be most closely related to the proportion of terraced housing and flats, while the social equity indicators affecting quality of life were related more strongly to intervening variables such as the proportion of local authority tenants in the town/city. Overall, the proportion of local authority tenants was the most important predictor of social equity: the higher the proportion of council housing, the better the social equity, especially if the drop in those employed in manufacturing is low. Perhaps this is because, to some extent, housing factors, including quality, location and form, are controlled by standards in the public sector. Social housing offers the opportunity to ameliorate some of the negative effects that the market would otherwise deliver to low-income groups. The findings also suggest that, altogether, as expected, housing tenure and structural changes in employment have a greater influence than compactness on social equity. Regional location also influences the effect of compactness on social equity, especially social and quality of life aspects.

Many of the specific social equity effects examined in the research proved in statistical tests to be more strongly related to compactness, or at least specific aspects of compactness, than to any of a substantial number of intervening variables. Close relationships with compactness were more obvious for some social equity indicators than others. For example, it was unsurprising to find that the amount of domestic living space per household is less in a compact city. However, it was rather more surprising to find that compactness indicators were the strongest predictors of performance on the health indicators.

Which forms of compactness are most beneficial for social equity?

There are several ways of assessing the relative merits of different aspects of compactness. For example, the evaluation may be based simply on the numbers of individual social equity effects influenced by each main category of compactness (density, mix of uses and intensification). From a cursory examination of Table 7, density appears to have the greatest influence on social equity, in that it is related to the widest range of social equity indicators. However, not all of these influences are positive. In contrast, intensification is related to only three social equity impacts, but appears to be positive for all of these. Table 8 summarises the differing influences of the three different categories of compactness.

Aspect of compactness	Significant influences no./14	Positive influences no./14	Balance of influence (no. of positive minus no. of negative influences)
Density	11	4	−2
Mix of uses	4	3	0
Intensification	3	3	+3

Table 8. The relative influence of aspects of compactness on the range of social equity effects.

High densities appear to be positive for four aspects of social equity: access to superstores, public transport use, lower death rates from mental illness and lower social segregation; mixed land uses for three: walking and cycling, general health and job opportunities; and intensification, for social segregation, job opportunities and affordable housing. However, although the high-density city yields the greatest number of positive influences, it may not be the most beneficial type of compact city, in that the positive influences are outweighed by negative ones. In terms of the balance of influence, intensification appears to offer the most potential. Furthermore, the possibility that other influences of intensification may become apparent over a longer time-period cannot be dismissed. This is encouraging for compact city proponents as it supports the validity of implementing the compact city concept in practice. In terms of individual indicators, it is impossible to identify any one aspect of intensification as most beneficial: nearly all the different types – higher densities, in-migration, non-residential development, and development on derelict land – are associated with greater equity in one form or another.

Although the mix of land uses has a neutral influence overall, there are certain aspects that seem to be mainly positive, namely the quantity of facilities within the city. In other words, the range and number of facilities is more beneficial than their geographical spread. There appears to be a complex set of relationships related to the mix of uses, stemming from subtle differences in the distribution of land uses around the city. Similarly, for density, while the balance of influence is negative, certain aspects appear to be mainly beneficial: in particular, the proportion of high-density housing forms such as terraces and flats.

The drawback of this evaluation is that it fails to take into account either the strength of each influence or the relative importance of each different social equity effect. It is impossible to derive unequivocal weightings for the 14 different social equity effects, as the significance of each will vary for each low-income household. As the basis for an alternative assessment, the compactness indicators were correlated with the overall/composite measure of social equity. From this, the only significant aspect of compactness that emerges is the quantity of newsagents in the city. This is not a key measure of compactness, but nevertheless seems to represent something important about the character of cities that are most supportive of social equity. As it belongs to the family of 'mix of use' indicators, it supports the theory that the mix of uses in a city is the most important aspect of compactness for social equity, contrary to the arguments above, but as the quantity of newsagents in an area is influenced by the nature of the predominant built-up or housing forms, there is a danger in reading too much into the relationship.

What seems to be clearer from the results is that the relative position of the poor (compared with the affluent) is better in a mixed-use city. Correlation tests show that mixed-use cities tend to be the most egalitarian: that is, the effects of compactness benefit the advantaged and disadvantaged equally. This was true also for the extent of variation in density across the city: the smaller the variation in density, the better the relative position of the poor. It is important to note, however, that these findings do not indicate that the poor are better off in an absolute sense or compared with their counterparts in other cities. In terms of earning capacity, cities with a high proportion of flats and terraced houses and a low proportion of detached and semi-detached houses appear to be the most supportive of social equity, confirming the importance of high-density housing. It is, perhaps, such individual components of compactness that should be the focus of attention in attempting to maximise the contribution of the compact city to social equity.

Conclusions

The compact city has been advocated as a sustainable form of urban development. The concept of social equity is an integral aspect of this argument, but an understanding of how it is influenced by compactness has been severely lacking. The quantitative methodology used for the research has gone some way towards redressing this deficiency through the provision of empirical evidence. Although it is impossible to conclude unequivocally that the compact city promotes equity, there are clear indications that in certain respects and with certain qualifications, it presents significant potential to do so.

While compactness appears to be positive for some aspects of social equity, it may be negative for others. Speculation alone would not have elicited these findings – many of the compact city claims were found to be untenable. The broader analyses suggest that the compact city may promote *equality* rather than *equity*, since it is more likely to improve the relative than the absolute position of the poor.

The goal of the research was to answer the question: does the compact city promote social equity? The results indicate that there can be no definitive answer; compactness may support equity in some respects but not in others. The research has shown that the potential of the compact city is unquestionably dependent on the form it takes. Certain dimensions appear to be more beneficial than others are: in particular, positive effects are emerging in response to re-urbanisation and development of previously derelict land. In general, the cities which most support equity are those with a large proportion of high-density housing, in the form of terraces and flats, and a large quantity of locally provided services and facilities, but at a more detailed level the forms of compactness most beneficial for individual aspects of social equity vary.

It should be noted that the cities used in the empirical investigation have evolved through periods of both explicit and implicit spatial segregation (of use, social class and housing type). In addition, since the 1920s, this has been coupled with policies, market opportunities and practice based on decentralisation: for example, peripheral development of private and social housing took place in the inter-war period. Therefore, until recently, these examples of relative compactness are unmarked by a positive intention to 'compact' or intensify. This is likely to affect the nature of the findings: the influence of compactness may have been more marked had it been possible to identify examples of more consciously compacted cities.

The importance of the findings lies not only in their contribution to the academic debate but ultimately in their implications for compact city policies, already in place in many countries. An improved understanding of the concept may allow the promotion of greater justice in its implementation. The research provides evidence to support the view that the compact city *may* support equity, but only if it is implemented in such a way that maximises the benefits and ameliorates the potential problems. Conflicts arise in attempting to identify future directions for policy, as forms of compactness that appear to be positive for some effects are negative for others. These contradictions need to be resolved if social equity is to be facilitated.

Note

For full details of the study, see *The Compact City: Just or Just Compact?* (Burton, 1997).

Katie Williams
Does Intensifying Cities Make them More Sustainable?

Introduction

The arguments relating compact urban form and sustainability are well rehearsed (Jenks *et al.*, 1996; CEC 1990; Breheny, 1992). The compact city is said to be beneficial for environmental, social and economic sustainability. Consequently, in the UK, urban intensification (see note 1) as a means of achieving higher densities, is now advocated in numerous land use planning policy and guidance documents (Williams, 1999). For example, there is now a national target for brownfield development, with 60% of all new development destined for re-used land in urban areas (DETR, 1998). Transport and housing policy guidance also strongly advocate intensifying development (DoE and DoT, 1994; DoE, 1992a), and new draft planning policy guidance on housing (DETR, 1999) suggests minimum housing densities should be set in urban areas. However, many of the arguments underpinning these policies are derived from assertion and theory (Jenks, this volume; Williams, 1998). Very little monitoring, if any, has been done of places which have been through a process of intensification to observe its effects.

The intention of the research presented in this chapter was to determine the impacts of intensification over a ten-year period in three London boroughs to assess whether compact city policies are meeting their objectives. This chapter presents the results of the parts of the research which:

- identified the objectives of national, regional and local intensification policies and compared these with what had happened 'on the ground' in Harrow, Camden and Bromley;
- identified the potential side-effects of these policies and traced evidence of them; and
- evaluated policy performance, based on these analyses.

Methodology

In order to facilitate the study, use was made of an Adapted Balance Sheet (ABS) devised for the then DoE to evaluate land use planning policy (DoE, 1992b). The ABS is a structure through which policy objectives and outcomes can be traced over time. It provides a framework through which to catalogue the interrelated aims, outcomes and effects of planning policies (Fig. 1). It does not provide any means of evaluating the data presented within it: this is the responsibility of the researcher. However, by setting out the data in a structured way, the evaluation process is open to reinterpretation.

The aim of the ABS is to set out information about planning's objectives and achievements. This is done by splitting the balance sheet into two sections: performance monitoring (columns 1–6 of the ABS) and strategic evaluation (columns 7 and 8).

Performance monitoring establishes the performance of planning against objectives, as set out in policies (column 1). This requires first collecting information on planning decisions (from planning inputs, such as local plans and national guidance, identified in columns 2 and 3). In the research, all planning decisions constituting intensification between 1987 and 1997 in the case study areas were analysed: these were the intermediate inputs (column 4). Then, the trends or patterns these decisions formed 'on the ground' were recorded in terms of, for example, development on derelict and vacant land, in the green belt or on urban open space (intermediate outputs, column 5). However, it was important that, along with a measurement of the intended outcomes of policies, there was an exploration of unintended consequences. The range of possible impacts was identified through a literature review. For each impact category, a number of 'indicators' were devised and qualitative and quantitative data was used to assess these (impacts, column 6).

The final stage of the ABS was the strategic evaluation. This used all the information gathered to allow a systematic account of policy effectiveness. It took place at two levels. First, there was a relatively simple assessment of whether the intensification policies' objectives had been achieved. A method was used which set out the objectives of policies and offered a rating of high medium or low achievement (column 7). This rating was based on whether the objective had been met, and what its impacts had been. Then, based upon this assessment, the achievements were considered across the scales of planning (column 8).

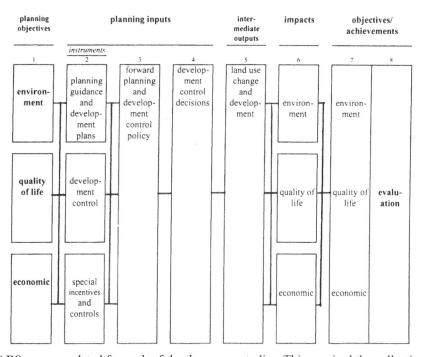

Fig. 1. The Adapted Balance Sheet.
Source: Williams, 1998, adapted from DoE, 1992b.

An ABS was completed for each of the three case studies. This required the collection of a huge amount of data from various sources (see note 2). It is beyond the scope of this chapter to present all the data, therefore it concentrates on the first and final stages of the ABS (columns 1 and 8). It presents the findings of the research which identified intensification policies, their objectives and potential impacts, and the final evaluation. In presenting these two stages, data is drawn in from the rest of the ABS (columns 2–7) and referred to in the text.

Throughout the ABS, policies are categorised (horizontally) under the three main interests in land use planning: *the environment, quality of life and economic.* Land use policies advocate intensification for reasons related to each of these interest categories. Therefore, the findings from the case studies are presented according to these groupings. Before the findings are discussed, a brief description of the case study areas and their policy approaches to urban intensification is given.

The case study boroughs

Harrow, Bromley and Camden (Fig. 2) were seen as appropriate case study areas for different reasons. Harrow experienced development pressures typical of an outer London borough throughout the 1980s and early 1990s. In particular, it saw a rapid increase in backland development, infill and conversions in its suburbs (Fig. 3), and continued pressure on its centre. Harrow had specifically addressed the problem of residential intensification in its local plans. Throughout the 1980s, continued pressure from residents forced the local authority to consider action against intensification in some areas but to promote it in others. Local opinions were well documented, as were the local authority's actions; hence this information was useful in tracing opinions back over time.

Fig. 2. Case study locations.
Source: Williams, 1999.

Camden is an inner London borough, and is markedly different in character from Harrow. It is sharply divided between some very affluent areas such as Hampstead and Bloomsbury, and neighbourhoods characterised by high proportions of social housing, high unemployment and overcrowding. Over the past decade it has witnessed intensification of built form and, significantly, large increases in both the numbers of people working in the borough, and visiting it as tourists (Fig. 4). The LPA's approach to urban intensification has been comprehensive, attempting to implement most of the policies set out in national guidance. In particular, it has tried to raise residential densities and reduce the need to travel by car.

Bromley is an outer London borough, but its circumstances are quite different from those in Harrow. It experienced intensification over the last decade which took the form, mainly, of redevelopment of existing buildings at higher densities (Fig. 5), conversions and some new build. However, in policy terms, it had a protectionist stance, especially in relation to open and amenity land. The local development plans were environmentally driven, and change was strongly resisted. Planners, more recently, have addressed the relationship between intensification and sustainability and are attempting to incorporate 'radical' policies into the revision of Bromley's Unitary Development Plan (UDP). The borough offered an interesting insight into intensification policy development and implementation in a preservationist policy environment.

Fig. 3. Intensification in the residential suburbs of Harrow – backland development.

Fig. 4. Activity intensification in Camden – more people living and working in the borough and visiting as tourists.

Fig. 5. Redevelopment at higher densities in Bromley.

Source: Williams, 1999.

The research findings

The environmental rationale for urban intensification in national policies

Environmental objectives drive intensification policies in the UK. Three key objectives are stated throughout planning policy. Table 1 summarises these objectives and shows from which national policy statements each emanates. It also shows the indicators used to investigate the achievement of each in the case studies.

Environmental objectives of urban intensification policies	Sources	Sources of data/information
To reduce greenhouse gas emissions by reducing the number and length of trips by modes of transport which are harmful to the environment, primarily the private car, and increasing trips made by other modes – walking, cycling and public transport	*Sustainable Development: the UK Strategy* (HM Govt, 1994); *Our Future Homes* (HM Govt, 1995); *PPG4: Industrial and Commercial Development and Small Firms* (DoE, 1994); *PPG6: Town Centres and Retail Developments* (DoE, revised, 1993a; revised, 1996); *PPG12: Local Plans* (DoE, 1988a); *PPG12: Development Plans and Regional Planning Guidance* (DoE, 1992a); *PPG13: Transport* (DoE and DoT, 1994)	Planning decisions for Harrow, Camden and Bromley, 1987–1997 (DETR); density of persons living within 800m of a major public transport interchange; no. of bus priority schemes; home-based shopping trips by mode; journey-to-work trips with origin and destination (LPAC, 1995); travel to work and net commuting by borough (OPCS, 1993, 1995); air quality data and planning permissions data (LPAs); residents surveys (e.g. DETR, forthcoming; LBC, 1994)
To use land in the most sustainable way by protecting the countryside, valuable rural land and green belt and concentrating development in urban areas, especially on derelict, vacant and contaminated land	*This Common Inheritance* (HM Govt, 1990); *Our Future Homes* (HM Govt, 1995); *Sustainable Development: the UK Strategy* (HM Govt, 1994) *PPG2: Green Belts* (DoE, 1988b; revised, 1995); *PPG3: Housing* (DoE, revised, 1992a); *PPG12: Local Plans* (DoE, 1988a); *PPG12: Development Plans and Regional Planning Guidance* (DoE, 1992c)	Planning decisions for Harrow, Camden and Bromley, 1987–1997 (DETR); area of green chains; areas of protected open space; areas of green belt and metropolitan open land accessible for public recreation; losses, gains and changes in quality of nature conservation sites; total area of boroughs that fits the DoE's definition of derelict land (LPAC, 1995); public open space in London (Llewelyn-Davies, 1992); *ad hoc* consultancy reports (e.g. Wootten Jeffreys Consultants, 1989)
To reduce energy consumption by providing building densities capable of supporting district heating and combined heat and power systems	*Sustainable Development: the UK Strategy* (HM Govt, 1994)	Local authority community heating schemes in London; combined heat and power and district heating generation in London (LPAC, 1995); planner interviews

Table 1. Environmental objectives of urban intensification policies, their sources and indicators of achievement.

First is the aim of reducing greenhouse gases and emissions by reducing the need to travel by energy-rich modes, principally the car. This is the main objective of *Planning Policy Guidance*

13: Transport (DoE and DoT, 1994), and is repeated in many other policies. The related aim of reducing traffic congestion to improve the quality of life in town and city centres is also increasingly significant. Policies to achieve this objective encourage development in locations which minimise the length and number of trips, and in locations which can be served by more energy-efficient modes of transport than the car.

Second is the objective of using land in the most sustainable way. This means developing urban brown land, protecting the countryside and keeping pressure off areas of environmental value. Policies suggest encouraging development in urban areas, especially on derelict or vacant land, but also restricting development elsewhere.

The third aim is to facilitate energy efficient technologies, such as combined heat and power (CHP) and district heating systems, through the provision of higher density developments. The aim is to ensure that in appropriate places, such as near transport nodes, and in inner urban areas, development is of a density sufficient to make such schemes viable. Policy guidance suggests that higher densities are preferable in enabling such technical advances.

The environmental consequences of urban intensification
Does urban intensification reduce the need to travel?
In the case studies, the relationship between intensification and travel behaviour was explored by comparing land use data and information on travel patterns. The data does not enable direct correlations, but illustrates general trends. Each of the case studies provided a different perspective on the relationship between intensification and travel patterns.

Camden had followed almost all the planning requirements set out in national policy to reduce trip-generation. It is a densely populated borough with a high concentration of mixed uses, which means that accessibility to many facilities and services is good for those who live and work in the borough (90% of the population live within 400m of a food shop). It also has low levels of car ownership (only 43% of households have access to a car), and is well-served by public transport. Furthermore, the LPA has successfully implemented higher density developments near transport nodes, and has approved car-free housing schemes. Given these circumstances, Camden should, according to national policy, be achieving benefits in terms of trip-reduction.

Nevertheless, traffic volumes on almost all routes in the borough have increased over the study period and traffic was reported by residents in two separate surveys as the worst element of life in Camden (LBC, 1994; DETR, forthcoming). Significantly, the borough's traffic problems are related to through traffic and commuters coming into the borough for work: more people work in Camden than live there. Conversely, 51.8% of those who live in the borough work elsewhere (OPCS, 1993). This said, roughly the same number of people use their car as use the bus for their daily work trip (170,000 each), which compares favourably with, for example, Harrow, where 160,000 work trips are made daily by car and only 15,000 by bus.

These findings support arguments that the relationship between urban form and travel patterns implied in policy may be rather simplistic (Banister, 1994; Breheny, 1995; Handy, 1992). In terms of work-related travel, Camden is part of London-wide and regional employment markets. Thus, whilst trips may be reduced for some locally provided jobs, there is unlikely to be any discernible change for more specialised employment. The same applies to leisure and shopping trips: they may be reduced for local needs, such as food shopping, but there is no guarantee that people will not travel further for different shopping experiences and leisure pursuits. Furthermore, the amount of traffic passing through the borough is likely to be unaffected by any changes in accessibility within it. And, while traffic remains at the current high levels, the environment for pedestrians and cyclists is so poor that the modal shift predicted in national policy has not occurred.

Both Bromley and Harrow are more car-dependent than Camden. Travel to work and shopping and other leisure journeys share a similar pattern. In Bromley 105,000 journeys per day are made by car for shopping, compared with only 19,000 by bus (LPAC, 1995). What is more, car use has increased over the study period, even though Bromley has been relatively successful in locating new trip-generating development, such as retail and offices, in central areas. Similarly, in all three case study areas, public transport use for commuting has decreased, contrary to the aims of intensification policies.

Most of the planners and councillors interviewed believed that improving the capital's traffic problems was a long-term aim, and agreed with writers such as Breheny (1995) in accepting that urban intensification is just one component of the solution. Major problems were identified in overcoming car culture and educating people about the strategic impacts of car use (see Nicholas, 1994). The consensus was that altering existing travel patterns is extremely difficult, but at least by refusing trip-generating developments in peripheral locations, and concentrating new development in existing centres, the infrastructure is in place for other trip-reducing policies to have an effect in the future.

Does urban intensification represent the most sustainable use of land?

Several components of the sustainable use of land were identified in policy. The first related to using urban land so that rural and agricultural land would be protected. As Camden is an inner-London borough, this objective does not apply, but Bromley and Harrow are bordered by the green belt. Both boroughs were successful in protecting this open land: only a handful of small-scale developments had been permitted. Planning policies suggest that such rigorous protection of the green belt will lever development towards brown field sites, especially those which are derelict or contaminated.

All three boroughs implemented this policy successfully. In Harrow only 0.1 ha. is classified as derelict and in Bromley no land is classified in this way. Camden also managed this policy well (only 9 ha. of derelict land), but it still has some underused land awaiting development. How much of this success is attributable to planning policies is difficult to determine, because the boroughs all have strong land markets. This said, policies to restrict peripheral development were seen as directing investment towards less desirable urban land, and in Camden and Harrow intensification policies, coupled with some financial support, made derelict land viable (planner interviews).

In central policies there were warnings that, by developing within existing urban areas, urban open space and habitats could be lost. However, evidence from the case studies shows that the amount of officially demarcated public open space increased over the study period. Between 1971 and 1991 the amount of official open space had risen by 30% in Camden, 22% in Bromley and 6% in Harrow. Although this data must be treated with care – the figures may disguise losses of informal open space (Bell, 1995) – it does suggest that because locally valued land was defined in local plans, green chains, metropolitan open land, green belt and public open space have been well protected.

Does urban intensification facilitate energy efficient technologies?

There was some evidence from the case studies that higher density developments, such as those in Camden, had facilitated the use of combined heat and power schemes. Camden achieved some high density new developments over the study period and in some of these the use of CHP was facilitated. Energy efficiency in many forms had been a policy priority in Camden, especially in the UDP (LBC, 1992). But the LPA's approach is to make the most of the existing built form and introduce energy-efficient design into new buildings, rather than manipulate built form to fit new technologies. Overall, Camden has 142 community heating schemes, covering 13,141 dwellings. Harrow and Bromley, however, did not make the link between higher densities and energy-efficient technologies in their UDPs, although this may be an issue which is considered in UDP reviews. Perhaps as a consequence they have a far lower incidence of community heating schemes: Bromley has only seven and Harrow five. Further research is needed to determine the specific influence of density on the take-up of energy-efficient technologies, but these findings seem to support the policy drive for higher densities as a prerequisite to take up (see note 3).

The wider environmental impacts
The literature review undertaken as part of the research identified several potential side-effects of intensification (Table 2). Evidence of these is presented below.

Potential environmental impacts	Examples of sources	Sources of data/information
Loss of greenery in towns, including trees, shrubs and greenery in private gardens	Breheny (1992); Bell (1995); Phoenix Group (1989)	Number and density of trees (LPAC, 1995); *Environmental Assessment of the Residential Areas of Harrow* (Wootten Jeffreys Consultants, 1989); local press cuttings; planner and councillor interviews
Upgrading of the local built and natural environment brought about by new buildings and high quality design	CEC (1990); Rogers (1995)	Resident surveys (e.g. DETR forthcoming; LBC, 1994); planner and councillor interviews
Increased environmental wear and tear – e.g. impacts on historic building fabric, production of litter and dirt	Phoenix Group (1989)	Resident surveys (e.g. of main environmental problems in Camden) (e.g. DETR forthcoming; LBC, 1994); planner and councillor interviews, local press cuttings

Table 2. The potential wider environmental impacts of urban intensification.

Three key environmental impacts were identified in the literature review. First was the issue of *loss of greenery*. The argument is that increasing development and densities in urban areas squeezes out space for greenery (Breheny, 1992). The research found that in Harrow, although the green areas with statutory protection had been well preserved, there had been significant losses of greenery, especially in suburbs where backland and infill development had meant the loss of trees and shrubs in gardens and public spaces. This deterioration was curtailed by the introduction of stronger policies protecting the leafy character of the neighbourhoods, and policies to ensure that new developments have a strong element of landscaping and greenery (see Wootten Jeffreys Consultants, 1989). Camden also managed to protect its trees and greenery. The borough is densely built-up, and new developments have tended to be at higher than average densities. Nevertheless, Camden still has only slightly fewer trees per hectare (35.26) than Harrow (35.8), and a third more than Bromley – the 'clean and green' borough (23.74). These figures are, of course, related to the amount of park land in the borough. Nevertheless, the conclusion is that intensification can, if not carefully managed, lead to losses of greenery, but if landscaping and planting are given priority by developers and planners from the outset of proposed developments, and policies are prescriptive about standards, then losses are not inevitable.

There was also the contention that *intensification could have an upgrading effect on the built environment and contribute to urban regeneration* (Rogers, 1995). Conversely, there are some who have commented that new development has been on such a large scale, or of such a poor quality and design, that it has had the opposite effect of disfiguring cities (Evans, 1990; Phoenix Group, 1989; see Hubbard, 1994). The research found that the effects were dependent on location, type and quality of development. A generalisation from the case studies is that development in mixed-use town centres was usually perceived to have a positive effect, especially in those areas which had subsequently implemented landscaping and urban design improvements. However, in the residential suburbs, infill developments were often seen as being of a poor quality and having a detrimental effect on the environment. Clearly, there were exceptions to this and the importance of defining the type of intensification acceptable to local residents and users of a given locality was the key to determining whether the effect of intensification was seen as positive (Williams *et al.*, 1999).

Finally, there was the contention that intensification would lead to *increased environmental wear and tear.* Councillors and residents reported complaints of littered and cluttered streets and roads which were in poor states of repair (councillor interviews; DETR forthcoming,). The problem was at its worst in Camden, where the local authority found it difficult to keep pace with maintenance and cleaning. This problem was being addressed in all three boroughs, and it was felt that better management and more resources were the solutions.

Conclusions on environmental policies

Urban intensification policies with environmental aims have had varying success. First, the case studies support the idea that intensification is a sustainable use of land. The use of brownfield sites, especially where they were contaminated, in preference to greenfield, was clearly beneficial, and intensification policies had helped divert development away from the urban fringe. Ecologically and socially valued urban open space had also been protected, although some losses of informal open space and habitats were apparent. Second, high densities had facilitated the use of fuel-efficient technologies: Camden's CHP schemes are examples of how such technologies can be applied.

Environmentally, the major failure of intensification policies appears to be their inability to reduce travel demand by energy-rich modes of transport, and therefore reduce greenhouse gases. The reasons for this policy failure had been foreseen by policy makers. The rate of change in built form is exceptionally slow, so it is difficult to make significant changes in the short term, especially with the development patterns inherited from past decades. Similarly, the growth in car ownership and diffuse life patterns are also trends which are difficult to influence through land use planning alone.

Overall, there are significant contributions to be made to environmental sustainability through intensification. However, there is also a danger that expectations of what it can achieve in influencing travel patterns are too high. It is likely that processes outside the land use planning system – such as more punitive measures, education and cultural changes – will be required to maximise the potential that compact urban forms can offer.

The quality of life rationale for urban intensification in national policies

Quality of life objectives surrounding urban intensification policies also focus on three related issues (Table 3). The first is the ability of urban areas to provide land to meet housing needs in the most sustainable way. One of planning's primary objectives is to ensure that there is a ready supply of land for housing. Building more homes in urban areas is argued to contribute to social sustainability through regeneration.

Quality of life objectives of urban intensification policies	Sources	Sources of data/information
To provide land in urban areas for housing, so as to meet housing needs in the most sustainable way and improve quality of life	*Our Future Homes* (HM Govt, 1995); *Sustainable Development: the UK Strategy* (HM Govt, 1994); *PPG3: Housing* (DoE, revised, 1992a)	Planning decisions for Harrow, Camden and Bromley, 1987–1997 (DETR); population mid-year estimates and projections; stock of dwellings 1994 (OPCS, 1995); population trends; Empty residential property (OPCS, 1993); number of dwellings in town centres; housing provision 1992–2006 (LPAC, 1995); London's housing capacity: large sites, including windfalls (LPAC, 1994)
To upgrade and improve towns and cities, and therefore foster civic pride, local identity, community spirit and safety	*Our Future Homes* (HM Govt, 1995); *Household Growth: Where Shall We Live?* (HM Govt, 1996); *PPG6: Town Centres and Retail Developments* (DoE, revised 1993a; revised, 1996)	Main problems in Camden (LBC, 1994); top issues improved or harmed by intensification 1987–1997 (DETR, forthcoming); planner and councillor interviews
To improve social equity by making services and facilities more accessible to all urban residents.	*PPG6: Town Centres and Retail Developments* (DoE, revised 1993a; revised, 1996) *PPG12: Local Plans*, (1988); *PPG12: Development Plans and Regional Planning Guidance* (DoE, 1992c)	Planning decisions for Harrow, Camden and Bromley, 1987–1997 (DETR); top issues improved or harmed by intensification 1987–1997 (DETR, forthcoming); percentage of population living within 400m of basic services (LPAC, 1995); availability of recreational and sporting facilities 1992 (OPCS, 1995); planner and councillor interviews

Table 3. Quality of life objectives of urban intensification policies, their sources and indicators of achievement.

The second objective relates to the ability of urban intensification to upgrade and improve towns and cities, and therefore foster civic pride, local identity, community spirit and safety. This goal is achieved by maintaining or increasing population densities which support local services and facilities. The consequent increases in activity are also claimed to reinforce the attractiveness and safety of urban areas, especially town centres, night and day.

The third set of objectives relate to improving social equity. These concentrate on the accessibility of services and facilities, and aim to make essential amenities accessible to all urban residents, regardless of their income, age or gender. The reasoning is that high population densities reach the thresholds which enable a mix of uses in the city to be supported locally. Therefore local services and facilities can be maintained within a short distance of residential areas.

The consequences for quality of life of urban intensification
Does providing more homes in urban areas lead to a better quality of life?
Measurements of quality of life are notoriously contentious (Findlay *et al.*, 1988), and when combined with the issue of density, become even more politically sensitive (Troy, 1996). The task here is to look for evidence of how urban intensification has affected the quality of life of urban residents, to see whether it makes urban living better or worse for those who live in

towns and cities.

In the case studies, most councillors and planners believed that intensification in existing centres had a positive effect on quality of life. People who live in the suburbs enjoy the accessibility of a variety of new facilities and the benefits of clustering trip-ends, but do not suffer bad neighbour effects. Those who live in the centres seem to appreciate increases in facilities and shops and environmental upgrading. Nevertheless, there are exceptions to this general finding. For example, when development in centres was judged to be unattractive, or there was additional noise and traffic, then intensification was seen to have had a negative effect on quality of life (DETR, forthcoming; LBC, 1994).

Conversely, intensification in suburban areas was consistently associated with a reduction in quality of life, whether due to perceptions of 'town cramming', a dislike of new people in the area, loss of character or more traffic (Wootten Jeffreys Consultants, 1989; DETR forthcoming). In Harrow, the effect of suburban intensification on quality of life was an important local political issue in the late 1980s and, in Bromley too, almost any new development in the suburbs was defended by well-organised networks of resident groups complaining of loss of amenity, overlooking, loss of light and so on. But again, there were exceptions. When redevelopment eradicated a local eyesore or unpopular use, this was seen as positive by local residents.

The conclusion from these findings is that opinions on intensification and quality of life are a reflection of how intensification changes the assets which people value in their neighbourhood. If they value vibrancy and liveliness, and intensification appears to add to them, then they will see it as positive. Conversely, if people value the quiet character of residential neighbourhoods, and intensification changes it, then residents will not be in favour. This finding sounds simple enough, but the difficulty of characterising public opinion in any given place is complicated by the diversity of perceptions in it (Healey, 1997). Not all people in a given space have the same values (for example, there are variations between existing residents and those housed in new developments), and choosing whose opinions take priority is a political decision.

Does urban intensification improve a city's vibrancy and culture, and lead to
a sense of community, local identity and safety?

As with the findings about housing location and quality of life, the findings concerning vitality, culture and community vary between mixed-use centres and residential suburbs. The town centres, where retail and employment activity had been concentrated, offered more cultural and entertainment facilities at the end of the study period, and were used more intensively during the daytime and in the evenings. Planning applications and approvals for restaurants, bars and clubs in all three boroughs have increased over the study period. This is, the planners believe, partly due to intensification policies, but is also related to changes such as alterations in social behaviour, increasing affluence (for some sectors of the population), the commodification of leisure and adaptation to the needs of tourists (Troy, 1996).

However, in suburban or predominately residential areas, it appeared that urban intensification had a negative effect on the sense of community and local identity (planner and councillor interviews). Residents almost always wanted to retain the social profiles of their neighbourhoods, not diversify them. This usually meant they wanted more home-owning families, and not small households, sharers or single-person households. These findings of antipathy to suburban intensification are completely at odds with the favourable view of the social effects in central policies.

Acceptance of the causal relationship which equates higher densities with safety, or perceptions of safety, is common in intensification policies (HM Govt, 1995; DoE, 1996). The reasoning is that more people in public places means that there is better surveillance and, therefore, less crime, and less fear. However, again, public perceptions are often the opposite of this, with cities commonly associated with violence and danger (Crookston *et al.*, 1996; McLaren, 1992). The research findings on this issue were mixed. Fear of crime is still very high: it ranks third in polls of residents' worries in Camden at both the beginning and end of the study period (LBC, 1994), and actual crime rates are almost impossible to relate to changes in built form. Councillors argued that people felt safer in lower density suburbs where they knew their neighbours. There was little support for the argument that intensification in residential neighbourhoods improved surveillance, or reduced fear of crime. There was some agreement that town centres now felt safer during the day and at night. This was attributed to a number of causes, such as security cameras, improved policing and the concentration of new entertainment facilities in town centres, which meant that people were attracted to the central areas. Again, it is difficult to know how much of this change is due to intensification and how much is a result of the other security measures.

Does urban intensification improve accessibility to services and facilities?

The equity alluded to in intensification policies is concerned with access to services and facilities for all urban residents, in terms of both 'physical' access (proximity) and opportunity. The contention is that intensified areas provide more facilities locally, which are within the reach of those without access to a car.

Determining whether intensification policies have improved accessibility is problematic. Certainly, in terms of locating new retail and employment developments in central locations, or on sites well-served by public transport, the three boroughs all improved their performance (Harrow has 218,957 m² of retail in town centres and only 4,631 m² in out-of-town locations, Bromley has 201,5000 m² and 54,674 respectively). In Camden and Bromley, surveys of residents found that access to shops was seen as the element of quality of life which had improved most due to intensification, followed by access to facilities – with approximately 40% of residents believing this to be so (DETR, forthcoming). Furthermore, the fact that in Camden – the most densely populated of the three boroughs – accessibility to local services is so good (90% of the population live within 400 metres of a food shop, compared with only 60% in Harrow), does provide some evidence of this relationship.

Yet, the conclusions here are similar to those about the relationship between intensification and travel patterns, in that the assertion that centralisation or intensification will improve accessibility in absolute terms should be questioned. This is because, whilst intensification did contribute to accessibility to some facilities and services, for example to shops for everyday needs, it did not appear to contribute to improving accessibility to more specialised jobs or retail, cultural or leisure facilities.

The wider quality of life impacts

The literature review identified a number of impacts on quality of life (Table 4). First, there was the contention that *intensification leads to reductions in private space* (Stretton, 1996; Evans, 1988, 1990). The research provided some evidence of this trend. New houses were smaller than the average size of the existing stock in Bromley and Harrow, although there was also a trend for some very large new houses (four bedrooms and above). The most common size for new units was two bedrooms. Conversions and subdivisions also meant new units were smaller than previous dwellings. There was also a slightly worsening situation of overcrowding: in Camden 10.4% of the population live at a density of more than one person per room. However, overall, the trend for smaller units was seen to contribute to sustainability by making the best use of resources, meeting the needs of one- and two-person households and giving more people access to housing, because smaller units are usually more affordable (planner interviews).

Potential quality of life impacts of intensification policies	Examples of sources	Sources of data/information
A reduction in private space, smaller houses and smaller gardens, or no gardens	Evans (1988); Stretton (1996); Phoenix Group (1989)	Planning decisions for Harrow, Camden and Bromley, 1987–1997 (DETR, forthcoming); dwellings completed, by bed spaces (LPAs); overcrowding in London boroughs (OPCS, 1993); planner and councillor interviews
Impacts of traffic, such as air pollution, noise and a generally poor environment for cyclists and pedestrians would be improved	Knight (1996)	Noise nuisance complaints by type of nuisance (LPAC, 1995); resident surveys (e.g. DETR, forthcoming; LBC, 1994); planner and councillor interviews
Potential bad neighbour effects of high density or mixed-use developments e.g. noise, disturbance and litter	Davison (1995); Knight, (1996)	Noise nuisance complaints by type of nuisance (LPAC, 1995); resident surveys (e.g. DETR, forthcoming; LBC, 1994); planner and councillor interviews

Table 4. The potential wider quality of life impacts of urban intensification.

The second suggested impact was that in intensified areas, because of the reduced need to travel and switches to non-car modes of transport, the *impacts of traffic such as air pollution, noise and a generally poor environment for cyclists and pedestrians would be improved.* In the case studies, however, no evidence of this benefit was found. As noted above, the predicted link between intensification and reductions in traffic was not verified. In fact, traffic volumes, and therefore traffic impacts, increased in all three areas. Conditions were so bad that air quality, noise, parking problems and road safety were ranked as the main detriments to quality of life by residents in all three case study boroughs (DETR, forthcoming; LBC, 1994).

The final impact was an alleged relationship between mixed-use, higher density developments and *bad neighbour effects.* There is some evidence of this relationship in the case studies. In Camden, for example, there was a higher than average number of complaints about noise from commercial and entertainment sources. In Harrow and Bromley, there were increases in complaints about noise from domestic sources, and complaints about smells from light industrial developments and new food outlets. However, in all three boroughs, most complaints were about noise from domestic sources (approx. 500 per year in all three boroughs) (LPAC, 1995). Again, determining the extent to which the problem is due to intensification and the proportion which is attributable to anti-social behaviour is difficult. But there is no doubt that intensification, especially in mixed-use areas, did increase the incidence of conflicting externalities.

Conclusions on quality of life policies
It is crucial that intensification brings about improvements to the quality of life or cities will be unsustainable, because those who can move away will do so (Smyth, 1996). This research has shown that in certain circumstances intensification can contribute to improving quality of

life. Benefits were identified in terms of better access to facilities and services, more shops, modernised urban centres, improved safety and increased liveliness. However, in other instances it was associated with overcrowding, reductions in amenity, increased air pollution and bad neighbour effects.

In the light of these findings, it is not possible to give a general conclusion on whether urban intensification improves quality of life, except to say that its outcome is dependent on the interaction of a number of intervening variables (Jenks, this volume). The type and magnitude of intensification are important, but different types and amounts affect quality of life differently, depending on how people define 'quality' in their lives. Perceptions of the impacts of intensification are also affected by how the side-effects or impacts of intensification are managed. The findings are bound up with issues of locality and personal preferences. The same degree and type of intensification can be seen as contributing to, or detracting from, quality of life in different areas, depending on their location and residents' and users' expectations.

The economic rationale for urban intensification in national policies

The economic reasoning behind intensification policies in the UK focuses on the leverage achieved by improving urban areas to attract businesses and new residents, and thus to aid urban regeneration (Table 5). The objectives are to make town and city centres more attractive places to live so that urban populations will be restored and use their spending power to support local businesses. The improved vitality and regeneration should, it is claimed, make urban areas more attractive to prospective employers looking for desirable locations for their businesses, and consequently an upward spiral of economic benefits should accrue. To achieve these objectives, national policies advocate the provision of land in urban areas for economically beneficial uses, and the restriction of development in other areas. This type of policy includes the sequential test for retailing (DoE, 1996). There are also policies aimed at improving local economic viability by achieving a mix of uses and diversity in urban areas.

The economic consequences of urban intensification

Does urban intensification contribute to vital and viable local economies?
The case studies suggest that intensification can bring about some economic benefits to urban centres. Since local policies advocated development in existing centres, and restricted development elsewhere, most of the major centres in the case study boroughs witnessed improved economic performance. Those that have not were judged to have been irreparably harmed by out-of-town retail developments or food superstores in nearby centres (planner and councillor interviews). Planners and councillors in the case studies felt that accommodating rising household numbers had meant that consumer services had been supported and were, therefore, viable. Rising business registration rates, employment levels and commercial occupancy rates could also be seen as an indication of this trend.

The success of local policies was obviously aided by national economic trends, but consolidation policies were also seen as important because they gave developers some certainty. This gave confidence in existing centres and encouraged inward investment. There are a host of intervening variables besides urban intensification which relate to an area's economic viability, but it appears that maintaining or increasing densities, and encouraging residential uses in mixed-use areas, do play a part in supporting and generating new local services.

Does intensification improve access to employment?

The case studies provided complex data on this relationship. In Harrow, more economically active residents now work in the borough than at the beginning of the study period. The UDP states that this is proof that accessibility to jobs has increased, and that consolidation policies are working (LBH, 1994). However, as more people also travel into the borough to work, more jobs have also been provided for those living farther away. Furthermore, a high proportion of Harrow's residents, especially skilled workers with specialised jobs, still work outside the borough. Similarly, in Camden, more jobs are available in the borough now than at the start of the study period, but many of the new jobs are in specialised fields such as medicine, media and marketing, whereas the unemployed in Camden are mainly looking for unskilled or semi-skilled work. This said, there have been increases in the numbers of jobs in the retail and hotel and catering sectors which have provided jobs for local people. In Bromley too, access to retail and office employment in existing centres has improved, but more than half of the borough's economically active residents still work outside the borough.

Overall, there appears to be some evidence that access to certain types of employment is improved by intensification. Accessibility to employment is most improved in the consumer service sectors, which benefit directly from intensification. Thus, the results show that access to office and retail employment improved, first, because there are more jobs in these sectors and, second, because physical accessibility was improved due to the proximity and availability of public transport services. For other types of employment, especially more specialised occupations, urban intensification does not appear to have a significant effect. People still commute long distances to enjoy the combination of home and work environment which they choose, or can afford.

Economic objectives of urban intensification policies	Sources	Sources of data/information
To improve vitality and viability of centres and contribute to regeneration – higher population densities provide a critical mass to support businesses, and planning policies help reduce competition from out-of-town developments	*This Common Inheritance: Britain's Environmental Strategy* (HM Govt, 1990); *PPG2: Green Belts* (DoE, revised 1995, 1988b); *PPG3: Housing* (DoE, revised, 1992a); *PPG4: Industrial and Commercial Development and Small Firms* (DoE, 1988c, 1994); *PPG6: Town Centres and Retail Developments* (DoE, revised, 1993a; revised, 1996)	Population trends in London boroughs; number and proportion of economically active population working within borough of residence; industry of employment (OPCS, 1993); gross retail floorspace (m²) in town centres and out-of-town centres; vacancy rates for industrial, retail and office premises (LPAC, 1995); shopping centres: national rankings (Hillier Parker, 1996); economically active (The Stationery Office, 1997); VAT registered businesses (The Business Statistics Office of the CSO, 1995)
Improved access to employment for urban residents because homes are located near workplaces	*PPG3: Housing* (DoE, revised, 1992a); *PPG6: Town Centres and Retail Developments* (DoE, revised, 1993a; revised, 1996)	Number and proportion of economically active population working within borough of residence; industry of employment (OPCS, 1993); economically active (The Stationery Office, 1997); VAT registered businesses, London boroughs (The Business Statistics Office of the CSO, 1995)

Table 5. Economic objectives of urban intensification policies, their sources and indicators of achievement.

43

The wider economic impacts

The main impact to be identified from literature was the *potential benefit to LPAs in terms of cheaper infrastructure provision* (Table 6). In other parts of the world (e.g. Australia) the arguments that infrastructure is cheaper to provide in compact settlements because less physical infrastructure (roads, street lighting etc.) is needed per household than in lower density suburbs has driven consolidation policies (Dunstone and Smith, 1994). However, in the UK it appears that LPAs are not concerned with variations in infrastructure costs between different development locations and forms (DoE, 1993b). The research found that the relative costs of infrastructure provision for different locational options were not considered by LPAs mainly because other issues were more important in determining a planning decision. Also, planners expected developers to pay for the majority of infrastructure in major new developments through planning gain, so cost was not a major deciding factor.

Table 6. The potential wider economic impacts of urban intensification.

Potential economic impacts of intensification policies	Examples of sources	Source of data/information
Benefits to LPAs in terms of cheaper infrastructure provision	DoE (1993b); Dunstone and Smith (1994)	Planner interviews

Conclusions on economic policies

Overall, the main aim of improving economic viability and vitality in centres appears to have had some success. Since major investments were made in these central areas, the potential to increase jobs by attracting new businesses and supporting consumer services has also been realised. What is more, these benefits have been achieved largely simultaneously with benefits to quality of life and to the environment (with the notable exception of increased traffic nuisance).

Determining the extent to which these benefits are a direct result of urban intensification, and how much they are the result of broader economic trends, is almost impossible (see Petrakos, 1992). Nevertheless, by providing a positive framework for investment in urban centres, and restricting competition from out-of-town locations, planning polices at least are harnessing economic benefits for urban areas as a whole, rather than allowing investment to disperse. This said, the fact that any broader economic consequences of intensification (such as infrastructure costs) are not considered in policy is a major drawback to achieving sustainability, as economic consequences affect the feasibility of intensification. Unless the full range of private and public economic costs and benefits of different development scenarios are explored, then the external costs of intensification may be under- or over-estimated.

Conclusions

The first and most obvious point to make in drawing overall conclusions is that the variety of components of intensification policies, and different aims, means that deriving conclusions is difficult. Some aspects of intensification, in some places, have contributed to sustainability, whilst others clearly have not. Yet there are some findings which are common to all three boroughs.

First, intensification did mean that land was managed in a sustainable way. In all three boroughs, policies had been influential in almost eradicating derelict land, and in steering development to less desirable brownfield sites. It also contributed to improved economic conditions in local centres. It helped make them more viable, lively and attractive and contributed to improving the quality of life for those visiting and living nearby. Higher densities also facilitated the introduction of sustainable technologies.

However, there were also common disbenefits. Reductions in traffic had not happened, and this was a serious problem in all three boroughs. It not only meant that one of the main environmental objectives was not met, but also that some quality of life policies were ineffective; there were no consequent improvements in air quality or reductions in noise. Intensification was also related strongly to environmental wear and tear and other localised environmental problems. In residential areas, there were also hostile reactions from existing residents keen to preserve the status quo of their neighbourhoods. In such places almost any development was seen, by definition, as unwanted.

Intensification did make some contributions to sustainability in certain circumstances; identifying these circumstances and relating them to policy content can best be achieved by undertaking a very detailed analysis of how certain types of intensification alter the existing assets of a given locality. This research found some crude generalisations relating types of intensification to central areas and suburbs, but even here no definitive conclusions could be drawn – there were exceptions which were dependent on how people valued their neighbourhoods. The side-effects of intensification policies also need to be given more attention: they may outweigh the benefits of policies in terms of sustainability, or it may be possible to manage them for beneficial results. Either way, to ignore them will jeopardise the future of intensified areas. Indications are that far more attention will have to be paid to identifying the exact implications for sustainability of different types and amounts of intensification in particular localities.

Overall, it seems that intensification policies were most successful where their objectives were related directly to land use. Planning performed well in meeting policy objectives concerned purely with the location of development. However, it fared less well generally (although it still had some success) when policies tried to achieve broader economic, social and environmental aims (see Reade, 1982). This is mainly because the policy outcomes are often reliant on a range of intervening variables, which are not within the control of the planning system. But it does seem that by achieving more intensive development, the planning system can be seen to have promoted a sustainable use of land. For most other aims it appears that it can provide urban forms which could potentially be used to facilitate sustainability objectives – but the resulting urban forms cannot be said to be sustainable *per se*. A term common in the sustainability debate refers to measures which are 'necessary but not sufficient' (Church, 1995). It seems that intensification policies could, in the main, be characterised in this way.

Notes
1. See Jenks, this volume, for the definition of intensification used in research for the DETR (forthcoming) and in this research.
2. Working with published data on the broad range of issues required for this research presented problems in terms of availability, timing and geographical spread. As the ABS allows an objective use of data, judgements had to be made in the evaluation about the strength of conclusions which could be drawn from the various data sets used. Qualitative data from interviews with planners and councillors supplemented the hard data.
3. See Rydin (1992) for optimum densities for CHP and district heating schemes.

Peter Newton

Urban Form and Environmental Performance

In 1968, Mumford stated that 'Nobody can be satisfied with the form of the city today' (p.108). Such statements, through to the contemporary, widening debate in the US (Gordon and Richardson, 1997), UK (Jenks *et al.*, 1996), and the Netherlands (Dieleman, 1997) concerning what constitutes desirable urban form call for more objective assessments of the performance of cities in relation to the organisation of land uses (different mixes and densities) and transport systems (modes and ownership). These assessments can be pursued via studies which draw upon empirical evidence from contrasting cities (or sections of cities), or from studies which model alternative land use/transport configurations for evidence of variability in performance or outcome.

This paper utilises the integrated land-use-transport-environment model, TOPAZ-2000 (Marquez and Smith, 1997; Trinidad and Marquez, 1998), to explore the nexus between urban form and key environmental performance indicators. These indicators are: transport energy consumption, pollutant emissions (CO, NO_x, SO_2, VOCs), air quality (ozone and particles) and greenhouse gas emissions. Several archetypal urban forms are examined in the context of their relative performance in accommodating population and employment growth and alternative types of transport infrastructure development in Melbourne, Australia, to the year 2011. The conclusion drawn from this study (see endnote) is that urban form does matter to the future environmental sustainability of large cities.

Alternative urban forms

What alternatives are there for the 'shape' or structure of our cities? Pressman (1985) and Minnery (1992), among others, have identified several archetypal urban geometries, described briefly as follows:

- *Dispersed city* – continued low-density suburban development of population, housing and jobs; infrastructure investment dominated by road transport; this, for the most part, is 'business-as-usual' in the context of contemporary Australian metropolitan development, despite recent attempts at urban consolidation (Troy, 1996; O'Connor, 1997).
- *Compact city* – increased population and density of an inner group of suburbs, with associated investment in public transport.
- *Edge city* – increased population, housing densities and employment at selected nodes within the city; increased investment in orbital freeways linking the edge cities.
- *Corridor city* – a focus of growth along linear corridors emanating from the central business district (CBD), supported by upgraded public transport infrastructure.
- *Fringe city* – additional growth predominantly on the fringe of the city.

46

For the most part, all urban forms, with the exception of the dispersed city, represent attempts to intentionally concentrate urban development in particular sections of the city. Each urban system or urban scenario also represents a relatively extreme possibility, deliberately selected in this study to identify the magnitude of relative shifts in environmental performance as alternative forms of city development are examined.

Appraising urban environmental performance

Since differences in urban development and urban form can be characterised by differences in transport and land use, the study described here uses the TOPAZ-2000 integrated land use/transport model as the tool for evaluating the environmental outcomes of alternative urban development scenarios.

Under the land use component, the city in question is divided into zones, with the list of land uses or activities specified (see Fig. 1). A scenario is then defined by specifying the population engaged in each activity within each zone, for a given time period. Values for link trips, energy use, and greenhouse and air pollution emissions are obtained by applying a transportation gravity model to the land use component. The gravity model generates and distributes trips between each pair of zones, depending on the trip generation and travel impedance properties of each pair of activities. The trips are then loaded into a road network to produce traffic flow. The level of congestion on each link determines the amount of emission produced for that link. For each land use scenario, the area-based emissions are obtained by multiplying the activity population with the corresponding per capita emission factor. Point-based emissions are then added from sources that fall within each zone. Emissions of volatile organic compounds (VOCs), nitrous oxides (NO_x), carbon monoxide (CO), sulphur dioxide (SO_2) and particulates of ten microns or less (PM_{10}) were modelled. The grid emissions are then passed on to an airshed model for dispersion analysis and an assessment of air quality (see Fig. 2 and Manins, 1995).

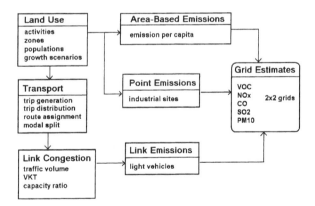

Fig. 1. Integrated land-use-transport-emissions model.

The example region used for this study was the Melbourne metropolitan area. The region was divided into 26 zones, as used in a 1991 national study of journey to work (Gipps *et al.*, 1997) (see Fig. 3). The zones in the outer ring or suburban fringe are large. However, the distribution of existing development within them is used as a basis for calculating trip lengths and zone centroids. Alternative future scenarios can then be distinguished largely by the type of future development that is assigned to each of the rings and their associated zones.

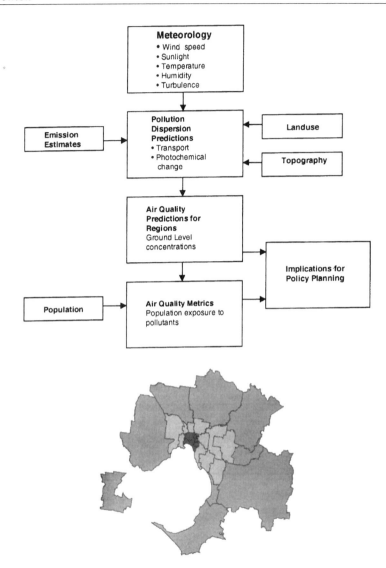

Fig. 2. Airshed model.

Fig. 3. The 26 journey to work (JTW) zones classified into inner, middle and outer rings for Melbourne.

Urban development scenarios

A range of scenarios that relate to alternative urban forms, defined in terms of land use changes and transport infrastructure improvement, were applied in modelling Melbourne's development to the year 2011. These alternative forms are described briefly below (their archetypal characteristics were outlined earlier). The key challenge is to accommodate an additional 500,000 people in Melbourne by 2011 to a base population of 3.2 million in 1991. The input data and assumptions for each scenario are summarised in Table 1.

Business-as-usual

In the business-as-usual scenario, the new half million population is distributed across the 26 JTW zones in the Melbourne metropolitan area (Fig. 3) in proportion to the 1991 base, as shown in Table 2 (see Gipps *et al.*, 1997 for a more detailed discussion of the base data).

Scenario	Transport		Population distribution			Employment distribution (%)		
	Infra-structure	Public transport (%)	Ring	%	Density (persons/ha)	Manufacturing	Producer services	Social services
Base case 1991	Existing network	20	Inner	7	28	22	53	32
			Middle	58	17	55	36	47
			Outer	35	2	23	11	20
Future to 2011	Upgrade		Growth			Growth		
Business as usual[1]		19	Inner	7		22	53	32
			Middle	58		55	36	47
			Outer	35		23	11	20
Compact city[2]	City freeway links	30	Inner	100	300	0	100	100
			Middle	0		33	0	0
			Outer	0		67	0	0
Edge city[3]	Freeway level ring road; radial rail	16	Inner	0		0	0	0
			Middle	86	80	33	83	83
			Outer	14		67	17	17
Corridor city[4]	Radial road/rail link upgrades	32	Inner	0		0	0	0
			Middle	0		0	0	0
			Outer	100	60	100	100	100
Ultra city[5] (including regional centres)	150 kph rail, freeways	31	Inner	2		7	16	10
			Middle	17		17	11	14
			Outer	11		7	3	6
			Regional	70	60	70	70	70
Fringe[6] (balance of homes and jobs)	Radial road/rail link upgrades		Inner	0		0	0	0
			Middle	10		10	10	10
			Outer	60		60	60	60
			Fringe	30	40	30	30	30

1. Increases density proportionally throughout the city – increasing congestion on existing road network, and travel times and fuel consumption as a consequence.
2. Concentrates growth in inner city well served by public transport.
3. Places new activities in edge city centres.
4. Similar to edge city but with growth channelled into growth corridors.
5. 70% of growth in regional cities (in separate airsheds) – linked by fast, electrified rail carrying 80% of cross-commuters (20% of new commuters). Electricity also generated in separate airshed.
6. Places 30% of new homes and service jobs in fringe corridor greenfield locations connected to radial highway/freeway and rail links. Balances new homes and jobs in each zone.

Table 1. Accommodating Melbourne's future population: scenarios and assumptions.

Zone	Land area (km²)	Residential population (000s)	Density (persons/ha)
Inner Melbourne	81.7	227.4	27.8
Middle Melbourne	1041.1	1831.8	17.4
Outer Melbourne	6708.5	1109.1	1.7

Table 2. 1991 Distribution of land and residential population in Melbourne.

This essentially continues a dispersed pattern of 'constrained' development within the confines of the Melbourne Statistical Division (MSD) – the entire built-up area of Metropolitan Melbourne – as presently defined, with population increased proportionately in each ring. The increase in outer Melbourne would be through greenfield development at the fringe, given the significant amount of land that remains available for residential or commercial development within the MSD. Consolidation trends associated with dual occupancy and infill development already under way would have some limited influence. Thus, this scenario models many of the current trends operating in Melbourne, including a slight increase in density.

Compact city

In this scenario, the new population is distributed to the eight statistical local areas that comprise inner Melbourne (see Fig. 3). The density of new residential development or redevelopment in these zones is designated at 300 persons per hectare, significantly above business-as-usual levels for the inner city. Higher densities are premised on the capacity of the transport and personal services in the 'transit city' section of Melbourne to accommodate such an influx of people. Public transport infrastructure in the inner city is enhanced in the context of the compact city scenario.

Multi-nodal or edge city

Here, all new population is allocated to six major district centres within the metropolitan area located on a major ring road. The district centres are located in zones situated within or close to the middle ring of Melbourne suburbs. The ring road is the same as in the base case except that, in this scenario, improvements have been made in order to bring it up to freeway status. The six nodes are also on radial rail networks centred on the CBD. These edge city zones are assigned medium-density housing up to 80 persons per hectare.

Corridor city

In the corridor city scenario, the new population is added to three corridor zones in the less developed outer ring of the city. The three expansion corridors – west corridor, north corridor, and south-east corridor – have each been allocated 70 square kilometres of land, carved out from the original (and larger) zones. The centroids of the three new corridors are roughly five kilometres out from the original zone centroids. The three corridors received transport infrastructure upgrades (of a radial nature) to both road and rail.

Fringe city

In the fringe city scenario, 30% of new population is added to the three development corridors in new greenfield sites on the urban edge – beyond the MSD boundary. Of the remaining 70%, 10% is added to the middle ring of zones and 60% is added to the outer ring. New manufacturing and service industries are also distributed to these same zones in the same proportions, providing a balance between new homes and new jobs. The timing of development of new homes and jobs will also be similar, increasing opportunities for selection of a home and job in the same local area, thereby increasing self-containment of commuting, as well as of shopping, and other trips.

The new corridor development and distribution to existing middle and outer zones is another variation of present and recent trends, except that there is no addition to the inner city zones. The new corridor fringe development is connected to the rest of the city with radial freeway/arterial links and with upgraded heavy rail links, thereby reducing travel times to these zones below what they would be without these upgrades.

Telecommuting (info-city)

In addition to the six urban form scenarios outlined above, it is also possible to 'superimpose' additional urban scenarios that relate to the form of work that sections of the population can be expected to be engaged in by 2011. It is anticipated that a higher proportion of the population will be engaged in telework than at present. Overall, this proportion may be as high as 20–30%, with some reduction in vehicle kilometres travelled (some being substituted by soft travel modes – walking and cycling – within local village contexts) and resultant emissions (see Newton and Wulff, 1998). The results from modelling this scenario are not presented here, but are available in Newton (1997).

Findings – urban form matters

Within the stated limitations and assumptions associated with the land-use-transport-environment modelling, the following conclusions related to urban form and environmental performance can be advanced.

Urban form and energy consumption

The compact city emerges as the most fuel efficient of all urban forms (see Fig. 4), with 43% less fuel consumption than a business-as-usual form of development. In the corridor city scenario, the fact that infrastructure investment was primarily radial in nature is the reason why higher levels of daily travel than in other scenarios were generated (that is, there are limited prospects for cross-town trips). The addition of a higher order ring or orbital transport network to the current corridor city infrastructure, however, could be expected to generate benefits in travel time and energy consumption.

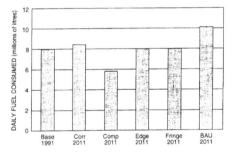

Fig. 4. Daily transport fuel consumption for base 1991 and five future scenarios.

Urban form and carbon dioxide emissions

Two of the key contributors to greenhouse gas emission by cities are demands from transport and electricity. For most Australian cities, electricity generation occurs in locations outside metropolitan airsheds, a trend that has occurred over the past 25 years as advances in transmission technology have permitted electricity production at greater distances from the market. However, the late 1990s are witnessing the emergence of a new set of forces in the electricity utilities industry in Australia (privatisation and deregulation of the gas and electricity industries) that may lead to an increase in the number of gas turbine generators embedded in the larger cities. This is likely to have a positive effect, overall, on greenhouse gas emissions, but a negative effect in relation to nitrous oxide emissions.

In this context, it is the link emissions that become the primary focus for reducing carbon dioxide from urban areas. In Fig. 5, it can be seen that compact city form delivers the lowest output of carbon dioxide emissions, due to greater use of public transport and fewer vehicle kilometres travelled (see Fig. 6), compared with other forms of urban development. A shift, by 2011, from business-as-usual urban development to a compact city form will produce savings in carbon dioxide emissions of the order of 11.5 million kilogrammes each day (11,500 tonnes).

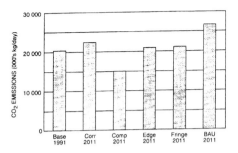 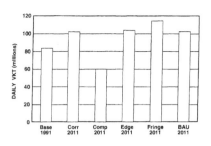

Fig. 5. Daily carbon dioxide emissions from link sources.

Fig. 6. Daily vehicle kilometres travelled for base 1991 and five future scenarios.

Urban form and pollutant emissions

The distinction between pollutant emissions and pollutant concentrations ('air quality') is fundamental. LUTE (land-use-transport-environment) models are used to estimate emissions for criteria pollutants on a fine grid basis across a metropolitan area. These emissions become inputs into airshed models (see Fig. 2) which forecast concentrations in pollutants (air quality) for particular areas, based on chemical mixing, meteorology and terrain. These airshed models generate air quality (ozone, particles) forecasts and population exposures.

On the basis of emissions, the more concentrated or 'directed' forms of urban development generate superior outcomes compared to the business-as-usual scenario (see Table 3).

Table 3. Percentage improvement in total emissions compared to the business-as-usual scenario (2011).

Future scenario	VOC	NO_x	CO	SO_2
Compact	27.3	25.6	39.7	3.8
Edge	23.0	17.7	31.8	2.3
Corridor	23.9	17.2	34.1	1.8
Ultra	22.4	15.2	31.2	1.5
Fringe	20.8	14.5	28.3	1.7

Urban form and air quality
Photochemical smog

Any one of several strategies designed to deliberately channel and concentrate additional population and industry into specific 'zones' within a large city such as Melbourne (for example, corridor, edge, and compact inner city 'zones'), when supported by the simultaneous installation or upgrading of appropriate transport infrastructure, will deliver environmental and efficiency benefits that consistently outperform those associated with a business-as-usual approach. In the case of photochemical smog, for example, a corridor model for Melbourne's metropolitan development in 2011 delivers a 55% improvement over the base situation for that city in 1991. Where new development is primarily concentrated at nodes on the fringe, within the inner suburbs or at key nodes within the city, the air quality enhancements are also significant (respectively, 39, 24 and 21% reduction in population exposure to smog compared with the base case). For business-as-usual development, the result is an increase by 71% in the population exposed to smog at levels above those considered appropriate by present Air NEPM Standards (national air quality standards).

Particle concentrations

Fine particle (PM_{10}) concentrations for the compact city scenario were little changed from the 1991 base model. However, since all the additional half million population gain proposed for Melbourne in this scenario is to be accommodated in inner suburbs, more people will be exposed to the 'umbrella' of particle emissions, given the pattern of dispersion of particle pollution forecast by the airshed models. Hence, considerably higher levels of population will be exposed to fine particles in the compact city. Indeed, the compact city delivers a 160% increase in population exposure to fine particles from the Melbourne base case (1991). For business-as-usual development, the level of increased population exposure is 61%. Edge, corridor and fringe developments all deliver improvements as far as population exposure to PM_{10} particles is concerned.

Conclusion

Urban form *does* matter – and not just for urban air quality. In relation to indicators such as greenhouse gas emissions and energy consumption, there appears to be universal concurrence from the land-use-transport-environment modelling that to maintain a business-as-usual model of urban development (that is, relatively *laissez-faire*, low-density, dispersed development) is to condemn the population and industry of the city to a sub-optimal living and working environment in the future. On most of the measures considered here, a trend to a more compact city, however defined – compact inner city, edge city, corridor city and so on – will lead to significant environmental improvements compared with business-as-usual.

Indeed, it is this type of strategic planning and evaluation which is notably absent at metropolitan and state government levels in Australia at present, as attempts are being made to chart the future infrastructure investments required for major metropolitan areas into the 21st century. By way of contrast, in the United States, a number of federal Acts are requiring a closer linking of funding, in areas such as urban transport, with a set of goals that include environmental performance criteria. Integrated land-use-transport-environment models represent the principal means by which impacts of proposed urban development can be evaluated – system-wide – across the spectrum of dimensions relevant to the key goals of economic efficiency, social equity and environmental sustainability.

Note

A more detailed account of this study, undertaken for the Federal Inquiry into Air Quality in Australian Cities, can be found in Newton (1997).

Michael Buxton

Energy, Transport and Urban Form in Australia

Introduction

In terms of the proportion of the population living in cities, Australia is one of the world's most urbanised countries. Over 60% of Australians live in metropolitan areas of over 100,000 people and 40% live in the two biggest cities, Sydney and Melbourne. About two thirds of population growth is occurring in the five metropolitan capitals (Armstrong *et al.*, 1995). The Australian Urban and Regional Development Review (Wettenhall, 1994) estimated that the postwar spread of Australian cities exceeded one million hectares and cost $4.2–$5 billion annually compared to the $3–$5 billion invested annually in new manufacturing plant and equipment.

Australia's high per capita energy consumption, low urban densities and high levels of road use make major contributions to very high per capita carbon dioxide emissions. Per capita motor vehicle travel is about 20% higher than the OECD average (ABS, 1994; OECD, 1994). The Australian National Greenhouse Gas Inventory has shown that over one quarter of Australia's greenhouse gas emissions arise from urban non-transport energy use and 12% from transport use. Transport accounted for 25% of Australian sectoral carbon dioxide emissions from energy use in 1990–91, with road transport making by far the highest contribution at 76% of the total transport emissions, in carbon dioxide equivalent terms (NGGIC, 1996; BTCE, 1995).

Nevertheless, Stretton (1996) has suggested that because energy savings of only 6–7% are possible through extensive changes to urban form and reducing car travel, other measures may be more cost effective. Similarly, Morris (1993) argues that since road transport worldwide contributes less than 5% of anthropogenic greenhouse gases, their reduction 'will have far reaching economic and lifestyle implications and will make only a small contribution to the global problem' (p.159). Others, however, derive different conclusions by concentrating on vehicle energy savings in the context of total potential urban savings. Pears (1995a, 1995b), for example, estimates that when emissions from waste and production of materials for urban infrastructure are included almost half of Australia's total greenhouse gas emissions and two thirds of emissions from energy are generated in urban areas or through energy conversion for urban use. The large contribution of Australian cities to transport emissions can be seen from the fact that 70% of national road transport kilometres occur in urban areas (Wilkenfeld *et al.*, 1995).

The ongoing controversy in Australia around the issue of whether cities should be dispersed or compact is intense because of the stage of development of Australian cities, particularly the two largest, Sydney and Melbourne. Populations in the inner and middle ring suburbs of Australian cities fell between the 1960s and the early 1990s and are continuing to decline in some cities, primarily because of declining household sizes.

Unlike many European cities, Australian cities have not experienced the development of high-density housing on the urban fringe. For most of the 20th century, the area taken up by Australian cities has expanded gradually through the building of relatively low-density detached housing. Since the 1970s, almost all new housing has been low density, single use, with a curvilinear street pattern and culs-de-sac, on the Canberra model. This subdivision pattern is similar to that of many postwar American cities, but in some respects there are major differences: in Australia, urban freeway construction has not generally dictated urban form; public transport infrastructure often remains in place; city centres remain strong cultural economic tourist and employment locations; inner city residential areas are vibrant and desirable; and many middle ring and inner suburbs are gaining population.

This chapter provides an overview of the current debate in Australia about preferred urban form, transport patterns and energy use, and their effects on each other. The debate is partly about facts and their interpretation but, ultimately, it is about values, about what cities ought to look like, what their shape should be, how they should function and develop, and what they ought to become. The debate will be examined around the themes of the dispersed city, urban consolidation, and the potential of self-containment around mixed-use, public transport oriented development. Then, the implications for this debate of the results of two major studies in Victoria – the Urban Villages Project and the Greenhouse Neighbourhood Project – will be discussed.

The dispersed city

Traditionally, land use planning has exerted strong strategic and statutory influences over the way Australian cities have developed. However, this traditional role is under threat from two sources. First, planned new infrastructure development, particularly urban freeway systems such as the planned outer ring road in Melbourne, appear capable of determining the direction and type of urban growth. Second, market decisions, particularly those concerning extensions to car-based regional shopping centres and incremental suburban office development, are capable of changing the traditional balance between city and suburban centres.

Many groups, representing government, the development industry, academia and the planning profession, strongly favour dispersal of city functions. For example, O'Connor and Stimson (1994, 1996) and McKenzie (1996) argue that the capital city of Melbourne should no longer be seen as single centred but as a multi-centred metropolis, functionally connected through an ever-widening commuter belt.

It is argued that, within the dispersed city, central city employment is proportionally declining, manufacturing has relocated to outer suburbs, employment and housing have dispersed, and outer urban population grown; this has led to dispersed commuter patterns, with shorter circumferential trips within the outer suburbs replacing longer radial trips to the central city, and leading to lower work trip times (Brotchie, 1992; Brotchie *et al.*, 1993, 1995; O'Connor, 1992, 1994, 1998; O'Connor and Stimson, 1994, 1996). To O'Connor and Brotchie, the transition to an information and global economy favours regionally self-contained suburban areas. An essential element in this concept is the need for new outer urban freeways to connect the dispersed centres, although Brotchie (1992) does not dismiss the value of improvements to public transport systems. Brotchie's model is based on increased urban productivity through decentralised, multi-functional suburban and industrial centres integrating production through a connected freeway system. This is precisely the model being implemented by the state government of Victoria and opposed by public transport and other community groups.

Others have contested this model of future urban development. Mees (1995) argues that the advocates of dispersal commonly confuse growth with decentralisation. The central city of Melbourne has witnessed an increase in its employment levels and its relative importance as a thriving cultural centre over time, and has declined in importance only in relation to its outer growth. Mees argues that ring freeways are unnecessary because of evidence of few long-distance circumferential journeys, a pattern of short radial journeys, and an inadequate public transport service. In addition, building ring freeways encourages use even though such use is unnecessary, and ultimately leads to lower travel times. Mees warns against replicating the American model of 'edge cities' (Garreau, 1991). His espousal of the need to maintain a dominant central city, supported by thriving housing and commercial areas and high quality radial public transport, and his criticisms of the suburbs forming a functionally separate ring linked by a circumferential freeway (Mees, 1994) have much in common with the work of Cervero (1986, 1989, 1997). Opponents of decentralised, road-based urban centres believe that such centres will reduce the importance of a central city area linked to its hinterland by efficient public transport, and lead to a counter-productive dependence on road-based transport, with its range of undesirable environmental and social effects.

Urban consolidation

There is still considerable debate over whether urban population and employment densities independently affect travel demand and modal choice. A wide range of studies suggests that transport energy use falls as dwelling density increases (Owens, 1986; Royal Commission on Environmental Pollution, 1994). Some of this work has been criticised, including Newman and Kenworthy's (1989) claims, made on the basis of inter-city comparisons, that transport fuel consumption rises as densities fall below about 30 persons per hectare. Common criticisms of Newman and Kenworthy's work are that income, car ownership and fuel price may be more important factors than population density in determining private vehicle use (Pucher, 1990; Kirwan, 1992a; Troy, 1992; Brindle, 1994).

It is claimed that mixed-use areas developed around public transport nodes within existing cities produce transport savings over outer-urban fringe area development (Banister, 1992; ECOTEC, 1993). There is considerable research to indicate that density and land use mix are both related to modal choice and that, as these increase, the levels of public transport use and walking rise, while single-occupant vehicle use falls. Increasing the level of land use mix at trip origins and destinations achieves the same results (Frank and Pivo, 1994). Localisation of employment and services, accessibility and high quality public transport are critical variables affecting results of studies. For example, higher density centres without these factors may be associated with an increase in cross-town vehicle use. After reviewing considerable research, the Australian Urban and Regional Development Review concluded that changing urban structure to emphasise compactness, concentration around a strong central city, increased density, public transport-supportive development, and localised employment and services can contribute to transport energy savings and, over a period of about 20 years, significantly increase the sustainability of cities (Armstrong *et al.*, 1995).

Conventional urban consolidation can occur through intensification of housing in the existing urban area, or on greenfield sites on the urban fringe, or through both. Consolidation is only partly aimed at reducing private vehicle use and transport energy consumption, and is justified on a range of other grounds, including cost savings compared to continuing outward growth, better utilisation of existing facilities and a range of social and environmental benefits. Intensification can occur in planned ways, usually through governments identifying suitable redevelopment sites, such as surplus public land or former industrial sites close to public transport and service centres. Or it can occur through incremental, market-led redevelopment of existing housing and building conversions. The three main growth areas of Sydney,

Melbourne and South Eastern Queensland deal with consolidation in different ways. The Victorian state government has amended all planning schemes to allow incremental apartment living anywhere in metropolitan areas, and has identified 620 redevelopment sites with a potential yield of 60,951 dwellings (Department of Infrastructure, 1997). The Victorian Minister for Planning's Projects Steering Committee estimated in 1993 that half the projected population increase of 280,000 by 2003 could be accommodated in established areas using a modest target of generally less than 5% population increase (DPD, 1993), not the 40% or 50% increases in some suburbs estimated by Self (1995). By 1996, the proportion of new housing starts on the urban fringe in Melbourne had fallen to 50%, down from 80% in 1994 (Department of Infrastructure, 1998a). Reynolds and Porter (1998) and the Department of Infrastructure (1998b) have shown from 1996 census results that in recent years inner city municipalities gained rather than lost population, a sharp reversal of past patterns of urban growth.

Other Australian governments have also begun to identify suitable redevelopment sites. For example, in Sydney, 487 hectares are being redeveloped in the inner south for eventual resident and workforce targets of 20,000 (Spiller, Gibbons and Swan Pty Ltd, 1998). Daly (1998), also drawing from the 1996 census, shows that inner Sydney suburbs now record both an absolute and relative population increase, and that, in comparison with middle and outer zones, a surge in property values has occurred. The New South Wales government is planning for an increase in Sydney in the proportion of new dwellings that are multi-unit from 42% in 1995 to 65% by 2001. At the same time, this government is planning to increase the dwelling density on the urban fringe from the current 11 per hectare to a modest 15 by the year 2011 (Holliday and Norton, 1995). The Queensland state government has adopted the same target for its south eastern outer urban growth area (Buxton and Searle, 1997; Minnery and Barker, 1998) and, soon after its election in 1992, the Victorian government removed a minimum density requirement of 15 dwellings per hectare for growth areas on the Melbourne urban fringe.

The figures for dwelling approvals also show a consolidation pattern. For several years, approvals for Melbourne's inner and middle ring suburbs have totalled about 10,000 a year, compared with 15,000 in outer and fringe area suburbs (Department of Infrastructure, 1998b). Between 1995 and November 1997, 8,143 dwellings were completed on the government's nominated redevelopment sites in inner and middle ring suburbs and only 828 in outer municipalities (Department of Infrastructure, 1997). Similarly, in Sydney, since 1990, a significant shift towards central locations has occurred in dwelling approvals, with inner areas accounting for about 25% of all new housing construction. In 1991, a Brisbane City Council task force recommended the development of a range of mixed-use, medium-density housing projects in four inner suburbs to address the 13% population fall from 1976–91 and to raise the population from 12,000 to 30,000 (Brisbane City Council, 1992). A substantial increase in the building of apartments in these areas has occurred, although between 1991 and 1996 only one inner suburb reversed the population loss, and that was only by 917 people (Minnery and Barker, 1998). In arguing that the main impacts of consolidation will be felt at the urban fringe, Self (1995) has misread the consolidation trend in the two largest cities, Sydney and Melbourne. Consolidation policies there are exerting greatest impact through higher densities in the older middle and inner suburbs. Traditional outward growth dominates the third growth area, South East Queensland.

There is a long history of opposition to urban consolidation in Australia by governments, planners, communities, academics and the development industry. Stretton (1996) and Troy (1992, 1996) argue in favour of conventional detached housing on relatively large plots on an extending urban fringe and criticise the arguments for consolidation, on environmental, economic, equity and lifestyle grounds. These and other critics, such as Kirwan (1992a, 1992b), often argue on economic grounds that urban consolidation will not reduce housing or land costs, or that the infrastructure costs of conventional fringe area subdivision have been exaggerated. Stretton and Troy claim that infrastructure costs associated with new housing on the fringe should be compared with the costs of expanding existing infrastructure capacity to cater for increased densities, although there is little evidence of insufficient capacity.

However, there is evidence that changes to the urban form of Australian cities could lead to substantial reductions to transport and housing energy use and infrastructure costs. Kinhill Engineers (1995) found that greenfield residential densities of 15 dwellings per hectare and higher street connectivity led to a 6% saving on infrastructure costs compared with a conventional 'sprawl' scenario using ten dwellings per hectare. The Kinhill study also found that infrastructure costs were likely to be inversely related to density. McGlynn *et al.* (1991) compared total annual transport energy use for Australia's capital cities under four scenarios: a base case involving expansion at urban fringes; a market-driven case with utilisation of spare capacity in established areas; a policy-forced case with more direct government-driven re-urbanisation; and the case of urban centres focusing all population and employment growth into established centres. All scenarios reduced growth in energy consumption compared with the base case (see Table 1 below). Non-transport infrastructure savings for urban centres compared to the base case ranged from $2.1–$4.2 billion.

Table 1. Energy use scenarios against a base case.
Source: McGlynn et al., *1991.*

Scenario	City total annual transport use 1988 and 2005 (petajules)		
	1988	2005	Increase (%)
Base case growth	382.8	518.3	35.4
Market-driven	382.8	502.2	31.2
Policy-focused	382.8	485.0	26.7
Urban centres	382.8	459.6	20.1

Different values lie at the heart of these disputes. Whereas Brotchie and O'Connor argue that the growth of an informational economy, the decline in manufacturing, job growth in finance, real estate and services areas, and in part-time and home-based work, favour urban dispersal to regionally self-contained suburban areas, Reynolds and Porter (1998) argue that these same influences benefit inner city areas most and lead to their renewal and growth.

Reynolds and Porter also argue that demographic changes, particularly the growth of one- and two-person households and the strong inward migration of young age groups, have helped increase the population of inner urban areas. However, Stretton, Troy and others justify conventional suburban development on the basis that it is the preferred choice of Australians, arguing that most could have chosen alternatives but 'are happy with where they live and how they live there, and specifically prefer their suburban houses and locations to denser housing forms or inner city locations' (Stretton, 1996, p.49).

Much of the research into housing preferences is biased, through the lack of meaningful respondent experience with housing alternatives. The rapid change in Australian housing preferences in recent years shows its shortcomings. In addition, until recently, consumer choice was very limited and governed largely by the large development companies. Choice at the lower end of the market is still packaged mainly as a choice between forms of conventional housing, and is determined by producers not consumers of housing.

Urban self-containment
Advocates of dispersal propose fundamental changes in the form and function of Australian

cities, whereas opponents of urban consolidation often focus primarily on dwelling size and lifestyle. The alternative to dispersal and conventional urban consolidation is an approach that proposes the redevelopment of areas close to public transport locations into centres with three characteristics. First, they must contain mixed uses and higher residential densities, incorporating significant local employment, retail, service functions and a density of 25–40 dwellings per hectare. Second, their design elements include interconnected street systems promoting walking, a range of plot sizes and dwelling types, protection of historic values, and energy efficient buildings. Third, the centres must be close to public transport systems as one of a number of ways to reduce motor vehicle use. This model seeks self-containment in centres, and integration between land use and public transport use. It contrasts with both the dispersal model, with its separated uses linked by road transport, and the conventional consolidation model, in which intensification occurs anywhere in existing or new suburbs, in an incremental manner.

Like the advocates of dispersal and conventional consolidation, Kaufman and Morris (1995) argue that urban villages are compatible with emerging economic and employment trends. Using Kemp's (1994) analysis, they emphasise the growth in producer and consumer services and the need for jobs close to the resident workforce, and the growth of home-based business, self-employment, and part-time work. They and others also pay great attention to physical design elements such as subdivision and street layout, access, building design, mixed or integrated building uses, parking and traffic consideration, and connections to public transport.

Calthorpe (1993) connects the physical determinist elements of urban village theory with social outcomes, arguing that 'the urban village is the search for a paradigm that combines the utopian ideal of an integrated and heterogeneous community with the realities of our time' (p.15). Advocates of urban villages argue that human-scaled, diverse, integrated neighbourhoods using public space and transport systems result in a more interactive, less individualistic and separatist, sense of self. Calthorpe (1993), for example, argues that communities must be redesigned to re-establish and reinforce the public domain. Again, this model is strongly underpinned by values, by firm ideas of what cities ought to look like and how they ought to function.

The features variously associated with the terms urban villages (Newman and Kenworthy, 1992), transit-supportive development (Calthorpe and Associates, 1992), and traditional neighbourhood development (Duany, 1992) can be grouped under the heading of New Urbanism (see Hasic, this volume). Katz (1994) has elaborated on the features of New Urbanism, and Kaufman and Morris (1995) correctly point out that they are associated with the traditional neighbourhood development characteristics of the inner suburbs of Australian cities developed prior to the invention of motor vehicles.

Some opponents of urban consolidation seem to reserve a special aversion to the concept of urban villages. Troy (1992) argues that encouragement of a 'stronger sense of community' by proponents of higher-density housing and urban villages is inconsistent with the realities of urban living and 'is built on a tragic – even deliberate – misinterpretation of village life ... not based on reality' (p.42). Whereas Calthorpe believes that higher-density, mixed-use living will encourage greater interaction and use of public space and resources, Troy (1996) believes it will foster individualism and separatism and 'provide the conditions for anonymity and withdrawal as people act to preserve their privacy and personal space' (p.164). Both Calthorpe and Troy refer to 'reality' in justifying their positions. Their value positions lead to very different pictures of what is real.

Troy also argues that urban villages are attempts to provide security and exclusive enclaves for the middle classes. In fact, conventional development now commonly occurs as enclaves.

The New Urbanists constantly stress the need for buildings to face, or be better integrated with, streets, and for diversity in household type, size and composition. Kaufman and Morris (1995) argue that the elderly, the young, mothers and the poor are assisted by New Urbanism, primarily through better access to services. The relocation of the poor to outer suburbs and the construction of gated or otherwise enclosed inner and outer suburban enclaves are contrary to New Urbanism principles.

Finally, Troy regards urban villages as a form of social control, repeating his accusation that a 'crude physical determinism' lies behind higher-density housing. However, the same accusation could be directed towards other land use interventions, including the planning systems that promote low-density urban expansion. Even planning systems, such as that recently adopted in the State of Victoria, which allow market decisions to determine the appearance and functions of cities, often require interventionist planning laws.

The practical options stemming from these three alternative approaches to urban form were summarised in a recent review prepared by the CSIRO, ABS and others (1994). Maunsell and Glazebrook and Associates (1994) have reviewed the effects of road and public transport oriented policies and have catalogued the benefits of integrating transport and land use planning around mixed-use activity centres. Australian examples of mixed-use, public transport oriented developments are outlined in *Better Cities* publications (Department of Housing and Regional Development, 1995), the Australian Urban and Regional Development Review publication, *Green Cities* (Armstrong *et al.*, 1995), and a recent World Bank publication (Buxton and Searle, 1997). Two other major Australian studies demonstrate the potential for reducing energy use and greenhouse gas emissions by altering urban form: the Victorian Greenhouse Neighbourhood Project and the Victorian Urban Villages Project. Each study will be examined in turn below.

Victorian Greenhouse Neighbourhood Project
This project, carried out in 1993, quantified the effects of increasing dwelling density and introducing mixed uses on energy use, transport patterns and greenhouse gas emissions, and associated infrastructure costs, in a new outer-suburban greenfield site. It demonstrates the significant impact of urban form on energy use. Three alternative residential neighbourhood designs were modelled on a site on the western metropolitan fringe of Melbourne:

1. The conventional subdivision of the 1980s, with a net density of ten dwellings per hectare, few local employment and retailing opportunities, a hierarchical street network, curvilinear street patterns, many culs-de-sac, mainly single-storey detached houses on standard plots with no particular regard for solar access.
2. Subdivisions shaped by the Victorian code for residential development (VicCode 1), with a net density of 15 dwellings per hectare, some mix of dwelling types, a more interconnected street network, some culs-de-sac and solar access to 70% of plots.
3. A traditional neighbourhood design (TND), with a net density averaging 25 dwellings per hectare, a greater mix of attached and detached dwelling types, a high level of local retail and employment opportunities with one job available for every two resident workers, a highly interconnected street network typical of the inner grid pattern areas of Melbourne, few culs-de-sac, good public transport services and solar access to 70% of plots.

The three major parameters considered in the study were housing energy use, transport energy use, and infrastructure costs. The study found that substantial savings in energy requirements and greenhouse gas emissions could be achieved through changes in urban form (see Fig. 1).

Use of the TND model, in comparison with conventional development practices, led to carbon dioxide emission reductions of up to 42%, by combining land use and transport related factors to reduce car travel, and by using dwelling siting and design to reduce heating and cooling related emissions.

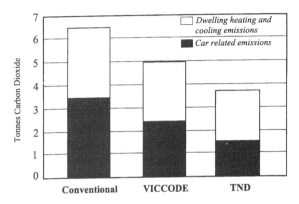

Fig. 1. Combined dwelling heating and cooling and car-related greenhouse gas emission reductions by neighbourhood type (tonnes of carbon dioxide per dwelling per year).
Source: Greenhouse Neighbourhood Project.

Savings of up to 57% in transport energy use could be achieved, primarily by increasing the proportion of local employment, retail and related land uses, which provided high levels of self-containment for daily activities. Increased residential densities alone led to more limited reductions in travel and emissions but remained important.

Energy savings of up to 26% over conventional detached housing could be made by designing houses to make the most of solar energy for heating and cooling, and using shared walls and floors like those in terrace or apartment housing. Density *per se* was less important than increasing solar access. As the degree of attachment between dwellings and storey height increased, energy requirements were reduced. A combination of improving solar access and thermal performance through attached housing forms appears to be the key to reducing dwelling heating and cooling energy requirements at higher densities.

The study also found that car travel time and distance travelled per dwelling reduced markedly with the increase in density from conventional to VicCode to TND neighbourhood types, as can be seen in Table 2. Increased density was a significant factor in reducing transport greenhouse gas emissions, but the greatest gains were made when there was a higher density in combination with a mix of land uses and local employment opportunities, leading to greater self-containment and fewer longer external trips.

| Residential density | Neighbourhood type | | |
(dwellings/ha)	Conventional	VicCode	TND
10	8.3		
15	7.6	7.0	
25	7.0		5.4

Table 2. Estimates of hourly morning peak car travel time per dwelling (minutes).
Source: Greenhouse Neighbourhood Project.

Local transport emissions were only slightly reduced in response to the higher degree of self-containment from conventional to VicCode to TND neighbourhood types. The number of local trips rose, though distances reduced markedly and trip times remained similar outside peak hours. The progressively increasing degree of directness and interconnectedness of streets in VicCode and TND types increasingly supported walking and cycling. Changes in the traffic management systems had some effect on reducing travel time, but the extent of change was not statistically significant. The number of people using public transport increased only slightly

61

from conventional to TND type as densities increased and land use mix and distribution changed. For urban infrastructure costs, as density increased, infrastructure costs per dwelling decreased from $11,745 for the conventional neighbourhood type, to $9,585 for VicCode and $5,300 for TND.

Victorian Urban Villages Project

The project, carried out in 1996, investigated the potential for redeveloping the existing urban area of Melbourne into urban villages, and developed detailed concept plans and site assessments for eight potential sites. Potential urban village sites were limited to those within a 400–800 metre radius of a public transport stop and capable of redevelopment into mixed-use centres with medium-density housing, local employment and street accessibility. In all 986 sites were identified, covering 27% of the metropolitan area in 1991. Projections were made of the capacity of urban villages to accommodate Melbourne's increased population to 2011.

The study projected that by 2011 Melbourne will require an additional 302,000 dwellings for an increased population of 478,800 people. Six scenarios were prepared, assuming in each that 800 urban village sites would be developed to varying extents. It is important to note the extent of current urban consolidation occurring outside these nominated urban village sites. If the 1994–95 consolidation rate is established as the trend, 110,000 additional dwellings would be built in the metropolitan area on 1991 boundaries between 1991 and 2011. A moderate urban village scenario, with approximately the same number of new dwellings in urban villages as in fringe housing would reduce urban expansion on the fringe by one third compared with consolidation on the 1994–95 level. Development of 800 possible urban village sites to their full potential would accommodate 230,000 additional dwellings or 76% of additional requirements by 2011. These results are summarised in Table 3.

	Distribution of projected additional dwellings in Melbourne between 1991 and 2011							Urban expansion	
Scenario	In the 800 urban village sites		In remainder of the established metropolitan area		Total for established metropolitan area	New development at the urban fringe		Growth of metropolitan area by 2011	
	No.	%	No.	%	%	No.	%	Ha	%
1. Urban consolidation at 1991/92 levels	25,200	8	42,800	14	23	234,000	77	41,100	21
2. Urban consolidation at 1994/95 levels	40,800	14	69,200	23	36	192,000	64	33,700	17
3. Minor urban village emphasis	60,400	20	60,400	20	40	181,200	60	31,800	16
4. Moderate urban village emphasis	120,800	40	60,400	20	60	120,800	40	21,200	11
5. Major urban village emphasis	181,200	60	60,400	20	80	60,400	20	10,600	5
6. 'Upper bound'	230,000	76	60,400	20	96	12,100	4	2,100	1

Table 3. Urban development scenarios and the extent of urban expansion by 2011.
Source: Urban Villages Project.

In addition to considering the capacity of urban villages to accommodate additional dwellings and residents, the Urban Villages Project also sought to assess the effect of urban village development on energy consumption and greenhouse gas emissions from the heating and cooling of dwellings. Estimates were made for the additional 302,000 dwellings projected to be required in Melbourne between 1991 and 2011. These suggest that redevelopment of metropolitan Melbourne on the basis of urban village principles, rather than continuation of urban consolidation at 1991–92 levels (Scenario 1), would result in significant energy and greenhouse gas savings. Under the most conservative scenario (that is, 'minor urban village emphasis'), a saving of 3% compared with Scenario 1 is estimated. The 'moderate urban village emphasis' is estimated to result in savings in energy and greenhouse gas emissions of 8.6% compared with Scenario 1, while the 'major urban village emphasis' would result in estimated energy and emissions savings of around 14%.

Four model runs were made on the LAND computer model to estimate the potential transport energy and greenhouse gas emissions savings. Results indicated that urban village development could achieve reductions in greenhouse gas emissions of between 21–27%, depending on the level of job self-containment assumed. Public transport passenger kilometres would increase significantly by between 90–100%.

Conclusions

The Victorian Greenhouse Neighbourhood Project provides further evidence that urban form can significantly reduce energy use and greenhouse gas emissions. The combination of higher residential densities, mixed-use neighbourhoods and public transport can lead to large reductions in transport energy consumption, travel times and distances, and infrastructure costs.

The Victorian Urban Villages Project quantified the potential for redeveloping sites near public transport as mixed-use centres of medium-density housing, service facilities and high local employment, the consequent reduction in the area of urban growth on the fringes of Melbourne, and related energy savings. The project also developed detailed concept and implementation plans for eight pilot sites, some of which are now being implemented.

Despite the growing interest in the concept of urban villages in Australia, most new housing in cities consists of either conventional urban consolidation, particularly in the inner and middle ring suburbs, or low-density, single-use housing on the urban fringes. Medium-density housing in established areas is largely incremental, often poorly located with respect to public transport, and increasingly being built as secure enclaves. The lessons of the two studies described here are not being applied.

Despite the potential of urban form to affect energy use and reduce car dependency, powerful political and market forces are assisting the dispersal of key city elements such as housing, offices, and retail and service facilities. This dispersal is likely to be aided by urban freeways. Freeways and suburban expansion of office and retail facilities are increasingly likely to determine the form and functioning of cities, reversing the traditional land use control of infrastructure requirements. Decisions on these issues in the next five years are likely to decide the future of Australian cities.

Mohammad-Reza Masnavi

The New Millennium and the New Urban Paradigm: *The Compact City in Practice*

Introduction

The search for the ideal city, the city form that would be able to express both the advantages of modern technology and the soul of rustic life, on the basis of enlightened ideas of social justice, has long been a major concern to many philosophers, social reformers, writers, architects and planners. This search which, in its historical roots, might be traced back to Plato, and his *Republic*, resulted in some contradictory socio-political and economic philosophies, and has influenced the development of different types of urban settlement throughout history. In the second half of the twentieth century, with growing awareness of environmental problems and ecological crises, the search has been transformed to address the question: what is the sustainable city? There are many uncertainties in the identification of alternative urban forms. This chapter examines two predominant and contradictory theories that are put forward as grounds for achieving sustainable city forms: the *compact city* and *urban dispersal*. A study of four different urban forms, which were selected and examined systematically in terms of their densities and land uses, is described (see end note).

Sustainable development, quality of life and the new urban paradigms: the compact city and dispersed urban development

It is predicted that, by the year 2000, almost half of the world's population will live in urban areas, where most resources will be consumed and most pollution and waste will be produced. Current patterns of urban development and human activity have led to environmental degradation, and have created a serious threat to continued human existence and to the sustainability of life on earth. It has been argued that there are strong links between urban form and sustainable development. Since energy consumption for transportation, and pollution, are two crucial issues in the context of sustainability, the question of the influence of particular urban forms on trip generation and travel patterns has attracted considerable attention from academics and governments as well as from town planners and architects.

Moreover, it has been widely recognised that the role of cities in terms of increasing sustainability is very important; hence, it is suggested that cities should act as a locus for solving global problems (Breheny, 1992a). However, despite the clarity of ecological/environmental crises and their outcomes, there is no common ground for an alternative urban design/planning paradigm (Breheny, 1992a; Jenks *et al.*, 1996). Two major and contradictory arguments in the late twentieth century are distinguishable:

1. urban dispersal (implying low density urban development); and
2. urban intensification (part of the compact city concept).

More recently, the majority of theories concerning urban development focus on the effects of

64

suburbanisation. In particular, some argue that decentralisation of housing and jobs reduces overall travel (Gordon *et al.*, 1989, 1991; Troy, 1996). Many others argue that low-density development, which is associated with decentralisation, can lead to increased automobile travel and fuel consumption (CEC, 1990; Elkin *et al.*, 1991; Newman and Kenworthy, 1992). Consequently, some have advocated the idea of the compact city as a solution, on the grounds that higher densities reduce energy consumption and, therefore, also pollution (Elkin *et al.*, 1991; Crookson *et al.*, 1996; Hillman, 1996). Whereas decentralisation tends to be advocated by theorists from Australia and the US, the compact city could be seen as the vision of European cities (Jenks *et al.*, 1996). Although the compact city idea is questioned, it has gained considerable attention and support (CEC, 1990; Elkin *et al.*, 1991; Breheny, 1992a, 1992b; UK Government, 1994; Masnavi *et al.*, 1997, 1998).

The compact city and quality of life

Much compact city theory focuses on the relationship between urban form and quality of life (QoL). It is claimed that urban intensification leads to safer and more vibrant urban areas, support for local business and services, greater social equity and social interaction, and better accessibility to facilities (Jenks *et al.*, 1996). This QoL theme is dominant in current moves towards planning 'neo-traditional' urban forms and 'urban villages' (Urban Villages Group, 1992). The compact city idea may be beneficial for the QoL of residents by creating places that are busy, convenient, attractive, energy efficient and supportive of public transport (CEC, 1990; Elkin, *et al.*, 1991; Newman and Kenworthy, 1992; Hillman, 1996; Scoffham and Vale, 1996; Masnavi *et al.*, 1997, 1998; Masnavi, 1998a, 1998b).

However, there are counter-arguments put forward predominantly by Americans and Australians. For example, popular demand may be seen to advocate urban dispersal and low-density development on the grounds that it leads to less congestion and pollution and that the QoL in this type of development is much higher (Gordon *et al.*, 1989, 1991; Troy, 1996). Jenks *et al.* (1996) argue that empirical research is required to resolve these contradictory arguments. In the research described here, indicators of QoL related to compactness were developed. These were identified as falling under the following categories:

- *Accessibility to facilities* – in terms of equity in access to the range of city facilities and services;
- *Reducing the need to travel* – in terms of journey length, particularly by private car;
- *Health* – in terms of improving public health, through reducing pollution, particularly that caused by emissions from vehicles; and
- *Social interaction* – in terms of opportunities for social contact in the neighbourhood's streets and public spaces, through more frequent use of these places and walking trips.

The aim of the research was to evaluate the travel and QoL-related sustainability impacts of four different urban forms through an empirical investigation in the West of Scotland. The following concepts and definitions were used:

Compact city: as defined by Elkin *et al.* 'must be a form and scale appropriate to walking, cycling and efficient public transport, and with a compactness that encourages social interaction' (1991, p.17). In practice, this suggests densities equivalent to those of the three- and four-storey urban street buildings found in most British inner-city areas (*ibid.*), and a form where 'it is still possible to provide each dwelling with its own front door to a public street, and to provide gardens for all family dwellings' (*ibid.*).

Mixed-use development: refers to a diversity of activity, such as the presence of retail functions and local industry in residential areas, and residential functions in retail areas (*ibid.*, p.21).

Single-use development: refers to the suburban and urban areas where most of the buildings are residential, and commercial activity is concentrated in town/city centres or retail parks.

Accessibility: refers to the distribution of the city facilities and the ease of access to destination points within the city/town. In this study, destinations were classified under nine major groups of activities.

Overall population density: refers to the population density of the whole urban area, tightly defined, and including all other land uses (expressed as persons per hectare – ppha).

Overall (gross) housing density: is equal to dwelling units per hectare, calculated over the whole of a residential neighbourhood, including roads, schools, workplaces and so on (expressed as gross dwelling units per hectare – dpha).

Average household size: is defined as the average number of persons per household.

Approach and methodology

The basic proposition of this study was that there is a relationship between urban form and accessibility, travel patterns and social interaction; and that urban forms with different densities and land uses will behave differently in terms of energy efficiency and quality of life. It was hypothesised that the compact city is beneficial in terms of QoL and energy consumption for transportation. To examine the research proposition and hypothesis, some sub-hypotheses were developed. The study then concentrated on the two physical characteristics of urban form, density and land use, as dependent variables, and their influence on energy consumption and social interaction, as independent variables.

Two levels of density were considered: high density and low density; while two types of land use were considered, mixed-use, and single-use. This suggests a two-by-two matrix or fourfold table to exemplify four urban types. This type of research design has been adopted by Handy (1992) and suggested by Greene and D'Oliviera (1989). This two-by-two design determined the selection of case study areas, each representing particular types of development in terms of land use and density.

The selection of case studies was based on an analysis of data for the former Strathclyde Region in Scotland (Strathclyde Regional Council, 1994, 1995). This led to the choice of Glasgow city, with an overall population density of 35 ppha, and East Kilbride New Town, with an overall population density of 7 ppha, the former representing a higher-density and the latter a lower-density urban form. Aggregate measures of population, economy, housing, land use and car ownership were calculated for 83 wards in Glasgow city, and ten neighbourhoods in East Kilbride New Town. Four case study areas were selected in the two settlements, as shown in Table 1. A range of sources of data was used for the investigation, including secondary data for the selection of case study areas, and primary data, from questionnaires and interviews with households, to test the research hypotheses.

Table 1. Case study selection matrix and identification of four different urban forms.

Types of land use	Levels of density	
	Compact (higher density) Glasgow inner city	*Dispersed* (lower density) East Kilbride New Town
Mixed-use development	Garnethill	East Mains
Single-use development	Hyndland	Stewartfield

Characteristics of the case study areas
The densities of the different areas vary considerably, as shown in Table 2.

	Garnethill	Hyndland	East Mains	Stewartfield
Total population	7,954	8,377	4,650	2,126
Total land area	72	86	138	144
No. of dwellings	3,285	4,163	1,989	731
Overall population density (average ppha)	110	97	34	15
Overall housing density (average dpha)	46	48	15	12
Average household size	2.2	1.8	2.3	2.9

Table 2. Overall densities of the four case study areas in terms of population density (ppha), housing density (dpha), and average household size (AHS).

Garnethill, Glasgow
Garnethill is located north-west of Glasgow city centre. It was developed from about 1820 as a more suburban quarter, and is now closely connected to the city centre. The structure of the area is based on a gridiron street pattern (Fig. 1) and all the buildings are three- and four-storey tenements (Fig. 2). The area is heterogeneous in terms of land use, with a mix of housing, shops, colleges, schools, nurseries and so on (often within the same structure – shops at street level and housing above).

Fig. 1. Garnethill, Glasgow.

Fig. 2. Tenement blocks of dwellings with street façades are mixed with a wide range of city facilities and services.

Hyndland, Glasgow
Located in the west of the city, Hyndland is one of the most homogenous neighbourhoods of Glasgow (Fig. 3). In terms of land use, it is almost totally residential, although there are some convenience stores and offices at the central axis of the neighbourhood. Most buildings (92%) are in the form of three- and four-storey tenemental urban blocks (Fig. 4). The area benefits from an effective public transport service.

Fig. 3. Hyndland, Glasgow.

Fig. 4. Three- and four-storey urban blocks of tenement buildings are dominant and create a homogeneous residential character in Hyndland.

East Mains, East Kilbride New Town
Designated in 1947, East Kilbride New Town was the first of five Scottish new towns built according to Ebenezer Howard's garden city ideas. Its original function was to assist in the

dispersal of population from the overcrowded areas of Glasgow and North Lanarkshire. East Mains is located north of East Kilbride town centre. It has expanded from an area that is called 'The Village' which, in 1947, functioned as a shopping centre for the emerging new town. The Village's function still exists but at the scale of the neighbourhood. East Mains is very close to the town centre and all its commercial facilities. The majority of the buildings are detached (16%), semi-detached (43%) and terraced (30%) houses, and are not more than two storeys (Figs 5 and 6).

Fig. 5. East Mains, East Kilbride.
Fig. 6. A typical street in East Mains with detached and semi-detached houses – the pavements are separated from vehicular traffic.

Stewartfield, East Kilbride New Town

Stewartfield is located in the north of East Kilbride. The area is fully residential and is made up of detached (83%) and semi-detached (15%) houses. Stewartfield benefits from a great amount of greenery and open space, and major commercial facilities are provided in retail parks or shopping centres and in the town centre (Figs 7 and 8).

Fig. 7. Stewartfield, East Kilbride.
Fig. 8. Detached and semi-detached are the predominant types of houses in Stewartfield, coupled with a great amount of greenery and open space.

Survey method

In order to examine relationships between factors such as density and land use, on the one hand, and accessibility to city facilities and the travel patterns of residents on the other, a questionnaire survey was conducted in each of the four areas. Questionnaires were distributed partly through the major schools, and partly through a random sample of addresses. A total of 327 completed questionnaires were collected for the four case study areas (127 from Stewartfield, 65 from East Mains, 75 from Hyndland and 60 from Garnethill) – this represented a response rate of, on average, 51.2% for the questionnaires distributed through institutions, and 71.4% for those distributed to a random sample of addresses. The samples were representative in terms of social class and employment in the two heterogeneous cases, except that the proportion of respondents from professional managerial groups was slightly higher than the average for the population in Garnethill and East Mains. The samples were also representative in terms of housing and car ownership characteristics. The female/male ratio of the respondents in some samples was nearly two times as great; however, since the questionnaire was presenting the overall household's views and not personal opinions, this was assumed to have little impact on the result.

In order to measure accessibility, major destination points were classified under nine categories of functions: work, daily shopping, weekly shopping, and visiting the city/town centre, friends and family, educational places, sports facilities, cultural facilities (for example, cinema and theatre) and entertainment facilities (for example, restaurants, pubs and bingo halls). In order to access these points, three modes of transport are generally used: walking, public transport or private car. Householders were asked how accessible the nine categories of destination points were to them, and were asked to give their main reasons for using the car, the frequency of that use, the distance travelled, and whether or not they were able to manage without a car. Respondents were asked to describe their social interactions within the neighbourhood and their level of satisfaction with living there. They were also asked a series of questions about their household's socio-economic characteristics.

Intervening variables

There may be many factors other than density and the mix of land uses contributing to energy consumption and social interaction in the case study areas. These intervening variables were controlled at two levels: first, through analyses of background data on housing, population density, car ownership, social class and so on. This allowed the identification of four areas which were as identical as possible in terms of socio-economic characteristics. Second, intervening variables were dealt with in the analyses of primary data. To control for the effects of some socio-economic characteristics, attempts were made to eliminate their effects through comparisons of the behaviour of matched households (for example, in terms of social class); or through frequency distribution control (for example, comparisons of households with children). In addition, the study employed other devices such as designing different sets of questions for one particular aspect of behaviour or attitudes (for example, the perceived degree of necessity for having a private car). Since these methods can control for only a small number of extraneous variables, there may be implications for the generalisability of the findings.

Research findings
Accessibility to city facilities
Residents were asked how accessible the nine categories of facilities were to them, in terms of travel on foot, by public transport, and by private car.

Accessibility of destination points on foot
Overall, the share of trips based on walking was significantly higher in Garnethill (69%) compared with Stewartfield (26%) (see Fig. 9). The variation in pedestrian trips is greatest for journeys related to recreational activities, daily shopping and education, and least for trips related to work, weekly shopping and visiting friends. Both the mixed-use areas had a higher percentage of walking trips compared with the single-use areas. This suggests mixed-use areas are more convenient for walking and have relatively easy access to destination points.

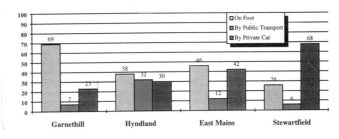

Fig. 9. Accessibility of city facilities by different modes of transport (% average of all trips).

Accessibility of destination points by public transport

To access the different facilities of the city/town, residents in the more compact, mixed-use area (Garnethill) did not use public transport very often. This might be because many trips could be made on foot, and because there are relatively short distances between trip points. Public transport was used significantly more in Hyndland (for 32% of all trips) – the high-density, single-use area – compared with Stewartfield (5% of all trips) and other areas, perhaps because use of public transport is related to distance from the city centre and the homogeneity of the area. The most common purposes in using public transport were to access the city centre and educational facilities, and the least common were for daily and weekly shopping.

Accessibility of destination points by private car

As shown in Fig. 9, the car was used significantly less in Garnethill (for 24% of all trips) than in Stewartfield (69% of trips). Residents in the two low-density areas, East Mains and Stewartfield, used private cars more frequently than did residents in the two high-density areas, Garnethill and Hyndland. This suggests a lower dependency on cars in compact areas than in dispersed areas. In the high-density, mixed-use area, the use of private cars was mostly for the purposes of going to work, weekly shopping, and visiting friends and family. This suggests longer distances between work and home in inner city areas due to decentralisation of jobs. The use of cars was not eliminated for certain purposes, such as bulky, weekly shopping, even in the compact area, although it reduced significantly the need for a private car, and therefore reduced transport energy consumption.

Characteristics of travel behaviour

Statistical tests were carried out to investigate differences in travel behaviour in the four different urban forms (see Table 3).

	Garnethill	Hyndland	East Mains	Stewartfield	
Frequency of using the private car, per week	11.87	9.78	13.91	15.72	**
Frequency of using public transport, weekly	3.38	3.80	4.78	0.89	**
Distance travelled by private car per week (miles)	76.00	169.00	132.00	214.00	*
Distance travelled to go to work (miles)	40.70	56.46	44.10	70.49	
Distance travelled for non-work purposes (miles)	35.30	112.54	87.90	143.51	*

Table 3. Travel behaviour in the case study areas, in terms of frequency of use of the private car and public transport, and the distance travelled by private car on a weekly basis.

* Significant at 0.001 level.
** Significant at 0.0001 level.

The tests showed significant differences between the mean frequency of use of the car in the high-density, mixed-use area compared with the low-density, single-use area. There were also significant differences between the mean use of public transport in the four areas. Although the mean frequency of use of public transport in Garnethill is higher than in Stewartfield, it is lower than in East Mains (the low-density, mixed-use area) and Hyndland (the high-density, single-use area). Mean use is greatest in East Mains, perhaps due to its closeness to the town centre. The mean distance travelled by car per week was found to be lower in Garnethill than in Stewartfield. The mean distance travelled per week for work trips is lowest in Garnethill and highest in Stewartfield. Further, the mean distance travelled per week for non-work trips is lower in Garnethill than in Stewartfield. These findings support the argument that there is a relationship between different urban forms and the amount of car travel undertaken by residents, both for work and non-work purposes.

In terms of residents' perceptions of being able to manage without a car, the findings showed a significant difference between the compact area and the low-density, single-use area (see Table 4). Nearly 80% of the respondents in the low-density, single-use area felt they could not conveniently access city facilities other than by private car.

	Garnethill	Stewartfield	Hyndland	East Mains	
Yes	51	38	39	21	**
No	49	62	61	79	
Total	100	100	100	100	

Table 4. Perceived ability of households to manage without a private car, by case study area (% of households' responses).

** Significant at 0.001 level.

The living environment and neighbourhood

General perceptions of the quality of the living environment

To investigate residents' attitudes to their environment, they were asked to give their opinions on nine different places/spaces (see Table 5). Residents were asked which of these places they considered the 'nicest' part of their environment.

	Garnethill	Stewartfield	Hyndland	East Mains	
Home	60	49	56	49	
Neighbourhood	35	74	54	78	**
Neighbourhood streets	10	9	31	17	**
Local park/square	38	22	23	36	*
City/town square	5	3	21	12	**
Entertainment places	15	33	15	16	*
City centre	48	13	15	20	**
High Street	5	4	2	0	
Other places	2	1	1	3	

Table 5. Residents' opinions about the nicest part of their environment (% of positive responses for each location).

* Significant at 0.05 level

** Significant at 0.000 level

In the two single-use areas, the neighbourhood was seen to be the nicest part of the environment, whereas, in the two mixed-use areas, the home was seen to be the nicest part of the environment. While 'home' and 'neighbourhood' were chosen as the two nicest parts of the environment in Hyndland, East Mains and Stewartfield, those in Garnethill recorded 'home' and 'city centre' as the two nicest places.

The quality of the 'neighbourhood's streets' was perceived to be better by the respondents in the two low-density areas (East Mains and Stewartfield) than it was by those in the two high-density areas (Garnethill and Hyndland). Entertainment places were identified by a relatively large proportion of respondents in Hyndland; the 'High Street' and 'other places' were seen as the least nice part of the environment, with less than 5% of responses. The four nicest parts of the environment in each area were as shown in Table 6.

	First preference	Second preference	Third preference	Fourth preference
Garnethill	home	city centre	local park	neighbourhood
Hyndland	neighbourhood	home	entertainment places	local park/square
East Mains	home	neighbourhood	neighbourhood streets	local park/square
Stewartfield	neighbourhood	home	local park/square	city centre

Table 6. Households' preferences for the four nicest parts of the environment.

Perceptions of safety

To examine the perceived safety of the areas for walking, respondents were asked about the period of hours during which they felt safe. Responses were similar in all the areas, although the situation was seen to be slightly better in Hyndland, particularly during the evening and night time. The percentage of respondents who stated that the area always felt safe for walking was significantly higher in Hyndland (the compact single-use area) (28% of responses compared with 3% and 9% in the other areas). One reason for Garnethill not being seen to be as safe as Hyndland up till midnight may be because the former area is very close to Sauchiehall Street, one of the major streets of Glasgow in terms of entertainment, restaurants, and pubs. This would have some impact on the streets of Garnethill, as they may be used by strangers for parking late at night. Overall, the results showed a better and safer environment for walking in the high-density, homogeneous area.

Social contact in the neighbourhoods

Although around half of respondents in all four areas were satisfied with their social contacts in their neighbourhoods, residents in Hyndland were slightly more satisfied than those in the other areas. Moreover, the proportion of 'very satisfied' respondents in Garnethill was slightly higher than in the rest (see Table 7).

	Very satisfied	Satisfied	Neutral	Very dissatisfied	Dissatisfied	Total
Garnethill	25	24	35	0	15	100
Hyndland	23	36	28	5	8	100
East Mains	21	30	36	3	9	100
Stewartfield	19	31	36	3	10	100

Table 7. Degree of satisfaction with social contact in the area or neighbourhood (% responses).

Conclusions

Analyses of socio-economic and demographic data in the four case studies revealed that the two homogenous case studies, despite their locations and densities, are similar in terms of the socio-economic characteristics of their residents; and both enjoy a more successful economy, which delivers better living conditions, compared with the heterogeneous case studies.

The research findings on accessibility overwhelmingly favoured the Garnethill neighbourhood – representing the compact city form – where over two-thirds of trips were based on walking. Evidence from this study therefore supports the research proposition that the compact city is associated with much greater accessibility to city facilities for residents. Through a mixed use of land, most facilities or services were accessible to the residents via short walking trips, leading to a clear reduction in the use of private cars and, hence, consumption of fossil fuel and production of harmful emissions from vehicles.

Conversely, results related to the quality of the living environment showed that the low-density areas, through aspects such as their greenery, open spaces and parks, provided a higher quality. However, there was no significant difference in terms of overall satisfaction with the neighbourhood among the four case study areas. In terms of other social issues, there were significant differences between the areas. For example, a greater satisfaction with social contacts was reported in the compact, single-use area (Hyndland). Again, in terms of safety and security, the results favoured the compact, single-use area, where a wider span of safe hours for walking was reported.

The evidence suggests that the compact city can reduce use of private cars by up to 70%, while at the same time reducing the distance travelled for non-work trips by 75%, compared with low-density, single-use urban form. Yet there is no evidence that the compact city can eliminate the necessity for using the car, since it was the form of transport used most frequently for going to work and for bulky shopping. There is also no evidence that compact, mixed-use areas are necessarily associated with an increased use of public transport. It appears that higher densities alone may not be the solution; a combination of higher densities and mixed land uses was generally most beneficial for sustainability. Nevertheless, deficiencies were observed in the compact city: for example, it suffered from a perceived lack of greenery, open spaces and parks, and a lack of privacy. These qualities were seen to be better in the lower-density environments. These deficiencies must be addressed if the compact city is to compete with the attractiveness of low-density areas. Physical improvements might be achieved through responsive architecture/urban design, which includes:

- sufficient greenery, open space and high quality local parks;
- appropriate pavements for safe, comfortable and convenient walking;
- adequate privacy of dwellings via appropriate design; and
- better design of back courts and the front gardens to ensure optimum use by residents.

Further research on the compact city is needed to clarify various issues. Since the compact city is a multi-dimensional phenomenon, detailed investigations might be necessary to address the quality of the social interactions with neighbours, privacy of dwellings, the use of public transport, safety and security of children in the neighbourhood, crime, and education and cultural aspects.

Note
Full details of the research can be found in the PhD thesis, *Urban Sustainability: Compact versus Dispersed in Terms of Social Interaction and Patterns of Movement* (Masnavi, 1998c).

Acknowledgements
The author is grateful for comments on this chapter from Prof. William. F. Lever at the University of Glasgow and Dr Colin Porteous at the Mackintosh School of Architecture, Glasgow School of Art. The research was sponsored by the Ministry of Culture and Higher Education of the Islamic Republic of Iran.

Peter Newton, Selwyn Tucker and Michael Ambrose

Housing Form, Energy Use and Greenhouse Gas Emissions

Introduction

Public policy for much of the postwar period in Australia has been oriented towards fulfilling the so-called Australian dream of every family owning its own detached house on a separate parcel of land in a 'garden'/suburban environment (Burke *et al.*, 1990; Berry, 1996).

Shifts in economic circumstances have occurred during this period, due to increased housing costs and issues of affordability, as well as a closer scrutiny of the manner in which governments provide (and subsidise) urban infrastructure to a spectrum of land uses, including housing. Environmental and equity considerations have also entered the housing debate. These shifts have resulted in a questioning of a range of contemporary practices and attitudes – and one which has been subject to continuing interest is that of Australians' attitudes towards the type and density of housing provision in particular and, more generally, the most desirable form for accommodating Australia's population.

Primarily in response to the negative economic aspects associated with low density suburban sprawl, most state governments in Australia have now introduced planning guidelines which facilitate an increase in the density of new residential development and redevelopment (for example, *The Good Design Guide for Medium Density Housing*, introduced by the State government of Victoria in 1995). This has subsequently generated much debate among academics (e.g. Troy, 1996) and local communities (via 'Save Our Suburbs' groups wishing to retain the existing style of housing). In 1997, another major stimulus for change to Australian housing emerged in the form of the Prime Minister's November 1997 Statement, *Safeguarding the Future: Australia's Response to Climate Change* (www.environment.gov.au) where it was stated that:

> The Government will work with the States, Territories and industry to develop energy efficiency codes and standards for housing and commercial buildings, appliances and equipment … We will expand the Nationwide House Energy Rating Scheme by including a minimum energy performance requirement for new houses and major extensions and we will work with the States, Territories and industry to develop voluntary minimum energy performance standards for new and substantially refurbished commercial buildings … These initiatives will take us to best practice standards in these important areas. If this voluntary approach does not achieve acceptable progress within 12 months, we will work to implement mandatory standards. (p.6)

To date, little has changed. Indeed, little is known about the energy efficiency (or otherwise) of Australian housing. This chapter summarises recent trends concerning the supply of, and demand for, different types of housing (differentiated primarily on the basis of density of development). The extent to which medium-density housing represents a more attractive environmental outcome – in energy and greenhouse terms – than low-density detached forms of housing is examined for typical examples of a single detached dwelling and an apartment.

Housing trends in Australia – demand and supply

Detached housing remains the dominant type of new dwelling constructed in Australia. However, this dominance is being challenged as a result of an increase in construction of semi-detached villas, apartments and town houses over the past 25 years. For example, in the late 1970s, detached housing represented 80% of new approvals; by the mid-1990s the level had declined to 70% (ABS, 1996). The typical profile for new dwelling construction in the 1990s is outlined in Table 1.

Type of dwelling	Average number of dwellings/year 1992–1998	
	Number	Percentage
Detached housing	109,363	70.5
Semi-detached, terraces, town houses:		
1 storey	16,092	10.4
2+ storeys	9,155	5.9
Flats, units or apartments in:		
1–2 storey buildings	7,205	4.6
3 storey buildings	4,975	3.2
4+ storey buildings	8,300	5.4
Total	155,089	100.0

Table 1. Profile of new dwelling construction in Australia in the 1990s.
Source: Australian Bureau of Statistics (Cat. no. 8731.0).

Consumer preferences in favour of medium-density housing have also shifted in favour of higher-density living, albeit gradually, as shown in Table 2.

	Very acceptable	Acceptable	Not very acceptable	Don't know
May 1995	9	52	34	5
August 1995	8	54	34	4
November 1995	10	54	32	3
February 1996	8	55	32	5
May 1996	11	56	30	3
September 1996	10	59	28	3

Table 2. Acceptability of medium density in the local area, by quarter, 1995–1996 %).
Source: Australian Housing and Urban Research Institute, Quarterly Housing Monitor, February 1997.

The various studies undertaken over the past 20 years into medium-density housing in Australia (Maddocks and PA Consulting Services Pty Ltd, 1978; King, 1981; Green Street Joint Venture, 1991; Leyshon, 1992; Wulff, 1992; Woodhead, 1994) suggest that demand for medium-density housing can be enhanced *vis-à-vis* detached housing, via:

- improved *design* (for example, greater privacy, better layout, and reduced noise propagation);
- better *location* (in relation to jobs, transport and services); and
- competitive *pricing* (medium-density housing currently attracts a cost premium).

Housing, energy and greenhouse

The environmental impacts of buildings over their life cycle have been little studied, particularly in relation to improvements achievable in energy performance through good design and management practices, material selection, and material re-use and recycling. According to Tucker (1996), a whole-of-life approach is required to obtain a balance between environmental impacts due to the contributions of the construction of a building and those due to its operation.

Within the housing industry, sources of carbon dioxide (the main greenhouse gas by quantity) are mainly due to energy usage. Energy is consumed both in the daily operation of the house (operating energy) and in the manufacture and supply of materials used in the construction and maintenance of the house (embodied energy). The activities that result in energy use due to construction and operation of a dwelling are shown in Fig. 1.

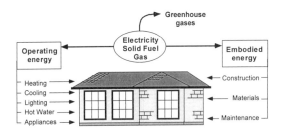

Fig. 1. Energy inputs of a typical house.

Embodied energy

It has been estimated that the energy embodied in construction in Australia is approximately 20% of annual energy consumption (Tucker *et al.*, 1998). This figure is comparable to the amount of energy used in the operation of buildings annually.

Reducing energy consumption through better design has been a goal of designers for many years, but the embodied energy portion of this consumption has largely been ignored. There are several reasons for this omission, including the absence of a clear assessment methodology, lack of data, lack of understanding and a common belief that the embodied energy portion of a building's energy consumption is insignificant. However, over recent years, the methodologies for assessment have improved, data reliability and access have increased and recent reports have indicated that the embodied energy portion may be as high as 40 times the annual operational energy of an office building and 15 times that of a house (Tucker *et al.*, 1993).

Embodied energy comprises all the energy inputs that are needed to manufacture the material elements of a house, such as flooring, glazing, roofing, fittings, and fixtures. It includes energy associated with extracting the natural resources as well as energy used in making the manufacturing equipment and in transporting raw materials and finished products. This is the process by which embodied energy is calculated in the case study dwellings described in this chapter.

Operating energy

For housing, operating energy is generally thought of as the energy – that is, electricity and gas – required to operate the dwelling. Technically, solar energy is also an energy source but, as it has no direct cost or impact on the production of greenhouse gases, it is seen as a positive energy source. Wood is sometimes used as an energy source for heating. It is those energy sources that rely on fossil fuels and consequently produce greenhouse gases that are of concern in reducing operating energy. Reducing a dwelling's need to utilise these direct energy sources helps lower the operating energy component of a building's life cycle energy. This is usually achieved through better design, orientation and selection of appliances.

The residential sector is estimated to account for around 13% of Australia's total end-use energy consumption, while the commercial building sector is estimated to account for approximately 5%. Space heating and cooling requirements constitute around 40% of this energy usage, water heating around 27%, refrigeration 11% and cooking 9%. The remainder is consumed in lighting and other appliances.

Typical energy efficient homes have been shown by computer simulation to reduce total annual energy usage by around 40%. This represents not only a significant financial saving to the residents, but also has the potential to deliver a significant reduction in Australia's overall energy consumption. Consequently, a reduction in Australia's greenhouse gas production is also possible.

There is a need, however, to take a life cycle perspective in considering energy consumption and greenhouse gas emissions within the housing sector, since the wider ramifications could fundamentally determine the sustainability of Australia's consumption-based culture. It is futile to design buildings that save either operational or embodied energy independently, as there are complex inter-dependencies. For example:

- materials need to be assessed in all relevant respects; that is, amount of material required, embodied energy coefficient and life expectancy. It is pointless using a substitute material with half the embodied energy coefficient, but which requires twice as much in, say, volume of material and needs to be replaced three times as often;
- life expectancy needs to be considered for the building item or element, rather than the material, as materials with long lives in building items with shorter lives will have their effective life reduced to that of the building item (see above); and
- embodied energy and carbon dioxide emission values should not be treated in isolation from other design concerns, such as reducing operational energy requirements through appropriate material selection. The typical example here is the concrete slab, which, although high in embodied energy and carbon dioxide emissions, provides excellent thermal mass and reduces dependence on heating systems, thus lowering operational energy usage.

Life cycle energy

Operating energy is an ongoing and recurrent expenditure. Initial embodied energy is a one-time only expenditure of energy associated with the creation of a building. However, it is important to remember that dwellings and all structures are, perhaps, among the most durable of all consumer goods. Dwellings routinely last upwards of a hundred years if properly maintained. The normal upkeep of a dwelling involves the routine maintenance and/or replacement of its components, as they wear out with age, exposure to the elements, or use. Thus, maintenance and replacement also add to the embodied energy requirements for the life cycle of the building.

Valuation services, insurers and a host of other related industries have developed sets of actuarial guidelines for most building components, including roofs, windows, and virtually all interior and exterior building elements, as well as the fixtures and appliances associated with dwellings. For the study outlined here, component life expectancies and maintenance schedules were derived from a CSIRO (Commonwealth Scientific and Industrial Research Organisation) study undertaken in 1993 for the National Public Works Council (Tucker and Rahilly, 1993). Hence, for the purposes of this study, the life cycle elements of dwellings are expressed as an additional energy and cost factor. Since operating energy is expressed as an annual value, embodied energy can be similarly reduced to a yearly value based on an industry average 80-`year lifespan of a house. The life-cycle aspect of structures can be accounted for by adjusting yearly embodied energy expenditure to reflect the periodic maintenance and replacement of various building components according to their average functional life and their relative share of total building cost.

Assessing life cycle energy in Australian housing

As Table 1 illustrates, there is a considerable mix of housing types in Australia, notwithstanding the dominance of the detached dwelling. In relation to the materials used in house construction, there is also a considerable range (for example, timber, single brick, double brick, concrete block, and fibro-cement), although the most recent statistics (1993–94) reveal a preference for brick (87%) over timber (6%) for outer walls – a significant reversal from earlier this century (1911) when 55% of dwellings had timber outer walls and only 25% brick (ABS, 1995).

Overall, then, there is a wide spectrum of choice available for new dwelling construction – in relation both to type of house and type of materials. The key question is: which is the most appropriate combination, from an energy and greenhouse perspective?

Modelling life cycle energy

In this chapter, two archetypal dwelling types are evaluated – a detached house and an apartment – using embodied energy models, operating energy models and life cycle analysis. The most common configuration, in terms of floor structure, external wall system, roof cladding and extent of insulation, was chosen for each type of dwelling in three different climate zones, where about half the population of Australia lives. Additionally, a low- and a high-performing combination of these elements for each type of dwelling were investigated for each climate zone. These few examples were considered to be representative enough to identify any major differences in life cycle energy for dwellings.

The application of the models establishes a general comparative benchmark between these dwelling types, and demonstrates the utility of the models for this type of analysis. Some indication of the relative energy costing and efficiency of flat or apartment buildings, relative to traditional detached dwellings, is a useful starting point for further and broader investigation of different dwelling types and styles, which are increasing in numbers throughout Australia. Life cycle energy analysis required the calculation of both embodied energy and operating energy, and both together.

Embodied energy model

To obtain the initial embodied energy totals for the various building designs, a prototype software package developed by CSIRO, with funding from the Energy Research and Development Corporation, was employed (Tucker *et al.*, 1998). The prototype embodied energy module utilises the APDesign software, an AutoCAD-based system tailored to creating 3D models of building designs using a large inventory of standard and custom building items. The module utilises APDesign's ability to estimate quantities of building elements, and disaggregates these into their material composition to calculate the total embodied energy and carbon dioxide emission values by material, material group, building element and the total building.

Operating energy model

The operating energy in this study is restricted to heating and cooling energy only as the other forms of energy consumption are essentially independent of the dwelling design. The heating and cooling energy was estimated using NatHERS (Nationwide House Energy Rating Scheme), a software product (NatHERS, 1998) developed in collaboration with CSIRO to provide quick, comprehensive and effective rating of different dwelling designs, materials, and sizes of home in various locations throughout Australia. The software produces a numeric and graphic representation of energy efficiency for a particular structure over a 12-month period and, by extension, over its entire operating life. It uses a five-star rating scheme of energy efficiency classification. The stars are regionally unique and defined in terms of the climatic character of the region.

The software is capable of evaluating the impact of different sizes of structure with individual footprint orientations, materials, and different insulation types, along with sizes and types of windows, roofing materials, and foundations. The software is sensitive enough to be able to factor in any savings resulting from the use of various exterior colours of building materials, due to their reflectivity. The software is user-friendly enough to allow its operator to suppress a variety of inputs, in order to assess the value of a particular basic element, or small number of basic elements, in the energy efficiency rating of structures across the country.

Case studies

The following sections outline the size, shape, and design characteristics of a typical detached house and apartment, as constructed throughout Australia. The designs selected have no specific energy efficient qualities above what is normally expected in an average display home.

Detached house

Based on an A.V. Jennings home plan, the single-storey detached home model is a 203 square metre, three-bedroom home (see Fig. 2). To determine energy efficiency, the orientation of the house was assigned to have the main living space (including kitchen and dining areas) facing north, and was constructed on a concrete slab with a brick veneer cladding and cement tile roof. Almost the entire area of the house was considered to be carpeted, with the exception of the entrance area and a gallery hallway, which are both tiled. The living area of the house includes three north-facing windows, along with two each towards the east and west. The main entry to the home is on the western façade.

To simulate various energy efficiency levels, varying degrees of insulation were included in the design. The standard house was considered to contain R2.5 insulating batts in the ceiling space and reflective foil insulation under the roof and in the external walls. For the high energy efficiency version, the insulating levels in the ceiling were increased to R3.0 batts, and R2.0 batts were placed in the external walls. The low energy efficiency version had all insulation batts removed. The impacts of these three principal variations (designated M, H, and L) on the energy efficiency of the detached house are outlined in the results section. Clearly, a range of other energy efficiency variables could have been modelled, but insulation is indicative of routes to superior thermal performance of dwelling units.

Apartment

A sample floor plan was chosen from an existing Becton City Properties project, as shown in Figure 3. The development is in a large complex of approximately 200 units. The structure is a three-level, concrete block, walk-up type building, with shared stairwells. The sample apartment is a two-bedroom unit of approximately 88 square metres. In the basic layout of the unit, the two bedrooms are located along a common long wall, with a bathroom between them. Each bedroom has one double-pane, sliding window. The other half of the apartment includes a dining/study area, along with a living room section.

As with the detached house, three variations were modelled to simulate different levels of energy efficiency. The standard apartment was considered to have concrete block walls with one wall being an exterior wall and the other being shared with an adjoining apartment and/or stairwell. The high energy efficiency model was considered to be an apartment in a mid-building location. The influence of adjacent units on either side, as well as above and below, would offer a sheltered insulation profile. The low energy efficiency model, again, has an exposed exterior wall, but the external wall structure was changed to pre-cast concrete, which has poor thermal performance

Fig. 2. One-storey detached house.

Fig. 3. Medium-density apartment.

Results

Life cycle energy

Housing energy consumption in Australia varies significantly from state to state, due to the different climate conditions. As a general rule, the warmer the climate the lower the operational energy, because of the reduction in heating energy required. Table 3 illustrates the annual energy usage for both a detached house and an apartment in three State capital cities and with three varying energy performance levels. Initial embodied energy remains the same for all climatic areas, as national values have been used, but heating and cooling energy values vary dramatically between the performance levels within each city and between the same dwellings in different cities.

The three cities selected were Brisbane, Sydney and Melbourne, all located along Australia's east coast, but at different latitudes. Brisbane is considered to be sub-tropical, Sydney is temperate and Melbourne is cool temperate. Brisbane is the best performer from the point of view of heating and cooling energy, due to its mild sub-tropical climate, resulting in little need for heating or cooling systems. Sydney's housing also performs very well, but Melbourne, with its colder climate, consumes significantly more energy, due to heating demand.

The embodied energy values increase slightly for each improvement in insulation level, due to the embodied energy of the insulating materials used. It is common to see an increase in embodied energy to achieve better operating energy values and it is usually accepted as necessary as operating energy is the largest contributor to a dwelling's total life cycle energy. However, it is not always necessary to increase embodied energy levels to achieve savings in heating and cooling energy. Changes in the design and materials used can result in lowering both embodied and operating energy. For example, in Brisbane, lightweight construction with good natural ventilation will perform well and is lower in embodied energy than the typical brick veneer construction.

Table 3 reveals that improving the thermal performance level of a dwelling can have a dramatic effect on its heating and cooling energy consumption. Sydney shows an impressive

70% reduction for the detached house when moving from the low performer to the high, while the general reduction for most dwellings in this study is around 50%. This energy saving not only translates as a cost saving for the resident through lower energy bills, but also helps reduce the amount of energy required to be generated, which reduces carbon dioxide emissions.

Location and level of insulation	Detached House				Apartment			
	Initial embodied energy (GJ)	Annual heating/ cooling energy (MJ/m²)	Life cycle energy (GJ/m²)	Life cycle energy (GJ/per occupant)	Initial embodied energy (GJ)	Annual heating/ cooling energy (MJ/m²)	Life cycle energy (GJ/m²)	Life cycle energy (GJ/per occupant)
Brisbane								
High	1027	42	12.8	898	445	48	12.9	652
Medium	1017	51	13.4	940	445	69	14.6	738
Low	993	115	18.3	1294	481	98	17.3	875
Sydney								
High	1027	47	13.2	926	445	47	12.8	647
Medium	1017	70	14.9	1045	445	78	15.3	774
Low	993	156	21.6	1515	481	111	18.4	931
Melbourne								
High	1027	143	20.9	1466	445	210	25.8	1305
Medium	1017	198	25.2	1768	445	283	31.7	1603
Low	993	273	30.9	2167	481	356	38.0	1922

Table 3. Annual dwelling energy performance.

The heating and cooling energy values for the apartment are similar to those of the detached house. However, it must be noted that these values are based on energy consumption *per square metre* and the apartment's total floor area is less than half that of the house. This is reflected in the embodied energy values, which are for the entire dwelling unit. As apartments, townhouses and units are generally smaller than detached houses, their overall energy usage, as a total dwelling unit, will be significantly smaller than a detached house, with the result that more compact living environments have significant potential for energy saving.

A more appropriate method of demonstrating the benefits of smaller, more compact living environments is to compare the energy use for both a detached house and an apartment against their respective occupancy rates. The occupancy rate for a typical detached house in Australia is 2.88 persons, while for a typical apartment it is 1.74 (ABS, 1996). Figure 4 shows the annual life cycle energy for a house and an apartment, based on consumption per occupant. In all cases, the apartments perform better than the houses, despite their lower occupancy rates. This is due to the relative size difference between the two dwelling types, with a general reduction in dwelling area of 55%, compared with the reduction in occupancy of 40%. These proportions of saving may not be achievable when all the other operating energy such as that used for lighting and appliances is taken into account; this should be investigated further.

Carbon dioxide emissions

Another important aspect of energy reduction is its impact on lowering greenhouse gas emissions, in particular carbon dioxide. Analysis of the life cycle energy consumption of a dwelling allows the relative carbon dioxide emissions to be estimated. Like energy, carbon dioxide emissions can be associated with both the construction and maintenance of a dwelling and the operating of the dwelling throughout its life. Table 4 shows the estimated carbon dioxide emissions for both case study dwellings over their life. The life cycle embodied carbon dioxide is directly proportional to the life cycle embodied energy and, as such, there is no difference between cities, but there are slight differences between the energy efficiency levels.

Location and level of insulation	Detached House				Apartment			
	Life cycle embodied CO_2 (t)	Annual heating / cooling CO_2 (kg/m²)	Life cycle CO_2 (t/m²)	Life cycle CO_2 (t/per)	Life cycle embodied CO_2 (t)	Annual heating/ cooling CO_2 (kg/m²)	Life cycle CO_2 (t/m²)	Life cycle CO_2 (t/per)
Brisbane								
High	171.99	5.67	1.30	91.69	71.46	6.48	1.33	67.29
Common	170.64	6.89	1.39	98.07	71.46	9.32	1.56	78.76
Low	166.05	15.53	2.06	145.20	74.88	13.23	1.91	96.56
Sydney								
High	171.99	6.35	1.35	95.50	71.46	6.35	1.32	66.74
Common	170.64	9.45	1.60	112.54	71.46	10.53	1.65	83.67
Low	166.05	21.06	2.50	176.41	74.88	14.99	2.05	103.66
Melbourne*								
High	171.99	12.39	1.84	129.59	71.46	36.75	3.75	189.76
Common	170.64	17.16	2.21	155.99	71.46	49.53	4.77	241.45
Low	166.05	23.66	2.71	191.05	74.88	62.30	5.83	295.10

Table 4. Life cycle carbon dioxide performance.

* Natural gas is the assumed fuel source for heating the detached house and electricity for the apartment.

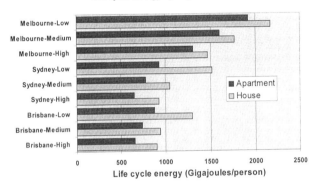

Life cycle energy by city and insulation level

Fig. 4. Life cycle energy per occupant.

Operational carbon dioxide emissions differ significantly from the operational energy values, due to the varying forms of fuel sources used to provide the energy for particular cities. Melbourne, with its cooler climate, uses predominantly natural gas for heating. Brisbane and Sydney use electricity, as their heating requirements are significantly lower, and so small electric heaters or reverse cycle air conditioners are used. These fuel sources have different levels of resultant carbon dioxide per megajoule of energy, electricity being 0.28kg/MJ and natural gas being 0.06kg/MJ (AGO, 1998). In addition, the appliances used to deliver heating and cooling have different levels of efficiency. When these factors are taken into account, it is possible to calculate the life cycle carbon dioxide emissions.

Figure 5 shows the life cycle carbon dioxide emissions for both the house and the apartment, again expressed in terms of the occupancy rates. As with heating and cooling energy, the apartment performs better in all cities. The significant levels of carbon dioxide emissions in Brisbane for the house are due to the need for significant amounts of cooling energy, which requires electricity. Design changes and a reduction in the use of cooling energy would see a dramatic drop in these values if natural gas heating were adopted.

Conclusions

Analysis of life cycle energy and the resulting greenhouse emissions for typical Australian dwellings has demonstrated the importance of considering the impact of dwellings on the environment from a whole-of-life point of view. There are three main conclusions from this study. First, the annual heating and cooling energy and embodied energy *per square metre* for the apartments are very similar to those for the detached houses, despite the total floor area of the typical apartment being less than half that of the typical house. However, when compared in terms of energy *per person*, the life cycle energy usage of apartments is significantly lower (ranging from 10% to 30% less) than for detached houses in all circumstances. This indicates that more compact living environments have significant potential for overall energy savings. Second, the life cycle carbon dioxide emissions *per square metre* differ considerably by climate zone because of the differing sources of energy used for heating and cooling. The significant levels of carbon dioxide emissions in Melbourne for the apartment are due to the use of electricity for heating. Melbourne houses predominantly use natural gas for heating, but this is uncommon in apartments. If this trend changed, a significant reduction in carbon dioxide emissions would result. Brisbane and Sydney use electricity, since their heating requirements are smaller. However, as for heating and cooling and embodied energies, emissions *per person* for apartments are generally very much smaller, ranging from 20% to 40% lower than for houses. Third, to transpose the gap in performance level beyond the individual structure of a dwelling to a wider perspective, a series of 'what if' scenarios for a city such as Brisbane demonstrate the following. What if, in 1999–2000 new dwelling construction in Brisbane shifted from the current profile of 30,000 detached houses, 5,000 semi-detached dwellings and 4,000 flats, units and apartments to 27,000 houses, 5,000 semi-detached dwellings and 9,000 apartments, to house the same population?

Life cycle CO₂ emissions by city and insulation level

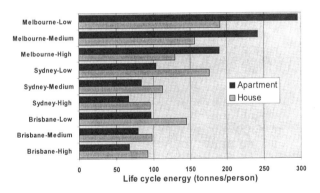

Fig. 5. Life cycle carbon dioxide emissions per occupant.

The results would be that for the lowest thermal performance-rated dwellings, the life cycle energy savings would be of the order of 2,115TJ and the greenhouse gas savings 206Kt; for the standard thermal performance-rated dwellings, the life cycle energy savings would be of the order of 1,733TJ and the greenhouse gas savings 160Kt; for the highest thermal performance-rated dwellings, the life cycle energy savings would be of the order of 3,527TJ and the greenhouse gas savings 414Kt. For a nation required, in the context of the Kyoto Protocols, to play its part in reducing greenhouse gas emissions and global warming, a reconsideration of the way in which it houses itself is certainly required.

Marina Alberti

Urban Form and Ecosystem Dynamics: *Empirical Evidence and Practical Implications*

Introduction

Urban growth and land conversion are major threats to ecosystems. They change natural habitats and species composition, disrupt hydrological systems, and modify energy flow and nutrient cycles. Since urban development alters ecological conditions (for example, species composition) through physical changes (for example, to patch structure), alternative urban patterns are expected to generate differential ecological effects. Patch structure (size, composition, persistence, and interconnectivity) is important to species survival, and the ecological conditions of any patch are related to patch characteristics. However, it is not yet understood how urban patterns affect patch structure in the urban ecosystem. Most ecological studies correlate changes in environmental systems with simple aggregated measures of urbanisation (such as the proportion of impervious surface). Urban studies, conversely, simplify ecological processes so much that they hinder their usefulness for understanding these relationships.

The hypothesis that alternative urban patterns have differential effects on ecosystems and their functions has been advanced by several authors (Howard, 1898; Lynch, 1961, 1981; Boyden *et al.*, 1981; Douglas, 1983; Owens, 1984, 1986; Owens and Rickaby, 1992; Breheny, 1992; White and Whitney, 1992; Jenks *et al.*, 1996). This hypothesis, however, has never been formally tested. Most studies have discussed how urban patterns affect resource flows directly, by redistributing solar radiation and mineral nutrients, and indirectly, by determining the resources needed to support human activities. Urban patterns also influence the feasibility of using alternative systems to supply resources and services to the urban population, thus indirectly affecting their ecological impact (Alberti, in press).

Landscape ecologists have started to document the impact of various arrangements of patch structure on ecosystems (Godron and Forman, 1982; Turner, 1989; Forman, 1995; Collinge, 1996). But various configurations of the urban structure imply alternative outcomes in the mosaic of patches, and thus differential effects on ecological processes. Three dimensions influence the relationships between urban patterns and ecological systems:

1. land use (purpose of use);
2. land cover (its actual manipulation); and
3. the biophysical and ecological conditions (effects on ecosystems).

The same land use (for example, residential use) can imply very different configurations of land cover. Likewise the same land cover (for example, deciduous forest) can be utilised for different purposes. Alternative land use/cover structures under different biophysical conditions may result in different ecological impacts. Land use and land cover categories overlap in ways that undermine their usefulness for studying the relationships between urban form and ecological impacts.

This chapter reviews empirical evidence on the impacts of urbanisation on ecosystem dynamics. First, a framework to examine the ecological impacts of urban form is presented. Then, the chapter systematically reviews the current evidence provided by urban and ecological literature on the relationship between typical urban pattern metrics (concentration, density, heterogeneity, and connectivity) and various indicators of ecosystem integrity. Finally, what we do and do not know about which pattern optimises ecological conservation potential is discussed. While current understanding of this relationship is limited, these studies help clarify the directions for future research and the implications for designing strategies to minimise urban impacts on ecosystems. This knowledge is critical to land use decisions and strategies for managing urban growth.

Impacts of urban growth on ecosystems (see end note)
Urbanisation affects the structure and function of natural systems both directly, through converting the land surface, and indirectly, by modifying energy flows and the availability of nutrients and water. The most apparent impact of urban growth on ecosystems is the rearrangement of the landscape and of its biophysical attributes that cause a variety of interrelated local and global effects (Godron and Forman, 1982). Changes in land cover affect biotic diversity, primary productivity, soil quality, run-off, and sedimentation rates. By altering the nature of the surface and generating large amounts of heat, urbanised areas modify the microclimate and air quality. The increase in impervious land area associated with urbanisation affects both geo-morphological and hydrological processes, causing changes in water and sediment fluxes (Wolman, 1967; Leopold, 1968). Since ecological functions and processes are linked with the landscape, urbanisation has important implications for ecosystem dynamics at the local and global scale (Alberti, in press).

Landscape ecologists have studied the effects of changing landscape on ecosystem structure (and functions) for quite some time (Risser *et al.*, 1984; Forman and Godron, 1986; Turner, 1989; Turner and Gardner, 1991; Pickett and Cadenasso, 1995; Gustafson, 1998). However, they have rarely studied the structure and function of populations, communities, and ecosystems under varying patterns of urbanisation and human activities (McDonnell *et al.*, 1997). Current knowledge is limited to gross measures of urbanisation. It is known that urbanisation affects patch structure by altering the size, shape, interconnectivity, and composition of natural patches. Each of these characteristics has dramatic consequences for habitat structure and species survival (Forman and Godron, 1981).

Urbanisation reduces the *size* of natural patches. Ecological studies have demonstrated that the number of native plant and animal species occurring in isolated patches decreases as patch size decreases. The effect of patch size on native species is both a direct effect of habitat loss and an indirect effect of interspecific interactions (Harris, 1984). Most studies have focused on the patch size effect on birds (Whitcomb *et al.*, 1981; Lynch and Whigham, 1984; Soulé *et al.*, 1988; Bolger *et al.*, 1991), although some have also documented its effects on mammals (Matthiae and Stearns, 1981; Dickman, 1987), insects (Faeth and Kane, 1978; Webb and Hopkins, 1984), and amphibians (Dickman, 1987). Furthermore, patch size affects plant species richness (Levenson, 1981).

Urban-induced fragmentation is also known to generate *edge* effects by increasing the length of the edge of patches exposed to disturbance agents. Ranney *et al.* (1981) have documented that edges have dramatic effects on the structure and dynamic of forests. Microclimate changes associated with fragmentation (for example, light, moisture, temperature, and wind) affect the increased edge of the forest patch. Moreover, they alter the remnant patch for tens of metres (Harris, 1984; Chen *et al.*, 1992). Edge effects are exacerbated in smaller patches, which have a large proportion of edge patch. They are also influenced by patch shape, which is a key factor in determining the proportion of edge and the effect of edge on native species (Forman and Godron, 1981).

Urbanisation is also blamed for homogenizing the landscape. The degree of habitat *heterogeneity* is considered a key factor in maintaining species diversity. Patches of higher heterogeneity support more species than more homogeneous patches. This is due to greater variation in microclimates, soil type, and topography, and thus greater variation in habitats. Patch heterogeneity, of course, interacts with patch size since large patches typically have more heterogeneous environmental conditions. Loss of heterogeneity may be more relevant for some species than others but certainly has significant effects on species richness (Newmark, 1987).

Another important factor for ecosystems threatened by urbanisation is landscape *connectivity*, which may mitigate the impact of urbanisation. Corridors that connect remnant patches are predicted to facilitate the movement of plants and animals, increasing their chances for survival. They also help maintain the integrity of other ecological processes. For example, the integrity of riparian corridors is critical to prevent soil erosion and protect water quality (Naiman and Decamps, 1990; Gregory *et al.*, 1991).

This knowledge provides a useful basis for exploring new patterns and interactions that occur in urban ecosystems. However, current evidence is inadequate to draw conclusions about the ecological performance of various urban forms. Further empirical research is needed before it is possible to assess the ecological sustainability of alternative forms. For example, the following questions need to be addressed:

- how do ecological conditions vary as a function of alternative urban patterns?
- at what scales are various ecological processes controlled in urban ecosystems?

Urban form

In spite of remarkable recent progress in studying urban ecosystems, urban ecology does not yet have an established set of urban pattern metrics to relate land uses to patch structure. As stated above, ecological studies generally correlate changes in environmental systems with simple aggregated measures of urbanisation, while urban studies, which use more disaggregated measure of urban form, simplify ecological processes so much that they provide little useful insight for understanding these relationships.

Four characteristics of urban patterns can be proposed to investigate the relationships between urban form and ecological conditions: urban concentration, land use intensity, land use heterogeneity, and land use connectivity (Alberti, in press). Urban *concentration* refers to the degree of centralisation of the urban structure. Land use *intensity* is the ratio of population or jobs to area. Land use *heterogeneity* indicates the diversity of functional land uses such as residential, commercial, industrial, and institutional. Land use *connectivity* measures the interrelation and mode of circulation of people and goods across the location of fixed activities. Each addresses some aspect of landscape structure, function, or change and can be useful in understanding ecosystem processes.

These measures are not exhaustive of all possible approaches to describing urban form. They indicate urban form characteristics that are relevant for predicting variation in ecological conditions, if links between the urban pattern and the ecological processes can be demonstrated (Turner and Gardner, 1991; Gustafson, 1998). Since these patterns can be measured, predicted and, to a certain extent, manipulated through land use policies, knowledge of their relationship with ecological processes is critical to improve our ability to design strategies to minimise the impact of urban growth.

Ecosystem processes

To assess the impact of urban form on ecosystems, a broad spectrum of ecological processes must be examined. The choice of indicators is of critical importance since there can be an infinite number of measurements but only a few might be important. Most landscape ecology studies use selected species. The debate on ecological monitoring and assessment points to the concept of ecosystem integrity. The term ecosystem integrity suggests that the attributes of ecosystem structure and functions should be metrics for measuring ecological conditions and impacts. Karr and Dudley (1981) have argued that biological integrity encompasses all factors affecting ecosystems. They define ecosystem integrity as 'the ability to support and maintain a balanced, integrated, adaptive community of organisms having a species composition, diversity, and functional organization comparable to that of natural habitat of the region' (p.56).

To assess whether urban structure and ecological conditions share spatial structure, selected studies of the impact of urbanisation on (1) plants, (2) birds, and (3) aquatic organisms are examined in the following sections. Each biological metric selected provides important information on various aspects of terrestrial and aquatic ecosystems. The studies examined explore correlations between an urban spatial variable, which describes the landscape patch structure, and an ecological variable.

Over the last decades, hundreds of empirical studies well outside the scope of this chapter have been carried out. In this review, the focus is on the treatment of urban and ecological pattern metrics. The evidence provided by current studies is systematically reviewed in order to investigate what is known about the relationship between urban patterns and ecosystems. Then, the practical implications of these studies for designing future empirical research are discussed.

Empirical evidence

Tables 1 and 2 summarize the results from several recent studies that directly or indirectly address the interactions between urban patterns and ecological processes in terrestrial and aquatic ecosystems. Apart from a few examples where land use activities are explicitly considered, all studies use aggregated measures of urban area. Most studies are based on patch structure and dynamics. Although patch structure can in principle be related to urban structure, none of the studies have explicitly addressed this relationship.

Hypothesis	Method	Urban pattern variables	Environmental variables	Major conclusions
Beissinger and Osborne, 1982				
Compared with natural areas, urban areas have lower species richness and diversity, higher biomass and density, and are dominated by a few species.	30 sampling sites were identified at 10m Habitat structure, vegetation volume.intervals on each side of two transects. Foliage height diversity and bird species diversity were calculated using the Shannon-Weaver and diversity indices.	Habitat structure, vegetation volume.	Avian density and diversity.	The urban community supports nine fewer species than the forest. Avian biomass is significantly greater in the town. The synergism of habitat structure and foraging factors favour a few species to dominate.

Blair and Launer, 1997

Butterfly species diversity can be used to assess the impact of development on natural habitat.	Experiment took place over two years. Six sites were selected to represent a rural–urban gradient. Surveys were taken for presence of species, type and amount of land cover, and human activity. Delphi technique used to rank sites; Shannon Index used to calculate species diversity; canonical correspondence analysis (CCA) used to determine how % land use coverage corresponded to species distribution and abundance.	Rural–urban gradient established by Delphi technique, using six sites. For each site, land cover was determined in terms of type and amount. Human activity at each site was also noted.	Butterfly species abundance and diversity was examined. Natural/ native habitat at each site was looked at.	Any development is detrimental to the original butterfly assemblage. Golf courses are not conducive to supporting native species. Residential area does not provide a refuge for butterflies.

Bolger *et al.*, 1997

To determine whether rodent populations within habitat fragments are viable over time. To ascertain whether species were differentially vulnerable to extinction, and if this is correlated to density.	Rodents were surveyed in 25 habitat fragments. Three control plots were used. Sherman live traps were used to trap rodents from 10/86–5/87, and then again in 1992. Relationship between species number and biogeographic variables was measured using both a stepwise logistic regression and a stepwise polychotomous logistic regression.	Fragment area and fragment age were looked at in relation to species presence.	Number of rodent species, both native and non-native, was measured to determine viability in fragments.	Fragments with no native rodents were smaller than fragments that supported rodent populations. Area is the primary determinant of species diversity. Negative effect of age on species number.

Bowers and Breland, 1996

Squirrel giving-up densities (GUDs) can be used as a functional, relativistic measure of the effects of urbanisation.	Research was collected at 78 sites in a 500 km² area in Virginia. Round plastic pans (35cm diameter, 10cm high) with 200 sunflower seeds mixed into 3l of sand were placed one per study site for 24 hours. The mean and median number of uneaten seeds were used to estimate the GUD. Multiple regression analysis was used.	Urbanisation gradient – city/town, suburban, agricultural, forest (near human), other, city park, forest (control) – was established to evaluate how grey squirrels used habitat.	Habitat usage patterns of grey squirrels – differences between urban and rural squirrels was determined.	Pans in city/town and suburbs visited more frequently and had more seed eaten than in forested areas. Grey squirrels are more abundant in urban than in rural or more natural settings.

Brittingham and Temple, 1983

High brood parasitism rates within isolate fragments of forest habitats reduce reproductive success of certain forest songbirds and may be responsible for their decline in near open habitats.	The cowbird population was indexed by a walk-and-stand transect method and recorded at 29 stations placed at intervals of 152m.	Distance to forest opening and amount of open habitat.	Occurrence of cowbirds, number of nests parasitised, cowbird eggs per nest, and interior distance of parasitised nests.	Cowbird parasitism is not the only cause of declines in songbirds. Cowbird populations are increasing.

Clergeau *et.al.*, 1998

Urban environments lead to new ecosystems with their own biological processes and particular species.	Urbanization gradients identified. Each plot mapped using Svensson method. Proportion of vegetated open space: human structures derived from maps, aerial photos, GIS. Cluster analysis performed using SAS average linkage method. Shannon-Weiner and Simpson indices of diversity used. Horn index used for similarity indices.	Levels of urbanisation – gradients based on plot location, % built-up area, and proportion of public and private gardens.	Structure and composition of bird communities. Seasonal changes in bird abundance and diversity along the urban gradient were quantified. Common attributes of the bird communities were identified.	The number of bird species decreases with level of urbanisation. The landscape setting of the city does not greatly influence the structure of the urban bird community. Local features are more important than regional ones for urban bird communities.

Fahrig and Paloheimo, 1988

The spatial arrangement of habitat patches affects local population size for species that do not move through dispersal corridors.	A mathematical model was created and tested against field studies.	Spatial arrangement of cabbage patches.	Local population size.	There is significant, though relatively small, effect of host patch spatial arrangement on local abundance in *P. ripae*.

Fahrig and Merriam, 1985

Population survival within a patch depends on the degree to which it is isolated from other patches.	Development and testing of patch dynamic model to *P. leucopus* (white footed mice) in southeastern Ontario.	Patch age and connectivity.	Population survival of *P. leucopus*.	*P. leucopus* populations in isolated woodlots have higher probability of extinction than in connected woodlots.

Germaine et al., 1998

By determining relationships between breeding birds and land cover variables, models can be developed to predict how the birds will respond to development-related habitat change.	334 plots were identified in the Tucson study area. Birds were censused for three months. Land cover was quantified using 19 variables. Gamma correlation analysis (= Kendall's Tau b + component that accounts for ties in the data) used to determine associations between bird species and land cover variables. Spearman rank correlation analysis used to determine relationship between land cover variables and bird community descriptors. Forward-stepwise multiple regression analyses used to develop predictive habitat models.	Land cover was looked at, specifically: type of vegetation, % cover by houses, % cover by paved or graded surfaces, and yards.	Species richness and abundance for breeding birds in study area was studied in relation to land cover.	Bird species formed several distinct groups based on their habitat relationships. Non-native birds were found more frequently as residential development increased. Some native birds seemed unaffected by land cover change, while others were very sensitive to the change.

Lynch and Whigham, 1984

Patch area, isolation, structure, and floristic characteristics significantly affect the local abundance of bird species breeding in the interior of upland forests.	Point survey method was used to quantify the occurrence and relative abundance of breeding bird species in the coastal plain province of Maryland.	Forest patch size, isolation, vegetation.	Index of occurrence and relative abundance of breeding bird species.	Forest isolation, plant diversity, and tree physiognomy were the best predictors of the local abundance of individual species.

Matthiae and Stearns, 1981

Landscape configurations affect mammal species richness of forest habitat patches.	Thirteen species of mammals were studied in 22 forested patches, ranging from 0.4 to 40ha, isolated by urban and agricultural land use in the Milwaukee metropolitan area, Southeastern Wisconsin, USA.	Patch size and land use.	Mammals species richness.	Species richness increases with patch size. Rural sites are more diverse. Patches in the urban–rural transition zone have lower species richness and abundance.

Rolando et al., 1997

There is little evidence to suggest adaptation of bird species has occurred with regard to urban ecology.	Eight different habitats were considered. Atlas types method for species detection and transect type method for species abundance were used. Shannon index used to determine habitat diversity.	Study areas were classified according to vegetation gradient, ranging from truly urban to completely wooded.	Pattern of habitat occupancy was observed.	The historical centre of the city had the lowest number of species and the least species diversity. Seasonal changes affected species abundance. Most species inhabit the city because of the presence of patches of their natural habitat.

Ruszczyk, 1996

Mortality factors of pupae can be identified in urban areas.	Fifty-five sampling sites were identified in Campinas, São Paulo, and % landcover was	Sites were grouped according to their positions along urban–rural gradient. % cover of various land	Pupal mortality factors were compared between *B. sophorae* and *O. invirae*.	There is higher survival potential for *B. sophorae* in urban areas. Parasite level is closely related to

calculated. Experiment took place over three years. Chi-square tests, multiple regressions, and ANOVA test were used to determine mortality and the relationship of mortality to urban variables. Pupal skins were examined to determine the mortality factor.	uses was looked at: vegetation, buildings and houses, streets and sidewalks, and open areas.			vegetation cover and may account for higher survival rate of *B. sophorae* in city centre.

Soulé *et al.*, 1988

Chaparral-requiring birds in isolated canyons have very high rates of extinction partly due to their low mobility.	The distribution of native chaparral-requiring bird species was determined for 37 isolated fragments of canyon habitat ranging in size from 0.4 to 104ha in coastal San Diego County, California.	Size of canyons, land cover, age of patches, disturbances.	Distribution of native bird species.	Chaparral-requiring species of birds have high rate of extinction in the San Diego area. Habitat area and time of isolation are significantly correlated with the number of surviving species. In the absence of large predators, smaller predators may increase the rate of extinction of birds. The effect of distance among patches is not statistically significant. Chaparral birds may be more vulnerable than forest birds because of their poor dispersal abilities.

Tilghman, 1987

Path characteristics of woodlands affect breeding bird communities.	Thirty-two sampling sites of woodland patches ranging from 1 to 69ha isolated by urban development were studied in Springfield, Massachusetts.	Habitat size, isolation, vegetation, number of adjacent building, density of shrub layer, and proximity to trails.	Number of bird species.	Patch size is the most important variable affecting the number of bird species observed.

Vizyova, 1986

Importance of habitat patch size, vegetation cover, and isolation affect number of species of land vertebrates in urban woodlands.	Species of land vertebrates were studied in 21 sites ranging from 0.6 to 47ha in Bratisiava, Slovak Republic.	Patch size, isolation and vegetation cover.	Species richness of land vertebrates.	Patch size is the best predictor of the number of species of land vertebrates. Patch size, isolation, and % vegetative cover account for 90% of the variation in species richness.

Table 1. Summary of selected studies of urban impacts on terrestrial ecosystems.

Hypothesis	Method	Urban pattern variables	Environmental variables	Major conclusions
Allan *et al.*, 1997				
The following factors are important influences of the landscape pattern on stream ecosystems: local vs. regional, and riparian vs. catchment-wide.	A case study of the River Raisin basin was performed to evaluate the influence of land use on stream integrity. The AGNPS model was used to explore how land use changes would affect non-point source run-off. The Index of Biotic Integrity (IBI) was used to assess the impact of land use change on habitat integrity.	Effects of land use within the catchment basin of the River Raisin in southeastern Michigan.	How land use affectsstream quality and habitat quality. Specifically, sedimentation yields were examined.	Water quality, habitat and biotic integrity of the river are strongly influenced by land use. Managing local and riparian conditions will provide some benefits to the environment, but it is more important to consider regional landscape conditions.
Kaufman and Marsh, 1997				
A new spatial and temporal classification should be used for edge cities. This can then be used to assess	A new classification of edge cities was developed based on a multiple-method case study approach.	Edge cities – 'urban places with at least 5 million square feet of office space, at least 600,000 square feet	Hydro-ecological impacts were evaluated, specifically changes in the hydrologic cycle, water quality and	Specific research is needed in the following areas: edge-city development forms, and data on stream

90

the hydro-ecological implications of fully developed edge cities.		of stores, a population that increases at 9am and is perceived as a single destination for job, shopping, and entertainment'. They occur in three locations: 1) interfluves; 2) valley floors; and 3) areas without any relationship to terrain. Highway location was also a variable.	stream flow. Habitat fragmentation was also considered, as was patch size.	flows, impervious surface, static groundwater levels, land use conversion, habitat fragmentation, and species diversity before and after edge-city development. The hydro-ecological impacts of edge cities typically extend beyond their own borders into neighbouring watersheds, ecosystems, and drainage systems.
Lammert and Allan, 1999				
Differences in land use among catchments account for differences in biotic integrity of streams. Scale in measurements affects the outcome of the analysis.	The Index of Biotic Integrity (IBI) and Invertebrate Community Index (ICI) were measured in six sites on three tributaries of the River Raisin watershed in Michigan, USA.	Land use and land cover at three landscape scales: entire sub-catchment upstream of site; 250m buffer area; and 100m buffer area.	Index of Biotic Integrity, Invertebrate Community Index (ICI), and in-stream habitat.	Land use immediate to tributaries predicts biotic integrity better than regional land use. The relationship between in-stream habitat variables and land use explains only a modest part of variability. Fish and macroinvertebrates respond differently to landscape configurations. Scale of analysis affects the strength of predictive variables.
Schlosser, 1991				
Identifying the relationship between the structural and functional characteristics of the landscape and stream-fish dynamics is critical to assess the impact of landscape change due to land use activities on population and community dynamics of stream fish.	Analysis of the life cycle of stream fish and the role that physical and biological processes play in regulating population and community dynamics. Analysis of the structural and functional characteristics of the landscape and fish-stream dynamics. Assessment of the influence of landscape change on these dynamics.	Land use in the drainage basin and physical heterogeneity of stream channel.	Life cycles and migration patterns, occurrence of fish species and size classes.	Land use activities result in significant alterations in population and community dynamics of stream fish. Various fish species and life stages require different types of physical habitats. Spatial heterogeneity and connectivity among terrestrial patches affect the reproductive success and survival of fish.
Wear et al., 1998				
Land cover changes are generally determined by topographic and locational features. Land cover regimes are influenced by position along the urban–rural gradient. Land cover changes differ between public and private lands at various positions along the urban–rural gradient.	Position along the u-r gradient was measured based on travel distance along road to the closest city. Empirical analysis was used to determine land cover change along the u-r gradient with respect to topographic, social, and locational variables. A simulation model was used to test for (1) differences in the implied equilibrium land cover at different positions along the u-r gradient and (2) implied changes in equilibrium land cover as development proceeds.	Land use changes along a rural–urban gradient were analysed in terms of both public land use and private land use.	Land cover change, especially from forested lands to non-forested lands, was looked at. Implications of land use change on water quality was then deduced.	Forest disturbance regimes and land cover changes are significantly related to site quality and location variables. Changes in land cover differ between public and private lands due to structural differences. Position on the u-r gradient influences land cover change regimes and could have a substantial influence on resulting landscape patterns. Potential water quality impacts are not spread evenly throughout the watershed, nor are they a simple decreasing function of distance from the city.

Table 2. Summary of selected studies of urban impacts on aquatic ecosystems.

Effects on plants

Fragmentation of natural patches is one of the best known impacts of human activities on the diversity, structure, and distribution of vegetation (Levenson, 1981; Ranney *et al.*, 1981; Brothers and Spingarn, 1992). Although the differential effect of alternative urbanisation patterns on plants is still not fully understood, it is known that converting natural or rural landscape into an urbanised landscape reduces the diversity of native plant species diversity in the urbanised region. However, species richness of non-native plants can also increase as a result of colonization of more tolerant plants. Levenson (1981) applied principles of island biogeography to woody vegetation in metropolitan Milwaukee, Wisconsin, and found that native species richness declined as patch size fell below 4.0 hectares.

The edge effect has been studied particularly in forests (Ranney *et al.*, 1981; Harris, 1984; Brothers and Spingarn, 1992; Murcia, 1995). Because forests are primarily vertical in structure, the removal of vegetation, and consequent exposure to natural and human disturbances, have important consequences on the structure and composition of plant communities. Ranney *et al.* (1981) have shown that deciduous forest edges in Southern Wisconsin contained more pioneer plants than the interior, and higher densities of shrubs and herbaceous vegetation for several metres into the forest patches. These plants also had higher species richness as a result of the invasion of non-native plants.

In addition to changes in species composition, urbanisation affects plant-environment interactions and vegetation functions in urban ecosystems. The urban forest influences the microclimate and the atmospheric concentration of pollutants and local carbon storage fluxes (Jo and McPherson, 1995). McPherson *et al.* (1994) estimated that in 1991 the tree cover in Chicago removed 17 tonnes of CO, 93 tonnes of SO_2, 98 tonnes of NO_2, 210 tonnes of O_3, and 234 tonnes of (less than 10 micron) PM. These trees also store 942,000 tonnes of carbon. Other important ecological functions of the urban forest include the mitigation of storm-water run-off and flood control. Many studies show, in addition, the role of urban vegetation in providing critical aesthetic values and community well-being.

While the evidence provided by these studies substantiates the hypothesis that urban patterns affect plant communities and vegetation functions in urban ecosystems, no one has yet systematically studied how alternative spatial urban structures influence conservation potential through various configurations of urban land uses and activities.

Effects on birds

Birds respond rapidly to changes in landscape configuration, composition, and function. Thus, they are excellent indicators of the effects of urbanisation on ecosystems. Urbanisation affects birds directly through changes in ecosystem processes, habitat, and food supply, and indirectly through changes in predation and interspecific competition (Marzluff *et al.*, 1998).

Most research on island biogeography has focused primarily on non-urban environments. Since Bond's 1957 study of area-sensitive birds, scholars have studied the effects of fragmentation on forest birds. But while most studies have focused on the effects of patch area on species composition (Moore and Hooper, 1975; Whitcomb *et al.*, 1981), a few have started to explore other factors and their relative contribution in explaining species survival. Robbins *et al.* (1989) have examined the effect of area, isolation, and vegetation characteristics on bird species composition in 67 forest islands in Maryland, Pennsylvania, and Virginia. They concluded that vegetation and isolation were consistently the best predictors of occurrence for bird species.

Lynch and Whigham (1984) studied the effects of habitat fragmentation on birds in the upland forest in the coastal plain of Maryland. They showed that the number of bird species breeding in the upland forests was significantly influenced by patch isolation, physiognomy, and floristic diversity. They stressed that the impacts of fragmentation on bird population are species-specific, but both structural and floristic characteristics of the forest were more important than patch size and isolation.

Recent studies of the impacts of urbanisation on birds provide more insight into the role of urban patterns (Beissinger and Osborne, 1982; Vizyova, 1986; Tilghman, 1987; Bolger *et al.*, 1997; Rolando *et al.*, 1997; Germaine *et al.*, 1998). These studies have started to document how urbanisation modifies the composition of urban avian communities through change in climate, abundant food and water supply, increased nest sites, and smaller predators. Native species decline in population because of reduced natural habitats and intolerance of human disturbances (Beissinger and Osborne, 1982; Rosenberg *et al.*, 1987; Blair and Walsberg, 1996).

A majority of bird studies in urban habitats were conducted in forested tracts. Habitat fragmentation creates edges and reduces vegetative cover with implications for food supply, nest placement, and predation. Beissinger and Osborne (1982) compared the avian community of a mature residential area in Oxford, Ohio, with two control sites in Hueston Woods State Park. The urban community supported nine fewer species than the forest, a difference explained primarily by vegetative cover and habitat patchiness. Tilghman (1987) studied the factors of urban woodlands that affect breeding bird diversity and abundance in Springfield, Massachusetts. She found that woodland size is the most important single variable explaining the number of bird species.

Soulé *et al.* (1988) studied birds that require native chaparral in 37 fragments of canyon habitat in coastal, urban San Diego. Focusing on the effect of isolation on species diversity, 90% of the variation in species richness across the fragments was explained by four variables: canyon age, total area of chaparral, total area of canyon, and predation. The absence of coyotes in urbanised environments allowed greater numbers of grey foxes and other avian predators (Soulé *et al.*, 1988). By eliminating large predators, urbanisation offset their capacity to control small predators and their impacts on birds.

Studies of the effect of fragmentation on birds are extensive and provide evidence of the effects of various degrees of urbanisation on community diversity and reproduction. However, it is not known how variation in the concentration, land use intensity, heterogeneity, and connectivity of urban development is correlated with the relative abundance and community diversity of birds and their chance of reproduction and survival.

Effects on stream ecosystems

Fish and benthic invertebrates have been proposed as useful metrics to assess the biological conditions of aquatic ecosystems and human impacts on streams (Kerans and Karr, 1994). The Index of Biotic Integrity (IBI) framework, initially developed for fish (Karr, 1981), is now also being applied to benthic invertebrates (Benthic Index of Biological Integrity, BIBI). Ecological studies have documented the impact of urbanisation on the B-IBI; however, the variability is only modestly explained by aggregated measures such as population density and total impervious surface. As well as being poor predictors of biological conditions, such aggregated measures of urban development provide little help to planners and managers.

Several authors hypothesise that the spatial distribution of impervious area in the watershed, and its connectivity to the channel, affect the hydrologic response of the watershed, and thus the biological conditions in a stream. Hence, alternative land use patterns may have differential effects on aquatic ecosystems. Beacause of the influence of biophysical and biological processes on fish stream dynamics, land use activities result in relevant alterations in fish population and communities (Schlosser, 1991).

Fish and macroinvertebrates have been used to compare the biotic integrity of streams in relation to various degrees of urbanisation in watersheds. The two taxonomic groups are used to measure both the biotic diversity and the pollution tolerance of species. But while fish reflect conditions over a large scale, macroinvertebrates may better reflect local environmental conditions. Evidence from current studies documents the relationship between land use/land cover and biotic integrity. Recent studies of macroinvertebrates have established that several local land use and habitat variables (for example, channel morphology) are superior to regional land use in predicting biotic integrity, and that predictive models are greatly improved by adding these variables (Richard *et al.*, 1996; Lammert and Allen, 1999).

The study of human impacts on stream ecology has raised the issue of scale. Several ecologists have demonstrated that the environmental variability affecting stream ecology occurs at multiple and temporal scales (Frissel *et al.*, 1986; Hawikins *et al.*, 1993). Great variations between the outcome of taxonomic groups suggest that the scale of investigation influences the strength of predictive variables. However, this hypothesis has not been explicitly tested in the urban environment.

Discussion

The literature on landscape ecology may contribute most to the study of the relationships between urban patterns and ecosystem dynamics. Building on island biogeography (MacArthur and Wilson, 1967) and metapopulation theory (Levins, 1969), landscape ecologists have been the first among the ecologists to conceptualise and synthesise the effects of spatially-explicit processes on ecosystem structure and functions. They have also been among the first to expose ecology to the study of human-dominated systems and highly transformed environments. This review raises important questions for urban research.

None of these studies directly addresses the critical question of what patterns of urban development best reduce ecological impacts and optimise conservation. All the studies reviewed use highly aggregated measures of urbanisation. They are helpful because they determine the mechanisms behind the relationships between spatial patterns and ecological processes, and the importance of gradients, and of spatial and temporal scale. Thus, they suggest some critical elements on which to build future empirical research.

A major methodological innovation will be required to integrate land use and land cover variables in the study of these relationships: a new classification system to meet both urban and ecosystem research needs. A recent review of land use classification systems by the International Geosphere Biosphere Program and Human Dimension Program of Global Environmental Change Programme indicates that current systems suffer from several problems (Turner *et al.*, 1995): lack of sound definition of the units of analysis; overlapping classification classes; absence of quantitative class boundaries (critical threshold values); combination of land use with other dimensions; and multiplicity of land use classification objectives. Since various urban patterns imply different land uses, land cover, and ecological outcomes, it is necessary to develop specific metrics of urban patterns. Urban patterns are influenced by two factors: how the land is used and how it is directly and/or indirectly modified. These patterns, driven by socio-economic factors, influence natural ecosystem dynamics. Three dimensions have been proposed to investigate these interactions (Turner *et al.*, 1995):

- How land is used – how does the land satisfy a specific human activity (for example, industrial, commercial, residential multi-family, residential single-family and so on)?
- How the land cover is manipulated – how is the land biophysically manipulated (for example, paving, cutting, drying, burning, planting and so on)?
- Biophysical and ecological conditions – what are the biophysical and ecological conditions under which land is used (for example, climate zones, soils, and so on)?

A second critical element is scale. To model land use/cover change dynamics, spatial and hierarchical scales must be crossed. Developments in hierarchy theory have demonstrated how landscape processes and constraints change across scales (O'Neill *et al.*, 1986). Since landscapes are spatially heterogeneous areas, the structure, function, and change of landscapes are scale dependent (Turner and Gardner, 1991). Spatial heterogeneity in both land use and land cover may affect the outcome of changes in driving forces only at certain scales (Turner *et al.*, 1995), yet current understanding of spatial scale links is still limited. Two scale issues must be addressed in linking land use and land cover change. First, each scale has its specific units and variables. Second, the relationships between variables and units change with scale. To tackle these issues, a nested approach needs to be developed.

A third element is the location on an urban-to-rural gradient. Urbanisation results in a complex pattern of intermixed high- and low-density built-up areas. Current evidence indicates that urban–rural gradients are not purely geographical, and cannot be described using a simple geographical transect from the urban core to ex-urban rural areas. Rather, they can best be described using a series of urban pattern metrics: some describe spatially aggregated variables (for example, land use intensity), and some describe spatial distributions of land use or land cover types (for example, heterogeneity). Each urban pattern metric describes an urban–rural gradient.

Implications
The transformation of the natural landscape into a highly human-dominated environment is expected to continue through the next century. Urbanisation cannot be prevented but it is possible to influence its direction and reduce its ecological impacts. The literature provides evidence of how human impacts on the landscape affect ecosystems. Studies of environmental change in urban ecosystems also provide a basis for new empirical research aiming to answer two questions that are critical for humanity: how can we manage urban growth to minimize its impacts on ecosystems?; and what patterns of urban development best facilitate ecological conservation? Land use is one of the most important factors influencing ecological processes and biodiversity, but there is still little understanding of how urban form affects ecosystem dynamics. In particular, how do changes in the extent and patterns of land uses affect various ecosystem processes? Urban patterns influence ecosystems via multiple disturbances operating at various scales. The interactions among disturbances at various levels can vary in relation to each urban pattern, yielding 'thresholds' in the relationship. These elements suggest implications for urban planning and management and directions for future research.

Prevention
Natural patch fragmentation has disruptive effects on ecosystems. While much research is still needed to understand the relationships between urban patterns and patch fragmentation, it is clear that the best way to prevent impacts on ecosystem functions and processes is to avoid fragmentation. Current ecological studies suggest that natural patches should be maintained as large and interconnected as possible.

Ecosystem approach
Species differ in habitat requirements and it is difficult to establish generic criteria and guidelines for all species. Furthermore, many elements of biodiversity, and the importance of organisms, are unknown. In studying and managing the impact of urban growth, an ecosystem approach can help protect millions of species and their critical functions, and avoid the mistakes of compartmentalised species-by-species protection strategies.

Adaptive management

Given the limited knowledge and uncertainty, adaptive management strategies may be most adequate. Adaptive management uses management intervention to strategically probe the functioning of an ecosystem. Interventions are designed to test key hypotheses about human impacts on ecosystem functions. Adaptive management identifies uncertainties, and then establishes methodologies to test hypotheses concerning those uncertainties. From this perspective, management is a tool not only to change the system, but also to learn about it.

Spatial metrics and scale

A number of spacial metrics can be proposed as measures of the ecosystem's ability to support important ecosystem functions. Urban patterns are scale dependent or are relevant to processes operating only at specific spatial scales. Since urban patterns are more significant at some scales than at others, the scale at which we predict, monitor, and manage ecological impacts is critical. This knowledge should inform the choice of the scale at which the interactions between urban patterns and ecological processes will be monitored and managed through spatial policies.

Cumulative effects and thresholds

Finally, to establish correlations between urban patterns and ecosystem dynamics, it is necessary to focus on ecosystem integrity and resilience rather than on specific indicators of pressure on environmental components. These indicators are likely to be the most difficult to incorporate in policy due to the scientific uncertainty and incomplete knowledge on the functioning of ecosystems.

In addition to the criteria suggested above for planning and managing urban growth, there are perhaps four critical areas for future research. First, it is necessary to define and measure urban patterns and establish metrics that better describe urban form. Second, long term empirical research is needed on the relationships between urban form and ecosystem dynamics in urban ecosystems to answer the questions posed in this chapter. Third, it is necessary to better predict urban growth and link predictions with models of ecological disturbances to provide decision makers with tools to explore impacts of alternative urban scenarios. Fourth, current monitoring programs are not designed to monitor ecological impacts of urban areas. For urban planning strategies to succeed, new datasets and more sophisticated monitoring programs need to be designed to assess progress towards a more sustainable urban form.

Note

The ecosystem is the whole complex of organisms and the physical environment they inhabit. The structure of an ecosystem refers to the distribution of energy, materials and species. The functions refer to the flow of energy and materials through the food chains and bio-geochemical cycles.

Acknowledgements

I am grateful to Elysian Mah and Pavinee Inchompoo for research assistance. This chapter has benefited from discussions with Kristina Hill, John Marzluff, Derek Booth, and Eric Shulenberger (University of Washington).

Ernie Scoffham and Teresa Marat-Mendes

The 'Ground Rules' of Sustainable Urban Form

Introduction

It is argued that urban form is only sustainable if it is acceptable to its inhabitants. This means it needs to be able to adapt to changing requirements over time. In attempting to find urban development solutions that will not alienate people, it is useful to examine those in history that have accommodated the pressures of technological and social change without alienation. The developed world was once developing, different parts of it at different times. Ancient Greece was developed at a time when the Roman Empire was developing, Rome was over-developed when Byzantine and Muslim cities were being established, and these, in turn, were museum pieces when medieval lords and merchants sought to encourage trading centres. The medieval town was overpopulated when Renaissance ideal-city planners formulated an elitist taste for an anonymous population, and Renaissance idealism was inadequate to deal with the population explosions of the industrial revolution. Nineteenth-century industrial squalor was the enemy of post First and Second World War reconstruction in Europe, and post Second World War rationalism has been savaged for its inhumanity.

From all these phases of developed and developing urbanisation there are survivors – towns that exhibit an ability to accommodate the changes of the next generation in an unselfconscious manner. It is this apparent historical regression that is emerging today in countries that find themselves the victims of overbearing rationalism, but critics who believe in a rational scientific approach to problem solving describe it as nostalgic romanticism. A dilemma is exposed: there is pressure to ensure rational argument prevails, but there is also the need to accommodate the apparently irrational nature of human behaviour, the popular banalities that educated taste seeks to submerge under an imposed pattern.

The patterns of development that have permitted educated taste and its wilful changes of fashion to live alongside popular choice are now worthy of examination. They are patterns that on one hand exhibit a seeming indifference to the environment, and on the other an environmental quality that transcends time by its neutral rationalism. The aim of this chapter is to identify the physical qualities, or 'ground rules', of such patterns, the dimensions of built form that, because they are adaptable, may be deemed to be sustainable.

Realisation of the potential of 'ground rules'

During the late 1960s and early 1970s the Centre for Land Use and Built Form Studies at Cambridge University (LUBFS), led by Leslie Martin and Lionel March, revealed a series of spatial, mathematical models which exhibited what could be described as a neutral rationalism (Martin and March, 1966, 1972) – 'relaxed simplicity' was the term used by Lionel March. LUBFS proved that the courtyard layout has a higher land use intensity, or plot ratio, than some other built forms. They suggested that linear ribbons of development enclosing squares achieve optimum density conditions. The principle of the 'fresnel' diagram, in which successive rings of the same area become narrower in proportion to the square of their distance from the centre, was the scientific base. The idea, common at the time, that high urban densities could only be achieved through high-rise blocks and towers was questioned. This questioning extended to Patrick Abercrombie's Greater London Plan (1944), on which postwar urban development policies had been based. Lionel March demonstrated his findings to the 1967 RIBA Conference, using the example of the abortive Hook New Town Plan of the London County Council. This had allowed 16 acres (6.48ha) of open space for every 1,000 people. By interpolation this meant that 20 acres (8.09ha) would be the requirement for 1,280 people. March revealed that this could be provided using a ribbon of three-storey houses, each with a small garden, surrounding the required open space. This would lead to a resultant net density of 200 persons per acre (494 per ha). The urban form would be similar in scale to Parker's Piece, a major public open space in Cambridge, and its surrounding terraced housing with simple road access (March, 1967). By locating open space in the centre of the 'fresnel' diagram, the effect of spaciousness between houses became increasingly pronounced as population targets required more open space.

Two housing projects in the London Borough of Merton demonstrated the practical validity of the LUBFS's work. At Pollards Hill, an exchange of land allowed recreational facilities to be placed in the centre of the site, so permitting unhindered perimeter development (*Architectural Review*, 1971; *Architectural Design*, 1971). The form of this perimeter development was an alternating series of P-shapes, one accommodating a short vehicle cul-de-sac, and the other some amenity open space between the three-storey housing blocks, arranged as a continuous terrace. A density of 116 bed spaces per acre (286 per ha) was achieved, each house having its own integral garage and private garden with immediate access to the open space. The second project, at Eastfields, used the same continuous terrace but with less convolution of the blocks and hence a lower density of 96 persons per acre (237 per ha) (*Architects' Journal*, 1974).

Compared with the majority of architecturally innovative postwar housing in Britain, and indeed elsewhere, these schemes are landmarks of built form design and planning. They have greater complexity, more advanced technology and, often, lower densities. The density of 116 persons per acre (286 per ha) achieved at Pollards Hill was greater than the density of London County Council's Roehampton Estates of 1952–57 (100 persons per acre, 247 per ha), where slabs and towers of two, four, eight and eleven storeys were used, none of the dwellings had integral garages and few had private gardens. The roads and much of the open space at Roehampton have now been appropriated by parked cars.

The LUBFS research had wide-ranging implications that prevail some 25 years later. Their exhortations to establish facts 'before rushing into producing exciting physical answers to non-existent problems' (March, 1972, p.378) attempted to prevent the kind of 'intellectual pleasure that is derived from a clever arrangement of inadequate space' (*ibid.*, p.378).

In 1974, LUBFS's ideas were investigated on a larger scale by MacCormac and Jamieson in a limited competition for the design and layout of 977 dwellings in Duffryn, South Wales. Whereas at Pollards Hill the intention had been to obtain the highest possible density with all houses on the ground, at Duffryn the density was prescribed at 70.8 persons per acre (175 per ha), so enabling house frontages to be 7.5 metres, twice the width of Pollards Hill. The convolution of the perimeter block was relaxed so that it could be modelled to the shape of the site (*Architectural Design*, 1977). A school was accommodated within the perimeter of housing, so the centre of the site was a huge, green, traffic-free area comprising all the open space of the project.

In his criticism of Duffryn, Peter Davey praised the ability of perimeter planning 'to extend to the working-class the benefits of living in individual houses in close contact with nature' (1980, p.214), stating that 'these are the kind of middle-class freedoms that Duffryn offers to its working-class tenants' (*ibid.,* p.214).

The intention of the design of housing at Fishermead, in the central area of Milton Keynes, was also not that of achieving a high density, but a conscious attempt to create street-facing housing with the benefits of car access and pedestrian activity. A perimeter development was built around the edges of 180 by 130 metre sectors, with flats on the corners and family houses along the sides. At the corners, provision was made for facilities such as a surgery, club, library, shops and offices. These perimeter buildings enclose an open space, 100 by 50 metres in size, with direct access from private gardens. Within this framework, houses are varied in frontage, height and type to achieve the required dwelling mix, while consistency of architectural form is maintained by uniformity of detailing. The first phase at Fishermead in 1972 uses a perimeter of three-storey terraces with three-storey corner units of flats and shops. Conniburrow is another sector in Fishermead style, while Downs Barn, further from the centre, consists mainly of two-storey houses on larger plots (*Architectural Design*, 1974).

Seen against the pattern of history where towns grew gradually, constantly changing to fresh pressures, being added to and renewed in phases, the rigidity of central Milton Keynes has been challenged. To an extent this criticism is answered through the ability of the urban framework to accommodate different housing requirements in different locations. The determined aesthetic and rigid geometrical order of Milton Keynes appears to defeat the attainment of a popular familiarity, through social intervention, that would give visual variety within the sustained framework – a characteristic of those towns in history that have survived social and economic pressures intact.

The perimeter block design principle appears to accommodate long-term objectives of adaptation and change without disruption of the original urban intention. The potential simplicity of the house plans, certainly the wider frontage ones, seems to satisfy the need for an amply dimensioned shell that permits renovation and adaptation to occur. The precedent for façades to be remodelled to accommodate changes in taste and style exists in history, but whether Milton Keynes' planners are so adaptable remains to be seen. While flexibility and adaptability were prime motives in the planning framework, they are translated at the level of physical provision, rather than as part of a developing social system – a pattern that will continue to develop while the physical framework remains the same. Richard MacCormac, architect for Merton and Duffryn, described a pattern that:

> confirms a satisfactory achievement of social equilibrium ... so that the need for individual expression in housing may be inverse to the acceptability of the overall image. (MacCormac, 1978, p.205)

Historical precedent

To Danish architect Steen Eiler Rasmussen, central Milton Keynes represents 'a continuation and a perfection of the special London pattern of the seventeenth and eighteenth centuries that was so different from all continental city planning of that period' (1980, p.141). The result was thus not new but the continuation of a tradition of built form planning that was reminiscent of the initial building and growth of the West End of London, where the grid of roads – like Milton Keynes, about one kilometre apart – guided the development of housing between them, and the introduction of squares and access to the English landscaped hunting parks of St James', Hyde and Regent's, within a comprehensive plan.

Significantly, the scale of the central Milton Keynes grid block of 1972 onwards is not too different from that of the grid block of New Salisbury, laid out in 1220, about which Tony Morris remarked, 'Its comparative regularity has proved well suited to mid-twentieth century city centre regeneration' (1979, p.109). This parallel exposes the increasing relevance of the theme of continuity of built form over a long period of time. New Salisbury accommodates an unselfconscious ability to adapt and change to social and economic pressures, an ability that is behind the motives, if not the reality, of central Milton Keynes.

This variability within a defined framework had been sought by Nikolas Habraken in the 1960s, at a time when the majority of European housing projects were being designed to precise specifications of dwelling size, mix and density. Habraken (1972) attempted to distinguish the constant elements of housing – structure, services, roads – from the variables – social mix, space standards, fixtures and equipment. His book, *Supports: An Alternative to Mass Housing*, is deliberately devoid of illustrations so avoiding any confusion that might be caused by the interpretation of visual preferences. Unfortunately, many of the projects based on his work demonstrated the prevailing tendency to translate such ideas through technological devices: structure and service frames, de-mountable partitions and interchangeable panels. What Habraken so eloquently described in words had been in existence for a considerable period of time, but could not be appreciated until the blinkered myopia of technology had been corrected.

Using his experience of self-build housing in South America, John Turner attempted to make this correction. He advocated a rearrangement of the knowledge we already have, to 'formulate practical performance standards for environmental design that would generate social and economic as well as physical harmony' (1976, p.101). Turner made reference to the new town plantations of Edward I in the Middle Ages, where a progressive development by individuals was allowed within an ordained framework. He described this as 'legislative planning', a setting out of the limits of what individuals were free to do, rather than the imposition of standard procedures to which they must adhere. The framework is one that has survived while the contents have changed with the passing of time – a framework that encouraged progressive development according to the 'will of autonomously organised people and communities' (Turner, 1976, p.101).

In his account of the *New Towns of the Middle Ages*, Maurice Beresford (1967) describes the intention of making towns 'to the greatest profit of merchants living there or coming to trade' (p.14). He also gives an account of a meeting of town planners at Bury St Edmunds in 1297, chaired by Edward I, at which their duties were 'to devise, order and array a new town' (*ibid.*, p.14). 'To devise' meant the selection and procurement of a site; 'to order' meant the recruitment of townsmen and their furnishing with privileges and legal security; and 'to array' meant giving the town physical accoutrements appropriate to its role (Beresford, 1967). With trade the prime function of towns, building frontage was a valuable commercial asset, especially near gates and market places. The resulting urban form, according to Tony Morris (1979), led to informally intense street scenes full of 'repeated visual surprise' (p.73). It was an apparently accidental result, yet he asserts that 'there was collective action more frequently than might be supposed' (Morris, 1979, p.73).

Winchelsea was laid out in 1292 by a merchant, Thomas Alard, at the behest of Edward I. Its plan was an irregular grid of broad streets defining 29 quarters of different and changing use. The river that brought Winchelsea its wine trade with Bordeaux silted up in the mid-fourteenth century and the town declined, yet today the remaining grid quarters survive to accommodate a very different town (Beresford, 1967). The model underlying Winchelsea can be seen in numerous medieval town plantations throughout England and Wales, and in the 'bastides' of Gascony – Montpazier being the most regular example. All of these towns are variations on a theme, relieved of the monotony that the plan apparently implies by local characteristics. According to Morris:

> only when each one [*medieval town*] is appreciated in the context of a number of others can its essential individuality be understood ... the limited vocabulary of planning components was ... adapted to each site in such a way that individuality of form was established from the outset. Time has enhanced the variations, with many sympathetic relationships of mediaeval and minor Renaissance buildings. (Morris, 1979, p.98)

Later medieval trading centres had more grand pretensions but were based on the same principles. What becomes noticeable is the gradual increase in space within the trading streets. The new towns of the Dukes of Zähringen, throughout what is now south-west Germany and western Switzerland, are notable examples, the most consistently impressive being Bern: originally 64 homesteads each with a frontage of 29.4 metres and a depth of 17.6 metres, which were later divided up into narrow frontage lots. All the Zähringen foundations (plantations) had common ground rules by the end of the twelfth century, among them being: a 22.0 to 29.4 metre wide market thoroughfare running the full length of the town, between the gates, no other interior spaces, the homestead as a planning module, a gridiron plan, public buildings located away from the market street, and a sewage system (Morris, 1979).

In the *Plan of the Three Canals* for Amsterdam in 1607, the trading motive brought an even greater spacing for merchant houses along the three principal canals. Development occurred against the background of a preconceived and existing canal network and a series of dimensional regulations that prescribed a distance of 47.1 metres between houses lining the main canals, an average frontage width of 7.7 metres for individual lots and a garden spacing between the backs of houses of not less than 35.3 metres. Along with other constructional regulations, these ground rules permitted the development and progressive modernisation of the inner city to that which is seen today (Morris, 1979). The dimensions are generous and far exceed those of Milton Keynes, New Salisbury and Winchelsea. Amsterdam was the mother city of a Dutch trading post at the mouth of the Hudson River (New Amsterdam), founded in 1618 upon a tract of land purchased from Manahatas Indians for scrap yard junk (Moholy-Nagy, 1968). During the next 300 years, New Amsterdam became New York, the largest city on earth; but its development beyond the boundary of Wall Street was to an altogether different set of ground rules, which did not include the provision of space.

Space was the major contribution of Renaissance planners in the evolution of development frameworks. The most significant aspect of this was the reversal of the medieval perimeter pattern of narrow frontage lots with ample rear gardens facing relatively narrow trading streets, and the exclusion of public open space except for market purposes, to the notion of the residential square around which houses were arranged behind formally designed façades. The motive for this was the accommodation of traffic, the coach and carriage trade that allowed Renaissance men and women to see and be seen. Later, in the case of London, the residential square became a public garden for the enjoyment of the inhabitants of surrounding houses. The inclusion of these garden squares among the speculative street façades of Mayfair, Bloomsbury and Belgravia formed the pattern of development that Rasmussen paralleled with the modern development of central Milton Keynes. The ground rules for Georgian London have been described by Summerson (1969): they were devised to encourage speculative development, under the authority of commissioners to allot ground for the rebuilding of houses. Frontages, at up to 8.8 metres wide, were generous by narrow lot standards, and encouraged the three-window façade that is familiar in Amsterdam, Bath, Edinburgh, the West End of

London and, indeed, most of the trading world. The 'shop house' of the Far East accommodates the intensive activities of trade, housing, workshop and storeroom behind its three-window, arcade façade. Ample windows were needed in Amsterdam to permit light to penetrate into a deep building form and this, in turn, encouraged the Dutch school of painting in its preoccupation with light, shade and perspective.

In summarising the Renaissance achievement, Morris (1979) argued that 'although its [*the gridiron*] Renaissance applications may have been unimaginative, the results generally had urban qualities, notably spaciousness, which were to be sadly lacking in the inhuman gridiron by-law housing of the industrial revolution' (p.126). In Britain, it was certainly the dismal legacy of nineteenth-century by-law housing that prevented appreciation of the ground rules by which its development had been controlled. Rightly, the tightly packed terraces, often of back to back houses, have been condemned for their inhumanity; but the more generously laid out terraces are part of a tradition that considerably pre-dates the industrial revolution. It is these examples that have accommodated the renovations and improvements brought about by the financial incentives of legislation during the 1970s and 1980s, and have also brought about an appreciation of the continuity of built form.

Soon after the renewal of confidence in urbanisation in Britain, following the restoration of the monarchy, John Lowther began the expansion of his coal mining and shipping interests at Whitehaven in Cumbria. Whitehaven grew to become the second port in Britain, by volume of trade, towards the end of the eighteenth-century and its growth, a hundred years before the industrial revolution, gave a foretaste of what was to follow. Successive generations of Lowthers controlled the development of the town by specific ground rules that recreated, in miniature and for a working class, many of the objectives of Georgian London, to which they constantly travelled on business and to attend parliament. These rules stipulated a 4.4 metre-wide house lot and a three-storey street frontage; two or more lots could be taken up, and double frontage houses were encouraged.

The layout of Whitehaven was so controlled that its dimensions enabled consultants Barnett Winskell, during the 1980s, to regenerate the original town by clearing overbuilding from back lots for the insertion of contemporary requirements, particularly the car. The Lowther plan has facilitated the insertion of new buildings alongside the old, while the old have been renovated for another generation (Fig. 1) (Barnett and Winskell, 1977).

Fig. 1.
Rejuvenation of a
grid block at
Whitehaven,
Cumbria.
Source: Barnett and
Winskell, 1977.

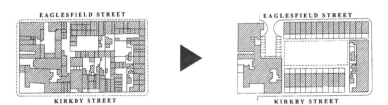

Stefan Muthesius (1982) has recorded the history of the English terraced house. He describes the various classes of houses intended for workers in London during the industrial revolution. Class 1 was 5.9 metres wide, had a three-window façade, was of four storeys and a basement, had a first-floor drawing room and an inside toilet; class 2 was 5.0 metres wide, had a two-window façade, was of three storeys and a basement, had a ground floor reception room and an inside toilet; class 3 was 4.7 metres wide, had a two-window façade, was of two storeys and a basement, and had an outside toilet; and class 4 was 4.4 metres wide, had a two-window façade, was of two storeys with no basement, and had an outside toilet. Significantly, with the improvement of conditions for the working classes due to increasing pressure from concerned philanthropists as the nineteenth-century progressed, the size of lots for the small- to medium-sized house in London and south-west England gradually increased. Around 1820, a two-storey house with basement in north London was 4.4 metres wide and 10.0 metres deep; around 1870, in east London, an equivalent house was 4.4 metres wide and 12.6 metres deep; by 1900, the standard plan was 5.0 metres wide and 16.5 metres deep; and, in the early twentieth-century, a standard type with no basement and back extension was 5.6 metres wide and 7.9 metres deep, whereas with a back extension and access to a garden it was 15.9 metres deep. The plot shows a similar expansion in size.

The turn of the century, however, brought fresh ideas and the publication of Ebenezer Howard's *Garden Cities of Tomorrow* (1945). Howard wrote that the average size of a lot should be 6.0 metres wide and 39.5 metres deep, and the minimum 6.0 by 30.5 metres. Lewis Mumford maintained that, when roads were allowed for, Howard's dimensions gave a density of 17–18 houses per acre (42–45 per ha), the density of the traditional town before over-building caused overcrowding (Mumford, 1945). Raymond Unwin's enactment of Howard's vision through the development of the garden suburbs of inter-war England was to 12 houses per acre (30 per ha), on the grounds that there was 'nothing gained by overcrowding' (Unwin, 1912). Milton Keynes is the final manifestation of a new town as Howard had intended. Its central area conforms to almost the same guiding principles that Edward I had in mind some 700 years earlier to encourage trade. This is the traditional town Mumford was referring to in his comparison of its density with Howard's utopia.

As Figures 2 and 3 show, there has been surprisingly little change in the frontage, although more in the depth, of the standard town house lot over a considerable period of time. The width of the houses at Fishermead in central Milton Keynes is little different from those at Whitehaven and New Salisbury. The larger examples of house lot, in Amsterdam and in Bedford Square, London, are also similar.

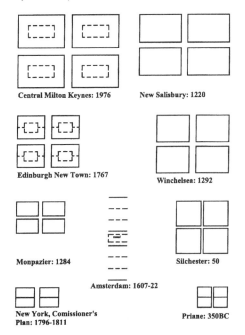

Fig. 2. Comparative regularised grid layouts to the same scale.

Interestingly, Howard's average lot size of 6.0 by 30.5 metres is exactly the same as that of the Commissioner's Plan for New York of 1811. The result, however, is the antithesis of the garden city Howard had in mind. This is explained by the dimension of the gridiron plan. With an area of 60 by 29 metres between roads, the land available for building is little different from that available in the Greek colonial city of Priene around 350 BC. Thus, it is not surprising that the only way to expand was upwards, and the only means of achieving this was by the use of technology. The grid of New York has permitted considerable and rapid changes since 1811, but in one direction only. Its resulting technological and real estate image has provided the model for most self-respecting cities throughout the world.

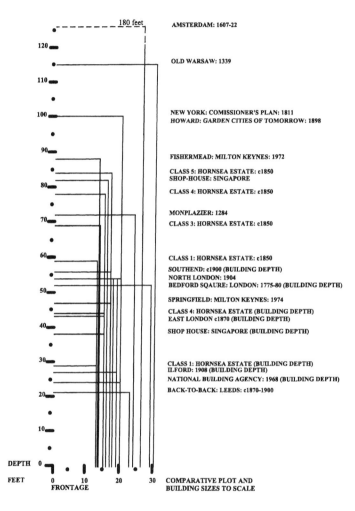

Fig. 3.
Comparative plot
and building sizes
to the same scale.

Case studies of Barcelona, Edinburgh and Lisbon

An ongoing analysis of three established examples of planned urban development seeks to identify some practical reasons for their sustainability, in the light of theoretical argument and historical precedent. The examples have been chosen because they appear to contain some contradictions. The plans for Lisbon's Baixa Pombalina of 1756 (Fig. 4) and Edinburgh New Town of 1767 (Fig. 5) were initiated within 11 years of each other and, while they are similar in their architectural determinism, they were based on very different dimensions. Ildefons Cerdà's plan for the expansion of Barcelona in 1855 (Fig. 6), while roughly similar to that of Edinburgh New Town in terms of dimensions, contained no such similarity in its determination of architectural, or even urban, form; within a rigid consistency of grid size, it proposed a variety of block configurations across one, two and four grid blocks.

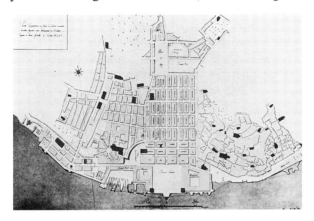

Fig. 4. Plan of the Baixa Pombalina, Lisbon, of 1756, by Eugenio dos Santos, Carlos Mardel and Elias Poppe.
Source: GEO, CML-CNIG, 1993.

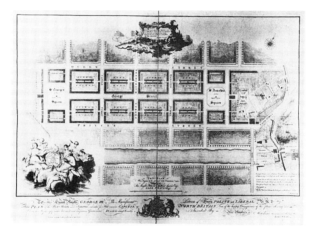

Fig. 5. James Craig's plan for Edinburgh New Town of 1767.
Source: Youngson, 1966.

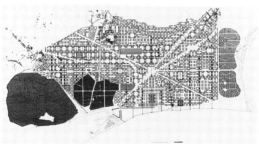

Fig. 6. Cerdà's plan for Barcelona of 1855, as proposed, with a variety of configurations within the same grid dimensions.
Source: Tarragó, 1996.

The case study areas were analysed to identify the changes that have taken place over time. Part of this analysis concerned changes of use and ownership, which do not necessarily manifest themselves in a physical manner. The relatively small grid size and predetermined architecture of Lisbon's Baixa Pombalina mean that each grid block forms almost an individual building, which the passage of time has enhanced. Only the small internal courtyard has been encroached upon (Fig. 7). At Edinburgh New Town, the predetermined elevations to surrounding main streets have remained mainly intact, but the larger grid size has allowed considerable modifications to the interior (Fig. 8). The majority of the physical changes have taken place along the original service road, now mostly pedestrianised. The intended variety of block configuration in Barcelona was never realised; the pressures of progressive development have ensured that each grid block has been maximised to its full potential, with buildings on all four sides and with subsequent infilling of internal spaces (Fig. 9). Nevertheless, the shape and size of Cerdà's grid were continued in the development of the Olympic Village of 1992, providing the framework for a fresh variety of built forms. Consequently, Barcelona has been able to accommodate considerable changes within its rigid framework of streets, with no apparent diminution in the quality of its urban life.

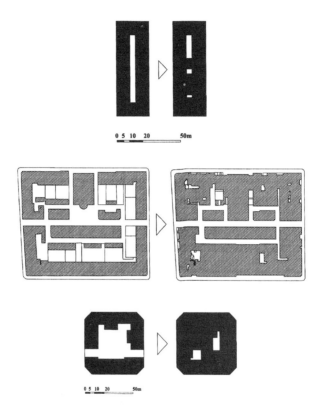

Fig. 7. A typical grid block of the Baixa Pombalina, Lisbon, in 1965 and 1987.

Fig. 8. The Assembly Rooms grid block of Edinburgh New Town, as developed by 1819, and the same grid block, from the Ordnance Survey map of 1998.

Fig. 9. A typical grid block in Barcelona, as developed by 1885, and the same grid block, as built over in 1996.

Conclusions

MacCormac's (1978) assertion that the desire for individual expression in housing is inverse to the acceptability of its overall image appears to be true in both Lisbon and Edinburgh, aided by conservation pressures to ensure that little is changed. Conversely, in Barcelona, constant participation has resulted in a quality of urban life that appears to be no less real and effective than in Lisbon and Edinburgh. Similarly, from her studies in the culturally different neighbourhoods of San Francisco, Vernez-Moudon (1986) maintains that small lots produce more predictable building forms and fine-grained grid block fabrics, and that large, deep blocks are intensified by the insertion of alleys and by subdivisions of the interior.

The dimensions of the urban layout thus appear to be all-important. Space is the asset that permits change to occur progressively and gradually, at low cost and with low expenditure of energy. Those historical examples that have enhanced the pattern of change by unselfconsciously adapting themselves to fresh pressures demonstrate a consistency in the shape and size of their irregular grids around which perimeter development has occurred. The ground rules for this would appear to be more universal than has hitherto been recognised.

Part 2

Urban Form and Transport:
New Dimensions
Introduction

Transport is a key issue in the 'sustainable urban form' debate. Arguments about the effects of urban form on travel patterns have provided perhaps the most dominant thrust to the move towards more compact urban forms. Policy makers have seen the manipulation of urban form as a tool to reduce travel demand. However, as with all issues in the sustainability debate, the arguments are not as simple as they seem. A number of dimensions to the urban form and travel relationship are only now beginning to be investigated and understood. Fortunately, research in this field is becoming more sophisticated. It is now beginning to get 'under the skin' of some of the basic assumptions about how urban form affects people's travel behaviour. In some cases it is questioning the universality of the existing wisdom (e.g. on the relationship between density and urban form), in others it is layering on information about variables and conditions to existing foundations.

The discussion on research in Part 2 begins with a chapter by Newman and Kenworthy, whose earlier work on density and gasoline consumption was a catalyst for research in the subject world wide. The authors focus on the car dependency aspect of sustainability. They present new data for 37 cities around the world and conclude that, whilst other issues are important, density still appears to be the dominant explanatory variable for the level of transport energy use. This conclusion prompts the authors to develop prescriptive measures for achieving a sustainable city from existing car-dependent urban areas.

Simmonds and Coombe then report on research which challenges Newman and Kenworthy's findings. They use a transport model to test various urban form and transport strategy scenarios. It compares 'compact city' and 'trend' (continue as normal) scenarios with 'Do-Minimum' and 'Do-Something' transport strategies, and finds that none of the scenario/strategy combinations tested eliminate growth in travel distance altogether. The authors then draw on other research, in conjunction with their own, and conclude that compact city strategies are not likely to have a great impact on total travel demand and car use, and will not necessarily increase the effectiveness of a transport strategy designed to reduce car use without restricting mobility in general. The lack of impact of more compact land use patterns is, they assert, due mainly to the fact that proximity has only a weak influence on travel choices.

This research raises issues about accessibility, which are studied by Reneland. He undertook research on the 45 largest towns in Sweden between 1980 and 1995 to see if accessibility to basic services (e.g. post office, schools and public transport) had changed, and if there were differences in accessibility between towns. He concludes that there are a range of influences on accessibility, but concurs with Newman and Kenworthy that the importance of population density remains. He also investigated the impact of the size of the city and found that small towns do not offer good accessibility to all services in comparison with larger towns.

Next, the influence of mixed uses on travel patterns is examined. Van and Senior report on research undertaken in Cardiff, based on US methods, to investigate the effect of mixed uses on a range of elements of travel behaviour. Their findings are that mixed land uses encourage walking and cycling and deter car use for light food shopping trips, and discourage car use for eating out. But there is little evidence that land use mix affects car ownership or mode choice for heavy food shopping and commuting.

The next chapters look specifically at the most sustainable location for future housing development at urban and regional scales. Titherdge *et al.* describe research based on a model that assesses the sustainability of proposed new housing location strategies in terms of personal travel demand and associated energy consumption and emissions. The chapter applies the model to test the sustainability of four alternative scenarios in Leicester and Kent: intensification, extensification, decentralisation and new town. The authors find that the intensification and new town strategies had some benefits in terms of trip lengths and energy consumption, depending on the mode and purpose of the visit, but that these findings are heavily dependent on future trends for journeys to work, shops and leisure facilities.

Headicar broaches the urban form/travel pattern relationship at the regional scale by questioning the outcomes of government guidance on transport in the UK. He explores the outcomes of planning policy guidance about strategic housing location to see if it brings about the claimed benefits in trip reduction. His research investigates policies to allocate housing in larger urban areas, to restrict housing development in villages and small towns and to avoid the development of small new settlements. He finds that the travel patterns are complex, and not related just to size of settlement: location, for example in relation to employment centres, is also important. Hence, he concludes that the principle of urban concentration needs to be applied more strategically – 'that is, allocating most new development to places in the vicinity of the largest urban areas or in corridors where closely spaced settlements provide for similar employment concentrations in aggregate'. In fact, he argues that 'By permitting – even promoting – the dispersal of new residential development throughout regions (albeit locally concentrated), existing planning policy is ... making its own contribution to the exploding city region'.

The chapters described above concern the relationship between various aspects of urban form and travel behaviour, but almost all of them also infer that socio-economic variables, such as car ownership and future employment trends, have an impact on their findings. The importance of socio-economic variables in comparison with land use and travel behaviour is the focus of research by Stead *et al.* They present the results of three recent research projects which find that socio-economic conditions often explain more variation in travel patterns than do land use characteristics. Influential socio-economic characteristics are: household car ownership, household socio-economic group and the proportion of working residents. But several land use characteristics are still important – such as the mix of uses. Stead *et al.* conclude that the influence of land use is perhaps lower than had previously been assumed.

Overall, the chapters illustrate that there are some areas of agreement, but clearly some issues remain contentious. Perhaps the most significant question still concerns the absolute significance of density on urban form. Although the weight of evidence suggests that higher densities yield reductions in trip frequency and distance, some important caveats and conditions apply, at both the urban and regional scales. Furthermore, the influence of socio-economic conditions and other aspects of urban form (such as mix of uses and size of settlement) need also to be considered.

Peter Newman and Jeff Kenworthy

Sustainable Urban Form: *The Big Picture*

Introduction

Sustainability is now a generic word to express the need for a long-term perspective where there is reduced demand on environmental resources and on environmental sinks; it also expresses the need to make the necessary changes in ways that are economically and socially beneficial. The approach taken in this chapter is to stress that cities cannot be considered sustainable if they are automobile dependent.

Automobile dependence exists where urban form and transport options are such that choices are limited to car use. Since this phrase was coined (Newman and Kenworthy, 1989), the policy agenda in many cities has been to try to overcome car dependence, although its links to sustainability remain contentious (for example, Gordon and Richardson, 1989; Troy, 1996). Car dependence is associated with a range of environmental, economic and social problems, as set out in Table 1.

Environmental	Economic	Social
• Oil vulnerability • Photochemical smog • Toxic emissions such as lead and benzene • High greenhouse gas contributions • Urban sprawl • Greater storm-water problems from extra hard surfaces • Traffic problems such as noise and severance	• External costs from accidents and pollution • Congestion costs, despite endless road building • High infrastructure costs in new sprawling suburbs • Loss of productive rural land • Loss of urban land to bitumen	• Loss of street life • Loss of community • Loss of public safety • Isolation in remote suburbs • Access problems for car-less and those with disabilities

Table 1. The problems of car dependence.

Perhaps the most central issue is how car dependence leads to heavy use of oil, the first of the fossil fuels to be reaching a production decline within a time frame well under the life of present suburbs, built in the 'Golden Age of Oil' (Campbell, 1991). As transport energy use relates to most of the other problems outlined in Table 1, it is generally used as the key indicator of car dependence.

This chapter seeks to provide new evidence on the influence of urban form, particularly density, on car dependence (Newman and Kenworthy, 1999). It also outlines a trend towards re-urbanisation, believed to be related to the information economy, which could help cities to become more sustainable; and concludes by suggesting the steps which cities will need to take if they are to overcome car dependence and achieve a more sustainable urban form.

New evidence on the influence of urban form

Table 2 presents new data on car dependence in 37 cities (see end note) (for further detail, see Newman and Kenworthy, 1999; Kenworthy and Laube, 1999).

Cities	Car use/capita (km)	GRP/capita ($US 1990)
Australian		
Perth	7,203	17,697
Adelaide	6,690	19,761
Brisbane	6,467	18,737
Melbourne	6,436	21,088
Sydney	5,885	21,520
Average	6,536	19,761
American		
Phoenix	11,608	20,555
Denver	10,011	24,533
Boston	10,280	27,783
Houston	13,016	26,155
Washington	11,182	35,882
San Francisco	11,933	31,143
Detroit	11,239	22,538
Chicago	9,525	26,038
Los Angeles	11,587	24,894
New York	8,317	28,703
Average	10,870	26,822
Toronto (Metro)	5,019	22,572
European		
Frankfurt	5,893	35,126
Amsterdam	3,977	25,211
Zürich	5,197	44,845
Brussels	4,864	30,087
Munich	4,202	36,255
Stockholm	4,638	33,235
Vienna	3,964	28,021
Hamburg	5,061	30,421
Copenhagen	4,558	29,900
London	3,892	22,215
Paris	3,459	33,609
Average	4,519	31,721
Wealthy Asian		
Singapore	1,864	12,939
Tokyo	2,103	36,953
Hong Kong	493	14,101
Average	1,487	21,331
Developing Asian		
Kuala Lumpur	4,032	4,066
Surabaya	1,064	726
Jakarta	1,112	1,508
Bangkok	2,664	3,826
Seoul	1,483	5,942
Beijing	351	1,323
Manila	573	1,099
Average	1,611	2,642

Table 2. Car use and Gross Regional Product per capita for 37 global cities, 1990.

From this data, it appears that there is no clear or systematic relationship between wealth and car use. For example:

- the car is used most in US and Australian cities, but European cities (which use cars 2.4 times less than US cities) are wealthier; and
- developing Asian cities have higher car use than the three wealthy Asian cities but are ten times less wealthy.

These results immediately call into question the long tradition of assuming that car use is an inevitable outcome of growing wealth (Rainbow and Tan, 1993). Whilst growing wealth may lead to higher car ownership, the extent to which this may be diverted to other expressions of wealth, or is not in proportion to car use, indicates that there are stronger factors determining automobile dependence.

Figures 1–5 show the broader patterns of automobile dependence for the regional groupings of cities, by several indicators: private passenger transport energy use; proportion of workers using public or non-motorised transport for the journey to work; public transport speeds compared with average traffic speeds; length of road per person; and urban density.

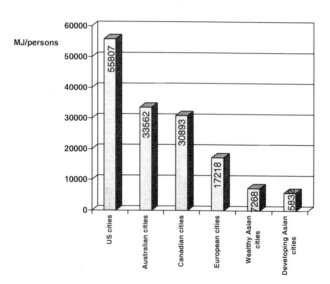

Fig. 1. Private passenger transport energy consumption per capita, 1990.

The two groups of cities that are most automobile dependent are low-density cities in the US and in Australia, with medium-density European cities distinctly less so. The wealthy and densely-settled Asian cities of Singapore, Hong Kong and Tokyo have very low automobile dependence, whilst the equally dense developing Asian cities of Bangkok, Jakarta and so on, are showing a new kind of automobile orientation. They are much more car using and congested than would be anticipated, with slightly higher car use levels than the wealthy Asian cities, but much lower wealth levels. The developing Asian cities are automobile dependent in the sense that they have few rapid public transport options and their public transport systems consist mostly of buses that are stuck in traffic; hence, anyone who has the income purchases a car as soon as possible to try to improve their travel speed. However, the data from our survey show that the public transport systems in some European and wealthy Asian cities have average speeds that are faster than the city's average car traffic speeds (Fig. 3).

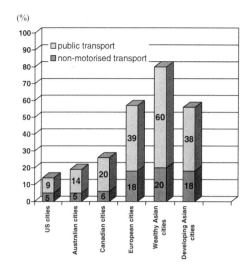

Fig. 2. Proportion of workers using public or non-motorised transport, 1990.

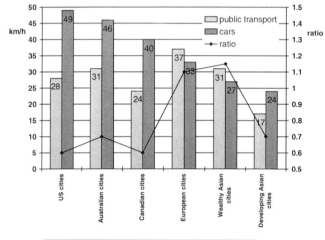

Fig. 3. Average public transport and car speeds and their ratio, 1990.

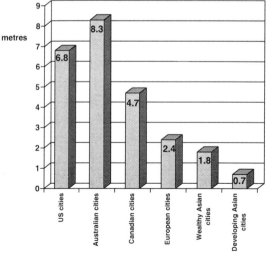

Fig. 4. Length of road per person, 1990.

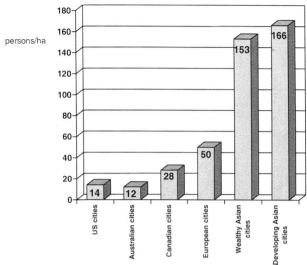

Fig. 5. Urban density, 1990.

Very strong correlations were found between the level of automobile use (or transport energy use) and parameters such as the level of public transport provision, public transport speed to traffic speed ratio, length of road and parking provision; but the strongest correlation is with urban density (see Fig. 6). Thus, in multiple regression analysis, density is the dominant explanatory variable for the level of transport energy use.

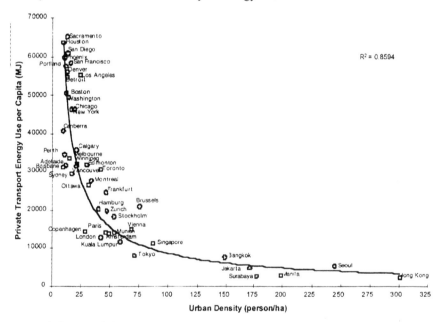

Fig. 6. Private transport energy use per person, by urban density, 1990.

As suggested above and shown below, there is obviously more to sustainability than increasing density (some dense Asian cities are still becoming car dependent or at least car-saturated). However, there is little doubt that density is a major factor in car dependence. Density, like car use, is not significantly correlated with wealth, either positively or negatively, as it depends on other, more important, factors. Nor can it be said that the close correlation between density and car dependence is only observable as a factor between cities.

Thus, achieving a more sustainable urban form inevitably involves the development of densities that can enable public transport, walking and cycling to be viable options. As shown below, this probably means building 'nodes and corridors' of high-density development rather than bulldozing the low-density suburbs of the car era. This strategy does not mean that other aspects of sustainability concerned with water, waste management and greening are jeopardised; on the contrary, most of the innovative experiments in urban ecology are occurring in denser urban environments, rather than in car-dependent suburbs (see Newman and Kenworthy, 1999).

Figure 7 demonstrates the significance of density in relation to city wealth (via the link to car dependence). It shows that the lower the density of the city, the more it costs to operate passenger transport systems.

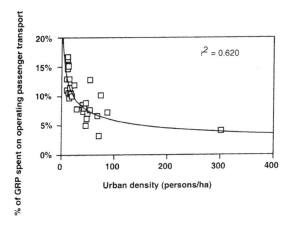

Fig. 7. The proportion of GRP spent on operating passenger transport systems in developed cities, by urban density, 1990.

These correlations and studies highlight the importance of increasing density within 'nodes' or 'urban village' sub-centres of a city as well as providing 'corridors' of viable public transport linking these nodes. It is also consistent with the need for information technology-based sub-centres.

The trend towards re-urbanisation – an opportunity for achieving sustainable urban form

The major economic change of the era – the onset of the information age – was once considered to inevitably lead to dispersed cities, making them more car dependent (Webber, 1963, 1964, 1968). More sophisticated theories have recognised that information technology has the ability to reform cities, based on the reduced need for face-to-face interchange in some activities, but that there is a continuing need for quality human interaction critical to economic and cultural processes (Castells, 1989; Castells and Hall, 1994,). After several years of being equivocal on this, Hall (1997) now states: 'The new world will largely depend, as the old world did, on human creativity; and creativity flourishes where people come together face-to-face' (p.89). Others have emphasised that 'local milieus' will emerge (Willoughby, 1994), or that local culture will be strengthened as globalised information makes national borders less relevant (Ohmae, 1990; Naisbett, 1994; Sassen, 1994), or that the importance of face-to-face contact will ensure centres emerge as critical nodes of information oriented production (Winger, 1997).

All the cities in the research sample are re-urbanising but the historic trend that the study has picked up is that all except two have reversed their trend downwards in density; measured as a combination of population and jobs, there has been a substantial shift towards increasing the amount of urban activity per hectare (Newman and Kenworthy, 1999). In US cities, the trend is to focus activity in outer suburbs through 'edge cities' and the inner areas continue to decline (apart from those cities where social and racial issues have been resolved). New data from New Zealand cities show that re-urbanisation is now well under way (Bachels *et al.*, 1998). Thus, rather than dispersing urban activity, the information-based technologies seem to be focusing it. In summary, the reasons for this are that:

- professionals require face-to-face interactions for creative project development work;
- community (especially youth culture) always needs face-to-face contact;
- de-industrialisation of inner cities is making them even more attractive for human-based work locations; and
- travel time budgets (1 hour/day) are being exceeded in fringe locations; hence, busy professionals are locating near work.

The information age seems to be favouring a multi-nodal city where the sustainable transport modes are increasingly important as they are more able to build the human-based centres critical for the new urban economy. The challenge will be to ensure that such sub-centres occur throughout the city, not just in wealthy enclaves; the role of light rail extensions into car-dependent suburbs, as a means of creating viable local employment and services centres, seems to be a growing agenda.

Achieving the sustainable city

The key ways in which land use patterns could be changed to be more sustainable and less car dependent, are expressed visually in Fig. 8, for a city that was initially highly automobile dependent. Several steps are required to change the 'car city' to a sustainable city:

1. Revitalise the inner city
2. Focus development around the existing rail system
3. Discourage further urban sprawl
4. Extend the public transport system and build new urban villages in the suburbs

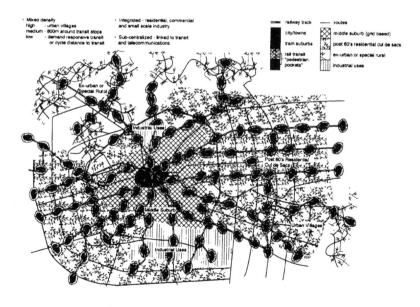

Fig. 8. A conceptual outline of the sustainable city, as it would develop from the car city.

Revitalising the inner city

In the inner city, there are already public transport oriented and walking oriented characteristics – that is, dense, mixed land uses with urban design conducive to face-to-face activity. So, here, it is possible to reach destinations with short trips, without a car, and to create walkable communities. In re-urbanising such areas, a city is extending into space that is not automobile dependent.

Re-urbanisation of essentially abandoned inner city areas has occurred in many cities around the world. Invariably, such successful revitalisation is closely associated with community processes that have developed a new vision for their area. Revitalisation is, thus, associated with processes such as historic building and streetscape preservation, street festivals and other community arts, the development of social housing to retain a mix of incomes, and investment by innovative entrepreneurs in new businesses. Finding the right spur for regeneration of some areas often requires great creativity and commitment from urban managers, but always includes significant community involvement.

Although there are now strong market forces encouraging the re-urbanisation process, little hope for regenerating the inner city will be found if there is a mood of fear on the streets produced by crime, or if schools in an area are inadequate. These problems have been major causes of the 'white flight', followed by the 'black flight' of middle class Afro-Americans, from US inner cities. Addressing this mood of fear is essential before urban regeneration can occur.

Measures that may generate investment and create a better environment for the community in the inner city include traffic calming and pedestrianisation, with reduced parking. These measures can help to begin the upgrading of an area, reversing the sense of decline, since they give people who live and work in the area a more positive attitude to their neighbourhoods. If traffic calming and street improvement is simply imposed on a demoralised community, it is likely to achieve little, but once a community has a new sense of its regeneration potential then improving the public environment can be the signal for broader revitalisation processes. The most obvious places to implement traffic calming measures are where the most intensive urban activity exists. Here, there is the greatest need to manage traffic. There may well be opposition from motorists and, for this reason, it is wise to include traffic calming as part of a community process to reclaim the city's streets. It is also advisable to implement traffic calming on an area-wide basis and to make it part of a general approach of reducing travel and shifting to other modes.

Copenhagen has carried out a 30-year programme of reducing central and inner area parking by 3% each year and, together with upgraded bicycle and pedestrian infrastructure and activities, the city has been able not only to cap traffic growth, but to ensure that central and inner areas have thrived.

Once the inner city is regenerating, a city can then begin to take its 'inner city' qualities to the suburbs. This can include traffic calming of neighbourhoods, but needs also to include a process of beginning to provide sub-centres that have 'inner city' characteristics, linking them up with good public transport.

Focusing development around the existing rail system

Even if a car city has a rail system, it may not have facilitated a market for higher-density, mixed-use development around its station areas, wherever they are – in the central business district (CBD), inner city or outer suburbs. This is a common failing in car cities, where zoning, inappropriate government land uses and lack of creativity often prevent such development. Cervero (1986, 1998) has shown that good rail transport will create such markets, but they can also be prevented by the planning system.

Joint development between public and private interests is, perhaps, the best way to optimise the use of land within a short walk of stations. Park-and-ride areas are not a good use of station environments, and were deliberately prohibited in Vancouver, Burnaby and New Westminster in order to maximise development potential. Park-and-ride sites do not promote active land uses and can be dangerous environments for public transport patrons at night. They can, however, be converted to urban villages later, so they may be an appropriate interim solution as a transport system is developing. Bike-and-ride facilities are more compatible with stations; the radius of those who can easily reach the train extends from 800 metres on foot to five kilometres by bicycle, and bicycle facilities do not interfere with essential pedestrian qualities of the station. There is also usually space for a bus interchange point at a station; if bus timetables are integrated with rail services, and feed in from both sides of a corridor, it is possible to provide cross-suburb transport. This extra activity makes it even more important that the station sub-centre or urban village offer an attractive walking environment, with mixed uses.

Bernick and Cervero (1997) and Cervero (1998) have outlined examples from around the world of such public transport-based villages, including a growing list in the US. Calthorpe Associates (1990) drew up guidelines for public transport oriented design, and Calthorpe (1993) has provided a number of examples of such developments, as have other New Urbanists (for example, Katz, 1994).

In California, there is a set of initiatives which establishes the legal basis of public transport-oriented development – the Transit Village Development Act of 1994 establishes all land within a quarter of a mile of rail transport stations as public transport village development districts, if applied for by a local authority. The area is then given the powers of a redevelopment agency and staffed to facilitate its transition into a mixed-use, high-density, pedestrian-scale urban environment. The district has first priority for funding from State and Federal innovative transport-land use programmes. The Act was introduced in response to growing public transport investment in California, and is aimed at ensuring there is a better link between public transport and land use on systems such as BART which has large park-and-ride areas around many of its stations.

In Melbourne, The Urban Villages Project has been drawn up. In this, over 500 urban village sites adjacent to tram stops and rail stations have been identified. The sites are all significantly under-developed and, hence, have been given special status for redevelopment. The local community is involved in the drawing up of plans to upgrade the areas. Calculations show that development in such areas may save up to 40% of transport and household energy/greenhouse emissions (denser developments use less heating as well as requiring less transport). They will be less expensive to build and will create opportunities for the local community through the shops, jobs, and child minding facilities that will be built there (Energy Victoria *et al.*, 1996). Significantly, up to 25 years of potential greenfield urban growth in Melbourne could be accommodated on such sites. This approach provides the basis, therefore, for curbing urban sprawl.

Discouraging further urban sprawl

Curbing sprawl requires a simultaneous process of cutting investment in highways that take people out of the city to greenfield sites, and in zoning processes that protect rural land on the urban fringe. It is almost impossible to prevent new sprawl through zoning alone if high-speed roads are still being built – they are like loaded guns pointed at rural land in their vicinity. At the same time, the goal of managing growth at the urban fringe is likely to be more acceptable if it is made known to people, expressed in zoning ordinances, and seen to be both a goal of sustainability and a market-based process.

The market for development of land in the inner city and around public transport stations needs to be underway if the third step of curbing sprawl is to be managed. Cities such as Vancouver and Portland, with active growth management and green belt strategies, could not hope to achieve their goals without a programme of re-urbanising around public transport stations. The same is the case in European cities.

Extending the public transport system and building new urban villages in the suburbs

There are large areas of suburban development with no real public transport service in most car-based cities. It is possible (particularly with joint development) to build state-of-the-art electric rail transport systems into these areas at reasonable cost – but, as a rule, only if it involves land development at stations to help pay for it. Through such systems, not only is it possible to develop the public transport service, but it also becomes more feasible to create the sub-centres or urban villages which these single-use suburbs generally lack. They ensure that many more local services can be provided, and allow good transport directly from the sub-centre to other cross-city destinations. Zurich has undergone a process of extending its light rail and building urban villages around stations. At the same time, the city has experienced declining car use whilst its public transport use has grown to over 500 trips per person per year, the highest figure in Europe.

This process may provide the essential means of reclaiming the car city. Many low-density suburbs need not be rebuilt, but could be given a less car-dependent form or structure, each with a nearby urban village as their focal point. They would, however, also need to be equipped with bicycle facilities, and could be provided with other state-of-the-art public transport, such as demand-responsive mini-buses for local services. Traffic calming would also play a key role in making such areas safer, more human in scale and suitable for walking and cycling. If such public transport-based sub-centres are built around or adjacent to current suburban shopping malls, then they can slowly begin to reclaim the acres of asphalt car park, as they begin to diminish the need for car access. The revival of delivery services from inner city supermarkets shows that a car is not essential for shopping.

There are few examples of this type of development so far, but they are beginning to happen. One has occurred in Mountain View, California, where a 1960s shopping mall has been replaced by a public transport oriented, mixed-use urban village (Center for Livable Communities, 1996). An even more impressive example has been built in Addison in Dallas, where a classic American 'edge city' surrounded by parking lots, freeways and collector roads has been transformed into a new town centre with 'a finely woven grid of narrow streets, with pedestrian-friendly sidewalks and public seating areas, shaded by trees' (*Livable Places Update,* November, 1997). The Addison Circle Master Plan provides buildings oriented to the street, ten acres of pocket parks, outdoor spaces for public events, and a mix of housing forms in a four-storey configuration around semi-private courtyards. The redevelopment will include a new light rail station by 2005.

In the US, groups other than the New Urbanists are attempting to reclaim the suburbs. A US Department of Transportation publication called *The New Suburb* (Rabinowitz *et al.,* 1991) outlines 34 innovative designs from recent US developments and a number from an international design competition (Beimborn *et al.,* 1991) promoting public transport corridor developments. Critical to all the designs is that, not only are they dense and mixed in use to allow pedestrian activity (and to be viable for public transport), they are also rediscovering the virtues of narrow streets, where people enjoy walking and where buildings are organically linked. The cul-de-sac housing estate, where buildings are hidden from each other, and the large undifferentiated open spaces typical of high-rise housing estates, have little place in a New Urbanist design. Nor have they had much favour in European urban design (Gehl, 1987).

The strong role of sub-centres with a commitment to information oriented services is universally recognised to be a feature of the 'Future City' (Castells, 1989; Brotchie *et al.*, 1995). Stockholm has built up its sub centres around its public transport system and has made the transition to an information oriented city whilst reducing car use, increasing public transport use and raising densities in the CBD, the inner area and the outer area (Cervero, 1998; Newman and Kenworthy, 1999). However, very few cities are as committed as Stockholm (and other Nordic cities) to using the new technological imperatives to help create or maintain a connected city of communities. Rather, they are using new technologies to maintain a disconnected city of individual households, as is found in car-based cities.

The characteristics of the sustainable city, in comparison with three other types of city – the traditional walking city, the industrial transit city, and the modern automobile city – are set out in Table 3 below.

	Traditional pre-modern walking city	Industrial transit city	Modern automobile city	Postmodern sustainable city
Economy (and technology)	Small household industries (local and small regional economy)	Larger industries, concentrated in parts of cities (national and regional economy)	Large scale industries scattered through city (national and regional economy)	Information and services oriented (global economy); heavy industries to rural areas and small towns
Social organisation	Person-to-person, community-based	Bigger cities losing person-to-person contact but still community oriented in rail-based suburbs	Individualistic and isolated	Local community-based, but globally linked
Transport	Walking (and cycling later)	Streetcars and trains (also walking and cycling)	Cars (almost exclusively)	Walking and cycling (local), transit (across city), cars (supplementary), air (for global)
Urban form	Walking city: small, dense, mixed, organic	Transit city: medium-density suburbs, dense mixed centre, corridors with green wedges	Automobile city: high-rise CBD, low-density suburban sprawl zoned to further separate functions	Sustainable city: local urban villages (high density) linked across city by transit, medium- and low-density areas around villages, no more sprawl
Environment • resources • wastes • nature orientation	Low Low Close to rural areas (dependent)	Medium Medium Some connection through green wedges	High High Little nature orientation (independent)	Low-medium Low-medium Close to nature

Table 3. Characteristics of four city types.

Conclusions

This chapter has shown that there are policies that can overcome car dependence in a way that helps a city environmentally, economically and socially. That there are cities that are thriving through their success at overcoming car dependence is an inspiration to those cities whose growth in automobile use seems to be inbuilt and inevitable. Such changes cannot occur overnight; a 30-year plan may be needed to ensure the steps outlined in this chapter are underway, and that progress towards the goal of sustainability is achieved.

Note

The data collected and analysed for Table 2 are part of several ongoing studies based on the initial work on 32 cities by Newman and Kenworthy (1989).

Acknowledgements

The authors wish to acknowledge with gratitude the considerable work of Felix Laube in compiling much of the comparative urban data in this paper and for preparing most of the graphics. We are thankful to Mark Bachels and Colin McKellar for their assistance on this paper. We also acknowledge the work of Paul Barter in preparing most of the data on developing Asian cities, as well as Chamlong Poboon and Benedicto Guia (Jr) for their work on Bangkok and Manila respectively. This work was partly supported through funds from the World Bank for which we are also very grateful.

David Simmonds and Denvil Coombe
The Transport Implications of Alternative Urban Forms

Introduction
This chapter presents and discusses some of the findings of a research project carried out for the Department of Transport in 1995–96 (MVA Consultancy *et al.*, 1996). The study brief was to compare the transport consequences of one or more compact city scenarios with a 'Trend' scenario reflecting the continuation of recent changes in land use distributions (see note 1). In this chapter, the model-based analysis is summarised; then, the results are discussed; these are compared with the results of other similar studies; and, finally, some conclusions are drawn.

Two points must be emphasised. First, the compact city scenarios tested are not intended to represent the policies of government or of planning authorities in the study area. In particular, they do not represent the combinations of land use and transport policies contained within *Planning Policy Guidance 13: Transport* (DoE and DoT, 1994). Second, the work concentrated on transport effects, and did not attempt to be comprehensive in its consideration of the compact city concept.

Modelling the scenarios
The transport model
The study used a transport model of the Bristol area originally developed by MVA for a consortium led by Avon County Council. The model provides an unusually complete representation of travel and responses to transport change, including choice of route, mode, destination, time of travel and frequency of travel. The modes include walking and cycling, and travellers' responses vary according to the purpose of their trips and their access to cars. The whole of a typical day is modelled. The characteristics of transport are varied both by congestion and by operator responses such as declining bus use leading to decreasing services. The model represents the study area of Bristol and its environs as 18 zones, illustrated in Fig. 1, plus six external zones to represent interactions with the rest of the world. Transport supply is considered in a correspondingly aggregate manner.

Further discussion of the modelling approach can be found in Roberts and Simmonds (1997). More on the Bristol context can be found in Barton (1992); what follows is to some extent complementary to that paper.

The use of the model
The modelling went through the following stages. First, a Trend scenario was developed, in which land uses continued to decentralise. This was tested with both 'Do-Minimum' and an initial 'Do-Something' (DS1) transport strategies. DS1 involved a reduction of parking in the central area, road pricing in the city centre, bus lanes, cycle lanes and park-and-ride provision (see note 2). Secondly, a compact city scenario was tested with three transport strategies: the

Do-Minimum, the initial Do-Something (DS1) and a more radical Do-Something (DS2). DS2 added an extensive light rapid transit (LRT) network to DS1. Thirdly, alternative compact city scenarios were tested under the DS2 strategy. This approach, which was adopted because of the limited number of model runs possible within the project, allows comparisons:

- between the forecasts (all for 2015) and the base year (1990);
- between the Trend and compact city scenarios, under either Do-Minimum or DS1; and
- between the compact city and its alternatives, under DS2.

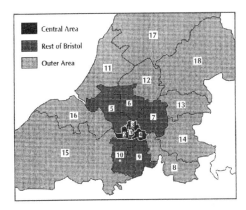

Fig. 1. Study area map.

The model produces a wide range of outputs, including measures of the environmental impact of the transport system in each test. We include here only the volumes of passenger travel by mode (Table 1). Other key results are mentioned in the following discussion.

Table 1. Model results: passenger travel by mode.
Source: MVA Consultancy et al., 1996, Table 5.2.

Mode	1990 base	Trend		Compact City			Scenario		
		Do-Min	DS1	Do-Min	DS1	DS2	A2	A3	A4
Car	29832.3	45131.8	44112.4	44106.7	43081.5	42981.5	43041.6	40701.1	40804.3
Bus	1045.0	826.6	916.3	806.4	890.8	673.0	597.0	865.2	764.1
Train	965.5	2000.2	1743.1	2095.8	1797.4	1739.3	1615.6	1764.3	1678.5
LRT	0.0	0.0	0.0	0.0	0.0	24.3	649.7	951.2	1096.3
P&R (car)	0.0	60.1	512.2	63.8	546.6	549.7	650.3	715.2	800.5
P&R (bus)	0.0	16.9	116.5	18.1	121.6	120.6	143.0	164.3	182.0
Walk	3352.5	3529.1	3650.2	3384.5	3513.9	3467.1	3532.3	3371.0	3435.9
Total	35195.3	51564.7	51050.7	50475.3	49951.9	50055.6	50229.4	48532.2	48761.7

The Trend/Do-Minimum forecast

The Trend scenario and Do-Minimum strategy produce large increases in travel, particularly by car. The total number of daily trips increases by 21% and the total number of daily trips by car increases by 34%. The total daily distance travelled increases even more, by 47%, and the distance travelled by car by 51%. The total volume of traffic increases by 53%, with marked variations between areas: there is less growth in traffic (+38%) in the central area and more in the outer urban area (+67%).

These changes are largely attributable to the continuing growth in car ownership. Continuing decentralisation contributes to faster growth of traffic in the outer area. The results demonstrate the extent to which urban transport problems are likely to get worse unless effective measures are introduced to deal with them. They also confirm that worsening traffic congestion is not enough to persuade car users to switch to other modes.

Compact city versus Trend

The dominant result of the compact city scenario, compared with the Trend, is that in terms of total trips, trip-kilometres and car use, the four sets of 2015 results are very similar to each other and very different from the 1990 situation. The Trend Do-Minimum represents a 47% increase in trip-kilometres over 1990. The lowest figure of the four, for the compact city scenario and DS1 strategy, only reduces this to a 42% increase, the equivalent of stopping the growth in total travel for about two years of the 25-year forecasting period.

The main effect of the compact city scenario, compared with the Trend, is that both trip-making and total person-kilometres go down fractionally, under either strategy. Under Do-Minimum, the compact city scenario reduces car passenger-kilometres by about 2.3%, bus-kilometres by 2.4% and walk/cycle-kilometres by about 4.1%. This compares with a reduction in car trips of 0.9%, an increase in bus trips of 3.2% and an increase in walk/cycle trips of 0.9%, which indicates that trips by all these modes have become slightly shorter.

The overall effect is therefore that the compact city scenario reduces lengths of trips slightly, but not the proportion made by car. It increases traffic in the central area by 6%, reducing it very slightly in the rest of the built-up area and reducing it by 6% in the outer area. These changes are small in comparison with the changes in land use that generate them. The effects of the change in transport strategy from Do-Minimum to DS1 are similar between the two land use scenarios. There is no indication that the compact city land use pattern makes the DS1 strategy any more effective in transferring demand from car to other modes.

The DS2 transport strategy

The light rail system added, in DS2, about 1% of the total modelled travel. It leads to a major decrease in bus use – about one-quarter of trips and of passenger-kilometres. There is a slight reduction in train use (about 7% of trips but only 3% of train-passenger kilometres). The proportional reduction in overall car use is tiny, at 0.2% of person-kilometres.

The alternative scenarios

The alternative scenarios discussed here are:

- A2 – concentrate employment in part of the central area best served by public transport;
- A3 – concentrate residence closer to the centre and along LRT lines; and
- A4 – concentrate both employment and residence (combine A2 with A3) (see note 3)

The alternative scenarios were all tested with transport strategy DS2, and all maintain the same totals of population and employment across Bristol itself.

Scenario A2 – employment concentration

The most marked effect of this scenario is the dramatic increase in the total volume of traffic (cars, buses and goods vehicles) in the central area, which increases by 43% – approximately in proportion to central area employment (see note 4). Overall, commuting distances increase slightly. Whilst it is relatively easy to reach central area jobs by public transport (in particular by LRT, the use of which increases by 30%), large numbers of commuters use their cars to travel there, producing serious central area traffic congestion and pollution.

Scenario A3 – population concentration

The total distance travelled by car is reduced by about 5%; within this, there is an increase in car travel to park-and-ride facilities. The total distance travelled by LRT increases by 81%, implying an increase in the average length of an LRT journey. This suggests a higher increase in the use of LRT by residents in outer zones (as a result of better access to stops), outweighing the effect of the general centralisation of the population. The distance travelled by bus also increases, by 28% (marginally less than the 30% increase in bus trips); this is probably due to the concentration of population in the inner zones, leading to net increases in bus use despite the improvements in access to LRT.

Scenario A4 – employment and population concentration
Scenario A4 combines Scenario A2 and A3 and produces a set of results whose relationship to the results of A2 and A3 is quite complex. A4 produces an increase in total commuting trip distance similar to A3 and a decrease in total shopping and other purpose distances similar to A4. In terms of traffic, A4 produces a slightly greater increase in the central area than A2 and a slightly greater reduction in the rest of the built-up area than A3. The combined effect of these is to leave the total volume of traffic over the entire urban area virtually unchanged, but more concentrated in the centre.

Summary of model results
The results of the modelling can be summarised as showing that:
- under Trend land use assumptions and a Do-Minimum transport strategy, substantial growth in travel and traffic is to be expected over 25 years;
- the main compact city scenario has only a slight impact on total travel, on car use or on emissions;
- the compact city scenario does not significantly increase the effectiveness of transport strategies aimed at encouraging the use of non-car modes;
- the alternative scenarios, if feasible, would have greater impacts but could cause much greater concentrations of traffic problems in particular areas; and that
- in terms of total travel and car travel, it is difficult for the land use scenarios to make much impact.

Discussion
The limited impact of the compact city
An initial point to note is that, because changes in land use are relatively slow, a radical reversal of trends, even over 25 years, is much less dramatic in terms of total population and employment. For example, the compact city scenario requires Bristol's population to increase by 4% instead of declining by 12% over 25 years.

Secondly, the compact city scenario modelled here results in *increased* average travel distances from some outer area zones. Commuting from outer zones to other, distant outer zones is markedly reduced, but so too is intra-zonal commuting; commuting from outer to inner or central zones becomes relatively or even absolutely more common. There are also increases in outward commuting, including increased commuting between central zones and external zones, instead of between outer area and external zones. Furthermore, average trip lengths from inner zones are not always shorter than those from outer zones.

The third and most important point is the distinction between 'need to travel' and 'desire to travel'. Discussion about compact cities or alternatives to them often focuses on reducing the 'need to travel', by arranging land uses so that residents can live closer to jobs, shops, schools and other destinations. The effect of such changes depends on the degree to which residents actually travel to the nearest job, shop and so on. The preference for going to the nearest destination was very weak in 1990 and will be further weakened by increasing car ownership. The authors believe this is realistic where travel costs are fairly low relative to incomes, and where there is a wide diversity of jobs, housing, shopping and so on. This diversity of skills, opportunities, and tastes means that the value of getting a particular job, going to a particular shop, and so on, far outweigh the additional costs of the extra travel. The model's hypotheses correspond with the findings of other researchers (including work by Farthing *et al.*, 1996, in the Bristol area) that more local provision of services will not in itself bring about changes in travel patterns.

What is called 'desire to travel' is therefore more accurately called 'desire to reach destinations that involve travelling further'. This distinction can be illustrated using the 'Brotchie Triangle' (see Brotchie, 1984, 1986, for the concept; Wegener, 1995, for another application), which highlights different relationships between the dispersion or concentration of activities and the dispersion or concentration of trips.

The Triangle itself is a graph, as shown in Fig. 2. The horizontal axis measures the concentration of employment, in terms of the average distance of jobs from the centre of the city. The vertical axis measures the average distance that residents travel to work. This distance is constrained by the relative location of residents and jobs. Hence:

- If all the employment is at the centre, the average journey to work must be equal to the average distance from the centre at which residents live, R. Such a city can be plotted as point A on the graph: this has zero dispersion of employment on the horizontal axis, and travel-to-work distance R on the vertical axis.
- If employment is as dispersed as residents are, the city can be anywhere along the line BC. If every resident takes the nearest job, the travel-to-work distance will be very small, as shown by point C. If residents are not at all concerned by travel-to-work distance, the travel-to-work distance will be much greater: point B represents the average distance if the matching of residents to jobs is completely random.

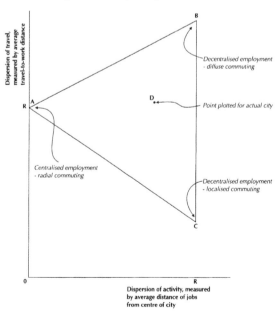

Fig. 2. The Brotchie Triangle: possible patterns of employment and commuting, given a population distribution.
Sources: Brotchie, 1986; Wegener, 1995.

The three corners of the Triangle therefore represent:
A – a city with wholly centralised employment, such that every working resident must commute to the centre;

B – a city with decentralised employment, and a highly dispersed pattern of long-distance commuting; and

C – a city with the same pattern of employment as B, but with every worker taking the nearest job, giving local concentrations of short-distance commuting.

For any given population distribution, the line AC can be interpreted as the minimal need to travel: this minimum travel-to-work distance decreases as jobs are decentralised to bring them closer to workers. The line AB shows that the same decentralisation of jobs allows travel-to-work distance to increase, if workers do not take up the nearest jobs.

Within the Triangle, a point D represents the dispersion of jobs and of trips to work for a given situation. Figure 3 shows the Triangle applied to the Bristol study area for the 1990 situation and for the 2015 Trend Do-Minimum test. This shows that:

- the Trend scenario does not significantly increase the dispersion of jobs relative to homes – the 2015 Trend point is only fractionally to the right of the 1990 point, which shows that jobs are already well dispersed (the 1990 point is closer to the BC line than to point A); and
- interaction between homes and jobs is already markedly dispersed in 1990 – the 1990 point is closer to B than to C – and becomes more dispersed by 2015.

All of the points D, describing the dispersion of employment and the forecast travel-to-work distance, fall within the rectangle shown in Fig. 3. This area is enlarged as Fig. 4. The first point to note is that for these two variables, it is not correct to conclude, as was found at the end of the modelling section, that the results for 2015 are all relatively similar when compared with the 1990 situation. It is still the case that the 1990 point is the lowest, indicating the shortest average journey to work, and that the 2015 Trend Do-Minimum is the highest. The other points, however, are well distributed between these two. They also show much greater horizontal differences – that is, the land use differences amongst the 2015 scenarios are much greater than the differences between 1990 and 2015 Trend.

By definition, points based on different transport strategies but the same land use scenario will be grouped into a vertical line. Hence, the Trend DS1 point shows a slight reduction in the length of the average journey to work, without any change in the distribution of activities from Trend Do-Minimum. The compact city Do-Minimum makes a slight reduction (relative to Trend Do-Minimum) both in the dispersion of activities (horizontal movement to the left) and in the dispersion of commuting trips (vertical movement downward). Introducing the DS1 strategy in the compact city case produces almost the same change as it did in the Trend. The DS2 strategy produces no perceptible movement of point D; that is, the introduction of the LRT system neither encourages nor discourages longer commuting journeys.

The A2 (centralised employment) scenario produces a further shift of point D leftwards and downwards. Point D for Scenario A3 (centralised population) is indistinguishable from that for the main compact city scenario with the same DS2 transport strategy. The point for Scenario A4 (combining A2 and A3) is indistinguishable from that for A2. This seems to illustrate particularly well that concentrating employment and population in the same or nearby areas does not reduce commuting distances unless there is a strong tendency or obligation for people to live near their work or to work near home. What we may conclude from Figs 3 and 4 is that in terms of travel to work:

- none of the scenario/strategy combinations tested eliminates growth in travel distance;
- there is some correlation in the measures plotted, that is between the dispersion of activities

and the dispersion of interaction, but not all of the changes intended to reduce travel actually do so; and

- the compact city scenario, and more particularly the variants that concentrate employment in the centre of the compact city, tend to move point D towards A rather than towards C – that is, towards the characteristics of a highly radial pattern of commuting rather than towards a highly localised pattern.

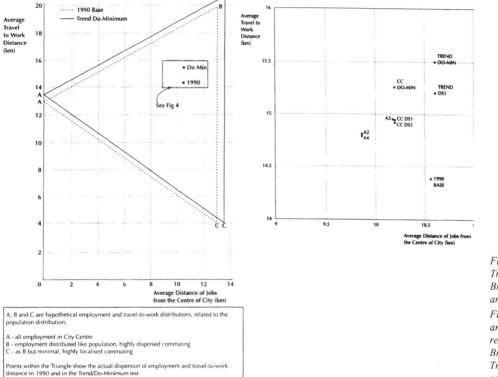

A, B and C are hypothetical employment and travel-to-work distributions, related to the population distribution:

A - all employment in City Centre
B - employment distributed like population, highly dispersed commuting
C - as B but minimal, highly localised commuting

Points within the Triangle show the actual dispersion of employment and travel-to-work distance in 1990 and in the Trend/Do-Minimum test

Fig. 3. Brotchie Triangles for the Bristol study area.

Fig. 4. Strategy and scenario results on the Brotchie Triangle: commuting trips.

Comparison with other studies

Comparison with the results of other studies is fraught with problems but it is nevertheless highly desirable to try to see how the results of the study described here compare with those obtained by other researchers.

Centralisation versus decentralisation

A number of previous studies were identified as giving quantified results for some form of compact city scenario, that is, one where the emphasis is upon stopping or reversing the trend towards decentralisation of population and employment. These are:

- the ECOTEC/TPA (1993) study of an unidentified urban area for the DoE and DoT;
- Still's (1992) research using a model of Edinburgh;
- Rickaby's study (1987) of alternative settlement patterns; and
- some of the results from the International Study Group on Land-Use/Transport Interaction (ISGLUTI) (Webster *et al.*, 1988; Paulley and Webster, 1991).

The ECOTEC/TPA and Still studies, like the present one, are based on changes in land use input directly to transport models. The Rickaby and ISGLUTI studies used integrated land use/transport models, which predict changes in the distribution of population and employment from changes in planning policy. Rickaby compared six different settlement patterns for an abstract study area, consisting of an archetypal English town and its hinterland, using a TRANUS model (De la Barra, 1989). The results considered here are for the 'concentrated-nucleated' configuration, compared with the base case.

The results from the ISGLUTI project are for two different models, IRPUD (Institut für Raumplanung Universitaet Dortmund) and LILT (Leeds Integrated Land-use/Transport), applied to the city of Dortmund. Descriptions of the models can be found in Webster *et al.* (1988), as can the IRPUD results. The LILT results are from Mackett (1990). The results quoted here compare a test in which growth was accommodated by peripheral development, with one in which peripheral development was largely or wholly prohibited. Table 2 attempts to bring together those results, which we believe, can, with caution, be compared. The objective here is to consider the transport results given the degree of centralisation shown, irrespective of whether this centralisation is input or output.

	Centralisation (increase within urban area, as % of urban area)		Centralisation (increase within area, as % of study area total)		Impact on travel by all modelled modes		
	Population	Employment	Population	Employment	Average trip length	Total distance travelled	Source
MVA/DSC CC/DM vsTR/DM	+18%	+12%	+8%	+7%	−2%	−2%	MVA Consultancy *et al.*, 1996
ECOTEC/TPA 1(central area expansion vs peripheral area expansion)	ns	ns	+10%	+10%	Car −2%	−3%	ECOTEC/ TPA, 1993
Still (Balanced vs Trend)	+2%	+7%	+1%	+5%	−3%	−2%	Still, 1992
Rickaby: Pattern 1 vs Pattern 0	+30%	+41%	+20%	+29%	−22%	−18%	Rickaby, 1987
LILT (Dortmund) Test 12.2 vs 12.1	ns	ns	+3%	+0%	−1%	−1%	Mackett, 1990 Webster
IRPUD (Dortmund) Test 12.2 vs 12.3	ns	ns	+5%	+8%	−1%	ns	*et al.*, 1988

Table 2. Summary of published results.

'ns' means not stated in published reports or papers

The figures show that the studies cover a range of degrees of centralisation. The LILT results produce a very small effect on population and no perceptible effect on employment. At the other extreme, Rickaby's are far more radical than any of the others, particularly in terms of employment. The results are unanimous in forecasting that centralisation of population and employment will reduce average travel distances and total distance travelled by all modelled modes. They can be grouped into Rickaby's, which shows reductions of around 20% in travel, and the rest, where the responses are in the range −1% to −3%. The greater scale of the impact in Rickaby's research is due to the greater scale of the scenario: a population increase in the town, at the expense of its hinterland, twice as great as any other of those considered here, and an employment increase six times greater. The results can be generalised as indicating that:

- only massive levels of recentralisation can produce substantial decreases in travel;
- reversing the trend towards decentralisation (ECOTEC/TPA, Still, present authors) produces decreases of only a few per cent;
- stopping further peripheral development (ISGLUTI) decreases travel by only 1% to 2%.

Intra-urban location

The effects of land use patterns within the city are now considered. Rickaby *et al.* (1992) tested several different patterns of intra-urban development, using a different application of the TRANUS land-use/transport interaction model mentioned above. The alternative patterns represented different strategies for accommodating 20% increases, over 20 years, in the number of households, the number of jobs and the amount of floorspace. Three of the patterns involved increasing densities within the existing built-up area, whilst the other two directed development into areas of peripheral expansion. This study found only slight effects: the option using least energy in transport used only 1.6% less than that using most energy. As in the present study, the differences in density implied by the alternative scenarios were quite slight.

Comparison with the following results is limited by the fact that Rickaby *et al.* did not consider an option of higher densities in the centre of their archetypal settlement. They perhaps felt that such densities would not be acceptable – the sample of towns from which their archetypal town was derived included historic centres such as Cambridge, Lincoln and York. The ISGLUTI results for Leeds can be summarised as follows (Mackett, 1991):

- the LILT model predicted a 3% shift of population and a 1% shift of employment into the inner area (central area plus inner suburbs, as defined for ISGLUTI);
- the MEPLAN model (see Hunt and Simmonds, 1993) predicted a 7% shift of population into the inner area but no detectable movement of employment;
- the LILT effects on transport (modal split, average distance and total distance) are all smaller than ±0.5%; and
- MEPLAN predicted small reductions in travel of −2% in total distance, −3% in average distance and in total distance travelled by car.

The general impact of intra-urban land use changes as forecast using land-use/transport interaction models is therefore very small. The authors' own results, with no feedback from transport to land use, and unconstrained by acceptability or feasibility, are likewise modest, the most significant being a 5% reduction in car use as a result of concentrating population (Scenario A3 compared with the main compact city scenario, both with the DS2 transport strategy). This produces a reduction in carbon dioxide emissions of between 2% and 3%.

The most quoted figure from the ECOTEC/TPA study is a 16% reduction in air pollution. This refers only to pollution from private vehicles during the peak hour, and is based on planning measures *in combination with* increased public transport. ECOTEC/TPA reported that 'it [was] not possible to distinguish the relative contributions made by the public transport investment and the land-use changes' (ECOTEC/TPA, 1993, Appendix 1, para. 18). This makes it difficult to compare it with other findings.

Comparison with other studies: conclusion

These comparisons have been limited to using readily available material. There is scope for much more analysis of the differences and similarities between the findings of these and other authors and their models. However, the authors believe that the results obtained from the present research conform to current professional thinking and analysis, and that this should increase confidence in using these results.

Conclusions

The main conclusions are as follows:
- Land use policy is generally a very slow-acting instrument; because rates of development

are slow, even radical changes from past trends produce only modest differences over a quarter of a century.

- A more compact land use strategy – changes in the broad distribution of activities between different parts of the city region – is unlikely in itself to have a significant impact on total travel demand and total car use, although the details of the strategy may have much greater consequences in particular locations.
- Such a strategy does not necessarily increase the effectiveness of a transport strategy designed to reduce car use without restricting mobility in general.
- The lack of impact of a more compact land use pattern is due mainly to the fact that proximity has a weak influence on travel choices under the range of conditions considered.

On the positive side, the more compact city does not in itself lead to a major worsening of travel conditions and related problems, as has sometimes been feared, though variants which involve particularly high concentrations of activity can produce concentrations of problems such as traffic congestion and associated pollution. Attention therefore needs to be given to: non-transport reasons why the compact city may be a desirable or undesirable urban form; whether other combinations of transport policies would be more appropriate and more effective within the more compact city; and other possible ways of influencing travel which might benefit from more compact cities.

The first of these points is clearly being considered in various streams of work, including those represented in the present volume and its predecessor (Jenks *et al.*, 1996). The second could be addressed, for example, through extensions of the policy optimisation approach pursued in the OPTIMA project (Shepherd *et al.*, 1997; May *et al.*, 1997); it also requires attention as to how different policy elements could practically be combined (for example, how to achieve high densities of office and shopping development, with very restricted parking provision and very high quality public transport). The third recognises that conventional ways of thinking about land use and transport may be inadequate to deal with the problems now faced, and that wholly new and as yet unrecognised elements to urban policy may be required.

Notes

1. The study described was carried out by the MVA Consultancy, David Simmonds Consultancy and the University of Leeds Institute for Transport Studies, under contract to the then Department of Transport (MVA Consultancy *et al.*, 1996). The authors of this chapter were Project Manager and Project Director, respectively. The views expressed, particularly in the conclusions, are entirely the authors' own, and the strategies tested were devised solely for the purposes of research.
2. Further research into transport strategies, based upon the same study area and a related transport model, can be found in a series of papers introduced by Coombe *et al.* (1997).
3. Two other scenarios have been omitted, but details can be found in the original report and in Simmonds and Coombe, 1997.
4. There is no hard limit on parking – it is assumed that people will always find a parking space, but will have to search, to queue and to walk further.

Acknowledgments

The model of the Bristol area was used by kind permission of the then Avon County Council. The authors would like to thank colleagues in their respective firms for their hard work on the model application and analysis.

Mats Reneland
Accessibility in Swedish Towns

Introduction

The increased mobility of modern society, brought about by developments in motor transport, has contributed to acidity in lakes, and increased air pollution and consumption of resources. The desired development towards a sustainable society demands that the needs of people and activities can be satisfied through long-term, sustainable mobility – that is, through using information technology, minimising the length of journeys and maximising the use of sustainable means of transport. From a sustainability perspective, walking and cycling are superior to other means of transportation.

The focus of policy in Sweden has shifted from issues of mobility and safety to the combination of accessibility, environment and safety. This has created the need for co-ordinated urban and transport planning, addressing both the location of buildings/land uses (housing, workplaces, services and recreation) and investments and restrictions in the transport network. An integrated urban strategy is necessary to maximise sustainability benefits, since changes in transport systems and changes in land use are interdependent. The qualities of the transport system, in terms of links and nodes, influence the ease with which people and goods can be moved from one part of town to another. Changes in the transport system of a town via changed accessibility create new land use structures, which, in turn, via the changed transport needs of people and activities, and the traffic flows thereby created, place demands on changing the traffic system.

This chapter addresses one important aspect of sustainable transport: accessibility. Good accessibility is crucial to achieving sustainable transport, since it may reduce the length of journeys or the need to travel by car, thus reducing carbon dioxide emissions and energy use. Sweden is still a thinly populated nation. Despite the migration from rural areas and villages to larger towns that has taken place and continues to take place, a large proportion of the population live in small towns and the countryside. In 1995, the five largest towns (over 100,000 inhabitants) contained just over two million inhabitants, the 14 towns with a population of between 50,000 and 99,999 contained nearly one million inhabitants, and the 33 towns with 20,000–49,999 inhabitants contained just over one million inhabitants. Altogether, 4,184,535 of Sweden's 8,837,496 inhabitants live in urban areas of more than 20,000 inhabitants. Providing the whole of Sweden with good accessibility could thus be said to be a difficult task.

This chapter outlines the first stage of a national-scale research project, *Accessibility in Swedish Towns.* Although the concept is wider, accessibility is defined, for the purposes of the research, in terms of the distance residents have to travel to certain types of service, such as food shops, post offices, chemists, libraries, primary, intermediate and secondary schools and public transport. For a more in-depth exploration of the concept of accessibility, see the

Swedish language project report (Reneland, 1998a). The research project makes comparisons between the years 1980 and 1995, and between the 45 largest towns in Sweden (excluding the Stockholm region). The proportion of the population, or the proportion of potential service users for particular categories of service, living within a theoretically possible distance of 400 metres of the nearest service or facility was calculated for various types of service, for the two years, 1980 and 1995. Through this, the project provides answers to the following two main questions:

- How has accessibility to each service changed for the population between 1980 and 1995?
- Are there any significant differences with regard to the distance of the population to the services studied between different towns?

In this chapter, only the findings in aggregated form for the towns in the population ranges 20,000–67,000 inhabitants and 79,000–480,000 inhabitants are presented.

Methodology
The aim of this research project was to provide empirically based knowledge about the form of Swedish towns, in particular the extent to which the population of Swedish towns is structurally dependent on the car.

The sample of towns investigated
Only the 45 largest towns were studied, excluding the capital city of Stockholm and some of the suburban towns in the Stockholm region. The towns in the research sample contained 20,000 or more inhabitants in 1990. Thus, from a European perspective, several are very small. In effect, the research looks at the level of accessibility to services for a little less than one third of the population of Sweden.

For the purposes of the research, the boundaries of each town were defined in accordance with the digital urban area boundaries for 1980 and 1995, as stipulated by the National Central Bureau of Statistics, Statistics Sweden (SCB). In summary, an urban area was defined as follows:

> An urban area encompasses all agglomerations of buildings with at least 200 inhabitants, on condition that the distance between these buildings does not normally exceed 200 metres. (SCB, 1996, p.6)

The types of service investigated
During the three-year duration of the project, accessibility to the following services was investigated:

- food shops and supermarkets (facilities controlled by several private or co-operative interests);
- post offices and chemists (services controlled by the state); and
- public transport, schools and libraries (services controlled by local authorities).

Research methods and uncertainties
The research project was carried out with the aid of GIS (Geographical Information Systems). Population statistics for each 'real estate' (see further explanation below), together with geographical data on public transport and different forms of service were added to digital

maps supplied by the National Land Survey of Sweden (Kartcentrum). A database was created and analysed using the GIS programmes, ArcInfo and ArcView, and the results were processed in Excel.

Details of addresses for the digitalisation of chemists, libraries and post offices in towns were obtained from telephone directories for the years and towns involved. Information about the public transport systems in each town were derived from timetables for the winter period 1980/81 and the corresponding period for 1995/96. The limitations and definitions in digitalising public transport are described in detail in the report entitled *Kollektivtrafikens Effektivitet* (Reneland, 1998b). Addresses for the digitalisation of food shops were purchased from Delfi MarknadsPartner AB.

The production of digital population statistics in Sweden needs some further explanation. Information about each resident is linked to the specific real estate (that is, specific parcel of owned land/development) where they live. Thus, different types of information about the population can be obtained from this real estate data, which can be loaded onto the centre points of respective real estates, defined by specific x and y coordinates. The real estate population information is normally aggregated to postcode areas, parishes, municipalities or other statistical districts. In this project, the population information was non aggregated, that is, linked to every real estate. For a real estate comprising only one single-family house, the real estate population information describes one household while, for a real estate comprising several multi-storey buildings, the real estate population information can describe up to several hundred households. A real estate with industrial use normally has no population information, as nobody lives there.

The real estate population information supplied by Statistics Sweden differ from the same organisation's table values (SCB, 1984, 1996). For both 1980 and 1995, the digital urban populations in all towns are less than those quoted in the tables. The average deviation for all 45 towns in the research sample was 4.18% for 1980 and 2.06% for 1995. This means that the trends towards extended distances between residents and service facilities from 1980 to 1995 found in this study are probably even more marked.

In the first phase of the research project, the focus is on the distance aspect of the concept accessibility. The intention is to continue with travel-time studies with regard to the public transportation and car traffic networks.

The measure of accessibility used in the research was the proportion of population of a town living within a theoretical distance zone of 400 metres from particular services and facilities. This zone corresponds to a walking trip of roughly five minutes or less at five kilometres per hour, and is used in Sweden to define a good standard for walking distance from the home to a bus stop (Statens Planverk, 1982). A distance of 400 metres or less to services and facilities may be considered an appropriate accessibility standard for both pedestrians and cyclists. This distance is conceived to be measured along footpaths and/or cycle tracks between departure and destination points. However, in this quantitative study it was unrealistic to measure distance from each service or facility in every town along actual pedestrian and cycle networks. Evidence suggests that there is a relationship between distance as the crow flies and real distance and, more specifically, that, as a rule, the latter is roughly 20–30% greater than the former (Statens Planverk, 1972; Statens Planverk, 1982). The GIS analyses were facilitated by estimating the actual distance of 400 metres to be 308 metres as the crow flies (the real distance between two points in the town was assumed to be approximately 30% longer than the distance as the crow flies).

In the analyses, the number of men and women living on real estates within a radius of 308 metres around each service/facility in each town was calculated. The percentage of the entire population of each town included in these distance zones was then determined. A further measure of accessibility, using average distances to facilities for the population as a whole in each town, was used but the results for this measure are not described here.

Findings
Accessibility to post offices – an example
By means of address details from the 1980 and 1995 telephone directories, the post offices were digitised as a layer on the digital town maps. Because the number of post offices was relatively small, automatic address matching was not used; instead, the addresses were found with the aid of conventional tourist maps, and digitised using the digital map's street network as a basis. Experience shows that automatic address matching creates errors that are difficult to discover and correct. For example, the address details used often contain abbreviations that the computer programme is unable to interpret correctly.

The digitised post offices were then provided with circular buffer zones with a radius of 308 metres. The layers of buffer zones intersect with the layers containing real estate population information. The sum of the population of the real estates within the distance zone was calculated. Because the population data at real estate level includes information on gender and age, it was possible to calculate, for example, the number of senior citizens (or women over 75) within 400 metres of the nearest post office.

Finally, data on the number of individuals within the 400 metre zones in each respective town were transferred to a calculation sheet in Excel, where the percentage of the total town population was calculated, and diagrams drawn up.

Figure 1 illustrates the significant differences between towns with regard to service provision. For example, the population of Eskilstuna (Fig. 1, left) is roughly double that of Uddevalla (Fig. 1, right), but the number of post offices is 6.5 times as many. This, of course, influences the proportion of the population within 400 metres. In 1995, this was 6.4% in Uddevalla and 26.0% in Eskilstuna.

Fig. 1. Urban area boundary, post offices and 400 metre zones in Eskilstuna (left) and Uddevalla (right) 1995.

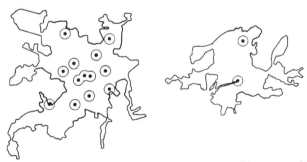

Changes over time are exemplified by Karlskoga, a town of just over 30,000 inhabitants, where the seven post offices in 1980 were reduced to only three in 1995 (Fig. 2). The effect was that the proportion of the population within 400 metres fell from 18.9% to 7.7%.

Summary of results
The data on accessibility obtained for the research was sufficiently detailed to allow in-depth analyses of the importance of the location and quantity of each type of service studied, in relation to the homes of the population in each town, in 1980 and 1995. It is likely that the long distances to services in certain towns are due to the low average population densities. In the case of other towns, they may be due to the natural topography, for example high hills and inlets from the sea.

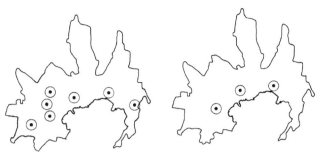

Fig. 2. Urban area boundary, post offices and 400 metre zones in Karlskoga, 1980 and 1995.

Table 1 presents the findings of the research in aggregated form. The detailed results can be found in the Swedish language project reports (Reneland, 1998c, 1998d, 1998e).

	Year	No. of services	Towns of 20,000– 67,000 residents	Towns of 79,000 – 480,000 residents
Urban population within 400m of the nearest chemist	1980	231	7.5%	15.6%
	1995	259	8.9%	15.1%
Urban population within 400m of the nearest library	1980	226	10.1%	12.2%
	1995	199	8.8%	10.4%
Urban population within 400m of the nearest post office	1980	442	18.9%	27.8%
	1995	348	14.5%	20.8%
Urban population within 400m of the nearest food store	1980	2076	55.2%	66.1%
	1995	1578	49.4%	62.2%
7–12-year-olds within 400m of the nearest school for their age group	1980	853	29.8%	41.7%
	1995	801	25.9%	37.4%
13–15-year-olds within 400m of the nearest school for their age group	1980	283	8.4%	14.7%
	1995	275	8.0%	13.6%
16–18-year-olds within 800m of the nearest school for their age group	1980	126	12.4%	10.6%
	1995	141	11.5%	12.8%
Urban population within 200m of the nearest public transport route	1980*		75.1%	79.0%
	1995		78.4%	84.4%
Urban population within 400m of the nearest public transport route with 20 min. frequency	1980*		47.8%	88.1%
	1995		48.2%	85.4%
Annual turnover in 1995 monetary value SEK per town inhabitant	1980		16,105 skr	13,895 skr
	1995		20,069 skr	15,678 skr

Table 1.
Aggregated
summary of the
proportion of
population within
200, 400 or 800
metres of the
nearest service/
facility, 1980 and
1995.

Net route length per inhabitant within 400m of the nearest public transport route	1980*	1.3m	0.9m
	1995	1.4m	0.9m
Street length per inhabitant	1995	5.9m	4.3m
Average density (residents per ha urban area)	1980	16.5	24.4
	1995	16.4	23.6

Göteborg is not included in these values

The trend between 1980 and 1995 with regard to accessibility to chemists in small towns, schools for the 16–18 age group in large towns and to public transport was that small increases in the proportion of population within 400 metres had taken place (Table 1). A possible explanation is that the number of chemists and the number of schools for 16–18-year-olds had increased, the latter as a consequence of reforms in school policy. The principal investment in the local authority sphere of public transportation was the creation of service routes (these are routes, often with light traffic, designed to link housing areas containing many elderly residents with various kinds of service facilities for older people, such as hospitals and health clinics). This is associated with increased route lengths per inhabitant, because such service routes often run parallel to the main routes, but with minor deviations.

The proportion of the population within short distances decreased for libraries, post offices, food shops and schools for age groups 7–12 and 13–15. The number of facilities for each respective service also decreased.

Overall, the research suggests that, for accessibility to the services studied between 1980 and 1995, distances became longer, and hence sustainability declined. The possibilities for walking or cycling to the services in question in both small and large towns deteriorated. Of particular concern are the changes within the competitive retail food trade. Although annual turnover per town inhabitant had increased considerably between 1980 and 1995, over the same period of time the number of shops fell by nearly a quarter. Annual turnover per town inhabitant was greater in the small towns than in the large, probably due to greater inflow of purchasing power from the surrounding countryside in the smaller towns. In spite of this, a lower proportion of the inhabitants had shorter distances to travel in the small towns than in the large.

The ongoing restructuring of the everyday commodities trade, from many shops located near the home to a small number of external shopping centres, in combination with petrol service station shops and small service shops offering limited variety and high prices, will probably encourage the population to use their cars more than they do at present for the purchase of everyday commodities. Closures of food stores may not be preventable by society but, through existing Swedish legislation, the location of new stores may be controlled. The predominant political philosophy, however, is that competition leads to advantages for the consumer in the form of lower prices. Discussions about the effects of external shopping centres on the length of shopping trips, choice of transportation and the environment show that competition is also seen to have impacts other than low prices.

Comparisons between the small and large towns show that the inhabitants of the large towns were those within the shortest distances of services and facilities (Table 1). The differences were considerable with regard to chemists, post offices, and schools for age groups 7–12 and 13–15, as well as for public transport routes with a service frequency of at least 20 minutes. It was only for schools for the 16–18 age group that the proportion within 800 metres was greater in the small towns in 1980. By 1995, through the expansion of this type of school, this situation had changed.

Surprisingly, the average street length per town inhabitant, calculated from the digital maps, was found to be noticeably shorter in the larger towns than in the small ones. A possible explanation for this is the higher population densities in large towns (Reneland and Hagson, 1994). In the case of post offices, the positive relationship between population density and the proportion of the population within the 400 metre zones was pronounced (see Fig. 3).

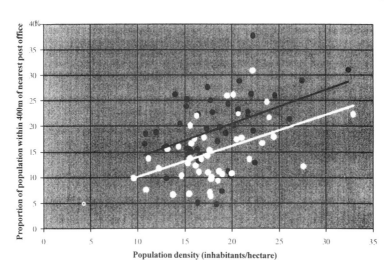

Fig. 3. The link between population density and the percentage of the population within 400 metres of the nearest post office (1980 shown in black and 1995 shown in white).

Regarding individual towns, there are also other important factors influencing the distances between homes and services, such as the shape of the town (see Reneland, 1998b), the overall provision of services (as in, for example, the comparison between Uddevalla and Eskilstuna), and the specific location of services with regard to centres of population.

Conclusions

There may be a range of influences on accessibility, but the importance of population density remains. A common notion today is that there may be a lack of services in small towns, because they do not have sufficiently large population bases, but the inhabitants generally live in relatively close proximity to all services. Since Sweden has become a member of the EU, it has been seen to be important to emphasise the country's structure of mainly small towns, so that not only the three largest cities, Stockholm, Göteborg and Malmö, receive attention from a European perspective. The National Board of Housing, Building and Planning has coined the term 'the moderate-sized town' with the objective of drawing attention to towns with a population of between 20,000 and 100,000 inhabitants (Boverket, 1996). The moderate-sized town has been associated with many positive qualities of a cultural and social nature, not least of which is proximity:

> The moderate-sized town … has everything one needs close at hand: shops, service, work, culture, entertainment, leisure time activities and other people. (Boverket, 1996, p.16)

There may now be reason to question this. The research outlined here suggests that although the small town has its advantages, it does not offer good accessibility to all services in comparison with larger towns. The research provides evidence that an increase in the number of services does not automatically lead to an increase in the proportion of the population within short distances of them. Neither does a reduction in the number of services lead to a reduction in the proportion of the population within short distances. This conclusion illustrates the usefulness of carrying out the geographical, GIS-based analyses used in this project. The findings are of relevance to service providers, particularly state-controlled ones. Such service providers often aim to serve some form of community function by offering the population an equal level of service, irrespective of where they live. It is clear that the proportion of the population within short distances of services differs widely from town to town. It is not always possible to understand the changes that have taken place with regard to the number and location of services and facilities between 1980 and 1995. Perhaps other criteria, such as annual turnover, number of customers and levels of rent, rather than proximity, have been the dominating forces behind these changes.

Uyen-Phan Van and Martyn Senior

The Contribution of Mixed Land Uses to Sustainable Travel in Cities

Mixed land uses and travel behaviour

Reducing the need to travel is high on the policy agenda, and land use planning is seen to have a prominent role in achieving this objective (Banister, 1997). In recent years, UK governments have claimed that mixed land uses can promote sustainable transport by reducing the need to travel by car. What evidence is there to support this claim? Some commentators are justifiably sceptical (Breheny, 1995) and there is some suspicion that politicians find proposed planning solutions to transport problems much more palatable than pricing ones.

This chapter first summarises the UK policy context, after which it is noted that, while there appears to be little empirical evidence from the UK, a number of studies have been undertaken in the US. These are reviewed and assessed. Then the chapter outlines a pilot empirical study, based on the US research, looking at travel behaviour in three neighbourhoods of Cardiff characterised by varying land use mix. The hypotheses of this research are that mixed land uses:

1. reduce the probability of using a car for commuting, shopping and leisure trips, as jobs, shops and leisure facilities are located nearby;
2. increase the frequency of short food shopping trips, since items can be purchased conveniently from local shops as and when needed, thereby reducing the frequency of longer food shopping trips typically involving a large number of items and often requiring the use of a car; and
3. encourage lower levels of car ownership, again because of easy access to local facilities.

In testing these hypotheses statistically, allowance is made, where relevant, for potentially confounding influences, such as density of development, number of employed persons and cars per household, distances travelled to work, to shops and to other facilities, and the adequacy of public transport.

The UK policy context

Sustainable development, mixed land use and design were central themes in the last Conservative government's approach to planning in the UK (DoE, 1997). The new Labour government has announced its intention to update planning guidance, and it is even more strongly committed to sustainable development and the integration of land use and transport planning (DETR, 1998).

Mixed land uses are seen as contributing to sustainable development objectives by reducing the need to travel, especially by car, and encouraging, instead, sustainable trips on foot, by bicycle and by bus. Indeed, *Planning Policy Guidance 13: Transport* boldly asserts:

By providing a wide range of facilities at the local neighbourhood level, the need for people to use cars to meet their day-to-day needs will be reduced. (DoE and DoT, 1994, para. 3.17)

Central government's advice on best practice (DoE and DoT, 1995a) talks approvingly of the 'urban villages' initiative (Aldous, 1992). However, only limited hard evidence on the sustainable transport benefits of mixed uses is quoted, namely evidence from a comparison of the new towns of Milton Keynes (England) and Almere (the Netherlands) (TEST, 1991), and from research on choices of transport mode for trips to local and other centres (ECOTEC, 1993). Even then, the ECOTEC report casts some doubt on the influence on travel of the intermixing of land uses, especially residential and employment. Moreover, an initial assessment of the implementation of PPG13 revealed local authority concerns about developers' willingness to invest in mixed-use schemes (DoE and DoT, 1995b). Yet this has not deterred the current government from expecting local authorities to use their planning powers to promote walking, cycling and public transport by ensuring a conducive land use mix (DETR, 1998).

Assessing US research
In the US, there has been a more substantial and vigorous empirical assessment of the influence on travel of mixed land uses (and of density and urban design), especially in the context of the debate over 'New Urbanism' in general and neo-traditional neighbourhood designs in particular.

Handy (1992) found that residents of mixed-use neighbourhoods made more walking and cycling trips to local retail stores than did those living in areas served by car-oriented retail developments. However, these trips did not replace, but were additional to, trips to regional shopping centres. Ewing *et al.* (1994), in a study of six communities varying from traditional higher-density, mixed-use forms to lower-density residential sprawl, discovered significant differences in travel behaviour, but not as large as expected. Residents lacking access to local facilities compensated by undertaking multi-purpose trip chains. Moreover, provision of local facilities in car-dominated communities appeared to be effective in reducing car trips. Thus, the community with the longest commuting trips also had the shortest shopping and leisure trips, because it had been planned as relatively self-contained, except for employment.

Other studies suggest that mixed uses influence commuting behaviour. Frank and Pivo (1994) found correlations between mixed land use and walking to work. Cervero (1996) supports this in a more rigorous and controlled analysis, but he notes that residential densities exert stronger influences in discouraging car commuting and encouraging public transport use. Cervero interprets his results in terms of trip chaining: local shops facilitate shopping on the way home from work, on foot or by public transport, while more distant retail facilities require a car. However, this interpretation needs to be confirmed by travel diary data to establish that such trip linkage does indeed occur.

Assessments of these studies (for example, Handy, 1996) have encouraged more searching analyses. Thus, Cervero and Kockelman (1997) take great care to distinguish the density, land use diversity and design dimensions of urban form, and use a range of indicators for each of these. They find that all three significantly reduce trip rates and deter car travel, but the strength of their influences are typically modest for land use mix and moderate for design aspects. Similar work, but with a stronger behavioural foundation based on consumer demand theory, is presented by Boarnet and Sarmiento (1998). Their analysis of non-work trip frequencies cautiously suggests that living in areas of higher retail-job density lowers trip frequencies by car, but that higher service-employment densities actually increase such frequencies. Using the same theoretical basis for their empirical work, Crane and Crepeau

(1998) find little evidence that land use affects travel behaviour in the ways suggested by the proponents of neo-traditional designs.

Although the evidence from the US does not provide consistent findings, there is increasing scepticism about the strength, and even the existence, of the impacts of land use diversity on travel behaviour.

Research design

The research design adopted for the study described in this chapter is an adaptation of that used by Cervero (1996). However, it is based on a small-scale survey and fieldwork, as the large-scale secondary data used by Cervero are not collected in the UK. Two wards in Cardiff were chosen. These have differing land use mixes, but similar average residential densities and socio-economic profiles and, thus, similar *propensities* for car ownership. The areas were not matched on *actual* car ownership, as this may be influenced by land use mix. The inner urban area of Canton was chosen to represent a relatively high land use mix. Using data from the 1991 Census on all the other wards in Cardiff, the adjacent area of Fairwater was found to have the most similar socio-economic composition to Canton (Table 1) and similar mean residential densities (Table 2). Much of Canton's housing comprises Victorian terraces and inter-war terraced and semi-detached properties, whereas Fairwater contains predominantly post-1945 private and local authority housing, varying from high-rise flats to semi-detached housing. While Fairwater is predominantly a residential area, except for a small sub-area of shopping and employment in the south, Canton has industrial, business, and hospital uses and an important district centre with office as well as retail land uses.

Socio-economic group	Canton	Fairwater	Difference
Employers and managers	11.01	6.69	4.32
Professional	3.72	2.25	1.47
Intermediate non-manual	16.52	12.64	3.88
Junior non-manual	21.70	22.33	−0.63
Manual	18.46	19.39	−0.93
Personal service and semi-skilled manual	13.44	14.89	−1.45
Unskilled manual	5.18	6.75	−1.57
Unemployed	9.96	12.07	−2.11

Table 1. Socio-economic composition of Canton and Fairwater (figures are percentages derived from the 1991 Census).

	Canton	Fairwater
Land area (ha)	297.5	300.9
Population density	44.1	42.2
Dwelling density	19.2	18.4

Table 2. Average residential densities (per hectare) in Canton and Fairwater.

Household and field surveys were conducted in three sub-areas exhibiting high, low and no land use mix. The main road running through Canton contains the local district shopping centre. Streets adjacent to the main road were randomly chosen, and dwellings were randomly selected from these. In Fairwater South, streets are arranged radially from a small shopping centre. Again, streets and then dwellings were selected randomly. In Fairwater North, the layout of housing is largely in the form of estates and culs-de-sac. Dwellings within three large estates were randomly chosen. The sample households were surveyed, using questionnaires, to obtain information on usual travel mode, frequency and distance for: work trips of the chief earner; light and heavy food shopping trips; and trips to eat out. Additionally, details of household car ownership, number of employed persons and whether the chief earner worked full- or part-time were collected. A land use survey was undertaken to record local housing types (and thus local density) and local non-residential land uses, including bus stops, within 400 metres of each responding household's home. The limit of 400 metres is arbitrary and raises the question of the geographical scale implied by the term 'mixed land uses'. Given this study's focus on local neighbourhoods and sustainable means of transport, 400 metres is considered a reasonable walking distance for a healthy adult to access local facilities, including public transport services. Indeed, only four respondents, all resident in Fairwater, did not have a bus stop within 400 metres of their homes.

The data were first examined to identify any contrasts in travel between the three sub-areas. Then, statistical analyses were used to assess the influence of land use mix, while simultaneously allowing for the effects of other factors. Logistic regression was considered an appropriate method for analysing choices of transport mode, and took the form:

$$log_e(probability\ car\ /\ probability\ not\ car) = b_0 + b_1\ X_1 + b_2\ X_2 + b_3\ X_3$$

Poisson regression was used to analyse car ownership and shopping trip frequency, as follows:

$$log_e\ Y = b_0 + b_1\ X_1 + b_2\ X_2 + b_3\ X_3\ ...$$

where Y = number of cars owned or frequency of trips made per fortnight.

The parameters, b_0, b_1, b_2, b_3 and so on, were estimated in GLIM (a statistical package for Generalized Linear Interactive Modelling – see Aitkin *et al.*, 1989) using the sample data from the household and field surveys. The hypothesised explanatory variables, X_1, X_2, X_3 and so on, are:

1. the mixed land use indicator (presence or absence of grocery store and other retail or commercial land use within 400 metres of a respondent's home);
2. residential density indicators (presence or absence of detached housing and presence or absence of flats within 400 metres of a respondent's home); and
3. other likely influences on transport decisions, namely, distance to work, shops or eating facilities (as appropriate), household size, number of employed persons per household and whether the chief earner works full- or part-time, and (for the analyses of travel mode and trip frequency) car ownership.

A comparison of household transport decisions in areas of varying land use mix

Table 3 summarises the transport attributes of households in the three sub-areas in Cardiff which exhibit varying degrees of land use mix. Generally, these data appear to suggest that mixed land uses may have partial effects on car ownership, mode choice and trip frequencies.

	Canton (high mix of uses)	Fairwater South (low mix of uses)	Fairwater North (no mix of uses)
Total households	66.00	28.00	36.00
Car-less households (%)	22.70	10.70	13.90
Households with 2+ cars (%)	31.80	32.10	33.30
Mean no. of cars per household	1.12	1.25	1.19
Commuting trips:			
by car (%)	67.80	87.00	87.50
by bus (%)	14.30	0.00	8.30

by foot/cycle (%)	17.90	13.00	4.20
Light food shopping trips:			
by car (%)	10.60	39.30	72.20
by bus (%)	0.00	7.10	5.60
by foot/cycle (%)	89.40	53.60	22.20
Heavy food shopping trips:			
by car (%)	63.70	89.30	91.70
by bus (%)	3.00	10.70	8.30
by foot/cycle (%)	33.30	0.00	0.00
Trips to eat out:			
by car (%)	43.30	80.80	88.60
by bus (%)	3.30	15.40	11.40
by foot/cycle (%)	46.70	0.00	0.00
by taxi (%)	6.70	3.80	0.00
Frequency of light food shopping trips:			
fortnightly (%)	0.00	3.60	11.10
once a week (%)	18.20	21.40	41.70
twice a week (%)	31.80	53.60	27.80
3+ times a week (%)	50.00	21.40	19.40
Frequency of heavy food shopping trips (%s do not sum to 100):			
fortnightly (%)	15.20	17.90	5.60
once a week (%)	63.60	75.00	88.90
twice a week (%)	10.60	3.80	2.80
3+ times a week (%)	4.60	0.00	0.00

Table 3. Car ownership and trip statistics for the three areas of varying land use mix.

The greatest degree of land use mix, in Canton, is associated with the highest proportion of car-less households, but the lowest percentage is not found in the single – residential – land use area of Fairwater North. Moreover, all three areas have very similar levels of multi-car ownership.

A clearer picture emerges for mode choices. Car use for commuting declines as land use mix increases. Yet, the gradient of this relationship does not seem particularly steep – over two-thirds of Canton's commuters travel by car, compared with 87% in the other two areas. The strongest evidence for the influence of mixed uses is for mode choice for light food shopping trips. In the questionnaire, these were defined as trips where items purchased could be carried relatively easily by hand, whereas for heavy food shopping trips this would be difficult. There are very strong contrasts between areas in car use and walking/cycling for these light food trips. Because of proximity to a district shopping centre in Canton, car use forms a very small percentage, and walking or cycling a very high proportion, of such trips. Even to the small shopping centre in Fairwater South, over half of all trips appear to be made on foot or by bicycle. Only for Fairwater North is the car the dominant mode for light food shopping trips. By contrast, for heavy food shopping trips, the car is the dominant mode in all three areas, with mode shares similar to commuting. However, a third of such trips in Canton are on foot or by bicycle, which may reflect access to the district shopping centre there. For trips to eat out, the car has the predominant role in both Fairwater South and North, but walking is slightly more frequent than car use in Canton.

Turning to shopping trip frequencies, a clear pattern of higher frequencies associated with greater land use mix is evident for light food shopping. The most frequent trips (three or more times per week) are the most common among households in Canton, two trips per week dominate in Fairwater South, and over half of all households in Fairwater North make weekly or fortnightly trips. There is a slight suggestion that the availability of shopping facilities in Canton and Fairwater South, which present opportunities for local residents to make frequent light food trips, encourages less frequent heavy food shopping trips there. However, the percentages for fortnightly heavy food shopping trips are not particularly high, and in all three areas the dominant trip frequency is once a week, with this frequency being most pronounced in the non-mixed-use area of Fairwater North. Canton has the highest proportion of households making heavy food shopping trips twice or more a week, perhaps suggesting that a minority of households, mainly those with no or one car, use the local district centre for both light and heavy food shopping.

Statistical analyses of the household and field survey data

The above comparisons might imply that land use mix is influencing certain transport decisions. The evidence seems strongest for both the travel mode and trip frequency aspects of light food shopping journeys. However, the interpretations so far can only be taken as suggestive, for at least four reasons. First, the household data has been aggregated by sub-area in Table 3. Second, the field survey details on local land use mix and densities around each respondent's home have not been used. Third, sample sizes are relatively small, so differences between the three sub-areas could have occurred by chance through the sampling process. Finally, even if these differences in travel are real, they could be the result of influences other than land use mix, such as car ownership. These issues are now addressed by using the statistical analyses outlined earlier, in which multiple influences on travel behaviour can be simultaneously incorporated. The technical results are summarised in Table 4 but, to facilitate interpretation, the significant influences on travel mode, trip frequency and car ownership are also portrayed graphically (Figs 1–6). Using the statistical goodness-of-fit criterion that standardised differences between travel observations and predictions should not be greater than an absolute value of two, all of the analyses give few, if any, poor predictions of household travel characteristics. Because no significant influences on trip frequencies were detected, frequencies of heavy food shopping are omitted from Table 4. It should also be noted that distances to work are used in the analysis of car ownership.

Table 4 reveals that only for mode choices for light food shopping trips is land use mix a significant influence. Figure 2 displays this effect of land use mix in the context of the simultaneous influences of car ownership and distance travelled; the spacing of the lines indicates that car ownership has a stronger effect on mode choice than mixed land uses.

The density variables are consistently insignificant across all analyses. By contrast, distance (reflecting the time and cost of travel) and car ownership (measured as number of cars per household or as a simpler car/no car classification) are always significant, except for the influence of car ownership on mode choice for trips to eat out. Additionally, the number of employed persons in households has a significant positive effect on car ownership, as does full- or part-time employment on mode choice to work. It is clear that the most marked influence of land use mix (on mode used for light food shopping) is being identified, but small samples are less likely to allow the statistical detection of less pronounced land use influences on travel which the data in Table 3 possibly hint at (see Cervero and Kockelman, 1997). This raises the question of whether analyses of larger sample datasets would have revealed wider impacts of land use mix and densities.

Explanatory variable	Commuting: mode choice of chief earner	Light food shopping: mode choice	Heavy food shopping: mode choice	Eating out: mode choice	Light food shopping: trip frequency	Car ownership
Number of employed persons	ns	ns	ns	ns	ns	0.2737 (0.080)
Cars in household	2.642 (0.730)	car/no car better	car/no car better	ns	− 0.1204 (0.0591)	not used
Car/no car	cars better	4.327 (1.537)	3.417 (0.791)	ns	cars better	not used
Full/part-time employment (chief earner)	2.262 (1.015)	not used	not used	not used	not used	ns
Distance travelled	0.9603 (0.300)	1.895 (0.382)	1.399 (0.318)	0.9424 (0.1886)	−0.131 (0.037)	0.0292 (0.012)
Density: detached housing < 400 metres	*1.339 (1.002)	*−0.488 (0.801)	*1.012 (0.801)	*0.107 (0.529)	*0.005 (0.103)	*−0.013 (0.1816)
Density: flats < 400 metres	*0.147 (1.262)	*0.500 (1.564)	*−0.668 (1.288)	*−0.524 (0.726)	*0.162 (0.153)	*−0.118 (0.204)
Land use mix: grocery store and other retail or commercial use < 400 metres	*−0.0133 (1.244)	−2.332 (0.858)	*−0.705 (1.280)	*−0.848 (0.720)	*0.167 (0.139)	*−0.153 (0.191)
Constant (b_0)	−6.415 (1.708)	−5.113 (1.717)	−3.762 (0.925)	−1.665 (0.4681)	1.676 (0.082)	−0.4041 (0.156)
% cases poorly predicted	1.9%	3.8%	2.3%	2.5%	0%	0%
Number of households used in the analysis	103	130	130	121	130	130

'ns' indicates a variable is not statistically significant at the 5% level.
* indicates that parameters are given for each non-significant land use or density variable included separately with the other significant variables.
Standard errors are shown in brackets.

Table 4. Logistic and Poisson regression analyses of household travel characteristics – parameter estimates (and standard errors).

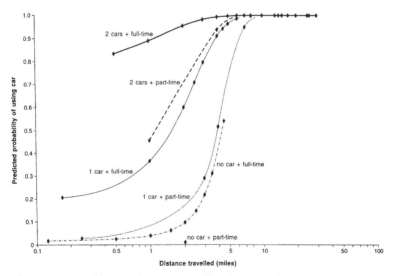

Fig. 1. Predicted car use for commuting.

Very tentative answers to this question are now offered by re-estimating the regression analyses using the significant variables plus one additional land use or density variable at a time (the estimated parameters are identified by a * in Table 4). If the parameters on the land use mix and density variables have the expected signs, and the ratios of their values to their standard errors are not too far below 2, the threshold for a significant variable, then it could be argued that larger samples might indeed detect significant effects. This argument can be immediately dismissed for the highly insignificant effect of mixed land use on the probability of car commuting; despite the expected negative sign, its parameter value is very small relative to the standard error. Unlike Cervero (1996), we find not even the remotest evidence that mixed uses influence commuting behaviour. However, of the two density variables, the one relating to detached properties has the expected positive sign and a parameter/standard error ratio of 1.33; thus, lower-density residential development may be encouraging car use for commuting. The influence of land use mix on mode of transport for light food shopping has already been found to be significant, but additional influences of density are unlikely, as both variables have unexpected signs and are quite strongly insignificant. For mode choices for heavy food shopping, land use mix and the flats density variable have the expected negative signs, but are clearly insignificant. A stronger case can be made for suggesting that low densities, as reflected in the detached housing variable, encourage car use for such trips. For eating out trips, land use mix is closer to statistical significance than the density variables, so a larger sample might detect a mixed-use effect discouraging car use for this trip purpose. A similar situation exists for the frequency of light food shopping trips, except that, here, land use mix may encourage higher trip frequencies, and the flats density variable may also have the same effect. Finally, for car ownership, the density variables are surprisingly strongly insignificant, and although land use mix has the expected negative sign, it, too, is quite insignificant. In any case, it would be expected that car ownership, as distinct from car use, would be relatively insensitive to land use mix as compared with such influences as household income, and quality and convenience of public transport.

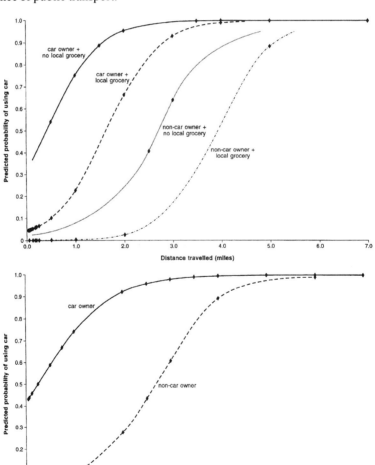

Fig. 2. Predicted car use for light food shopping.

Fig. 3. Predicted car use for heavy food shopping.

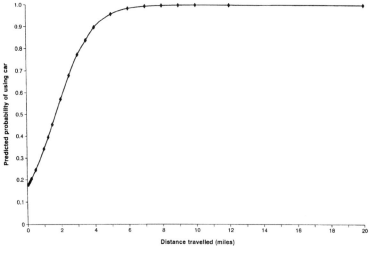

Fig. 4. Predicted car use for eating out.

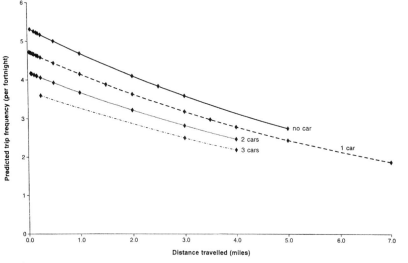

Fig. 5. Predicted frequency of light food shopping trips.

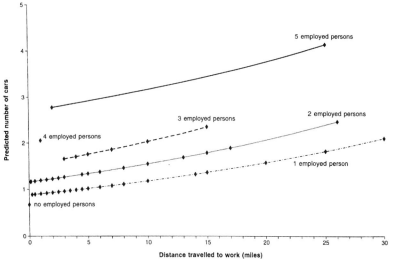

Fig. 6. Predicted car ownership.

Conclusions and recommendations

The clearest conclusion from this study is that mixed land uses encourage walking and cycling, and deter car use, for light food shopping trips. Much more tentatively, it is suggested that such land uses may prompt higher trip frequencies for this purpose too, and discourage use of the car for trips to eat out. There is little evidence that land use mix affects car ownership or mode choice for heavy food shopping trips and especially for commuting. Thus, our results reinforce the sceptical tone emanating from recent research in the US.

However, further research is needed to confidently accept or dismiss policies of land use mixing aimed at influencing travel behaviour. Handy (1996) has already pointed the way. It should be emphasised that it would be desirable to acquire detailed records of household members' activity and travel behaviour over time-spans of a week or more, and correspondingly detailed inventories of land uses around respondents' homes and possibly their workplaces. The geographic scales at which land use mix is recognised and which may influence behaviour require further investigation (Boarnet and Sarmiento, 1998); and the behavioural basis of people's travel and locational decisions would benefit from more rigorous scrutiny.

Finally, it should be stressed that any findings that residents of mixed-use areas adopt more sustainable travel behaviour cannot necessarily be generalised to those who currently do not live in such areas, but might be persuaded to. Past, unsustainable travel habits might not be relinquished easily when residential relocations occur. An investigation of the travel behaviour of residential movers is, therefore, one of the most important research needs. However, this may be a difficult task as the dominant preferences for decades now have been for low-density, single-use, residential areas (Breheny, 1995).

Helena Titheridge, Simon Hall and David Banister

Assessing the Sustainability of Urban Development Policies

Introduction

The concept of sustainable urban form has been, and still is being, widely debated. Alternatives include the compact city (Commission of the European Communities, 1992), decentralised concentration (Rickaby, 1987, 1991), remote new settlements (Breheny *et al.*, 1993) and multi-centred cities (Owens, 1987, 1991; Mensink, 1990). Banister (1992) and Blowers (1993) propose balanced communities with a good range of facilities, services and job opportunities so that enforced dependence on the car and long distance travel are minimised. Much interest in promoting sustainable urban form has focused on potential sustainability benefits related to transport. The first stage of enquiry into the relationships between transport and urban form has now been replaced by more sophisticated investigations. Initially, a second stage explored the links between transport, energy use and urban form at the national (Banister, 1992) and local levels (Banister *et al.*, 1997). Such studies revealed the difficulties in determining the nature of relationships, due to the many variations in urban form, whether the urban area is considered in terms of the labour market area or a city within a region, and the influence of socio-economic variables. Patterns of energy use and transport vary both within and between urban areas, and over time. Categorisation and comparison helped in the understanding of some of the relationships but not the underlying processes at work. The third (and current) stage extends the analysis to include emissions, together with a clear spatial representation of the relationships. The aim of this stage is to test the impacts of different policy actions on urban form, transport, energy and emissions levels.

Perhaps the most important decision now being faced by planners in the current round of structure plan reviews concerns the siting of new housing developments. Government projections predict that at least 3.8 million new dwellings will be needed between 1991 and 2016 to meet the country's housing needs. Pressure has been placed on local authorities to identify suitable sites for this housing and to consider the transport implications of these new developments. With no clear rules that can be generally applied, local authorities need clear guidance and methods to assess the consequences of adopting different development strategies.

A number of transport models are commercially available or under development, ranging from complex network flow models to simple spreadsheet models, but many are unsuitable for explicitly assessing strategies to reduce personal travel through alternative land use and development policies. A number of models have been developed specifically for assessing strategic decisions and require much smaller amounts of data. These include the TPK spreadsheet model of Hampshire settlements (TPK, 1996), the JET city-based spreadsheet (Banister and Esteves, 1995), the DREAM model (Titheridge *et al.*, 1996) and the DOS-based regional model, TEMIS (Fritsche and Rausch, 1993). However, none of these models are spatially based, nor do they model the trip patterns generated by a specific region.

Research is currently being carried out (see note 1) within the Bartlett School of Planning to develop a model which will assess the sustainability of new housing developments in terms of personal travel demand, and associated energy consumption and emissions. This research has identified an appropriate structure for a tool that could prove invaluable to local authority planners and policy makers in making difficult choices about the best location for new housing developments. This chapter describes the model (called ESTEEM – see note 2) in its current state and then illustrates how it could be used by local authorities. Discussions with several local authorities have produced favourable comments about the timeliness and usefulness of such a tool.

The model stands out from other transport models currently on the market for a number of reasons. First, it has been designed to use readily available datasets and will not require costly travel surveys and traffic counts. Second, the model has been designed to link with a GIS programme – ArcView – which has been shown to be one of the more popular GIS programmes currently in use within local authorities, and therefore requires minimal transfer of data. Third, the model is windows-based and menu driven, and thus easy to use.

Model structure

ESTEEM consists of two modules – a travel module and an emissions module. The two modules have been developed within different packages – the travel module currently exists as a C executable programme, whilst the emissions module is in spreadsheet format. The modular structure allows local authorities to enter actual travel data, or their own estimates of expected travel patterns derived from other transport models, into the emissions module. The modules operate as separate, but dynamically linked, models. Data from the travel module output are captured by the emissions module, allowing the effect of changes in travel patterns on emissions to be seen immediately. Eventually, users will be able to interact with both modules using solely the GIS interface.

ESTEEM not only allows planners to see the effects of different developments on individual travel modes and purposes, but also allows them to visualise and evaluate the effect on different areas within the county. This visualisation dimension has been achieved through maps showing the changes in modelled mean trip distance travelled by residents of each enumeration district (ED). The values for the ED centroids are interpolated to produce complete surface coverages.

The travel module

The travel module operates as an add-on to ESRI's ArcView GIS package. ArcView was selected following a review of GIS packages, considering their functionality and extent of use in local planning. The purpose of this review was to ensure model development in a package compatible with those used by local authorities, thereby maximising its potential use. The review comprised two elements. The first was an analysis of the Association for Geographic Information's *Local Government GIS Survey* (AGI, 1995). The results of this survey were based on responses from just over 70% of UK local authorities in September 1995. This information was updated by the second element of the review, a telephone survey of GIS use in county councils, carried out in November 1997.

The travel module currently simulates, using an origin-constrained gravity model, travel patterns for education, work, personal business and retail journey purposes, by car and bus. This covers approximately 60% of all personal journeys by motorised transport (DETR, 1997). Each travel mode is modelled with a generalised cost function based on distance. Two versions of the travel module have been developed. The more sophisticated version uses network distance, while the simpler version uses euclidean distance and is aimed at those local authorities who are relatively new to GIS, as it does not require the purchase of network data. This chapter outlines only the euclidean version of the module. There are no vehicle capacity constraints in either model version; thus, the complex trip assignment procedures often required by transport models are avoided. This limitation has the disadvantage of requiring crude procedures to take account of congestion, but this is not a great problem as the model operates on an annual basis.

All trip purposes use ED centroids as origins, with appropriate population-based census variables as production units. The number on school roll (NOR) and the number of people with a workplace in each ward are used as destination attraction indices for education and work trips respectively. Footprint floor space was used to generate a destination attraction index for shopping and personal business trip purposes.

The split of total trip production between different modes has been incorporated by applying factors (derived from the *National Travel Survey 1994/6,* DETR, 1997) to the production values. Modal split is currently constant for all trip production units (EDs) and does not take into account differences in either the socio-economic or accessibility characteristics of the EDs. Modal split elasticities will be incorporated into the model during the next phase of development.

Emissions module

This module calculates energy consumption and emissions (CO_2, CO, VOC, NO_x, PM, SO_2) related to personal travel within an Excel spreadsheet. Numbers of trips per year, by mode and purpose, are entered into the model to derive total travel. The module output includes total and per capita vehicle-kilometres, passenger-kilometres, fuel consumption and emissions.

All journey purposes and modes are included in the emissions module. Average trip length for those purposes and modes modelled within the travel module are fed into the emissions module via a dynamic link. Average trip lengths for the remaining purposes and modes, derived from local or national statistics, are entered directly into the spreadsheet. External trips are also included at this stage (external trips are defined as those trips whose destination is outside the study area).

Travel-related energy and emissions are calculated using factors derived mainly from COPERT II (Ahlvik *et al.*, 1997). The emissions module takes into account fleet characteristics, such as vehicle age, engine size and type, as well as estimates of average journey speeds and cold start distances. The module also includes algorithms for calculating emissions from alternative powered vehicles such as electric, CNG and LPG vehicles. In addition, future emissions limits for cars and buses have been included where possible; for example, the emissions limits for new cars, which are proposed for 2001 by the European Commission under the recent directive resulting from the auto-oil programme (Directive 98/69/EC, CEC, 1998).

Calibration

The euclidean version of the travel module was applied to Leicestershire (including Leicestershire, Leicester and Rutland administrative areas) and calibrated using travel survey data (CALTRANS) for 1995. The travel module was run for each mode/purpose combination. In each case, the distance-decay exponent was adjusted until the modelled mean trip distance and CALTRANS mean trip distance converged, to create a series of sub-models (one for each mode/purpose combination).

To support this calibration, a sensitivity analysis was carried out for each sub-model. The distance-decay exponents were varied by ±5% and ±10%. For each run, the modelled and CALTRANS mean trip distances from each origin were compared using the Standardised Root Mean Square Error (SRMSE), chi square and Pearson product-moment correlation tests. For each sub-model, the distance-decay exponent that provided the best fit with the observed data, and that gave a mean trip distance within the 95% confidence interval of the CALTRANS mean, was selected. Due to the nature of the model, the results of the statistical tests cannot be used to accept or reject the model but merely as a guideline for comparison of the different model runs.

The education sub-models within the euclidean model gave the greatest SRMSE (0.89 for car trips and 0.66 for bus trips). This is partly because secondary and primary schools are included within the same sub-model, and the catchment areas for these types of school are often very different. Separating these out into two sub-models would probably improve the model calibration results; unfortunately, the local travel survey data used to calibrate the model could not be separated.

The calibration results for work and retail trips were better (a SRMSE of between 0.40 and 0.49), with the smallest SRMSEs given by the retail sub-models (0.43 for car and 0.40 for bus). The work trip sub-models included the most comprehensive coverage of possible destinations, but as for education trips there were inaccuracies in the model, as no distinction was made between different occupation types. Retail sub-model inaccuracies occurred, since smaller local services and facilities were not included within the Goad data (see note 3) used to provide the location and attraction indices for this purpose.

The bus sub-models showed better calibration results than the car sub-models. At present, the model uses a generalised cost function based on distance. This simplification works better for buses than for cars, as distance is a better proxy for cost by bus, due to the smaller variation in journey times and speeds.

Validation

In order to test whether the same values for the distance decay exponents could be used for different counties, the model was applied to Kent. The sub-models were applied using the same distance decay exponents that had been calibrated for Leicestershire. The modelled mean trip distances using these Leicestershire distance decay exponents were found to be substantially different from the mean trip distances derived from a travel survey carried out in Kent in 1995. It was therefore necessary to recalibrate the sub-models for Kent. The same process was used for Kent as had been used for Leicestershire.

The calibration results for Kent were not as good as those for Leicestershire, with much greater values for SRMSE, ranging from 0.41 to 1.17. However, it was possible to establish an optimal value for the distance decay exponent for all modelled mode/purpose combinations within the 95% confidence limits of the overall mean trip distance derived from the local travel survey data. For some of the Leicestershire sub-models, the minimum SRMSE occurred when the overall mean trip distances fell outside the 95% confidence limits.

As for Leicestershire, the bus sub-models provided better calibrations than the car sub-models. However, there were some differences between the two counties. For Kent, the education-car sub-model calibrated with the worst results while the education-bus sub-model provided the best calibration. For Leicestershire, the SRMSEs for both education-car and education-bus sub-models were large compared with the other sub-models. This difference between the two counties can possibly be explained by the different policies of the local education authorities (LEAs) involved.

Model application – Leicestershire and Kent travel patterns, 1995

The calibrated models were run using all ED centroids within the county as origins to produce an estimate of current travel patterns within each county.

Total travel per capita for Leicestershire was found to be 12.9 thousand kilometres per person per year (Table 1). This is slightly above the figure of 11.2 thousand kilometres per person per year given in the National Travel Survey 1994/96 for the rest of England and Wales, although there is likely to be a great deal of variation between the different counties included in this figure. However, it is possible that the data in the model for Leicestershire slightly overestimate external trip lengths, as these are based on data from the CALTRANS travel survey, which covered an area in the centre of Leicestershire. For Kent, travel per capita was found to be 12.6 thousand kilometres per person per year (Table 2). The National Travel Survey 1994/96 gave a figure of 12.6 thousand kilometres per person per year for the South East (excluding London).

Although annual travel per person was less for Leicestershire than for Kent, the annual energy consumption per capita due to personal travel for Kent (21.92GJ) was slightly greater than the annual energy consumption per capita in Leicestershire (21.90GJ). This difference in energy consumption per kilometre is due to differences in average trip distance by car and by rail between the two counties. In Kent, the average length of a car trip is much longer than in Leicestershire, whilst the length of the average trip by rail is much shorter in Kent than in Leicestershire.

For Leicestershire, it was found that for retail trips the mean trip lengths for bus and car journeys were similar. This may be because the Goad data used focuses mainly on town and large district centres and does not include all out-of-town retail parks, therefore limiting car users to the same selection of facilities as bus users. The mean length of work trips by bus was shorter than that for work trips by car, as would be expected. However, the mean length of educational trips by bus was greater than that for education-related car trips. This is thought to be partly due to the effect of LEA provision of school buses for journeys over a certain length.

	Annual travel per capita ('000 km)	Annual energy consumed/ capita (GJ)	Annual emissions of pollutants per capita (kg)							
			CO	NO$_x$	VOC	PM	CO$_2$	SO$_2$	Pb	
Base	12.87	21.90	75.29	12.88	13.95	0.52	1,445	90.78	8.76	
IN	12.86	21.88	75.23	12.86	13.94	0.52	1,444	90.69	38.71	
EX	12.86	21.89	75.28	12.86	13.94	0.52	1,444	90.75	38.75	
DC	12.88	21.91	75.33	12.89	13.95	0.52	1,446	90.83	38.78	
NT	12.86	21.91	75.31	12.88	13.95	0.52	1,445	90.81	38.78	

Table 1. Leicestershire travel, energy and emissions per capita for the base model and four strategies. See below for explanation of the four strategies.

	Annual travel per capita ('000 km)	Annual energy consumed/ capita (GJ)	Annual emissions of pollutants per capita (kg)							
			CO	NO$_x$	VOC	PM	CO$_2$	SO$_2$	Pb	
Base	12.64	21.92	78.80	12.63	14.53	0.42	1,362	92.34	41.27	
IN	12.62	21.88	78.60	12.58	14.49	0.42	1,358	92.04	41.14	
EX	12.63	21.90	78.64	12.59	14.50	0.42	1,359	92.12	41.18	
DC	12.65	21.94	78.74	12.62	14.52	0.42	1,362	92.31	41.25	
NT	12.63	21.93	78.72	12.62	14.52	0.42	1,361	92.26	41.24	

Table 2. Kent travel, energy and emissions per capita for the base model and four strategies. See below for explanation of the four strategies.

Mean trip lengths by car for both education and work purposes were substantially longer in Kent than in Leicestershire. This is probably due to differences in the distribution of settlements within the two counties. Kent has a dense, almost linear band of smaller settlements along its northern boundary which then curves southwards following the east coast, whilst Leicestershire has a strong radial pattern, with Leicester sitting in the centre of the county, surrounded by a ring of smaller settlements. Mean trip lengths by bus for education and work purposes were also longer in Kent than in Leicestershire, but to a lesser extent. Retail and personal business trips were, on average, longer in Leicestershire than Kent. Kent has a large number of retail centres of similar size, so journeys tend to be made to the nearest centre, whilst Leicestershire has a much more hierarchical structure, with Leicester attracting shoppers from much greater distances.

For Kent, it was found that the mean length of bus trips for work purposes was substantially shorter than the mean length of car trips. This is possibly explained by the greater level of access to motorways and 'A' roads within Kent compared with Leicestershire, encouraging car use for longer journeys. Similar effects are seen for retail journeys, though to a much smaller extent.

Figures 1 and 2 show how mean trip distance changes across the county for Leicestershire and Kent respectively, with the shortest mean trip lengths occurring close to the centres of the main towns.

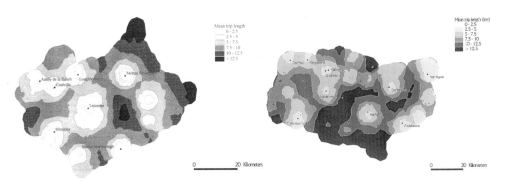

Fig. 1. Modelled mean trip length for Leicestershire by origin, 1995.

Fig. 2. Modelled mean trip length for Kent by origin, 1995

Modelling the development strategies

To illustrate the use of the model in preparing structure plans and development plans, a series of four development strategies for both Leicestershire and Kent were devised. The strategies were kept as simple as possible in order to isolate the effect of the location of a new development (or set of developments) on travel, energy and emissions. For each strategy, an additional 10,000 households were accommodated according to the different development policies within the county. It was assumed that these households would have the same characteristics as the county average. Additional employment and school places were also included, close to the new housing, at a level which would maintain the current (1995) job ratio and availability of school places (that is, places per child). Finally, it was assumed that the development would take place during 1995 and, therefore, the fleet characteristics used in the strategies remained unaltered from the 1995 base model. A brief description of each strategy is given in Table 3.

Leicestershire

The four strategies were found to have different effects on each of the travel module sub-models (Table 4). The intensification strategy resulted in the smallest increase in total car travel for work purposes, with mean trip length decreasing from 5.31 to 5.26 kilometres. For commuting trips by bus, the extensification strategy resulted in the greatest reduction in mean trip length, from 4.27 kilometres in the base model to 4.24 kilometres. For education, retail and personal business trips both by car and by bus, the new town strategy resulted in the greatest reductions in average trip lengths.

Development Strategy	Description
Intensification (IN)	Housing and employment developments were concentrated within the main urban areas, increasing both the residential and employment densities of existing towns. No new retail centres were created.
Extensification (EX)	Housing and employment were concentrated around the periphery of the main urban areas. As for the intensification strategy, no new retail centres were created.
Decentralisation (DC)	Housing and employment developments were located in rural villages throughout the county. Again, no new retail centres were created.
New town (NT)	All new housing and employment developments were located in a single new settlement located in a relatively rural part of the county. A new retail centre was created to serve the population of the new settlement.

Table 3. A brief description of the four development strategies.

	Mean trip distance (km)					
	Education		Work		Retail and personal business	
	Car	Bus	Car	Bus	Car	Bus
Base	1.68	3.51	5.31	4.27	3.90	3.90
IN	1.68	3.50	5.26	4.27	3.86	3.86
EX	1.69	3.53	5.30	4.24	3.96	3.96
DC	1.67	3.51	5.31	4.27	3.88	3.88
NT	1.66	3.46	5.52	4.34	3.79	3.79

Table 4. Mean trip distance for internal trips within Leicestershire by mode and by purpose.

Considering the results of the sub-models together, the intensification strategy (IN) resulted in the smallest increase in total travel (Table 5), with total passenger-kilometres increased by 2.7% above the base model (the total number of passenger trips for all the strategies increased by 3.0% over the base model). For strategies EX, DC and NT, total passenger-kilometres rose by 2.8%, 2.9% and 2.8% respectively. Similarly, the intensification strategy resulted in the smallest increase in total energy consumption and emissions. However, although both the extensification strategy and the new town strategy resulted in an increase of 2.8% in total annual travel, the extensification strategy resulted in an increase in annual energy consumption of 2.8% whilst the new towns strategy resulted in a greater increase of 2.9%. This means that, whilst only the decentralisation strategy resulted in an increase in annual travel per capita, both the decentralisation and new town strategies resulted in an increase in annual energy consumption and annual emissions per capita (Table 5).

	Total annual travel (million passenger-km)	Annual energy consumed/ (TJ)	Annual emissions of pollutants (thousand tonnes)						
			CO	NO_x	VOC	PM	CO_2	SO_2	Pb
Base	11,371	19,352	66.53	11.38	12.33	0.463	1,277	80.22	34.25
IN	11,682	19,880	68.38	11.69	12.67	0.476	1,312	82.41	35.18
EX	11,689	19,894	68.41	11.69	12.67	0.476	1,312	82.46	35.21
DC	11,702	19,912	68.45	11.71	12.68	0.477	1,314	82.54	35.24
NT	11,689	19,907	68.44	11.70	12.68	0.477	1,313	82.52	35.24

Table 5. Leicestershire annual modelled travel, energy and emissions for the base model and four strategies.

Note: the travel increase represents the 10,000 new households allocated around the county according to the rules stated in Table 3 for each development strategy.

Intensification (IN) of Leicester had little effect on mean trip lengths within the city and its immediate surroundings (Fig. 3). However, mean trip lengths around the other main towns decreased as a result of this strategy. The higher levels of employment opportunities and facilities associated with the increased population seem to attract trips away from Leicester.

The extensification strategy (EX) resulted in shorter mean trip lengths around the edge of the towns, in line with the location of the new development, as was expected. However, the mean trip lengths of those living in inner Leicester and Loughborough increased – attracted by the out-of-town business parks.

Spreading new housing and employment across the rural areas of the county in the decentralisation strategy (DC) had the effect of reducing mean trip lengths of the rural residents, due to greater employment opportunities closer to home. Nevertheless, only a small proportion of the total population of Leicestershire was affected by shorter journey lengths, due to the lower densities of the rural areas.

In the new town strategy (NT), a new town of 10,000 dwellings was located to the east of Leicester – an area of high mean trip lengths. The settlement was designed to be self-contained, providing jobs, schools and other facilities for its residents. Trip lengths within the new town area decreased substantially compared with those of the base model (Fig. 4). Conversely, mean trip lengths for those living to the east of the new town increased substantially – attracted away from the smaller centres. Trips to Leicester from the west of Leicester were unaffected.

Fig. 3. Change in modelled mean trip length from the base model for Leicestershire intensification strategy.

Fig. 4. Change in modelled mean trip length from the base model for Leicestershire new town strategy.

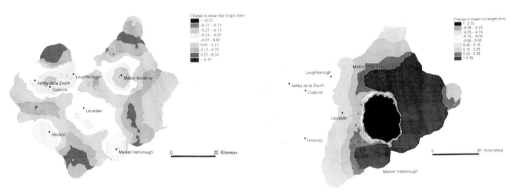

Kent

As was the case for Leicestershire, the strategies were found to have different effects on each of the travel module sub-models (Table 6). The intensification strategy resulted in the lowest mean trip length for work journeys both by car and by bus. For education, retail and personal business trips by both car and by bus, the new town strategy resulted in the greatest reductions in average trip lengths.

Table 6. Mean trip distance for internal trips within Kent by mode and by purpose.

| | Mean trip distance (km) | | | | | |
| | Education | | Work | | Retail and personal business | |
	Car	Bus	Car	Bus	Car	Bus
Base	3.66	4.00	10.37	4.29	4.91	4.07
IN	3.63	3.96	10.26	4.29	4.88	4.04
EX	3.65	3.98	10.34	4.34	4.88	4.05
DC	3.69	4.03	10.47	4.27	3.88	3.88
NT	3.62	3.95	10.71	4.33	4.77	3.97

Adding the results of the sub-models together for Kent, again the intensification strategy resulted in the smallest increase in total travel (Table 7). Total passenger-kilometres increased by 1.50% above the base model (the total number of passenger trips for all the strategies increased by 1.7% over the base model). This was slightly smaller than the increase in total travel resulting from the extensification strategy (1.54%). The intensification strategy also resulted in the smallest increase in total energy consumption and emissions.

	Total annual travel (million passenger-km)	Annual energy consumed/ (TJ)	Annual emissions of pollutants (thousand tonnes)						
			CO	NO$_x$	VOC	PM	CO$_2$	SO$_2$	Pb
Base	18,236	31,362	113.71	18.22	20.97	0.60	1,965	133.23	59.55
IN	18,509	32,091	115.45	18.48	21.29	0.61	1,994	135.20	60.43
EX	18,520	32,117	115.51	18.50	21.30	0.61	1,996	135.31	60.48
DC	18,554	32,180	115.66	18.53	21.33	0.61	2,000	135.58	60.60
NT	18,530	32,168	115.64	18.53	21.33	0.61	1,999	135.52	60.58

Table 7. Kent total annual travel, energy and emissions for the base model and four strategies.

Intensification of Kent's major towns caused a decrease in mean trip lengths originating from them and their surroundings (Fig. 5). This effect was expected, as an increase in facilities and employment opportunities promote local trips. In rural areas, mean trip lengths increased, suggesting that the towns attract trips from these areas. Between the areas of increased and decreased mean trip lengths are bands of no change. This implies that much travel from these areas was originally to the towns.

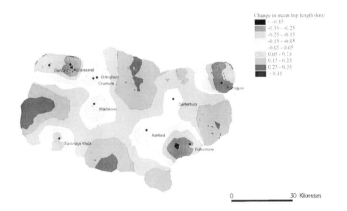

Fig. 5. Change in modelled mean trip length from the base model for Kent intensification strategy.

The extensification strategy produced a similar pattern to that of intensification. The developed areas caused a decrease in mean length of trips originating from them. Trip lengths increased from other areas, attracted to the new developments. Again bands of no change were apparent.

The decentralisation strategy (DC) had the effect of decreasing mean trip lengths from rural areas, most markedly in the southern, central region of Kent, which exhibited high travel distances (Fig. 6). The development appears to have produced more trips to local facilities and jobs in these areas. The mean lengths of trips originating in the towns increased slightly, indicating that some travel was also attracted from these areas.

The new town strategy (NT) placed the development just south of the centre of the county, in an area associated with high mean trip lengths. This option reduced the travel distances originating from it and in its surroundings. The new town also attracts travel from more distant areas, demonstrated by their increased mean trip lengths. This influence diminishes with distance.

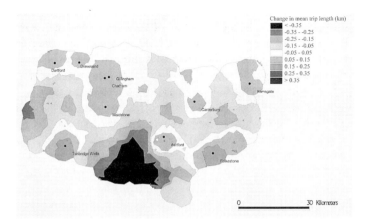

Fig. 6. Change in modelled mean trip length from the base model for Kent decentralisation strategy.

Conclusions

The analysis above suggests, at first glance, that of the four strategies tested for both Leicestershire and Kent an intensification policy would be the most sustainable policy to adopt, in terms of travel, energy and emissions. However, the results are dominated by the effect of each strategy on journeys to work by car. Between 1985 and 1995, the distance travelled per person per year to and from work increased by 18%, whilst the distance travelled per person per year for shopping and personal business purposes increased by 35% (DETR, 1997). During the course of a year, the average person travels as far for shopping and personal business purposes as he or she does for commuting – 1204 miles per person per year, as compared with 1265 miles per person per year (DETR, 1997). As the balance between commuting and other purposes changes, so too will the locations of the most sustainable developments.

The analysis shows that developments have marked effects on neighbouring areas, affecting not only travel patterns but also possibly the vitality of these areas. These findings may be important when considering the wider implications of development location and not just the implications for traffic reduction.

Overall, the impression given is that the resulting changes are small, but it should be remembered that only 10,000 additional households have been allocated. It has also been assumed that jobs, services and facilities will be provided in the new locations in a similar pattern to those already available. If no new jobs, services and facilities are provided, then the trip lengths and energy use will increase substantially.

The results presented here only really reflect the initial development and testing of the methods. The approach is currently being further developed with the network-based travel model and a more sophisticated modal split element based on the actual strategies being adopted by these two counties.

The decisions being made now on the allocation of substantial new housing within the counties will have a significant impact on future travel demand and patterns of sustainability. ESTEEM will allow strategic planners to test quickly a large number of possible options for new developments, at a very early stage in the structure plan and unitary development plan review processes. Many decisions about housing location are currently based on intuition. By providing a model which uses a familiar windows-based interface, together with the means to link it to local authorities' own data, some of the questions about which settlement options are more or less sustainable in transport terms will be answered.

The model has the potential to test a much wider range of options. As already noted, the model allows the location of services and level of service provision to be altered, as well as the bus, road and other transport networks serving them. This means that the model could be used, for example, to model the effects of adding bus services to the network or building an additional railway station on a line. Local authorities and housing developers could use the model to examine the level of facility provision within new developments, improving the attractiveness of the developments as well as reducing the need to travel.

ESTEEM provides a practical tool to aid decision making at the strategic level. The model has substantial potential in the structure plan review process, in the testing of county strategies, and particularly in assessing the implications of integrated land use and transport policies. The model can assess these strategies in terms of their transport consequences (through distance travelled and mode used), together with estimation of energy use and a range of pollution emissions.

Notes
1. Phase 1: funded by EPSRC Sustainable Cities Programme, October 1997 to December 1998. Phase 2: funded through the EPSRC LINK – Inland Surface Transport Programme, January 1999 to December 1999.
2. ESTEEM – Estimation of Transport, Energy and Emissions Model.
3. The GOAD data was provided by Experian and includes footprint floorspace of retail outlets in shopping centres (including town centres and some out-of-town locations).

Peter Headicar

The Exploding City Region: *Should It, Can It, Be Reversed?*

Introduction

The title of this chapter is deliberately provocative. It sets out to question the conventional wisdom that the trend of exploding city regions has unsustainable travel consequences and should therefore be reversed. In the UK, this view is enshrined in PPG13 – the planning policy guidance on transport issued by Central Government to local planning authorities (DoE and DoT, 1994). This advocates a combination of land use and transport policies aimed at reducing the need to travel and increasing the choice of non-car modes.

In relation to housing development, PPG13 includes the following principles to be applied at the strategic (county structure plan) level (*ibid.*, para. 3.2):

- Allocate the maximum amount of housing to existing larger urban areas (market towns and above).
- Avoid any significant incremental expansion of housing in villages and small towns where this is likely to result largely in car commuting to urban centres.
- Avoid the development of small new settlements (broadly those unlikely to reach 10,000 dwellings within 20 years).

The reason for questioning these principles is to seek evidence that they are in fact well founded. The need to do this arises because the evidence on which they were originally based (ECOTEC, 1993) was not as conclusive as the PPG's sharp change in policy direction implied.

This chapter therefore begins by reviewing briefly the trends in population distribution and travel within the UK, and examines the evidence from national sources about the possible relationship between them. It then reports on a series of local research exercises conducted in the Oxfordshire area, which have sought to examine more precisely the links between the location of residential development and the amount of car based travel. Evidence from both sources is drawn on to offer a critique of contemporary UK policy, particularly as it applies to non-metropolitan areas.

Trends in population distribution and travel

The 'exploding city region' refers to two spatial trends working in combination. 'Counter-urbanisation' is the net shift in population downwards in the urban hierarchy – from larger cities to medium and smaller towns and from more to less urbanised regions. 'Deconcentration' is the shift *within* any urban region from inner to outer parts of the core built-up area and from this area as a whole to the surrounding country ring.

During the 1980s, the functional urban regions that form the heart of conurbations experienced an average fall in their population of 0.9% whilst regions centred on free-standing towns and cities experienced an average increase of 5.8% (Champion and Dorling, 1994).

The largest rates of increase (around 8%) occurred in the latter regions but outside their core settlements. This type of location – typically a village or small town within a shire county – is now home to about a quarter of the nation's population.

Counter-urbanisation can also be depicted using the OPCS (Office of Population Censuses and Statistics) classification of local authority districts, by identifying the net change in population between the various district types. During the 1980s, all the more urbanised types of district experienced a relative loss of population, and amongst Outer London and the provincial metropolitan districts an absolute loss (Table 1). The largest absolute increase occurred in the 'mixed and accessible rural' category. Many districts in this category (including those in Oxfordshire discussed later) have their administrative areas overlapping the outer suburbs of neighbouring cities. In these cases, the net in-migration will have a strong component of urban deconcentration – that is, deriving from population movements within the same functional region as well as from outside it.

	1991 population	% change from 1981	Natural change	Migration
London				
Inner	2,566.4	0.6	112.3	−96.1
Outer	4,255.4	−0.4	129.7	−148.5
Metropolitan districts				
Principal cities	3,401.6	−4.2	59.0	−207.6
Others	7,704.5	−1.3	155.1	−254.0
Non-metropolitan districts				
Cities	4,620.3	0.9	99.7	−57.3
Industrial towns	6,851.3	2.1	166.9	−25.5
New towns	2,379.1	8.8	116.2	76.0
Resort and retirement	3,633.9	7.9	−158.5	423.6
Mixed and accessible rural	10,000.9	5.3	235.7	264.7
Remote, mainly rural	5,560.2	8.4	−30.9	459.9
Total, England and Wales	50,954.8	2.7	885.2	435.3

Table 1. Population change 1981–91 for OPCS urban types.
Source: after Breheny, 1995; from OPCS, 1992.

Accompanying these changes in population distribution have been large increases in the volume of travel. During the two decades from the mid-1970s, the annual travel distance per person increased by more than a third (Table 2). Part of this arises from a greater number of journeys but the majority is due to a lengthening of the average journey distance. This in turn can be related to the increased share of journeys by car (as driver or passenger). Significantly, the overall increase in travel time was only half the increase in distance travelled. Journeys in the 5–10 and 10–25 mile bands 'surged' disproportionately (Potter, 1996) – distances that would typically involve travel *outside* a single settlement and consist of journeys to or between neighbouring urban areas.

	All modes (%)	Car driver (%)
Number of journeys	+13	+49
Total distance	+38	+66
Average journey length	+24	+12
Total time	+19	+53
Average journey time	+5	+5

Table 2. Changes in travel (per person per year) 1975/76 – 1993/95.
Source: National Travel Surveys.

During the period 1991–2016, the number of households in England is projected to increase by 3.8 million. Nationally, land in urban use is projected to increase by only about half the rate of household growth because of the recycling of urban land (Bibby and Shepherd, 1995). Counties with the projected highest rates of urban growth form a belt extending north-eastwards across southern England into an arc around the northern side of the London Metropolitan Region, together with an adjacent area encircling the southern half of the West Midlands.

In terms of future traffic volumes, the central estimate of total vehicle distance is an increase of 46% between 1996 and 2021 (DETR, 1997). In contrast with previous forecasts, recent government figures (DETR, 1997) incorporate the effects of growing congestion on the nation's highway network and the annual increases in fuel duty begun in 1993. They also take account of a study of the effects of planning policy guidance and increasing congestion on land use patterns (Oxford Brookes University and WS Atkins Ltd, 1996). Within the overall increase there is considerable variation in the traffic growth anticipated at different types of location and on different types of road. This arises from a combination of different rates of future population and employment growth and different degrees of spare capacity in the existing highway network.

Possible links between development location and travel growth

Since development predetermines trip ends, it is logical from a sustainability viewpoint to explore whether particular spatial arrangements lead to more efficient travel outcomes: that is, to shorter average trip lengths and a higher proportion of less energy intensive modes.

Theoretically, the differing degrees of specialisation amongst human activities implies a hierarchical urban structure, with residential areas nested within successively larger clusters containing facilities requiring greater catchment populations. At each level, the centralisation of facilities provides for a concentration of movement which facilitates multi-purpose journeys and the provision of viable public transport. Concerns to limit journey lengths and to provide conditions conducive to walking and cycling as well as public transport lead to the rejection of low-density development. At the same time, excessive centralisation and densification are to be avoided because of consequential congestion.

These arguments lead to 'decentralised concentration' as the preferred urban form (Owens, 1986; Rickaby, 1987), and the rejection of the single 'compact city' model advocated by the European Commission (CEC, 1990; Breheny, 1992). The travel efficiency of any settlement pattern is, however, highly dependent upon prevailing fuel prices. Under a relatively low fuel price regime, the poly-centred functional region has the potential disadvantage of 'encouraging' longer distance movements between settlements when more local opportunities are available. This is particularly important in countries like the UK where conditions for inter-urban car journeys are relatively favourable. However, uncertainty about the external influences upon travel compared with the permanence of development and transport infrastructure gives 'decentralised concentration' the advantage of robustness.

The translation of these theoretical arguments into practical policies is bedevilled by three main obstacles:

1. There is immense variety in the settlement and travel patterns which local planning authorities have to take as their starting point. No standard model can be specified and each authority has to determine the best arrangement for its area. Unfortunately, the technical resources available to individual authorities typically do not allow for the systematic generation and assessment of options; instead, a much looser, more political process, involving trade-offs with other planning objectives, is likely.

2.   The units of local government through which this process takes place have only a partial relationship to the form and functioning of contemporary urban regions. Councils inevitably assess development options in terms of outcomes for their particular *administrative* areas (that is, for their political constituency). This works strongly against the integrated treatment of spatial issues at the level of the functional region.

3.   There is a lack of empirical evidence that demonstrates conclusively the merits of any one patterning of settlement over another. This constrains the formulation of national and regional guidance but it also leaves local planning arenas vulnerable to pressure group activity focused on more tangible environmental impacts and the protection of private territorial interests. It is to the issue of empirical evidence that this chapter now turns.

Empirical evidence – national

Evidence is available from two main sources. Personal travel is sampled in the National Travel Survey, with the location of respondents' homes coded according to the OPCS classification of urban areas (DoT, 1996). This enables tabulations to be produced for main regional groupings and by size of urban area. Personal, household and travel-to-work attributes are surveyed comprehensively in the decennial Census of Population. England-wide analysis has been undertaken on the 1991 dataset to identify 'Urban Trends', as between local authority district types (Atkins *et al.*, 1996).

There are several difficulties using these sources to investigate the relationship between urban form – in this case the size and patterning of settlements – and personal travel. They arise in connection with the classification of location.

The first difficulty is the obvious one that the spatial units used in the two sources are not the same and therefore the findings from them cannot directly be linked (nonetheless, an attempt to do this is reported below). The second difficulty is that neither unit of classification – the built-up area in the National Travel Survey and the local authority district in the Census analysis – contains any information about the relationship of the 'home' town or district to any other. In practice, this will have a major influence on its functioning and hence the travel behaviour of its residents. A third difficulty is that neither of the statistical units used is a very 'pure' version of what it purports to be. The administrative overlapping of suburban areas by 'rural' districts has already been highlighted. The definition of 'urban areas' on the basis of physical rather than functional connections creates similar problems. In both cases, any relationship between settlement characteristics and travel behaviour will be muddied by these 'anomalies'. With these provisos, the evidence from the two sources will now be summarised.

In relation to the National Travel Survey, use can be made of the tabulations generated by ECOTEC (1993) and Potter (1997). The remarkable feature in ECOTEC's tabulations is how weak is the apparent link between population size and either distance travelled or the proportion of journeys by car as far as the mass of urban areas of 3,000–250,000 population size are concerned (Table 3). Nevertheless, the longitudinal study by Potter suggests that the differences are widening over time (Table 4). However, in both cases it is necessary to consider the possibility that the differences may not be due to the size of settlements as such but to differences in the characteristics of their populations. For example, the number of work journeys per head has fallen over the last 20 years, yet amongst the work journeys which *are* made the average journey length is increasing twice as fast as for journeys as a whole. Thus, the distribution of the population in work is particularly important.

	Distance (km per person per week)			Percentage of distance	
	Work	Non-work	All purposes	Car	Rail and local bus
London (Inner/Outer)	45–58	96–108	141–167	54–68%	33–19%
Other conurbations	20–47	63–103	89–136	54–69%	26–15%
Other urban >250,000	37	104	141	66%	14%
Urban 100,000–250,000	49	112	161	72%	12%
Urban 50,000–100,000	45	109	155	72%	13%
Urban 25,000–50,000	50	101	151	73%	12%
Urban 3,000–25,000	52	124	176	76%	9%
Rural (<3,000)	66	145	211	78%	6%
All areas	49	111	160	71%	13%

Table 3: Distance travelled by purpose, and mode share, by settlement population size.
Source: after ECOTEC, 1993, from National Travel Survey, 1986.

Data excludes trips under 1.6km; travel by modes other than car and public transport.
'Other conurbations' shows the range of figures for the six urban areas of West Midlands, Greater Manchester, West Yorkshire, Glasgow, Liverpool and Tyneside.

Table 4: Distance travelled (1992/ 94) by purpose, and mode share, by settlement population size and change from 1975/76.
Source: Potter, 1997, from National Travel Surveys.

	Distance (km per person per week)			Percentage of distance	
	Work	Non-work	All purposes	Car	Rail and local bus
London	36 – 2%	126+36%	162+25%	70%+9	22%–4
Other conurbations	31+14%	133+42%	163+35%	78%+11	12%–11
Urban > 100,000	40+38%	146+47%	185+45%	80%+11	10%–8
Urban 25–100,000	38+31%	156+45%	194+42%	82%+12	9%–9
Urban 3–25,000	50+39%	180+54%	229+50%	84%+8	7%–5

Table 5 shows the variation in the proportion of adult males in employment. The figures quoted are the difference in percentage points between the average for the particular district type and the all-England percentage given at the foot of the table. There is a difference of 13 percentage points between the lowest and highest, with the district types at the extremes of this range – 'principal metropolitan cities' and 'urban and mixed urban districts' – having a combination of factors which work in opposite directions.

	Proportion of adult males in employment	Proportion of households with a car
Greater London		
Inner London	−1.7	−21.5
Outer London	+4.0	+0.4
Metropolitan districts		
Principal cities	−7.0	−15.7
Other districts	−3.8	−6.9
Non-metropolitan districts		
Large cities	−2.6	−8.3
Small cities	−2.5	−5.2
Industrial districts	+0.3	+0.7
Districts with new towns	+2.9	+3.4
Resort, port and retirement	−5.6	+2.7
Urban and mixed urban/rural	+6.0	+12.3
Remote mainly rural	+0.2	+10.4
All (actual percentage)	63.1%	67.6%

Table 5: Variation in population characteristics between local authority district types.
Source: adapted from Atkins et al., 1996.

Table 5 also shows the even larger variations in household car ownership between the district types. Car ownership is a key factor in travel generation, in addition to the income differences that it represents. Statistical analyses conducted by ECOTEC, using car ownership and urban size variables, showed the former to have a much stronger and more significant role in explaining differences in travel behaviour (ECOTEC, 1993, Appendix 4).

These and similar analyses reflect the social polarisation which is endemic to much counter-urbanisation. From a research perspective, it bedevils attempts to generate empirical evidence about the significance of the purely physical attributes of settlement size and type. Given the extent of socio-economic variation, it is perhaps surprising that the locational differences in travel behaviour reported thus far are not in fact greater.

Given the differences that exist between the extremes of the settlement size spectrum, one would expect the trend of counter-urbanisation to have been accompanied by a substantial increase in travel, particularly by car, with adverse consequences for energy consumption. However, an analysis carried out by Breheny, linking the National Travel Survey and Census data sources, has indicated that over a 30-year period to 1991 the redistribution of population made a difference of only 2% in the amount of energy consumed, and an even smaller reduction in overall travel distance (Table 6).

OPCS district category	National Travel Survey settlement type/size	Population difference '000*	Travel distance per head/ week (km)	Energy consumed per head/ week (Mj)	Total travel difference m km/wk	Total energy difference m Mj/wk
Greater London						
Inner	Inner London	1,357	141.3	140.4	191.7	190.5
Outer	Outer London	749	166.6	182.5	124.8	136.7
Metropolitan districts						
Principal cities	Metropolitan areas	1,793	112.7	119.1	202.1	213.5
Non-metropolitan districts						
Cities	Urban 100–250k	586	160.5	180.6	94.1	105.8
Industrial districts	Urban 50–100k	−278	154.5	173.1	−43.0	−48.1
New towns/resort	Urban 25–50k	−1,160	151.0	170.8	−175.2	−198.1
Mixed urban/rural	Urban 3–25k	−1,680	175.7	203.4	−295.2	−341.7
Remote, mainly rural	<3k	−935	211.0	248.0	−197.3	−231.9
England & Wales						−98.0	−173.3
actual total					7,814.0	8,774.0
% change					−1.3%	−2.0%

Table 6: Estimates of change in travel and associated energy consumption arising from the redistribution of population 1961-91.

Source: adapted from Breheny, 1995.

* 1961 share of 1991 population minus actual 1991 population.

As the author comments, this result is 'surprising':

> [It] challenges the validity of the fundamental assumption upon which much of the emerging conventional wisdom on urban sustainability in the UK is based ... There may be other benefits from urban containment, of course, but the suggestion here is that energy savings [in travel] should not be a prime motivation in promoting such a policy. (Breheny, 1995, p.428)

It should be emphasised that these observations only refer to population changes at the district level. There will be additional effects due to suburbanising movements of population within individual districts and to changes in the location of non-residential uses – these will be subsumed within the overall travel increase during the period. The administrative units being used are also likely to mask the degree of change that is actually taking place, particularly in peri-urban areas. Ideally, therefore, one would wish to examine situations in which:

1. the locational characteristics of the populations being compared were more precisely defined; and
2. socio-economic attributes relevant to travel propensity were controlled.

These properties can be achieved in specially designed local studies and the evidence from this type of research will now be explored.

Empirical evidence – local data

Investigating travel behaviour at the local level normally involves having to use a variety of data sources, which makes comparison difficult – see the local studies by ECOTEC (1993) and by Banister *et al.* (1994). The discussion that follows draws instead on a group of research exercises conducted in the Oxfordshire area. Several were led by the author and share common definitions, methodologies and so on.

Oxfordshire, as a study area, is interesting for a number of reasons:

- It is located in the Outer South East, within the arc of rapid population expansion referred to earlier.
- Its geography is that of the classic city region, dominated by Oxford City but with a number of second order free-standing towns.
- The local housing market and travel-to-work patterns are also affected by the 'overspill' effects of the London Metropolitan region.
- As in many other areas, residential growth at the periphery of the principal city (Oxford) has deliberately been restricted, in this case by means of a formal green belt.
- For many years planning policy has been to concentrate new development on the larger free-standing towns beyond the green belt (the so-called 'country towns' policy).

The main features of the Oxfordshire area are shown in Fig. 1. The City of Oxford itself occupies a central geographical position and has a population of around 115,000. The nearest urban areas of similar or larger size are all beyond the county boundary some 30 or more miles from Oxford City. The edge of the Greater London conurbation is 45 miles away to the south-east.

Oxfordshire employment and travel to work

Oxfordshire has an overall balance between jobs and resident workers, although the job/worker ratio varies considerably within it (Table 7). Oxford City and, to a lesser extent, Banbury have dominant employment positions. Elsewhere, the ratio of jobs to workers is mainly within the 0.65–0.75 range. The ratio improved in almost every individual area during the 1981–91 decade, yet the overall county ratio deteriorated slightly. This reflects the 'downward' shift in population that took place between the two largest towns and the rest of the County.

The Census Workplace Statistics show that, in Oxford and Banbury, at least three-quarters of resident workers have workplaces in the same town. For the other towns, the proportion is in the region of 35–45%. As one would expect, Oxford has major significance as a workplace for residents in the immediate green belt ring and, to a lesser extent, for residents in nearby Abingdon and Witney.

In terms of travel mode, there is surprisingly little difference in the proportion travelling to work by car in Oxford compared with the other main towns, as far as 'home town' journeys are concerned. Banbury is an exception arising from a particularly polarised land use pattern. More notable is the difference between home town journeys as a group (where the car proportion varies from 38% to 60%) and journeys to workplaces elsewhere (76% to 88%). Except within Oxford City, public transport also has a more important role for work journeys outside the home town.

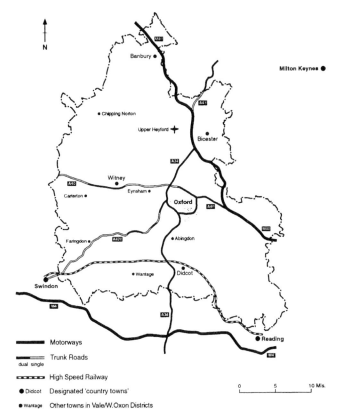

Fig. 1. Main features of the Oxfordshire area referred to in text.

Home location	'81	'91	Balance jobs/workers		Mode% residents' work trips by car 1991		Destination of residents' work trips					
			Home town	Elsewhere	Home town* % trips		Oxford City % trips		Rest of Oxon % trips		Outside Oxon % trips	
					'81	'91	'81	'91	'81	'91	'81	'91
Oxford City	1.68	1.79	38	77	–	–	88	86	9	8	3	6
Abingdon	0.70	0.76	46	84	34	37	28	23	34	31	5	9
Central Oxon (exc.Oxford City and Abingdon)	0.65	0.68	42	77	28	29	55	47	13	16	4	7
Bicester	0.68	0.73	45	86	38	40	12	17	42	26	8	18
Didcot	0.55	0.63	44	76	32	29	11	11	47	45	10	15
Witney	1.09	1.01	41	84	55	45	20	22	21	28	4	5
Banbury	1.27	1.37	58	85	78	75	3	3	10	9	8	12
Outer Oxon (exc. four country towns)	0.78	0.77	60	88	54	51	13	11	14	16	19	22
Oxfordshire	0.98	0.97	50	84	–	–	–	–	–	–	–	–

Table 7: Job/ worker balance, residents' travel to work mode and destination of work trips by main sub-areas of Oxfordshire, 1981 and 1991.

Source: Census Special Workplace Tables prepared by Oxfordshire County Council.

* For Central Oxfordshire and Outer Oxfordshire 'home town' represents all workplace destinations within these areas, *not* within a particular town.

Travel from estates in Oxford and the designated 'country' (expanded) towns

Households on estates in Oxford and the country towns have been surveyed using a methodology which controls for some of the non-locational variables likely to influence travel behaviour (Curtis and Headicar, 1994). In addition, to offset the differences in composition between one estate and another, the results presented here have been standardised using the average household mix for all estates.

Surveys were conducted in 1993–94 in both recently developed and established housing estates. The selected locations were on the edge of Oxford and in the three country towns of Bicester, Didcot and Witney. Although the towns are much the same size and have a similar relationship to Oxford City, they are different in their relationship to the London Metropolitan Area. Bicester lies close to the M40 London–Birmingham motorway whilst Didcot is served by high-speed rail services on the Great Western main line. Witney, by contrast, lies on the far side of Oxford, as far as access to London is concerned, and has no high-speed connection with it.

The travel behaviour of households in these surveyed areas is depicted in Fig. 2 (see note 1). In terms of *numbers of trips*, the estates are very similar. The average of 29 regular trips per week is split almost equally between work and non-work purposes (see note 2). In terms of *car driver trips*, the share by residents of the new estates is 16 points higher. On the new estates, this proportion does not vary overall between work and non-work, but on established estates there is a 12-point difference. Comparing the towns, the car driver share is highest in both cases in Bicester and lowest in Oxford. In terms of *distance travelled*, work journeys account for three-quarters of the total. The distance for regular journeys is 36% higher on the new estates with almost all of this (71 miles a week, on average) being attributable to differences in work travel. Comparing the towns, Bicester residents travel from 35% to 40% more than their counterparts in Oxford. This is made up of a greater difference in their work travel offset by less difference in non-work.

These differences in travel distance compound those in mode share so that the variation in *car driver distance*, both between locations and between new and established estates, is even more marked. Overall, the new estates generate 44% more car mileage per adult and both the Bicester estates 60% more than their Oxford counterparts. Again, these overall figures mask the much greater disparities in work compared with non-work travel.

In the other towns, Witney has similar, though slightly less pronounced, features to Bicester. Didcot has very different characteristics arising from its location on the high-speed rail line – overall, car commuting is less, and average car driver distances on Didcot's new estate are actually lower than on the established one because rail is used more for long-distance work journeys.

There are a number of socio-economic variables not controlled in the survey design, which could contribute to the observed differences in travel behaviour. Further analysis showed that household income, car ownership and availability of an employer's car were all significant factors (Headicar and Curtis, 1998). However, comparison of people in the same income and employer's car categories revealed that those living in estates on the edge of Oxford City owned fewer cars and made shorter trips, with a higher proportion by non-car modes. The combined effect was that their car distance per adult (for *all* journeys on an average weekday) was around 30% less than in the country towns.

Population characteristics are also relevant to the observed differences in travel between residents of new and established estates. Further investigation of the Bicester data has shown that there are statistically significant differences in income, length of residence, car ownership and employers' cars (Higgitt, 1998). Nevertheless, when the data is standardised for these attributes, the households on the new estate continue to exhibit higher car driver mileage of 25% or more.

Differences between residents of new and established estates can also be seen in their previous home location and in the places they considered moving to (Table 8). In the country towns, over two-fifths of households on the established estates previously lived in the same town. By contrast, the largest single category amongst households on new estates came from outside Oxfordshire altogether. In terms of possible housing location, the options considered by people eventually moving to the new estate also ranged over a wider area.

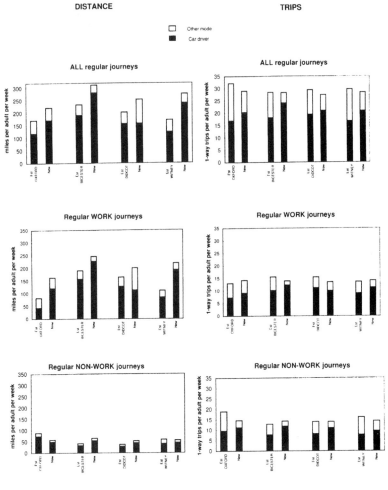

Fig. 2. Travel distance and number of trips per week (regular journeys) by purpose, mode and location (per adult amongst selected households on surveyed established and new estates in Oxfordshire).

| | Where lived previously | | | | | | Places considered* | | | | | |
| | Bicester | | Didcot | | Witney | | Bicester | | Didcot | | Witney | |
	Est.	New	Est.	New	Est.	New	Est.	New	Est.	New	Est.	New
Home town	41	22	55	26	42	32	54	43	63	47	72	50
Oxford City	2	11	4	4	8	5	7	2	1	2	0	4
Rest of Oxon	30	21	20	29	32	33	29	34	31	35	25	41
Outside Oxon:												
Metropolitan**	8	17	10	24	5	14	7	7	2	11	2	3
Elsewhere	22	29	10	18	14	16	3	14	2	5	0	2

Table 8. Previous home location and places considered for moving to (% of households by surveyed estate).

* Up to three possible places were recorded; the data here shows the sum of all responses.
** 'Metropolitan' is Greater London plus the sector of the Outer Metropolitan Region between it and Oxfordshire.

Workplaces and travel from other locations in Oxfordshire

A further survey of the same kind was conducted on a new housing estate in Banbury – the fourth of Oxfordshire's country towns – in 1996. Banbury provides an interesting comparison with the other country towns in that it is larger, geographically more isolated, and further from Oxford City and from the London metropolitan region.

Additional evidence is available from surveys of smaller recent housing developments by two of Oxfordshire's District Councils – West Oxfordshire (Webster, 1998) and the Vale of the White Horse (Graham, 1998). These two districts occupy the western half of the county (Fig. 1). The surveys involve a number of settlements that in size and location occupy a broader spectrum than simply Oxford and the country towns.

The 'villages' included in the two surveys are very different. Those in West Oxfordshire (the Witney/Chipping Norton area) are typically rural in character and location whereas the bulk of responses from the Vale are from two more suburbanised settlements either side of Abingdon close to Oxford and Didcot respectively.

The District Councils' surveys are similar to each other and attempt to provide information on *all* households. However, their published results do not include controls for household composition or adjustments for response rates. Consequently, comparison of their findings with those from the new estates needs to be approached with caution (Table 9).

	Workplace*						Journey to work**			
	Urban area resident population 1991	Dist. from Oxford (miles)	Home sett. inc. at home (%)	Oxford City (%)	Rest of Oxon (%)	Outside Oxon (%)	Avg trip dist. (miles) all modes	% trips car driver	Avg trip dist. car driver trips	Avg car driver trip dist./ worker
Established estates										
Oxford (New Marston)	119	2	76	home sett.	16	8	6.3	56	6.0	3.4
'Country towns'										
Bicester	22	13	45	18	22	15	12.3	67	15.1	10.1
Didcot	*16*	15	32	10	43	15	10.7	73	11.3	8.2
Witney	20	12	45	20	32	4	8.3	66	9.3	6.1
New estates										
Oxford (Botley)	119	3	66	home sett.	21	13	11.4	64	13.3	8.5
'Country towns'										
Bicester	22	13	26	23	20	31	17.6	88	18.5	16.3
Didcot	*16*	15	24	12	35	29	14.9	74	11.4	8.4
Witney	20	12	26	28	33	13	15.5	80	17.1	13.7
Banbury	40	23	56	8	10	26	15.6	72	19.3	13.9
New developments										
Eynsham	*5*	7	23	41	26	11	10.7	*75*	13.1	9.8
Carterton	*12*	18	28	16	49	8	12.7	*84*	14.4	12.1
Chipping Norton	*5*	21	20–30	11–13	46–49	11–20	13.7	*80*	16.1	12.9
W Oxon villages		11–24	0	15–44	25–73	10–33	10.2–24.4	*79– 91*	11.3– 27.9	8.9–25.4
Abingdon	35	7	30	29	32	9	6.6	69	*5.2*	*5.5*
Wantage/Grove	*17*	16	19	8	56	17	7.9	81	*7.0*	*7.2*
Faringdon	*5*	17	13	11	47	29	11.1	87	*10.3*	*10.6*
VOWH villages		4–17	6	22	48	24	11.6	79	*9.6*	*10.2*

Table 9. Workplace distribution and journey to work characteristics amongst surveyed developments within Oxfordshire.

The surveyed estate at Botley is here classed as part of Oxford although administratively it is outside the city. The data for 'new developments' is derived separately from the established and new estates and is not directly comparable: see explanation in text. The figures in italics are (close) estimates.
* Excludes workers with no fixed workplace.
** Of those with a fixed workplace who travelled to work, i.e. excluding those working at home.

Overall, the smaller housing developments provide evidence of a pattern in which trip length and car share increase with distance from Oxford and reduce with settlement size. This much is not unexpected. Dependency on Oxford as a workplace also declines with distance, and is mostly counterbalanced by greater use of workplaces elsewhere in the county rather than outside it. Faringdon is an exception as it functions increasingly as an 'up-market' dormitory to Swindon, only 12 miles away.

In the case of the villages, many show an unusually high dependence on Oxford considering their distance from it. They also have a relatively high proportion of workplaces outside the county, although some of this arises 'naturally' from their more peripheral location. Nevertheless, from some West Oxfordshire villages, the generation of car mileage per worker is extremely high.

Commentary

The Oxfordshire evidence shows that, at the local level, there is much greater variation in travel behaviour relative to settlement characteristics than aggregated national statistics would imply. This arises even in a county which only has a limited range of settlement sizes and which has representation of only two of the OPCS urbanisation categories.

In relation to settlement characteristics, the size and job/worker ratio of the home town has a strong influence on the proportion of people working locally and hence – all other things being equal – on average commuting distances and the degree of car use. However, the significance of this is greatly conditioned by the alternative opportunities that are available in the surrounding region. The free-standing expanded towns of 20,000 or so in Oxfordshire only act as home town workplaces for a fifth of residents on new estates and less than a half on established ones. This applies even in Witney, which has a numerical job/worker balance. Much therefore depends on how far people travel who do not work in their home town – or, looked at from the other direction, how far people with workplaces elsewhere have to look to obtain a house which meets their requirements.

Comparison of Banbury and Abingdon provides a clear illustration of this. Banbury performs well in terms of self-containment on account of its size, its favourable job/worker ratio and its geographical isolation. However, the commuting distances of residents who do not work in the town are necessarily large and this greatly reduces its performance in terms of travel generation overall. By contrast, Abingdon has a less favourable jobs/worker ratio (and is much less self-contained) but is situated centrally in relation to the concentration of employment located in Central Oxfordshire along the A34 corridor. As a result, the average length of non home town journeys is relatively short and its overall performance much better.

The relative significance of settlement size and alternative employment opportunities can also be seen in the results for villages in the Vale (most of which are located in or close to the same A34 corridor). Although the villages themselves supply little local employment, their car commuting is generally no greater than from free-standing towns further afield, and actually less than from the country towns.

The more peripheral location of the country towns (including Banbury) means that their functioning is potentially more subject to housing and employment opportunities in adjacent sub-regions. Bicester, Didcot and Banbury all have a significant dormitory function in relation to these other major urbanised areas. Even Witney's performance seems to be conditioned by its greater accessibility to the trunk road network compared with other towns in West Oxfordshire. This points to a serious conundrum for planning authorities contemplating locating major new housing development in free-standing towns. Attracting employment to these towns to avoid them assuming a solely dormitory role is likely to depend on their inter-regional highway accessibility. Yet this same accessibility provides the means (and the incentive) for people to choose to live in these towns and commute elsewhere.

In relation to the scale of new development, evidence of the greater commuting distances by residents of the large new estates raises the question of whether there is something intrinsic to the planning and marketing of these estates, which encourages such behaviour. The accessibility that these towns enjoy (and which provides the opportunities for people, once moved, to commute out) also provides ease of access for house-hunters working elsewhere to consider moving in. There may also be lower average house prices on the large estates, which encourage households to locate there and travel further.

In relation to trends in home location and travel behaviour, the evidence from new and established estates offers insights into the way changes occur over time. What appears in aggregate to be a gradual change in behaviour can be viewed better as a changing balance between two quite different sets of people – one (mostly older) with local origins and affiliations and the other (mostly younger) without such links whose housing and workplace choices range over a wide area, and for whom a high volume of car use is endemic to their lifestyle. For planning purposes, it is the behaviour of people moving to the new estates which should be the basis for assessing the effects of proposed developments and not the less travel intensive habits of their town's indigenous populations.

Conclusion

Counter-urbanisation is generally discussed in relation to functional regions centred on conurbations and industrial cities where reversing trends depends very much on urban regeneration. But counter-urbanisation is also occurring in other regions, not primarily because of decline in their main towns (and hence not remediable by regeneration) but because of disproportionate growth in small towns and rural areas.

The approach to be followed in such counties is important because of the scale of projected housing requirements and because a relatively large share will have to be accommodated on greenfield sites (Breheny and Hall, 1996). Most would-be residents are not committed to their choice of home town and so planning authorities should, in principle, be able to exert a substantial influence on travel outcomes through housing location policies.

At present, regional planning conferences divide the projected housing requirement for their area between constituent counties who in turn allocate this between their constituent districts on a more or less *pro rata* basis to existing population levels – an approach which owes as much to political expediency as to planning logic. This approach can be reconciled with the formal requirements of PPG13 in that within each administrative unit the bulk of new development can be allocated to 'larger' urban areas. However, it contradicts the spirit of PPG13 in that, within the overall spectrum of settlement sizes, many of the towns identified for growth are relatively small. The travel patterns associated with new developments in Oxfordshire's country towns in effect provide 'advance notice' of the consequences of the present application of PPG13 pursued over a period of 20 years.

The conclusion is therefore that the principle of 'urban concentration' needs to be applied much more strategically – that is, allocating most new development to places in the vicinity of the largest urban areas or in corridors where closely spaced settlements provide for similar employment concentrations in aggregate. Since such places are unevenly distributed within a region, it follows that the primary element of a regional strategy should be to identify suitable opportunities where they exist – for example, the unofficial proposal for three new city clusters in South East England (Hall and Ward, 1998).

Elsewhere, in counties such as Oxfordshire, where there are significant sub-regional concentrations of employment, the appropriate policy is *not* to follow the 'dispersed concentration' which PPG13 in combination with PPG2 (planning policy guidance on green belts, DoE, 1995) currently provides for. Instead, new residential development should be located close to the major employment concentrations. This could take the form of peripheral expansion of the principal city and/or smaller new settlements and settlement expansions on transport corridors linking it with nearby free-standing towns. This accent on location rather than size is a fundamental departure from the guidance currently found in PPG13.

New settlement proposals in relatively isolated locations (which PPG13 also allows for) should be excluded too. During its last structure plan review, Oxfordshire County Council had to face down its own example of such a proposal at the former US air force base at Upper Heyford (between Bicester and Banbury). The research reported in this chapter was used to demonstrate that the travel consequences of this would have been even worse than continuing with the country towns policy (Headicar, 1997).

'Urban concentration' as currently articulated in PPG13 is only appropriate to a third type of area – the most rural ones well away from any major centre of employment. Because of limited opportunities and their innate propensity to greater car use, only a small proportion of development should be allocated to such places anyway, irrespective of the presence of small or medium free-standing towns.

By permitting – even promoting – the dispersal of new residential development throughout regions (albeit locally concentrated), existing planning policy is thus making its own contribution to the exploding city region. Fortunately, reversing this influence is in principle straightforward. Unlike urban regeneration initiatives (which need to be pursued in parallel in the older city areas), the change does not require large public investments to make development viable in the favoured locations. It does not have to work against market forces or counter social trends. But it does require vision, a genuinely strategic approach to spatial planning and a willingness to confront 'protectionist' interests in the areas identified as most suitable for development. Whether this makes it any more feasible is a moot point.

Notes

1. The graphs refer only to adults' 'regular journeys'. A much fuller report and analysis of the findings from the new estates can be found in Headicar and Curtis (1998).
2. Because of the control on household composition, all households contained two adults of whom at least one was in full-time employment. Overall, 88% of adults were in work.

Acknowledgement

The author would like to thank the many people who have contributed to the Oxford Brookes University work reported here, particularly Carey Curtis, Jillian Anable and Martin Higgitt.

Dominic Stead, Jo Williams and Helena Titheridge

Land Use, Transport and People:
Identifying the Connections

Introduction

This chapter examines the extent to which land use planning can influence travel patterns and how planning might be able to reduce travel. Although other studies have examined this issue before, many have only examined the influence of a small number of land use characteristics and most have not taken account of any socio-economic reasons for the variations in travel patterns in different areas. Previous research has often assumed that there is a simple cause and effect relationship between land use and travel patterns, in which various land use characteristics (such as density, population size or the presence of local services and facilities) directly influence travel patterns.

However, the spatial distribution of the population is not homogeneous: for example, the characteristics of residents of high-density, large urban areas are quite different to those of residents of low-density rural areas. It is likely that there is a complex interaction between land use and travel patterns, as shown in Fig. 1a. The chapter examines the evidence for a three-way relationship between travel patterns, land use and socio-economic characteristics (Fig. 1b).

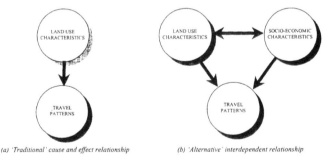

Fig. 1. The interaction between urban form and travel patterns.

(a) 'Traditional' cause and effect relationship   (b) 'Alternative' interdependent relationship

To do so, the effects of a large number of socio-economic characteristics, as well as a range of land use characteristics, on travel patterns are examined. The results of three recent, related research projects carried out by the authors are reported (see note 1). These projects draw on a range of UK information sources, including both national data (from National Travel Surveys and Censuses of Population) and local data (from travel surveys carried out in Kent and Leicestershire, for example).

The chapter is divided into three main sections. Recent studies of the interaction between land use, socio-economic characteristics and travel patterns are reviewed in the first section. The methodologies of the three studies reported in this chapter are described in the second section and, in the third, the findings of the three studies are outlined.

Interactions between land use, socio-economic characteristics and travel patterns
This section reviews the wide range of research concerning the interaction between land use and travel patterns and between socio-economic characteristics and travel patterns. The interactions between land use and socio-economic characteristics are also discussed.

Relationships between land use and travel patterns
A number of land use characteristics, ranging from strategic to local in scale, may affect travel patterns (Fig. 2). At the strategic level, the location of new development (in relation to existing towns, cities and/or other infrastructure) may affect travel demand. The size and shape of new development and the type and mix of land use may affect travel patterns. At the local level, the extent to which land uses are mixed, and the extent to which development is clustered or concentrated into nodes, is likely to affect travel demand. At the local and neighbourhood level, the density and layout of development may also affect travel patterns.

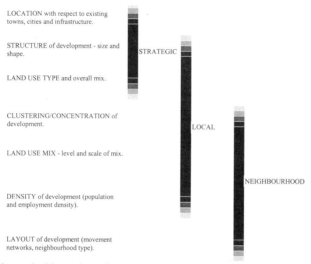

LOCATION with respect to existing towns, cities and infrastructure.

STRUCTURE of development - size and shape.

LAND USE TYPE and overall mix.

CLUSTERING/CONCENTRATION of development.

LAND USE MIX - level and scale of mix.

DENSITY of development (population and employment density).

LAYOUT of development (movement networks, neighbourhood type).

STRATEGIC

LOCAL

NEIGHBOURHOOD

Fig. 2. Land use characteristics that may affect travel patterns.

The proximity of households to the urban centre
The proximity of households to the urban centre is likely to influence travel distance since many jobs and services are in urban areas. Very long distances from urban centres may also influence the frequency of journeys, particularly for more discretionary journeys (such as social or entertainment purposes). Spence and Frost (1995) show how commuting distance changes with increasing distance between home and the urban centre in London, Manchester and Birmingham. In London, commuting distance increases almost linearly with distance between home and urban centre. At a distance of 20 kilometres from the centre of London, commuting distance continues to increase with increasing distance from the centre of the city. In Manchester and Birmingham, however, the relationship is different. Commuting distance in Birmingham first increases with increasing distance between home and the urban centre, but at a distance of around seven kilometres from the urban centre commuting distance reaches a plateau. At a distance of around nine kilometres from the centre, commuting distance begins to decrease as distance from the urban centre increases. Commuting distance in Manchester first increases with increasing distance from the urban centre. At a distance of around five kilometres from the centre, commuting distance reaches a plateau and does not increase much thereafter. Gordon *et al.* (1989a) describe the changes in average travel distance in the US between 1977 and 1983 of people residing inside and outside cities. In various sizes of city,

both work and non-work journey distances in 1977 and 1983 were almost always lower for residents inside cities, than for residents outside cities.

Næss *et al.* (1995) identify a statistical relationship between distance from the urban centre and total travel distance per person in Oslo. They found that the distance between home and the urban centre, along with factors such as car ownership and accessibility to local facilities, is an important determinant of total travel distance. Car ownership was found to have the greatest influence on transport energy consumption, followed by the distance between home and the urban centre, accessibility to local facilities from the home, income per capita, and various other socio-economic factors.

In a study of travel patterns in five new housing locations in and around Oxford, Curtis (1995) shows that the distance between home and urban centre may be linked to average work journey distance. A link between average non-work journey distance and the distance from home to urban centre is much less apparent. Local planning authorities can exert a major influence on the amount of car-based travel. The average figure of 27 miles travelled per adult each weekday varies by location, but this variation is not affected by accessibility or by socio-economic attributes. Headicar and Curtis (1994) conclude that the income differences between residents of new housing locations are not the primary source of the variations in work related car travel between the five locations. Variations in travel have traditionally been based on the differences in household characteristics (principally income), but the importance of location on travel patterns must be understood if sustainable mobility objectives are to be strengthened.

Mogridge (1985) demonstrates a near linear relationship between distance from home to the urban centre and transport energy consumption. The relationship is shown to be very similar in both London and Paris. On average, residents living at a distance of 15 kilometres from the urban centre consume more than twice the transport energy consumed by residents living five kilometres from the urban centre. Similarly, Newman and Kenworthy (1988) identify a relationship between transport energy consumption and the distance from the central business district in Perth. It is reported that residents living at a distance of 15 kilometres from the central business district consume approximately 20% more transport energy than residents living five kilometres from the central business district do.

Settlement size

Settlement size is a key factor influencing the range of jobs and services that can be supported and may influence the range of public transport services that can be provided locally (Williams and Banister, 1999). Thus, in small settlements that are unable to support a large range of services and facilities, local residents may be forced to travel longer distances to access the services and facilities they require. However, very large, centralised settlements may generate longer travel distances as the separation between homes and the urban centre increases. Large settlements with a wide range of jobs and services may also attract people living long distances away to travel to them. Thus, it is unlikely that there is a simple relationship between settlement size and travel patterns (for more detailed discussion, see Owens, 1986; ECOTEC, 1993; Banister *et al.*, 1997; Williams and Banister, 1999).

According to analysis of data from the various National Travel Surveys of Great Britain (DETR, 1997), total travel distance is highest in the smallest category of settlements (containing fewer than 3,000 residents), and lowest in large metropolitan areas (excluding London) (Banister, 1992; Breheny, 1995). The average journey distance by car is also lowest in conurbations and highest in rural areas, even when the variations in travel by car ownership are controlled for (Banister, 1997). Similar results have also been found in more detailed studies of Gloucestershire (Williams, 1997). Research by Gordon *et al.* (1989a) shows no easily identifiable relationship between urban population size and modal choice. In a study of commuting patterns in the ten largest urbanised areas in the US, the proportion of car journeys was found to be least in New York (which has the largest population of the areas studied) and highest in Detroit (which has the sixth largest population of the areas studied). However, public transport has never accounted for a very substantial proportion of travel in the US, so one would not expect a great variation. Williams and Banister (1998) suggest that settlement size does influence modal split both nationally and at county level in Gloucestershire. In larger settlements, use of non-car modes is far greater than in smaller, rural settlements where the use of the car predominates.

The mix of land uses
It is argued that the mixing of land uses may affect the physical separation of activities and therefore influence travel demand, although some evidence suggests that this influence is not as strong as that imposed by density (Owens, 1986; ECOTEC, 1993). Nevertheless, the level of mixed use may contribute to travel demand, particularly through the decentralisation of less specialised employment, and it is commonly measured using job ratios – the ratio of jobs in the area to workers resident in that area. In research undertaken in the UK (Banister *et al.*, 1997), a significant relationship between job ratio and energy use per trip was established in one of six case studies (Oxford), but not in the others (Liverpool, Milton Keynes, Leicester, Almere in the Netherlands, and Banbury).

Evidence from the US finds only weak evidence of links between job ratio and travel. Ewing *et al.* (1996) report that there is no statistically significant relationship between the balance of homes and jobs and journey frequency and, in a study of commuting patterns in San Francisco, Cervero (1989) reports a weak negative relationship between job ratio and the proportion of journeys undertaken on foot or by cycle – where there are many more jobs than houses, the proportion of journeys on foot or by cycle falls. Giuliano and Small (1993) question the importance of job ratio on travel patterns and present the results of a commuting study in the Los Angeles region to show that job ratio has a statistically significant, but relatively small, influence on commuting time. They conclude that attempts to alter the metropolitan structure of land use are likely to have small impacts on commuting patterns, even if jobs and housing became more balanced.

The provision of local facilities and services
The provision of local facilities and services may clearly reduce travel distances by encouraging more locally-based activities, which can be reached easily by non-motorised modes. Little evidence has been collected on this subject – it is currently under investigation (see below). Winter and Farthing (1997) report that the provision of local facilities in new residential developments reduces average trip distances but does not significantly affect the proportion of journeys on foot. Evidence from the same study indicates that the provision of local facilities reduces the average journey distance by car (Farthing *et al.*, 1996). ECOTEC (1993) report from neighbourhood case studies that clear relationships emerge between the distance from a local centre, the frequency of its use and average journey distance. Hanson (1982) reports similar findings, showing that proximity to local facilities is positively associated with average distance, after taking into account the effects of various socio-economic differences of the areas studied. Hanson also shows that the provision of local facilities is associated with increased journey frequency, although the effect of increasing journey frequency is not as strong as the effect of reducing trip length.

Population density

Population density may be linked to travel patterns for several reasons. First, higher population densities widen the range of opportunities for the development of local personal contacts and activities that can be maintained without resort to motorised travel. Second, higher densities widen the range of services that can be supported in the local area and reduce the need to travel long distances. Third, higher density patterns of development tend to reduce average distances between homes, services, employment and other opportunities, and, fourth, high densities may be more amenable to public transport operation and use and less amenable to car ownership and use, which have implications for modal choice. Average journey distance by car, bus and rail decreases with increasing population density, whilst the average journey distance on foot is more or less constant, regardless of population density (ECOTEC, 1993; Hillman and Whalley, 1983). These findings are supported by the most recent data from National Travel Surveys. Ewing *et al.* (1996) report that there is no significant statistical link between trip frequency and population density.

It has been shown that with increasing population density, the proportion of trips by car decreases, whilst the proportion of trips by public transport and on foot both increase (ECOTEC, 1993). Car trips account for 72% of journeys in low-density areas (less than one person per hectare) but only 51% of trips in high-density areas (more than 50 persons per hectare). There is a fourfold difference in public transport trips and almost a twofold difference in walk trips between very low-density areas and very high-density areas (Banister, 1997). The proportion of both shopping trips by public transport and commuting trips on foot are positively linked with population density (Frank and Pivo, 1994), even after accounting for socio-economic differences (Kitamura *et al.*, 1997). Evidence from the US (Gordon *et al.*, 1989a) suggests that there is no clear relationship between the proportion of car trips for work journeys and population density, but this may be explained by the researchers' definition of population density in terms of workplace rather than residential locations. The correlation between urban population density and transport energy consumption is demonstrated by Newman and Kenworthy (1989) in their study of 32 cities around the world. Research by Næss (1993) in Sweden also identifies a link between population density and transport energy consumption.

Proximity to main transport networks

Proximity to main transport networks may also influence travel patterns, and consequently travel distance, by increasing travel speeds and extending the distance which can be covered in a fixed time. Headicar and Curtis (1994) report that proximity to major transport networks has a substantial effect on work travel distance. They conclude that proximity to either a motorway or a main road is associated with longer travel distances and a higher proportion of car journeys. They also report that proximity to a railway station is associated with long distance commuting but fewer car journeys. Kitamura *et al.* (1997) report that the proportion of car journeys increases and the proportion of non-motorised journeys decreases with increasing distance from the nearest bus stop; and the proportion of rail journeys increases with increasing distance from the nearest railway station. Cervero (1994) shows how the proportion of rail journeys decreases with increasing distance from the railway station. Residents living at a distance of approximately 900 metres from the nearest railway station in California are likely to make only about half the number of rail journeys than residents living within approximately 150 metres of a railway station. This pattern was found to be similar in Washington, Toronto, Edmonton and California.

Availability of residential parking

Limited availability of residential parking may discourage car ownership and use, particularly if finding a parking space close to home is difficult. Evidence from Kitamura *et al.* (1997) shows that availability of residential car parking is linked to both trip frequency and modal choice. As the availability of residential car parking increases, the average number of trips per person decreases: an observation that is perhaps counter-intuitive. Kitamura *et al.* suggest that residents with more parking spaces make fewer and longer journeys, whilst residents with fewer parking spaces make more journeys but these tend to be short. It is also reported that, as the availability of residential car parking increases, the proportion of car journeys increases. This would imply that residents with more parking spaces not only make fewer and longer journeys but also that these journeys are more car based. Conversely, the research implies that residents with fewer parking spaces make more journeys but these tend to be short and less car based. Balcombe and York (1993) identify a correlation between the availability of residential parking (expressed as the ratio of vehicles to spaces) and the proportion of car owners making short journeys on foot (in order to retain their parking space). Their research indicates a greater tendency to walk in areas where residential parking is limited. Similarly, Valleley *et al.* (1997) suggest a relationship between the modal split of commuting and parking provision at work.

Relationships between socio-economic characteristics and travel patterns

The identification of relationships between land use characteristics and travel patterns is complicated by the fact that different land use characteristics are often associated with different socio-economic factors, and that socio-economic characteristics may also affect travel patterns. The variation in socio-economic characteristics increases the difficulty in establishing the precise relationships between land use characteristics and travel patterns, and complicates the comparison of travel patterns in different areas. A large number of socio-economic factors may influence travel patterns and there is a substantial amount of literature on the subject. The effects of a number of socio-economic characteristics on travel patterns are reviewed below (for a more comprehensive review, see Damm, 1981; Hanson, 1982).

Household income

Hanson (1982) reports that trip frequency is linked to household income: people in higher-income households make more journeys than those in lower-income households. Cervero (1996) shows how commuting distance increases with increasing income, and Næss and Sandberg (1996) identify a positive link between household income and total distance travelled per person. Transport energy consumption is reported to increase as household income increases (Næss, 1993; Næss *et al.*, 1995), and Flannelly and McLeod (1989) show how income is linked to the choice of mode for commuting. Income is also linked to land use patterns, which may explain some of the variation in travel patterns in different locations. Mogridge (1985), for example, shows how average incomes in Paris and London increase with increasing distance from the city centre, with the exception of residents in very central locations (within approximately four kilometres of the city centre).

Car ownership

Hanson (1982) reports that trip frequency increases with car ownership, whereas Prevedouros and Schofer (1991) contend that car availability does not explain the variation in trip frequency. Total travel distance is reported to increase with car ownership (Næss and Sandberg, 1996), as is transport energy consumption (*op. cit.*) and the proportion of car journeys (Næss, 1993).

Flannelly and McLeod (1989) show that the number of cars per household is linked to the choice of mode for commuting, and Ewing (1995) reports that travel time increases as car ownership levels increase. Like income, car ownership is also linked to land use patterns, and may explain some of the variation in travel patterns in different locations. Gordon *et al.* (1989a), Levinson and Kumar (1997) and Næss *et al.* (1995) identify links between car ownership and population density. Higher-density areas tend to have lower levels of car ownership. According to evidence from the US presented by Gordon *et al.* (1989a), car ownership tends to be lower in larger cities. Other studies show that car ownership increases as the distance from the city centre increases (Mogridge, 1985; Næss and Sandberg, 1996).

Flannelly and McLeod (1989) show how the possession of a driver's licence is linked to the choice of mode for commuting. People who use the bus are likely to come from households where fewer members have a driver's licence. Interestingly, it is reported that people who share cars to work are likely to come from households with more drivers' licences than average (*op. cit.*).

Employment status, gender, age and household size

Prevedouros and Schofer (1991) report that employment status does not explain variations in trip frequency, although Ewing *et al.* (1996) report that journey frequency increases as the number of workers per household increases. Ewing (1995) reports that average travel time per person increases as the number of workers per household increases, reflecting the fact that where there is more than one worker in the household, home location may not be near to the workplace of each worker.

Hanson (1982) reports no difference in total trip frequency according to gender in Sweden, while Gordon *et al.* (1989b) report that the frequency of non-work trips is higher for women than men in the US, and that women have shorter work trips than men, regardless of income, occupation, or marital and family status.

Hanson (1982) reports no difference between trip frequency and age, while Prevedouros and Schofer (1991) report that age explains some of the variation in trip frequency. Evidence from Flannelly and McLeod (1989) suggests that age has no significant effect on the choice of mode for commuting, although Næss *et al.* (1995) report that transport energy consumption increases with increasing age, and Banister *et al.* (1997) report a negative correlation between transport energy consumption and the proportion of children within each survey group.

According to Hanson (1982), journey frequency increases as household size increases, and evidence from Ewing *et al.* (1996) supports this finding. Ewing (1995) reports that travel time per person increases as household size increases. Banister *et al.* (1997) report that household size is negatively correlated with transport energy consumption.

The treatment of socio-economic variables in research

Several of the studies of land use and travel (reviewed above) do not explicitly recognise that different land use characteristics are associated with different socio-economic factors, which also have an effect on travel patterns. Consequently, they do not attempt to differentiate between the effects of land use characteristics and socio-economic factors. Other studies recognise the effect that socio-economic factors may have on travel patterns but employ a research method that does not differentiate between the effects of land use characteristics and socio-economic factors. ECOTEC (1993), for example, recognise the relationship between population density, lifestyles, income and car ownership but do not attempt to identify the separate effects of socio-economic factors and land use patterns.

Several other studies recognise the effect of socio-economic factors, and employ research methods that attempt to hold socio-economic variables constant in order to observe the effects of land use characteristics. These studies tend to have been carried out within the last decade. Two methods have been employed to hold socio-economic variables constant. The first and more popular approach uses multiple regression analysis, in which socio-economic variables and land use characteristics are treated as explanatory variables (examples include Cervero, 1989; Ewing, 1995; Ewing *et al.*, 1996; Frank and Pivo, 1994; Kitamura *et al.*, 1997; Næss, 1993; Næss *et al.*, 1995; Næss and Sandberg, 1996; Prevedouros and Schofer, 1991). The method allows identification of the main socio-economic and land use characteristics that are associated with certain travel patterns, but does not, however, allow the identification of causal relationships. A second method employed to hold socio-economic variables constant involves the selection of case study areas that have similar socio-economic profiles but different land use characteristics. In this way, socio-economic differences are minimised and the variation in travel patterns is assumed to be the result of land use characteristics (examples include Handy, 1992; Curtis, 1995).

Relationships between land use and socio-economic characteristics
The interaction between land use and socio-economic characteristics may be two-way. First, socio-economic characteristics may be influenced by land use. Some residential locations (and land uses) may be undesirable or unaffordable for certain socio-economic groups. Decisions about residential location depend on a range of factors including affordability and accessibility (to work, friends, shops and so on) which are determined by socio-economic characteristics such as income, car ownership and work status. Second, land use may be influenced by socio-economic characteristics. Areas with high levels of car ownership and use may, for example, be more prone to new development that is car oriented, with high levels of parking and extensive road infrastructure. Evidence for these type of interactions between land use and socio-economic characteristics is very limited.

Summary
In addition to the interactions between land use, socio-economic characteristics and travel patterns, which add complexity to the study of land use and travel patterns, it is also likely that there is further complexity due to interrelationships between different land use characteristics. Settlement size, for example, may be linked to population density, the distance to the urban centre or the availability of residential parking (Fig. 3). Similarly, there may also be interrelationships between different socio-economic factors. Household income, for example, may be linked to employment type and working status. This may influence car ownership and use. Car ownership and use may be influenced by the possession of a driver's licence, age and gender (Fig. 4). Regression analysis allows some of these complex interactions to be disentangled (see section below).

Research methods
The three studies reported in this chapter have used different sources of data but have employed similar research methods to disentangle some of the interactions between land use, socio-economic characteristics and travel patterns. Multiple regression analysis has been used in all three studies as a way of identifying the extent to which land use and socio-economic characteristics explain the variation in travel patterns (and the extent to which socio-economic characteristics explain the variation in land use, and *vice versa*). Stead (1999) has examined the effect of a range of socio-economic and land use characteristics on total travel distance per person using data from a series of National Travel Surveys of Great Britain (see note 2)

and local travel data from Kent and Leicestershire. The analysis was carried out at the individual level and at the ward level. Titheridge *et al.* (1999) have examined the effect of land use and socio-economic characteristics on travel to work patterns using the 1991 Census data. The Local Based Statistics (LBS) from the Census provided data on resident population, car ownership, employment and other socio-economic characteristics at ward level, and the Special Workplace Statistics (SWS) provided detailed journey-to-work information, including travel between wards. A number of additional variables were derived from other sources such as public transport timetables. Analysis was carried out at the ward level and the settlement level (using the Census based Urban Area Key Counts). Williams and Banister (Williams, 1997; Williams and Banister, 1998) have used data from National Travel Surveys (see note 3), the 1991 Census and a variety of other sources to establish facilities provision in Gloucestershire, including information from GOAD, Yellow Pages and Urban Area Key Count data. Analysis was carried out at the ward level and at the settlement level. Table 1 summarises the levels of analysis and characteristics examined in the three studies.

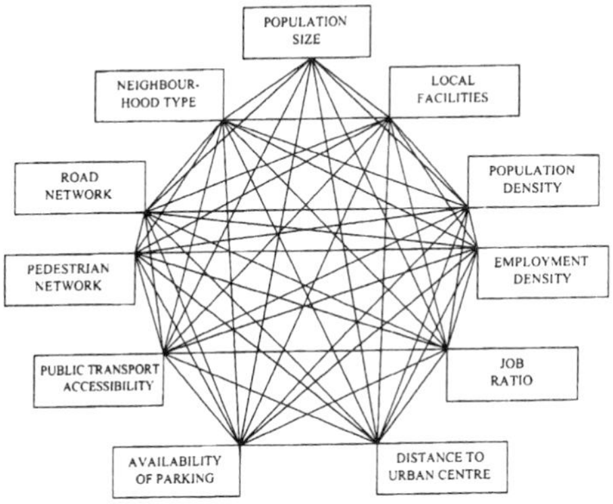

Fig. 3. Possible interactions between land use characteristics.

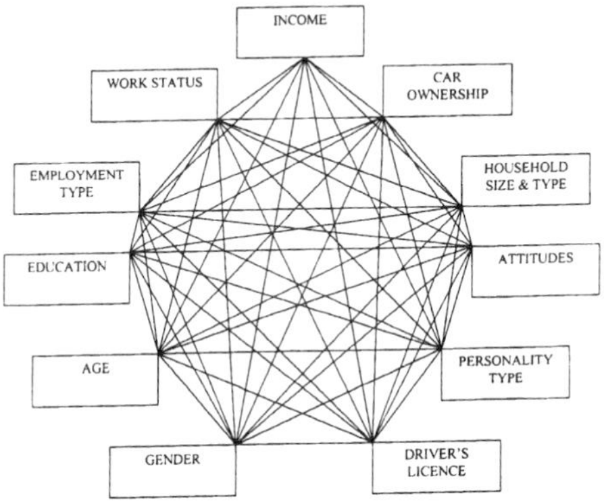

Fig. 4. Possible interactions between socio-economic factors.

	Stead (1999)	Titheridge *et al.* (1999)	Williams and Banister (1999)
Level of analysis			
individual level	✓		
ward level	✓	✓	✓
settlement level		✓	✓
Travel patterns			
total travel distance per person	✓		✓
travel to work distance		✓	✓
travel to work mode (a)		✓	✓
Socio-economic characteristics			
socio-economic group	✓	✓	✓
car ownership	✓	✓	✓
possession of a drivers' licence	✓		
employment status	✓	✓	✓
gender	✓		
age	✓	✓	✓
household structure (size and composition)	✓	✓	
income			✓

Land use characteristics

---

distance from the urban centre	✓	✓ (b)	
'rurality'		✓ (c)	
settlement size	✓	✓	✓
the mixing of land uses	✓ (d)	✓ (e)	
the provision of local facilities	✓	✓	✓
the density of development	✓	✓	✓
proximity to the nearest bus stop	✓		
frequency of the nearest bus service	✓		
number of local bus services		✓	
proximity to the nearest railway station	✓	✓	
frequency of rail services at local stations		✓	
proximity to a motorway junction	✓		
the availability of residential parking	✓		

(a) Analysis of travel to work mode includes consideration of the proportion of work journeys by car, rail, bus, on foot and by cycle.

(b) Titheridge *et al.* (1999) examined the effect of distance from the centre of London and distance from the nearest settlement containing at least 10,000 persons (South–East wards only).

(c) Titheridge *et al.* (1999) examined the effect of 'rurality' using the proportion of the ward classified as urban.

(d) Stead (1999) examined the mixing of land use in terms of the job ratio (the ratio of jobs to employable residents).

(e) Titheridge *et al.* (1999) examined the mixing of land use in terms of the proximity to local employment (expressed as the number of jobs within 1, 2.5, 5 and 10 kilometres of home).

Table 1. Levels of analysis and characteristics examined in the three studies.

Research results

All three studies examined the effect of both land use and socio-economic characteristics on travel patterns. Two of the studies also identified (in less detail) some possible interactions between land use and socio-economic characteristics. The interactions identified in the three studies are summarised below.

Both land use and socio-economic characteristics were found to explain the variation in travel patterns in all three studies. Socio-economic characteristics often explain more of the variation in travel patterns than land use characteristics do. Stead (1999) estimated that socio-economic characteristics typically explain half of the variation in travel distance per person across different wards. Land use characteristics often only explain around one third of the variation in travel distance per person. These results are reasonably consistent with research reported by Gordon (1997) who estimates that a third of the variation in transport energy consumption per capita is attributable to socio-economic characteristics and a further third of the variation is attributable to land use factors. The results are also consistent with the research of Goodwin (1995) who reports that socio-economic factors are responsible for more of the variation in car use than location factors are.

Stead (1999) identified a number of 'key' socio-economic characteristics, which appear to be the most important socio-economic determinants of travel distance per capita at the ward level. These comprise household car ownership, household socio-economic group and the proportion of working residents. Williams and Banister (1999) report similar socio-economic determinants of travel distance per capita, and also identify income as another important determinant (Table 2). Titheridge *et al.* (1999) found land use factors exerted more influence than socio-economic factors on journey to work distance, but that car ownership

183

levels and socio-economic profiles were also significant. The results of the research by Stead (1999) and Williams and Banister (1999) on travel distance per capita correspond with research in Canada showing that high transport energy consumers come from larger households with high income levels and high levels of car ownership (McDougall and Mank, 1982). Williams and Banister (1999) and Titheridge *et al.* (1999) identify similar socio-economic influences on travel-to-work mode: important socio-economic characteristics include car ownership, employment status and age.

	Total travel distance		Travel-to-work distance	Travel-to-work mode	
	Stead, 1999	Williams and Banister, 1999	Titheridge *et al.*, 1999	Williams and Banister, 1999	Titheridge *et al.*, 1999
Socio-economic characteristics					
Socio-economic group	✓	✗	✓	✗	✓
Car ownership	✓	✓	✓	✓	✓
Employment status	✓	✓	✗	✓	✓
Age	✗	✓	✗	✓	✓
Household structure (size and composition)	✓	n.a.	✗	n.a.	✗
Income	✓	✓	n.a.	n.a.	n.a.
Land use characteristics					
Distance from the urban centre	✗	n.a.	✓	n.a.	✗
Settlement size	✓	✓	✗	✓	✗
Mixing of land uses	✓	n.a.	✓	n.a.	✓
Provision of local facilities	✓	✓	✓	✓	✗
Density of development	✓	✓	✗	✗	✗
Frequency of the nearest bus service	✓	n.a.	✗	n.a.	✗
Proximity to the nearest railway station	✗	n.a.	✓	n.a.	✓
Availability of residential parking	✓	n.a.	n.a.	n.a.	n.a.

Table 2. Relationships between travel patterns, land use and socio-economic characteristics.

✓ signifies an interaction identified; ✗ signifies no interaction identified; n.a. signifies interaction untested.

Although socio-economic characteristics explain more of the variation in travel patterns than land use characteristics do in many of the analyses in the three studies, there are, however, several land use characteristics that are still important in explaining the variation in travel patterns. Characteristics such as the mixing of land uses appear to explain variations in both travel distance and mode. Other land use characteristics, such as the provision of local facilities, explain variations in travel distance but do not explain variations in travel mode. Evidence for the influence of other land use characteristics on travel patterns remains unclear. Some results suggest interactions whilst other results do not. Ongoing research by Williams and Banister (Williams, 1997; Williams and Banister, 1998) suggests an interrelationship between settlement size, local provision of services and facilities, and travel patterns.

In addition to examining the ways in which both land use and socio-economic characteristics might influence travel patterns, Stead (1999) and Williams and Banister (1999) have also examined how land use and socio-economic characteristics interact. Stead (1999) looked at the effects of land use on car ownership and showed that land use characteristics may explain up to 40% of the variation in car ownership in different areas. Two of the more important land use characteristics linked with car ownership are proximity to a railway station and the frequency of the local bus service. Car ownership is lower in areas with high frequency bus services (more than four per hour) and in areas within a 44-minute walk from the nearest railway station (which is approximately equivalent to three miles or five kilometres). Thus, the availability and frequency of public transport may clearly influence household decisions about the need for a car. Stead (1999) claims that land use characteristics, such as proximity to a railway station and the frequency of the local bus service, are potential (indirect) levers to reduce travel distance (see above). These results suggest that locations where car ownership may best be suppressed are those within reach of frequent public transport. Such locations are most likely to be urban or inter-urban and on transport corridors, since other locations are less likely to be able to support frequent public transport. This accords with current planning policy guidance on transport and land use (e.g. DoE, 1994).

Evidence from Williams and Banister (1998, 1999) suggests that settlements of differing size exhibit particular socio-economic characteristics. Socio-economic variables that vary considerably with settlement size include economic activity and car ownership. These socio-economic characteristics are likely to influence travel patterns. Thus, in larger settlements where economic activity and car ownership is lower, travel distances are lower and there is less reliance on the car. The reverse is true in smaller settlements.

Williams and Banister (1999) also report that socio-economic variables (mainly income related) also influence level of provision of facilities and services in a settlement. This in turn affects both modal split and total distances travelled in a settlement. It would also appear that feedback loops exist between socio-economic characteristics, settlement size and the local provision of facilities and services. Williams and Banister (1999) assert that settlement size is a key variable influencing travel patterns, both directly and indirectly. However, the relationship is complicated by the interaction between settlement size, socio-economic variables and levels of facilities and services provision. Thus, it seems that there are interactions between land use and socio-economic characteristics, although only a few have been examined to date. It is often difficult to establish cause and effect relationships in these interactions: socio-economic characteristics may influence land use and/or land use may influence socio-economic characteristics.

Conclusions

There is a substantial amount of empirical evidence for the link between land use and travel patterns. However, many studies have not considered how the variation in socio-economic characteristics may also explain the variation in travel patterns across different areas. A review of socio-economic influences on travel patterns shows that there are several ways in which socio-economic characteristics might be responsible for the variations in travel patterns in empirical studies. The research reported in the chapter has been framed by a view of the land use transport interaction that is more complex than traditionally supposed. Rather than assuming a simple cause and effect relationship between land use and travel patterns, a set of interactions between land use, socio-economic characteristics and travel patterns has been assumed. The chapter has then attempted to identify the extent to which both land use and socio-economic characteristics influence travel patterns.

It appears that there are a number of socio-economic reasons for the variation in travel patterns across different areas. However, land use characteristics also explain some of the variation. Socio-economic characteristics often explain more of the variation in travel patterns than land use characteristics do. Important socio-economic influences on travel patterns in an area include the socio-economic and employment profile, car ownership levels and income. Socio-economic characteristics typically explain half of the variation in travel distance per person across different wards, whereas land use characteristics often only explain around one third of the variation. There may also be interactions between land use and socio-economic characteristics, although research in this area has so far been fairly limited. Thus, there is evidence for a three-way relationship between travel patterns, land use and socio-economic characteristics (for fuller discussion, see Stead, 1999; Williams and Banister, 1999).

Clearly, the extent to which land use might influence travel patterns may be lower than other studies have previously indicated (where they have not taken socio-economic characteristics into account). However, this does not mean that land use does not have an important role to play in influencing travel patterns. Neither does it imply that the compact city cannot contribute to more sustainable travel patterns. It does suggest that the apparent success of compact cities (in terms of shorter distances travelled and shifts towards non-car modes) may result as much from the socio-economic characteristics of the inhabitants, as from the urban land use and form characteristics of the cities themselves.

The results of the three studies reported in this chapter indicate that land use characteristics such as the mix of uses, settlement size and the provision of local facilities have a role to play in promoting more sustainable development. Furthermore, combinations of several land use measures may have significant effects on travel by creating synergies between measures, and the use of other non-land use measures (e.g. fuel taxation or public transport provision) may complement the effect of land use policies.

Notes

1. The three projects were carried out at the Bartlett School of Planning and funded by the Engineering and Physical Sciences Research Council (EPSRC). They comprise: Planning for Less Travel – (see Stead, 1999); the TRANSZ project (Transport Sustainability: A Study of Small-Zone Data) carried out by Professor Peter Hall, Helena Titheridge and Simon Hall (Titheridge *et al.*, 1999); and the Urban Sustainability and Settlement Size (URBASSS) project carried out by David Banister and Jo Williams (see Williams and Banister 1997 to 1999).
2. Stead (1999) examined National Travel Survey data from 1978/79, 1985/86, 1989/91 and 1991/93, supplied by the Data Archive at the University of Essex.
3. Williams and Banister (1998) examined data from the three most recent National Travel Surveys, supplied by the Data Archive at the University of Essex.

Approaches and Strategies for Achieving Sustainable Urban Form
Introduction

The previous two parts (1 and 2) offered some clarification of what sustainable urban form might be. They tested a number of possible forms against a host of sustainability variables and advocated a number of different scenarios. Given the apparent multiplicity of potential sustainable forms, or pathways, it seems appropriate that the chapters in this part should reflect that variety in the aspects of urban form they address. The chapters outline strategies and approaches devised to *deliver* more sustainable urban forms than at present exist. They outline ways of integrating the complex interpretations of a sustainable future into development practices. To achieve this integration, the authors grapple with definitions of both sustainable urban form and of urban processes at the broadest level. In so doing, almost as many problems arise as opportunities are revealed. Nevertheless, collectively, the chapters offer an insight into how practice is evolving, and how researchers, policy makers and practitioners are working towards delivering a more sustainable future.

The first three chapters represent broad strategic thinking about how a more sustainable future might be reached. In the first, the idea of development and demonstration as adaptive strategies is reviewed. These are posited as methods for the transformation of both the institutional structures governing the delivery of urban environments and social and technical conditions. Van Vliet argues that innovation towards sustainable development is currently constrained by multiple barriers, but that the 'adaptive approach can loosen deadlock with surprising outcomes'. He gives examples of innovative development schemes in Denmark which were influential in countering the 'crises of conventional urban development in achieving sustainable urban form'.

The next chapter, by Crilly and Mannis, also challenges the ways in which urban areas are perceived. Their aim is to develop a method which will enable people to think holistically about the development and management of complex urban systems. A locally specific approach to understanding and communicating urban systems, which is helpful to a variety of urban decision makers, is suggested. The specific solution they develop is a Sustainable Urban Management System (SUMS), the basis of which is an understanding of needs, applications and means of communication amongst those with a role in the management and planning of urban areas. The authors give examples of GIS based SUMS which are effective because they can 'spatialise' information about changing urban form. Hence, this is a key way of facilitating communication with a wide range of interest groups.

Ravetz then presents a review of the fundamentals of sustainable urban form (what are cities and how do they work?), the findings of which he applies to a worked example: Manchester. He explores what the consequences would be of applying the key elements of sustainable urban development to typical housing and neighbourhood structures. He finds that a fixed blueprint for future development is inappropriate, and a more flexible approach, which adapts to changing needs and demands, is required. Consequently, in an argument similar to that presented by Guy and Marvin (Part 1) '... this suggests a concept of sustainable urban form as a dynamic process of physical change which interacts with economic and social pressures and demands'. Ravetz's analysis of the feasibility of various 'pathways' towards sustainable development results in some keen observations about the way that urban problems are approached. He asserts that solutions are often 'one-dimensional', with fixed objectives, yet should be more robust, self-organising systems, with multiple balancing interactions.

One of the key elements of sustainable urban form is urban compaction. As previous chapters have shown, compactness is a multi-faceted quality that fails to supply universal sustainability benefits, and can have some distinctly unsustainable side-effects. But evidence still suggests that it may – at some scale of application, and with careful management – be a component of sustainable urban form in the future. If this is the case, then there are some key associated problems that need to be solved. Two such problems are addressed next.

De Roo develops an approach for dealing with environmental problems in compact urban areas. By focusing on environmental policy in the Netherlands, and using the US policy system as a comparison, he identifies ways of decision making to deal with environmental issues, based on typologies of environmental conflicts. He concludes that a distinction could be made between simple, uniform conflicts which can be solved by implementing centrally defined standards (as has been done in the Netherlands), and more complex ones. Complex conflicts, which are strongly linked to local context, are better understood by local authorities and local people, and require a different approach – akin to that used in the USA. Hence, he concludes that local authorities should make decisions about which approach should be adopted depending on the complexity of the conflict.

Jenks addresses the key issue of the acceptability to urban residents of higher densities and urban compaction. He builds his arguments around findings from research for the British government which points to tensions between strategic sustainability measures and their impact on local populations. Jenks introduces the concept of 'social capacity' – a measure of limits to intensification, defined in terms of urban residents' attitudes – as a companion to existing measures of physical and environmental capacity. He describes how a decision support mechanism, which uses the research findings in combination with an assessment of a locality's character, could be used to determine acceptable intensification. In essence, Jenks' work offers an example of the type of urban management system that Crilly and Mannis advocate: it is derived from locally-based knowledge, and adapts to accommodate differences between localities.

The final chapters are examples of documented strategies to achieve sustainable urban form in the UK. They concentrate on environmental issues, design and strategic land allocation. Howes explains how the Environment Agency – one of the UK government's environmental bodies – hopes to promote sustainability in the Thames Region, through a strategy for land use planning. Raymond then outlines the processes involved in producing a design guide for the county of Kent, which embraces sustainability and improves the quality of development. Finally, Zanré describes Wycombe District Council's strategy of 'sustainable site selection' for future residential development. This was achieved by devising a 'comparative site assessment – goals achievement matrix' – which tested potential sites against sustainability criteria. By using this method, the local authority was able to meet its housing targets and also earmark sites for future phased development.

The chapters in this part present a snap shot of approaches and strategies for sustainable urban form, either under development or in use. How successful they are will become clear only in time. What is important is that by showing how to overcome problems, or prescribing new paths of action, they turn theory into practical solutions.

David van Vliet

Development/Demonstration: An Adaptive Strategy

Introduction

Demonstration is posited here as a key, if not necessary, strategy for the transformation of both institutional structures governing the delivery of urban environments and the principles and requisite conditions – social and technological – that can define sustainable urban development. This chapter addresses projects as means for policy development. It refers to the rich history of urban demonstration, giving examples from current practice. The key features of demonstration projects are outlined along with an expanded conception of the role of demonstration. The chapter argues for employment of an adaptive approach to strategies for integrated urban development with greater sustainability characteristics. In many municipal contexts, there is the experience of innovation lethargy, due in part to the existence of multiple barriers and a degree of uncertainty in all jurisdictions. Such a socially constructed stalemate can be undermined by the social dynamism of learning. The 'adaptive approach can loosen deadlock with surprising outcomes' (Lee, 1993, p. 58), and is needed if scientific, professional and political uncertainty is not to frustrate socially timely action.

Barriers and transition

Examples of urban development considered to be sustainable are still very few. This implementation gap is attributed in part to the existence of numerous entrenched barriers within the residential community delivery system. Barriers are those factors appearing to limit society from turning knowledge into action. A list exceeding 150 barriers to sustainability implementation within the North American and European municipal planning contexts were compiled in recent research (van Vliet, 1999). These divide into the following categories:

1. Perceptual/attitudinal/behavioural
2. Institutional structures and capacities (political, regulatory, procedural, legal)
3. Economic/financial
4. Others

Often there are multiple barriers to widespread adoption of any innovations, and a different configuration of barriers will exist for different behaviours or changes. The focus on barriers is a strategic focus on opportunities. Focusing on the barriers directly is a helpful tactic to identify and discern sources of resistance, and focus on the relationships – the implicit norms and power relationships – within which they are embedded (Senge, 1990). Barriers are not formidable walls nor an excuse for inaction. Their identification is not to provide an explanation for why things do not happen, but to understand opportunities for overcoming them. 'The concepts associated with creating sustainable communities are not difficult; it is the process of bringing them to fruition that is challenging' (Moore, 1997, p.176). There are general commonalities of barriers experienced in most Western policy and implementation contexts. In addition to the shared task to respond to the challenges of sustainability, the jurisdictions (in regard to municipal development conditions) are similar in a number of key dimensions:

- They share organisational and societal institutions – local government with comparable departments and corporate mandates, state government with equivalent general mandates and responsibilities.
- The planning system and housing delivery system have many matching players and roles.
- The issues of site development, servicing standards, codes, procedures and so on are shared by all municipal jurisdictions.
- Public sector bureaucratic cultures tend to share certain common characteristics and tendencies regardless of location (Osborne and Plastrik, 1997). These include: rules, which shape their cultures; the fact that they are creatures of the political sector, and are thus targets of public demand through elected officials and undergo scrutiny from legislators, interest groups and media; the fact that they are hierarchical – with order givers and order takers and a concentration of power; that they are bureaucratic organisations – where thinking, research and doing are often separated; and the fact that they are near monopolies – facing little pressure from customers or competitors.
- The fundamentals of politics, hierarchy, bureaucracy and monopoly give rise to organisational cultures in which the inhabitants have a tendency to: blame rather than take responsibility; live in fear of making mistakes rather than innovating; and resist or observe change rather than adapt to it.
- Many of the social technologies for community responsibility, acting locally, and user engagement have parallels in many environmental and urban development affairs.
- The planning and design professions and research groups among countries are positioned to offer technology and other capacities for establishing innovative demonstration projects of similar character.

Sustainable urban development emphasises an integrated approach, a long-term perspective and, importantly, builds on active community participation. That is, by combining technological innovation, public regulation and organisational innovation, it can contribute to reducing resource throughput and achieving modified, yet improved, social and economic conditions. When applied in a deliberate and adaptive way, it involves a process of comprehensive transition over time, where the existing built urban environment undergoes positive transformation. This transition involves the ongoing identification of barriers to applying and developing sustainability solutions, to ensure that these approaches can be included more extensively in urban development activity. The tensions between planning and implementation in pursuing sustainable urban development need to be managed, and this can be revealing. The act of implementation provides the necessary signals of what does not work, thus identifying what requires modification in the more centrally developed plan. Without such action this is not evident, or remains speculative. An adaptive search for sustainability learns from demonstration practice, and thus implementation can help to identify barriers and decentralise power. In the urban environmental arena, where policy makers regularly face uncertainty, this can be a highly advantageous approach. It is, however, not without costs. Barriers to its use are the need for information gathering, the political risks incurred by having clearly identified failures, and the problem of how to persuade taxpayers of the value of learning. Social learning, as a public good, is to be paid for by government (state and local). However, if government officials are seen to be open to possible discredit by unfulfilled promises, their willingness to invest – for the sake of learning – declines (Lee, 1993).

Demonstration

Demonstration has been advocated by various authors and agencies to promote alternatives that are not otherwise emerging (see note 1). It is an area of activity closely associated with sustainable community assessment and monitoring of performance, occurring in both the formal and informal sectors over the past years (NRCan. 1994, 1998). Compared with other parts of the world, the European Community has been developing a favourable policy environment for sustainable urban development initiatives, in which research and demonstration are considered to be two of the main instruments of action (CEC, 1993). It is recognised that research, demonstration, and training to develop improved methods and techniques of urban management can have wide benefits. Therefore, financial support is offered to such experimentation, through demonstration and pilot projects, which might serve as models for wider application thereby playing an important role in the dissemination of information about the practical results obtained. The success of demonstration projects in several countries indicates the viability of this approach to overcoming barriers in implementing sustainable urban development concepts (see note 2).

Demonstrations and their results provide experience and inspiration for work with new building and community design projects. The knowledge accumulated by, and available to, the city and the development industry grows. The intention should be to ensure that urban ecology solutions could be included more extensively in urban development, whether in new development or urban renewal. In this chapter, a demonstration project is defined as an area-based, site-specific planning and design process and built project, which has a cluster of innovations (new/better technologies, systems, designs, methods or programmes) that shows potential adopters the benefits of employing these innovations. Demonstration in various ways can increase dematerialisation (by reducing resource throughput, including re-conceived processes and demand, and increasing natural capital), re-socialisation (increasing social capital, equity, participation), help to develop policy, change regulations and so on. Depending on the type of innovation, demonstrations can increase productivity, lower production costs, raise quality of living and deliver social services more efficiently. Following from a survey of built projects, the key features of demonstration are outlined below (see Perks and van Vliet, 1994; van Vliet, 1999).

They are built under terms of innovation sponsorship.

- There is a commitment to build and experiment with new practices or new norms of development.
- Sponsoring agencies are variously municipal corporations, departments and institutes of the national government, private foundations, private companies, universities and community-based organisations. Partnership between them is common; project implementation is often multi-sectoral. It is also multi-jurisdictional (city, region, and state levels of government) and multi-disciplinary, involving expertise and approaches from architecture, engineering, planning, ecology, health, landscape, biology, sociology, and local people.

Their sponsorship entails some form of resources support, such as:

- architectural design competitions with awards that lead to commissions for built projects;
- provision of land for demonstration building sites, at favourable terms of sale or lease;

- defraying the costs of research and development or non-customary planning and design services (usually grants for project-specific research and design, and publications to disseminate information and new ideas);
- incentives, by which more state-funded housing units can be allocated to private developers' projects in which sustainability experimentation is undertaken; and
- workshops and seminars for designers, developers, builders, residents and municipal officials.

Demonstration projects are invariably tied into some form of public exhibition.
- Exhibitions are organised to present 'a window on the future'. They provide a medium not only for public education and awareness-building but also serve to convene experts for evaluative research and appraisal of the projects and dissemination. Typically, constructed houses, street blocks or neighbourhoods will comprise the exhibition site. In addition, drawings, plans, equipment and materials will be displayed. Company and agency promotions, conferences, workshops, and tours of individual demonstration project sites will take place.

The idea of demonstration is to show what can be done and what needs to be done. Public learning occurs through manifold processes – doing it, seeing it and experiencing the demonstration in its fully-formed presence in an environment. Demonstration residential community projects are, in essence, research and development. Research and development is called for because there is a gap between 'what we know' and 'what we need to know' regarding sustainable urban development. Although demonstration projects may evolve from experimental and pilot phases, they must be designed to advocate and test the adoption of innovation. In short, more and better integrated examples of improved practice are needed. Projects demonstrating greater sustainability illustrate a type of urban planning founded in community performance goals rather than a mechanistic translation of land use planning principles, codes and site development standards. This approach shares with conventional municipal planning practices normal requirements, such as providing a land use setting and infrastructure systems. Conversely, urban ecological planning projects, both built and contemplated, are centred on concerns for stipulating the performance of the built environment, the performance of its open spaces and habitats, and the performance (or roles) of the community and its individual inhabitants. Fully featured demonstrations are a matter of both technical and social-political innovation and application. Solving sustainability problems in an urban context requires a diffusion of available innovative approaches – technical, social and political. Too often, experiences from experiments and demonstration projects have failed to be diffused into larger scale utilisation. 'Diffused' implies the new ideas are communicated, utilised and developed for the market, or transformed into new regulations, principles and procedures for building and planning.

Hence, an improved understanding of the role of demonstration is needed. Usual references to the role of demonstration follow the dictionary definition: demonstration 'as outward exhibition, logical proving, ... thing serving as proof, ... exhibition and explanation of specimens and experiments as way of teaching' (Allen, 1992, p.309). This conception, as a product for education and to support adoption of innovations, has been the main function of demonstrations within their long history in urban planning and architecture, and continues in projects focusing on resource conservation.

The best among the built projects investigated and surveyed by the author in Europe and North America were conceived as 'development' – trying to realise a new set of considerations using new approaches to build capacity – and as 'demonstration' – to be visible, instructive, educative, experiential examples.

Ecologically-based proposals in the residential development sector have tended to be smaller scale and diverse, rather than large-scale projects. These smaller initiatives have seldom significantly influenced design or infrastructure arrangements more broadly, and many proposals have failed to be realised. Obtaining development capital, even for small projects, has been an ongoing struggle. In view of this, 'demonstration projects with environmentally conscious design which can assist with the spread of knowledge about improved practice [appear to] have a key role in innovation to resolve these tensions, both in terms of approach taken and built form outcomes' (OECD, 1996, p.45), and should be supported.

Congenial models for more sustainable, community-building experimental projects, investigated and reported in literature, indicate a diversity of type, scope and size. The development principles differ in important methodological and conceptual respects from current assessment (and environment management) type practices focused on negative impacts, measures of protection, preservation and mitigation. A number of projects demonstrate deeply innovative planning and design principles that draw on economic, environmental science, conservation and regeneration principles.

Danish demonstration – Egebjerggård

Although progress toward goals of sustainability differs significantly between the EC member states, certain countries are showing considerable advancements in good practice. Denmark is noted for its strategies and instruments, and Danish municipalities are considered among the lead agents. Significant features of Danish municipal planning are the numerous pilot and demonstration projects in local communities for developing and promoting the operational principles of sustainability (see Munkstrup and Sørensen, 1995). Among the best practice examples are the urban renewal scheme in Kolding (see case study by van Vliet and Gade, this volume) and a new neighbourhood in Ballerup, briefly described below.

Egebjerggård is a 782 unit, 38ha, mixed-use urban extension and neighbourhood intensification project located in the municipality of Ballerup (50,000 population), 15km northwest of København. A new pattern for 'integrated neighbourhoods' emerged through experiment, public debate and an innovative system of planning guidelines and regulations. Egebjerggård was the venue for an international building exhibition in 1996. Construction of dwellings had started in June 1988, and by the end of 1997 the planning was complete and the housing schemes in the urban quarter's four stages were nearly finished. Some limited selective infill is still to occur on a few sites reserved for commercial or institutional use. The project and results were monitored during the course of construction (see van Vliet, 1999). Figure 1 shows a site plan of the Egebjerggård scheme and Table 1 summarises its main elements.

The author's research (van Vliet, 1999) concerned the planning of demonstration community projects as a strategy to alter the dynamics of the delivery system context toward building capacity, developing policy and expanding practices for sustainable urban development. The inquiry addressed the question, 'Can demontration projects be useful as a social learning device and in elaborating planning design policy alternatives towards sustainable urban development?' The focus was on the diffusion of innovation, as well as on problems and potentials in policy and practice. The hypothesis was that a demonstration project can be a pathway to overcoming barriers, and a locus for policy development, contributing to changing attitudes and actions of authorities and citizenry to the requirements of sustainable urban development.

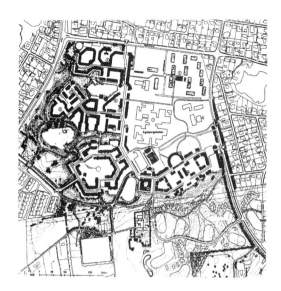

*Fig. 1. Site plan
of the
Egebjerggård
scheme*

Owner/client – The former brickyard site was municipally purchased and subdivided according to local plans. Building lots were sold to a mix of private landlords, housing societies, municipality and individual owners.

Area

Gross area	388,654m²	38.8ha
Floor area	95,944m²	9.5ha
Common open area	117,984m²	11.7ha

Built/planned – 1986–94 (Phase I, 1989–90; Phase II, 1990–91; Phase III, 1991–92; Phase IV, 1993–96). Selective infill will occur in the future.

Housing units – 782 units in four phases of a mixed area, including housing, shops, school and institutions Housing is a combination of public, young persons, elderly, co-operative and private.

Density (gross) – 24 housing units per gross ha (9.6 units per acre), % coverage for area is 25%.

Net density – In phase I, II, III, and IV the site area is 17ha for 732 units (43 units per ha, or 17.2 units per acre). Net density does not include the large environmental reserve space or the school.

Population (1996) – 928 units (51 persons per ha). Average persons per unit is 2.15.

Age demographics for residents – % ages between 1–4, 5–9, 20–24, 25–29, 30–34 years is higher than the Ballerup norm. Other age groups are lower than average. This is typical of a new housing area.

Intended programme – Social housing 65; co-operative housing 20%; private housing 10%; accommodation for students and the elderly, co-housing, learning disabled, craft studios, commercial and semi-industrial 9,900m².

Realised programme – Social housing 56%; co-operative housing 15.5%; private housing 14%; accommodation for students and the elderly 6%; co-housing, learning disabled, craft studios, commercial and semi-industrial 3,000m².

Plan-design – Ballerup Municipal Planning Department.

*Table 1. The main
elements of the
Egebjerggård
scheme.*

Town planning – Hæstrup, Dybbro and Haastrup Planning Consultants, the Town Planning Department (part of Technical Division, Ballerup municipality).

The Egebjerggård case provided a situation where the implementation process and the overcoming of barriers to sustainability could be studied, making it possible to conduct both micro and macro level analysis, by means of an examination of the institutional mechanisms and relationships that connect and shape what happens at both levels. The investigation traversed levels from the national political economy to the city, to local levels and micro project features. The project proved to be a suitable vehicle for conveying ideas and concepts on how to integrate environmental, social and economic concerns in city planning and related politics. The findings from research into the project's documentation, interviews with key informants and analysis provided strong evidence that the process of transition to more sustainable urban development can be speeded up by means of a sufficiently integrated project. Evidence for the diffusion of innovations was documented in other municipal initiatives, in national policy, and in other projects in Europe.

Based on attempts to plan innovative urban infill neighbourhoods in Canada, the commonality of barriers and community planning principles was argued as the basis for relevance and generalisation of the findings to the Canadian municipal context. Public policy directions and specific initiatives (in their early stages) for community scale demonstration projects with multiple sustainability characteristics were identified in the cities of Calgary and Vancouver. The characteristics necessary for a demonstration project to have a sufficiently developmental role in these contexts were speculated.

The research shows that analysis of leading practice can contribute to a better understanding of the potentials and constraints for advancing sustainable community planning policy, design and implementation at neighbourhood and city levels. Such analyses might also offer practical guidance for undertaking initiatives in Canada and elsewhere. They call for a national programme of demonstration and exhibition, outlining a three-armed strategy along with the potential benefits and costs and the inferred effect on identified problems. The potential for education and policy development, in combination, make demonstration an important part of a sustainable development strategy.

The value of an experimental approach

The development of Egebjerggård was a strategic move to change the process and form of development. Discovering how to do this required experimentation. The 'experimental' term in urban development is often misapplied. Some argue that much of contemporary urban development has been, and continues to be, an uncontrolled 'experiment' at an unprecedented scale. While municipal officials and practitioners may refer to a certain policy or initiative as an experiment, it is incorrect to characterise many initiatives as even quasi-experiments. An experiment intends to answer a question in a systematic way, where the validity of the results depends on the competence of the experimenter (see note 3). The approach is less applicable to community design, being a type of field science, or field art. The community 'laboratory', whether new or established, far from being a controlled setting, is a dynamic context of human actions and natural fluctuations.

In spite of this, real learning can occur in a community, and it is possible to speak about an experimental framework for implementation and action. When an alternative set of conditions exist in community planning and design, where there is good understanding of the intentions behind them, then evaluations and comparative data analysis can be undertaken. In this way, a built demonstration community can be seen as an opportunity to have a one-to-one context for comparative study, for analysis *in situ*, where enough of the variables present are understood (see note 4). This 'concreteness' is a key reason why site specific projects are important. People can more readily come to a choice when they are directly involved in practical actions and decision making, particularly availed to precedents and visualisation support. As Jantzen states, 'It is first in experimental situations that participants are drawn into close contact with existing practice and existing boundaries are tested and adjusted – or completely overthrown on the basis of reasonable arguments, should these boundaries be in the way' (1994, p.6).

Securing reliable knowledge is an essential part of any strategy. Given the complicated relationships in urban development, experimentation would seem to be an important precondition for developing new knowledge. Without experimentation and demonstration, reliable knowledge accumulates slowly – as most cities are witnessing – and without reliable knowledge there can be neither social learning nor sustainable development. Since the uncertainty inherent in complex urban systems makes errors and surprises inevitable, experimentation is recommended as an effective strategy for sensing surprise and for recovery from error. Considering planning in terms of experiments has important sociological consequences, wherein surprising results are to be seen as legitimate rather than as signs of failure. Unexpected information becomes an essential ally rather than something to be feared. Importantly, in the process of implementation, surprising resources and opportunities (human and material) can come to the fore and encourage further development.

Adaptive polices and urban management

Because there is an inherent unknowable and unpredictable quality to sustainable development, solutions are more likely to be discovered through field attempts rather than central command. Evolving systems require policies and actions that, in addition to meeting social objectives, achieve a continually modified understanding of evolving conditions, and provide flexibility for adaptation to surprises. This is the essence of active experimentation through management at the scales appropriate to the questions. Otherwise, exploitive development or 'development that impoverishes' (Daly and Cobb, 1989), is inevitable, where increasingly brittle ecosystems, rigid management and dependent societies lead to crises (Holling, 1992).

Adaptive urban policies define experiments probing the behaviour of the urban system. An adaptive management approach deals with the unpredictable interactions between people and urban and ecological systems as they mutually evolve. The approach treats initial policies as hypotheses (simply stated predictions about how important community components will respond), and design and management as a set of experiments from which planners and other responsible agents can learn. If the practice succeeds, the hypothesis is affirmed; if it fails, the adaptive approach will still permit learning, so decisions can proceed from a better basis of understanding (Lee, 1993).

This differs from conventional urban development practice by emphasising the importance of feedbacks from the urban environment in shaping policy, followed by further systematic (non-random) experimentation to shape subsequent policy, action and so on. The process is iterative, based on social and institutional learning. Urban development can proceed by design that simultaneously allows for tests of different management policies and emphasises learning by doing. It is an inductive approach, relying on comparative studies that combine urban ecological theories with observation, local knowledge and active human interventions (Gunderson *et al.*, 1995).

Because an experimental demonstration project is an operational model, planning can and should act as a lead agency. Operational practice often leads formal policy rather than drawing up policy and political decisions to then initiate practice. Formalised policy adoption will then follow, well informed by attempts, experiments and experiences.

While this approach is relatively new, it is common-sense logic that emphasises learning by doing. In breaking down barriers between research, design and management, the adaptive approach resembles aspects of traditional – as in pre-formal planning or vernacular – urban systems. Because it proceeds in a stepwise fashion, responding to changes and guided by feedback from the urban landscape, community features and residents, adaptive management allows for institutional learning (Gunderson *et al.*, 1995). Like incremental practice, this relies on feedback and learning, and on the progressive accumulation of knowledge, often over long periods, However, the adaptive approach has the advantage of systematic experimentation and the incorporation of research into the overall process and scheme, while it also benefits from the considered experience from active study of precedents.

> Admonishing people to improve their learning will do little good; we will have to design social structures that nourish it. Developing a learning society will require many years of criticism, social experimentation, failed experiences, and a great deal of thinking and discussion. (Milbrath, 1989, p.88)

The approach involves double-loop learning (Argyris and Schön, 1978), requiring an adjustment of the norms that govern the action process – specifically, change in the actor's theory of reality, values, and beliefs – as a major cognitive reframing with far-reaching practical consequences for self-image, human relations, formal authority, and the ultimate distribution of the costs and benefits of action. A neighbourhood scale demonstration, where action informs strategy to overcome resistance, should be an environment for such learning. Friedmann (1987, p. 182) describes a model where social learning results from four combining elements:

1. action (purposeful activity, ongoing events to change reality); plus
2. political strategy and tactics (which tell us how to overcome resistance); plus
3. theories of reality (tell us what the world is like); plus
4. values (that inspire and direct the action); equals a form of social practice.

Demonstration project implementation with the intention of influencing planning and delivery system change is a profound form of social practice. Without concerted action, experience is not gained and learning does not occur. An innovative social learning system structure should:

1. enhance the probability of innovation
2. increase the opportunity for social practice
3. increase the opportunity for dialogue and face-to-face relations (Friedmann, 1976).

Undertaking a demonstration project sets up an important condition of bounded conflict for adaptive policies. The demonstration project is limited in its scale, content, applications and responsible agents. This can be seen as a pragmatic application of politics protecting the adaptive process by bringing a degree of discipline to the inevitable discord that arises from unavoided error. That is, adaptive project implementation can identify, challenge and force operational and structural change in very specific ways, but these are contained by the particular conditions for conflict established around the project. Complete consensus is not required or desired; conflict is bounded, so breakdown is unlikely and avoided. The focus on particular choices being articulated can open up alternatives not previously conceived, revealing a way forward. Planners help to inform new ways of thinking and all play a role in enlightening other participants in the process and problems.

Learning about the behaviour of urban systems is possible from interventions into populations and landscapes. Clear results can only be derived from experimentation when these interventions are large enough to bring about measurable change – incrementalism does not have this effect. Such larger changes can be expensive, risky and controversial, and therefore require negotiation and sound planning. Adaptive interventions should not be system wide. Rather, in learning about urban systems, an important strategy is to identify those interventions that can be quickly informative from small scale experiments and actions. This is consistent with the urban ecology approach as it more often deals with the specific local area but by strategic means. In other words, initiatives are often undertaken as priority projects within the framework of an overall plan and are exploratory to determine best approaches. For example, the Japanese refer to the production of demonstration areas as a strategy to a have a 'strong point', explaining that these are 'places to materialise the idea and aim of a green city' (City of Funabashi, 1994, p.14).

Demonstration has costs. While this planning approach has appeal at the operational level, from the political viewpoint the approach is challenging. Is our society willing to make sacrifices now to secure the future? Are our municipal organisations and communities prepared to invest in adaptive learning and experimentation? These questions need to be considered in contemplating demonstration action. Potential failures following public investments of time and resources are feared, in spite of the growing recognition that the predominant patterns of development have wide impacts and are evident failures. Investment in social learning is a strong, but under-recognised, indicator of directive change. As Lee states, 'How much social learning can be afforded in particular times and places affects how quickly development can become sustainable' (1993, p.113).

Describing the characteristics of a social and political climate that will support such experimentation, and how these characteristics, barriers and challenges can be encouraged, needs further verification. Postulates for the current condition of slow implementation of sustainable community planning and design practice can be found in the crisis, conflict, innovation lethargy and gridlock of cities where the problem and responses continue to have the following characteristics:

- piecemeal policy and many single, often unrelated, targets (codes, standards, regulations);
- a single scale of focus, typically short term and site specific;
- no recognition that all policies are experimental; and
- rigid management with no priority (and an underdeveloped capacity) to design interventions as ways to test hypotheses underlying policies.

This condition (pathology) can be overcome when community planning is seen not as a procedural issue of industrial control, but as a strategic process of adaptive management, undertaken at the appropriate scale, with a better understanding of human behaviour. Holling (1995, p. 9) advises that reorientation requires:

- integrated policies, rather than piecemeal ones;
- flexible, adaptive policies, rather than rigid locked-in ones;
- management and planning for learning, not simply for economic or social 'product';
- monitoring as a part of active interventions to achieve understanding and to identify remedial responses, not monitoring for its own sake; and
- citizen involvement and partnership to build 'civic science' (Lee, 1993), not public information programmes to inform passively.

In the previous sections, experimental planning and design projects, their characteristics and performance features have been considered, and justification for an experimental and adaptive approach has been identified. An expanded conception of demonstration is outlined next.

An expanded conception of demonstration

The conception of a demonstration as a product for education and to support adoption of innovations has a long history in urban planning and architecture. Examples are Crystal Palace in 1851, the garden city at Letchworth (see note 5), the Berlin IBA in 1987, Ecolonia in 1994 and Emscher Park in 1999. These functions continue in the many projects focusing on eco-efficient production and eco-sufficient consumption sectors, with efforts concentrated within the areas of energy consumption and supply, water consumption and waste water, waste handling, indoor climate, environmentally-friendly materials, life cycle analysis, full cost pricing and planning tools. This conception of demonstration has been referred to variously as (see van Vliet, 1999):

- providing a medium for public education and awareness-building and serving to convene experts for evaluative research and appraisal of projects;
- a model for an exemplary medium- to high-density residential community;
- a powerful form (with design competitions) of technology transfer – giving experience and providing inspiration;
- a complex communication medium for diffusion of innovation;
- generating substantial interest within the design community and construction industry, leading to many practitioners 'buying in' to new ideas – providing the necessary performance data to convince sceptical designers and owners;
- testing of innovative designs, which can be refined prior to broader replication;
- serving to develop and verify performance standards within experimental projects, and to develop design components that can be incorporated into future projects;
- a means to make visible and available many kinds of information;
- a context or platform for trialability;
- speeding adoption of 'green' technologies and field test performance requirements; and
- assisting with the spread of knowledge about improved practice.

Blowers declares such projects 'more effective than writing and talking in changing attitudes and improving standards generally as a practical example in which theory is tested and opportunities provided for experiment and for generating new ideas' (1993, p.204).

As important and necessary as this view of demonstration continues to be, the study findings (van Vliet, 1999) point to an expanded conception of demonstration. The Egebjerggård research shows empirically how a demonstration project can be an effective development instrument as a 'staging area' or 'halfway house' for organisational change, policy development and improved practice. It is a good example of development demonstration, because the process of its implementation changed the very systems and means to realise the ends. It was a transformation process, not only a production process, directed toward the marketing of better practices. The example showed how a neighbourhood can be built to integrate environmental considerations while bridging traditional professional disciplines, administrations, the public and private sectors, residents and authorities, and how municipal planning can be used and developed as a suitable tool for setting priorities for general plans for the urban environment. Undertaking the demonstration within an experimental framework became a process of discovering what is possible and how to change processes and operations using new approaches to build capacity, and to provide visible, instructive, educative, experiential examples. In this regard, demonstration has been referred to specifically as:

- a zone for innovation and developmental learning, for institutionalising intelligence through collective action;
- an opportunity to develop tools and processes for conceptualisation and testing ideas in practice and for practising the cycle of thinking, doing, evaluation, and reflecting; or stated otherwise theory, strategy, vision and action;
- a way to influence system change towards more sustainable community planning and design as an example of a profound form of social practice;
- a form of consensus, as it results from the process of planning, design and realisation;
- a part of a social movement promoting alternatives (innovative sustainability features) that are not emerging otherwise in a particular context (depending on its ingredients and the extent of diffusion);
- a more psychologically sophisticated approach to altering resource consumptive behaviour than the 'rational-economic model' of human behaviour and conservation curtailment directed at the individual;
- part of a process of individual and social learning, with its intended function to speed social change, on a large scale;
- a needed institution that integrates decision making on economic and ecological issues together and are open to popular participation;
- an initiative to bring the future into the present (by doing things now that anticipate a possible and appreciable tomorrow);
- an opportunity for inter-sectoral action that can be implemented by private public partnerships;
- a viable tactic to alter the dynamics of the delivery system context and one having a sufficiently developmental role to contribute significantly to overcoming barriers to sustainability; and
- a strategy for confronting barriers and deriving more consistent gains than former practice.

While the above set of descriptions share some redundancies, they can be seen as mutually consistent and complementary, serving to broaden the substantial developmental role for demonstration. This role appears to be poorly understood and is seldom acknowledged in community planning in many countries. These functions, in combination with the potential for education and policy development, make demonstration an essential part of a sustainable development strategy. They suggest that demonstration projects will be a critical catalyst in developing an improved and restructured planning framework.

Sustainable development will only occur where it is a deliberate strategy. A basic assumption in this chapter is that urban ecosystem management is necessary, requiring fundamentally different approaches, not mere tinkering with current models and practices. The social-ecological practices, mechanisms and principles identified have the potential to improve conventional urban development by providing: insights for designing adaptive demonstration projects and management systems that flow with nature; novel approaches to site planning, housing, streets, open space, energy and water; lessons for developing systems of social interactions and sanctions, and successful implementation and enforcement of more sustainable practices; means to avoid surprises caused by conventional approaches; and experience in managing fluctuations and disturbance. Learning from local social-ecological systems, and combining insights gained in adaptive approaches through demonstration, may counteract many of the prevailing crises of conventional urban development in achieving sustainable urban form.

Notes

1. For example, Aldous (1992) recommended 'urban village' developments as model projects, emphasising mixed use, mixed occupancy, house type diversity and good urban design as ways to influence developers, the financial community, planners and conservationists.

2. This is not to say that the type and extent of support in Europe has been adequate to the task, only that it has begun, which is not the case in, for example, Canada. This is due in part to the nature of the supra-national level of spatial policy development, and to the lack of direct links between spatial and environmental planning in North America.

3. With built projects, and with the extent of innovation, the comparison with experiments is difficult as they are not carried out with a neutrality of outcomes. Longer-term actions require commitment. They are abandoned only when their unworkability is clearly evident, and even then the failure might be compromised by seeking the reason for failure elsewhere. However, it should be more widely understood that validation in science is a dynamic social process, not the dispassionate practice most assume (Goldsmith, 1992).

4. There is controversy about the number of measures that should be included in a community scale project. The evaluation of Ecolonia (Novem, 1995) states that where many innovations are introduced at the same time, it is difficult to quantify the effects of each measure, and when residents' attitudes are involved, it is difficult to determine accurately which measures are reproducible and which are not. Conservatives suggest a few clear features, while others say this makes a project less informative. Lee (1993) feels that when experiments are involved, the bias should be to explore as many hypotheses as possible, where each experiment is designed inexpensively. Lee states that 'Given the scarcity of current knowledge, more can be learned from crude experiments probing different aspects of ecological [and urban] systems than can be learned from refined measurements of theories that may turn out to be irrelevant even if correct' (p.177).

5. Raymond Unwin, responding to the propositions of Ebenezer Howard, drew up 'Letchworth, the first garden city attempt, a demonstration project undertaken by a private association' (Mumford, 1938, p.399).

Michael Crilly and Adam Mannis
Sustainable Urban Management Systems

Introduction

The authors explore the dynamic aspects of urban change and definitions of sustainable urban form in the development of a low-level Geographical Information Systems (GIS) framework for spatial urban design indicators and a linked methodological 'tool kit'. The aims of such a framework are to think holistically about the development and management of complex urban systems and to suggest a locality specific approach to understanding and communicating the totality of the system in a way that is beneficial to a variety of urban decision makers. The resulting urban management tool is tested in a number of different urban archetypes and policy/application scenarios to provide case-study evidence of practical local sustainability.

The nature of urban planning, management and decision making
Theoretical context

The roots of current problems associated with our understanding of sustainable urban form lie in the notion of 'separation'. Continuing work in the area of sustainable development has emphasised the holistic nature of the concept but has then gone on to compartmentalise, sectorise and separate individual issues, specific scales of investigation and the substantive response from the analytical and procedural theories. The continuing conceptual evolution of sustainability paralleled with the dynamic nature of physical, socio-economic and demographic change within cities have also been considered in isolation from urban form. As a result there is *confusion* over meanings and definitions, *contradictions* between topic-based advice, and *conflicts* with competing and incomparable trade-offs. Overall, our response and thinking has been sub-optimal rather than systemic.

Most importantly, there is separation between research and practice (Clark *et al.*, 1995). Academic work on sustainable urban form is instigated on an expert rather than a multidisciplinary basis. Evidence of integration is between similar physical empirical issues and, excluding a few noticeable exceptions, work is typically prescriptive, generic, thematic and requires end-users to integrate the findings into their own wider context, thus requiring a certain level of expert knowledge for any useful application of the research findings.

Urban policy makers and decision makers approach the challenges of the sustainable city from a very different starting point. They are constrained by time, resources (staff and financial), institutional frameworks and statutory responsibilities. They increasingly tend to be more concerned with making decisions, both reactive and proactive, on a basis of overall effect, and there is often an uncritical acceptance of generic research findings despite variances in local contexts, conditions and communities (Crilly *et al.*, 1999).

The development of a practical framework for sustainable urban form requires recognition of such 'separations' and needs to identify ways in which they can be reconciled. The basis for a framework for improved decision making is an understanding of the needs, applications and appropriate means of communication of individuals and organisations who have a role in the planning and management of urban areas. A 'bottom-up', populist and non-empirical approach to designing and testing a framework for sustainable urban form based on these requirements is the theoretical basis of a Sustainable Urban Management System (SUMS).

Practical context and end-user prerequisites

The first requirement for a practical framework of urban planning and management is the recognition that a basic understanding of our complex urban systems and the interconnections between issues is more productive than in-depth investigations into any singular aspects of physical design (Alger, 1990; O'Regan and Moles, 1997). The need for a comprehensive overview is also central to the holistic nature of sustainable development. Thus, we argue that systemic thinking is the central practitioners' prerequisite for operationalising the concept of sustainable urban development. A systems based approach allows us to go beyond the question of what we build, and link issues of 'goal-setting' and processes with those of physical urban form. When we begin to consider the totality of urban systems we tend towards real-life scenarios, where decision making is based on spatial systems rather than thematic concerns. 'Understanding ... (the urban system) ..., how it is structured, how it changes and impacts on peoples lives, is "policy-relevant"' (Smith and Timberlake, 1995, p.94). The characteristics and advantages of thinking systemically about a framework for urban decision making are:

- Our understanding of urban systems will be based upon a multi-variant and integrated reflection of real-life complexity (Goldsmith, 1978; Clayton and Radcliffe, 1996).
- Responses will be locality specific (Smith and Timberlake, 1995), non-prescriptive and non-scale dependent.
- Understanding the co-evolution of sustainable development and non-linear urban systems will reflect the temporal/dynamic aspects to meeting needs, changing definitions and emphases within sustainable development, thereby avoiding 'end-state' planning.
- Any decision making framework will be flexible/adaptable to ensure feedback mechanisms between process and product.

The rationale of a SUMS is to think systemically and overcome current problems of separation by starting from a *consensus* at a conceptual level; a consensus based on the meaning of sustainability rather than the implementation of the concept. It is an analytical/flexible rather than a substantive and prescriptive staring point. It then has a framework able to reflect the *complexity* within urban systems, and adapt during *consultation* with end-users to ensure feedback over the usefulness and functionality of the framework. In effect, it suggests adopting a 'bottom-up' approach to urban systems focused on the specific requirements and geographical scales of decision makers, breaking down the notion of deterministic theories and replacing them with non-generic responses – responses that by nature must be criteria based and design-led. The framework is intended to provide responses to issues of sustainable urban form that will be policy relevant (Local Agenda 21, statutory land use/spatial planning), reactive to changing needs, participative, accessible, understandable and meaningful. A SUMS stresses the importance of the utility of an approach that is based upon an understanding of 'real world complexity' (Goldsmith, 1978, p.306) rather than the behaviour of a mathematical model.

In balance, there are limitations of a systems approach to developing an urban management tool. Ultimately, it is a 'technocratic diversion' (Ferguson, 1975) to empirically model every aspect of a system as complex as a city. Within any overview there will be concerns over data error and reliability, information 'gaps' and limitations (often caused by empirical and public domain bias). Additional concerns include metadata (precision and reliability), objectivity and attribute weighting, data practicality and resource implications. However, many such concerns over systems modelling are also applicable to a critique of sub-optimal modelling.

System rationale for a new type of urban model

Some of the concerns of a systems approach can be addressed by developing a SUMS as an urban 'model' aimed at improving our understanding of complex and dynamic urban systems rather than being a predictive tool.

Rees has argued that we need to rethink how we define our urban areas '… conceptually and in spatial terms' (1997, p.308) in a way that recognises the city as a 'parasitic subsystem' within any spatial hierarchy. We require conceptual tools and methodologies to improve knowledge and understanding of interaction and dependence between different levels of spatial abstraction – natural ecosystems, city-region/urban hinterland, urban neighbourhoods and households. These 'concepts' of urban systems should allow us to map linkages, trends and relationships. Concepts of cities as 'multilayered networks' of resource flows (Smith and Timberlake, 1995), 'ecosystems' and polycentric communities all have similar components. In this context, commentators have argued that sustainability demands a new type of urban model – one that: is flexible and non-determinate, being more of '… an interactive methodology rather than a model' (Clark *et al.*, 1995, p.85); has a spatial dimension (Wallner *et al.*, 1996) where boundaries, as the interfaces between different systems, help us determine structure and interactions internal and external to the specific area being modelled; and values monitoring, and links forecasting with feedback to check 'homeostasis' (system diversity and resilience) and to correct errors (Grossman and Watt, 1992). Ultimately, we require an urban model that aims to improve understanding and decision making rather than being concerned with a representation of reality. The system, in use, must be systemic, flexible, simple to use and objective. Information within the model will be based on the principle of 'Best Available Data Not Entailing Excessive Costs' (BADNEEC).

Spatial indicators of sustainable urban form

System requirements and limitations/concerns can best be met by the use of indicators – proxy measures of sustainable development packaged together to meet the requirements of thematic scope, linkages between issues and ease of communication/understanding. A 'package' of indicators can raise public understanding of sustainable development by providing an overview that highlights many of the links between the different facets in a manner which shows correlation if not also causality.

The spatial representation of indicators of sustainable urban design is a means of representing the nature of the urban system; ensuring a direct significance to issues of quality of life, physical design and urban form, while ensuring objectivity in highlighting linkages. It allows end-users to recognise patterns, 'hotspots' and connections between two or more indicators – addressing the prime concern that indicators are integrated and understood as a set of measures. A complex spatial systems model can allow us to '… describe the connected behaviour of sub-systems' (Allen, 1997, p.107), linking existing modelling and areas of policy work through an adaptable framework for spatial indicators of sustainable urban design. It can also help identify repeating patterns at micro and macro scale that are linked (Wallner *et al.*, 1996) and coexistent (Allen, 1997).

System design
Establishing a framework for spatial indicators of sustainable urban form

An understanding of complexity within our urban systems and a bringing together of concepts implicit and explicit in the chronology of institutional, governmental and academic ideas within both the analytical and procedural debates forms the conceptual basis for the linked attributes and choice of spatial indicators. The SUMS adopts a semi-hierarchical structure of these broad concepts, attributes and measurable spatial indicators (Table 1). There are many overlapping indicators with shared attributes within this framework where the significance is the breadth and range of indicators (including goal setting and procedural/management indicators) and their presentation and integration on a spatial basis.

Commonality of concepts	Attributes specific to urban design	Range of possible spatial indicators
Holism Self-sufficiency Carrying capacity Social justice Participation	size/critical mass, economic and social diversity, energy and food production, important habitats, new forms and features, designing out crime, recycling and waste reduction, energy efficiency, hierarchy of protection, traffic congestion, urban carrying capacity, range and diversity of facilities and services, accessibility and levels of permeability, healthy and safe environments, social limits as 'contextual absolutes', aesthetics and beauty, urban quality, reducing inequalities, emphasis to the disadvantaged, decentralised decision making, individual choice, political acceptability	impact upon surrounding communities and ecosystems, planning policy context, size and limit, sustainable energy strategy, building/block height and depth, open space provision, sacred structures as critical assets, parking space standards, segregation of public/private open space, subdivision of spaces, control and personalisation, mixed uses, densities and space efficiency, accommodation, access, robustness and resilience, availability of public transport, active frontages, transport road use, barrier free environment, urban image/townscape, 'sense of place', local identity/urban quality, participation and feedback,

Table. 1. A conceptual presentation of spatial indicators of sustainable urban design.

The transference of this adaptive framework for spatial indicators into an operational context poses a series of questions relating to system design. Significant elements are dependent upon the nature and availability of data being used. Ideally, a hierarchical data structure would be adopted where the level of detail increases as scale reduces – effectively, using 'information subsidiarity' where there is a match between the level of abstraction, form of spatial data and the user needs at their appropriate scale of decision making. However, data availability, in terms of thematic extent and spatial abstraction, constrains the basic starting point to applying a SUMS as a conceptual framework.

Data collection tool kit
The practicality of a SUMS as a conceptual framework is that it can link to a range of appropriate low-cost data collection methodologies. If the framework is to be useful then it must be possible to gain the breadth of indicator data within acceptable cost, time and technical constraints. This means a pragmatic approach to the adaptation of existing data collection methods to suit the area under investigation.

In the application and testing of the SUMS, pilot projects set within a range of urban typologies were undertaken to test the range of data collection methods appropriate for the 'tool kit'. In all of these, the first task was to systematically undertake a basic *inventory* of secondary information sources and public domain data comprising data source, time series/ trend availability, spatial scale/resolution (vector or raster) and the possibility of geo-referencing non-spatial data, comparative figures and cost of acquisition. This process highlights data gaps where primary data collection is required to ensure the broad thematic scope of sustainability is achieved and to avoid the trap of being limited by existing data availability. The identification of data 'gaps' can be thematic, scale-dependent or due to problems of data reliability.

The findings from the pilot projects and applications suggest that the key areas of omission of data relevant to urban design are *qualitative* and *spatial*. Public data collection is dominated by the needs of empirical monitoring, and fails to address key areas of qualitative research, such as perceptions and attitudes and their links with individual household behaviour. In addition, spatial referencing is based on institutional boundaries, creating problems in disaggregating data at a scale appropriate to an urban designer or a community organisation. These limitations have implications for spatial database structures and design.

There are differences between three-dimensional grid/spreadsheet data (normally regional/ sub-regional datasets based upon externally defined administrative areas) and geo-spatial data models (physical and cognitive elements) that include user-defined areas of concern and levels of data abstraction. A SUMS requires a range of mixed data collection methodologies appropriate to the technical and resource limitations of the end-user organisation to help fill the identified data 'gaps', both qualitative data and spatialisation. A number of qualitative data collection methods – customising traditional sociological methods, using complementary mixed and multi-method tools (mixed scanning) – have been used within the pilot projects.

Understanding the spatial and qualitative dimensions

The focus of the system is on rigorous ways of understanding the totality of relationships within urban systems and *describing* and *communicating* spatial attributes as a precursor to any sub-system applications. The framework should be descriptive '… without expectation of causal explanation' (Stake, 1995, p.38) and be constructed using mixed (qualitative and quantitative) methods. Adopting a variety of methods, both numerical and non-numerical, can help in overcoming difficulties in data availability, and is a reflection of epistemology in methodology.

Qualitative urban design scale indicators need to link methods of collection to data representation on a spatial basis. An audit of subjective design issues and aesthetics can include an appraisal of the physical context or policy environment (designations and/or planning decisions). A common thread in suggestions for a conservation/design checklist has been a reliance on the description and assessment of qualitative factors in empirical form (Guise, 1995) or a local adaptation of traditional townscape analysis techniques – in the form of annotated maps (Bentley *et al.*, 1985). Such approaches have been adapted in the pilot projects to be supplementary and complementary to quantitative datasets but have been extended to cover issues of attitudes and perceptions (Table 2).

Within the framework, the exact choice of methods and primacy of results is purely pragmatic and will relate to local circumstances, constraints and choices. This is a pluralist approach that recognises that choice has to be exercised in data collection, as not all techniques will be appropriate or possible within any local context. This is particularly true when working within real-world constraints of time and money. As the nature and scale of urban communities are unique, the theoretical basis is influenced by *grounded theory* (Glaser and Strauss, 1967) which argues for contextualism as a means for integrating a variety of methodologies and linking meaning to complex situations/events on a case study basis. Essentially, this means the choice of what to collect, and where and how to sample are factors grounded in the researcher's (individual's, community group's or local authority's) understanding of the locality. The actual methodological approaches adopted will be varied and may only emerge when applying the conceptual framework: the selection of the appropriate methodology should be seen as a dynamic process where the applicability of the results and the needs of the end-users are the prime concerns. According to Philip '... freeing up epistemological space frees up methodological space, creating room for combined-methods research' (1998, p.263).

Examples of data collection techniques and methodologies	Key references and examples for adapted methodology
'Planning for Real' and community visioning	Wates (1996), Poterfield and Hall (1995), LGMB (1996), Levett (1997)
Narrative and content analysis (including the use of texts as secondary sources)	Burgess and Bryman (1994), Denzin (1972), George (1959)
Discourse analysis (unstructured qualitative data from interview text and other verbal accounts)	Spradley (1980), Finger and Kilcoyne (1995)
Cognitive mapping	Lynch (1990), Downs (1982)
Participant observation (active and passive)	Foot-Whyte (1943), Hester (1987), Perkins (1988)
Photographic survey (physical and historical/cultural)	Lynch (1990), Appleyard (1981)
Phenomenological questioning (open-ended questioning focusing upon meanings)	Bogan and Taylor (1975), Rowland (1973)
Neighbourhood mapping	Lee (1976)
Social networks	Frankenberg (1966), Golledge (1978)

Table. 2. A tool kit for spatial and qualitative data collection within a given epistemological position concerning the nature of urban systems and the needs of policy relevant applications.

It seems that most practitioners and applied researchers have followed a similar, necessarily pragmatic path that is not confined by epistemology and which is, in essence, a revision of Etzioni's (1967) *mixed scanning* approach to methodology. The central concerns are: a contextualisation of the community; generating an understanding of diversity within the community; and issues of decision making and management (Kaufman and Jacobs, 1987). What is new in this revision is an application starting at a community level and thus allowing for the inclusion and integration of many subjective and behavioural elements which can only be obtained from individuals.

Objectivity in data collection

There is a distinction between *hard* (empirical) and *soft* (qualitative) forms of research as distinct paradigms, and different weight is given to each within decision support frameworks. The focus of *soft* qualitative research is on meaning and understanding. From a review of approaches adopted, it is clear that an additional split can be made between *collection* and *analysis* of qualitative data (Okely, 1994). *Collection* methods for qualitative data are characterised by informality and open-endedness in the scope of sources used and in the manner of interviewing, participant observation and/or content analysis. Methods of *analysis* are more intuitive, descriptive, creative and ultimately personal, in spite of attempts at objectivity. Other, apparently positivist, approaches to analysis, as characterised by empirical indicators, are still derived from the analysis of the measurable attributes of qualitative fieldwork and as such do not surpass subjectivity.

In practice, it must be recognised that qualitative inquiry is subjective and while total objectivity is desirable it is unachievable. Ultimately, a range of data collection methods (formal and informal) and analytical approaches (empirical and descriptive) should provide a clearer understanding of the social process under investigation. For example, a range of information relating to household energy use, activities, attitudes and values/concerns is more meaningful than a single figure for energy use for linking to activities aimed at changing behaviour. Adopted research methods should be mixed and appropriate. Epistemological concerns surrounding objectivity and attribute weighting are typical of much qualitative social research and should not on their own suggest any priority should be placed on empirical data or the translation of qualitative sources into empirical results. There is the danger of losing meaning when an attempt is made to quantify qualitative data. The preferred alternative is to acknowledge any subjectivity and improve methods of qualitative data collection, including spatial and visual techniques, and communication to aid understanding. As Stake comments, 'There are times when all researchers are going to be interpretive, holistic ... and uninterested in cause, and then, by definition, they will be qualitative inquirers' (1995, p.46).

Developing a common basis for integration and analysis

The development of a comprehensive holistic model for understanding urban systems poses an additional question concerning the integration of the social and psychological dimensions with the geophysical on a basis that allows for comparison and analysis. This is best achieved on a constant spatial basis where Cartesian maps of geophysical attributes are integrated with maps of social processes and cognitive constructs with attached geo-referenced attributes relating to these soft systems. This spatial integration is both 'graphical' and 'intellectual' (Stringer, 1999). This conceptual model of overlying spatial attributes comes with the significant proviso that issues of individual/collective data, map errors and dynamic factors are adequately addressed through methodology selection and design.

> It means that our map of the city has to have overlapping layers to show its physical, social and psychological geometry at the same time. This is consistent with socio-spatial approaches in social philosophy, urban geography, urban sociology and architecture which address these dimensions simultaneously and focus on the dynamic interrelationship of these aspects. (Madanipour, 1996, p.87)

Figures 1 to 4 show spatial and qualitative data collection methods tested in real life case studies as part of a 'tool kit' of techniques.

System operation
Information needs and technological developments

The development of user friendly information services, shared information sources, the strengthening of electronic networks, and better use of indigenous knowledge has become recognised as central to Local Agenda 21 activities '... in the broad sense that includes data, information, appropriately packaged experience and knowledge' (UNCED, 1992, p.284). Local Agenda 21 places special emphasis on the transformation of existing information into forms more useful for decision making, and on targeting information at different user groups, through the application of information technology (IT).

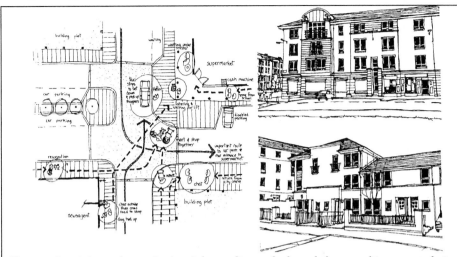

The use of participant observation/spatial recording methods, and photographic survey techniques at Crown Street, Glasgow – Participant observation/spatial recording methods (after Hester, 1985, 1987) and photographic survey techniques (after Lynch, 1990) were used to investigate social interaction and urban change within the redevelopment of the Crown Street 'Urban Village', Glasgow. This provides a record of physical layouts and how the resultant streets and space are used, making social interaction, meaning and activities spatial indicators.

Fig. 1. participant observation/ spatial recording methods provide a record of physical layouts and how the resultant streets and space are used.

Increases in computing power and storage capacity, alongside falling prices in real terms and dramatic reductions in the size of installation, have been the major changes occurring in the hardware sector over recent years. Every year, more computing power is available to the average user at lower cost, making hardware more easily available to many individuals and most institutions. This increased power has resulted in a broadening range of users of GIS technology. GIS is no longer seen as the high-level preserve of scientists, academics and engineers, being increasingly used for low-level applications in planning, resource management, economics, teaching, landscape and urban design.

Integration and digitisation

The integrated approach to decision making, as argued for by both high- and low-level users, can be facilitated by GIS. GIS improves '… the use of data at all stages of planning and management, making systematic and simultaneous use of social, economic, developmental, ecological and environmental data, as well as stressing interactions and synergisms in analysis' (UNCED, 1992, p.66). Integration by GIS provides 'information synergy' since disparate data sources (information of different scales, sources, construction/system design) can be linked together on a common basis. The key to the application of GIS technology is the underlying database structure – containing both geometric data (co-ordinates, shapes and topological information overlays) and associated attribute data (information describing the properties of spatial objects – numerical, string and Boolean).

GIS have been defined as systems for capturing, retaining, checking, integrating, manipulating, analysing and displaying data which are referenced spatially to the earth (DoE, 1987). From an urban designer's viewpoint, the most significant advantages of GIS, compared with traditional mapping packages, are:

- The potential to store and integrate, on a consistent basis, large amounts of spatially referenced information and data from a variety of sources.
- The unique spatial presentation of information in a form which is more comprehensible to decision makers and a wide range of end-users (who may not be able to readily or rapidly distil knowledge from pages of tabular data).
- The ability to simulate the impact of policy choices.

However, the potential role of GIS is more than as a common denominator in linking datasets, it provides a framework for the attribute data that can be worked interactively to reveal new patterns and relationships between attributes.

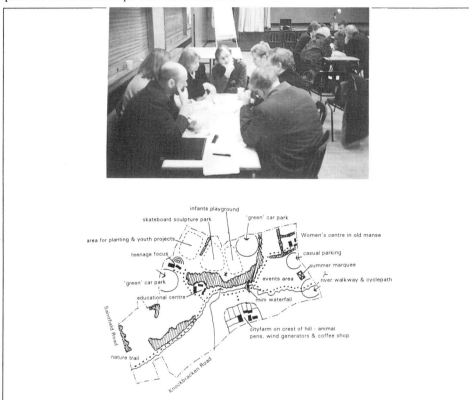

Fig. 2. The Cairnshill Residents' Association taking part in a Planning for Real exercise and part of the resultant masterplan.

The use of subjective and spatial data collection methods in Community Visioning and Planning for Real events by the Cairnshill Residents' Association – Subjective and spatial data collection methods can be combined in participative approaches to urban design such as community visioning and Planning for Real events, where group working can produce collective rather than individual spatial constructs. Approaches to mapping neighbourhood objectives and aspirations can be tailored to the limitations and requirements of a community organisation. On the periphery of the Belfast urban area, the Cairnshill Residents' Association, with the assistance of the Irish Sustainable Housing Association, adopted such an approach to produce a community master plan for use in a local planning inquiry, addressing both the primary use of the 'whiteland' (to rectify local under-provision of open space and community facilities) and as a pragmatic alternative to developer led schemes and the inadequate indicative layout suggested by the local planning authority (DoE NI, 1996). This was in addition, and complementary, to figures relating to housing need, community facilities and open space provision and the findings of a household survey on development preferences.

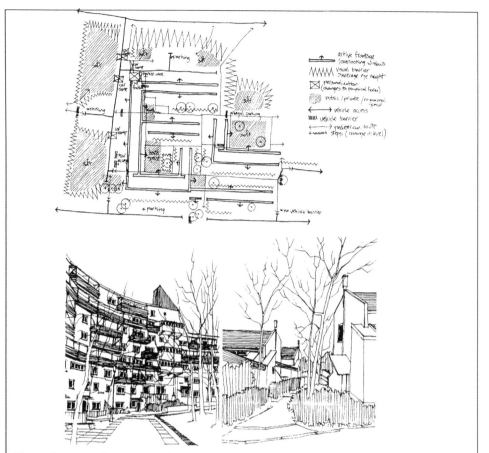

The application of indicators of 'social environmental learning' by individuals and community representatives from the inner city Byker Estate, Newcastle upon Tyne – The application of indicators of 'social environmental learning' (Finger and Kilcoyne, 1995) (levels of involvement, transformation, adaptation and community building) can give a picture of linked social and physical change, related to the number and range of actors involved in an urban redevelopment and how attitudes and perceptions develop over time. These dynamic issues of adaptability and resilience are given a spatial dimension and documentation, as described and mapped by individuals and community representatives on a walking tour of the inner city Byker Estate, Newcastle upon Tyne.

Fig. 3. Mapped responses by individuals and community representatives on a walking tour of the Byker Estate and sketches of the Estate.

Technocratic analysis

The development of indicators of sustainable development throughout a range of UK local authorities has provided the impetus for a number of GIS projects, concerned with illustrating linkages between individual indicators and investigating the distributional effects and implications for social equity. Lancashire County Council's (1997) *Green Audit 2* shows how indicators vary across the county, utilising polygon (ward based socio-economic measures), point (wildlife areas) and line (rivers) based attributes. Similar indicators developed by Cardiff City Council (LGMB, 1995) are being linked to a GIS based model for energy and environmental planning (Jones, 1996). GIS is being used as an information retrieval system, helping to explore some of the existing relationships between the spatial indicators and defining new data relationships. Recent developments in quantitative (or mathematical) geography are increasingly adopting GIS for statistical analysis (Philip, 1998) and the investigation of distributional effects.

211

Quality and Density of Development

A — 3-4 storey modern townhouses (approx. 30 dwellings per acre)

B — 2-3 storey Victorian terrace (20-25 dwellings per acre)

C — 1960's 3 storey flats (approx. 25 dwellings per acre)

D — 2 storey modern terrace (15-20 dwellings per acre)

E — 2 storey Victorian terrace (approx. 20 dwellings per acre)

F — 1970's 2 storey terrace (15-20 dwellings per acre)

G — Modern detached bungalows (10-12 dwellings per acre)

H — Inter-war detached bungalows (8-10 dwellings per acre)

J — Post-war detached bungalows (approx. 8 dwellings per acre)

Fig. 4. An extract from a qualitative household survey undertaken in the development of a SUMS for Carrickfergus.

A qualitative approach to assessing the built environment in Carrickfergus – The illustrations above are an extract from a qualitative household survey undertaken in the development of a SUMS for the historic commuter town of Carrickfergus (approximate resident population 35,000), nine miles north of Belfast. Stated preference and open-ended questions were combined to link perceptions and attitudinal responses to urban design, quality and residential density.

The exploration of existing spatial relationships is possible because GIS allows for objects (single point) and fields (continuous surface) to have multiple attributes that share the same data structures. This is useful within a policy context where a GIS project can use traditional geographical analytical tools and methods applied to spatial data sets to correlate and quantify a relationship between attributes. Walford (1995) has argued that GIS is the most appropriate tool for defining new data relationships and understanding their spatial patterns. Techniques and methods such as point/line density and distribution, adjacency and nearest neighbour analysis, and line connectivity (trees and circuits) can be used to integrate data sets within a GIS project. The role of GIS as a data integrator is further enhanced when it is linked to statistical computer packages such as SPSS (statistical package for the social sciences) (albeit with only the 'table' as a basic data model) where the analogy between the systems is valid.

However, the application of expert analytical tools and the linking with predictive models within GIS can have the effect of making the technology appear technocratic, and the specialist remit of designers, geographers and planners. We need to remember that however we structure and analyse our data, 'geometric reality' will only ever be a representative model of reality. It will be limited in its ability to add dynamics or temporality to spatial databases, investigate three dimensions in a two-dimensional framework (for example, the land use applications of Webster, 1990) and by the lack of availability of reliable data (Burrough, 1992).

In this context, Fedra (1993) argues that it is more important to ensure the GIS tool is useful to the policy maker within an easy-to-use decision support framework, rather than to attempt to overcome the technical problems associated with the GIS computer architecture required to allow for fully integrated spatial modelling. Most of the limitations of GIS in environmental modelling relate to high-level problem solving and not to supporting policy decisions and other low-level applications.

Democratic communication

At the level of policy making, it is most desirable to integrate predictive environmental models into the decision making process by using GIS as a means of data capture and/or visualisation, where the output is displayed on a spatial/map background. The European CORINE (Co-ordination of Information on the Environment) programme is one example where GIS has been used for data presentation rather than for the use of its analytical facilities (Allen, 1996). The development of a GIS based model for Cardiff (Jones, 1996) is linking a series of existing sub-models (prediction of building energy use, SATURN transport model, traffic emissions) through a common spatial framework. Again, the major role of GIS software is in the presentation: axial and thematic mapping of the various attributes under investigation. Similar work in Swindon (Steadman, 1996) is also concerned with linking existing energy and transportation models through the medium of GIS. Where data manipulation and analysis has occurred wholly with a GIS environment, it has tended to be simple models based on specific query building which in turn provide simple answers in the form of single words and/or numbers (Nyerges, 1993). Again the limiting factor in the development of these models is the extensive data collection required and this suggests that the more successful GIS projects are those with the flexibility and adaptability to become tailored to make best use of public domain data and incorporate low-cost primary data.

Theoretically, the scale of GIS investigation is only constrained by data availability and the IT skills of the end-user. Yet the potential of GIS has been significantly under-utilised at a community level and in the investigation of urban design relationships. It is at this scale that a SUMS operates and at this scale that the limitations of data collection experienced at higher levels of application, abstraction and analysis can be most easily overcome. The low-cost approaches outlined in the methodology 'tool kit' are appropriate for the use of non-experts such as community groups, schools, local business and special interest/civic organisations. The processes of indicator definition, data collection and system design in developing a SUMS can be beneficial for consensus-building and raising awareness of sustainability. It is an accessible framework that can be useful for improving local democracy as well as providing a framework for data analysis at a high-level application.

A SUMS sets in place a common spatial (digital) database to be used for design, assessment/

evaluation and monitoring of urban systems – becoming a fully integrated, multi-use/stage decision making tool for a range of different end-users at a variety of data abstraction levels. A SUMS utilises data collected by local interests, and benefits from GIS capabilities as a '... "toolbox"... for geographic data manipulation' (Martin, 1996, p.185), becoming dynamic in its operation and updating, linking traditionally discrete stages in policy planning and design, providing synergy, and highlighting overlapping concerns between different interest groups.

The interactive dimension

Multi-media products present information in an interactive way, by combining digitally processed text, speech, sound, graphics and video. Applications of multi-media have increased substantially in recent years, due in part to the effects of increased hardware performance at reasonable cost, and the development of accessible software. A SUMS merges multi-media with GIS by providing geo-referenced 'hotlinks' to a range of multi-media files, which are made up of qualitative data sources. A SUMS then becomes an important 'map-based' interface that makes a common spatial database accessible and easy to use for a variety of environmental monitoring, assessment, design, and didactic applications.

Concerns have been raised over the power of maps to persuade (Wood, 1992) and the fear that '... the digital medium inevitably carries more authority than the paper' (Martin, 1996, p.160) because it represents both data and the results of complex spatial analysis of the data. If it is true that more weight in decision making is due to the use and application of GIS and IT, we need to be aware of who controls the technology, how accessible it is and how it is understood. One response to these concerns is the adoption and continuing development of a non-expert interface to GIS (Yoshikawa, 1997) where '... the map of the future [*may*] be manipulated, interrogated, and analysed using Virtual Reality tools' (Taylor, 1996, p.20). In each case there is a premise that improved visualisation of data can help to open up the planning system and decision making to greater public scrutiny and understanding. A SUMS demonstrates the benefits and potential for this approach in improved urban management at the local, community based level. GIS is a tool for integrating, communicating, interacting with and analysing overlying spatial indicators.

Summary and conclusions

Sustainable urban form is influenced by the dynamism of complex urban systems and the changing nature of definitions of quality of life. In this theoretical framework, decision makers are more concerned with understanding trends and linkages than predictions. One means of integrating disparate data sets, each representing separate attributes (qualitative and quantitative indicators) of an urban system, is to spatialise the information. This approach has a number of benefits in helping to communicate information to a range of interest groups, including simplicity in understanding the nature of the data and many of the linkages between attributes. The approach also poses a number of research challenges, principally in qualitative data collection and the spatial representation of non-physical attributes. The authors argue that as these challenges are met, such a conceptual approach to understanding urban systems can begin to link analytical, substantive and procedural considerations and help us to understand the temporal and dynamic elements of sustainable urban form.

Acknowledgements

This paper is based on research jointly funded by the Economic and Social Research Council, UK and Sir Norman Foster and Partners, London. The authors also acknowledge the assistance of Cairnshill Residents' Association, Belfast; Janet Croft Residents' Association, Byker, Newcastle Upon Tyne; and Carrickfergus Borough Council.

Joe Ravetz

Urban Form and the Sustainability of Urban Systems: *Theory and Practice in a Northern Conurbation*

Introduction

> One of the legacies of the City's rapid and uncontrolled growth is the conglomeration of mixed uses of property ... industrial, commercial and residential buildings exist side by side ... the unravelling of these mixtures of conflicting uses is one of the principal aims of the Development Plan. Not until it has been entirely cleared of its slums, has had its entire major road system remodelled and its central area redeveloped on modern lines ... will the Manchester of the future reveal itself for what it is ... (Nicholas and McWilliams, 1962, p.261)

There could not be a clearer message on 'sustainable urban form' from half a lifespan ago, at the time of the great plan for a great city. And now? Definitions of sustainable urban form may be as many as the people in the city. There is a loose consensus on reinventing many of the features lost and zoned out – the 'new urbanism' model – and this perhaps has as much to do with cultural trends as technical or environmental issues. But such a model could easily end up housing the rich who cause their environmental damage elsewhere – or housing the poor in clusters of poverty and crime. It might be obsolete within a decade, or it might linger on as a burden to future generations. It might be energy efficient and socially dysfunctional, or even *vice versa* – there are so many variables it is difficult to tell.

So the first aim of this chapter is to begin to unravel the tangled question of sustainable urban form, with a review of the fundamentals of sustainable urban development – in other words, what are cities for and how do they work? The second aim is to apply such thinking to a worked example – a demonstration of the prospects in housing and neighbourhood structure for a typical conurbation in the UK. For this we draw on a unique case study, the 'sustainable city-region' project in Greater Manchester (GM), which provides a breadth and depth of evidence on the prospects for a dynamic and problematic city (Ravetz, with the Town and Country Planning Association [TCPA], 1999).

What we find is that the linkages between urban form and its environmental impacts are generally complex and indirect, and dependent on the social and economic context. Clear linkages between transport and land use are hard to find, for instance because each is implicated in larger and more complex systems (Stead *et al.*, this volume). Likewise, the linkages between urban form and social-economic well-being are complex and hedged with intervening factors. And then in historical context, each generation tends to see its problems in terms of visible solutions – a century ago a major transport problem was horse manure, and the internal combustion engine was seen as the solution.

Manchester, in its postwar plan, aimed with the best of intentions, to sweep away huge tracts of housing and industry to create a modern city with spacious highways. Even the town hall was to be replaced in concrete with a boulevard down to the river (City of Manchester, 1945). In the event, the planned depopulation of the city coincided with the unplanned decimation of its industrial base, with disastrous results for communities and local economies. The city's tradition of radical innovation, in urban design as in other areas, ended up with some successes and many failures – creating new opportunities in the regeneration game, where industrial 'dereliction' is transformed into professionals' 'delectation'.

The upshot of putting theory into practice is that sustainable urban form, if it means anything, is not so much a fixed blueprint or imposed product, but more a continuous adaptation of physical forms and spatial patterns to changing needs and demands. The street-café model is an active theme and aspiration in urban policy, but is far from a universal solution, and a portfolio of complementary patterns and incremental processes is needed in a fast-changing world. Time will tell how current models perform in the light of demands and pressures which are barely foreseeable at present and, if there is any conclusion, it is the need for modesty in claims for sustainability.

Urban systems and sustainability
Urban environmental sustainability
Let us for a moment step back to first principles, bypassing theoretical debates, taking 'urban' to mean a city or regional unit of activity, and cutting through a jungle of definitions with a simple equation:

- *urban environmental sustainability* – the long term balance of human activities in urban systems with their environmental resource base (as each of these is constantly changing, 'sustainability' is a direction rather than a fixed goal)   +
- *urban development* – the evolution and restructuring of physical and human urban systems in their global context (also a direction, not an end-state)   =
- *sustainable urban development* – actions which steer urban development towards the moving goals of environmental sustainability   +
- *sustainable urban form* – the physical and spatial forms which are both cause and effect of sustainable urban development (not necessarily simple or fixed patterns)

In practice, nothing is so simple: environmental sustainability raises many political and ethical questions, 'urban development' is a one-way journey towards an unknown destination, and 'sustainable urban development' has countless interpretations. To put in context its urban form counterpart, we can visualise land use and spatial structure as one intersection between many overlapping systems (Fig. 1).

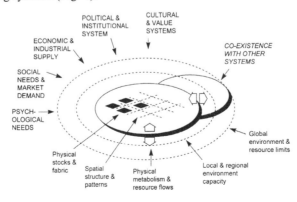

Fig. 1. Urban systems: outline of many interacting systems in cities or regions.
Source: Ravetz with the TCPA, 1999.

216

Starting with what is most tangible, the city's physical metabolism involves large stocks and flows of materials and energy, which like an engine can be tuned or re-engineered for greater efficiency. But for most cities there is a huge mismatch between such flows and the available resources or capacities. These mismatches point towards some basic goals for environmental sustainability:

- higher energy efficiency, with four-to-tenfold reductions in carbon emissions and other impacts;
- greater material efficiency, with reductions in throughput of a factor of four-to-ten; and
- improved environmental efficiency, to reduce risks and enhance quality in air, water, ground, soil, biomass and biodiversity.

Each of these relies on steering current trends towards a more fundamental restructuring of the physical metabolism. But cities are also complex and self-organising systems where each part is linked to the others. Restructuring of environmental systems then depends on restructuring of other dimensions in turn:

- technological restructuring, to enable innovation and best practice in environmental efficiency;
- economic restructuring, for competitiveness, equity and non-monetary activity;
- social restructuring, to enable greater cohesion, opportunity and inclusion;
- political restructuring, for effective governance and empowerment of communities;
- institutional restructuring, to enable better management, co-ordination and investment;
- cultural restructuring, to enable greater welfare with less material consumption.

And then each of these is implicated as both cause and effect of urban form at various scales:
- spatial restructuring for qualities such as accessibility, efficiency, viability, security and amenity; and
- physical restructuring of the fabric and metabolism of buildings, streets, space and utility networks.

Such restructuring might work well for a self-contained island, but cities are by nature intensive hubs of activity, transforming resources into goods and services, with continuous flows of imports and exports. For a conurbation such as GM, the volumes are huge, with flows of up to 0.2% of the world total, and the overall efficiency or ratio of primary to 'useful' materials is less than 5% (World Resources Institute, 1997). Such resource flows tend to disrupt natural and self-organising 'eco-cycles' as natural resources are sucked in and pollution and wastes are pushed out. A city or an urban form which contains its own resource flows and eco-cycles tends to be less vulnerable, less damaging and *de facto* more sustainable – one example would be a city which grows food locally and returns its nutrients to the soil from whence they came.

Such resource flows and eco-cycles exist within certain environmental capacities. But eco-systems are interconnected and continuously changing and, even for simple issues, causes and effects can be complex – the link between a smoky chimney and ill-health can be obvious but difficult to prove. To tackle this there are many methods for capacity assessment at local and global scales, as the basis for environmental targets and criteria:

- *carrying capacity* – levels of pressure or consumption which maintain environmental quality.

- *ecological footprint* – notional land area needed to supply basic resources (Rees and Wackernagel, 1995).
- *environmental space* – equal distribution of resources and assimilation capacity (Carley and Spapens, 1997).
- *ecological rucksack* – the ratio of material consumption to useful outputs of goods or services (Sachs, 1998).
- *urban capacity* – acceptable pressures and thresholds in the physical, environmental, social and economic environments and functions of cities (Entec, 1997).

Each of these capacity measures can be seen in terms of stocks, flows and pressures, and most accounting and indicator systems relate to such tangible features. In practice, equally as much depends on 'patterns' (the organisation of processes and activities in time and space, such as street patterns, landscape or eco-system patterns) (Mollison, 1991). Such patterns in cities – in other words, urban form – are much harder to measure than stocks or flows, but are just as crucial in forming resources and opportunities, for instance in enabling neighbours to talk to each other, or children to play in the street (Alexander, 1986). In practice, there is often a large but invisible gap between the 'measurers' of quantities, and the 'designers' of patterns, frequently overlooked in debates on sustainable development.

Urban development
Urban form itself is both a cause and effect of urban activity and the world around it, and of course the world itself is in a hectic state of flux. Each city marks a stage along certain 'long waves' of development, a combination of technology, communications and economic innovations (Brotchie *et al.*, 1987). Parallel to this is another structural transition in human activity and employment itself, from 'primary' resource-based sectors, to 'secondary' manufacturing, to 'tertiary' services, to 'quaternary' knowledge-based and cultural sectors. For several centuries, primary and secondary activity was the basis of the industrial city, of which GM was arguably the first. Local and imported materials were processed via labour, land and capital. Economic specialisation and hence its urban form could be defined in terms of the city-region's resources as a 'material processor' (Fig. 2) (Solow, 1970).

Fig. 2. The city as a material processor: general system flows in a typical industrial city-region, based on geography of Greater Manchester.
Source: Ravetz with the TCPA, 1999.

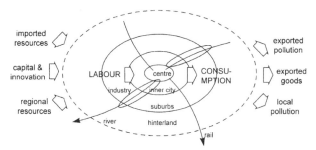

Such a model is now in transition to a more post-industrial 'city of flows' (Borja and Castells, 1997). An extended city-region functions more as a node in a global 'hypergrid' – a network of motorways and airports for movement of people and goods, and a network of satellites and wires for movement of capital and information. Many patterns of urban activity are turning inside out, as the growth nodes of production and consumption migrate to the urban fringe or 'edge city' – airports, retail, leisure and business parks linked to the hypergrid (Fig. 3) (Garreau, 1991). The city itself, and its people's reasons for being there, centre on services and consumption, with a cultural 'cachet' which competes in a global hierarchy. Likewise, the city's physical forms and spatial structures are pressed to serve entirely new functions and technologies, with obvious mismatches: high streets become traffic junctions, and terrace houses become IT centres.

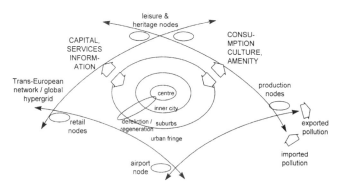

Fig. 3. The city as an information processor: general flows for a post-industrialised city-region.
Source: Ravetz with the TCPA, 1999.

There are many paradoxes in such a transition. In GM, for instance, there are nineteenth and twentieth century cultures and economies side by side. While production and consumption is globalised, there is a counter trend of 'localisation', a new kind of 'place advantage' through cultural amenity (Dicken, 1998). In physical terms, edge cities are formed through counter-urbanisation, while historic centres are re-urbanised and industrial areas regenerated. In social terms, 'uneven development' creates clusters of unemployment and exclusion alongside enclaves of privilege. In environmental terms, the bulk of a city's impacts are channelled through the global hypergrid, which is increasingly privatised and deregulated, and where environmental management becomes increasingly complex.

Sustainable urban development

Fitting such urban development transitions to the environmental sustainability agenda is a major challenge, but one approach is through the triangle of interactions between economy, environment and society. For economy–environment interactions, a very simple analysis is shown by the identity $I = P \times A \times T$ or:

environmental impact = population × affluence level × technology factor

This shows simply that doubling average levels of affluence, while halving environmental impact, requires a 'factor of four' increase in material efficiency (von Weizsacker *et al.,* 1997). The implications for urban form are far-reaching. Rising affluence and population levels are bound to increase environmental impacts, unless technology can be improved even more rapidly: up to now, for instance, rising energy efficiency in buildings has been outweighed by rising comfort standards (Evans and Herring, 1989).

For the environment–society linkage, the logic of this equation can be extended loosely to a human 'needs' interpretation of affluence levels, as dependent on social and cultural factors:

human needs × cultural factors × fulfilment ratio = affluence level

The upshot is that urban systems which enable and encourage non-material needs are more likely to be environmentally sustainable (Max-Neef, 1992). For instance, the UK climate emission targets could be met tomorrow, in the unlikely event that the entire population wore thermal clothing at all times. A similar case applies to high-density zero-energy healthy buildings, which could solve many environmental problems, if only social and cultural forces would allow them. For the third leg of the triangle – society–economy – it is clear that co-operation and mutual aid is crucial for many aspects of sustainable urban form, such as high-density housing, public transport, urban ecology and others. Where people can share gardens with friends, for instance, more satisfaction is gained from less space (Ravetz, 1998). This in turn depends on social cohesion and shared cultural values, each of which are implicated in the urban form which contains them. Such deep-rooted demand factors can be seen at one end of a chain of causal linkages, while the other end leads towards environmental impacts and outcomes (Fig. 4).

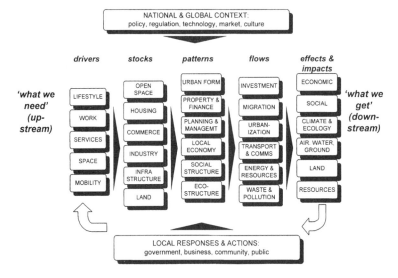

Fig. 4. Urban form and development: integrated assessment mapping of multiple needs and outcomes.
Source: Ravetz with the TCPA, 1999.

Such an integrated assessment chart shows many possible linkages: between lifestyles on the demand side, urban form and infrastructure, technology on the supply side, environmental pressures and impacts, and many kinds of outcomes, from social exclusion to climate change. It shows the sustainability of the system as a dynamic balance between multiple needs and outcomes, rather than a fixed formula. For instance, the social need or demand for shelter and territory needs to be balanced with the environmental and human impacts of space provision. Lifestyle shifts on the demand side can be as important as provision on the supply side. Likewise, indicators of sustainable urban form can be seen as a linked chain of 'intensities' in the welfare-impact balance of housing (Levett, 1998):

- human welfare per unit of internal space
- internal space per unit of environmental impact
- environmental impact per unit of human outcome

In practice though, human welfare is notoriously difficult to evaluate – the first question being about the fuzzy distinction between 'need', 'demand' and 'greed'. This can be seen with the 'extensification' dynamic of households and housing: nearly half the projected national household growth is due to population, with the rest down to demographic and lifestyle factors. The people are both expanding and spreading out, as the average household unit contains fewer people but more space per person. Whether from need or greed, this perhaps reflects another set of long-wave social–economic trends (Ravetz, 1998):

- life cycle expectations in personal space and territory – material desires with cultural roots, where people growing up in two-room terraces tend to aspire to something bigger;

- the dynamic of sub-cultures, or the desire to share spaces with like-minded people (where the affluent leave the poor behind the effect is polarisation into class and income bands);
- individuation and empowerment, as reflected in material engagement and space demand (many people now require home, workspace, workshop, garage, equipment storage and so on); and
- the perennial human desire to have one's cake and eat it – to combine good access to amenities, jobs and services (the best balances tend to be found at the suburban fringe and other locations with the highest prices).

Do such dynamics conflict with the case for sustainable urban form, and are they in themselves sustainable? There is no simple answer to this. Stronger urban containment would protect land and help to revitalise cities, but would also put pressure on the less affluent and those in housing need. An opposite policy might provide more and larger units but at the expense of countryside, local services and transport impacts. Virtuous circles and win–win solutions are rare in reality, and the fact that all policies may have mixed results for winners and losers, in an uncertain system where multiple needs produce multiple outcomes, is an essential foundation to the discussion below.

Sustainable urban form in a city-region

All this suggests a concept of sustainable urban form as a dynamic process of physical change which interacts with economic and social pressures and demands. To demonstrate how such thinking would apply to an actual city, the TCPA's sustainable city-region project looked at the prospects for long term sustainable development in GM (Ravetz, 1996). With a strategic view of the dynamics of the city-region over 25 years, it looked at the totality of current trends, environmental impacts, future targets and viable actions, mapping out strategies for each sector and area of the city, with a focus on their linkages and conflicts in physical, economic and social terms.

A fair share of urban problems can be seen in GM, where industrial restructuring has left widespread dereliction and contamination in 10% of the urban area, a quarter of all housing is over 100 years old, and 40% is unfit or in poor condition. The people have departed from many inner areas, leaving large gaps in the urban fabric, while the pressure for development mounts at the periphery and beyond. The building stock produces climate change emissions of a tenth of 1% of the world total and, for this and similar problems, improved efficiencies are overtaken by rising demand for space, mobility, comfort and consumption. If a clear urban structure of neighbourhoods and local centres is integral to quality of life, then a comparison of London and Manchester shows that the latter's abnormal suicide rate may have some connection with the degradation and disintegration of much of its urban area (Hebbert, 1998).

There are many approaches to such a tangle. One is to look for holistic patterns, both human and physical, which set up virtuous cycles of reinvestment and regeneration. Some basic human patterns can be seen in the location trade-offs for individuals or organisations, for instance with privacy and territory in balance with the need for public spaces and services (Fig. 5a). Different physical patterns, such as suburban or urbanist models, can shift the balance point one way or the other, both in physical form and in human expectations. This approach underlies a series of 'patterns in urban form' in the following sections. These are generic spatial arrangements which self-organise with an internal logic, and are cause and effect of the multiple functions of the built environment.

a: Needs, demands & conflicts in location aspects of human settlements at any scale
Adapted from Alexander 1985: Mollison 1991

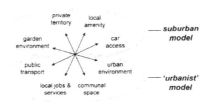

b: General requirements & system patterns for conurbation forms:
Based on Geddes 1915: Howard 1898

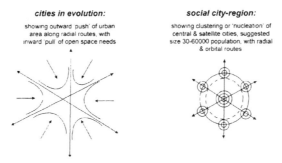

c: General patterns for single neighbourhood units
Based on Jacobs 1965, Alexander 1986, Calthorpe 1994

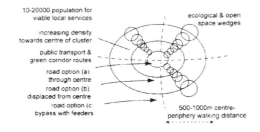

d: Alternative patterns for multiple overlapping neighbourhood units
Based on Jacobs 1965, Alexander 1986, Calthorpe1994

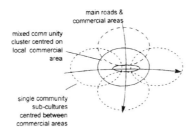

e: General patterns for combinations of neighbourhood units within urban grid: to l
adapted to local circumstances. Based on Alexander 1986: Rapaport 1987

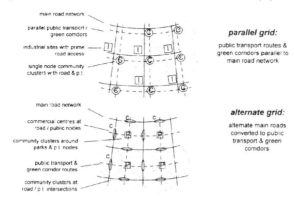

f: General patterns for street and block layout and section
Based on alexander 1986, Urban Villages Forum 1998

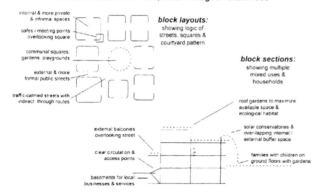

Fig. 5. Patterns in urban form.

The shape of the city

With a clear core and satellite structure, GM is a classic industrial city. Some of the mill towns and suburbs around the periphery are still distinct units, while others have merged into a large mass around the regional centre. The density of the urban area is 45 persons per hectare (pph) gross, with average net housing densities of 25 dwellings per hectare. Open land is urbanised or developed at nearly 1 square kilometre per year, although 80% of all development in GM is on 'brown' urban sites. However, development of 'white' land not in the green belt is over 1% of the total per year, with about 80 years' supply to go.

Pressures on size and density are determined largely by economic growth – housing and commercial floorspace appear to increase at 1–2% per year, and site area rather faster (Fothergill *et al.*, 1987). The resulting outward spread is both cause and effect of area decline, waste of land, and increased car dependency. For GM, after decades of de-population, there is a clear policy goal to provide for the current population and its projected increase of 2% per decade (DoE, 1995). However, the conurbation already has the highest urban density in the UK outside of London and, while brown and derelict land is plentiful, high quality amenity sites and open spaces are more scarce. The current UK target for 60% of development on brownfield sites is not so relevant to GM which, as stated above, already achieves 80% and still has problems (DETR, 1998). The sustainable solution would seem to be to re-use wasted assets in the urban area while protecting critical assets on the fringe, but such a solution would need to

223

shift consumer expectations on the demand side, and the constraints of developers and agents on the supply side. Possible measures include levies and subsidies on greenfield and brownfield sites, a new contamination regime, business rate reform, powers of land assembly, the return of betterment and extension of planning controls to density and tenure (TCPA, 1998).

Many urban form discussions focus on the linkage of density to transport demand and, while the evidence is sketchy, the optimum pattern appears to be in free-standing, medium-sized settlements of about 80–100 pph net, or 40–50 pph gross – in fact, this is already the average density of GM (Ecotec, 1993). Its travel intensity or distance per person per week is 10% less than London, 50% more than Merseyside, and 15% less than the UK average for towns of 250,000 population. Its satellite pattern and mixture of uses are also similar to the recommended 'dispersed nucleated' structure (Breheny *et al.*, 1994). So it might be difficult to influence travel demand much further at this macro-level; such opportunities may lie at more local levels.

Land and land uses

The urban area in GM takes up 43% of the total and, within this, housing accounts for over half, transport 13% and open space 10% (GMR, 1995). At current trends, 30 square kilometres of rural land would be developed by 2020, and the entire stock of urban and fringe vacant land would be used up. The projected growth of land for services, employment and transport would take nearly half the current vacant land.

To maintain the overall size and shape of the urban area while providing for development needs, multiple and diverse land use is one approach (Nijkamp *et al.*, 1992). There is an opportunity in transport-related land, as traffic calming will enable much road space and parking to be used as public space. Housing land may intermingle with employment via teleworking, and spare land on industrial and institutional estates can be cultivated. Land policies and management practices should aim to use available space more efficiently, equitably, and with increased added value.

The other key resource is vacant and derelict land, currently at 10% and 7% respectively of the urban area, not counting numerous leftover corners attached to other uses. Vacancy and dereliction are by-products of industrial restructuring, and some vacant land is inevitable while land uses change. Even if all vacant land was developed for housing, at current densities it would provide for less than half of the requirement, and in practice much of it is unsuitable for housing. But vacant land is a valuable resource in the consolidation of neighbourhood units and services. It enables the clustering of housing to cater for household growth, and can provide green corridors and 'necklaces' for wildlife and cultivation.

The 3,200 hectares of derelict land has stayed level for two decades, as reclamation has been balanced by new dereliction. Much is concentrated in former industrial areas such as East Manchester, where the negative value and image are huge barriers to development. If a 25-year programme was to reduce dereliction to a third of current levels, assuming that new dereliction continues at its current rate, total reclamation activity would need to double. In the meantime, each derelict or vacant site is a resource in its neighbourhood strategy (see below) and, where its future is uncertain, temporary and short-life uses should be investigated.

Urban form and capacity

In the wider view, the question of urban form is much more than simple density and brown/green choices, it is about the spatial structure of human activities. This is not a new theme – a century ago, the garden city concept aimed at planned communities as a response to the overcrowding of cities and deprivation of the countryside (Fig. 5b) (Howard, 1898). The agenda for the post-industrial world is now not so much about new settlements, as about restructuring existing cities for social and ecological goals – the theme of clustering for viability and cohesion, or organisation out of chaos, is equally valid. At present, there is much debate on the urban capacity for absorbing development, and the North West region is studying new methods (NWRA and Llewellyn-Davies, 1997). This is both a technical and social issue – development viability depends on the social acceptability of densities, mixed uses and other factors, and many European cities show that much higher densities are viable with the right combination of lifestyle and kinship, housing tenure, housing finance, and public facilities. Urban capacity depends on a creative and shared vision of the future city (Ravetz, 1998).

Human scale neighbourhoods

One starting point for such a creative vision is at the neighbourhood level, but in reality most neighbourhoods contain many communities, and most communities are spread over many neighbourhoods. While networked communities and sub-cultures are part of the richness of the city (Comedia and Demos, 1999), the physical quality and human scale of local neighbourhoods are equally important in public perceptions (Robson *et al.*, 1994). So the principles of human-scale neighbourhoods are nothing new, but it seems they have to be re-interpreted for the post-industrial city (Jacobs, 1965). The starting point is the linkage between homes, jobs and services. Viable education, retail and other services require a 10,000–20,000 population range, and a viable walking distance for most people is about 400–1,000 metres, depending on the quality of the environment.

Both these ranges can be achieved by clustering higher-density housing and mixed employment around local centres, in mainly pedestrianised units of up to one kilometre radius. Clusters of neighbourhood units can be arranged around public transport loops and district centres with specialised services, with an interlocking 'eco-structure' or matrix of green spaces. Highways should be in a tree pattern with restricted through routes – walking or cycling within the neighbourhood, and public transport between neighbourhoods, should be the first choices (Fig. 5c) (Calthorpe, 1994).

In practice, the neighbourhood unit, 'pedestrian pocket', or 'transit-oriented development' is only a starting point for a complex conurbation such as GM. Urban vitality and richness may not be optimum with a single choice for local services and, for many, 'local shop' now means the nearest retail park. For the crucial question of road access, there are alternative strategies, from a route through the centre to an external bypass, and each of these brings problems and opportunities. For social communities, perhaps the most complex of any urban patterns, there are several options for multiple overlapping community units. An economic unit is generally centred on existing roadside commercial centres, while a cultural or ethnic unit might also be contained within the cells of the highway network (Fig. 5d) (Rapaport, 1987).

Urban grain and texture

If these generic patterns for individual neighbourhood units are applied to a large urban area, there are interesting possibilities for urban 'micro-form' or texture (Fig. 5e). Public transport routes and green corridors may be parallel but removed from the main road network, as in the upper diagram; or alternate to the road network, as in some new towns. Each has implications for accessibility, commercial services, the diversity of communities, and the 'richness' of the city. While such generic patterns have to translate to a complex and messy reality, the theme of overlapping nodes and communities is a useful approach for inner and outer urban areas.

Average distances from dwellings to local centres in GM are estimated at 750 metres, or twice the modern acceptable walking distance (Ravetz, 1996). A policy of doubling average housing densities within 400–500 metres of local centres could accommodate up to half of all new development within this radius by 2020, depending on land availability, and the population contained would increase to an average of 5,000, or half the catchment. Such a scenario is closely linked to traffic reductions which enable pedestrianisation on alternate routes, and residential traffic calming will increase pedestrian travel and the effective catchment. A similar rate of restructuring over the next 50 years would see three quarters of the population living within easy walking distance of local centres. This is, of course, dependent on local centres serving viable functions, and other economic and political measures outside our scope would be needed to ensure this.

Translating such goals into the reality of a city such as GM is a daunting prospect. Physical restructuring may take decades, local priorities are overridden by external actors, and most people have little desire to 'bunch up' (Hooper, 1994). One approach is in fostering self-organising processes at neighbourhood level, through local regeneration, business and voluntary activity. Another approach is the integration of neighbourhood strategies to other city-wide strategies for transport, ecology, employment and so on, each of which aims to turn problems into opportunities:

- problems of household growth, with solutions through local densification;
- problems of viability of local services, with solutions in local economic measures;
- problems of traffic growth, with solutions in traffic calming and integrated transport strategy;
- problems of security and liveability, with solutions in fostering social cohesion and mutual aid; and
- problems in funding area improvements, with solutions in reinvesting appreciation of values.

Housing need and demand

At least half of the neighbourhood agenda revolves around housing, where the first question is that of the 40% of housing in GM which is unfit or needing repair, combining with social stress, unemployment and ill-health. At the same time, 'levelling up' and provision of new housing to current standards on the scale needed would have large land use and environmental impacts. For the future, there is a very big question – 'where should the people go?' (TCPA, 1996). The average size of household in GM is projected to reduce from 2.45 to 2.14 people per household, and the number of households may rise by 140,000–210,000 over the next 25 years (Fig. 6). Accounting for replacement of unfit housing, a quarter of all dwellings in the conurbation could be new by 2020. Much of the older stock will also be near the end of its life and needing large-scale renewal, putting further pressure on housing land. Most of the new households will be for single persons, whereas most of the supply is in larger family dwellings. However, the industry suggests that smaller households do not necessarily want smaller dwellings, and demand for space is likely to increase with new patterns of teleworking and a localised social economy (HBF, 1996).

The projections themselves can be questioned and there are many more unresolved arguments on tenure, social housing investment, affordability, equity, and the benefit system (Bramley and Watkins, 1996). The obvious goal of densification to accommodate demand may well conflict with psychological desires for personal space and the general conservatism of the property industry (Rydin, 1995). The challenge is to turn a problem into an opportunity via the clustering of housing in mixed uses around local centres, aiming at quality rather than quantity of space per person. One possible scenario for housing shows how the projected demand could be met almost entirely within the urban area by a combination of clustering and conversions (Table 1).

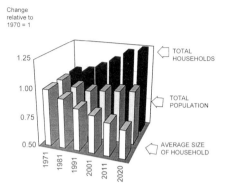

Fig. 6. Trends and projections in households and population in Greater Manchester, with extrapolation 2016–2020.
Source: GMR, 1995 and DoE, 1995.

	Land area (ha)	Average density (dwelling/ha)	Units
Local centres infill	200	100	20,000
Local mixed development	200	75	15,000
30% of urban vacant land	1,000	50	50,000
60% of peripheral vacant land	1,500	30	45,000
50% vacant space over shops/offices			10,000
50% vacant industrial conversions			5,000
Larger house subdivisions			10,000
Rural ecological housing	500	30	15,000
Total	3,500		175,000
(mid range estimate requirement to 2020)	(7% of urban area)		

Table 1. Housing development scenario: approximate estimates for new housing supply to 2020 (vacant land areas include for projected new vacancies to 2020).
Sources: Based on GMR, 1995 and AGMA, 1995.

Housing forms and layouts

The increase in single person households coincides with the need to increase housing densities, but such housing needs to be adaptable to current trends such as home-working, teleworking, extended families and subdivision, as in the '21st century homes' concept (Rudlin and Falk, 1999). Meanwhile, the effects of rising disposable incomes are likely to increase the demand for space, both internal and external. Such demand can be met by design approaches and 'patterns' which increase space efficiency and added value, while maintaining privacy, external space and 'defensible' space. Plan forms such as courtyards, and sectional forms such as maisonettes and stepped forms can be seen in further 'patterns' of urban form, which aim at mixed uses, mixed households and mixed tenures within a hierarchy of external and internal space (Fig. 5f).

In London and most European cities, land prices and cultural differences make higher-density living both necessary and viable, and while GM is for the most part a low-rise city, a combination of development strategy and rising land prices would tend to encourage the 'urbanist' market. Such demand hinges on the added value of location, as seen in waterfront development. Younger mobile households, for instance, are attracted to housing close to local centres or cultural facilities with a 'happening' nightlife. The housing numbers challenge is in fact a challenge for creative 'urbanist' strategies (Ravetz, 1998).

It is also clear that cultural and lifestyle shifts are crucial in enabling people to live in proximity with added value, sharing collective space and facilities. This may need a re-think of current housing tenure, investment and benefit systems. The former model of nuclear family owner-occupation is in many ways outdated in an age of career and domestic mobility, and there is a case for portable finance packages which allow flexibility between locations and tenures. As a positive alternative, co-operative and self build tenures should encourage sharing and multiple uses, with both appreciation on investment and flexibility of occupation (Rudlin and Falk, 1999).

Conclusions

This is a brief sketch of some key concepts behind sustainable urban form, and a review of their application in an actual city-region. In the space available the focus has been on land use, neighbourhood structure and housing, as the tangible surfaces of the demands and activity patterns behind them. Less has been said about those activity patterns, and their other dimensions such as transport, pollution, energy, economy, employment, services and so on.

The broader spatial trends, both for individuals and organisations, show growing tensions between localisation and globalisation. Each of the European historic city cores which inspire the 'urbanist' model is surrounded by a sprawl of estates and business parks – as though the two kinds of form are complementary. And both the historic core and the business parks are driven by economic development as both cause and effect of increasing choice, specialisation, labour markets and customer catchments. The typical sunrise business now operates on a European or global scale, and whether its front office is in or out of town is not necessarily a key issue. In GM the opening of the Trafford Centre in 1998, then the UK's largest shopping mall, caused outrage and predictions of doom for adjacent centres. But here the issue is not only displacement of trade, but the invention of a new retail experience – a cathedral-like orgy of materialist fantasy – with half the UK's population in its catchment. This and similar cases show different types of balance between changing activity patterns and urban forms, at every scale from local to global.

With such an overview, we can draw some general conclusion, not so much about physical forms, as about the way in which problems are approached. The failures of redevelopment and the large estates, and the current failures of some regeneration programmes, highlight problems at the systems level – in other words, one-dimensional 'solutions' with fixed objectives, rather than robust self-organising systems with multiple balancing interactions. In contrast, some of the more stable and variegated suburbs and inner neighbourhoods in GM, as elsewhere, seem to sustain themselves and their populations with relative ease. As yet, they may not sustain the global environment, and bringing such wider objectives into the picture may change the pressures and demands on a future generation of urban forms. In particular, they will have to deal with new patterns of work and leisure, networks and subcultures, age and kinship structures, information and communications technology systems, transport modes and accessibility demands, and environmental priorities for biodiversity, energy efficiency and material minimisation. In the face of such rapid changes and uncertainties, future forms for more sustainable urban settlements are there to be invented in a creative process.

Gert de Roo

Compact Cities, Environmental Conflicts and Policy Strategies: *Complexity as a Criterion for Decision Making*

Introduction

During the 1980s and 1990s there was a rise, and then a fall, of the compact city as a spatial concept, and as a concept that contributes to sustainability. At first, the compact city was thought of as a sound answer to pressing urban difficulties; it did not prove, however, to be an answer to all of them. Contrary to what once was expected, new spatial and environmental conflicts have been created due to compact city policies. Currently, attention has shifted to other, complex, difficulties which some call the 'dilemmas of the compact city'.

Dilemmas of the compact city can arise due to conflicts in decision making. Against general expectations, it proved rather hard to achieve dense urban development, while enforcing strict environmental rules. As a result, authorities everywhere are developing strategies, methods and standards to cope with environmental issues in dense urban areas. This chapter is about these developments. It focuses on The Netherlands as an extreme in environmental policy making, and uses the US policy system as a comparison.

Developments in policy making are investigated in order to learn, from practice, how to cope with environmental issues in dense, and therefore complex, urban areas. The aim is to find a general approach to identifying ways of decision making to deal with urban environmental issues. This approach will be based on typologies of environmental conflicts in compact cities, with complexity as the key to this approach.

Urban environmental conflicts

As long as there are cities, there are environmental conflicts. Urban environmental conflicts are caused by human activity: polluting one's own nest seems to be the inevitable by-product of development and 'progress'. Even in Roman times courthouses had to deal with complaints about environmental pollution, such as smoke from workshops (Brimblecome and Nicholas, 1995).

There are numerous environmental conflicts affecting almost everyone's daily life. These conflicts are related, in the main, to environmental quality. Poor environmental quality in cities is mainly the result of waste and environmentally intrusive emissions. Besides street litter, waste in Western countries is almost entirely reduced to a logistic problem. Emissions to soil, water and air are therefore the main factors influencing the quality of the local environment. In Western parts of the world, sewer systems and water treatment plants take care of most dirty water, and emissions to soil are often strictly forbidden. Unfortunately, concentrated emissions to soil have taken place in the past, and are now seen as environmental disasters, stagnating spatial developments. Even more common, and not always as easy to avoid, are environmentally intrusive emissions into the air. While soil contamination is almost entirely chemical, air pollution can be the result of a wide range of pollutants, such as toxic, carcinogenic or radioactive substances, dust, electromagnetic radiation, and – probably the best known – noise and odour (Miller and de Roo, 1997). Recently, visual hindrance, excessive light, shade, wind effects around buildings, and inner-city climatic effects have also been recognised as environmental pollution (Hough, 1989; Miura, 1997; O'Riordan, 1995).

Most of the time, the severity of these conflicts depends on the distance between a function or activity and its unintended environmental effect. These unwanted distance-dependent effects, which have spatial consequences, are usually defined as externalities (Marshall, 1924; Mishan, 1972; Pinch, 1985). Keeping enough distance from the polluting sources is, therefore, a natural potential solution for preventing environmental spillovers. It is, however, a strategy that is space consuming too, and may not always be in line with the principles of the compact city.

Environmental conflicts and urban structure
Most urban environmental conflicts are related to only a limited number of types of location. At least, this can be concluded for issues in and around Dutch cities. A number of studies point out typical locations where environmental quality and spatial development are in conflict with each other (Bartelds and de Roo, 1995; Blanken, 1997; Borst *et al.*, 1995; Kuijpers and Aquarius, 1998; VROM, 1996). Amongst these locations are industrial and harbour sites, particularly those which have to be revitalised, sites with soil pollution, areas around railway stations, the immediate surroundings of roads and railroads, and inner cities. Kuijpers and Aquarius (1998) point out that almost all these locations are undergoing a process of restructuring. Although it is far from easy to get a precise picture of the size and character of these locations, there are enough indicators to give a reasonably good idea about the causes and consequences of environmental conflicts on and around them.

Industrial sites are responsible for a substantial proportion of environmental disturbances, particularly in nearby housing areas. In The Netherlands, around 4% of the population is 'severely' affected in one way or another through environmental intrusion caused by industrial activities (VROM, 1993). Six per cent of the Dutch population is affected by industrial noise (VROM *et al.*, 1998).

The restructuring of *industrial, harbour, railway and military sites*, which are or will become redundant, is interesting from a 'compact city' point of view. Reasons to restructure these sites are related strongly to the urban structure and the way this structure is influenced by past developments. Most of the time, these sites are surrounded by residential areas. Often they are poorly accessed, and since this is hard to improve within reasonable costs it is necessary to restructure the site. Restructuring is seen as an option in upgrading the site, turning it into a more dynamic area which could include housing. Even if these sites are abandoned, land contamination is often a common barrier to new developments. If not abandoned, there are other complications: lack of occupancy; an economically weak stock of companies on the site; poor image of the site; and poor environmental quality all make restructuring a pressing issue. Furthermore, uncertainty about the intentions of remaining intrusive activities reduces the possibilities to redevelop these sites.

Alongside roads and railways, environmental pressure is increasing for a number of reasons. Car mobility is still increasing. The railway network is expanding rapidly too, and is even showing signs of congestion. The distance between living and working has hardly lessened, and the dynamics of living and working are becoming more and more independent. The number of two-earner households with different work locations is increasing, and recreational traffic has increased. In the meantime, restructuring measures and pricing policies have proved relatively ineffective in reducing car use, and infrastructure for bikes and public transport remains poor.

Inner city areas are also under strain. The aim of inner city policy, known as city centre management, is to keep inner cities lively and attractive to a variety of people. It focuses on multi-functionality and high quality in terms of recreational and residential facilities. However, the function of the inner city as a node in a transport network is decreasing, and shifting towards the fringes of city centres; but this does not mean that traffic congestion in inner cities is no longer an environmental issue. In addition, many widely differing intrusive facilities and functions, such as bars, cafés, shops, car parks and garages, outdoor recreation and festivals, and inner city construction are not easy to manage at an acceptable level of liveability. Combining these functions with housing is one of the most difficult tasks facing city centre managers.

Finally, there are the *development areas*. These are meant for residential purposes and are located just outside existing city boundaries. The conception that these areas can be regarded as empty, and can be treated as such, is anything but true (Kreileman and de Roo, 1996). Too often, environmentally intrusive facilities – such as energy carriers and road infrastructure – are already in place, preventing substantial parts of planned developments from happening. These development areas are located at the edge of the city, where busy ring roads and most of the industrial sites can be found (Koekebakker, 1997). Frequently, this results in environmentally intrusive spillovers, which restrict the use of development areas.

In functional terms urban environmental conflicts arise due to distance related effects from above ground environmental intrusion. Also, urban environmental conflicts are caused by location-bound effects, such as soil contamination. These conflicts are partially the result of existing urban situations and of changes that take place within the spatial structure. Keeping an effective distance from polluting sources or avoiding polluted locations might be an obvious solution for these urban environmental conflicts. However, in the light of the urban structure resulting from compact city policies, it would also be a fairly one-sided solution. Within a compact city context, keeping a safe distance – a functional-rational solution – might be too simple a strategy to cope with all the concerns related to urban environmental conflicts.

Framing environmental urban conflicts

If a functional-rational solution – a solution based on direct causal relationships – such as keeping a safe distance between source and environmentally sensitive functions, is not always the best solution for all interests concerned, one might wonder which solutions are. To answer this question, four different approaches in decision making are introduced. Two of these approaches, the *standards* and *objectives* approaches, are goal oriented, and concern the effectiveness of planning. The other two approaches, the *hierarchy* and *consensus* approaches focus on organisation, communication and co-ordination, and are therefore institution oriented. The institution oriented aspects of planning touch on the efficiency of planning. The four approaches are presented here as interrelated extremes that encompass the different concepts of decision making (see Fig. 1).

The standards approach is based on single, fixed targets, which should lead to an optimum result for one particular environmental issue. The use of standards as a tool for environmental policy is common in most parts of the Western world. Standards are not seen as a means only, but are meant to be goals, aimed at by environmental policy to restrict environmental pollution. Since the early 1970s, it has been common policy in The Netherlands to develop goals for decision making based on quantitative standards of acceptable environmental conditions. In the US too, standards were used to mitigate environmental pollution. Although policies differed from state to state, they were mainly source oriented. Source oriented policy is designed to improve the performance of activities responsible for causing pollution. Well known are the far-reaching and successful initiatives taken by the State of California in the 1980s to reduce car emissions. In The Netherlands, source oriented policy was preceded by effect oriented policy. Effect oriented policy aims to shield or protect environmentally sensitive activities from being affected by pollution and hazards.

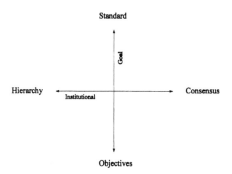

Fig. 1. Four approaches in environmental planning.

Traditionally, effect oriented policy in The Netherlands was based on fixed standards which are translated spatially into contours. These contours differentiate areas where environmental intrusion is acceptable for certain polluting activities from areas with environmentally sensitive land uses. The areas which are enclosed by these contours can be designated as environmental zones. Policy that leads to different environmental actions, depending on the areas bounded by the contours, is called environmental zoning. It emphasises protecting impacted areas by regulating how they may be developed and used. In a way, the use of environmental standards relates environmental policy, policy for mitigating local land uses, and physical planning. It is a policy that focuses on the direct causal relationships between source, transport from source to area of impact, and impacted area. The rationality behind this is strongly functional in character.

The standards approach often goes hand in hand with the so-called hierarchy approach. The hierarchy approach is synonymous with top-down or central control. According to this approach, the decision maker dictates and directs developments, and expects everyone to comply. This approach is based on the idea that the decision maker is aware of the 'ins and outs' of the conflict, and is able to predict the effects of the policy that is meant to tackle the conflict.

However, the hierarchy approach has restrictions. For example, it concentrates on general effects. As a result, hardly any attention is given to the unique character of specific and local difficulties. This could mean that although most conflicts are dealt with in the way that was initially expected, this policy might have a contrary effect on some of the conflicts. These will no doubt be the more complex and uncertain conflicts. Consequently, dealing with these kinds of conflict lead to less predictable outcomes. In line with this argument, there is another restriction of the hierarchy approach. It can only be successful if the various intentions of the decision maker do not interfere with each other. The hierarchy approach leads easily to the exclusion of interests by emphasising single-issue policies.

The hierarchy approach is opposed to what can be called a consensus approach. The consensus approach is based on participation and on more-or-less equal interactions between interests and people involved. Instead of central decision making, participatory interaction is seen as a way to define conflicts, to acknowledge different interests, and to generate commitment to the outcome of the decision making process. This approach becomes interesting when hierarchy and local autonomy are inefficient or lacking. Instead, there is mutual dependence between the participants involved. Policy making through an interactive process becomes more necessary when the number of relevant actors, all with different interests, is relatively high. Interactions within these kinds of setting are characterised by great uncertainties and dynamics. The conflicts are increasingly complex. In this situation, policy will be established through a process of evenly matched mutual influence: tuning in on the planning process, rather than controlling it, becomes an important activity. Processes are required which develop a mutual understanding of the present situation, shared visions of a better society, realistic strategies to achieve these visions, and comprehensive practical activities (Amdam, 1994).

In situations that are uncertain and complex, approaches which are functional–rational in character become less apparent. An objective view on the issue is almost impossible because of a lack of hard facts. Subjective judgements are becoming increasingly legitimate in making decisions. According to Friedmann, 'the problem is no longer to make decisions more "rational", but how to improve the quality of the action' (1973, p.19). In these situations, the decision making process shifts from a 'closed' to a more 'open' procedure. Also, 'object oriented' planning is shifting towards 'process oriented' planning, emphasising inter-subjective relations. To understand these shifts in decision making, functional rationality is no longer sufficient. Instead, communicative rationality is seen as a way of thinking to understand what is happening (Dryzek, 1990; Healey, 1992; Innes, 1995). Communicative rationality is heavily influenced by the thoughts of Habermas, who states that:

> far from giving up on reason as an informing principle for contemporary societies, we should shift perspective from an individual, subject–object conception of reason, to reasoning formed within inter-subjective communication. (quoted in Healey, 1992, p.50)

By this way of thinking, definitions, proposals, plans, scenarios and solutions are no longer starting points in planning: they are results of decision making processes.

While direct causality is the basic principle of functional rationality, the basic principle of communicative rationality is an alienated causality between cause and effect. The assumed 'mechanic' relationship will be replaced by a more statistical causality (Prigogine and Stengers, 1990). Chance and choice and surrounding influences – the context – become essential in understanding what is happening. A 'optimum' outcome of the decision making process can no longer be guaranteed, but the aim will be to optimise the possibilities that the planning process is offering.

In a way, communicative rationality is a particular form of rationality specifically meant to explain institution oriented aspects in planning. However, as already stated, planning is also goal oriented. The standards approach was identified as one of its functional–rational representatives. The objectives approach was introduced as its opposite. The objectives approach represents the goal oriented aspects, within a complex environment. Within a complex environment, with several interfering interests and many different actors, a conflict can no longer be treated as if it stands on its own. Instead, it has to be seen within an ongoing process that is oriented to a variety of difficulties and issues that change over time. Cohen *et al.* (1972) speak of a 'garbage can', which is filled with problems, solutions and targets. Linking these at the right moment should contribute to the optimisation of the decision making process. Linking different issues and conflicts, combining strategies and aiming for multiple goals is what the objectives approach represents. It is an approach that should increase the effectiveness of planning in complex situations.

Environmental zoning, a traditional approach to solving urban environmental conflicts
With the above mentioned four different approaches, a theoretical framework can be put
together as a tool for decision making. In Fig. 2, a diagram is shown that represents the four
approaches, placed in extreme positions. This theoretical diagram also represents an outline
of the current debate in The Netherlands on how to improve the effectiveness and efficiency
of urban environmental policy making. Since the end of the 1980s, a shift from the hierarchy-
standards quadrant (left, top) towards the consensus-objectives quadrant (below, right) has
been under discussion as a response to the uniqueness and complexity of environmental
conflicts in dense urban regions (Fig. 2).

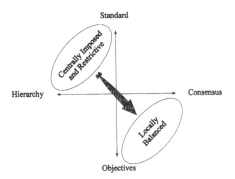

*Fig. 2. Policy
characteristics
and changes in
Dutch
environmental
planning.*

As mentioned above, in The Netherlands, environmentally intrusive activities are separated
from environmentally sensitive areas by keeping enough distance between the two. Quantitative
environmental standards were introduced by central government to be translated at the local
level into spatial zones. The use of fixed, central standards as an environmental policy
instrument was announced by the Dutch government in the 1972 *Urgency Report on the
Environment* (VM, 1972). In this report, the national government stated that the quality of the
environment was cause for concern, and drastic measures might have to be taken to keep air,
water and soil clean.

The use of centrally formulated standards became particularly popular after the successful
introduction of the Noise Abatement Act in 1979 (Tan and Waller, 1989). This act was
noteworthy not only because it facilitated the possibility of translating environmental standards
into spatial zones, but also because it mentioned spatial consequences which had to be taken
into account if spillovers reached environmentally sensitive areas. The implementation of the
Act proved easy – if expensive – since this type of nuisance is often a clearly defined and
local issue. Therefore, it is hardly surprising that more standards were drawn up during the
1980s to deal with other types of nuisance. Interim standards were suggested for odour, and
guidelines were constructed dealing with risks from exposure to chemicals and radiation.
Standards expressing the quality of soil were introduced after a number of cases of soil
contamination, which resulted in the demolishing of whole neighbourhoods. All this legislation
was initiated by the national government, leaving the translation of standards into spatial
zones, the abatement of local intrusive sources, the issuing of permits and the implementation
of these zones to provincial and municipal authorities (Borst *et al.*, 1995).

The top-down use of environmental standards excludes hardly any distinctions in differences
between local situations, and little attention is paid to local spatial consequences and side
effects. The hierarchy-standards approach results in a strict environmental policy framework,
which imposes its rules on other policy sectors such as spatial and physical planning (Miller
and de Roo, 1996). In 1989, a major improvement to this centrally oriented standard approach

was suggested. The Dutch Ministry of Housing, Spatial Planning and Environment introduced a system for integrating sectoral environmental standards and their related spatial zones into one integrated environmental zone around complex industrial sites (VROM, 1990a). Tan, the IEZ project supervisor, saw integrated environmental zoning as a 'natural ending of sectoral environmental legislation and a logical move towards integrated legislation' (in Nieuwenhof and Bakker, 1989, p.11).

The IEZ methodology has been tested in 11 pilot projects around The Netherlands. It reduced and minimised the impacts of environmental spillovers, by using the designation of zones based on levels of pollution remaining after reasonable abatement effects, and integrating spatial and environmental policy. The methodology involved measuring the spatial distribution of noise, odour, toxic and carcinogenic forms of air pollution, and hazards from manufacturing activities including fire and explosions. Measurements for these five environmental spillovers are normalised and combined to provide a single index for the combined environmental impact on every location in the urban area. Associated with each of these combined environmental impact scores are a set of restrictions which limit land use options, especially when an area is heavily impacted (Miller and de Roo, 1996).

For the first time, an integrated overview of environmental conditions was available. Unfortunately, in several pilot projects, it was discovered that pollution over a wide area was greater than had been anticipated, and application of the regulations required either that factories be closed, with unacceptable losses of manufacturing jobs, or that residents of whole neighbourhoods be relocated (Borst *et al.*, 1995). For example, the pilot projects in the cities of Arnhem, Dordrecht and Zwijndrecht (Boei, 1993; Stuurgroep IMZS Drechtsteden, 1991; Voerknecht, 1993) concluded that large portions of these urban areas would need to be demolished and the land use changed, if the IEZ programme were to be implemented.

The results of these pilot projects called into question the appropriateness of central government imposing a single set of standards and regulations on localities throughout the country. The conclusion that the centrally developed directives of the innovative IEZ programme were not practical in all local situations, and were contrary to the fundamentals of the compact city concept, indicated a need for additional strategies. In line with this, the increased focus on mitigating the effects of pollution while replanning affected areas, rather than only controlling pollution at source, has made integrating environmental policy and spatial planning an urgent concern. Also, the one-sided environmentally oriented perception of urban environmental conflicts had to change.

Differences in complexity of urban environmental conflicts
Although the IEZ pilot projects made clear that centrally imposed environmental policy based on a strict use of standards can have potentially devastating effects, research on urban environmental conflicts showed that in most cases environmental standards can be implemented locally without a decline in spatial quality (Bartelds and de Roo, 1995; Borst *et al.*, 1995; VROM, 1996). Furthermore Borst *et al.*'s research (*ibid.*) made clear that in only a small number of urban environmental conflicts will the use of standards cause a negative result, due to the complex context of the conflict. This research focused on conflicts around industrial sites with heavy industrial activities. There are 1,700 of these sites in The Netherlands: 257 of them had two or more environmentally intrusive spillovers, affecting their surroundings. In the majority of cases, noise and odour were involved. These sites are the most intrusive industrial sites in The Netherlands (SCMO-TNO, 1993). A rough estimation shows that 59 of the 257 sites have a relatively low impact on their surrounding, affecting 1,000 people or less per site. Against this are 99 sites responsible for excessive environmental load to between 1,000 to

10,000 people, while 77 sites affect between 10,000 and 50,000 people. There are 22 sites in The Netherlands that affect more than 50,000 people (SCMO-TNO, 1993). In general, the environmental impact of these sites on their surroundings is substantial. It makes one question if 'distance keeping' as a formula to end excessive exposure from environmentally intrusive loads is sufficient.

To answer this question, from the 257 sites with a multiple environmental load, 35 sites were selected (in Borst *et al.*, 1995) in order to look at the spatial consequences of environmentally intrusive emissions. These sites included 11 IEZ pilot projects; the other 24 sites were selected at random. For each of these, the number of intrusive sources per site, the spatial impact of the different environmental loads, the spatial structure of the surroundings of the site, and the spatial dynamics of the area were studied. This analysis resulted in the identification of five different categories, which were differentiated mainly by the relationship between spatial structure and the size of the integrated environmental load (Fig. 3).

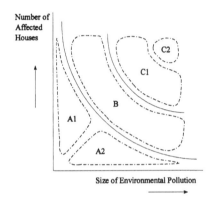

Fig. 3. Categories of environmental conflicts around industrial sites (A, B, and C).

Identified is a group of industrial sites (A) with hardly any impact of pollution on environmentally sensitive residential functions. Within this group a differentiation can be made; there are sites (A1) which have excessive spillovers, but are without impact due to an absence of residential uses in the locality. There are also sites (A2) which are surrounded by residential areas, but have only minor spillovers outside the site itself. It is obvious that in these situations the use of centrally issued and boundary conditioning standards will create a 'sustainable' separation between these sites and residential areas.

With another group of industrial sites (B), it is more difficult to implement environmental standards. Environmental emissions from these sites affect a relatively large number of environmentally sensitive functions. Implementation of environmental standards is still an option, and it will not affect the local spatial quality negatively; however, it is advisable to use some flexibility in implementing the standards. Furthermore, local differentiation in the use of standards, or compensation for excessive load, might be possibilities.

The last identified group of industrial sites (C) is characterised by extensive environmental spillovers in addition to a complex spatial structure, including a mix of residential and industrial functions. Within this group, a few so called 'hot spots' can be identified. The urban environmental conflicts that these hot spots create are almost impossible to solve by implementing environmental standards. The side effects would be too substantial to consider; factories would have to close and neighbourhoods be demolished. Hence, as Borst *et al.* state, 'Other solutions have to be found to get an optimum and realistic result' (1995, p.219).

Based on these distinctions, a differentiation can be made between relatively simple (A), relatively complex (B) and very complex (C) urban environmental conflicts. To get an idea about the 'ratio' between the three types of conflicts the analysis of the 35 selected industrial sites with a multiple environmental load has to be extrapolated to the 257 sites. In this way, about half of the most polluting sites in The Netherlands can be viewed as relatively simple. The environmental conflicts around these sites can be solved using fixed and centrally formulated standards. About 100 sites face a more complex situation. Flexibility is needed when implementing national standards. This means that about 25 sites are considered very complex, with only a handful identified as hot spots. In these cases, functional rational solutions are not appropriate, so solutions have to be found which take into account unique, local and complex interwoven aspects. Here, implementation of fixed standards is out of the question. These are the more complex environmental conflicts which have been targeted heavily by critics. These conflicts were the final blow to the IEZ programme, and put the Dutch environmental policy structure and its environmental standards system under great pressure.

The American way – communicative action
Although in The Netherlands the IEZ methodology has been put aside as too controversial, it was welcomed by the New York City Department of Environmental Protection. This department was looking for ways to manage environmental problems in residential areas. The Dutch IEZ methodology was used to produce a Baseline Aggregate Environmental Load (BAEL) Profile. This profile is to be used 'by policy makers and citizens in designing and implementing effective abatement and pollution prevention strategies for areas with aggregate, multi-source and multi-media environmental problems' (Osleeb *et al.*, 1997, p.2).

While IEZ failed as a policy instrument in The Netherlands, the policy impact of BAEL within a completely different policy setting is intriguing. BAEL is not meant to be an instrument imposed from above; on the contrary, it is meant to be a tool contributing to local action. The fact that the IEZ methodology was developed by the Dutch government to protect residential areas underlined its attractiveness. As Blanco states, 'This differs from the way the suitability analysis has been typically used in the US, where the concept [of] "environmentally sensitive areas" has been reserved for natural resource areas, such as wetlands' (1999, p.163). The environmental loads which are considered within BAEL include air emissions, noise, odour and environmental hazards from the storage or use of highly flammable, explosive or toxic substances. In contrast with the Dutch IEZ methodology, it is not meant to have direct spatial consequences. It is meant to make people – citizens and policy makers – aware of local environmental conditions and their possible effects.

Currently in the US, local authorities can allocate activities mainly through land use zoning or performance zoning. Although environmental regulations are referenced in certain zoning resolutions' performance standards there is little, if any, co-ordinated enforcement between land use control and the spatial implications of environmental policies. Externalities are not taken into account to separate environmentally intrusive activities from residential areas (see Anderson *et al.*, 1997). Hence, the reason why the New York City Department of Environmental Protection embraced the IEZ methodology to construct its BAEL is obvious. It is, in part, a response to the undesirable situation, whereby some districts are heavily burdened by environmental impacts (such as in Greenpoint-Williamsburg, see Blanco, 1999). It is also to help provide local environmental information which is desperately needed to support the policy making process and citizens in their actions. The situation is that lack of environmental information and policy instruments leads to local action for change.

In The Netherlands, in contrast to the situation in the US, national and local authorities are primarily responsible for the local environment. In addition, the lack of information about local environmental quality is not so much of an issue. The spatial implications that follow from this information – if taken seriously – are what cause substantial resistance. Strangely enough, this resistance is mainly the result of local authorities worried about the impact of top-down environmental legislation restricting their power concerning local land use planning.

This means that the critical issue is not the instruments – IEZ and BAEL – but the context in which the instruments have to operate. In the US, BAEL gives information about the local environmental situation. This information should support local participation among citizens, the business community and the authorities. In The Netherlands, citizens and the business community are not expected to take action, since the government is 'taking care' of all their environmental needs.

Obviously in The Netherlands, solving conflicts between environment and spatial developments is heavily regulated (direct regulation); through top-down policy all urban environmental conflicts are treated alike, despite the fact that there are many differences at the local level. In the US, the role of government is reduced to the minimum, to avoid interference with the social interplay of forces. Society has to take the initiative, which eventually results in communicative action and local participation (self regulation).

The most obvious difference between the environmental policy systems in The Netherlands and the US is who has primary responsibility. In The Netherlands, the authorities are responsible: in the US, the authorities are not primarily responsible, but will support and organise people in their efforts to solve a conflict. From a complexity point of view, in The Netherlands, the most common and relatively simple environmental conflicts are dealt with satisfactorily, while extreme cases do not fit in with the system. In the US, people liaise with each other in a process of communicative action, usually only in the most extreme cases. So, what is there to learn from this comparison?

Complexity, a touchstone for decision making?

If we consider differences between urban environmental conflicts on the basis of their complexity, it is not totally unrealistic to suggest that traditional Dutch environmental policy is suitable for relatively simple urban environmental conflicts, while US policy is more suited to very complex conflicts. It is a fact that some local environmental conflicts are more specific, individual and complex than centrally defined solutions can resolve, and that an approach other than centrally imposed regulation might be needed. However, a complete shift towards self-regulation ignores the fact that the majority of urban environmental conflicts can be solved without too much effort, using centrally imposed standards.

Therefore, perhaps a distinction could be made between relatively simple and uniform conflicts and far more complex ones. Relatively simple conflicts can be solved by implementing centrally defined standards. The more complex conflicts, which are strongly linked to local context, and are understood better by local authorities and local people, require a different approach, more like the US model. If this is so, it would mean that decision making becomes complexity dependent (see Fig. 4). But what are the consequences if we accept this suggestion?

From a theoretical perspective, it will mean that complexity is no longer used as an excuse for not dealing with an issue, for being uncertain, for being unable to handle a problem, or for being wrong. On the contrary, complexity can become a means to differentiate planning and policy making according to the size and character of the issue. It means that although an issue is regarded as complex, we are still facing a reality that can be known and can be acted upon.

Most of all, choice becomes important. If a conflict is seen as relatively simple, the issue can be divided into a number of distinct parts. The relationship between the identified parts can then be seen as direct causal. It is a functional-rational line, recognisable in the hierarchy and standards oriented environmental policy of The Netherlands. It results in a high level of predictability in terms of the outcome. A consequence of standards as fixed rules is an almost mechanical procedure that will more or less automatically result in the goals set up at the beginning of the procedure. Unfortunately, this mechanical procedure, while emphasising one interest in particular, often ignores possible related interests.

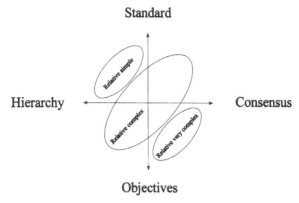

Standard

Hierarchy ← Relative simple / Relative complex / Relative very complex → Consensus

Objectives

Fig. 4. Complexity in relation to approaches in environmental planning.

In contrast, one might choose to regard an issue as very complex and dynamic. No longer will all the attention go to individual parts of the issue. The relation between the issue and its context becomes far more important. In this case, the basis for certainty, and therefore the predictability of the outcome, is rather weak. Instead of a strongly guided process, a more open form of planning is required. There will also be a shift from pre-defined goals to process related aspects. No longer will the issue or conflict itself be emphasised: instead, the issue is described, and the support this description receives from everyone involved in the issue is important. This is a communicative rational line, which does not take logical deducted knowledge as a starting point, but knowledge that is agreed upon by the parties concerned (Woltjer, 1997). Although there is hardly any certainty in this kind of process, it might lead to numerous possibilities. As mentioned above, instead of optimising the outcome, the planner's task is to optimise the use of the possibilities that are being developed.

Another important issue is who makes the choice regarding the complexity of an urban environmental conflict. In the US, each conflict is seen as unique, which more or less excludes choices based on differences in complexity. In The Netherlands, an urban environmental conflict is treated as a 'joined' problem. Therefore, below, we continue to look at The Netherlands.

Shifts in Dutch environmental policy making
This somewhat theoretical discussion leads us to question which direction developments in Dutch environmental policy making will take. IEZ, as the peak of traditional Dutch environmental policy making, resulted in unexpected environmental profiles of Dutch cities. A number of the pilot projects appear blacked-out in IEZ maps, which indicates that if source reduction is insufficient to reduce environmental spillovers then new spatial developments cannot be allowed, and – in the worst cases – existing neighbourhoods and industrial activities have to be relocated. These are almost unacceptable outcomes from a policy perspective. The IEZ results suggested that a debate was needed about the potential for change within the Dutch environmental policy system. Will there be a shift from one extreme – top-down regulation on the basis of environmental standards – to another extreme, which will depend entirely on self-regulation? Using 'complexity', will it be a shift from a policy which was focused on relatively simple conflicts to one focusing on very complex conflicts? Or will

there be a notion that differences between environmental conflicts demand a far more flexible approach, taking the complexity of the conflicts on board? It looks as if the Dutch have decided to go for the latter (VROM, 1995). Although this move might seem an acknowledgement of the idea of complexity dependent decision making, in practice the relationship with complexity is far from explicit.

Developments in Dutch environmental policy show us a move towards a position somewhere in between the two extremes – the hierarchy-standards approach and the consensus-objectives approach (de Roo and Miller, 1997). Specifically, proposed changes in noise and soil abatement legislation represent change (IPO, VNG and VROM, 1997; MIG, 1998). In terms of Fig. 4, it would mean that the point of attention within environmental policy moves to relatively complex conflicts. It is a position which makes it relatively easy to move to a policy which suits relatively simple or very complex conflicts. Central government is still issuing environmental standards, although these standards are no longer seen as fixed, and are no longer the only possible way to go. Also new is that local authorities can decide if they are willing to adopt the national guidelines or not. It means a shift in responsibility for urban environmental issues from national to local authorities. When a conflict is considered simple, national legislation will be implemented, using national guidelines as strict environmental standards. But when a conflict is considered relatively complex, local authorities will set their own standards, depending on the local situation and other interests. For extremely complex issues, strict national standards or even national guidelines have no use in the short term. A process of local interaction between all parties involved is needed to define the conflict, the planning procedure and the actions to be taken.

Consequences of thorough local policy making
If local authorities do decide to disregard national standards, they will have to compile a well thought-out local policy themselves. This policy will not only require a new set of standards that is better suited to local conditions, but will have to be imbedded within a strategic plan as well (Fig. 5). It should include a clear explanation of why the authority has decided to go its own way. This is the official proposal, but it is further complicated when complexity is taken into consideration.

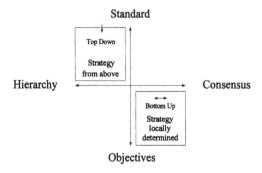

Fig. 5. Policy approaches in relation to strategic planning.

As long as local authorities implement centrally imposed environmental standards, it is clear to everyone what the strategy is, what the consequences are, and which roles different actors have to play. Most importantly, the rules, as well as their results, are clear to everyone. This changes when local authorities decide they need a more flexible and locally initiated policy to solve conflicts. When authorities view local environmental conflicts in a wider perspective there will be consequences. First of all, local authorities will have to set up a new policy framework to replace central government's planning strategy. A strategy should be designed in a way that relates conflict-related knowledge with a more abstract view of local environmental planning. It should also relate to other issues, such as local land use planning and traffic management, which are partially interwoven with the topic concerned. Objectives based on this wider perspective have to be well defined. Experiences in cities such as Amsterdam and Rotterdam (see Peters and Westerdiep, 1993; VROM, 1990b; Amsterdam 1994a, 1994b, 1995; Rotterdam, 1994) show that local strategies which include the 'grey' environment require substantial investments in knowledge, time and people.

Also important are the changes in thinking needed in local organisations dealing with uncertainty, complexity, and the consideration of which other parties should be involved in the decision making process. One of the main reasons why a conflict increases in complexity is because of the high number of people and organisations related to it. In such cases, authorities are no longer in a position to make decisions entirely on their own. Many interests are involved, and therefore other parties need to be included in the decision making process to improve its effectiveness and its efficiency. Then, consensus and participation strategies should be taken into consideration. In The Netherlands, this will mean a change in the traditional role that authorities are accustomed to. Their role will change from regulator to stimulator and participant. Authorities will have to accept a role more or less equal to other parties involved. This is a consequence of an unwritten rule that goes with the use of consensus strategies: the interests of different parties should be more or less equal, otherwise the strategy will fail (Teisman, 1992). However, local authorities' desire to create more flexibility should not be mistaken with the desire to have fewer rules. Every approach has its own rules, explicit or not, and its own possibilities and consequences. Therefore, local authorities that are willing to take responsibility to solve urban environmental issues should be aware of the consequences of their choice.

Complexity as a bridge between extremes
Complexity dependent decision making means that one general approach is not the answer to difficulties concerning urban environmental conflicts. More interesting is a move towards a position in which authorities can make a decision determining which approach should be adopted, depending on the complexity of the issue, and considering the options and consequences. In practice, this development is more or less taking place in The Netherlands, although not explicitly on the basis of complexity. From a theoretical viewpoint, the fact that choices have to be made about the nature of conflicts means that there is a bridge between functional rationality and communicative rationality. That bridge is complexity.

Mike Jenks
The Acceptability of Urban Intensification

Introduction

Few would dispute the fact that cities are a major concern in the context of achieving sustainable development. Cities have a significant global impact. Within 25 years it is predicted that over 60% of the world's population will live in urban areas (WRI, 1996). Cities are the largest users of renewable and non-renewable resources, and are responsible for the largest proportion of unsustainable development (White, 1994). The scale of the potential problems would appear to be vast, and difficult to define, yet tackling them would help to solve 'the most pressing global environmental problems' (CEC, 1990).

Since 1987, when Brundtland (WCED) raised an awareness of the problems, the response has been remarkable. Policies to deliver sustainable development have been widely adopted (Breheny, 1997). There has been considerable debate about the relationship between urban form and sustainability (Jenks *et al.*, 1997, 1996a; Urban Task Force, 1999; Breheny, 1992; Haughton and Hunter, 1994), much of which advocates compact, mixed-use settlements (Sherlock, 1991, 1996; Jenks *et al.*, 1996b). This work represents a significant area of theory and empirical research about urban form, and promotes the concept of the 'compact city'. Its basis is the idea of urban containment to protect valuable amenity and agricultural land from suburban sprawl (CPRE, 1996; HM Govt, 1996). The concentration of development within urban areas is claimed to reduce travel distances and thus emissions of harmful greenhouse gases (ECOTEC, 1993) and to encourage more sustainable modes of travel (DETR, 1998). Higher densities, it is suggested, would lead to more social vitality and economic viability for urban areas and more energy efficient land uses (e.g. Elkin *et al.*, 1991).

In existing urban areas one of the principal means of achieving the claimed benefits of the compact city is through a process of urban intensification – using urban land more efficiently and intensifying development and activity (see Table 1). Intensification is a process that has been recognised generally within European policy (European Commission, 1996; CEC, 1990). In the UK, there is a range of national planning policies to 'intensify' the use of existing towns and cities (Williams *et al.*, 1996; Williams, 1998). These policies assume greater significance in the light of projections for household growth, which predicted that 4.4 million new homes were needed by 2016, now modified to 3.8 million by 2021 (Urban Task Force, 1999, p.35). The government's response was to initiate discussion on where these new homes should be located (HM Govt, 1996), and the outcome was a policy for at least 60% of the projected new households to be accommodated in urban areas (DETR, 1998).

Yet the ideas of the compact city, and of urban intensification, are not fully tested and their effectiveness is at best open to debate. Many of the benefits claimed for intensification are at the strategic level, yet most of the impacts are local, and often likely to be negative (Williams *et al.*, 1996; Williams, this volume). Intensification is a cumulative process that takes place over time, and it is difficult to define the limits beyond which it may become 'over-development' (Burton *et al.*, 1996). The idea of environmental or development capacities has been developed using measurable indicators (UK Round Table on Sustainable Development, 1997). While there is broad consensus that 'an environment has a limit or capacity up to which it can absorb activities without irreparable harm' (Entec UK Ltd, 1997, p.25), there is less agreement as to these measures' utility, and they largely ignore the social dimension (Williams *et al.*, 1999).

Intensification of built form
- development of previously undeveloped urban land
- redevelopment of existing buildings or previously developed sites (where an increase in floorspace results)
- subdivisions and conversions (where an increase in the use of buildings results)
- additions and extensions (where an increase in the built densities or an intensification of the use results)

Intensification of activity
- increased use of existing buildings or sites
- change of use (where an increase in use results)
- an increase in numbers of people living in, working in, or travelling through an area

Table 1.
Definition of
intensification.
Source: DETR,
forthcoming

One of the most serious challenges to the claims for urban compaction has been raised by Breheny (1997), who suggests they should be subject to three tests. These are veracity (will the environmental benefits be delivered?), feasibility (can the market forces for counter-urbanisation be reversed?) and acceptability (will people affected accept it?). The evidence for the first two tests is not conclusive and questions still remain, especially about the feasibility of delivering a solution to the placing of a high proportion of the 3.8 million new households on existing urban land. The third test of acceptability until now has suffered from a lack of evidence (e.g. Breheny and Ross, 1998; Levett, 1998). From the evidence available at the time, Breheny suggested that policies for urban compaction or intensification are likely to be deeply unpopular. But is this true?

This chapter presents new evidence on the acceptability of intensification gathered from research into the perceptions of urban users. The attitudes of local people, and the factors affecting acceptability, are discussed, and the concept of *social capacity* is introduced. Social capacity is a 'measure' of limits to intensification in terms of local acceptance. It is proposed to be used alongside the physical measures of environmental and development capacity noted above. A decision support system is then suggested as a means to translate research findings into policy. It is shown that although intensification can have both positive and negative impacts, if understood and managed well, the process can be acceptable, and provide more sustainable urban areas in which to live.

Acceptable urban intensification
Research into intensification was carried out at Oxford Brookes University (with Entec UK Ltd) for the UK government (see note 1), and provided a key source of objective evidence about sustainable urban form (DETR, forthcoming; Jenks *et al.*, 1996b; forthcoming). A national survey of all local planning authorities was undertaken, followed by 12 case studies investigating the type and form of intensification, and the impacts this had on different stakeholders – residents, visitors and urban professionals. The research showed that the impacts of intensification varied from place to place and between the different groups involved, and that acceptability was dependent on a range of local factors. Various combinations of the

characteristics of an area, its socio-economic make up, and the type of intensification could lead to either negative or positive impacts, and predicting the impacts was context specific.

The findings pointed to the tension between the strategic measures designed to achieve sustainability and the impact they have on local populations. The proponents of urban compaction, and policies being implemented, suggest that intensification will be acceptable and that local people will change their behaviour to promote the wider public good (e.g. by giving up cars to live in high-density, car-free housing developments, or re-populating cities instead of suburban locations). The counter arguments are that market and social trends demonstrate the reverse, and intensification will not be accepted by the people affected (Breheny, 1997). So what is the evidence?

Attitudes towards intensification

There is no straightforward answer to whether or not intensification will be acceptable. Intensification is not a homogeneous phenomenon as every intensified area manifests a unique combination of different qualities and socio-economic characteristics. Even so, in general, local people clearly notice intensification and believe it affects them. They draw a clear distinction between the different forms it takes. Overall, more than half of local residents believe that increases in development either make no difference or make their areas better (Table 2). This contrasts with their views about increased activity, where the majority felt that the area was made worse as a result.

	Development (%)	Activity (%)
Much better	6	1
Better	22	10
No difference	29	16
Worse	30	54
Much worse	9	16
Don't know	4	3

Table 2. Perceived effects of increased development and activity on the local urban area. Source: drawn from DETR, forthcoming.

But a key issue is how satisfied local people are when living in intensified, or compact, denser urban areas. A housing attitude survey carried out for government (DoE, 1994), representative of all housing types, locations and densities, provides a marker against which the intensification survey can be compared. Most people in intensified areas are happy with their area as a place to live (78% are very or fairly satisfied), but they are not as content as the population generally (85% are very or fairly satisfied) (Table 3). However, these figures mask considerable differences. The housing attitudes survey was undertaken in areas ranging from low density rural locations where, overall, 89% of residents were satisfied with their area to suburban and residential areas (86% satisfied), and to higher density urban and city centre locations (76% satisfied). Overall, the intensification survey was comparable, with 85% expressing overall satisfaction in suburban areas, and 72% in urban areas. But in detail, the suburban/urban distinction found in the housing attitudes survey was not borne out in the intensification survey, as some urban areas were more highly rated than certain suburban areas. However, broad comparisons between the national figures and the intensification survey indicated little difference in overall satisfaction, so it seems unlikely that intensification will have accelerated counter-urbanisation trends.

Certainly those affected by intensification also perceived benefits. Better public transport and shopping facilities, and improvements to the appearance of an area through well-designed buildings and general upgrading were common themes. At the same time, there were problems, mostly related to traffic congestion, but also concerned with air pollution and noise, as well as worries over the loss of green space. Traffic is a particular problem in all urban areas, and equally, if not more so, in intensified areas. However, the research indicated slightly lower increases in levels of car ownership in intensified areas than nationally, suggesting that intensification might contribute to a modal shift away from the private car.

	Housing Attitudes Survey [1]	Intensification Survey [2]
Overall satisfaction [3]	85	78
Neutral	5	11
Overall dissatisfaction [4]	10	11

Table 3. Overall satisfaction with the area of residence – national housing attitudes survey and intensification survey.

1. Source: DoE, 1994.
2. Source: drawn from DETR, forthcoming.
3. 'Very satisfied' and 'fairly satisfied' categories combined.
4. 'Very dissatisfied' and 'fairly dissatisfied' categories combined.

The research does not support the view that intensification of the use of urban land will be generally unpopular, and therefore unacceptable. For those who choose to live in urban areas, increases in development are reasonably acceptable, but there are problems caused by increased activity from larger numbers of people living, working in and visiting their areas. Nevertheless, the vast majority of local people are generally satisfied with intensified areas.

The local acceptability of intensification

The broad aims for intensification and sustainable development are only likely to be successful if the process can be managed and implemented in a way that is acceptable to local people. While the research shows complexity and area differences, analysis across all the findings indicates that there are certain types and combinations of factors that are both acceptable to, and positively valued by, residents. These relate to the type of intensification, the type of the area within which it takes place and the social characteristics of the people experiencing it. Taking account of these factors and balancing the local and strategic level benefits is the key to achieving acceptable intensification. It is a basis for assessing the 'social capacity' of an area.

Type of intensification

The intensification of development can take the form of new development, redevelopment, conversions and extensions. Forms of intensification that are well-designed and predominately residential will generally be viewed positively. This is especially so if previously derelict or vacant land is developed. Small-scale and incremental intensification is also seen as acceptable, and small extensions in back gardens are hardly noticed at all. Conversely, large-scale, non-residential development, and the loss of amenity land, are viewed negatively. There is a strong preference for development that is in keeping with the character of the local area. Intensification tends to be unpopular when it is badly designed, out of keeping, or if redevelopment involves the loss of historic or traditional buildings.

Increased activity stems from the increased use of buildings and sites, and from more people using the area for living, work or leisure. The intensification of activity is frequently seen negatively (see Table 2). Particular dislikes are where newcomers change the social make-up of the area, especially if changes are perceived to affect property values. Some new uses, such as clubs, are seen as anti-social, adding to noise and disruption. However, more people in an area for more hours can help revitalise some urban areas and the evidence showed an increase in people's feelings of security. Again, the research indicated the variability of local circumstances. It indicates that many of the arguments for the vibrancy of urban living and the 24-hour city are valid only in some locations, and produce problems in others.

Type of area

Intensification is a process of change that takes place over a period of time. Not surprisingly, the existing character and quality of an area is highly significant in how intensification is received. In established high status areas, which have more to lose from changes, intensification is less readily accepted. These areas generally have a predominance of social classes I and II, and a high proportion of home and car owners. People living in more suburban or primarily residential areas often seek to protect the peace, quiet and space of their areas, their primary concern being about environmental quality.

By contrast, people in mixed-use, central urban areas appear to be tolerant of change. In these locations the increased activity and vitality achieved through intensification is generally positively received. It is the more run-down areas that tend to benefit most from the process. These areas often contain a large amount of derelict or vacant land, and new business, investment and housing can be an effective means of regeneration.

The intensified areas covered by the research tended to be at the higher end of the density spectrum, and the research did not reinforce national findings suggesting sharp distinctions in preferences for suburban over urban living. The density of an area has little to do with whether or not residents are content with their neighbourhoods: Table 4 shows there is no discernible trend in the data comparing density of persons per hectare and overall satisfaction of residents. The concern is more about any significant *changes* in density, although there may be limits beyond which increases in density become problematic. Residents are concerned that increases in density may change valued characteristics of the area rather than that they may make the area more built up, and so it appears that density *per se* is less important than the form and quality of development. Assessments of physical capacity of an area are, thus, unlikely to be a reliable indicator of whether or not intensification will be acceptable. Acceptability depends on a more complex set of issues that takes account of the social capacity of the locality.

Table 4. Density of intensified areas and overall resident satisfaction.
Source: drawn from DETR, forthcoming.

Density persons/ha.	Overall satisfaction % responses
5 < 20	93
20 < 40	72
40 < 60	77
60 < 80	89
80 < 100	75
100 +	68

Social characteristics

The social make-up of an area is significant. The research tested for the significance of age, social class, length of residence and tenure. The evidence provides some support for the idea of different levels of acceptance for different stages in people's lives. For example, the young and mobile, who rent rather than own their dwellings, have more positive views about intensification – an optimistic finding in relation to predicted increases in single-person and small households. However, older people, especially those who have lived locally for many years, and those in social classes I and II, are likely to be most negative about the changes resulting from intensification.

Indicators for social capacity

There is no one solution to achieving acceptable intensification. It is a complex process that depends upon a unique combination of the type of intensification, and the characteristics of the area and the people who live in it. The evidence briefly outlined above was subject to statistical analysis to identify key relationships between the significant factors affecting acceptability. These form the basis for indicators of social capacity identified in the research, and some examples, categorised by type of area, are presented in Table 5. However, these cannot be used alone. To be useful in predicting the social capacity of intensification they would need to be incorporated into an assessment method that takes account of the relationships between the indicators and is responsive to the combination of factors unique to each area. How, then, can the findings from research be used in practice?

Any area

- Activity intensification is likely to be more problematic than development intensification, although fewer people notice activity increases than notice development intensification.
- Intensification which causes negative impacts associated with 'outsiders' (e.g. commuter parking, through-traffic, litter brought in by visitors) is the greatest concern for local residents.
- Residential development is less problematic than non-residential development: new housing may reduce under-used space in the town or city, thereby improving perceptions of safety; or it may knit together physically fragmented communities.
- Non-residential development leads to more concentrated traffic problems and bad neighbour effects.
- Development on derelict or vacant land is unquestionably more popular than development on previously recreational or public land.
- Opposition to intensification is greater where it threatens the perceived assets of an area, such as its quietness, traditional character of the local buildings, or amount of open space. For this reason, redevelopment is more acceptable where it replaces buildings that are considered unattractive rather than buildings that are of local value.
- Increases in population tend to be more negatively received than increases in households. Population increases – where housing becomes more densely occupied – are often associated with overstretched facilities and lack of care for property, while greater household densities are perceived as supporting local facilities and services.
- Intensification that significantly changes the social make-up of an area causes concern for local residents, particularly homeowners.

High status areas

- Intensification is generally less favourably received in high status areas, because residents have more to lose from changes.
- High status areas usually contain a high proportion of social classes I and II and a high proportion of homeowners and car owners; these are the social groups that are likely to be the most concerned about intensification.

Suburban areas

- Intensification is more problematic in suburban areas than in more 'urban' locations. Again, this is probably because of its threat to the perceived assets of the area: privacy, open/green space, gardens, low density housing. Residents are often worried that intensification will erode the peace and quiet of the area or that it will change its residential character.
- As suburban areas are predominantly residential, non-residential development is particularly disliked.
- In lower density areas, local concerns revolve predominantly around issues of environmental *quality*.

City centre, mixed areas
• These areas tend to have the ability to absorb changes relatively easily. Because their assets are generally different from those of more suburban locations, the threats posed by intensification are not so great. People may choose city centre living for the vitality, activity and range of facilities it can offer and for the chance to be free of dependence on car travel.
• Many of the potential benefits of intensification (improved facilities, public transport, upgrading, increased prosperity) occur more frequently in these areas.
• Housing development in commercial areas can increase perceptions of safety, as can intensification involving promotion of the 24-hour city concept.
• Intensification which increases the number of visitors to an area has the potential to increase local prosperity and support local businesses.
• Car ownership levels are lower amongst city dwellers; therefore, some of the traffic problems caused by intensification are less likely to concern them (e.g. parking difficulties), while the potential benefits to public transport are more likely to be appreciated.
• Environmental problems caused by intensification in these areas revolve around the quantity rather than quality of space – i.e. loss of light and privacy, feeling hemmed in.
Inner urban, run-down areas
• Unsurprisingly, these areas are the ones most likely to benefit from intensification, because of its potential to upgrade and improve their general image and appearance, especially where derelict land is used for development. Such changes in turn may generate greater confidence in an area, attracting new businesses and investment and encouraging existing trade to flourish.
• Households in these areas are more likely to be renting their accommodation and are more likely to lack access to a car. Both factors are associated with greater acceptance of intensification.

Table 5. Potential social capacity indicators. Source: DETR, forthcoming.

Decision support for acceptable intensification

The European Commission (1996) recognised that systems for managing and accessing information which are user-defined, relevant and serve democratic ends are an important component in helping to make cities more sustainable. This gave an impetus to the development of a decision support system to put the findings from the intensification research into a workable tool. The system stems from a tentative exploration of a paper-based Intensification Assessment Method (IAM) developed in the research. It drew on the full range of information within the research, including correlation data, scaled judgements about the qualities of any urban area, assessments of issues that affect sustainability such as transport and design, and policies and examples of good practice.

The issues involved in urban intensification are clearly complex. As the process is characterised by differences, with each site having a different combination of factors, many possible solutions and alternatives will need to be explored. From its early beginnings, work is being undertaken on the IAM to develop a decision support system that takes into account social capacity indicators for use by the stakeholders involved in the intensification process (see note 2). The proposed decision support system takes account of the multiple objectives of different stakeholders, the complexity of the decision-making process, and should support a wide range of possible solutions (e.g. Bertuglia and Rabino, 1994). Such complexity is characteristic of many urban problems addressed by existing models. It is the reason why models have evolved from one method for decision support (e.g. GIS) to the development of multi-criteria decision aids, which link operational to spatial data (Wood and Rodriguez-Bachiller, forthcoming; Timmermans, 1997; Brandon *et al.*, 1997; Wegener, 1994; Batty, 1994).

The system is designed to be easy to use, and to enable users to deploy either judgement, and/or data, to make it work. Its output will identify possible impacts through exploring alternative solutions and scenarios. There are three potential user groups: local authority planners responsible for land use and development control; community groups, users and residents wanting to know the impact of proposals to intensify their local areas; and designers and developers who may wish to explore proposals for intensification that are financially feasible, and test out alternative designs in the local context. The decision support system, as it is being developed, uses a process which has a common base, but which can access different forms of information. Three stages are required:

1. Definition of the type of intensification and area (the types of intensification that will take place, and the area's social and environmental characteristics, i.e. its social capacity).
2. An assessment of the likely impacts of the particular intensification typologies.
3. Provision of guidance on making judgements and taking action.

The three-stage process is based on indicators (stages one and two) with supporting information on call in graphical and/or statistical form and, in stage three, on guidance and examples of good practice being presented that relate most closely to ameliorating negative impacts, or encouraging positive ones (Table 6).

Stage	Aim	Derivation
1	Determination of intensification typology	From 71 indicators used in 12 case studies
2	Assessment of likely impacts of particular intensification typologies	Statistical analysis of data obtained from case studies – some 50 significant impacts
3	Guidance on making judgements and taking action	From interview, and analysis of policy documents, practice and literature

Table 6.
Derivation of an intensification assessment method.
Source: Jenks and Gerhardt, 1998.

Object-oriented database technology is used to integrate systems through dynamic data exchange and object linking and embedding. It can be made to work with incomplete data, and still yield useful results. The 'objects' include the complex data, or judgements, that can be made about the physical and environmental characteristics of an area, the types of intensification that are happening, or which are proposed, and the socio-economic data either from census or local knowledge. The database will also be able to hold local and strategic policies for achieving sustainability, and examples of good practice that can be used for guidance.

The design allows several applications and users to share the same information at several levels of abstraction, supported by advanced object database technology (Essenius *et al.*, 1998). The system offers generic modelling functionality for design, planning and assessment of a proposal, as well as for the re-design, planning and assessment of existing areas. The impacts of changing designs and plans are simulated, linking physical to socio-economic characteristics. The developed system will be used at either a site specific or neighbourhood scale to facilitate discussion on the consequences of urban intensification in a given area. It will not show an 'optimum' outcome, but will allow an accurate exploration and elaboration of development alternatives (Jenks and Gerhardt, 1998).

Conclusions

This chapter has presented some of the evidence that suggests that intensification *can* be an acceptable process, and one through which more sustainable urban forms might be achieved, but only in certain circumstances. It has also outlined a way in which the complexities and local differences inherent in the process might be incorporated into practice through a system for decision support. Of course, such a system is only one way forward, and at present it is under development: but it does explore an important aspect of intensification. To be successful, the process needs to be managed in a way that is not deterministic and does not prescribe simple solutions. Alternatives need to be explored, and discussion between various stakeholders should take place to enable acceptable decisions to be reached.

Far from being the wholly unpopular option that many critics argue, intensification can be beneficial, and can contribute to making some urban areas more sustainable and livable. The evidence suggests that intensification may help reduce pressures for outward expansion, and may help to attract at least some sectors of the population back into urban areas. But it is not a universal panacea. A range of different environmental and socio-economic factors can combine in different ways, cause different responses to intensification and lead to different impacts – which may be regarded as positive or negative. With careful urban management and policies that take account of the range of factors identified in the intensification research, many of the impacts can be managed to achieve local benefits (Williams, 1997).

Understanding and responding to local differences is the key issue. The idea of social capacity suggests that there are limits in terms of types and amounts of intensification beyond which the process will become unacceptable, and therefore, in the long term, unsustainable. These limits can only be locally determined, and those managing the process will need to balance these limits against their broader, strategic aims for sustainable development. The key is in interpreting the research findings to draw from them the types of intensification likely to be seen as beneficial in different locations.

The research gives some cause for optimism. Although intensification will not reverse the flight from cities, it can certainly make a contribution to accommodating a proportion of the predicted growth in households, especially since so much of that growth is expected to be among the young and single and is planned to take place in inner urban areas. The research shows that it can be achieved beneficially at the local level, and that it can in certain circumstances be acceptable. If this is so, then intensification will help achieve a measure of urban compaction in ways that will forward the broad objectives of sustainable development.

Notes

1. The research studied intensification over a 13-year period from 1981. It was carried out for the Department of the Environment (now DETR), and the final report submitted in 1998. The work was carried out by Oxford Brookes University (with Entec UK Ltd), and was written by E. Burton, K. Williams and M. Jenks of the Oxford Centre for Sustainable Development. The opinions expressed in this chapter are those of the author, and do not necessarily represent those of the DETR.
2. The decision support system is being developed in collaboration with Professor Waltraud Gerhardt at the Technical University Delft and Steve Race of D'Arcy Race, Oxford.

Hugh Howes

Sustainable Development Comes of Age:
The Thames Environment 21 Experience

Introduction

Thames Environment 21 – The Environment Agency Strategy for Land-Use Planning in the Thames Region (The Environment Agency) was published in March 1998. It provides an approach to achieving sustainable development in the most congested part of England. It sets out the key environmental issues that the Agency wishes to see addressed through the land use planning system in the Thames Region, and indicates the enhancement and mitigation measures that are required from developers if the environment is to be protected and improved. It provides a method for assessing the impact of development on the environment and demonstrates to all those involved in the planning process how this impact can be managed, and a better environment achieved.

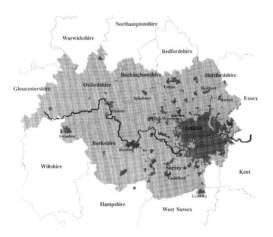

Fig. 1. The Thames Region.
Source: The
Environment Agency.

The *Thames Environment 21* strategy has three main messages. First, it stresses the need for close working between local planning authorities, the development industry, water companies, environmental and economic interest groups and the Environment Agency. Second, it promotes an appraisal methodology to assist strategic planning authorities in selecting sites that are most appropriate for major developments. Third, it gives advice on how the stock of environmental assets can be enhanced through the development process.

The role of the Environment Agency in the town and country planning system is that of a statutory consultee. It has the right to be consulted on development plans and on a range of planning applications. It is entitled to comment but the local planning authorities take final decisions. Accordingly, there is a premium on persuasion and influence to ensure that environmental issues are addressed properly. The Agency is refocusing the emphasis of its planning work towards influencing regional planning guidance and development plans. Success in securing sustainable development is most likely to be achieved through proactive involvement in forward planning by specifying environmental objectives at an early stage in the development process. This chapter sets out the techniques that the Agency has developed to ensure that it makes a positive contribution towards achieving sustainability, at both strategic and local levels, through the planning system.

The challenge of achieving sustainable urban form in the Thames Region

The Thames Region is already intensively developed and continues to experience high levels of growth. It contains nearly a quarter of the population of England and Wales, generates more than a quarter of the gross national product and a similar proportion of all construction work. The region is at the forefront of new industries such as information technology, biotechnology and advanced engineering. No less than 88% of the working population in the region is employed in the service sector. The Government's Green Paper, *Household Growth: Where Shall We Live?* (HM Government, 1996), suggests that current planned levels of growth will be exceeded by approximately 10% in the period to 2016.

Thames Environment 21 provides an approach to achieving sustainable development in the face of some challenging development pressures. These include: a more dispersed pattern of development and growth in traffic; growth in the number of households; industrial and commercial development; disturbance of contaminated land; mineral extraction; and waste production and disposal.

Thames Environment 21 contains three sections. The first outlines the role and responsibilities of the Agency, and gives an overview of the environment within the Thames Region, and an outline of the Agency's vision for the region. The second describes the Agency's six sustainability principles, and how they relate to the Agency's concerns for the region. The third considers how these principles can be applied to land use planning.

Sustainability principles

The six sustainability principles devised by the Environment Agency aim to:
1. manage ground and surface water resources to achieve the right balance between the needs of society and the requirements of the environment;
2. manage floodplains and flood risk for the benefit of people and the natural environment and the protection of property;
3. maintain and, where possible, improve the quality of air, land and water through the prevention and control of pollution, and by applying the 'polluter pays' principle;
4. achieve reductions in waste through minimisation, re-use and recycling, and improved standards of handling and disposal;
5. conserve and enhance the natural, cultural and historic value of river corridors, their landscapes, and biodiversity; and
6. retain, improve, and promote water and waterside land for the purposes of navigation, appropriate recreational use, and public access and enjoyment.

These principles cover the environmental factors which the Environment Agency believes should be taken into account in land use planning. They should guide the nature and location of development within the region.

Thames Environment 21 includes a series of planning strategy tables that contain issues which planners should consider when reviewing policies and proposals in order to promote the Agency's sustainability principles. The tables also include environmental indicators to monitor each principle, and possible mitigation and enhancement measures which can be implemented to improve environmental conditions.

The economic consequences of introducing environmental enhancements into the development process

The development process provides significant opportunities for physical solutions to achieving sustainable urban form. *Thames Environment 21* shows several examples. Success is most likely where both the Environment Agency and the local planning authorities specify environmental enhancements at an early stage in the development process. This may be through a local planning authority's development plan, a planning brief, or a planning agreement between a landowner and a local planning authority.

Figure 2(a) shows how the developer bases his or her calculations on the market value of the completed development. From this the development costs, finance costs and an element of profit are subtracted. Unless the developer is aware of a requirement for environmental enhancement, the residual sum will be the maximum he or she is prepared to pay for the site. Clearly it is too late at this stage for the Environment Agency to require a substantial mitigation package. Figure 2(b) demonstrates what happens when the Environment Agency specifies its requirements for environmental enhancements in advance. In this case the developer takes the environmental enhancements into account during the financial calculations and offers correspondingly less for the site. The landowner will make less profit on the sale but, as the environmental enhancements are the key to releasing the development value of the land, he or she is still better off than if the land had been held back. Figure 2(c) shows that the environmental enhancements are likely to increase the value of the completed development and that they are, in any case, likely to partially finance themselves. Figure 2(d) reflects the situation where planning policies are seeking to divert development pressures to the redevelopment of brownfield sites. The value of the development to the purchaser is unlikely to be greater than if the development had taken place on a greenfield site. Furthermore, there are additional site costs to be taken into account and there may therefore be less scope for the Environment Agency to seek substantial environmental enhancements. Nevertheless, there are many examples of successful enhancements being included in development schemes, particularly where planning permission has been granted for retail development which results in a substantial increase in site value.

It should be noted that whilst the Agency plays a valuable role in advising the local planning authority on required or desirable environmental enhancements, it is the planning authority that negotiates the package of benefits (including environmental enhancements) which will be required of developers.

Achieving sustainable urban form at the strategic level

The objective of *Thames Environment 21* is to secure a strategic enhancement of the quality of the environment of the Thames Region by:

- ensuring that new development contributes to the quality of the environment
- preventing further erosion of the region's rich heritage
- promoting restoration of damaged environments and
- contributing to sustainable management of the region's natural resources.

An environmental appraisal process has been used to analyse strategically the cumulative environmental impacts of major development at a number of locations across the region. An integral aspect of this work has been the development of a profile of environmental constraints and opportunities for each county within the region and for London. These will be updated to reflect changing demands and will aid the Agency in its discussions with local planning authorities.

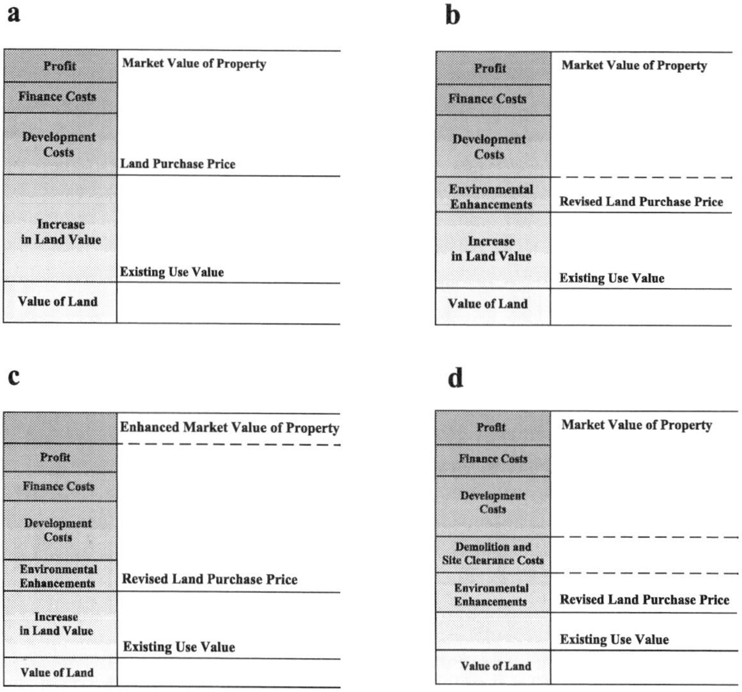

a

b

c

d

Fig. 2. Costs and benefits: developers' calculations.
Source: The Environment Agency.

The process has been applied in London, Hampshire, Surrey, Swindon and Stevenage and will be applied in other parts of the region to support the Agency's role in the preparation of development plans and in its contribution to planning inquiries. The process is based on a simple matrix which analyses the potential impact of a proposed development in terms of the sustainability principles set out above. The impacts are shown as potential effects – major positive, minor positive, major negative, minor negative or no significant effect. The analysis is supported by a significant amount of descriptive material.

Table 1. Environmental appraisal technique.
Source: Thames Environment 21 (The Environment Agency, 1998).

Key pressures	Potential environmental constraints and opportunities	Sustainability principles					
		1	2	3	4	5	6
Transport and dispersed development							
Housing growth							
Industrial and commercial development							
Contaminated land							
Mineral extraction							
Waste							

The analysis makes it possible to assign development sites to one of three bands (Table 2). Most sites fall into Band 2. The studies provide the opportunity for the Agency to provide a detailed specification of the mitigation and enhancement measures at a very early stage in the planning process, with a correspondingly greater chance of success. In this way these studies provide a focus for forming partnerships with organisations involved in land use planning to identify and appraise environmental constraints and opportunities.

Band no. of site	Site characteristics
1.	Sites where there is an overriding environmental objection.
2.	Sites where there are either potential or known major environmental issues but where there is scope for mitigation and enhancements.
3.	Sites where there are no significant environmental constraints.

Table 2. Site categorisation technique.

The household forecasts (DoE, 1995), which state that, if current demographic trends are projected into the future, then 4.4 million new households will be created by 2016, have placed additional pressures on local planning authorities to identify further sites for development. The Environment Agency is using the process outlined above to assist them in selecting the optimum sites for development. The following two examples demonstrate the versatility of this approach to strategic environmental impact assessment. The first demonstrates how the technique helps assess the relative merits of alternative sites, whilst the second illustrates how environmental enhancements can be promoted for a single site.

The prospect of providing dwellings for up to 10,000 additional households adjacent to Swindon – a large town in the south west of England – is likely to have significant environmental effects which are of concern to the Agency. Swindon Borough Council held a consultation exercise based on three development sites and a further two long-term options. Using the method shown above, the Environment Agency was able to provide an analysis of each site and the impact of development on it, in terms of the sustainability principles. The Borough Council then took these environmental considerations into account in reaching a decision on the most appropriate location for future development.

Hertfordshire County Council has resolved to develop land to the west of Stevenage in the south east of England for housing development. The initial development is of 3,600 houses but enough land has been allocated for a long-term total of 10,000. The site is to be developed within the 'Garden City 21' programme, a key element of which is sustainability. This programme involves a partnership of five organisations reflecting interests from local authorities at a county and district level. The Environment Agency commissioned a study to provide a concise statement of the Agency's interests and concerns relating to the site and to make recommendations on how these might be addressed in the development. They include:

- supply of water resources
- the effects of urban surface run-off on flood risk and water quality
- the available capacity of sewage treatment works
- potential pollution of the chalk aquifer
- the effects of development on river corridors
- the lack of spare landfill capacity
- the effects on air quality

The study treats each of these issues both as a concern and as an opportunity, and includes a range of appropriate mitigation measures.

Achieving sustainable urban form at the local level
In addition to working at a strategic level, the Environment Agency is also involved, at a local

level, with individual site developments. The protection and enhancement of the environment relies on good working relationships between the Environment Agency, local planning authorities and developers. The Agency is keen to promote its plans and proposals through working closely with all agents involved in development. Co-operation can offer significant benefits to the environment and to the community. Developers can likewise benefit from an enhanced environment. Partnerships can therefore be an efficient and effective method for promoting the interests of all parties.

One of the primary pressures on the Agency will continue to be the environmental impact of new development. It is therefore essential for Agency staff to identify, at various stages of the planning process, how the Agency's interests can be protected and furthered through partnerships with external bodies, including local authorities, industry and environmental groups. Partnerships have resulted in the achievement of a wide range of environmental enhancements. A few such enhancements are described below. They are examples of schemes that the Environment Agency has secured through the planning system.

Soho Mill, Wooburn, Buckinghamshire – Soho Mill on the River Wye is located in the village of Wooburn, approximately 3km upstream of the confluence with the Thames. Following the closure of the mill, the site was redeveloped for industrial use until this ceased in the 1980s and the buildings were demolished. The river through the site was left largely unaltered from its previous condition when the mill was working, and included a two-metre weir drop through the old mill race, together with restrictive brick channels and arches. The developer wished to redevelop the main body of the site as a warehouse, and a new scheme of river works was designed. He was keen to enhance the river environment fronting his new premises, as were the local authority. A new design included splitting the weir into two smaller ones to lower a section of the river, and constructing a fish pass. Improvements to channel capacity were also included. The scheme is an excellent, small-scale example of multidisciplinary work. It demonstrates the benefits of working in partnership with the local authority through the planning process and with an enthusiastic developer.

Restoring a river as part of a major residential development at Aylesbury, Buckinghamshire – The Fairford Leys development consists of 70 hectares of housing on the edge of the built up area of Aylesbury. In addition to a large flood compensation area to be excavated, and landscaping on the edge of the River Thame floodplain, considerable work is being carried out to restore the formerly heavily engineered main rivers to a more natural state. This involves reforming the watercourses as multi-stage channels within enhanced river corridors, which vary in width between 35 and 90 metres. The low-flow channels will be aligned with a natural sinuosity and provided with pools and riffles. This development is an important milestone for the region as it represents the first major river restoration project achieved in co-operation with, and funded by, private development.

A superstore at Wokingham, Berkshire – The hard, impermeable areas associated with development can result in undesirable consequences in terms of the rapid run-off of surface water. This can result in poor quality water entering watercourses and a risk of local flooding. The Agency is therefore promoting a range of measures for dealing with surface water as close to its source as possible. The car park at this superstore demonstrates several such measures, and is an excellent example of a more sustainable approach to development. A permeable pavement prevents the rapid run-off of surface water, which is filtered through pipes in the surface and discharged for filtration through a reed bed. A two-stage channel restricts the rate of discharge into the local watercourse.

Redevelopment of Bell Green gasworks site, South East London – Former gasworks present a considerable challenge both to local authorities and the Environment Agency in terms of their high levels of contamination. The former Bell Green gasworks site has a long history, stretching back to the nineteenth century. The Pool River interrupted the operational requirements of the works. To overcome this, the river was contained in a straight concrete culvert three metres below ground level.

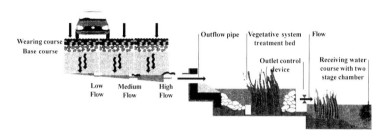

Fig. 3. A cross-section of the car park at the Tesco superstore showing sustainable urban drainage techniques.
Source: The Environment Agency.

In the late 1980s British Gas Properties (BGP) began to investigate and consider the viability of redeveloping the Bell Green site. From the earliest stages BGP worked closely with the London Borough of Lewisham and the National Rivers Authority (now the Environment Agency) to identify a regeneration strategy that would have a beneficial impact on both the economy and environment of the local area. Part of the site was redeveloped as a superstore and part was laid out as public park to contribute to the policy of providing 'green chains' through London. Over 100 years of gas manufacture had left a legacy of contamination in parts of the site. Contaminants were either removed or contained within the site. The Pool River could have remained in its existing position. However, the creation of a park with the river as its focus in an open channel was preferred. The river has been enhanced with a sinuous channel, cascades and riffles, all of which help the passage of fish. This significantly enhances the ecology of the river and provides an educational and leisure resource for the local community.

Conclusions

In recent years the Environment Agency has made great progress in translating the theory of sustainable development into practice. This chapter has suggested an approach towards achieving sustainable urban form. *Thames Environment 21* looks at the region-wide challenges for achieving sustainable development in the context of substantial additional pressures for development stemming from the household projections (DoE, 1995). It defines sustainable development and provides a methodology for ensuring that all new development includes mitigation and enhancement measures that will add to the environmental capital of the region.

The Agency has been involved in a wide range of environmental enhancement schemes involving partnership arrangements with local planning authorities, developers, water companies and amenity groups. Examples of such schemes have been described, including cases where land contamination has been an issue. The statutory system of town and country planning offers opportunities for securing a range of environmental enhancements. The challenge is to recognise these opportunities and to maximise their potential.

Acknowledgements

The author wishes to thank the Environment Agency for permission to contribute to this book. The views expressed are those of the author and are not necessarily those of the Agency. Hugh Howes was project manager for *Thames Environment 21: The Environment Agency Strategy for Land-Use Planning in the Thames Region.*

Abigail Raymond
The Kent Design Initiative:
Towards a Sustainable Future

Introduction

Good design is not simply a matter of what buildings look like but how they function and relate to each other. The spaces between buildings are also important in the creation of quality environments. While, in the UK, structure plans and local plans consider where new development should go, design guides inform how development should take place, offering decision makers the parameters by which to judge proposals, and giving developers advice on how to meet design objectives. New development represents only a small proportion of the built environment but it can make a significant contribution to promoting sustainability by demonstrating good practice and raising awareness of environmental issues.

Historically, design guides have tended to focus on aesthetic and highway considerations. Promoting sustainable development creates a particular challenge for a design guide in that many sustainability principles, such as resource management, have not tended to figure prominently within the planning process, or fall outside planning control.

The aim of the Kent Design Initiative (KDI) was to produce a design guide that embraces sustainability, while at the same time raising the quality of development. To meet these objectives it was recognised that all the key stakeholders involved in development in Kent would need to be given the opportunity to influence the principles to be included in the guide. In the context of producing formal supplementary planning guidance this is a fundamentally progressive approach.

This chapter sets out the processes that have been established to take the KDI forward. It presents some of the KDI's preliminary findings and refers to the constraints identified in promoting sustainable development and the potential for overcoming these constraints. The chapter also reports on some of the related activities being promoted by the KDI, including research, education, marketing and demonstration projects.

Background to the Kent Design Initiative

The last *Kent Design Guide* (KDG) (Kent County Council) was published in 1995. It offered advice on a range of design issues but concentrated on residential development, and was dominated by highway design standards. It has been largely superseded by major shifts in government policy, especially those relating to sustainability and transportation issues. For example, its focus on residential development did not address the relationship between uses, which has become so crucial to the sustainability agenda. One of the key criticisms of the KDG was that there had been insufficient consultation on the proposals contained within it: this had undermined its credibility and was one of the reasons why it was not well used. The desire to produce a new KDG was also influenced by the poor quality of many recent developments which are dominated by highway layouts, and lack convenient facilities. This has led to an increasing dependence on private cars.

There have also been a number of significant developments in policy and guidance in recent years, particularly at the national level, which have had a bearing on design and highway matters and influenced the decision to revise the KDG. Some of the most influential documents are listed below.

- *Planning Policy Guidance 1: General Policy and Principles* (DoE, 1997a) – gives increased weight to sustainability and design issues, seeking to encourage mixed-use developments and local distinctiveness.
- *Planning Policy Guidance 7: Countryside* (DoE, 1997b) – acknowledges the need to enrich, as well as safeguard, the character of the countryside.
- *Planning Policy Guidance 9: Nature Conservation* (DoE, 1994a) – recognises that Britain's wildlife is an integral part of towns, counties and coast, and not confined to statutory sites.
- *Planning Policy Guidance 13: Transport* (DoE and DoT, 1994) and the Transport White Paper *A New Deal for Transport: Better for Everyone* (DETR, 1998) – advocate a shift from car usage to walking, cycling and public transport.
- *Planning Policy Guidance 23: Planning and Pollution Control* (DoE, 1994b) – gives advice on the relationship between control over development under planning law and pollution control legislation. The aim is to avoid duplication and encourage consultation. This guidance states that the potential for pollution is capable of being a material planning consideration.
- The CEC directive on the conservation of natural habitats and of wild flora and fauna (CEC, 1992) – requires member states to endeavour to encourage the management of landscape features which are of major importance for wildlife and flora.
- The Quality in Town and Country initiative launched by the DoE in 1994 (DoE, 1994c), and the Urban Design Campaign in 1995 (DoE, 1995) – aim to stimulate debate and encourage best practice in good quality urban design, sustainable development and community responsibility.
- *Circular 5/94: Planning Out Crime* (DoE, 1994d) and *Advice Note: Secured by Design* (Association of Police Officers Project and Design Group, 1994) – aim to encourage the building industry to adopt crime prevention guidelines in commercial and residential design.

In the light of these policy and guidance changes, and as a response to local concerns, the KDI was launched. This was done at a major conference in October 1998, where a wide range of development interests were represented.

Organisational structures
The KDI is a partnership led by the Kent Association of Local Authorities (KALA) including the 12 Kent District Councils, Medway Unitary Council and Kent County Council. It is overseen by a steering group whose experience, ideas and advice helps guide the overall campaign. Day to day management is the responsibility of a project management group made up of representatives of the Kent Planning Officers Group (KPOG) and Kent Technical Officers Association (KTOA). Working groups were established to develop ideas and provide a technical input during the first stage of the campaign. A project team was set up to co-ordinate and administer this process and to draft the new KDG.

Steering group
The steering group meets quarterly to direct and review the progress of the KDI and to provide feedback on any documents produced: numerous local and national organisations are represented (see note 1).

Working groups

The role of the working groups has been to identify the broad principles and practice that might be carried forward into the design guide. Individual working groups identified their own work programmes and the issues to be researched. They received presentations from specialists within the groups and from external organisations, including representatives from water companies, architectural practices and planning and development consultants such as Ove Arup, David Lock Associates and Llewelyn-Davies. Topic papers were prepared setting out the main findings of each group and proposing a number of principles to be carried forward into the KDG.

The Sustainability Working Group

The Sustainability Working Group identified the following broad principles as important for the KDG:

- reducing the need to travel
- reducing the consumption of natural resources
- safeguarding landscape and built features of importance
- maximising the use of land
- increasing biodiversity
- minimising pollution of air, soil and water
- minimising the production of waste by re-using and recycling
- minimising the consumption of natural resources
- involving local people – promoting greater choice for consumers to achieve more sustainable lifestyles

Innovation in Design Working Group

The role of the Innovation in Design Working Group was to identify how innovation and innovative techniques could be used to promote sustainability objectives. It considered five broad issues: highways, construction, water demand management, mixed-use development and community safety. The key findings of the group are summarised in Table 1.

Achieving Good Design

The Achieving Good Design Working Group examined both how to attain better quality design and the constraints that currently work against it. The group recognised:

- The value of a multi-disciplinary approach to schemes, and early involvement of local councillors on major schemes.
- The importance of good preparation before negotiations.
- The importance of the local authority setting out their requirements in a comprehensive manner early in the process, for example, in local plan policies and development briefs.
- The need for adequately skilled designers and controllers to embrace innovation and address its implications.
- The need for adequate and timely public consultation and involvement of councillors.
- The importance of environmental education.

The working group format provided a useful means of developing ideas, sharing expertise, and identifying constraints and ways of overcoming them. A number of suggestions for action emerged that went beyond the scope of the KDG from the working groups, such as support for public transport. The KDI will have to consider how to take forward these issues, for example through lobbying of central government.

Issue	Recommendations
Highway design	Car use should be discouraged by reassessing highway and parking standards; for example, by looking at historic precedents for less dominant road layouts, encouraging public transport by providing the necessary infrastructure, and promoting walking and cycling by providing convenient, safe and attractive facilities and reducing vehicle speeds through innovative highway design.
Water demand	Designers should be encouraged to develop schemes that management facilitate the use of recycled water, minimise the use of water, maximise water collection and protect water quality (NRA, 1995; Environment Agency, 1998).
Community safety	Safety can be enhanced by providing natural surveillance, ensuring public spaces are well maintained, populating streets by encouraging activity and movement on foot, differentiating between public and private space and providing CCTV in vulnerable locations (e.g. remote parking areas).
Construction	New technologies and techniques should be encouraged where they promote sustainable development. This might include the use of solar energy, recycled materials and energy efficient appliances and practices. It should be recognised that new eco-buildings can be attractive, and that sustainability features can be incorporated within traditional designs. A key role that the KDI could play might be to promote both the submission of sustainability statements – detailing the measures taken to reduce resource consumption – and the use of environmental rating schemes such as BREEAM (The Building Research Establishment Environmental Assessment Method) (BRE, 1995, 1998).
Mixed-use development	Drawing on the work of the Urban Villages Forum, the value should be acknowledged of bringing complementary uses together and providing convenient and safe routes between work, homes, shops and entertainment facilities. The new KDG should give advice on how to safeguard against conflicting uses and address market resistance to the concept of mixed-use development. It is also important that an appropriate range of uses and supporting community facilities are delivered at a suitable time in the process.
Landscape and nature conservation	Following the work of the Countryside Commission (1996a, 1996b), the importance was recognised of responding to site characteristics, protecting sensitive sites, minimising the impacts of new development and identifying appropriate mitigation for lost habitats. The creation of a network of open space and wildlife habitats and assurance that all residential and commercial developments are readily accessible to green space was also seen as vital to the success of a development, as was the need to address the long term maintenance of any proposed landscape and nature conservation areas.

Table. 1. The Innovation in Design Working Group's recommendations.

Environmental education

The North Kent Architecture Centre is currently running a series of highly successful architectural and regeneration initiatives in Kent and is leading the development of an educational project, linked to the KDI, intended to develop awareness amongst school and college pupils of design and sustainability issues. It is planned that the education project will be launched in conjunction with the publication of the new KDG. Potential elements might include producing computer games with a planning and design content, involving students in producing designs for local sites, and establishing an Internet page for schools.

Best practice from other guides

A number of design guides have recently been produced which have helped to inform the work and direction of the KDI. Such guides have been developed in Essex (Essex County Council, 1997), Norfolk (Norfolk County Council, 1998), Lincolnshire (Lincolnshire County Council, 1996), Leeds (Leeds City Council, 1996) and Suffolk (Suffolk County Council, 1993).

The Essex Guide *(op. cit.)* gives a detailed assessment of design principles such as site appraisal, spatial organisation and building form. It seeks to reduce the emphasis on the private car and reduce vehicle speeds. It provides a series of potential layouts for different types of development. Norfolk's Guide *(op. cit.)* gives emphasis to local character and traditional design, and contains a sustainability checklist. The *Lincolnshire Design Guide (op. cit.)* also places considerable emphasis on detailed design issues with the text supplemented with numerous drawings and photographs to demonstrate good practice. The *Sustainable Development Design Guide*, published by Leeds City Council *(op. cit.)* gives detailed advice on reducing resource consumption, designing and constructing environmentally sustainable buildings and giving priority to pedestrians, cyclists and public transport. It contains advice of a strategic, rather than site specific, nature and does not explicitly address aesthetic or local design issues.

Research

Concerns have been expressed by the Kent Design steering group that the public, as consumers, may not be prepared to accept some of the proposed changes advocated by the KDI. In response to this, the working groups took advice from the Kent Institute of Art and Design on a potential research project which would provide a benchmark of the sustainability of existing lifestyles. It would use consumer groups to test public attitudes to some of the principles from the KDI and to central government policy, such as reducing reliance on the private car and promoting higher-density urban development. It is envisaged that this research will inform how the principles contained within the KDG might be best marketed to professionals in the development industry and to the public.

Marketing strategy

It is important that all involved in development in Kent are aware of the new KDG and the principles contained within it. A marketing strategy has been developed which seeks to identify the target audience, for example, developers, planners, consumers, schools and government departments, within Kent. The new KDG should also be of benefit to other organisations outside the county as an example of good practice.

A conference is planned to launch the publication of the KDG at the end of 1999, and a series of seminars for user groups and community workshops will follow. As well as promoting the KDG, it is intended that the conference will help reinforce the principles contained within it through a series of lectures, exhibitions and design competitions.

Demonstration projects

In order to explore the practical aspects of some of the emerging principles, a number of demonstration projects have been identified. A proposal to expand the village of Iwade near Sittingbourne in Kent seeks to incorporate the principle of mixed-use development and give priority to movements on foot and cycle. This proposal is based on a design brief written in partnership with the developers. The project is being monitored by the University of Greenwich. Other potential projects demonstrate energy-saving building design, sustainable construction practices and innovative solutions to highway design.

Role of locally elected councillors

Councillor involvement and endorsement is seen as being an important component of the KDI. The KDI is led by the KALA, in which each Kent local authority is represented by its chief executive and council leader who receive regular updates on the KDI. Each local authority will also have an opportunity to formally report on the KDG to their respective committees, with the objective of seeing it adopted as supplementary planning guidance.

The sustainability and design agenda presents a major challenge to locally elected members who are keenly aware of the concerns and aspirations of their constituents, for example in respect of mobility, security, safety and amenity. A series of tours have also been undertaken to illustrate good and bad practice in recent developments and to introduce councillors to some of the innovative ideas under consideration.

Constraints

The KDI has exposed the tensions between sustainable development and the realities of the market place and decision making processes. Consumers have concerns about high-density and mixed-use development, such as the potential loss of privacy and the increase in nuisance from neighbouring activities. Developers are also wary of investing in products, such as water recycling infrastructure, when the market for them is not evident. Some have a similar reluctance to embrace more innovative housing designs, particularly when their market research suggests people prefer traditional styles. Similarly, current highway policies which rely on standard road layouts can inhibit the development of attractive and intimate communities which require a more flexible approach to highway design. However, change is resisted, partly because of liability issues associated with untested road designs. The inclusion of better quality landscaping to create an attractive environment can also raise concerns because of the maintenance burden that might be imposed on the local community.

The KDI has sought to tackle these constraints by exploring examples of good practice and encouraging practitioners to share expertise and develop advice for inclusion within the KDG. The KDG may, for example, advocate that maintenance issues are addressed more fully at the planning application stage rather than at adoption.

Summary of emerging objectives

Previous design guides for Kent have tended to adopt fixed standards and traditional design solutions. The new KDG needs to be flexible enough to respond to a range of innovative approaches, whether these relate to new highway layouts or to more sustainable building techniques. The new KDG is therefore likely to put a greater emphasis on objectives than standards. It will illustrate how to achieve these objectives by giving advice and examples of best practice, but allow sufficient flexibility for developers to meet the objectives in other ways and to respond to the specific characteristics of a site.

In order to reinforce the principles of sustainable development, it is envisaged that the KDG will also include a sustainability checklist. The emerging key objectives are outlined below. They aim to:

- Adopt a proactive and collaborative approach to development proposals to achieve the best solution for any site.
- Promote innovative solutions.
- Improve quality of life by bringing residential, commercial, retail and community uses together in a manner which reduces the need to travel.
- Provide a safe and secure living environment for people and property.

- Minimise the consumption of natural resources in the layout, construction and on-going use of a development.
- Embrace local distinctiveness, promote quality and protect existing features of cultural, visual and historical importance.
- Conserve, create and integrate landscape and natural habitats to mitigate the impact of development.
- Promote the movement of people by walking, cycling and public transport, to reduce dependency on the car.
- Conserve water resources and minimise consumption.
- Maximise the use of land by encouraging the development of recycled land and increasing density.
- Ensure appropriate maintenance arrangements for highway and landscape areas.

Conclusions

The KDI set out to be a broadly based campaign, primarily to give those with a vested interest in development within Kent an opportunity to contribute to the process and take ownership of the KDG when it is produced. The concept has already reaped considerable benefits with 25 bodies represented on the steering group, 60 organisations on the working groups and more than 100 additional contributors to conferences, seminars and workshops. The expertise, time and enthusiasm which have been made available to the KDI has produced a wealth of ideas and provided an invaluable testing ground for the principles that might be carried forward into the KDG. There has also been positive feedback from partners, relating to the pace and quality of the work that has already been produced.

The KDI has emphasised the interaction between different aspects of design; for example, it has recognised the role that landscaping can play in creating a safer environment as a traffic calming tool and in creating new wildlife habitats. A similar interrelationship exists between the desire to encourage more walking and cycling in order to reduce pollution and to populate the streets in order to promote community safety.

The KDI has recognised that sustainability is not an end in itself. It is important not only to market the principles of sustainable development but also to give practical advice to developers on how these principles might be implemented. The KDI did not set out to re-invent the wheel, but to draw on best practice wherever possible. While some of the ideas that have been promoted by the working groups may no longer seem particularly innovative, the uniqueness of the KDI is in the effort that is being taken to explore how the goals of sustainable development can be translated into a workable and enforceable design guide, embraced by all those with an interest in development in Kent.

Perhaps the KDI's greatest strength has been the constructive dialogue between traditionally opposing sectors. The KDI has already raised awareness amongst organisations and authorities within Kent of the value of sustainable development. Parties have been able to recognise and discuss each other's respective positions in a constructive fashion. The involvement of the Government Office for the South East has been valuable to the KDI because it enabled the national debate on sustainability to be furthered at the local level.

The ultimate test for the new KDG will be how developers and controllers respond to the challenge offered by more flexibility. There are some concerns that objectives rather than standards may be more difficult to enforce, and that any case studies and illustrations may be interpreted as new standards. The success of a more flexible approach is certainly dependent to a large extent on the willingness of all partners in the development process to collaborate and invest in the design process. That investment includes making the necessary time, skills and resources available to ensure that real improvements can be seen, both in terms of physical development and people's actions.

Notes
1. Kent TEC, Council for the Protection of Rural England, English Heritage, Government Office for the South East, House Builders' Federation, Institute of Civil Engineers, Kent County Council, Kent Developers' Group, Kent Institute of Art and Design, Kent Planning Officers Group, Kent Technical Officers Association, Landscape Institute, Royal Institute of British Architects, University of Greenwich, Women's Institute, Kent Police, Soroptomist International, Kent Federation of Amenity Societies.
2. The views expressed in this paper are those of the author and not necessarily those of Kent County Council or the KDI.

Giuseppe Zanré

Review of the Wycombe District Local Plan: *Comparative Strategic Site Assessment – The Goals Achievement Matrix*

Introduction

Local plans can make an important contribution to the achievement of sustainable development in the UK, a fact recognised in the requirement for local authorities to produce environmental appraisals as part of their local plan preparation. Such appraisals ensure that environmental issues are central to the local plan preparation process, and that local plans address all the necessary issues as consistently and effectively as possible.

Wycombe District Council's (WDC) commitment to sustainable development is part of its wider commitment to the environment. The techniques adopted in the review of the presently adopted *Wycombe District Local Plan* (WDC, 1995) and thus the preparation of the *Wycombe District Local Plan to 2011* (WDC, 1998), which will guide development in the District into the new millennium, have been designed to reflect this commitment, and to ensure that the new local plan addresses sustainability as fully as is possible.

Background

Wycombe District is in South East England and covers extensive rural areas together with the major urban centre of High Wycombe, the riverside town of Marlow, the rural settlements of Princes Risborough, Stokenchurch and Lane End, and many villages and communities, each with distinct identities. Extending to approximately 32,360 hectares, the District is subject to considerable development pressures in both urban and rural areas. This is because of its attractive environment, its location in the South East, its proximity to Heathrow Airport, and its position on the national motorway network.

One of the District Council's principal planning tasks is to reconcile development pressure with the protection and enhancement of the environment. Much of the countryside in Wycombe is within the metropolitan green belt, and the majority is within the Chilterns Area of Outstanding Natural Beauty (AONB). The District's residential areas are varied and attractive. There is a large number of conservation areas. These mostly centre on a village or hamlet, but also cover historic centres of the larger towns. The District has numerous listed buildings and archaeological sites, and a rich diversity of wildlife habitats. The River Thames along the District's southern boundary, together with its tributary, the River Wye, is a significant environmental and recreational resource.

The economic base of the District centres on High Wycombe and Marlow. The traditional industries are furniture and paper production. Modern service industries have been attracted to the District, and include nationally known firms such as Dun and Bradstreet, Saab, Volvo and Rank Hovis McDougall. Agriculture is important locally and many small firms have developed in association with it. Overall, the local economy is strong and diverse and is modernising to meet market conditions. New development is directed mainly to sites used previously for employment, and opportunities for new employment sites are limited.

266

Buckinghamshire County Council's (BCC) 1994-based population projections expect a 1% drop in the District's population between 1991 and 2011. The Registrar General's mid-year estimates indicate that Wycombe's population rose from 159,800 in 1991 to 164,100 in 1995, but fell in 1996 to 164,000. This indicates that the expected reduction in the population by 2011 is likely to take place, mostly as a result of net out-migration. The County Council predicts a change in the age structure of the population, with a reduction in the number of children and young people (under 18 years) and an increase in the number of people over retirement age. In 1991 people over retirement age accounted for 15% of the population, while in 2011 they are expected to form 23%.

Despite this fairly static population, the County Council, taking account of national household projections, has calculated that, if locally generated housing demands are to be met, the resident population of Wycombe will require 12,200 new homes to be built between 1991 and 2011. However, due to environmental constraints and the inadequacy of local transportation systems, the adopted Buckinghamshire County Structure Plan (BCC, 1996) (which provides the strategic context for the new local plan) has identified that only 60% (7,200 homes) should be provided during the plan period to 2011. By April 1997, 2,017 homes had been built.

Planning considerations

The 1990 Town and Country Planning Act (as amended) places a duty on local authorities to prepare a unitary or district local plan. These identify how the housing, transport, environmental and other needs of their communities are to be met. Like many other local authorities in the UK, WDC is facing difficult decisions about the location of future development and how to best deliver a development strategy which promotes sustainable development.

The District Council has a housing and employment allocation which has to be addressed within the new local plan for the period up to 2011. This allocation must satisfy the requirements of WDC, BCC and central government. Policy H2 of the *Buckinghamshire County Structure Plan* (BCC, 1996) establishes that a new strategic housing allocation of between 1,500 and 1,700 dwellings is required in the High Wycombe urban area between 2001 and 2011. A further 700–900 dwellings are to be allocated in the remainder of Wycombe District over the same time period.

Achieving sustainable development

In order to find sustainable locations for the dwellings required to meet local needs, WDC embarked on a process of sustainable site selection. The first stage in this process was the completion of an environmental appraisal of the *Wycombe District Local Plan* (*op. cit.*). This appraisal highlighted the key issues to be addressed in the production of the new local plan, and was the starting point for the development of WDC's appraisal methodology.

The results of the appraisal exercise were used, together with guidelines and advice set out in *Sustainable Settlements: A Guide for Planners, Designers and Developers* (Barton *et al.*, 1995), to inform the development of criteria for the initial assessment and selection of the new local plan's strategic housing sites (later published in the *Pre-Deposit Issues Paper*, WDC, Planning Policy Unit, 1997a), and it was at this time that the broader emphasis on sustainable development was introduced. This emphasis was confirmed in the following statement, approved by the Planning, Environment and Transportation Committee:

> The overall vision for the review of the local plan is to create a sustainable planning framework that contributes positively to the pattern of development in the District, balancing the needs and well being of the District's residents for homes and employment

growth with environmental constraints. The self-sufficiency of communities should be improved and, by so doing, the need to travel reduced. (WDC, Planning, Environment and Transportation Committee, 1996)

Sustainability testing involves the consideration of economic, social, equity and cultural issues, as well as environmental ones, and enables them all to be considered within the same assessment framework. Therefore, the initial site selection criteria (WDC, Planning Policy Unit, 1997a) were refined for use in a Comparative Site Assessment – Goals Achievement Matrix, which incorporated issues raised in responses from the public to the *Pre-Deposit Issues Paper* (*op cit.*). In all, WDC received 2,000 responses with the following major concerns.

- There was a desire for existing urban land to be used before greenfield sites were considered.
- The fact that some potential sites were in AONB or green belt was problematic.
- Respondents felt that development in some areas might add to traffic congestion and strain local services.

The Comparative Site Assessment – Goals Achievement Matrix was also adapted to reflect WDC's strategic plans. New criteria were added, and structured in accordance with the District Council's strategic vision for a caring and thriving community, a healthy environment and value for money.

Urban capacity study

At a meeting of WDC's Planning, Transport and Environment Committee in November 1997, it was resolved that:

a comprehensive review of brown field housing sites and employment land availability be carried out with a view to investigating in further detail the alternative development sites suggested in responses to the consultation exercise. (WDC, Planning Policy Unit, 1997b)

In response to this resolution, a comprehensive urban capacity study was undertaken (WDC, Planning Policy Unit, 1998a) to review the ability of existing built-up areas in the District to accommodate housing development. In particular, this was done with a view to investigating alternative development sites suggested in response to the public consultation mentioned above. The urban capacity study provided an opportunity to identify vacant, derelict, and underused land within urban areas which, if developed, would not compromise urban quality.

The study contained two elements: a primary investigation into urban site potential, and an evaluation of suggested alternative sites. The study divided sites into three broad categories, as shown in Table 1. This technical exploration provided an objective basis through which potential sites of 0.4 hectares or more, with a reasonable and sustainable relationship with the built-up area, could be assessed.

The urban capacity study identified 937 sites from the following sources:

- suggested alternative sites in response to pre-deposit public consultation in 1997 (204 sites);
- sites within the built-up areas of Wycombe District identified for further investigation by WDC's Policy Unit of the Planning, Transport and Development Directorate (225 sites);
- sites suggested by the development control teams of WDC's Planning, Transport and Development Directorate (106 sites);
- scattered employment generating sites and/or badly sited users (328 sites); and
- designated green spaces (74 sites).

Size of site (hectares)	Status of sites for future development
< 0.4	In accordance with *Planning Policy Guidance 3: Housing* (PPG 3) (DoE, 1992), these sites were not progressed through the study. Annex B, paragraph 10, states that studies should not normally attempt to identify small sites, and that an aggregate allowance for such sites should be agreed and clearly justified by evidence of the contribution which sites have made to housing provision in the area over recent years.
0.4–1.0	In accordance with PPG 3 (DoE, 1992, annex B, para. 10) every effort was made to identify such sites and a sensitivity test applied to assess their contribution to meeting 'windfall' projections.
> 1.0	In accordance with PPG 3 (DoE, 1992, annex B, para. 11), sites were assessed for development potential, for which allowance had not been made in earlier studies.

Table 1. Status of sites for future development (by size).

The next stage of analysis involved the removal of all duplicated sites within the above listed categories, sites within the green belt, sites within the Chilterns AONB outside established settlement boundaries, and sites of less than 0.4 hectares. This left 88 sites between 0.4 and 1.0 hectares, and 71 sites over 1.0 hectares, making a total of 159 sites. A further stage of analysis removed those sites which: were designated as green space, and were located within an area of critical public open space deficiency (as identified in *A Review of Public Open Space Needs and Provision in Wycombe District* [BDP, 1996]); were not suitable for residential development on the basis of compatibility with surrounding land uses; had access problems which could not be mitigated against easily; would not become available during the life of the new local plan because of ownership or existing planning consents; contained statutory or critical landscape and/or nature conservation designations; and were less than 1.0 hectares. This left 23 sites within the High Wycombe urban area and nine sites in the rest of the District. These were then reviewed in the light of technical information and responses from sources outside the Planning Policy Unit (Table 2).

- In-house information from WDC Directorates – Leisure, Health and Community, Property and Housing.
- BCC Departments – Environmental Services, Highways and Education.
- Statutory bodies including the Farming and Rural Conservation Agency (FRCA, 1998), Ministry of Agriculture, Fisheries and Food (MAFF), the Environment Agency and Thames Water.
- Consultants' reports on public open space (BDP, 1996), landscape quality (Gillespies, 1997) and Housing Needs (Fordham Research Services, 1996).
- A transportation study of all the strategic sites (Halcrow Fox, 1998).
- The public consultation exercise, as reported in the *Pre-Deposit Issues Paper* (WDC, Planning Policy Unit, 1997a)

Table 2. Sources of information for the review of 32 potential development sites in Wycombe District.

At the end of this investigation, four sites remained. These were then added to the sites already identified as strategic sites in the *Pre-Deposit Issues Paper* (*op. cit.*) and were put forward for comprehensive sustainability testing using the Comparative Site Assessment – Goals Achievement Matrix.

The Comparative Strategic Site Assessment – Goals Achievement Matrix
The Comparative Strategic Site Assessment process constitutes a highly comprehensive sustainability testing of the 22 remaining sites. Thirteen of the sites are within the High

Wycombe urban area and nine are within the rest of the District. Each of the sites was subjected to a detailed assessment against the Goals Achievement Matrix. The Goals Achievement Matrix reflected WDC's existing strategic plan goals, and concentrated on four key goals.

- A caring community – which incorporates leisure issues
- A thriving economy – which includes housing issues
- A healthy environment – which includes transport issues
- Value for money – which includes local democracy issues

By using the Goals Achievement Matrix, each if the 22 sites was tested against 32 individual sustainability objectives, ranging from a 'self-sufficient communities' objective to a 'public opinion' objective. The performance of a site against each of the four main goals, measured through the sustainability objectives, was tested further against three broad measures, derived in accordance with advice from Barton *et al.* (1995). This publication suggested the use of five measures, which were condensed for the purposes of the Comparative Site Assessment – Goals Achievement Matrix into three measures (Table 3).

Type of measure	Definition of measure
1. Critical constraint	where development would result in the loss of a critical asset, or performs badly against an individual objective and/or conflicts with national and regional planning policy.
2. Negotiable/transferable constraint	where development would lead to a specific issue which would need to be addressed either through negotiation, or by transferring, substituting or replacing the issue off-site.
3. Development opportunity	where development would deliver benefits, or performed particularly well in relation to an objective.

Table 3. Measures of constraint and opportunity used in the Comparative Site Assessment – Goals Achievement Matrix.

These three broad measures were developed in more detail in relation to each of the 32 objectives. They were also colour coded for the testing procedure of each site. As in the case of the *Urban Capacity Study* (WDC, Planning Policy Unit, 1998a), a number of sources of information, apart from the District Council's own records and site surveys, were used to provide detailed technical information in order to test each of the sites.

Comprehensive sustainability testing was successfully completed for each of the 22 sites, using the Comparative Site Assessment – Goals Achievement Matrix. The full testing for each of the 22 sites is outlined in more detail in individual site schedules (WDC, Planning Policy Unit, 1998b).

Results of the Comparative Strategic Site Assessment – Goals Achievement Matrix
Following the completion of the study, the results of which are summarised in part in Table 4, 11 of the sites that were tested were recommended to the District Council's Planning, Environment and Transportation Committee for inclusion within the *Wycombe District Local Plan to 2011* (WDC, 1998) as sites that would meet the *Buckinghamshire County Structure Plan* (BCC, 1996) housing requirement for the District, to 2011.

The following two case studies are examples of, first, a site which was recommended for inclusion within the list of 11 allocated sites and, second, a site which was rejected.

Wycombe Marsh Sewage Treatment Works, High Wycombe, Buckinghamshire – Occupying an area of 14.2 hectares, with a guideline figure of 300 dwellings, the site forms part of a development area which includes Wycombe Marsh Paper Mill. The site is located on the eastern transport corridor of High Wycombe, and offers an opportunity to provide a new residential environment as part of a mixed-development proposal. Development of the site would make the best use of existing brownfield land and would involve the relocation of the existing sewage treatment works on the site to Little Marlow. Of the 22 sites tested and of the 11 sites allocated for residential development, the Wycombe Marsh Sewage Treatment Works site performed best when assessed against the 32 sustainability objectives. It was therefore proposed that the site be one of the allocated sites for the new local plan.

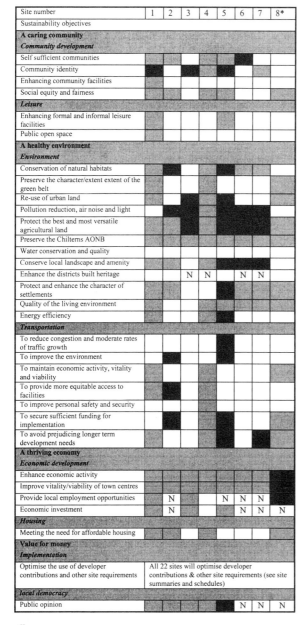

Site number	1	2	3	4	5	6	7	8*
Sustainability objectives								
A caring community								
Community development								
Self sufficient communities								
Community identity								
Enhancing community facilities								
Social equity and fairness								
Leisure								
Enhancing formal and informal leisure facilities								
Public open space								
A healthy environment								
Environment								
Conservation of natural habitats								
Preserve the character/extent extent of the green belt								
Re-use of urban land								
Pollution reduction, air noise and light								
Protect the best and most versatile agricultural land								
Preserve the Chilterns AONB								
Water conservation and quality								
Conserve local landscape and amenity								
Enhance the districts built heritage			N	N		N	N	
Protect and enhance the character of settlements								
Quality of the living environment								
Energy efficiency								
Transportation								
To reduce congestion and moderate rates of traffic growth								
To improve the environment								
To maintain economic activity, vitality and viability								
To provide more equitable access to facilities								
To improve personal safety and security								
To secure sufficient funding for implementation								
To avoid prejudicing longer term development needs								
A thriving economy								
Economic development								
Enhance economic activity								
Improve vitality/viability of town centres								
Provide local employment opportunities		N			N	N	N	
Economic investment		N				N	N	N
Housing								
Meeting the need for affordable housing								
Value for money								
Implementation								
Optimise the use of developer contributions and other site requirements	All 22 sites will optimise developer contributions & other site requirements (see site summaries and schedules)							
local democracy								
Public opinion						N	N	N

Key
- Development opportunity
- Critical constraints
- Negotiable/transferable constraints

Notes: Sites are 1: Wycombe Marsh, 2: Abbey Barn North, 3: Abbey Barn South, 4: Ercol, 5: Gomm Valley, 6: land north of Pimms Close, 7: Ashwells, 8: Axa/Sunlife.
* All 22 sites could not be included in this table; it shows only the first 8 listed.
'N' represents a case where it was deemed inappropriate to test a site against a certain criterion.

Table 4. A section of the Comparative Site Assessment results of testing.

Longwick Village Site, Longwick, Buckinghamshire – Occupying an area of 3.4 hectares, with a guideline dwelling capacity figure of 50 dwellings, the site at Longwick Village is identified as having the worst transport infrastructure of all the sites tested, owing to the lack of public transport facilities, and the inability of the site to support a commercially viable bus service. The results of the sustainability testing concluded that further development would not provide a sustainable form of development in comparison with other development opportunities within the District. The site did offer some environmental benefits, due to its location outside both the green belt and the Chilterns AONB; nor would it involve the loss of good agricultural land if developed. However, these comparative benefits were outweighed by the site's poor transport performance, which would not accord with the local plan's sustainability objectives. It was therefore proposed that the Longwick Village site not be allocated as development site for the new deposit local plan.

Recommended housing strategy

At the Planning, Environment and Transportation Committee in April 1998, members were presented with the detailed results of the sustainability testing which had taken place on the 22 sites. By developing the 11 recommended sites, the Government's requirement that at least 60% of all new development should be developed on brownfield land can be achieved by WDC, as 68.4% of dwellings should be on such land. The County's target up to 2011 could also be achieved. The assessment identified a list of high performing sites which were not required to meet the *Buckingham County Structure Plan* (BCC, 1996) allocation, but which were defined by the Planning, Environment and Transportation Committee as safeguarded land to meet development needs post-2011.

Conclusion

Following the District Council's Committee resolution in April 1998, the 11 sites were formally allocated for residential development in the *Wycombe District Local Plan to 2011* (WDC, 1998) via Policy H2 of the Housing chapter. The comprehensive sustainability testing carried out by WDC through the Comparative Strategic Site Assessment – Goals Achievement Matrix had therefore achieved the District Council's objective of achieving the County's housing allocation in a sustainable way.

Note

The views expressed in this chapter are those of the author and not necessarily those of Wycombe District Council (October 1998).

Part 4
Built Form and Design Solutions
Introduction

The chapters in Part 4 describe built or planned sustainable urban form 'solutions'. They give examples of where the problems of defining and implementing sustainable urban form have been worked through to the design and development stage, and where designers, clients or researchers believe that sustainability has been achieved. The solutions presented are chosen deliberately to illustrate the contrasting solutions emerging from attempts to achieve the common goal of sustainability. They give an insight into the varying interpretations of a sustainable future, by offering high and low-tech designs, and small- and large-scale developments and solutions derived from looking to the future alongside those drawing heavily on what has worked in the past.

The chapters by Thompson-Fawcett, Dumreicher *et al.* and Kalamaros describe 'urban' scale solutions: an urban village, a 'Sustainable City Implantation' and a large-scale infill project. Thompson-Fawcett introduces the urban village, as promoted by the Urban Villages Campaign in the UK, as a reply to 'modernist planning and the urgency of environmental and social sustainability'. By highlighting the aims of the campaign and presenting two case studies – Poundbury, a new settlement, and Crown Street, an urban regeneration project – she unravels the contributions that urban villages might make in moving urban development closer to a sustainable urban form. She concludes that although there are ideological goals which may fall foul of the managerialist nature of the campaign, the Urban Village does have some social and environmental merit and is an improvement on standard urbanisation processes in the UK.

Dumreicher *et al.* then describe their vision of a 'Sustainable City Implantation' (SCI), which is a modernist view of the sustainable city. They start from familiar definitions of sustainability, but develop a new urban form. They take the Italian hill town as a model, but change the 'city-on-a-hill' concept to a 'city-as-a-hill'. This model is developed for a site in Vienna. The authors outline how the workings of a dense, 'ant-hill' development will be managed by a computerised 'sustainability engine', which acts as the automatic nervous system of the city, reporting if it is out of balance. The SCI sits in a 'partnerland', which enables it to be self-contained in terms of resource use and environmental impact. This new urban form will, the authors believe, 'complete the agenda of modern architecture'.

The next example is of a large-scale infill project in West Los Angeles, named Playa Vista. Kalamaros describes developers' attempts to balance environmental, economic and community concerns and meet market criteria. He describes how every stage of Playa Vista's development was guided by a set of guidelines and principles covering building materials, recycling and waste, energy, domestic water, power signal and control, adaptability, landscape and transportation. These guidelines contain recommendations, measures and performance metrics, and lists of sources of technical information. Kalamaros describes the scheme as 'an example of a substantial demonstration of the viability of sustainable urban form in an American city'.

The next chapters take the urban 'block' and describe how it can be redeveloped, or developed, in a more sustainable way. Fauset reviews the 'Homes for Change' development at Hulme, Manchester, a self-contained community development with a shop, offices, workshops and housing, among other uses, which was constructed using sustainable materials. This is offered as a model for housing design in the future, in an age when most housing development is highly conservative and built for relatively wealthy homeowners, rather than for those seeking to rent.

Van Vliet and Gade offer two examples of sustainable renewal of urban blocks in Kolding, Denmark. The first, the Fredensgade block, focuses on making the water cycle visible to urban residents, and thus engendering support for rainwater collection and waste water treatment. The scheme incorporates a bioworks – an impressive pyramid building in the centre of the block – which not only enables the water to be treated, but also creates a unique and striking shared space for the residents. The second example is the Solgården block, which has been adapted to harness the sun's energy. By integrating a large photovoltaic system, the use of fossil fuels should be reduced. Both schemes are examples of bold and imaginative renewal, and have won international acclaim. It is hoped that they will act as demonstrations, and force a revision of current renewal practice by municipal departments and development partners.

The final three chapters address the scale of the 'dwelling'. The issue of sustainable social housing is addressed by Morgan and Talbot. They outline how a housing competition which used a 'sustainable housing assessment method' enabled two schemes to be chosen on the basis of their contribution to sustainability. The schemes have since been built in Glasgow. The authors explain how sustainable design was achieved without the need for trade-offs in other aspects of housing quality.

Hasic then presents his own vision of sustainable housing, derived from an expanded version of the principles of New Urbanism. The model is an apartment block called the 'Sustainable Urban Matrix'. It is four stories high, with four apartments on each floor, and can be multiplied by factors of four to form groups of apartments, or neighbourhoods. Such neighbourhoods adhere to some of the key principles of New Urbanism in terms of walking distance, size, mix of activities, building types and so on.

Finally, Heath explores whether the adaptive re-use of buildings for residential use should be perceived as a valid means of achieving sustainability. By reviewing recent building re-use initiatives and examples he draws the conclusion that re-use is sustainable because: it can be considered as re-cycling – use is made of embodied energy of buildings; it contributes to 'living in the city', and thus sustaining vibrant urban centres; and it meets certain housing needs, especially those of smaller households. However, he points out there are significant constraints to re-use which need to be overcome before it can be implemented at a significant scale.

These chapters illustrate clearly that there are a number of different routes through which sustainable urban form could potentially be achieved. They are examples of very different processes – from community-led solutions to computer-generated designs – and products – from the modernist city-as-a-hill to the more recognisable urban village. They outline schemes that have attempted to deal with one key aspect of sustainability, such as the water or energy cycle, and schemes that have addressed a multitude of social, economic and environmental criteria. Collectively, they are examples of competing, but not necessarily mutually exclusive, visions of sustainable urban form.

Michelle Thompson-Fawcett
The Contribution of Urban Villages to Sustainable Development

Introduction

The British Urban Villages Campaign was launched in June 1992. Stimulated by indefatigable architectural critic, HRH the Prince of Wales, it was a campaign born out of disillusionment with conventional development practice. Campaign protagonists' solution was the dedicated creation of 'urban villages' within the built environment. These villages are forms of development characterised by economic, environmental and social sustainability. In particular, according to the Campaign, they should include:

- A variety of uses, such as shopping, leisure and community facilities alongside housing.
- A choice of tenures, both residential and commercial.
- A density of development that can help encourage the use of non-housing activities.
- A strong sense of place, with basic amenities within easy walking distance of all residents.
- A high level of involvement by local residents in planning and managing the development. (http://propertymall.com/uvf/forum.html)

Throughout the 1990s, the Urban Villages Campaign has advanced with astounding momentum. It has built up a large body of discourse, infiltrated national and local planning policy, fostered construction projects, and turned its nomenclature into popular parlance.

The urban village idea was derived from a concern with traditional aesthetics. However, the Campaign has come to realise that its thinking is closely aligned to much of the rhetoric being espoused on the sustainability issue, particularly as it pertains to compact cities, self-sufficiency, transportation, building durability, and the use of local materials. As a result, at the instigation of the campaigners, there has been a merging of their urban village idea with the ill-defined concept of sustainability. There are few unequivocal imperatives relating to urban sustainability. While leaning toward options for urban compactness, the Urban Villages Campaign compromises between the centrist and decentrist alternatives. Largely, the Campaign's stance is realist in nature. It takes elements of the centrist (such as containment and urban regeneration) and decentrist (such as controlled nodal decentralisation) positions and combines them into something with a measure of palatability and practicality.

In this chapter, I do not attempt to reach any conclusions about the ultimate sustainability of an urban village option. I present a case to acknowledge the type of contributions that urban villages might be expected to make in moving urban development slightly closer to a sustainable form. I do this, first, by outlining the ambitions of the Urban Villages Campaign, and second, by presenting two case studies of recent urban village developments. Both case study projects are assessed in terms of the way in which they meet their creators' intentions (and urban village objectives), and their replicability. From this, a conclusion is drawn as to the value of the contribution of urban villages to future urbanisation.

The evidence provided in this chapter is the result of an analysis of Urban Villages Campaign texts and rhetoric, and development documents from the two case study areas. In addition, much use has been made of intensive interviews conducted with more than 50 key informants closely involved in the Campaign and the case study projects (see note 1).

The ambitions of the Urban Villages Campaign

The first *Urban Villages* report (Aldous, 1992) commences by establishing a context for the Campaign's concerns about urban development. Listing a range of qualities that the Campaign believes proper in urban areas (including diverse architecture, a legible layout, mixed uses, community commitment and sustainability), the report then lays the blame for their absence on the structural pervasiveness of urban monoculturalism (especially land use zoning). The concept of an urban village is introduced as a riposte to monocultural planning. Its fundamental characteristics (such as its compact size, self-sufficiency, organic nature and resident mix), siting options, and potential for complementary polycentric groupings are presented as not only sensible urban management, but also socially advantageous and financially viable. Further, the Campaign's first text is not limited to an elaboration of a physical design concept. Rather, it encompasses many issues of process, such as those related to consultation, statutory planning, estate management and financing.

Physical characteristics
Size
A notional area of 100 acres (40 hectares) with a combined resident and worker population of 3,000–5,000 is suggested for an urban village. The proposed aerial extent, if based roughly on a circular shape (having a diameter of just over half a mile or 900 metres) with no remote corners, is intended to enable anywhere in the village to be reached on foot in ten minutes or less. This is equated to the size of neighbourhoods like Soho, Covent Garden and Clerkenwell in London. It is small enough to allow easy access to local resources and to allow a degree of familiarity (even if just by association) with those living and working in the village. In addition, the proposed size of an urban village is intended to have 'sufficient critical mass' (Aldous, 1992, p.47) to inspire commercial confidence and make the provision of a wide range of functions and amenities economically feasible. Through an intended community strength and business vitality, it is anticipated that an effective local democracy will flourish and defend the interests of the neighbourhood.

Integration
It is fundamental that urban villages should not be produced as isolated elements. They are meant to integrate with other urban villages and with adjoining neighbourhoods, linked by cycle and footpath networks as well as public transport. New urban villages should complement the facilities of the bordering areas and also cater for any deficiencies in those places. At the larger scale, the polycentric grouping of urban villages is encouraged wherever possible.

Self-sufficiency
A mixing of uses is promoted within each village in order to encourage self-sufficiency, both within street blocks and, in the case of the more densely built-up main streets and central area, within individual buildings as well. Overall, there should be a balance between housing units and workspace. The aim is 'a theoretical 1:1 ratio between jobs and residents able and willing to work' (Aldous, 1992, p.30).

Occupancy mix

A more overtly social aspect of the Urban Villages Campaign agenda is the desire to see a diversity of housing and employment unit types and sizes. Related to this is a policy of offering a wide variety of tenancy arrangements, ranging from owner-occupation to rental to equity-share for homes, and from freehold to leasehold (including initial low, non-commercial rents) to easy in/easy out licenses for businesses. The ultimate aim is to encourage the early and continued provision of local services, including small independent enterprises, and a diversity of residents in terms of income, ethnicity, age and household type. There is an express objective here to encourage people to meet with social difference, in order to enable an understanding of, and empathy for, heterogeneity, and thereby enhance community civility and democracy.

Architecture and landscaping

Architecture and landscaping are the urban village characteristics that receive the greatest degree of attention in the Urban Villages Campaign's first report (*op. cit*). As a point of departure, the report advocates that an urban village should 'focus on a public square or place of sufficient size and quality to give people a sense of place' (Aldous, 1992, p.48). Maintaining a strict building hierarchy is advised. Points of focus within the square and a sense of enclosure are features considered imperative architecturally. Elsewhere, there should be a broad mix of different building types and sizes. Large, important buildings should always be placed in key locations offering visual impact. It is also important that the streets and squares have a comprehensible layout and respond to existing landscape and historic features. Finally, parks, gardens and other public spaces should be small but abundant throughout the urban village. These need to be designed as an integral part of the village, with appropriate lighting, seating and other embellishments to reinforce the village identity. The implementation of a series of codes under the guidance of a master plan is advocated in order to fortify the above principles.

Transportation and access

A readable, plain arrangement of streets, lanes, pedestrian paths and public spaces, which radiates out from the small blocks surrounding the central square to the larger blocks on the village periphery, should be provided for the benefit of walkers, cyclists and drivers. Traffic calming, combined with physical measures to acknowledge pedestrian priority, can be used to tame motor vehicles accessing the central square. Those activities which generate high vehicle movements and freight should be sited on the periphery of the village, preferably in the spaces that separate one urban village from another, accessed by designated boulevards.

Collaboration and partnership characteristics

A commitment to effective multilateral participation in planning and management processes related to the establishment and maintenance of urban villages is a further goal of the Urban Villages Campaign. From the outset, the Campaign has been candid about the fact that the public involvement foreseen is not an attempt to ask 'the public to "design" the village' (Aldous, 1992, p.40). It is an opportunity for the community 'to find out what is envisaged, offer information and comment, feel they are helping to shape the development' (Aldous, 1992, p.40). It may also give community members a direct role in the planning, implementation and management process. In particular, the establishment of a community development trust is recommended when creating an urban village. Such a trust would be consulted during the planning process, would advise on implementation, and would be an equity partner in the long-term management of the urban village.

The Urban Villages Campaign's unique offering

Despite the discussion of the urban village concept presented in the previous sections, it remains difficult to distil the unique contribution of this notion to contemporary urbanisation. Certainly, in a physical sense, it would be virtually impossible to detect an urban village solely by viewing its plan or built appearance. The urban village is posited more in the form of a cloudy paradigm than a prescriptive model, making it especially vulnerable to liberal interpretation. Consequently, it is also frequently subject to complaints of ambiguity. Furthermore, many outside the Campaign claim that certain aspects of the Urban Villages agenda are fulfilled in urban developments not associated with the Campaign.

Anchored in its multidisciplinary platform, the Campaign takes the organic, holistic, urbanistic, polycentric, and aesthetic nature of pre-industrial city quarters and villages, combines them with the community and management ideals of late nineteenth century and early twentieth century utopian models, and then integrates these with current objectives for sustainability, compact cities and collaborative planning. The potential for realising this vision *in toto* is recognised by Urban Villages Campaigners as limited, and even described as 'myth' or 'fantasy' by some (author's interviews). But their task is to commence a change in this direction as opposed to remaining content with conventional contemporary urbanisation.

Building urban villages

From disclosures obtained during interviews, and supported by evidence drawn from Campaign newsletters and reports, the projects under construction that offer the best current examples of urban villages are the Poundbury project in West Dorset and the Crown Street regeneration project in inner city Glasgow.

Poundbury case study

As an example of an urban village, Poundbury closely replicates the physical, social and employment outcomes sought by the Urban Villages Campaign. It also demonstrates elements of the preferred partnership, management and early consultation objectives of the Campaign. Where the project departs from Campaign ideals is in its lack of a formal mechanism for effective long-term community input and in its decision not to maintain the freehold to the land as a long-term management tool.

Poundbury is a 20-year, staged development for 5,000 inhabitants. Covering a site of 158 hectares, the project will ultimately provide four discrete mixed-use quarters. Construction began in late 1993 and, to date, most of the first quarter has been completed and work on the second quarter is under way. The Duchy of Cornwall (see note 2) is managing the project, under the watchful eye of its steward, the Prince of Wales, and his adviser and master planner, Leon Krier.

Aims of the project

Each of the project's four urban quarters has been conceived of as a traditional Dorset town for 500–800 households, with a permeable layout covering no more than 40 hectares, and using traditional building types and materials. In this way, it was anticipated that the quarters would mature into distinct communities that nurture their historical and cultural continuity with the rest of Dorset. The quarters are intended to provide local education, employment, shopping and leisure facilities.

The master plan is being implemented via a series of ground plans and a building code. The ground plans for each urban quarter delineate first the individual plots for each block, then the shape of spaces and buildings, and finally the pattern of streets and squares. The building code monitors implementation over time. It is a mechanism for ensuring that the project's main tenets are adhered to, and that consistently high standards of design and construction, in keeping with the scale, proportions and materials of traditional Dorset urban areas, are achieved. The code is a 23-page document detailing performance standards and prescriptive requirements in relation to the following matters: external walls of buildings, roofs and chimneys, windows and doors, building and subsidiary elements, gardens, garden walls and fences, accessibility, and environmental targets.

At its heart, the Poundbury scheme is an attempt to use the instruments of architecture and collaborative planning to forge a development that is distinctly urban (not suburban and not zoned). It is to comprise decipherable neighbourhoods linked into the existing fabric of Dorchester, but with a high degree of self-containment, courtesy of their rich mix of uses. By virtue of the neighbourhoods' urbanity and design, it is anticipated that vitality in terms of street life, and the development of a sense of place, identity and community, will be encouraged. In addition, by limiting the size of the neighbourhoods to a human scale and by providing a range of housing types and tenancies, it is hoped that a high degree of neighbourly interaction will take place between diverse people. A feeling of community ownership and responsibility will consequently be engendered, promoting an active local democracy. Finally, a related but slightly secondary tenet is that the development should emulate the historical Dorset vernacular in terms of traditional market town scale, pattern, design, materials and decoration.

At a less lofty level, there are a large number of objectives devised to assist in the realisation of the above goals. Most of these objectives relate to matters of urban design and architecture. They include the desire to achieve: a clear urban boundary; compactness; layout, building and space variety; a building hierarchy; simplicity in housing design; an attractive and interesting public realm; unique focal points; architectural unity without uniformity; priority provision for the pedestrian and cyclist; and a re-prioritisation of design relating to the car in terms of street layout and private parking.

Evaluation of the Poundbury process and outcome so far
Achievement of creator ambitions
It is too early to make a useful assessment of how well project objectives, particularly long-term ones, are being achieved. Even so, in their enthusiasm, a number of those interviewed for this research offered a cautious but favourable interpretation of some of the wider ambitions. Two particular aspects that were highlighted were the social mix and the developing sense of community identity. Several promoters of the project argue that community identity, a sense of place and local pride are evident amongst the new Poundbury residents (author's interviews). This viewpoint is also apparent in the myriad of newspaper and magazine articles about Poundbury, which often incorporate brief interviews with local residents.

However, reservations were expressed in regard to the future social mix and community interaction envisaged at Poundbury. Originally, it was intended that the 20% of housing dedicated to the Guinness Trust (the social housing provider) would be relatively evenly distributed throughout the development, but the concentration of social housing in the opening stages of phase one construction altered this balance. Now there will be very few Guinness units erected in section C of the first quarter because the social housing allocation for this phase has almost been reached. One wonders whether this spatial imbalance might lead to the very sort of social stratification that the project had intended to avoid.

However, a more fundamental task at the moment is ensuring the development actually continues to progress. With the flat economy of the mid-1990s, the Duchy was legitimately concerned that the project should not slow down to the point of token progress (author's interview). Maintaining momentum is a high priority. Any looming success in their own terms cannot be based solely on what has been constructed so far. As a minimum, unless the whole of each quarter is completed, then the development will automatically be considered a failure.

Assessment of the achievement of Poundbury's urban design and architectural objectives is easier than assessment of the longer-term aims. The application of the broad master plan, its ground plans, and the building design code makes it almost impossible not to achieve these aims at least initially. This is further bolstered by the co-operative efforts between Poundbury's implementers and the District and County Councils. Photographs help to demonstrate how the various objectives are being concretised. They highlight key design features, including: prioritisation of pedestrian movement (Fig. 1); and winding roads around housing (Fig. 2).

Fig. 1. Prioritisation of pedestrian movement via car-less lanes.

Fig. 2. Slow winding roads around housing.

Project replicability

In considering the Poundbury project as an example of an urban village, or an example of an alternative to conventional development, one of the most telling questions is whether it is reproducible. Scepticism abounds when the promoter is a prince, and his instigators are a generously resourced royal institution. Even the creators themselves acknowledge the project's peculiarity, dubbing it a 'unique', 'unusual', and 'special' development (author's interviews). Nevertheless, from the outset, a primary objective of the many players has been to ensure that Poundbury is repeatable (author's interviews).

Several factors detract from Poundbury's replicability. The most obvious is the way the Duchy has been able to deal with financial arrangements. Although the Duchy operates under demanding Treasury constraints, it is a large and well-endowed organisation capable of adequately supporting the development and biding time for monetary reward. There is no doubt that the project has a large and costly crew working for it, paid for out of the Duchy's coffers. As well as reducing the size of the development team, there are several other areas where costs could be reduced for future projects attempting to adapt a Poundbury model. By limiting the materials specified and simplifying the road pattern, the same objectives could be achieved at less expense. The publicity surrounding Poundbury, which presumably would not be so unwavering for any other development, has not assisted with such matters. The team has felt the need to be especially meticulous.

Another factor affecting replicability is the Duchy's use of small, local building and architectural firms to carry out most of the development to date. The use of these firms, which have good local links, and a thorough knowledge of Dorset materials and their availability, means that it is easily possible to produce buildings of varied design, built with regional materials. Such an outcome would be much harder to achieve by working with major national house building companies who would rely on in-house architectural technicians and operate within very tight profit margins.

Another unusual factor has been the relatively potent influence of the master planner, via his royal patron. Normally a master planner would have less authority in the implementation of the plan. However, because of the peculiar role of the Prince in relation to the Duchy, Krier has been able to wield considerable power. It could well be much harder to maintain adherence to such a plan's precepts in light of other priorities (especially financial) in any other projects. As has happened in the US, this could result in new developments which copy superficial architectural motifs because of their market popularity but replicate none of the associated urbanist, community or collaborative principles (Bressi, 1994; Langdon, 1994; Scully, 1994).

A final significant difference between Poundbury and likely future development is its sheer magnitude in terms of land area, projected population, and time frame. However, its division into four separate, relatively self-contained, neighbourhoods means that its principles are still relevant for adaptation to different contexts, even if its extent is not duplicated.

There are four main factors that might encourage the replication of Poundbury elsewhere. First, the project has been financially viable and the returns are increasing with time (author's interviews). Even though the Duchy is an affluent property owner, it has still had to perform within the Treasury's restrictions and without government subsidy. Second, the development is a market winner. For whatever reason, and it may be partly that traditional architecture has popular appeal at present, Poundbury houses have sold successfully even during poor economic times. Third, the development has demonstrated the high quality and architectural variety possible for social housing while operating within Housing Corporation guidelines. This means that it is possible for future projects to take a similar approach to pepper-potting social housing that is physically indistinguishable from private housing, and still receive a Housing Corporation grant. Finally, although Poundbury to date has been limited to traditional vernacular architecture, a wide variety of responses have been allowed to its building design code in comparison with those of other smaller traditional developments at places such as Abbotsbury and Broadwindsor. The latter examples have been much more architecturally disciplined and limited in their design palette.

Therefore, although there are unique features associated with Poundbury, its principles of collaboration, design and project management have potential for adaptation and improvement in subsequent developments. Poundbury's masterminders believe they are influencing other development already. With the publicity Poundbury has received, large numbers of developers, planners, architects and others from within Britain and abroad have been drawn to take a look at the scheme. The major national developers have been keeping tabs on Poundbury as a possible indicator of the direction of change in the industry. Furthermore, all those interviewed allege that a variety of projects now under way have transferred elements of Poundbury's principles to their sites. They point to examples and proposals in Cambridgeshire, Somerset, and elsewhere in Dorset.

Poundbury is already meeting most of its acknowledged objectives. Much of the credit for this is due to the scheme's careful implementation through a foundational master plan, evolving ground plans, and the performance standards and restrictions contained in the building design code. As built, the development reveals a compact and interesting layout, a variety of spaces and buildings, a modest residential architecture, a grander public and key-site architecture, prioritisation of pedestrian and cyclist movement over that of the car, a merging of social and private housing, and a small degree of mixed activities. Primary concerns in terms of achieving the project's goals as it progresses include the continuing needs to ensure a tenure mix, enable integration with the existing adjoining community, and keep the development progressing so that a full range of community, retail, commercial and industrial uses are realised.

Crown Street case study

The Crown Street regeneration project closely mirrors urban village partnership, management and social ideals. However, it only partially meets criteria related to physical characteristics, falls short of the standards for community involvement, and relies more heavily on the public sector for project finance than the Urban Villages Campaign recommends. Even so, it is a credible example of the Urban Villages Campaign's first preference type of urban village: an inner city regeneration of a brownfield site.

Launched in 1990, the Crown Street regeneration project aims to breathe new life into the infamous Gorbals district of Glasgow by creating 800 accommodation units of assorted tenure, blending commercial and community activities, and attracting back a social mix of residents and private investment. Three-quarters constructed, this renewal of inner city brown land is hailed as visionary, innovative and transferable by its proponents.

A multi-agency partnership was established to bring about this project. Members include the Glasgow Development Agency, Scottish Homes, Glasgow District Council, and the local community. Each of these members contribute to the steering group that manages the project. Against the background of previous renewal failure, one of the first tasks of the project's steering group was to draw on the lessons from the earlier 'solutions' for the Gorbals and develop a transparent set of objectives for the new development. Critical features the steering group highlighted were lack of family accommodation in the vicinity, absence of a supermarket nearby, and the unattractive and inadequate nature of the adjoining local shopping centre. In response, the group decided upon a goal of encouraging families and young people into the area to balance the existing aging population and help to sustain community life, and on a goal of providing more than just houses so that the community actually 'live' in the area, not just sleep in it. Beyond this, the group set itself a broader challenge to improve the social, economic and environmental qualities of the Gorbals, and thereby also benefit the wider Glasgow image. The project was not envisaged as a narrowly based, housing-led scheme. Short-term fixes were not on the agenda, nor was gentrification. Rather, in addition to the physical redevelopment of the site, long-term regeneration of the location and its economy was desired. Furthermore, it was intended to be an initiative that would have an impact beyond its own bounds (EDAW, 1997).

To this end, the steering group set itself five overriding objectives (Crown Street Regeneration Project, 1995) and three guiding principles (EDAW, 1997) for the project to adhere to. The objectives are to:

- Make the Gorbals a place in which people want to live.
- Develop a new and positive image for the Gorbals as a popular, balanced community.
- Assist in bringing new energy and growth into the Gorbals economy.
- Integrate the new development into the social, economic and physical fabric of the existing community.
- Provide solutions that stand the test of time.

The related guiding principles are:

- The redevelopment of the site will seek to apply the highest attainable quality of development.
- The site will not be developed in isolation from the surrounding area, but become a cohesive and integrated part of the Gorbals both physically and socially.
- The development will exploit where possible the opportunities for improving the local economy of the Gorbals.

In response, when the master plan was developed, it emphasised the following design concepts:

- creation of the livable, urban city
- reinvention of the tenement block
- reversal of the road hierarchy and reintroduction of the shopping street
- redefinition of the grid pattern with linkages into surrounding communities

Evaluation of the Crown Street process and outcome so far
Achievement of creator ambitions
Crown Street, the showpiece
The project partners have relied very heavily on the urban form and architecture of Crown Street to achieve their ambition of a showpiece redevelopment. In so far as they have produced a distinctive urban layout with a varied and unique architecture compared with contemporary development elsewhere in Glasgow and the rest of Britain, they have succeeded in creating a modest showpiece. The new development is generally considered by the project partners to have made a significant contribution to changing local attitudes about the Gorbals, improving its image and potential (EDAW, 1997).

Integrated social and economic regeneration
The long-term focus of this aim means that it is premature to judge its success at this time. Nevertheless, it is possible to point to a number of factors that suggest a change in the desired direction. First, the project has been instrumental in installing the Gorbals Initiative. The Gorbals Initiative has now firmly established itself as a key organisation in promoting local economic development and enhancing local access to employment and training. A second factor has been the attempt by the project partners to encourage the use of local contractors, and to ensure training and construction employment opportunities have been maximised for local people during the development of the Crown Street project. EDAW (1997) estimates that 112 full-time equivalent jobs have been created through the scheme. Of these, approximately 15% have been taken by local people, which compares well with figures from national studies concerning the proportion of local people normally employed on such projects. The mixed-use emphasis of the project has stimulated private sector investment and local work opportunities. The biggest impact has been that of the supermarket shopping centre, which involved an investment of more than £1 million, and the employment of 50 on-site staff. Furthermore, the supermarket company is following a policy of local recruitment for all its vacancies except senior management.

Another objective the project partners have begun to achieve is that of attracting first-time buyers into Crown Street – a high proportion of the phase one owner-occupiers are in this category (EDAW, 1997). The purpose of this objective was to secure social diversity and to increase the income levels of the neighbourhood in order to help support a range of local amenities. However, whether these new owner-occupiers are choosing to spend their income locally has not been quantified.

Even less certain are the Crown Street project's outcomes in terms of addressing integration with adjoining communities, and improvement of the local social climate. Despite the east–west connections anticipated in the project's new road layout, Crown Street remains an island on its own in the Gorbals. In part this is a result of a number of persistent physical barriers, including the Laurieston Road dual carriageway, the numerous adjoining vacant sites, and the undesirable Queen Elizabeth Square shopping precinct. Several steps could be taken by the project's partners to eliminate some of these hurdles which lie beyond the site, especially given that much of the land involved is in public ownership.

The social barriers to integration are a much more complex issue. Within Crown Street itself, residents' and tenants' associations have been formed and are functioning well in each street block (author's interviews). However, they prevail as separate enclaves from the rest of the vicinity. According to one informant (author's interview), there is a 'kind of two tier Gorbals. There's the real Gorbals, which still has all of the problems; and then [there] is Crown Street'. While the 'balanced' social mix achieved to date in Crown Street is impressive, one wonders how long it will continue without Crown Street residents feeling the necessity to build a protective wall around themselves.

The inadequacy of the community participation process has been a major factor in the project's difficulties with regard to any attempt to improve the social climate of the Gorbals. Throughout the planning and construction phases of the project, there has been an acknowledged failure to bring local citizens in as equal partners. Inevitably, this has reinforced the lack of identification that the surrounding district has had with Crown Street right from the start (EDAW, 1997).

Thus, while some progress has been made in Crown Street in terms of achieving private sector commitment to the site, the project has not yet stimulated additional investment in the vicinity or noteworthy social interaction.

Stable and balanced population

Closely tied to the two goals considered above is an objective devised to help fulfill them both, that of increasing the long-term social mix within the Gorbals. In particular, in a consummate piece of social engineering, the project partners sought to reduce the public sector monopoly over housing in the area and its predominance of elderly and vulnerable tenants, and reintroduce owner-occupied accommodation aimed at local residents, young families and those on higher incomes. It was hoped that this would add a liveliness and stability to the area, nourish diverse social interactions and neighbourhood cohesion, and help sustain community and schooling facilities.

An analysis of phase one, carried out by the Gorbals Research and Information Team (EDAW, 1997), indicates that a mix of people from different backgrounds has taken up the Crown Street housing. A total of 34% of households in phase one had previously lived in the Gorbals. Such households accounted for 93% of new social housing tenants and 20% of new owner-occupiers. In terms of household type, just over a third of phase one housing was occupied by single-person households, nearly a third was occupied by couples with no children, and just under a third was taken by families that included children. In terms of the combined employment and household type characteristics, the two largest groups represented were single professional or managerial households and families headed by a skilled manual worker.

While these outcomes meet the project partners' objective almost completely, there is concern that the results in later phases may not be so favourable. Two factors have given rise to this fear. First, with the increasing market success of the private housing and corresponding higher value sales, there is the real possibility of the value of owner-occupied units increasing beyond the price range of local residents. Second, at the same time as the private sector housing has been built and sold ahead of schedule in response to demand, the provision of social rented housing has lagged behind. This has reinforced claims that existing Gorbals residents are alienated from the scheme and unable to benefit from it, especially in so far as taking up the new housing is concerned. This has further fuelled the polarisation debate. In addressing the latter worries, the project partners have placed pressure on Scottish Homes to ring-fence their funding to the housing association, guaranteeing social housing provision will be made an urgent priority on the site. However, it is not known how (or whether) the project partners intend to deal with the matter of rising house prices over the long term.

An affordable high quality environment
The emphasis placed on this objective within the design briefs is oriented primarily towards housing quality in terms of 'variety of design, construction and finish' (Crown Street Regeneration Project, 1994, p.7). Residential quality is one ambition that has clearly been achieved in the phases of Crown Street already erected. There is an architectural variety in Crown Street that is matched by high standards of construction and external cladding, along with traffic calmed boulevards (Fig. 3), convenient communal gardens (Fig. 4), abundant artwork and semi-mature trees. The accent on quality has been judged a success by the partners (EDAW, 1997) and developers (author's interviews) in terms of attracting residents to the area.

Fig. 3. Traffic calmed boulevards.
Fig. 4. Convenient communal gardens.

Of course, this affordable, high quality environment needs to be sustained in order to meet the intentions of the project's creators. There is little guarantee that this will be the case. Considerable potential for the long-term maintenance of quality rests with the community trust that will administer the project area over the long term. How vigilantly this task will be undertaken depends entirely on the local community. Less potential exists for ensuring owner-occupied housing in the area remains affordable. While Scottish Homes can exert pressure to keep low prices for the sale of units from the developer to the first customer, future sales are open to the market.

The reintroduction of a recognisable, urban scale built environment
This objective has given considerable weight to the reinvention of the tenement building with its classic Glasgow 'big windaes' (large vertical windows) and the revival of the grand, linear street, with the support of subsidiary traditional features such as interconnected buildings forming enclosed communal areas within each block, a responsive grid road pattern, street-fronting shops, and a range of community and business activities.

The application of Crown Street's master plan in conjunction with detailed design briefs for each street block on the site has meant that this objective has largely been achieved in the phases completed thus far. The mid-term review of the project applauds the 'strong urban character' that has resulted (EDAW, 1997, p.11). Maintaining the project's momentum is the paramount issue for completely achieving this objective. If the project stalled, not only would it harm new occupier confidence, but it would also damage market interest, especially relating to the provision of non-residential uses (such as the hotel, licensed premises and offices).

Project replicability
Both the project partners and the Urban Villages Campaign uphold the Crown Street scheme as an example of what is possible, but not conventional, in contemporary development. But how repeatable is the project? In its own mid-term review, doubt about replicability was expressed (EDAW, 1997). Many of the developers and architects involved in the project are

even more blunt in their assessment. They describe Crown Street as a definite 'one-off' undertaking that does not lend itself to repetition (author's interviews). Nonetheless, given similar funding circumstances, the various developers, architects and the housing association all said they would be prepared to be involved in such an endeavour again.

The high level of public subsidy is the single biggest factor that would diminish any easy translocation of Crown Street development practice. The Crown Street regeneration project is an £80 million venture (based on 1991 prices). The share of the costs is split approximately 63% private sector, 12% Glasgow Development Agency and 25% Scottish Homes, with the City Council also contributing in terms of the provision of road realignment and a public library. There are a number of aspects of the project that would be very difficult to transfer elsewhere without this high proportion of public assistance.

In addition, there are a number of other factors that developers and architects working on the project argue would not be transferred to future schemes. First is the concept of the tenement. Despite the market success of the new Crown Street tenements, there was general cynicism about the potential of this housing form for twenty-first-century living amongst both developers and architects. Another feature of Crown Street that developers suspected would not be taken up in future schemes was the inclusion of retail units on the ground floor of housing blocks (author's interviews). The long time taken to let the shops, even with Crown Street's relatively quick housing up-take, further dampened the developers' enthusiasm.

Notwithstanding the above obstacles to Crown Street being a useful model for contemporary practice, there are some elements that could be easily brought into existence in other schemes. Further, Crown Street demonstrates the potential of a master planning approach. Plainly defined physical outcomes were outlined in the master plan and detailed in the design briefs. This meant that the site could be divided into manageable parcels and development implemented relatively expeditiously by a variety of developers and architects. Hence, a range of architectural responses have been welcomed, from quite traditional to very modern, while still maintaining a coherent urban form interwoven with common tree-lined boulevards.

Finally, attention could be given to the potential for providing a mixture of rental accommodation and affordable owner-occupied and shared ownership housing for local residents of inner city areas, and of constructing medium-density urban (as opposed to suburban or high-rise) dwellings in central city areas. Both these aspects of the Crown Street project were successful in terms of their popular appeal. Granted, the large public funding input meant that such goals could be achieved with high quality results for a minimal cost to the initial end-user. However, the degree of success begs the question of whether mixed tenure affordable housing for local citizens and overtly urban building design would still be in demand even if a more financially modest approach was employed. Following these matters up would require public agency commitment, because the private sector would not act on them of their own volition. But it may be plausible to significantly reduce the level of subsidy.

From the outset of the project, Crown Street was destined to be a lavish, although not ostentatious, masterpiece. The public agencies involved made a deliberate choice to concentrate effort on one small portion of the Gorbals rather than spread their labours more evenly. As a consequence, one of the most notable features of Crown Street is its high quality. However, the very high proportion of public aid used to bring about this result, at a reasonable price for the project's residents, diminishes any likelihood of replicability. Undoubtedly, the collaborative planning and implementation process and the master planning approach could be adapted and improved in future developments with relative ease.

Conclusion

Poundbury and Crown Street illustrate varying degrees of commitment to the many facets that comprise the loosely bound urban village vision. In these two developments, it is possible to view the concrete application of the ideas of the Urban Villages Campaign amidst the influences of other factors involved in urban change. At the most cursory level, the Urban Villages Campaign presents an argument for environmental benefits via compact, self-sufficient, diversely populated, traditionally designed, high quality neighbourhoods, which are integrated into surrounding areas, and planned and managed by multilateral partnerships. Beyond this surface interpretation there is also a fundamental ideological goal. The physical design, and its development process, is an instrument for achieving a social agenda. This agenda upholds the 'traditional' nuclear family; neighbourliness and decency; community commitment, responsibility and self-policing; and orderly social relations. Combined, the Campaign's physical and social agendas are expected to reduce environmental and societal costs, although their claims of social sustainability may be overstated.

The legitimacy of the Campaign's action is reinforced by the way in which it dovetails into fashionable debates within the wider policy making community. To a degree, the Campaign synthesises and symbolises through its paradigm many popular currents in late twentieth century British environmental and planning dialogue. In particular, it is one of many possible pragmatic replies to deliberations over the adequacy of modernist planning and the urgency of environmental and social sustainability. A reiterated neo-traditional urban form and modified environmental and social orders are being envisaged and constituted via the urban village discourse. Furthermore, the approach is winning favour. The continuing pressure to reconsider urban patterns and conditions on those charged with managing the city has led to widespread adoption of principles such as those rendered by the Urban Villages Campaign.

However, the urban predicament in the late twentieth century is very complex. The Urban Villages Campaign takes a managerialist line, believing that it is possible to manage the city, to control the city, in order to improve the urban condition. Minimal recognition is given to the influence of extensive structural forces and the reasons behind the seeming poor state of the city. Instead, the Campaign concentrates on the potential for itself as an agent to influence the re-allocation of resources, largely ignoring the meaning of the mal-distribution in the first place as well as the continuing powerful forces of capital.

Even so, the urban village is an entity that cannot be written off as a hollow right wing project. Although a discordant and double-dealing contributor to urbanisation, the urban village has some social and environmental merit, and conceivably presents improvements on standard urbanisation processes and outcomes in terms of effecting sustainable urban form.

Notes
1. References to 'author's interviews' throughout this chapter relate to qualitative research undertaken between 1994 and 1998. For full details see Thompson-Fawcett (1998).
2. The Duchy of Cornwall is a landed estate founded to provide the Heir to the Throne (currently HRH the Prince of Wales) with an income from its assets.

Heidi Dumreicher, Richard S. Levine, Ernest J. Yanarella and
Taghi Radmard

Generating Models of Urban Sustainability: *Vienna's Westbahnhof Sustainable Hill Town*

Introduction

The dawning millennium beckons us with a future offering enormous promise and unparalleled risk. Like the age of Dickens' two cities, the twenty-first century presents opposing faces. It will be either the century of sustainability or the century of ecological collapse. It will be the century where the continuation of the unsustainable economic practices of today precipitate irreversible catastrophes. Or it will be the century where small local successes in implementing sustainable practices and processes proliferate and transform the entire global economy into a balance-seeking relationship with our natural ecosystem. It will be the century where the analytical, reductionistic methods of science and industry that are the sources of both our progress and our increasingly unsustainable way of life will continue as the central economic paradigm: or it will be the century where a new integrative economic paradigm emerges which promises to reconcile humankind with the natural environment, whose health is the precondition for all human activity.

We are thus confronted with the ecological and social choice of either continuing our descent into the realm of unsustainability, while denying that it is the consumerist/materialist path that is the problem, or shifting to a new emerging paradigm. Unfortunately, few recognise that a real alternative exists to the prevailing path. Therefore, the primary challenge facing our generation is to develop a real and viable alternative to decline, not merely on a theoretical basis, but in a real place: the sustainable city.

Urban sustainability is an idea whose time has come (Yanarella and Levine, 1992b). While the required change may seem enormous, it may actually take very little to precipitate such a paradigm shift. It took only one steam engine, one light bulb and one photocopying machine to trigger previous social and technological revolutions. So too, it may take only one city operating within the limits of its resources and its environment to prove to all others not only that sustainability is possible, but that it is the only possible way cities and their economies can be designed and managed to ensure their long-term survival. Fortunately, an operational theory of the sustainable city is in place and has been embedded in the *Charter of European Cities and Towns Towards Sustainability* (European Sustainable Cities and Towns Campaign, 1994). Many towns and cities are attempting to implement the Charter in programmes and urban projects.

The focus of this chapter is Vienna's Westbahnhof project, an ambitious undertaking now in the third phase of its conceptualisation and design at the Centre for Sustainable Cities at the University of Kentucky, in association with Oikodrom in Vienna. Because the underlying framework of this project departs in significant respects from conventional approaches to sustainability, the chapter begins with an extended outline of its theoretical underpinnings and design elements, as well as the historical model and precursor to its 'city-as-a-hill' design.

288

Then, through text and illustrations, it explores the fundamental effort to integrate urban architectural design with strong sustainability principles into a programme for implementing a Sustainable City Implantation (SCI) upon and over the present Westbahnhof site. The purpose is to demonstrate not only that sustainability in a place is imperative, but that it is possible and realisable. When completed, the implantation may become the first project in Europe to fully implement the principles of the Aalborg Charter and, in so doing, become Europe's first modern sustainable city.

The sustainable city of the past

The sustainable city is not a new phenomenon. Historic towns and cities around the world did not have a choice. If they existed for any length of time it was only because they were able to develop and maintain a continually re-balancing relationship among their internal social and economic activities and with their wider natural and agricultural landscape (Levine, 1987). Ironically, it is a tribute to our genius that we have been able to create an artificial economic system and larger 'second nature' that have been able to operate on a new unsustainable basis for many generations. We have been able to do this because of the brilliant ways we have contrived to export the problems we have created either to poorer, less defensible regions or to future generations. But the fact that those problems cannot be indefinitely forestalled, and that cascading effects of that unsustainable future are rapidly mounting is becoming increasingly clear.

The sustainable patterns of past cultures are very similar to the ways in which a natural ecosystem operates. Like an historic town, a natural ecosystem is a strong local economy working as an interconnected network, typified by regenerative cycles of energy and material flows. In nature, processes turn on themselves and return to their roots; there is no waste. Over time, the diversity, resiliency and, thus, stability of the ecosystem increases. Indeed, as Redclift (1987) and others (Yanarella and Levine, 1992a) have pointed out, complex ecosystems, like tropical rain forests, achieve eco-sustainability or homeostatic balance, or what natural ecologists call 'climax systems' of high diversity, large biomass, and high stability through protection from rapid change and 'through shifts of energy flows away from production and towards the maintenance of the system itself' (Redclift, 1987, p.18). By contrast, human settlements typically seek to stall such ecosystems in early stages of ecological succession, where the yield of products is high, but where the stabilising elements of organic matter and biomass fail to accumulate. High production within these ecosystems then comes at a high price. The result is a state of arrested development in social systems.

The good news is that the sustainability movement is growing and is a worldwide phenomenon. The Earth Summit in Rio in 1992 and the Climate Change Conference in Kyoto in 1997 are just two of the many international activities striving to confront our growing environmental problems. The bad news is that the principal vehicles employed in this movement are the largely analytic, reductionistic methods that have arguably created the very problems that the movement is struggling to address. This overwhelmingly quantitative approach insists that we must commit ourselves to do more with less and less. While this approach offers successful initial steps (recycling aluminium, changing to fluorescent fixtures, more tightly insulating homes and so on), subsequent steps become successively more difficult, more expensive, less popular, and less effective, until a point of diminishing returns is reached long before sustainable balances have been achieved (Levine and Yanarella, 1994). Equally troubling is that this pervasive quantitative approach is also a top-down approach starting at the global level (e.g., Rio) and working its way down to regional, national and local programmes of restriction and regulation. Such an approach is fraught with the inevitable controversy and conflict (who is to make which sacrifices and on what basis?) that are likely to breed dissension and division, and defuse any initial momentum. In any case, as the Rio Plus Five conference indicated, the record has not been promising.

An alternative approach exists that, while less visible in the US, has achieved greater momentum in Europe. A major embodiment of this approach is seen in the *Charter of European Cities and Towns Towards Sustainability* (The Aalborg Charter) which, in contrast to the reductionist approach, is holistic, process oriented, and place centred (i.e. the city). This puts the Charter squarely in the realm of architecture and urban design and promises to extend both the nature and influence of those realms. As principal architects of the Charter, we are pleased that this document has been ratified by more than 300 of Europe's most progressive cities.

What is sustainability?

At least since the late 1980s, the sustainability movement has been organised around a minimalist, consensus definition advanced in the UN through the Brundtland Commission's report, *Our Common Future*, namely, that sustainable development is development that 'meets the needs of the present without compromising the ability of future generations to meet their own needs' (WECD, 1987). Instead, an alternative course is proposed: a complete theory and process for generating and operating a sustainable city/region. It is based on Oikodrom's 'compass of sustainability' and The Aalborg Charter, which in turn derive from our 'five operating principles for the sustainable city'. Here is the complete definition: sustainability is a local, informed, participatory, balance-seeking process, operating within an equitable ecological region, exporting no problems beyond its territory or into the future.

Sustainability is a local ...

Sustainability needs a place in which to happen. Although problems aggregate and become manifest on a global scale (e.g., ozone depletion, global climate change), offences to the environment are produced locally. These offences are not necessarily the work of ill-intentioned people, rather they are often simply the by-products of productive and desirable activities. The further these offences travel from their source, the more diffuse and intractable they become. Yet when dealt with locally as part of the production process, the neutralisation or re-use of all negative by-products can be considered part of the price of doing business.

'Local' is to be read as city/region (Levine *et al.*, 1998). The earlier history of our civilization is the history of city/regions' largely autonomous towns which gained virtually all of their material needs from their local countryside and had to maintain the quality of the countryside in order to sustain their way of life.

Sustainability cannot happen at the scale of the family – we are far too interdependent for that. Sustainability cannot happen at the global scale – that is far too vast to be knowable or controllable. It is the scale of the city/region that is the largest scale capable of addressing the many urban architectural, social, economic, political and other imbalances besetting the modern world, and simultaneously the smallest scale at which such problems can be resolved in an integrated and holistic fashion.

Sustainability is a local, informed ...

In order to be able to maintain the quality and the productivity of the local region and its countryside, it is necessary to understand the consequences of the metabolic activities occurring within the city/region. Earlier towns operating within a largely closed system received rather rapid feedback as to the consequences of their activities. When imbalances threatened the city system, they were noted and adjusted locally. In the modern world, there are effectively no local boundaries, and positive activities at a small scale may well have negative consequences at larger scales. By using modern means, however, we gain powerful tools both to design and monitor major energy and material flows and to model the projected implications of different processes we might choose to include in our city/region.

As part of the Westbahnhof project, we are currently working on something called the Sustainability Engine, a computer-based utility providing feedback on local cause and effect (Levine, 1994, 1996). The idea is that instead of a local culture evolving slowly over many generations through a process of trial and error (the historic precedent in, for example, medieval Italian hill towns), many different scenarios may be tried on the Sustainability Engine before anything is actually implemented. The Engine, which is a combination of computer aided design (CAD) and geographic information systems (GIS), augmented by a strong database and a systems dynamics utility, makes it possible to try out a variety of alternative strategies and scenarios relating to the city/region (Levine *et al.*, 1991). It provides many different kinds of feedback as citizen stakeholders explore various 'what if' scenarios, and indicates the extent to which the various proposals are bringing the city/system towards, or further away from, balance. It thereby becomes the design and management utility for building urban scenarios, economic activity scenarios, and process scenarios (energy and material flow scenarios). It is also the feedback tool to inform stakeholders of the various consequences of their design ideas and lifestyle choices.

Sustainability is a local, informed, participatory ...

Sustainability is a process by which a local community can decide how it will afford to live within its natural budget and the limits of its own creativity. If we are living beyond our means, it is always possible to limit our activities through treaties and legislation or through the restrictions of authoritarian regimes. With the prospect of top-down regulation we are already beginning to hear the expression 'eco-fascism' being levelled at proposals limiting our consumerist way of life. It seems clear that, short of dictatorial restrictions, sustainability can only be achieved through a process that engages the participation of all stakeholders. However, representative democracy is difficult enough. How can one hope to create a process that engages a wide spectrum of people and interest groups on a range of issues upon which they are sure to disagree?

Several factors make a sustainability process workable. First of all, such a process starts with the principle that the sustainability process is non-negotiable while, in principle at least, everything else is negotiable. That means that all participants in the process must agree that the health, equity and viability of the city/system is the precondition for any other decision. In other words, the sustainability process begins as a 'sustainability game' that the participants gradually learn to play. The nature of the sustainability game is to try to satisfy one's individual self-interest while maintaining the viability of the city/system. As an individual, an industry or a sector will be incapable of satisfying its own needs alone or in isolation, it becomes necessary to engage others and to correct for the imbalances caused by the satisfaction of their needs. Using the Sustainability Engine, each stakeholder will attempt to satisfy his or her needs and interests through a variety of different scenarios, each involving different strategies and different partners (Levine, 1994, 1996).

Strategies that throw the city/system out of balance are eliminated quickly, or are re-balanced by introducing new ideas or processes with different attributes. Over time, more favourable strategies are built upon and elaborated while less favourable strategies are set aside. Developing scenarios are favoured and pursued when they satisfy multiple interests, when they bring the city/system toward balance, and when they hold the promise of fostering equity for all the stakeholders.

As the sustainability game proceeds, the stakeholders increasingly realise that they share a common destiny and that significant synergies will result from their creative encounters, negotiations, and co-operation. Over time, it becomes less of a game and more a real economy and urban system. Eventually, the players become partners and become more focused on building common wealth.

Sustainability is a local, informed, participatory, balance-seeking process ...

The problem with our existing economic system is that it has no built-in mechanism to ensure its own long-term survival. In fact, because it demands growth and expansion, it is designed to put pressure on the physical and ecological limits of our planet. As noted above, natural ecosystems in early stages of succession are also designed to maximise production at low levels of diversity, but as such systems mature, and organic material accumulates, the emphasis shifts away from production and toward maximising diversity, resiliency and maintaining internal balances. This needs to be a characteristic of human ecosystems. Using the Sustainability Engine to create different models of an emerging sustainable city/region, the stakeholders become engaged in such a balance-seeking process.

Yet if the city/system is close to balance, any major intervention is almost certain to throw the system out of balance. The problem is then to seek the means to bring the city/system back toward balance. Even a city/system that has been thrown far out of balance presents an opportunity for major interventions. In this game, there are no inherently bad moves. On the contrary, if the city/system should ever come exactly into balance, then in a sense the game would be over and such closure might actually be undesirable or at least premature. In any event, the design and management of the city/system is an ongoing process. At some point in the process, when all the stakeholders are working in harmony and the economic systems and opportunities have developed, it would be appropriate to build the SCI.

Sustainability is a local, informed, participatory, balance-seeking process, operating within an equitable ecological region (EER) ...

In the past, nature was assumed to be so vast as to be able to comfortably absorb any and all offences that humankind's activities dumped onto it. This was far from true: it is now clear that we have exceeded many of nature's capacities. What then may we be permitted? What is our ecological budget? The EER is our concept for the natural budget in land area, available for each city/region to support its way of life (Levine *et al.*, 1998). It is an important, precise concept, which gives us a clear picture of where we stand in relation to sustainability. A preliminary determination of the EER for a city/region is simple to make: a country's total land area is divided by its population and multiplied by the number of people in the city/region, yielding a certain number of hectares per person. This will not be the final EER. The actual budget may be considered from a variety of points of view, and the way in which it will finally be calculated is a matter to be determined in the future.

The point is that we have been appropriating environmental space in many cases far beyond what we can afford and far beyond what we are entitled to. EER is an equitable method for permitting us to understand what we are entitled to and what we have to work with. Once the land and its resources have been identified for a given city/region, the informed, participatory, balance-seeking process can proceed.

In looking at existing city/regions, it is obvious that many do not have an adjacent land area available to constitute their EER. In such cases (and this may well become the rule rather than the exception), it will become useful to contract with a rural partner region or regions whose needs and resources complement their urban counterpart. In such a case, the city and its mutually dedicated partner regions will have closed their ecological cycles within their equitable ecological footprint.

Sustainability is a local, informed, participatory, balance-seeking process, operating within an equitable ecological region, exporting no problems beyond its territory or into the future

A key idea is that when the prior part of this emerging definition is realised, such a city/region will effectively export no problems beyond its territory or into the future. However, even this circumstance is negotiable, given the fifth of our 'operating principles for sustainable cities', which states that 'imbalances are to be negotiated outward' (Yanarella and Levine, 1992a). This means that in some cases an imbalance may be exported from the city/region, but only if its re-balancing can be accounted for by an agency beyond the scale of the city/region.

Another aspect of the fifth 'operating principle' is based on the realisation that an island of sustainability cannot exist for long in a sea of unsustainability. It indicates that a successful sustainable city must become the inspiration for the proliferation of other sustainable cities, until the contagion is complete. This means that even in its early stages the principles and processes of sustainability must find a place and a space for possibilities to grow. By adopting this theoretical framework as the basis of regional management, a city/region will be able to operate within the realm of sustainability. Once the viability of such a sustainability process is demonstrated, the success of that example will be a catalyst to the proliferation of sustainability to the countless other city/regions of the planet.

This definition has profound implications for the future of the design professions. The challenge of our times is to forge an equitable way of living on this planet, within the limits of nature. This challenge can be seen in part as a design problem, a major part of which are urban and architectural design problems, along with urban management issues. More importantly, the methods to be used in the sustainability process derive from and are much more akin to traditional architectural design methods than they are to science and its analytical methods.

Sustainability is seen as a process for transforming society from an exploitative, consumerist enterprise to an equitable society where the balances between human enterprises and between humankind and nature are negotiated locally. Although such a process derives from traditional design processes, a new expanded architectural design process is envisaged. Instead of relying solely upon the 'hoped for' genius of individual architects, the sustainable design process will also benefit from the collective genius of all the individual stakeholders in the equitable ecological city/region (Levine, 1987, 1989). In spite of the fact that the sustainability design process will require working in a highly interactive way with other professionals and stakeholders, the architect will be located in a more critical position than conventional practice affords. Thus, for the architect, both challenges and opportunities will greatly increase in the design and management of the sustainable city of the future.

The Westbahnhof Project – the sustainable city of the future

The city of Vienna, Austria, is considering building a SCI as a solution to a long-standing urban problem: the need to build over a major train yard at the Westbahnhof. Developed conceptually through numerous architectural design studio projects and field studies, the SCI is inspired by the historic medieval European hill town (see Figs 1, 2 and 3). This city-as-a-hill prototype, rendered through the Sustainability Engine, presents a new, holistic, people centred, urban vision. In the SCI, sustainability is non-negotiable. This means that all major material flow processes are regenerative and the implantation is completely powered by solar renewable resources.

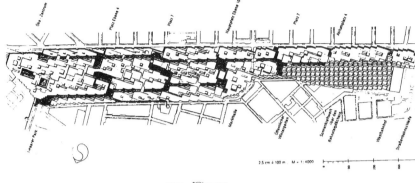

Fig. 1. Site plan of Westbahnhof SCI showing network of sloped streets and piazzas (see end note).

Fig. 2. Transverse section through city-as-a-hill, looking west.

Fig. 3. Transverse sectional elevation showing visual aspect of urban fabric.

Theory and practice – form and counterform

Having established a coherent, consistent and complete theory of the sustainable city/region, the question remains how to proceed from theory to practice. In fact, the evolution of the theory has been paralleled by the co-evolution of a new urban form. In seeking an appropriate form and structure for the sustainable city of the future, the aim is not to identify means of solving the problems of existing cities, but to synthesise a new model where the problems of the modern city never appear, and the above process definition of sustainability can be strongly adhered to. In the iterative, trial and error process known to all designers, numerous different concepts are proposed and studied. Unproductive directions are eliminated and promising models are saved. By circling around the problem over and over again, a locus of mutually supportive relationships slowly emerges. It is not just a question of seeking a 'perfect form', but of determining and developing a family of forms with the flexibility and responsiveness to accommodate a variety of possible local preferences.

Thus, structures are chosen at a variety of scales, which have mutually supportive tendencies that can be associated with the needs and possibilities of sustainable cities. From the definition of the sustainable city/region, a number of strong tendencies can be inferred. The definition suggests a dense, compact city with a dynamic balance between community and privacy. It suggests a community rich in form, public space and individual and collective opportunities. It suggests a city with a strong sense of itself as a place, a clear and defined form and a common destiny. It suggests a human-scaled environment, not one that is over-scaled and sized to accommodate vehicles, industries and faceless institutions. Yet it also suggests a city able to find appropriate space for the various larger-scaled industries and infrastructure necessary to accommodate the metabolic and economic processes of a modern city.

The city-as-a-hill – a new urban model

In seeking to discover an urban structure with the above characteristics, our proposal for a new type of city district combines some of the most compelling aspects of the medieval European hill town with the best of modern processes and technology. Instead of the medieval city on a hill, this proposal is for a city-as-a-hill whose outer surface resembles, in scale and texture, the pedestrian-scaled medieval towns. Using advanced computer modelling software, which allows for the possibility of generating many varieties or models of such SCIs in an interactive and participatory manner, this new urban configuration creates many opportunities not possible in the modern unsustainable city (Levine and Radmard, 1990; Levine *et al.*, 1991). In our city-as-a-hill model, the outer surface of the city contains all of the dwellings and neighbourhoods, the smaller-scaled commercial and institutional activities and the network of public buildings and public spaces, that is, the streets, walkways, stairs and squares which give historic medieval towns their life-affirming, pedestrian character. Inside the city-as-a-hill, daylit by courtyards and light wells, is a series of concourses and gallerias, along which are located the large-scale commercial, institutional, and industrial spaces, as well as the infrastructure and other activities necessary to support them.

Over the years in which these models have been developed, their structure and complexity have increased. A new, flexible, concrete structural system, the Coupled Pan Space Frame, which generates a complex family of building geometries, is being used as the framework for both spanning the train tracks and for creating the inner hill and the urban fabric above ground level (Levine, 1982; Dumreicher and Levine, 1996). This frame permits the negotiation of both level and sloping streets on the constructed hill, giving it the sort of three-dimensional, organic character rarely seen in modern architecture and modern cities.

Vienna's sustainable city implantation

Behind the Westbahnhof lies a train yard 1.5km long by 200m wide. For many years, this yard has been a scar on the city, dividing a neighbourhood and creating near slum conditions on either side of the yard. There have been many proposals to build over the yard but none has been either a suitable economic proposition or acceptable to the city. The present proposal (Dumreicher and Levine, 1995, 1996) is for a glazed, vaulted train shed behind the terminal building at the east end of the site. It is, in part, in the tradition of the early glass train sheds found in many major European cities, except that the glazing contains integrated photovoltaic (PV) collectors that deliver a substantial percentage of the implantation's energy requirements, while modulating the climate and quality of light entering the terminal.

A pedestrian street extends from the terminal and runs the length of the site to the west, parallel to the tracks, rising up the city-as-a-hill at a gentle six per cent slope. As it rises, it crosses other horizontal floor levels and at every third level (levels four, seven, and ten) it passes through a public square or piazza. A streetcar runs along this otherwise pedestrian street and, after passing through the main piazza (Hauptplatz) at level ten, it descends through piazzas at levels seven, four, and one to join an existing track at ground level.

On the surface of the constructed hill is a human-scaled town with networks of streets, stairs, piazzas and paths, weaving between three- to five-storey neighbourhoods of dwellings and a variety of shops and services. Also on the hill's surface is a winter garden, growing food year round, and a network of south-facing greenhouses. At the west end is an east–west exchange centre which is roofed by a large, terraced, ecological park, connected to the existing technological museum. At this end of the site is another sloping street which is more like a linear park, culminating at the level ten Hauptplatz. By this main square is a fountain, which is also an energy gnomon (the height of the fountain is an indicator of the rate at which the implantation is exporting renewable energy to the larger city of Vienna). Overflow from the fountain trickles down through the linear park, feeding various ponds and other green areas along its course. The roofs of the outer city are either glazed greenhouses or flat surfaces which are all utilised either as private or semi-private terraces, gardens, courtyards or public parks, playgrounds or piazzas.

Running almost the length of the site is a three-story galleria. Levels four and seven, as the major horizontal circulation levels, connect courtyards in the outer city to each other and to the piazzas, as well as connecting to the inner gallerias. Along the gallerias, daylit through courtyards and light wells from above, are all the major institutional, commercial, and industrial activities as well as infrastructure, service, parking, tracks and transportation – activities, whose bad neighbour effects and large scale often disrupt the integrity of a traditional urban fabric, but which are necessary to sustain an urban economy. In the city-as-a-hill, they fit in well, providing maximum accessibility without compromising the small-scale, village character. The sustainability enhancing features of the SCI are summarised in Table 1.

The SCI is a totally urban construction, which multiplies value, in part because it multiplies real estate. Railroad services occupy almost the entire site at the original ground level, but there are additional levels of developable real estate in the framework above, with their own appropriate functions and activities. Because it is completely urban, and has no open ground of its own, the implantation is to be linked with a rural partnerland, which is dedicated to re-balancing the city/region. On this land, most of the agriculture and energy from solar/regenerative sources would be negotiated with its urban counterpart. The implantation, together with its rural partnerland, would constitute an equitable ecological region.

The partnerland principle

Numerous references have been made in this case study to the relationship between urban implantations and rural partnerlands for the exchange of goods, materials, energy and social and cultural opportunities and benefits. However, it is one thing to create theoretical models of how this might work and quite another to create the social and political space to enable it to happen. To create a fertile ground out of which the Westbahnhof SCI can rise, the whole Fifteenth District is appropriated as the urban region to be utilised. It is being partnered with Mistlebach, a sparsely settled agricultural region in the Weinviertel to the north of Vienna near the Czech border, which has approximately the same overall population (70,000).

Within the Fifteenth District, an extensive network of social, ecological and economic initiatives and enterprises already exists, but the actors are unaware of their importance and the value or extent of this network. Individuals often consider themselves as a powerless minority who, at most, can only overcome some of their more pressing shortcomings. In the process of establishing the network, the actors come to see the relationship between their own small spheres and the dynamic and increasingly powerful whole.

In activating the city/region principle, a first step has been to establish partnerships between well defined structures in the town district (Wien 15) and the region (Mistlebach), including the political, administrative, cultural, economic and agricultural institutions. The concept of a market place is extremely useful in the establishment of new opportunities. The market place of ideas, as well as of goods, services and cultural exchanges becomes the generator of an expanding social network for the creation and utilisation of available goods and services. Such a programme has already been put in place, involving, for example, the farmers of Mistlebach and the grocers of the Fifteenth District.

The partnership concept represents a first small step in the reconstruction of the global economy on a sustainable basis. The essential operating goal of any sustainability regime is to assure that the movements of materials, energy, goods and services are activated by the larger, more comprehensive forces of supply and demand which include ecology and equity as balancing influences on traditional economic forces. The 'partnerland' concept is a novel way of implementing a first operational step at the scale of the city/region.

Sustainability feature of the SCI	Description of feature
Humanly-scaled urban form	An urban form small enough to be easily walkable and to eliminate even the desire for a car, yet large enough to provide the variety of opportunities and services required for a rich urban life.
Density and compactness	A complete and well articulated structure that permits virtually all needs and services for the majority of inhabitants within the SCI.
Three-dimensional urban fabric	A clear form and boundary, and a legible, yet complexly woven, three-dimensional structure that coalesces into a continuous urban fabric.
Physically secure public spaces	A structural design such that no large mono-functional buildings front onto public paths, where they would create 'dead' or dangerous zones.
People oriented scale	An urban design enhancing the public spatial realms while providing for many scales of private realm, offering pathways that build in a continuity of walking surface.
Self-balancing	A green city implantation that works toward internal balance-seeking while striving to absorb more material and energy flow problems from the surrounding unsustainable city, thus exporting ecological, equity and economic benefits to that city.
Complex and flexible urban	A robust, but malleable and open-ended concept/system capable of different articulation of urban sustainability derived from participatory processes spanning design, governance and management.
Spaces for possibilities	A flexible architectural/urban structure, which creates the sense of an equally pliant and secure social space where physical, social and economic characteristics of the city can be negotiated.

Table 1. Sustainability enhancing characteristics in the Westbahnhof SCI and prior design studies.

Conclusion

In subsequent stages of development of the SCI, the city models and their parts will become the framework for the integration of other systems including: mechanical, electrical, material and infrastructure systems, facilities management, information, energy and material flow models, economic activity, imports and exports (input/output) to the city, and the modelling of the ecological balances within the city and between the city and its rural partnerland. This will be done on the Sustainability Engine. The Sustainability Engine is the 'autonomic nervous system' of the SCI. Both during the design process, and in the governance and management of the city, the Sustainability Engine houses the energy, material flow and process models that are studied and tested in order to progress the development of the city. As the city, its processes, and industries are studied, the Sustainability Engine provides frequent feedback on the ongoing state of the system and indicates the sectors where it is out of balance.

Urban sustainability thus promises to create the next major transformation both in architecture and in our cities. In many ways, the sustainable city may represent the rebirth of Modern Architecture. The Athens Charter became a disaster for our cities. Because of the mechanistic ways in which it separated functions and activities, it reinforced the economic tendencies toward unsustainability. In contrast, the sustainable city will demand a dense, diverse, highly integrated urban fabric. It will demand a whole new range of architectural and urban forms and structures. It will put architects and architecture at the centre of a participatory process demanding the skills and creativity of all participants. In short, it will complete the agenda of Modern Architecture.

Note

Because the design of the Westbahnhof SCI is an ongoing project, subject to continuous interaction, modification and negotiation throughout the design, construction, and maintenance process, designs should be regarded as ongoing studies. There are already many different (often conflicting) residential plans, neighbourhood plans and site plans, with differing levels of detail, responding to different needs and design considerations. The few studies such a limited chapter permits are taken from different series of design studies.

Acknowledgements

The research reported in this chapter was carried out by Oikodrom – Forum Nachhaltige Stadt, Vienna, Austria, and the Centre for Sustainable Cities, University of Kentucky, Lexington, USA. Financial support for the Westbahnhof project has been given by: Wien MA18/23, Oesterreichische Nationalbank, Jubilaumsfonds, Bundesministerium für Wissenschaft und Verkehr, Bundesministerium für Land - und Forstwirtschaft, Land Niederosterreich, Urban-Buro Wien, and the University of Kentucky.

The architectural, scientific, and social scientific team was composed of: Heidi Dumreicher, Oikodrom; Richard S. Levine, Centre for Sustainable Cities; Florentine Astleithner, Oikodrom; Harald Fenz, Oikodrom; Bettina Kolb, Oikodrom; Frederike Konig, Universitat Graz, Verein Sustain; Christian Krotscheck, Universitat Graz, Verein Sustain; Michael Narodoslawsky, Universitat, Graz, Verein Sustain; Reinhard Paulesich, Wirtschaftsuniversitat Wein; Richard Perfler; Claudia Pichl, WIFO, Wien; Veronika Prandl, Oikodrom; Taghi Radmard, Centre for Sustainable Cities; Friedrich Schneider, Universitat Linz; Robert Snyder, CADD Concepts; Otto Schulz, Österreichische Vereinigung für agrarwissenschaftliche Forschung (OVAF); Claudia Schwab, Oikodrom; Horst Steinmuller, OVAF; Ernest J. Yanarella, Centre for Sustainable Cities; Rob Nickol, Scott Fleming, Nathan Smith, James Black, University of Kentucky; and Matt Fox, Ball State University.

Alexander E. Kalamaros
Sustainable Development in Southern California: *The Case of Playa Vista*

Introduction

Over the past decade, planning and development professionals have recognised the importance of balancing environmental, community and economic concerns in their decisions about urban land use and development. Drawing on principles of sustainable development, an attempt to achieve this balancing act was made at the development, commenced in 1998, at Playa Vista ('beach view'). This large scale infill project comprises 1,087 acres of underdeveloped land in densely populated West Los Angeles. Worth in excess of US$5 billion, the project is significant for its simultaneous consideration of profitability and the natural and social environments in which it is situated.

Beyond its underlying community responsiveness and the market discipline enjoyed by the private nature of its ownership, Playa Vista maintains a fundamental commitment to environmental stewardship. Virtually every decision to be made regarding the project's design has been subject to the scrutiny of a decision making process that seeks to be sensitive to the environment, without sacrificing profitability. Although work on Playa Vista will continue for some time, early marketing efforts have demonstrated a favourable response.

To provide a complete picture of the Playa Vista project, this chapter comprises several sections. First, the regional context in which the project is situated is considered, as it informs the choices of components selected for the project. Next, the details of the Playa Vista plan are discussed. The final section describes what the project seeks to accomplish, through the use of an example of how sustainability principles are implemented in practice at Playa Vista. The example, taken from a set of guidelines for sustainable performance in residential development, illustrates the legacy the project seeks to leave behind, in addition to its physical form.

The local context

As sustainability can be understood best as a local phenomenon, it is useful to consider how the regional context influences the choices made about the components of the Playa Vista project. Southern California, and Los Angeles in particular, is often pointed to as a primary example of unfettered 'suburban sprawl', referring to the postwar proliferation of low-density single-family housing and strip mall development at the urban fringe, typically settled exclusively by middle-income families. 'Suburb', in this context, means a dormitory community with a collection of homes whose residents use freeways to commute to their work in the central city. 'Sprawl' specifically refers to the preponderance of this form of development stretching for many miles. Developers consumed open space purely as a function of the use of land for suburban housing, assuming the role of the central city would remain fixed over time.

While at least a portion of the region may deserve to be described as sprawling, developers in the vicinity of Playa Vista did not all conform to this pattern of land planning and consumption. Other parts of Los Angeles take the form of carefully planned, denser than average, self-contained communities, built near dispersed centres of industrial production, and fuelled by decades of defence spending. At the time these areas were developed in the 1940s, there were no multi-lane freeways running to them from the central city. Nearly all the surrounding land was used for agricultural purposes, and the primary market for homes was a heterogeneous mix of factory workers and executives. The developers at the time recognised the importance of the workplace–residence link. Historian Greg Hise describes several of these communities, including nearby Westchester:

> They were not the sprawling in-fill of isolated residential neighborhoods projected along mass or private transit routes. These nodal developments were dynamic hubs of manufacturing and job creation, the foundation necessary for operative builders' experiments in communities of balanced living. (Hise, 1996, p.261)

In the same manner as developers at that time responded to prevailing economic and geographical conditions, Playa Vista responds to current conditions. The area around Playa Vista, including nearby Culver City, has replaced much of its defence employment with jobs in the entertainment industry. The builders of Playa Vista are experimenters of sorts too, as they work to demonstrate that environmentally sensitive buildings can be just as profitable as more conventional forms of development.

The Playa Vista plan
Playa Vista is located in West Los Angeles just north of Los Angeles International Airport (see Fig. 1). The site is bordered by Marina Del Rey to the north, Westchester to the south, the San Diego Freeway to the east, and the Pacific Ocean to the west. The complete Playa Vista plan contains 13,000 residential units, a 2.9 million square feet Entertainment Media Technology District, 1.9 million square feet of commercial space, 600,000 square feet of retail space, 750 hotel rooms, 11 acres of public facilities and a new 30-acre boat basin adjoining Marina Del Rey. Occupancy of the first residential units is expected in 2000.

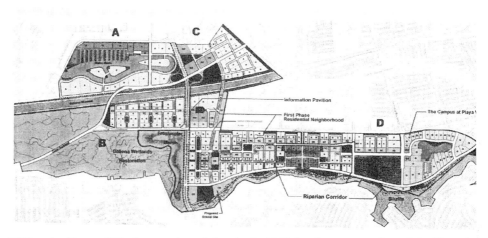

Fig. 1. The Playa Vista plan.

Billionaire Howard Hughes purchased the site in 1941 for the construction of the Hercules HK-1, the 'Spruce Goose'. The Entertainment Media Technology District noted above will feature sound stages and production offices including the historic Spruce Goose hangar. After

300

Hughes' death in 1976, initial attempts to gain approval to develop the site failed until Maguire Thomas Partners won approval of the current plan in 1993. A recession and a series of court challenges held up the project for five years. Since 1998, the project has been managed by a group of Wall Street investors, operating as Playa Capital Company LLC, although Maguire maintains a minority interest.

The project is expected to contribute 31,600 permanent jobs, and to generate $125 million in combined fiscal benefits annually, to the City and County of Los Angeles and the State of California. Over the next 15 years, more than $720 million in sales and personal income tax to the State is expected. Over that same period, the Entertainment Media Technology District is expected to contribute $117.8 million to the City of Los Angeles, $45.8 million to the County and $361.6 million to the State.

Half the project will be set aside as open space. Integral to the development's commitment to its environment is the restoration of the Ballona Wetlands into a nature reserve area of more than 340 acres. A 190-acre saltwater marsh will be included, as will a 26-acre freshwater marsh system, a 25-acre restored riparian corridor and 100 acres of dunes, uplands and surrounding habitat. $12.5 million has been committed to saltwater marsh restoration.

Offering a 'balanced community of low- to mid-rise buildings with a strong emphasis on the provision of a generous public realm' (Katz, 1994, p.180), the design of Playa Vista seeks to reduce time spent on California's freeways by providing a mix of uses, and by allowing residents to complete many of their daily errands on foot. Pedestrian orientation is crucial to the Playa Vista plan, and will be important, if not essential, to a region that expects to see continued growth over the coming decades.

Implementing sustainability

When the environmental movement emerged in America, grass roots action turned attention to breaking the habit of polluting. Since then, vehicle emissions standards have improved and industrial pollution control measures are in effect. But the prospect of bringing an appreciation of the environment into the popular marketplace is still largely unrealised.

Individuals who found the more extreme elements of environmentalism too radical in the 1970s found a new voice with the popular emergence of the principles of sustainable development in the 1980s. This new population demographic, widely recognised in the American LIVES study (Ray, 1997), demonstrated that public desire to utilise environmentally sensitive products had grown, and is likely to continue to grow steadily.

Playa Vista's future is fundamentally linked to its responsiveness to the community and to its natural environment, but the project extends beyond an exercise in conservation and planning. Playa Vista maintains the underlying discipline of market viability. In so doing, it will facilitate the mainstreaming of sustainable development ideals. Even so, the market mechanisms related to environmentally sensitive products are not yet widely understood. Furthermore, housing construction methods are largely unchanged since World War II. Playa Vista's answer to these constraints is to draw upon the considerable body of knowledge of green building methods at every possible opportunity. As the construction of Playa Vista proceeds, project workers at every level will be asked to consider the simultaneous objectives of creating an environmentally sensitive, livable community that is also economically viable.

The development of sustainability guidelines

In preparation for commencing the first stages of residential construction, the Playa Vista management team prepared of a set of guidelines relating to the project's objectives of environmental awareness and sensitivity (Playa Capital Company, LLC, 1998). In addition, the guidelines include a number of mitigation measures required in the project's entitlement, as well as a number of standards required by municipal ordinance. The guidelines cover eight major categories:

1. building materials
2. recycling and waste management
3. energy
4. domestic water
5. power signal and control
6. adaptability
7. landscape
8. transportation

Each category contains information for building contractors regarding the mandatory requirements the project must meet, the sustainable design issue involved, recommended on-site measures for construction teams, performance standards for material selection, references to related documents and application notes.

One example of the guidelines at work is the Building Envelope Guideline, one of six components of the Energy category (Playa Capital Company, LLC, 1998). The guideline raises the issue of heat transfer as the basic design issue related to sustainability of the exterior 'skin' of the building. Heat transfer related to the sun's energy is considered to have more effect than mere insulation. Therefore, window design takes on added importance. The guideline suggests that windows should be designed to allow ambient daylight, whilst also limiting heat gain. The guideline consists of: a guiding principle; mandatory requirements, such as the percentage energy use reductions required and the need to provide shading and glazing modifications on glass windows and doors; recommended measures, such as the beneficial use of reflective surfaces; performance metrics, which set out aspirational targets in terms of, for example, air changes per hour; and application recommendations. In combination, these elements of the guideline ensure that developers meet acceptable sustainability standards in the building envelope.

Conclusion

According to Dowell Myers, exactly what is meant by quality of life in our cities changes over time (Myers, 1989). Rapid development in Southern California once compounded pollution problems. New development was seen as a threat to quality of life and led to the imposition of growth controls. In the decades it has taken to plan and approve the Playa Vista project, at least one serious economic downturn reminded Angelenos of the benefits of growth. As Playa Vista's approval in 1993 came in the midst of a recession, there was an apparent change in the local definition of quality of life. At Playa Vista, quality of life means a balance of community livability, environmental sensitivity and economic viability. If Playa Vista meets these objectives, it will provide a substantial demonstration of the viability of sustainable urban form in an American city.

Peter G. Fauset

The Hulme Estate and the 'Homes for Change' Development:
Britain's First Major Sustainable Housing Project

Introduction

The Hulme Estate was a notorious, huge, high-rise, inner city, residential area built between 1964 and 1972. Most of the 5,000 dwellings were in the form of maisonettes, mainly in six-to eight-storey deck-access blocks, using heavy concrete panel construction. The estate suffered severe social problems, a high crime rate and a rapid deterioration of the building fabric. This chapter explains how, in 1991, Manchester City Council and AMEC, a large private developer, secured a grant from the government to regenerate the area. It outlines how a strategy plan for the redevelopment was drawn up by a distinguished local architectural practice that included a unique urban design code to control the design of all new developments.

It then explains how part of the Hulme Estate was transformed, as the sustainable 'Homes for Change' development was conceived and constructed. This self-contained community development, including a shop, offices, workshops, studio theatre, café and 50 co-operative maisonettes and flats, was constructed of sustainable materials, and is now a model of sustainable development.

Background

Situated south-west of Manchester city centre, Hulme is an inner city area which has mainly housed the poor, and suffered different forms of depravation during its life (see Engels, 1844). Originally developed during the Industrial Revolution by speculative landlords, Hulme consisted of a gridiron of streets with poorly built, mainly two-storey, terraced housing, constructed to a density of over 150 dwellings per hectare. Following the clearance of the slums, Manchester City Architects' Department designed a new estate incorporating all the latest fashionable housing ideas of the 1960s (Manchester City Planning Department, 1965). Largely inspired by anglicised versions of Le Corbusier's housing projects, the estate was characterised by its free-standing towers and deck-access blocks (see note 1). The new plan proposed accommodation for about 15,000 people at a density of about 37 dwellings per hectare, with plenty of open space which had not been provided in the original nineteenth century layout. About 5,000 dwellings were eventually built, 3,000 of which were in the form of seven-storey deck-access blocks, with most of the remaining dwellings arranged in short, four- or six-storey blocks of maisonettes and a small number of thirteen-storey tower blocks of flats. Industrialised heavy concrete panel construction was used for building virtually all of the housing blocks. The most distinguishable part of the estate, however, was formed by four enormous seven-storey crescent blocks containing deck-access housing, each about half a kilometre in length, designed by local architects, Wilson Womersley. The inspiration for the footprint of these blocks was clearly Woods' Georgian Royal Crescent in Bath, but there the similarity ends.

Almost as soon as the estate was completed, it suffered acute social problems and severe deterioration of the fabric of the buildings. In 1975, after the death of a child falling from one of the decks of the crescents, the tenants forced Manchester City Council to accommodate families only on the ground floor; in effect, this meant moving them to other estates since most of the ground floor of the Hulme blocks comprised garages. Crime – such as murder, mugging, burglary, drug taking and pushing, vandalism and graffiti – made Hulme the least safe place in Manchester. A large part of the reason for this was explained by Oscar Newman in his seminal book, *Defensible Space* (1973). The extensive use of open, public, unsupervised spaces – such as the vast parkland, play areas, decks, lifts and lobbies – was the main reason for Hulme's failure. In addition to this, the adoption of maisonettes and flats 'up in the air' for families was alien to the English culture of single-family houses with private gardens.

The health and safety of Hulme's residents was also at risk as structural defects became apparent. There were problems in the jointing of concrete slabs and panels; condensation due to the lack of insulation, and the inadequate and expensive heating systems; cockroach infestations due to damp, warm conditions, and a network of ducts and cavities; and dangers caused by the extensive use of carcinogenic asbestos in walls and panels. The estate deteriorated rapidly, many families fled the area and vacant units were either occupied or vandalised. Various attempts were made by the Council to eradicate the problems, but these were mainly cosmetic. The enormity of the problems and the cost of rectifying them was so overwhelming that by 1992 it was decided, finally, to demolish the estate.

Regeneration

The impetus to demolish Hulme and regenerate the area had begun in 1991 when the Secretary of State for the Environment announced the introduction of the 'City Challenge' programme. The aim of the programme was to regenerate England's worst inner city areas by comprehensively dealing with all their problems, including housing, employment, education and crime. In a competition process for government grants, 57 'urban priority areas' were selected for regeneration. As part of the competition process for City Challenge, the applicants had to demonstrate that substantial private investment would be included in the process of regeneration. The government grants paid to each urban priority area were worth £37.5 million each, and were to be paid over a five-year period. In the bid for Hulme, Manchester City Council formed a joint venture with AMEC, who envisaged approximately £230 million of private investment over the first five years of the redevelopment. Following the successful bid, a small independent private company was set up – Hulme Regeneration Limited – which was to co-ordinate the redevelopment of the area.

An early enlightened initiative by Hulme Regeneration Ltd was to commission the distinguished local modernist architectural practice of Mills Beaumont Leavey Channon to produce a strategy plan and urban design code for the area. The strategy plan for the regeneration proposed 'a straightforward and robust street pattern which reflects the original grain of the area, links back to surrounding neighbourhoods and provides the overall structure for the future' (Hulme Regeneration Ltd, 1994). In essence, the plan is a grid pattern of streets and squares which re-establishes some of the important streets that existed prior to the 1960s, yet also knits these streets into the surrounding area. A hierarchy of streets was proposed, with the more important streets containing mixed uses, with shops and businesses and other commercial activities at ground level to give a street life which is necessary for the rejuvenation of the area. Building blocks follow the gridiron pattern of streets and are generally arranged around internal landscaped courtyards for exclusive use by the residents. The new plan envisaged a much higher housing density than the previous estate – 75 to 85 houses per hectare – though with the provision of a park this was lower than the original nineteenth century Hulme (Fig. 1).

150 DWELLINGS/HA   37 DWELLINGS/HA   75-87 DWELLINGS/HA

Fig. 1. Figure ground plans showing the changing pattern of Hulme from the nineteenth century (left), the 1960s (middle), and the 1990s Strategy Plan (right).

In view of the large numbers of disparate developers, from both the public and private sectors, likely to be carrying out building projects in the area, Hulme Regeneration Ltd felt it needed to establish some form of planning guidelines for the developments. Mills Beaumont Leavey Channon suggested that a planning control system developed in North America – an urban design code – be instigated at Hulme. The code was a more detailed extension of the work the architects had carried out on the strategy plan and provided guidance to developers under ten different headings.

1. *The street* – This section emphasised the importance of street-dominated layouts in the regeneration of Hulme and proposed that streets should be closely defined by buildings in the traditional manner. It also suggested that streets should be the main form of communication for pedestrians and that they should not be dominated by the motor car.
2. *Integration* – The emphasis here was that Hulme should be integrated into the city and that only mixed-used developments be encouraged, rather than the 1960s' pattern of separating or zoning different land uses.
3. *Density* – To foster a wide range of facilities close to dwellings and create a street life, it was suggested that housing should be at an average density of 90 dwellings per hectare.
4. *Permeability* – Encouragement was given for all streets to lead somewhere and be connected to other streets, rather than be in a cul-de-sac form which is anti-urban.
5. *Routes and transport* – The promotion of public transport, the reduction of traffic speeds, on-street car parking, reduced car parking standards, traditional crossroads and cycle routes were advocated.
6. *Landmarks, vistas and focal points* – These were considered necessary to give a sense of place and to aid orientation. Emphasis was given to creating street-corner buildings, public art and street furniture.
7. *Definition of space* – In order to create a sense of urbanity in the new Hulme, recommendations were made with regard to the ratios between the height of buildings and the distances apart they should be – across streets, squares and parks.
8. *Identity* – The code suggested that each development should have its own identity through its response to location, use of different building materials and finishes.
9. *Sustainability* – Various issues of sustainability were addressed in the code, such as flexibility of buildings for non-housing uses, long-life buildings, retention of existing streets and high quality landscaping, recycling of materials, avoidance of harmful gas emissions and energy conservation.

10. *Hierarchy* – A hierarchy of streets with corresponding building heights and street widths was set out.

In order to ensure that developers and their consultants complied with this code, it was necessary that Manchester City Council adopted it for all planning applications at Hulme. However, a number of the code's recommendations were contrary to some of the Council standards, notably with regard to highway engineering, crime prevention, parking standards, density and distances between buildings. Fortunately, after much persuasion, the Council agreed to adopt the code in full. Interestingly, all planning applications for Hulme are also passed on by the Council to Mills Beaumont Leavey Channon for comment. The code has clearly had the desired effect of producing truly urban housing that is oriented towards the street and planned around courtyards, and has fortuitously prevented the characteristically British, suburban, intestinal cul-de-sac form of layout favoured by most developers. Although some developers and architects have criticised the code for being too prescriptive, the variety of resulting built forms and architectural styles is amazingly diverse. Perhaps it is too diverse, since on some streets – notably where two separate developers have constructed housing on opposite sides – there is little unity between them to 'hold the street together'. When the whole of Hulme is complete, the excessive variety may result in visual chaos. Perhaps the code should have gone further and specified a limited palette of walling and roofing materials. While one could envisage developers bitterly complaining that this would have made development too restrictive, at least Hulme would then have had more of the harmony found in, for example, Woods' Bath or Craig's Edinburgh New Town.

'Homes for Change'
Although a number of housing schemes have already been completed at Hulme, and several more are under construction or are being designed, the most interesting so far is, without doubt, the Homes for Change development. This project came to life through the collective energy of a group of 'alternative', educated, ecologically-minded, articulate Hulme residents who had very firm ideas about what sort of community they wanted to build. Central to their philosophy of design was a desire to be able to live and work in the same complex; in effect, to create an '18-hour-a-day' building. Interestingly enough, in the new development they sought to incorporate some key features from the former Hulme Estate, such as maisonettes, deck-access and six-storey buildings, though with increased security and a different image.

Before appointing the architects, Mills Beaumont Leavey Channon, the co-operative had already prepared a detailed brief for the new development to consist of 1,500 square metres of workspace, a wholefood shop and café, a 130-seat studio theatre and 50 dwellings. The co-operative also wanted to be actively involved in the design process, and a series of weekly workshops was organised to develop the design. In order to help the co-operative explore and understand the organisation of the building, different model-making techniques were used, such as the use of plasticine for investigating the massing of the building and cardboard to construct full-sized rooms so residents could appreciate the size and layout of their future dwellings.

Homes for Change is a registered co-operative who design, own and manage the building. The £3.6 million project received finance from several sources, notably the Housing Corporation, European Development Fund, City Challenge, Guinness Trust and some ecological charities. The Manchester based Co-operative Bank was used for deposits and loans on the scheme, and the rental income pays off the interest charges to the bank. Approximately 60% of the residents work in the building in about 30 new 'start-up' businesses, such as a wholefood shop, a recycling workshop, a potter's studio and an urban consultant's office.

The complex is planned in a U-shape around a central landscaped courtyard and is surrounded by streets on three sides (Fig. 2). The open side of the courtyard faces south and a second phase of the development will eventually be built along the southern boundary. Situated on the ground and first floors along the north and west sides of the complex are the workshops, studios, offices, theatre, shop and café (Fig. 3). Above these facilities are maisonettes, the northern block of which is six storeys in height while the west wing is mainly four storeys, except at the junction with the west wing which is five storeys (Fig. 4). The east wing consists of six storeys of maisonettes, including six larger family units at ground and first floor levels. An interesting result of the design workshops was that some of the residents needed to distance themselves a little more from the communal parts of the scheme; also, it was felt that the noisy recycling workshop needed to be separated from the bulk of the building. This resulted in two separate buildings at the southern end of the site which are linked by bridges to the west and east wings.

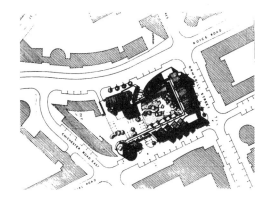

Fig. 2. Site plan.

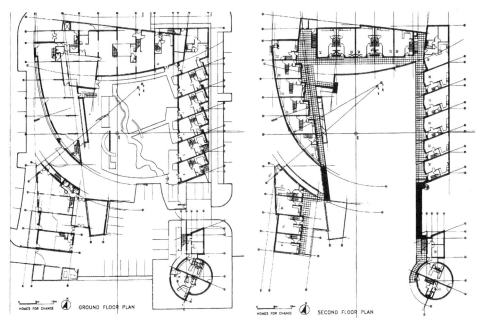

Fig. 3. Ground floor plan, with main entrance and studio theatre at the junction of the north and west blocks, workshop space in the north and west wings, and family maisonettes in the east wing.

Fig. 4. Second floor plan, with maisonettes and roof gardens.

307

In the plans of the buildings, the geometries are constantly shifting, breaking away from the orthogonal and providing stimulating tensions. In the east wing, the maisonettes are angled towards the south-west to achieve more solar gain and better views from the tight courtyard (Fig. 5). The detached block linked to the east wing is circular in plan since it is at the hinge point to the next phase of the development. In the western wing, the street façade curves inwards towards the courtyard, again to achieve more solar gain to the dwellings in this part of the scheme (Fig. 6).

Access to the scheme is principally from one controlled entrance at the north-west corner of the building. From here, a lift and staircase provide access to the maisonettes via decks at second and fourth floor levels on the courtyard side of the building. Five small roof gardens are also provided in the scheme for communal use by residents.

Considerable interest and variety has been achieved in the development through the choice of diverse building materials and finishes (Fig. 7). The predominant material is a buff coloured facing brick, although render, horizontal weather-boarding and smooth concrete have also been used. Stainless steel has been used extensively for the balustrades to the decks, bridge link structures, fire escapes, balconies, lintels over longer span openings, spiral stairs, cladding panels around the lift tower and curved roof sheeting. The main structure for the walls, floors and flat roofs is a combination of precast and *in-situ* concrete. Party wall construction consists of two precast concrete panels filled with reinforced *in-situ* concrete in the cavity. The floors and flat roofs use precast concrete planks with a structural concrete topping. All the exposed precast concrete wall and roof panels have such a smooth finish that they may be decorated with varnish, paint or wallpaper by the residents. Machine sanded timber boarding was selected for the floor finish to the maisonettes and can be varnished or covered with carpets or rugs.

Fig. 5. East wing facing the courtyard, with decks at second and fourth floor levels, and roof garden.
Source: Len Grant.

Fig. 6. Street façade of west wing.
Source: Len Grant.

Fig. 7. Courtyard side of north wing.
Source: Len Grant.

Many sustainability principles have been used in the choice of building materials and environmental services in the development. These choices were mostly made by members of Homes for Change and supported by associated ecologically minded organisations (see note 2). The design workshops established the environmental targets for the scheme, and cost checks were carried out on their application, to test viability. Various alternative systems were explored by the client and consultants, such as passive solar energy, water recycling, and natural ventilation by the 'stack' effect. Regrettably, the high capital cost of some of these innovative ideas, and difficulties associated with receiving statutory approvals, prevented them being realised. However, the scheme does incorporate a remarkable number of sustainable features, such as:

- Recycled building materials – for example, the concrete blocks were made of 80% recycled materials including 60% pulverised fuel ash (from power stations), and the roads incorporated crushed concrete from the former Hulme Estate.
- Locally produced building materials to reduce transport costs – such as the facing bricks which came from south Manchester.

- Avoidance of the use of building materials which contain chlorofluorocarbons (CFCs) and hydrochlorofluorocarbons (HCFCs) which damage the atmosphere.
- Use of timbers from sustainable forests.
- Super-insulation standards for walls and roofs – equivalent to U-values of $0.2\ W/m^2\ K$ – and use of special heat-reflecting glass.
- Lower energy costs – space heating costs reduced to less than £1 per week.
- Solar gain and maximisation of natural daylight – large living room and bedroom windows, angled as near as possible to face south, and small windows facing north.
- On-site recycling of waste materials – collection of unsegregated waste is less than 50% of a typical UK household.

Conclusions

Homes for Change is without doubt one of the finest and most innovative housing schemes to have been produced in Britain since the late 1970s. That it should have taken so many years for an alternative form of housing to have emerged in Britain can only be explained by understanding the previous government's dogmatic antagonism towards public housing, and the innate conservatism of British private housing developers. The government's reliance on the private sector as the only provider of housing has resulted in an acute shortage of dwellings for certain groups of people. Fluctuations in supply and demand together with economic recessions have seriously affected the mobility of many people and have resulted in a large number of repossessions. Private housing developers provide mainly out-of-town, suburban, ultra-conventional houses for middle-income families, or flats in exclusive residential areas for wealthy people (Fauset, 1994). Since the late 1970s, social and economic changes have resulted in conditions which require a different approach to housing to deal with new household groups, such as single people, young couples, single parent families and old people. Also required are developments in inner urban areas to bring new life to the city, to reduce the consumption of rural land and avoid our dependence on the motor car, and a mixing of housing with workspaces and other communal facilities. This new approach needs also to include sustainability, to slow down the depletion of the Earth's natural resources. In view of this, the Homes for Change development is a remarkable achievement; it undoubtedly signals a new way forward and is a model for housing design in the future.

Notes
1. The deck-access form of housing, sometimes referred to as 'streets in the air', was first projected by Le Corbusier in his Algiers Project (1930–34) although the first housing constructed along these lines was Park Hill in Sheffield (1957–61) which had a major impact on the design of public housing in Britain in the 1960s and 1970s.
2. Associated with this development was the Urban and Economic Development Group (URBED), who helped to establish the environmental targets for Homes for Change. The scheme was used as a demonstration project in an URBED report by David Rudlin and Nicholas Falk (1995).

David van Vliet and Torben Gade
Sustainable Urban Renewal:
Kolding, Denmark

Introduction

Urban renewal is a good example of recycling. The greatest concentrations of human and economic resources are found in our cities, making these important areas to begin with in the task of regeneration. Many elements must be considered to effectively integrate the social, economic, cultural, ecological and physical dimensions of renewal. How to do this, and at what scale, needs to be considered for many differing conditions and circumstances. This chapter describes two recent urban renewal schemes in Kolding, a progressive provincial town with a population of 45,000, in south Jutland, Denmark. While Kolding has had a housing renewal programme for many years, in 1992, as part of its emergent debate on *Green Ideas for Kolding* (Fisker, 1995), the Municipality changed priorities in its renewal policy. Rather than continue the limited programme of upgrading selected housing blocks in an area, it chose to develop and test new environmentally sound investments in a more integrated way. It did this first with an entire block at Fredensgade and Hollændervej. This project is outlined here as the first case study. The nearby Solgården block, a later scheme which is near completion, is the second case study.

Each project addresses a different period of built form, using differing approaches and combinations of elements, from micro to meso scale, dealing with the structure, interior renovation, site and common outdoor areas. Rather than being one-off projects, they represent a new phase in an urban renewal strategy that is now influencing the next stage of district urban renewal. While both blocks are comprehensive renewal schemes, the first focuses on the water cycle (rainwater collection and waste water treatment in a solar aquatic/bioworks at the centre of the block). The second concentrates on energy, integrating a large photovoltaic (PV) system.

Renewal in the area was planned on the basis of the Danish legislation, 'Urban Renewal and Housing Improvement', a subsidy programme for building modernisation, open space improvements and re-housing. The National Building and Housing Agency directed experimental support to a series of specific ecological measures. The aim was to combine accumulated experience with new developing themes, and gain experience with known techniques by testing them at a larger scale, and in an urban context. This is a step in developing a future urban renewal model, where ecology and resources are taken into consideration as a norm. Each block is described and conclusions are presented below.

The Fredensgade block

Cities are commonly criticised for their linear and hidden resource streams. For example, the most that many residents see of the water cycle is the 20cm from their tap to the plug hole. Ecologically sustainable design introduces cycles in the flow of resources and shows people the consequences of their ways of living. This project explores how to make visible to residents, through urban renewal, the consequences of profligate water use.

The pendant shaped block consists of 40 properties, each three or four storeys (all with a basement), containing 129 dwelling units, six business properties and two social club premises (Table 1). The owners and tenants responded positively to ecological initiatives recommended in information meetings and discussions during the planning process.

Address	Fredensgade and Hollændervej, Kolding, Denmark
Client	Kolding Municipality, Building and Housing Council, Ministry of Housing, Byfornyelsesselskabet Danmark (Urban Renewal Company Denmark)
Building dates	1993–96 two new infill buildings (others mostly from 1900–1920, four from 1930–39 and three from 1940–49)
Area of block	11,688m², of which 7,635m² is unbuilt. Plot sizes vary from 176m² to 915m² Total floor area is 12,424m² 10,476m² is residential and 727m² (or 5.8%) is commercial/industrial or institutions
No. of units	129 units prior to renovation, 143 after, 250 residents. Density of block is 122 units per ha or 214 persons per ha
Architect	Gruppen for By-og Landskabsplanlægning Aps
Engineer	A/S Samfundsteknik, Kolding

Table 1. Characteristics of the Fredensgade block.

Renovation/new construction

A building inventory confined demolition and new infill to only two sites at opposite corners of the block. Both are now greener buildings well integrated with the block. The new corner building at Sydbanegade/Kongebrogade, for a co-operative housing society, now contains eight units (50–79m² each). The infill on Hollændervej (six units, each 57–61m²) is constructed using a high percentage of recycled materials (brick, wood, glass and crushed concrete) from local demolition sites. The renovation of the apartments started in August 1994, and a number of resource conserving initiatives have been carried out. Energy measures include improved insulation, windows and doors, more effective heating systems, automatic controls and, on some units, solar panels for domestic hot water. New water conserving fixtures were installed. Differing solutions have been used in modifying the rear façades such as adding glazed balcony enclosures providing passive heated outdoor rooms to extend the living areas. On a former flat-roofed building, new units and a large attractive rooftop greenhouse for the residents' collective use have been added.

Energy and water

Domestic water for some of the buildings is heated using solar energy. All buildings in the block are connected to the regional district heating net (co-owned by the three local municipalities), based on surplus energy from industries, waste incineration and CHP (combined heat and power) plants. Rainwater from all roofs is directed to a pond and cistern to be pumped to all dwelling units for use in washing machines and toilets. To keep the water fresh, it is recirculated over a water cascade along a stream and back to the pond (see Fig. 1). In case this supply is inadequate, city water can be automatically supplemented.

Special importance has been given to the treatment of the water to emphasise its value as a vital resource, and to demonstrate that waste water can be treated locally. At the centre of the courtyard is the bioworks, formed as a glass pyramid (21m × 21m × 13m high), which was completed in August 1994 (see Figs 2–5). The bioworks form provides a simple volume, having reduced surface area for energy conservation, and takes into consideration solar exposure, shading and views from surrounding apartments. Waste water from the flats (kitchens, bathrooms and toilets) is directed for biological treatment. The first stage in treatment occurs outside in below-grade tanks where sludge settles, bacteria decompose nutrients, and germs and pathogens are killed using ultraviolet light and ozone. Inside the bioworks, water is led through a series of concrete tanks containing algae, plankton, mussels and fish respectively, in a natural food chain. The water moves to an outside root zone marsh before it seeps through a filtration system under a 1000m^2 area to groundwater or is absorbed by plants and trees. Then, when efficiency and hygienic performance have been documented, the purified water can be directed to the rainwater pond to complete the cycle. The process itself is not unusual; it is a modification of solar aquatic systems used in an increasing number of locations. What is unusual is the urban context, immediate residential proximity and scale of operation.

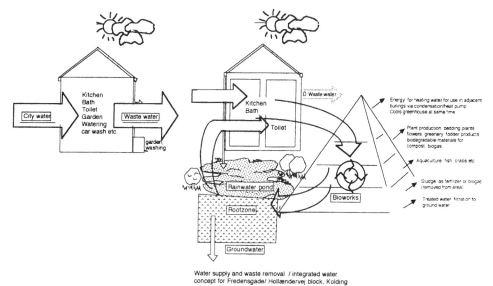

Fig. 1. The Fredensgade block water concept – before and after.
Source: D. van Vliet.

Fig. 2. The Fredensgade block: the bioworks is complete, flat renovation is under way, but new infill buildings are not yet started.
Source: Holmgaard and Rudolph.

Fig. 3. The bioworks with pond, wild flowers, root zone (right) and new glazed balconies (right).
Source: D. van Vliet.

Water supply and waste removal / integrated water concept for Fredensgade/ Hollændervej block, Kolding

Inside the bioworks, it is warm and humid. There are sounds of circulating water and vents and roller shades opening and closing in response to changing cloud cover and temperature. Profuse green plants line the edges of the tanks, and on the water surface duckweed mingles with reflections of the surrounding colourful apartment façades and the pyramid structure. Insects and fish skim the surface. Light filters down through the three metal grid floors, where water is directed from the last tank, supplying nutrients to 15,000 plants in easily movable trays on roller tables. These plants in turn contribute to the purification of the water while

312

producing a marketable commodity. A central stair connects the horticultural levels, and a platform hoist is used to move plant trays up and down. The bioworks is leased to a nurseryman, who grows seedlings, plants and flowers and looks after the area.

The cost of cleaning water in this manner has proved to be the same as in other modern plants at the village or town scale. However, it is more expensive than large centralised facilities.

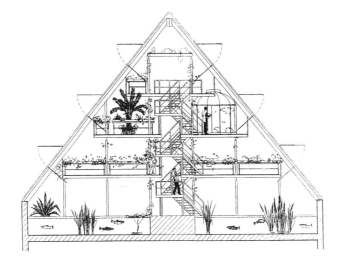

Fig. 4. Section through the bioworks, showing water tanks and the three levels for plant production.
Source: T. Gade, Gruppen for By-og Landskabsplanlægning Aps (GBL).

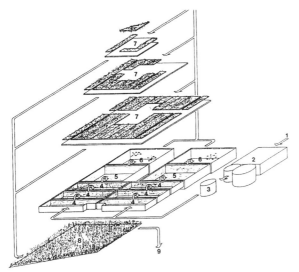

1. Waste water from the apartments (sinks, baths, showers, toilets)
2. Sludge settlement and pre-treatment by bacteria
3. Hygienic sanitation by UV-rays and ozone (clean, pure, decontaminated)
4. Tank with algae feeding on nutrients in water
5. Plankton feed on the algae
6. Fish and mussels feed on algae and plankton
7. Horticultural area with plants nourished by the water
8. Root zone marsh for final treatment of the water
9. Filtration to the ground water

Fig. 5. The bioworks – identifying the process stages.
Source: T. Gade, GBL.

Courtyard

Before the renewal of the block, almost 70% of the block area was unbuilt, the private rear yards were neither functional nor attractive. Remarkably, a negotiated common area equal to about one half of the inner area has been carved from the former maze of fence lines marking the individual properties. To realise this alternative semi-public realm in the midst of the city is an admirable accomplishment. It is no wonder that most of the concerns expressed by residents and owners during the planning process were about how much private and public space there would be. The terrain slopes two metres across the block, providing interesting views and changes in levels. Private yards are defined by stone retaining walls and robust wooden fencing and planting. Details include traditional rural craft techniques and natural finishes. Portals between or through the perimeter buildings access a new path network leading through the common area and beyond. Along one path, rainwater babbles from a flowform fountain and forms a brook, which passes a pergola, a play area that integrates the water, a place for an open fire and a little waterfall into a pond. There are diverse spaces dedicated to small gardens, recycling and composting, drying clothes, sitting, playing and so on. Trees are preserved and the area is planted in low maintenance, hardy, edible and diverse species. On the other side of the bioworks is a multi-purpose area for maintenance, vehicle parking, play, car washing (using grey water) and resident parking (with a recharge point for electric cars). On its roof are 36 PV panels with an installed output of 3,000kWh. The annual production, 2,050kWh, covers about two-thirds of the power for lighting the yard and pumping water for the brook.

Waste

Recycling depots, or 'environment stations', have been established in three locations for sorting many types of paper, metal, glass, chemicals, batteries and reusable items for exchange. There are two composting areas with all-season composters. Due to the effective waste handling programme, there has been a dramatic sevenfold increase in the amount of materials recycled. The remaining waste has been reduced by over 50%, decreasing the total tenant charges for refuse removal by 40,000 DKK per year.

Economy

The programme required all ecological measures for reduction of energy consumption and treatment of rainwater, sewage and refuse to be economically viable. That is, any increased investment in ecological measures should produce a corresponding long-term return in savings, through reduced energy consumption, recycling and reduced or eliminated taxes and rates. Negotiations with the public utility suppliers in the Municipality of Kolding were therefore necessary. An agreement to waive drainage rates was reached, since sewage and rainwater from the block are no longer led into the public system. The exemption period is currently ten years; however, the property owners would prefer it be extended. Budget calculations now indicate there is a balance between financial costs and savings for the tenants. That is, there are no additional costs here compared with other newly renovated areas. In fact, the residents actually save a little, due to the individual savings from using rainwater, conserving fixtures and energy economies which are not included in the calculation. These economies of return are possible due to the strong public policy framework of eco-taxation in Denmark, raising unit resource prices to aid resource conservation to complement efficiency targets. Total investments in the block were approximately 65 million DKK: the two new infill buildings cost 10 million, the renovation of 129 units 40 million, the bioworks and water systems 12 million and the open areas 3 million. Fifteen million DKK of subsidies were gained for experimental components (bioworks, and the additional elements in renovations and the open space).

Completing the project, getting the systems up and running and monitoring the results have been the continuing responsibility of the firms involved. Six months of negotiations prepared the homeowners' association to take over the courtyard in early 1997. The bioworks remains the property and the responsibility of the municipality.

Conclusions

Residents and owners consider the block to be a very attractive place to live, providing a basis for a more meaningful existence. In a 1997 municipal survey, residents responded 'very positive' or 'positive' to all questions about the scheme, except those regarding the extent of their influence on the layout of the outdoor areas. Although recommendations in the early planning and design meetings were wide-ranging, the residents' main concern at that time was the size of the private garden areas. The rest of the layout came to be determined by the project designers and the renewal company, in consultation with the property owners. The chairperson of the block's council has expressed a positive view about the project. The residents are proud of what has been accomplished, and recommend that 'What we learned from this project we must use in the next urban ecology projects' (Madsen, 1998, p.6).

The project has received wide attention, garnering considerable popular and professional press in Denmark, and was selected as a good practice example in the Danish report to Habitat '96. It has been referred to often in the extensive debate on urban ecology. The Ministry of Housing considers the project to have had a huge pay-off in terms of public education about water conservation in Denmark.

The Solgården block

There is wide agreement that the consumption of fossil fuels must be reduced dramatically in the near future in order to reduce carbon dioxide emissions. An approach identified as having long-term potential in this process is the expanded use of PVs, however a number of uncertainties and barriers – both economic and technical – have limited their use to date. The renovation of the Solgården block has demonstrated how PVs can become a central strategy in urban renewal (Table 2).

Address	Kongebrogade, Kolding, Denmark
Client	Kolding Municipality, Building and Housing Council, Ministry of Housing, Byfornyelsesselskabet Danmark Amba (Urban Renewal Company Denmark)
Building owners	Ejendomsselskabet ASX 2226 ApS. National Building and Housing Agency. Municipality of Kolding
Building dates	1996–1998 (a 1939 five-storey building with a basement, 80 units), one replacement building (56 units for young people) and 4 new infill buildings (24 flats)
Area of block	Total floor area of the Solgården building is 5,681m² (55 two-room flats, 25 three-room flats and four small businesses)
Project group	Urban Renewal Company Denmark (research management and business management). Engineer, Rambøll A/S (mechanical and construction). Engineer, C. J. Kjærby ApS (electrical engineering and PVs). Architect, Roskjærs Tegnestue ApS (building Solgården). Architects, Kjær and Richter A/S (solar system and balcony enclosure). Gruppen for by-og landskabsplanlægning aps (town planning and open space site plan). Engineer, Benno Nielsen (construction management)

Table 2. Characteristics of the Solgården block.

The work, from 1996 to early 1998, consisted of comprehensive building improvements to all flats in the block, the addition of elevators, the installation of prefabricated bathrooms, the establishment of an improved large common open space and provision of attractive new housing units on adjacent sites.

Energy

The Solgården block, built between 1939 and 1940, is a good example of international modernism. It was identified as being well suited for a solar experiment due to its orientation, form and size. Even its name translates as 'Sun Court'. To promote the initiative, a project prospectus was prepared and distributed to inform decision makers, advisors and others about the possibilities for using PV technology as a part of future energy and resource conscious urban renewal. The objectives for the PV system were to:

- demonstrate various possibilities for PV in a multi-storey residential property;
- adapt to the problematic architectural and technical challenges of integrating PV panels in different building types;
- clarify the extent to which the annual energy use in a large residential building can be met by PV energy;
- realise methods to reduce, by half, the use of fossil fuel in a large residential property; and
- gain experience about the operation of a large-scale system, in terms of performance, maintenance, durability, consumer response and accounting principles.

The PVs are in two locations. The roof system consists of four continuous bands of semi-transparent, monocrystalline PV panels on a steel gallery. It has 846 PV modules (757m^2) with a maximum output of 89.5kW. The eight glass balcony towers have 80 PV modules (175m^2) with a combined maximum output of 16.5kW. The output is 230 volts of alternating current used primarily in Solgården, with surplus sold to the local electricity utility. Originally, the purchase and sale of electricity generated and consumed in Solgården was to follow three rates at three different prices, depending on time of day or night, to provide an economic structure that would derive benefit from off-peak usage. PV systems offer an advantage with this method of accounting, as their electrical production occurs during the day, reducing the need for peak demand energy. The objective was to encourage residents to modify their behaviour, responding to the variation in electrical prices, in order to optimise the payback on the PV system investment. However, to keep the arrangement simple for the residents, one rate has been applied. Residents can realise savings by adjusting their electrical usage to that produced directly during daylight hours. To support this, a PV-meter is installed in each flat informing the residents whether they are below or beyond their 'share' of electricity produced by the system.

The increase in consumption is mainly due to the new elevators, ventilation systems and electrical cooking. As predicted, the PV production is 70–75% of previous consumption, and 60% of post renovation consumption. These reductions directly reduce carbon dioxide emissions and consumption of fossil fuel. Previously, the electrical source was from a coal fired CHP plant on the regional district heating network. The energy consumption for heating the building was 3,200GJ/yr, in 1993: in 1998, it is expected to be 2,700GJ/yr (see Table 3). This is approximately a 15% reduction.

Renovation/new construction

The renewal concept for the site required selective demolition. The site inventory identified preservable structures and salvageable materials. Apartments for young people are now completed. Figure 6 shows the large south facing windows daylighting the common room, with integrated solar collectors at its perimeter. Four urban villas (each three storeys high with six flats) for the elderly are being built adjacent to a stream. The site plan creates good outdoor areas, possibilities for activities and access to parking serving both the existing and new buildings. Moreover, there is provision for flood protection from the stream.

Electrical consumption in 1993 (before renovation)		138,000kWh/yr
households	94,000kWh	
gas for cooking equivalent to	12,000kWh	
common areas	22,000kWh	
commercial areas	10,000kWh	
Expected electrical consumption after implementation.		175,000kWh/yr
Actual electrical consumption in 1998 (after renovation)		168,000kWh/yr
households	112,000kWh	
common areas	43,000kWh	
commercial areas	13,000kWh	
Expected electrical production from system on roof		89,500kWh/yr
Expected electrical production from the enclosed balcony system		16,500kWh/yr
Expected total electrical production for solarcell system		106,000kWh/yr
Electrical energy production from PV (est. after 9 months production)		100,000kWh
Energy used for heating before the improvements carried out		3,200GJ/yr
Expected energy used for heating after improvements carried out		2,700GJ/yr

Table 3. Previous, predicted and actual figures for energy consumption in Solgården (September, 1998).

Fig. 6. The Solgården block (August, 1998) showing large PV array on the roof and new glass balcony enclosures. Courtyard and new housing are still to be developed.
Source: Holmgaard and Rudolph.

Bringing the building and housing up to a modern standard required a number of improvements, including (those receiving special financing are in italics):

- Strengthening the inadequate foundation. The site is part of a fill area near the harbour. The building was supported on spruce piles up to 8m long.
- Renovation of the roof, façade, balconies, staircases, basement, entry areas, and sewage, waste and water installations.
- *Enclosure of the south facing balconies with glazed structures with integrated PV panels.*
- Increasing the thermal insulation in the roof, gateway portal and basement; and replacement of the heating system.
- *Installation of new elevators, at each staircase.*
- Ensuring all water fixtures are of the water conserving type.

- Complete renovation of all kitchens and bathrooms. Removal of existing fixtures, and *installation of energy conserving electric ranges/hotplates.*
- Renovation of the electrical services, and *expansion to provide for the connection of electric ranges/hotplates and ventilation systems.*

As elsewhere, there is a pressing need to fit older housing stock with elevators, and a requirement for developing efficient methods to achieve this. Residents now have eight new elevators, serving all floors including the basement. New shafts were cut through the building, walls built, then the casing, doors, electrical installations and elevator cars assembled by lowering them through the roof.

Proper renovation of bathrooms is usually a difficult task in such renewal. Here, this was facilitated through the installation of prefabricated bathrooms, factory-delivered in separate modules. Installation was fast and effective, resulting in a rational arrangement and quality finish, with no additional expenditure compared with other methods of renovation.

Economy
Urban renewal funding was arranged jointly by the Ministry of Housing, Municipality of Kolding, and the owners and tenants. Grants for the experimental components were from the Ministry of Housing. In addition, support for experimentation was provided by the Building and Housing Agency's 'Project Renovation'. The total cost of the renewal was 76 million DKK.

Evaluation of the scheme
While monitoring is in place, it is too early to present full performance results. These will be published later to inform decision makers, advisors and others about the possibilities for using PV technology as an integral part of energy and resource conscious urban renewal. This is one of northern Europe's largest architecturally integrated PV systems. This project too has received many visits, and the group responsible for the project was awarded the Danish part of the highly regarded Solar Prize.

Conclusions
The two projects are remarkably comprehensive, in terms of their sustainability features, and well integrated considering their confinement to a single block. It is usually considered more feasible to implement sustainable community objectives effectively, and with a higher degree of integration, within a programme of larger-scale settlement than on single sites. Size brings with it certain efficiencies, with greater direct and indirect positive environmental effects. The scale of projects undertaken is important to allow proper testing and social learning in the system. These projects should, however, be sufficient to force a review of resource dedication, requiring that development partners and municipal departments appreciate some of the contradictions and differences that exist in their agendas.

James Morgan and Roger Talbot

Sustainable Social Housing for No Extra Cost?

Introduction

> Sustainable development is the challenge of meeting the growing human needs for
> natural resources, industrial products, energy, food, transportation, shelter and effective
> waste management whilst conserving and protecting environmental quality and the
> natural resource base essential for future life and development. (US Green Building
> Council, 1996, p.1)

If sustainability is to be achieved there must be a recognition that meeting long-term human
social and economic needs will be impossible unless we also conserve the Earth's natural,
physical, chemical and biological systems (Advisory Group on Sustainable Development,
1997)

For some time now, governments in the UK have accepted the need 'to make sustainable
development a touchstone of ... policies' (DoE, 1994, p.5). Building regulations, pollution
controls, waste minimisation legislation and energy taxation measures will progressively
penalise developments which fail to address sustainability issues. Projects which take a
proactive approach to environmental protection and look to provide both social gain and
economic opportunity will correspondingly reap major benefits in terms of cost savings, reduced
liability, workplace health and social approval.

Agencies funding social housing landlords are taking increasing account of this policy
direction but their traditional, cost-driven systems of development funding often constrain
housing quality and sustainability. There is currently a great deal of tension in the system
between these two opposing pressures. However, sustainability is set to become the major
driver of the design and construction process at the start of the next millennium. In this chapter,
some of the first fruits of this within social housing in Scotland are examined.

Scottish Homes (the national housing agency in Scotland) sponsored 14 design competitions
which sought to bridge the gap between the potentially conflicting aims of cost efficiency and
sustainability. Two innovative housing association (HA) schemes in Glasgow, which were
winners of these competitions, and were highly rated by newly developed housing quality
and sustainability assessment methods, are considered here.

First, we provide a brief introduction to the role of HAs as developers, and the context of
the two Glasgow schemes used here as examples of sustainable development. Then, we discuss
the concept of sustainable housing and how this has informed the development of the new
assessment method used in evaluating the Scottish Homes, Housing Association Grant (HAG)
Competition. We then consider how the winning schemes proposed by CUBE HA and
Shettleston HA achieved high levels of sustainability. Finally, we look at the influence of
location on the creation of sustainable communities.

Housing associations and sustainability

HAs have been the main providers of new socially rented housing for the past 20 years and, by 1995, they owned over one million dwellings in Great Britain (Wilcox, 1997). Their development is funded by a mix of private finance and a decreasing level of government grant. While often praised for the quality of their developments, HAs have only recently begun to focus on sustainability. Acknowledging that housing is a major contributor to carbon dioxide and other environmentally damaging emissions, and to the depletion of resources through its production, use, demolition and replacement, funders now wish to promote sustainable design (DoE, 1997; Scottish Homes, 1996a). A life cycle approach to housing has begun to be explored (e.g. Eco-Logica and Williams, 1996).

Nevertheless, there is some evidence that competition for grants has led to reductions in quality such as reduced space standards (Karn and Sheridan, 1994). For Page (1993), the quality of new HA developments is linked to the sustainability of communities. He has argued that poor design and quality have played a part in HA estates becoming run down very quickly and exhibiting many characteristics of the local authority sink estates of the 1970s. Page sees the lack of variety of tenants, who are predominantly families with children, as a factor in neighbourhood unsustainability.

However, HAs have always had a role in providing housing for older people and for those with special needs, and there is a growing trend for people with various abilities to be housed in mainstream association developments. Provision of barrier free housing is now a condition of receiving grants in Scotland (Scottish Homes, 1995a, 1995b) and the 'lifetime homes' concept, encompassing accessibility and adaptability for the needs of people with a range of abilities, is being championed by the Joseph Rowntree Foundation among others (Brewerton and Darton, 1997). Given the increasing complexity of patterns of household composition, it is coming to be recognised that flexible and adaptable housing design can help sustain communities where otherwise people would have to move on as the composition of their household changed (Rudlin and Falk, 1995). These trends encourage the development of more mixed communities and also imply that the location of sites should be in close proximity to retail, health, education and leisure facilities, and public transport.

A major priority for most communities is making and reshaping their habitats. In its broadest sense, construction embraces housing, land use policy and transport infrastructure, and the regeneration of cities and towns. Land use and planning processes both respond to, and shape, the way we live and the way in which resources are used. Effective planning can limit demands on land and the environment and reduce the need to travel, especially by car. In a wider sense, construction planning should seek to integrate economic, environmental and social factors in decisions about where to locate homes, jobs, shops, leisure facilities and so on. To the extent that HA developments recognise the importance of locational factors and the existence of suitable infrastructure for nurturing and serving the communities they seek to build, they can help to create sustainable, diverse neighbourhoods often in brownfield sites as recommended by the Urban Villages Group (Aldous, 1992) and government policy (e.g. DoE and DoT, 1994; Scottish Office, 1996).

The schemes discussed in this chapter are, as noted above, being built by Shettleston HA in the Shettleston area and by CUBE HA at Charing Cross, both in Glasgow. Shettleston HA is a community based HA (CBHA). While CUBE HA is not community based, it does have a structure of area committees which are predominantly composed of local residents. Since the introduction of Housing Action Areas under the Housing (Scotland) Act 1974, CBHAs have successfully rehabilitated many of Glasgow's older, inner areas where the main house type is the four-storey Victorian tenement, often with shops on the ground floor. The retention of popular, high-density, mixed-use neighbourhoods has been particularly successful, and HAs operating in inner areas are now building on gap sites to increase the range and type of housing in these neighbourhoods, and to complete their regeneration (Scottish Homes, 1996b). HA inner city new build has been focused on gap sites, in part because these sites are unattractive to private developers and because they are located within the areas of operation of the territorially based CBHAs.

Shettleston's scheme involves the reclamation of a former laundry site on the boundary between two-storey housing and the tenemental area rehabilitated by the association. CUBE's scheme is on a gap site where rehabilitated tenements meet high quality public and commercial buildings on the edge of the city centre. A crucial element of the discussion in this chapter is the extent to which these locational factors impact on the type of development, and how sustainable communities can be developed in different areas.

Sustainable housing

The processes and products of construction provide a vital part of the life-support systems upon which communities depend (DETR, 1998a). The form in which, and the quality with which, we choose to construct our cities, towns and villages have a huge impact on our quality of life. At a strategic, as well as at an operational, level architecture – and housing design in particular – offers a critical, though under-appreciated, mechanism for community building by helping to deliver some of the social, cultural and economic needs of a sustainable community.

Such needs include, but are not limited to, affordable housing providing affordable warmth, reduction of poverty, good health, accessibility to services and recreation, environments for learning, economic opportunities and opportunities for social inclusion. In this context, a partial definition of sustainable housing can be offered as an approach to the planning, design, construction and use of housing which contributes to community building, to social justice and to economic viability at a local level.

At this point we confront a paradox. Whilst the products and processes of the construction industry manifestly provide a major part of the very life-support systems and infrastructure upon which strong, healthy and sustainable communities depend, they are just as clearly contributing to the wholesale destruction of the resource base and the pollution of the environment in ways which are wholly unsustainable (DETR, 1998b). Of special significance are those changes in the structures and distributions of populations that have led to increased demands for housing and business development with their associated infrastructure for shopping, energy supply and transport.

Built facilities can be seen to impact on the natural environment in four specific ways (Engineering Council, 1994):

- through the spatial displacement of natural ecosystems and loss of land to other productive purposes;
- through the impacts resulting from human use of the built environment;
- through the depletion of mineral and energy resources from natural ecosystems during the construction and use of the facility; and
- through the generation of large amounts of waste material over the whole life cycle of a development.

The consequence is that the construction industry is directly and indirectly responsible for 50% of UK energy consumption, whilst energy for buildings is responsible for in excess of 330 million tonnes of the carbon dioxide released in the UK annually (DETR, 1998a).

Overall, in the UK, the construction industry uses about six tonnes of material per person per year, and is responsible for the quarrying of 250–300 million tonnes of material annually (*op. cit.*). Extraction of these primary resources implies major environmental impact from the loss of habitats and elements of the ecosystem, damage to landscape, potential subsidence and release of methane. Some 70 million tonnes of construction waste are generated every year in the UK (DoE, 1995). All this waste is ultimately returned to the environment with significant environmental impact, whatever the method of waste management adopted (SEPA, 1997).

Issues of sustainable building and construction extend beyond resource base problems. They include the toxicity of the processes through which materials are extracted, manufactured and used. Thermal efficiency standards are especially low in rural areas with consequent higher fuel bills for households, many of whom are already amongst the lowest income sectors (Scottish Homes, 1998a). Construction sites provide major sources of noise and nuisance. At another level, the way we choose to develop and manage our cities can have a profound effect on the protection – or destruction – of wildlife habitats, and hence biodiversity.

It is obvious that we need to extend our provisional definition of sustainable housing to take account of the fact that, in order to become sustainable, the processes of building design, construction, use, replacement and maintenance must be fundamentally transformed. Such transformation should lead to a drastic reduction in the amount of energy and material consumed at every stage of development, and the elimination of the adverse impacts on both environmental and human health.

A model we can look to for guidance on how to produce, consume and live in sustainable ways is provided by natural ecological systems. Nature produces little or no waste, relies on free and abundant energy from the sun and uses resources wisely, efficiently and sustainably (Capra, 1996). From an ecological perspective, the overall effect of any human development on the environment should ideally be the same as if we were not present. Ecologically, this means that we should mimic the natural context we displace as closely as possible. Through such a strategy, human settlements would become ecologically invisible by becoming, in effect, part of the flow and change of matter and energy which occurs naturally in the biosphere – not separate from it (Rodger, 1997).

To achieve these results – to transform planning and building into an ecologically sound, eco-efficient process – requires a systems approach. It demands thinking in cycles (closing loops) and requires an integrated, multi-disciplinary approach which brings together indoor, local and global environmental considerations across any development's full life cycle.

Key principles of sustainable housing

Combining the two aspects of sustainable housing outlined above, namely ecological and social/economic sustainability, leads us to conclude that an ecologically informed approach to housing design should, as a minimum, satisfy the following basic principles:

1. eliminate waste, not just incrementally reduce it; but
2. manage any inevitable waste as efficiently, effectively and safely as possible;
3. reduce energy and material resource requirements by effective demand management techniques – a process known as dematerialisation;
4. substitute non-renewable resources with natural sustainable ones and increase the use of renewable resources in construction;
5. utilise essential energy and material resources – including water – as efficiently as possible;
6. adopt a design philosophy which makes use of passive solutions in preference to mechanical solutions;

7. source materials, energy supply and skills locally;
8. pay special attention to how the building will be used over its lifetime, and assess potential changes of use and future adaptations and extensions;
9. incorporate maintainability into the brief as a key issue;
10. take full account of the ecological context for the development;
11. ensure sensitivity to the local socio-economic, cultural and climatic context of the development;
12. implement a partnering approach to any development so that client, consultants, contractors and end-users work together as a design team;
13. practise integrated building design as a cornerstone for developing sustainable buildings that are efficiently combined systems of co-ordinated and environmentally sound products, systems and design elements;
14. select design team members on the basis of commitment to the project vision, a willingness to work as part of an integrated design approach and an ability to think beyond their own speciality;
15. recognise and realise economic development opportunities within the local area for which the new development can serve as a catalyst; and
16. acknowledge that buildings (since we spend on average 90% of our time in them) can, and should, offer a major opportunity for educating the community about sustainability.

The sustainable housing assessment method

These key principles provided the basis for a new evaluative tool, known as the Sustainable Housing Performance Assessment Method, which was developed by the Edinburgh Sustainable Architecture Unit and used by the authors as part of an evaluation of the 'sustainability rating' of schemes entered for the Scottish Homes HAG competition in 1997/98 (Scottish Homes, 1998b).

The 16 principles were used to generate a total of 106 systematically selected sustainability performance criteria for housing developments. Collectively, the criteria were intended to provide a comprehensive description and assessment of the housing's performance measured on a scale of sustainability. Existing methods of assessment were found to be inadequate for this task. The performance criteria were then organised under 14 major performance categories, across four life cycle stages, as shown in Table 1.

Life cycle stage	Performance category
1. Pre-design stage categories	• brief building and appointment of consultants • strategic land use and the development of the site • transport planning and accessibility
2. Design stage categories	• energy in use (form and fabric) • energy in use (systems) • the indoor environment • the outdoor environment • maintenance and adaptability
3. Construction stage categories	• process of construction • specification of materials (resources) • specification of materials (emissions)

Table 1.
Performance
categories for
different life cycle
stages

4. Occupancy stage categories	• facilities management
	• household waste management
	• water management

The process of evaluation

The evaluation comprised two processes:

- Assessing whether the quality of competition entries exceeded that achieved in normal HAG funded developments at comparable cost levels.
- Analysing the competition process and estimating the costs involved.

In the overall evaluation process, sustainability was one of six housing quality dimensions which included space standards, functionality and flexibility of space, barrier free design, security conscious design, the design of private and communal space, and architectural quality. To carry out the evaluation, the researchers devised an innovative methodology for assessing the multiple dimensions of housing quality. In the case of the sustainability dimension, the method, based on principles of multiple criteria analysis and best practice, involved the weighting, assessment and aggregation of individual performance criteria within each of the 14 performance categories. The aggregate score determined the overall assessment of the performance in each of these categories as excellent, good, satisfactory or unsatisfactory.

The results were presented visually on a 'radar diagram' and the development assigned an overall sustainability rating of excellent, very good, good, very satisfactory, satisfactory, partly unsatisfactory or unsatisfactory according to the average performance category score (see Fig. 1).

Shettleston

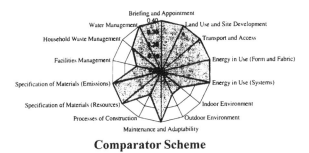

Comparator Scheme

Fig. 1. 'Radar'
diagrams of
sustainability
performance for
Shettleston and a
typical housing
association
comparator
scheme.

Key

0.10 - Unsatisfactory
0.20 - Satisfactory
0.30 - Good
0.40 - Excellent

The sustainability assessment method proved to be a demanding one and asked many questions of even the best of the competition winners. All competition winning schemes scored 'satisfactory' or better, but only three schemes scored 'good' or 'very good'. The main results for two of these latter schemes are presented below. None of the eight comparator schemes, selected as some of the best examples of 'normal' HA developments, achieved better than partly satisfactory, indicating that there was a clear difference between the comparators and the competition winners.

Examples of sustainability assessments

Shettleston Housing Association – Shettleston, Glasgow

The Shettleston scheme was ranked 'good' or better in ten out of the 14 performance categories, making it one of the top performing developments in the competition programme. The key to success was clearly the fact that environmental sustainability was considered from the outset as a key driver and determinant of design – in terms of both products and processes – and was then carried through comprehensively and systematically.

The procurement process recognised the importance of open consultation with user groups and of a partnering approach between clients, consultants and contractors. Effective use of land was made by the selection of a brownfield site, and the design included proposals to re-use some parts of existing buildings within the new development. A car free development was proposed, and this is still a radical typology in Scotland. The south-facing aspect of the design allowed for the location of solar panels on parts of the roof, whilst house types were selected to maximise the energy efficiency of the whole development. High levels of insulation using warmcell as part of a timber frame breathing wall construction were specified.

Greater quality and efficiency of resource use was facilitated by an emphasis on off-site prefabrication. An innovative ventilation system taking preheated air from the void between roof tiles and sarking was proposed. Special interest in the Shettleston scheme derives from the specification of a geothermal energy system taking advantage of a disused coal mine deep under the site (see Fig. 2).

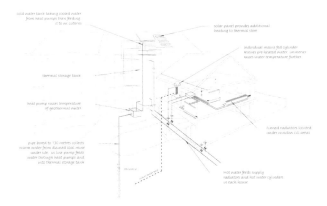

Fig. 2. Shettleston scheme showing innovative geothermal heating system.
Source: John Gilbert Architects.

The scheme scored 'excellent' on aspects of sustainable construction, both from a materials selection perspective, and through the strong emphasis on the re-use, re-usability, recycling and recyclability of building components. The scheme performed exceptionally well in respect of domestic waste and water management systems, with a number of innovative features incorporated. The scheme had few weak points, but fully deserved its overall rating of 'very good'.

CUBE Housing Association – Berkeley Street, Glasgow

The scheme was ranked 'satisfactory' or better in all of the 14 performance categories. Here, the key factor lay with the extent to which the procurement process as a whole reflected the HA's concern with integrating the development fully in the local community – a prime requirement for sustainable community building. The use of focus groups was especially emphasised, as was the importance of partnering and teamwork. An estimated SAP rating of 95 confirmed good energy efficiency performance, achieved in part by the specification of low U-values and passive stack ventilation systems. Sustainable construction was an excellent feature of the scheme. The selection of a building system characterised by long life and low maintenance, and which allows for ease of disassembly and repair, was an outstanding feature of the design. The concern for resource efficiency and safe specification was followed through with commendable consistency. The scheme was found to exhibit positive domestic waste and water management features.

Building sustainable communities – social inclusion, urban form and location

The two schemes discussed above are examples of sustainable development in two very different locations within the city: Berkeley Street is in the city centre and Shettleston is in a working class suburban area. Each scheme addressed many of the issues involved in creating a local environment which is inclusive, and enhances the quality of life of the residents while contributing to the vibrancy of the neighbourhood. In other words, an attempt was made to establish a sustainable and enriched habitat within the city. The schemes tell us a great deal about the relationship between sustainable communities, urban form and location. Here, we highlight three aspects of the schemes: social inclusion, car free development and site layout, and relate these to location.

An inclusive community – access and flexibility

Inner city Glasgow, at its best, offers a model for high-density, mixed-use communities. However, the inner city tenement is a difficult model to adapt for the needs of people with mobility difficulties. If the city is to be a community with a variety of housing suitable for people of all ages and abilities, these problems must be overcome.

The Berkeley Street development had to be accessible, and fit within a high-density city centre location. The design brief incorporated the lifetime homes concept developed by the Joseph Rowntree Foundation (Brewerton and Darton, 1997). In principle, a lifetime home can give increased accessibility, even to many wheelchair users, without appreciable increases in either space or costs (Sangster, 1997). While this allows the construction of housing at the suburban scale which is almost indistinguishable from traditional houses, the city centre location requires an altogether more massive building to fit with the surrounding urban form. A four-storey building provides the appropriate scale at Berkeley Street and therefore a lift was needed if all of the homes were to be accessible (see Fig. 3) . To absorb the extra costs which a lift entailed, thus giving costs per unit which were acceptable to the funders, the design had to maximise the number of flats served by one lift. The designers felt that this could only be achieved on a corner site and the search for a suitable gap site in a corner location began.

In Shettleston, the defining characteristics of the location are different. The site is in a suburban area. In this setting, the scheme is developed in a very different way to achieve the aims of social integration, community building and enhancement of the townscape. The resulting development is primarily two-storey in height (with a three-storey flatted building toward the boundary with the tenemental area) and has a mix of eight flats and eight houses of one to three bedrooms. One flat is built to wheelchair standards and all of the ground floor areas are barrier free. The suburban location makes it easier to plan space and access for barrier free, ground floor accommodation. The location did not lend itself to a building large enough to make a lift financially viable, so the upper floors are reached by stairs and are not entirely barrier free. Nevertheless, spaces on the upper floors are designed to be accessible and usable by visitors with restricted mobility.

Fig. 3. CUBE scheme at Berkeley Street showing appropriate urban scale of socially inclusive housing.
Source: Chris Stewart Architects.

In both developments, the principle of inclusion was carried through by ensuring that internal spaces allowed accessibility and flexibility. The living spaces at Berkeley Street are thoughtfully designed with exceptional consideration of space standards and functionality, for example in tenant choice of open plan or enclosed kitchen. Both developments also perform well in relation to flexibility, with removable party walls, optional door positions and the option of a bed space in the living area. Detailing, such as the audible, visual, tactile and Braille indicators on all lift controls, is also well thought out.

Car free development

As mentioned, both developments were designed to be largely car free. Aside from the direct environmental benefits in terms of reduced car journeys, this aids the design of the scheme in a number of other ways. In the very tightly bounded Berkeley Street scheme, space would not have allowed parking to be included in any case. Car free living in the city centre is only really viable in conjunction with the continued health and vitality of city centre facilities. It can support, and is supported by, the expansion of food and other retailing which caters to the needs of city centre residents. Good city centre transport links and employment opportunities also contribute to the success of car free development, and this is particularly true of an inclusive development such as Berkeley Street.

Although the Shettleston scheme is in a suburban location, it is close to shopping, leisure and health facilities, schools and public transport – by bus and rail – and this has enhanced its feasibility as a car free development. The wheelchair accessible house has been provided with an in-curtilage car port in accordance with the principles of barrier free housing. The Shettleston scheme demonstrates the potential conflict between inclusiveness and car free development and the importance of transport links and services, again highlighting the importance of mixed-use neighbourhoods in nurturing sustainable development.

Issues of sustainability in site layout

The success of a development in supporting a sustainable community involves not just the buildings themselves but also the site layout: the way in which the external parts of the scheme can enhance its enjoyment by residents, and its contribution to the character of the wider neighbourhood. Both of these schemes demonstrate how good design can provide aesthetically pleasing, sustainable and usable environments.

Car free design opens up the possibility of using the external space in a creative manner. In place of the bland and forbidding areas of car parking often associated with new development, external spaces can be created which enhance the environment and encourage social interaction. Where capital resources are at a premium, the money saved by not making car parking provision can also help with the costs of landscaping. The challenge for the designer is to create an external space which promotes a subconscious sense of ownership, encouraging its use and discouraging misuse and vandalism. At Shettleston, a pleasant, high quality semi-private space, including a safe water feature, is planned where the car parking might otherwise have been.

The logic of providing this semi-private usable space has been carried through in the development of the Shettleston scheme as a whole. The three-storey building has been designed with a south-facing glazed atrium, where deep planting beds are provided to allow creepers and vines to grow on the glass and walls. The atrium is wide enough for people to sit in and provide informal support and interaction rather than simply being a stairwell.

At Berkeley Street, as there is little opportunity for landscaping at ground floor level, the design includes a roof garden which is accessible by lift. As at Shettleston, the careful choice of plants, including native species, promotes biodiversity by providing food for birds and insects. The roof garden at Berkeley Street has the potential to be a sanctuary in the middle of the city, enriching the experience of urban living.

Conclusions

Sustainability should be a core dimension of housing quality and central to the development process as a whole. As conceived and implemented in this demonstration project, sustainability becomes a major factor in community building and a determinant of the real costs-in-use for the occupant over the lifetime of the building. At the same time, ecological sustainability offers a vital concept for ensuring a reduction in the throughputs of energy and materials throughout the development process and for reducing the impact of any development on both environmental and human health.

The barriers to change in the development process to allow for the full integration of sustainable building principles and practices are shown to be primarily neither economic nor technical but relate to levels of awareness and to the mindset of clients, funders and consultants. Sustainable solutions do, however, demand increased flexibility in funding as they are often costed differently, although they do not necessarily cost more. Partnering, as endorsed by the Egan Report (DETR, 1998c), is shown to offer many advantages in both the design and procurement processes, whilst performance based contractual arrangements with consultants and contractors, linked to environmental probity, would seem to offer the way forward to better design and construction quality.

Building homes which do not exclude people on the grounds of disability is a key aspect of building sustainable communities. These schemes have shown that this can be achieved in a variety of building types which are compatible with a range of urban locations. It is essential that inclusive, sustainable development responds to the place in which it is built and takes advantage of the unique factors of the location.

Reduction in car use is an aim of public policy. Both of these schemes have demonstrated that car free development is an option in areas where there are good public transport and local facilities. They have also demonstrated that designing for people rather than cars can allow spaces to be developed where people can meet and interact with one another in a way which should support neighbourliness and a sense of community.

Sustainable design can be achieved without the need for trade off in other aspects of housing quality such as adaptability and barrier free design. On the contrary, sustainable design, as defined here, naturally embodies such issues as key elements of sustainable housing at no extra cost.

Tigran Hasic

A Sustainable Urban Matrix: *Achieving Sustainable Urban Form in Residential Buildings*

Introduction

This chapter is about how we could house ourselves, and live, in a more sustainable way. The context is an urban one, which draws on the ideas of neo-traditional development, or ideas known as 'New Urbanism'. But this chapter goes a step further than New Urbanism's ideas by introducing a new context for urban and suburban housing development – a sustainable urban matrix (SUM) model.

This model is an apartment block housing unit which attempts to consolidate the neighbourhood in a more socially and spatially sustainable way than at present. The chapter also shows that the ideas of neo-traditional development have no boundaries, they just have regional and local contexts. The eternal or timeless values, goals and ideas enshrined in neo-traditionalism remain the same regardless of where they are implemented.

There is a continual need for dwellings through which people can integrate their own values, form social links and bonds, and become 'anchored' in a positive way. Although this sounds simple, perhaps even old-fashioned, they are goals which have to be revisited if sustainable urban form is to be achieved. People should feel happy and proud to be living in their homes. Alexander *et al.* describe urban residents' homes in an emotive way when they state: 'They are their [*urban residents*] houses – homes, they are the product of their lives, it [*their home*] is everything to them, the concrete expression of their place in the world, the concrete expression of themselves' (1985, p.14). Similarly, Norberg-Schulz states that 'Home is the most sacred place to every being, a place of retreat, dignity, privacy, identification, a place where he/she [*the resident*] "expresses and gathers memories" which make up his/her very own, special personal world' (1993, p.13).

Quality of 'dwelling life' is not therefore simply concerned with having a roof over one's head and a sufficient amount of living space, but also with social and psychological satisfaction. Sustainable physical design can contribute to quality of life (Hasic, 1997). However, the social and behavioural components of housing design are central to the overall success of any sustainable residential environment. It is essential, when seeking solutions to sustainable urban form, to look at five key social and psychological aspirations: satisfaction, territorial definition, personalisation, privacy, and social interaction (Anderson, 1982). These aspirations are also components of some fundamental human needs, or, perhaps, needs in relation to housing. These needs are for shelter, security, comfort, socialisation, self-expression, work, economic rewards, political stability and aesthetic or visual quality (Hasic, 1997).

One fundamental factor appears constantly to link these psychological issues and human needs. It is 'living space': the places in which we live our lives, and that offer the potential to live in a sustainable and enjoyable way. The focus here is on forming a framework, in this case a model, for something that could be called sustainable housing. This is defined as housing that has the ability to endure, by transforming and adapting itself over time, by retaining its attractiveness and value and by providing an enjoyable, pleasant and sustainable place to live (Hasic, 1997).

The concept of neighbourhood, one of the fundamental organising elements of New Urbanism, is the key focus of this work. Planning ideas need to be rethought so that neighbourhood cores, dwellings, institutions, leisure places and gathering places can have a better chance of developing, and giving heart to a community (Langdon, 1997). One of the crucial issues here is to achieve a balanced life-cycle mix – to develop places containing people of varied ages and incomes. In other words, a broader and more complementary mix of housing is needed, so that more complete sustainable communities can be attained. In some instances these could be completely self-sustaining, but interdependent nonetheless. This does not have to be achieved exclusively by mixing different housing types. It can be achieved by only one type of housing; this is where the arguments presented in this chapter differ from the ideas of New Urbanism.

New Urbanism principles apply equally to villages, towns and cities. Most of the principles can even be applied to places of very high density. The SUM model can also be applied in both urban and suburban areas. The intention of this chapter is not to delve deeply into the architectural design of the SUM model, but rather to discuss it as a conceptual urban form.

New Urbanism revisited (see end note)

The four most important conceptual frameworks of New Urbanism – the planning and design approaches – are emphasised and adopted in the SUM model. They are:

1. The centre of each neighbourhood should be defined by a public space and activated by locally-oriented civic and commercial activities.
2. Each neighbourhood should accommodate a range of household types and land uses.
3. The importance of cars should be kept in perspective.
4. Architecture should respond to the surrounding fabric of buildings and spaces, and to local traditions (Katz, 1994) (Figs 1 and 2).

These principles have been given different labels, such as neo-traditional planning (NTP), traditional neighbourhood development (TND) and transit oriented development (TOD) (Kunstler, 1996). They can all be seen as cornerstones of New Urbanism, and are added to here in an attempt to define the SUM model framework.

Fig. 1. Low density sprawl versus traditional planning.
Source: Duany and Plater-Zyberk, 1991.

Fig. 2. Transit oriented development.
Source: Calthorpe, 1993.

Both figures courtesy of A. Duany and. P. Calthorpe.

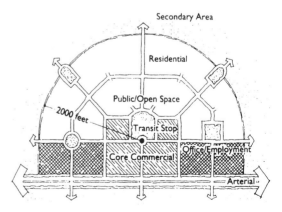

The basic spatial and social unit of planning is the neighbourhood. This unit, if it stands alone, can be a village or a town. A cluster of neighbourhoods can also form an urban village or a town. Clusters of a large number of neighbourhoods become a city. Their population density can vary, depending on local conditions, but they should offer a balanced mix of dwellings, workplaces, shops, civic buildings and parks. The dwellings, however, can be designed at a large scale.

The neighbourhood should be limited in size, with a well-defined edge, and a centre. The size of a neighbourhood is defined by a five-minute walking distance. Hence the neighbourhood should not exceed 400–500 metres from edge to centre. So the boundary will be ten minutes from edge to edge, or half a mile. The centre is the locus of the neighbourhood's civic life. Public buildings, shops, a post office, bank, convenience store, daycare centre, school and other buildings and functions should be situated in the centre. They can also be integrated within the neighbourhood, either at the edges or within predominantly residential neighbourhoods. To guarantee sustainability, communities and neighbourhoods may have to become smaller.

The limited size of the neighbourhood means that all residents are within walking distance of many of their daily needs. Neighbourhoods must contain public transport stops for an express bus service, while a larger neighbourhood should have a more substantial link, perhaps to a light rail network, or to part of a larger transport network. The stop's location, amongst other neighbourhood services and within walking distance of home or work, makes the transport system more convenient. Ten minutes is also the maximum time which people are typically willing to walk prior to a mode change. Cars and other wheeled vehicles are permitted in the neighbourhood and should be integrated in a pedestrian-friendly way. Reliance on cars should be reduced.

The neighbourhood should have a balanced mix of activities, and provide for different types of people, for example with a range of incomes, backgrounds and ages. Buildings for a variety of functions should be provided, but they should be compatible in size and orientation with the street. Commerce and shopping is integrated with residential, business and, in some instances, industrial uses, though not necessarily all on the same street. Living spaces are permitted above ground level, as well as adjacent to shopping and workplaces.

Buildings should be characterised by their use, density, form and aesthetics. Architecture is deeply bound within the culture of regions and countries. Building types, not building styles, should be the source of historical continuity. New design and development should be based on research that establishes the viability of historic, regional and local types, and also suggests newly created or imported types that may have local applications. The buildings should also be ecologically sensitive in their use of materials and energy, and be designed with enough material and technical quality to allow their continuity, renovation and re-use.

Streets should be conceived as the essential fabric of the public realm. They are not the dividing lines within an urban context. They are, on the contrary, communal rooms and passages. The street pattern should be a network which creates the greatest number of alternative routes from one part of the neighbourhood to another. Streets should be seen as the interconnecting network to all the interesting routes within the urban fabric. They can exist in a hierarchy, from broad boulevards to narrow lanes and alleys. There are four characteristics which can help to define streets: pattern, hierarchy, figure and detail.

- Pattern – A single street is always part of the wider street network. Connectivity and continuity of movement within such a network can encourage a mix of uses in the city.
- Hierarchy – A variety of street sizes and scales exist depending on the pedestrian and vehicular movement required.

- Figure – The architectural character of streets is based on their configuration in plan and section.
- Detail – The design of streets should support their use by pedestrians. Neighbourhood streets of varying types should be detailed to provide equitably for pedestrian comfort and car movement.

Streets should provide a setting for casual meetings that form the bonds of community, and contribute towards a better quality of life, strengthening the sense of place. Streets should play an important role in the creation and distinction of public and private spaces and places. They should be designed to be comfortable, safe and interesting for pedestrians.

Civic buildings, including town halls, religious buildings, schools, libraries, and so on, should be placed on preferential sites such as the frontages of squares, neighbourhood centres, and where street vistas terminate. They should serve as landmarks, and should symbolically reinforce their civic importance. Cultural and commercial activities should be focused close to public transport stations to develop a usable, integrated and enjoyable system of spaces and functions.

The optimum neighbourhood size, with five-minute walkability, will enable residents to visit on foot many different types of services and activities, such as shops, pubs, schools and cultural events. This may also help promote small-scale, locally owned businesses, in turn leading to community prosperity, civic benefits and casual socialising – instead of small town provincialism and isolation. Community facilities are assigned special positions in the neighbourhood, underscoring the importance that both institutions and public places play in community life.

'Corridors' form the boundaries between neighbourhoods. These corridors are simultaneously connectors and separators of neighbourhoods and districts. They can include natural and man-made elements. They can be parks, nature reserves, travel corridors, railway lines or a combination of all of these. They are urban elements characterised by their visual continuity. They are defined by the districts and neighbourhoods around them, and provide entry to them. Corridors serve connection and mobility. They represent a regional link, and are therefore extremely significant to the relationships between regions.

In towns and cities, a neighbourhood, or parts of neighbourhoods, can form a district. Districts are composed of streets or ensembles of streets where special activities dominate. It is urbanised areas that are functionally specialised (shopping, entertainment, tourism, retail, education etc.). The specialisation of a district still allows multiple activities to support the primary one. The optimal situation is a combination of all activities in one district which enables dynamic, livable, social and sustainable public life. Interconnected circulation also supports pedestrians, enhances transport viability, and improves security. Attention to the character of the public spaces creates a sense of place for its users, even if their home is elsewhere. The SUM model incorporates all of the above principles, which have been drawn from the New Urbanism movement, and added to by the author.

The Sustainable Urban Matrix model
Rather than being seen as just another apartment block, the SUM is envisaged as an integrated, coherent spatial neighbourhood unit. It enables residents to have more sustainable social and physical relationships with the environment, as well as with each other. This is achieved by the SUM's unique modeling. The SUM is a spatial and social unit which is not so large that it cannot develop and sustain personal contact, nor so small that it suppresses difference and variation. More specifically, it is a unit which is an apartment block, four stories high (with, additionally, the ground level and roof-top), with four apartments on each floor (Fig. 3).

This type of unit can be multiplied by four, creating a SUM group, with a maximum of 256 inhabitants (64 families). Anthropological evidence, recent studies, and a millennium of experience indicate that the optimal population for a neighbourhood is between 500–1,500 inhabitants (Alexander *et al.*, 1977). The unit of 1,000 inhabitants (four SUM groups), which we can, in 'pattern language' (Alexander *et al.*, 1997), call a Close Neighbourhood Group (CNG), corresponds to the size of a traditional European village. Taking into account the aforementioned criteria derived from New Urbanism's ideas about an 'ideal' neighbourhood, this is also an optimal size for inhabitants at different points in their life-cycles. So 16 SUM's would comprise a CNG group, which can be multiplied by four to create an urban village or a smaller town, with approximately 4,000 inhabitants. This could represent a sustainable community, a place with major public and civic activity and a transport nodal point. All of this matches the criteria of a quarter of a mile walking distance from the edge to the centre. This is achieved in the CNG and in the SUM model. Therefore, SUM and CNG groups can result in a form that can be called an urban village or a town neighbourhood (Fig. 4 and Table 1).

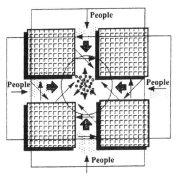

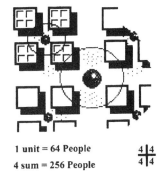

1 unit = 64 People

4 sum = 256 People

Fig. 3. The Sustainable Urban Matrix model.
Source: Hasic, 1997.

Fig. 4. The Sustainable Urban Matrix Model multiplied to form a Close Neighbourhood Group (CNG).
Source: Hasic 1997.

As noted above, it is not the purpose of this chapter to go in to depth about the urban and architectural design of this model. Nonetheless, some key design elements which relate to spatial and social issues will be explained to clarify the potential of the SUM.

Key elements of the SUM

A special feature of the SUM model is that it offers a multitude of spaces for human interaction. As can be seen from Fig. 5, it is made up of spaces that can be considered as interior and exterior socialising places, open for neighbourly contacts as well for other activities, and of semi-private spaces for the residents themselves. It also provides places in which the culture of small neighbourhood communities can develop, for example places for specialised shops, daycare services, community facilities, recreation, and so on. Hence, streets that are interesting and livable and which offer vitality, attachment to place, security and personal comfort can be created by the SUM model.

SUM provides other places for meetings too, for example squares, streets and environmental and social nodes. These are places where people can develop links and contacts. They are also places that create a sense of home and unity for residents.

Throughout the neighbourhood groups, or matrixes, it is possible to perceive axial relationships between social structures and public, semi-public, semi-private and private spaces. The SUM gives order and structure to places, while still retaining variety and new experiences. This is something that most residents want. Recognising the place and space of one's neighbourhood, and yet having the capacity to be surprised by it, are key characteristics of the SUM. Elements of consistency, variety, order and security all come together to create a place that is active but not overly complex. These spaces, even though geometrically rigid at first glance, are actually very flexible. They are adaptable to people's needs, values, beliefs and habits. The SUM's apartments should allow residents flexibility so they can adapt the internal space according to their needs, while retaining the structural elements.

Sustainable Urban Matrix (SUM)	One SUM unit	Four SUM units
type of SUM unit	four floors and entry level and roof top	× 4
size of the SUM apartments	various: 40m²–120m²	various × 4
number of households/families	16–20 max.	64–80 max.
	16–20 max.	64–80 max.
number of apartments	various: studio, 2-	various: same as
SUM apartment types	bedroom, 3-bedroom, duplex etc.	in one unit
interior apartment flexibility	yes	yes
number of persons	48–56, 64 max.	192–224, 256 max.
life-cycle mix	various	various
income and other background	various	various
socialisation spaces	interior/exterior	interior/exterior/ square
walking distances from centre	5–10 minutes, 400–500m.	5–10 minutes, 400–500m.
and to/ from transit nodes and civic centre	from the edge max.	from the edge max.
transport nodes	walking/cycling	walking/cycling/cars
sustainable water and waste management	yes	yes
sustainable energy supply and use	yes	yes
integration of environment/ecology	yes	yes
services and other functions	yes	yes
parking spaces	underground–boardwalk	underground–boardwalk

Table 1. Optimal characteristics of the SUM.
Source: Hasic, 1997.

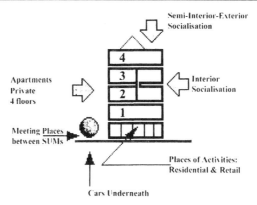

Fig. 5. The Sustainable Urban Matrix: a spatial and social model.
Source: Hasic, 1997.

It is important to emphasise that the SUM model can also be ecologically sustainable. It can help abate environmental problems, such as air pollution, greenhouse effects and depletion of energy sources, natural resources, habitats and open spaces. It is also socially sustainable in that it can accommodate a mix of age groups, socio-economic classes, ethnicities and household types (Kelbaugh, 1997).

The importance of cars is kept in perspective. Parking should be in places where pedestrian activity is least affected. The SUM offers, as one solution, space under boardwalks, which are semi-hidden garages between the SUM groups. The model's design, land use patterns, street layouts and density should make walking, cycling and public transport viable alternatives to driving.

The beauty of the SUM concept is that it can be applied in different-sized settlements, partly because it achieves a balance of housing, shops, recreation and culture. Each SUM unit can have its own identity, but cumulatively they could also create a local identity for residents, which in turn could engender an attachment to place and a sense of belonging. Clusters of SUMs could provide lively, rich environments, with services, amenities and civic activities in the centre. A special quality of the SUM model is the continuity of activity. Not only is the centre of the unit clusters a busy place, so too is each unit, which has a life of its own with activities inside and out. Each unit can exist by itself, but it is also dependent on other units, so a livable and coherent organism is created. This model, like New Urbanism's principles, can be applied almost anywhere. It does not have to be limited to new building. The model, or at least most of its characteristics, can also be applied to neighbourhoods which are in a process of renewal.

Conclusions and discussion

It is useful to review what the SUM model contributes to sustainable urban form. First, it unites new, progressive, positive, sustainable ideas of human settlement development. Second, it is not an exclusive single-family housing type for one social group, with a massive exploitation of land, nor is it a 'sardine packed' living machine. It is a model which can be successfully applied to new collective housing development, but also to urban reconstruction, and renewal of existing housing areas. Third, the SUM is adaptable to different regional, cultural, traditional, local and human needs. It draws heavily on the ideas of New Urbanism, but also goes further by revisiting and reformulating some of the principles. It is, perhaps, not an ideal form, but it is a step towards more sustainable housing – towards achieving a more sustainable urban form.

The main elements of the SUM model, and the changes it brings, can be summarised under ten headings:

- high quality spaces, inside and out
- social interaction and vibrant neighbourhood life
- sense of, and attachment to, place
- rich mix of uses and activities
- walkability and livability
- integration of spaces and framework of streets
- cars in perspective and transport in focus
- traditional values for contemporary needs
- sustainable and eco-living for the future

The SUM model also incorporates the concept of futurity. By reducing dependence on vehicles and embracing the rapid development of information technologies, people may be looking for self-contained, energy-efficient and transport-friendly communities in which to live. Places that can offer residents a work space adjacent to their home will be popular. Advances in telecommunications and changes in the way people live and work are beginning to take shape today. These developments will continue to foster rapid growth in home-based enterprises in the coming years. Technology will soon allow a greater number of people to combine living with work, and hence create more sustainable and livable communities (Cervero and Bernick, 1996). The SUM is ready for that challenge, ready to create a better place to live.

The SUM brings together a community where housing, and all of the facilities needed to meet the daily needs of residents, are close together. SUMs can be designed so that people can live and work in close quarters and comfort. They should provide housing which offers variety, security, stability, attachment and quality and, above all, is enjoyable to live in.

Energy conservation integrated into building design is another goal. SUM enables strategies such as natural ventilation and simple shading to be employed. Intelligent building configurations and landscaping are crucial (Calthorpe, 1993). The SUM goes further than New Urbanism in that it can employ ecological design techniques, for example passive solar gain, and provisions for reducing water consumption, as well as more energy efficient land use planning (Roseland, 1998; Edwards, 1996).

Another key characteristic is human scale. The SUM respects the intricate relationships between residents, their apartments, buildings, streets, and man-made and natural elements. By concentrating on this scale, special places which bring people together and create a vital, fresh and renewing sense of community and a strong attachment to place are created (Figs 6 and 7).

Fig. 6. and Fig. 7. Friendly, attractive and enjoyable neighbourhoods – locus amoenus.
Source: Congress for New Urbanism, 1998.

Finally, the SUM aims to create, and recreate, places that are liked, loved and enjoyed. It incorporates timeless values, measures and standards, and human needs. It values qualities often overlooked in contemporary developments, such as space for cultural expression, safety and security, local identity and social interaction. In short the SUM is a socially, economically and environmentally sustainable urban form.

Note

The ideas in this section are derived from the protagonists of the New Urbanism movement. The list of principles is a compilation of their ideas, which have been articulated in a number of publications. They are taken primarily from Peter Calthorpe (1993), Howard Kunstler (1996), Doug Kelbaugh (1997), Peter Katz (1994), Andres Duany and Elizabeth Plater-Zyberk (1991), Todd Bressi, Stefanos Polyzoides and Elizabeth Moule (in Katz, 1994), Philip Langdon (1997) and Robert Cervero and Robert Bernick (1996). Christopher Alexander's ideas are always there as a leitmotif (Alexander *et al.*, 1985, 1977), and there are also some original contributions by the author.

Tim Heath

Achieving Sustainable Urban Form through the Adaptive Re-use of Buildings for Residential Use

Introduction

Two of the most important issues facing society in the Western World at the end of the twentieth century are how to accommodate substantial growth in the number of households and how to recreate vital and viable city centres. One solution advocated by policy makers is to increase the number of homes within city centres. Indeed, too many cities, as we reach the next millennium, are typified by Hirst's description:

> There is an eerie silence in the city – towering offices dominate the streetscape but no one appears to be in them. A distant mechanical hum and the fluttering of litter in the wind shows the only evidence of occupation. (1996, p.8)

Cities play a pivotal role in bringing people together as a focus of social and economic activity. Town and city centres are multi-functional places providing an organic mix of functions, acting as a shopping and market place, an arts, cultural and entertainment centre, a business and transport hub and, once again, increasingly a place to live and visit. The contraction and rationalisation of many of the traditional roles of the centre such as industry and commerce has provided the space for this renaissance in the provision of dwellings in city centres. This is in sharp contrast to the over-riding trend in Britain during this century for the dispersal of population away from traditional centres. The public's perception of urban areas has been very poor. However, in recent years there has been a resurgence of interest in urban living (URBED, 1998). In addition, since the mid-1990s, there have been television programmes and numerous articles in newspapers and magazines extolling the virtues of living in the city centre. Indeed, in November 1996, *The Observer* announced that 'urban life is sexy again' (Harrison, 1996, p.12).

This chapter supports the idea of creating sustainable cities through centralisation and containment rather than dispersal and low-density development. As URBED argue:

> Policies to attract people back to cities have the potential to kill three birds with one stone. They could reduce the loss of countryside and promote more sustainable patterns of development, while at the same time addressing the root cause of urban decline by making the inner city into somewhere which people no longer wish to escape. (1998, p.15).

This chapter explores whether the adaptive re-use of buildings for residential use should be perceived as a valid agent or tool for the attainment of sustainability. Four sections explore: first, the demand for, and virtues of, city living; second, the opportunities, types and constraints of adaptive re-use; third, the sustainability of providing this type of accommodation; and fourth, how to break down barriers to adaptive re-use and build upon existing constructive processes.

Living in the city

Recent household projections for the UK predict the need for 3.8 million new homes by 2016 (DoE, 1995). Many have claimed that this figure should be nearer to 5.5 million and that dramatic measures are necessary if this need is to be met (URBED, 1998). There are various ways of accommodating this projected housing need. However, in terms of more sustainable development and urban form, it is arguable that existing buildings and/or areas need to be used as much as possible. Indeed, URBED argue that:

> Re-using existing housing as well as vacant commercial and industrial buildings would reduce the resources needed for construction and make use of urban infrastructure. (1998, p.17)

One solution advocated by policy makers is to increase the number of homes within city centres. Indeed, policies at European, national and local level are all promoting housing within existing urban areas. At the press conference for the launch of the discussion paper, *Household Growth: Where Shall We Live?* (DoE, 1996a), former Secretary of State for the Environment John Gummer reaffirmed the government's commitment to urban regeneration by saying that:

> For centuries, towns and cities have been the engines of civilisation ... It is therefore right and proper that we should seek to enhance them and their vitality by providing new homes within the existing urban fabric with facilities and services readily available. With the right commitment to standards of environmental quality and the provision of homes, jobs and services, urban regeneration can offer a highly sustainable option for future settlements. (Gummer, 1996)

More people living in the city centre can create a healthier, richer, more sustainable urban environment which has minimal impact on the existing environs. It is strongly believed that increasing the numbers living in city centres will achieve a whole range of social, economic and environmental goals. In city centres, especially outside normal retail and office hours, residents help to create a 'living heart'. They contribute to vitality by bringing a crucial 24-hour life to the city centre, which creates a demand for an increasing variety of uses. Sherlock stresses the importance of a residential component in this mix by arguing that 'Any long-term solution to the dreariness of central business districts must ... involve the return of housing' (1991, p.164). In addition, an indigenous population can help to create a safer environment with passive or natural surveillance reducing the level of opportunistic crime and vandalism. The benefits of concentrating residential development within existing urban areas and the positive impacts upon the quality and vitality of these places are widely recognised, notably in the European Communities' *Green Paper on the Urban Environment* (CEC, 1990). Indeed, Breheny notes that:

> The EC Green Paper broadened the debate because its advocacy of the compact city rests not just on strictly environmental criteria of energy consumption and emissions, but also on quality of life grounds. (1992, p.139)

Haughton and Hunter (1994) identify that higher densities may help to make the provision of amenities and facilities economically viable. Increasing the resident population will make it easier to maintain or re-establish important services such as schools and shops which are dependent upon there being an adequate catchment population. *Planning Policy Guidance 6: Retail and Town Centres* stresses that 'Residents and workers stimulate shopping, restaurants and café's, and other businesses to serve them, and so in turn add vitality' (DoE, 1996b, para. 2.13). The re-use and upgrading of existing buildings can also have a positive effect on the image of the city. Their adaptation is important in terms of eradicating blight, highlighting activity and promoting the city centre as a destination for residents, visitors and investors. Residents in city centres can also enhance the viability of public transport services and reduce reliance on private cars, which in turn reduces both the need to travel and journey lengths.

The demand for urban living

Secretary of State for Transport, Environment and the Regions, John Prescott, has stated that he wants 'to see a renaissance of our cities. That will mean using existing empty houses, offices and warehouses for new affordable flats – not just for City yuppies' (1998, p.20). However, the crucial question with regard to city centre living is whether there is any demand for such living: do people want to live in city centres? Davidson argues that:

> Perhaps we divide naturally into two types: those for whom cities are vibrant and exciting, a focus for human activity; and those for whom they are dirty, noisy and dangerous. (1995, p.iii)

Significantly, new patterns of housing demand have emerged since the early 1990s, with some households seeking accommodation closer to places of work as transport costs and congestion increase. Smith explains the phenomenon of a:

> trend toward fewer children, postponed marriages and a fast-rising divorce rate, younger homebuyers and renters are trading in the tarnished dream of their parents for a new dream defined in urban rather than suburban terms. (1996, p.52)

The potential significance of the conversion of city centre buildings is increased by the rising demand for accommodation because city living is becoming more fashionable again (RICS, 1998).

Especially relevant is the composition of the additional households required by 2016. Approximately 75% of the households are expected to consist of one or two people (DoE, 1996a). The type of residential unit produced by conversion is generally non-family housing and therefore likely to be desired by smaller households. Furthermore, these groups may be more likely to be attracted to city centre living and be prepared to trade-off disadvantages traditionally associated with urban environments against the benefits of a central location. To date, the majority of new city centre residents are young single professionals, students and temporary residents during the working week (URBED, 1998). However, increasingly there is evidence that the over-50s and empty-nesters (people whose grown-up children have moved away) are also being attracted back into city centres. The provision of public transport, facilities, amenities and the accessibility to employment, friends and family are major factors in this trend (Kelly, 1998). City centre accommodation may not be appropriate for everyone throughout their life cycle. However, it is already providing a convenient and attractive form of living for many, and there is clearly both the potential and demand for these numbers to increase.

Policy initiatives

A primary aim of government policy for over 20 years has been to regenerate urban areas. Since the mid-1990s, the UK government has produced a number of White Papers and policy guidance documents that have been increasingly supportive of initiatives to revitalise town and city centres, particularly through the promotion of residential uses. Initiatives such as the Single Regeneration Budget have implied an examination of the potential of commercial buildings to meet housing as well as employment requirements. Additionally, *Planning Policy Guidance 15: Planning and the Historic Environment* recommends residential use on upper floors for several reasons:

> Bringing vacant floors back into use, particularly residential use, not only provides additional income and security ... It meets a widespread need for small housing and helps to sustain activity in town centres after working hours. (DoE, 1994a, para. 4.11)

The DoE's document *Our Future Homes* states that, 'Encouraging more people to live and work in our cities helps support our environmental policies' (1995, p.15). The report goes on to say that meeting the increased demand for housing in a sustainable way requires the use of the planning system and public investment to encourage people to live in cities. Similarly, the concept of the conversion to residential use fits well with the principles set out in *Sustainable Development: The UK Strategy* (DoE, 1994b) which advocates making the most efficient use of existing urban areas through making them more attractive places to live and work. Planning advice in *Planning Policy Guidance 13: Transport* also recommends 'allocating the maximum amount of housing to existing urban areas' (DoE and DoT, 1994, para. 3.2). In addition, the government's White Paper, *A New Deal for Transport: Better for Everyone* (DETR, 1998), gives advice to local authorities to provide more homes in towns and cities and along public transport routes as part of an initiative to integrate land use planning and transport. With regard to housing, the document says that new planning guidance will emphasise the benefits of providing new homes in towns and cities and making the most of places or vacant buildings which can be well served by public transport, or reached easily on foot or by bicycle.

Opportunity for change and potential for re-use
All cities are in a state of transition. The processes involved can be so slow as to hardly be apparent or they can happen extremely rapidly with dramatic effects. The physical form of our cities is not timeless and the fortunes of urban spaces and buildings often correspond to those of the economy or changing technologies. Indeed, Ratcliffe and Stubbs highlight how:

> Fluctuating economic conditions, new legislative frameworks, political and social swings, advances in information technology and communications, and innovations in management theory and practice, all conspire to create a climate of constant change. (1996, p.ix)

Changes to existing towns and cities that result in obsolete buildings open up opportunities for entrepreneurs to exploit the legacy of the past to meet the needs and aspirations of the present.

When a building is commissioned and built, it is usually 'state of the art' in terms of its functional requirements. It will also be built to the contemporary standards of construction and be appropriately located with regard to its function. Nevertheless, from its conception, a building starts to become obsolete. There are several interrelated dimensions of obsolescence, some being attributes of the buildings themselves, while others relate to the area as a whole. For each dimension, the degree of obsolescence will be different for each building or area. Equally, 'obsolescence is a relative term with regard to the terminal state, obsolete, which may never be reached' (Lichfield, 1988, p.22). For example, unless a building was designed for a very specific purpose it is difficult to conceive of it having no residual physical utility and being impossible to convert to another use. Thus, a state of total obsolescence is rarely reached. An important distinction must be drawn between the obsolescence of a building in its current use and the building being obsolete for any use. It is this process which opens up the opportunity for adaptive re-use to take place. Indeed, Jacobs identifies that:

> Time makes the high building costs of one generation the bargains of a following generation. Time pays off the original capital costs, and this depreciation can be reflected in the yields expected from a building. Time makes certain structures obsolete for some enterprises, and they become available to others. (1961, p.189)

Conversion of redundant buildings to residential use is not a new idea – most cities have examples of buildings that have been successfully re-used. In the early 1970s, it became popular to live in former manufacturing spaces that were converted to residential use in some older industrial cities of Western Europe and the United States (Zukin, 1989). In the UK, the trend for converting obsolete commercial space into residential was started by people like The Manhattan Loft Company who imported the New York loft idea to London. Gradually, bigger players like Barratt Homes, Berkeley Homes and St George were attracted to the concept and now many old buildings that become available are considered suitable for conversion.

There are three primary sources of residential conversions in towns and cities. First, most settlements have abandoned or under-used space on the upper floors of shops and banks. Second, many former industrial cities have a substantial legacy of former industrial buildings and textile mills. Third, most cities have an abundance of obsolete office buildings that are a legacy of the 1960s and 1970s. Re-use of each of these types complies with the government's policies of promoting sustainable development and concentrating new development in urban areas to provide the benefits outlined above.

Residential accommodation over shops initiatives

Every city in Britain has a significant amount of vacant or under-used space above its shops. A number of government initiatives since the late 1980s have encouraged the repopulation of town centres through re-inhabiting space over retail units. *Planning Policy Guidance 6: Town Centres and Retail Development* states that: 'occupation of flats above shops can increase activity and therefore personal safety, while ensuring buildings are kept in good repair' (DoE 1996b, para. 2.13). Initiatives have included Living Over The Shop (LOTS), Flats Over Shops, and Social Housing Over Shops (see DoE, 1997). These projects provided financial incentives to bring redundant space over retail units back into use. A similar initiative, the Nottingham City Council-led Quality Houses from Shops initiative has helped to finance the conversion of a number of vacant and derelict retail premises (see Fig. 1). The LOTS initiative, spearheaded by the University of York, has helped bring vacant space over shops back into use and improve the economy and vitality of towns through increased residential population (see Petherick and Fraser, 1992; Goodchild, 1998).

Fig. 1. Flats created from redundant space over shops on Derby Road, Nottingham.

Between 1991 and 1994, the LOTS initiative provided over 2,000 residential units in various town centres (LOTS, 1994). There have been a number of success stories to date in towns and cities such as Stamford, Rippon, Huddersfield and Newcastle. However, conversions that have occurred have been on a relatively small scale, despite the obvious potential. Nevertheless, Ravetz argues that 'All this wasted space could contribute half a million units to our total housing stock of 19 millions' (1995, p.136). Similarly, the *Dwelling In and Over Shops* (LPAC, 1998) study suggests that vacant shops and floors above shops could contribute between 25,000 and 54,000 dwellings to London's housing. To date, one of the greatest barriers to housing over shops projects has been the traditional prejudices and conventions of the commercial property sector. Nevertheless, a number of local authorities and some large property owners, notably the National Westminster Bank and Boots the Chemists, set up their own initiatives and the DoE also set up a pilot scheme called Flats Over Shops between 1992 and 1995.

Conversion of industrial and mill buildings

The conversion of nineteenth century industrial buildings since the 1970s has been important in demonstrating that it is possible to create attractive housing that sells successfully in new locations (see Fig. 2). Currently, a romance and charm – together with a certain social cachet and air of distinction – attaches itself to living in former industrial spaces. However, they have not always been considered chic nor comfortable:

> Until the 1970s … making a home in a factory district clearly contradicted the dominant middle-class ideas of 'home' and 'factory', as well as the separate environments of family and work on which these ideas were based. (Zukin, 1989, p.58)

Nevertheless, beginning in New York, a desire for loft living has arisen. The initial loft spaces in SoHo had been raw industrial spaces that the first tenants adapted to residential use. These 'unfinished' spaces could be tailored to individual requirements. This idea of 'loft living' is proving extremely popular and loft apartments are being created in old warehouses throughout the UK. Such buildings can often provide appealing spacious accommodation with high ceilings and an attractive external appearance (see Fig. 3). There are individual developments in cities such as Birmingham, Sheffield, Liverpool and Leeds and there are clearly identifiable quarters of such schemes, like Shad Thames and Clerkenwell in London, Whitworth Street in Manchester and the Merchant City in Glasgow (see Tiesdell *et al.*, 1996). Since the mid-1990s the media have continually hyped loft living, and this has clearly helped to create a demand for this new residential type.

Fig. 2. The conversion of a harbour-front warehouse in Toronto as part of a waterside regeneration initiative.

Fig. 3. The legacy of the nineteenth century textile industry at Nottingham's Lace Market offers an opportunity to create a unique living environment.

Offices to flats

The conversion of postwar office space to housing is a relatively recent phenomenon which, in the UK, has been largely confined to London, where a great demand for residential accommodation is combined with an oversupply of office space. Nevertheless, office to residential schemes are common in cities such as Toronto, Melbourne and Sydney. Gradually, such developments are emerging in towns and cities in the UK such as Birmingham, Leicester and Portsmouth. The opportunity has arisen from a restructuring within the office sector which has resulted in large surpluses of office accommodation, built mainly in the 1960s and 1970s, which does not meet contemporary requirements. As Hirst states:

> The downturn in the office market – caused by lingering effects of the recession, company decentralisation, down-sizing, and the new spatial demands of computer technology – means that hundreds of city centre offices are lying empty and lifeless. (1996, p.8)

Recognising the potential for office to residential conversions, the Joseph Rowntree Foundation commissioned Barlow and Gann (1993) to explore the technical aspects of this phenomenon. This building type is often characterised by large, 1950s and 1960s curtain wall buildings of up to 12 storeys in height, situated in secondary or fringe locations that typically command lower rental values within the central business district (see Figs 4 and 5). In the early 1990s, many property analysts were writing off these postwar edifices as the most problematic part of the commercial building stock, with no future at all. However, the very design and specification of these offices often makes them highly appropriate technically for conversion. Initially, conversions were seen purely as a solution to the oversupply problem after the dramatic property slump. However, significantly, it is predicted that over 100,000 residential units are likely to be created from such conversions by 2016 (URBED, 1998).

Fig. 4. The conversion of Marathon House, Marylebone Road, London has created 106 luxury apartments from an obsolete 11,000 m^2 postwar office building.

Fig. 5. The adaptive re-use of the former Independent newspaper offices in London offered the opportunity to re-clad a poor 1960s office block to a modern apartment building which relates more successfully with the street.

Constraints to re-use

The opportunities for adaptive re-use are clearly available, with the Empty Homes Agency estimating that, in the UK, 800,000 of the required new homes could be provided by converting existing buildings (Cooke, 1998). However, the capacity to undergo change is dependent on both factors concerning the building itself, such as its structure and fabric, and external factors, such as its surroundings and the local infrastructure. Despite the volume of conversion activity to date, it must not be assumed that all, or even a majority of, obsolete buildings can automatically be converted to residential use. The conversion process is more complex than new build, with more limitations and unknowns. The existing building defines what can and cannot be done, and in principle conversion and refurbishment are not as attractive to developers as new build.

There are also constraints that can cause the development pipeline to dry up. These include: the effect of interest rate rises; the effect of overseas – particularly Far Eastern – economies on property investment in the UK; and the implementation of onerous planning gain by local planning authorities (HBF, 1998). The market, which works through a combination of cost, value and risk, is therefore the key to unlocking capacity. Any government policy that tries to work against the market is destined to fail, or at least to have limited impact. These areas are intricately tied up in the workings of the planning, grant and taxation systems. However, there is no simple formula for a successful conversion, rather it depends on the positive outcome of a wide range of social, political, economic and technical variables (Barlow and Gann, 1996). If any one variable fails, then in all likelihood it will jeopardise the proposed scheme.

The sustainability of adaptive re-use
Dealing appropriately with the legacy of the past is a challenging problem for many cities. Indeed, there is a lot of real and symbolic committed capital in city centres. Alongside cultural and social explanations are a series of closely related economic arguments. Blowers states in relation to sustainability and the built environment that:

> Resource conservation requires patterns of development that minimise energy consumption, maintain the productivity of land, and encourage the re-use of buildings. (1993, p.7)

The conversion of buildings may be seen as a more sustainable approach than new build in that re-use constitutes the conservation of scarce resources, a reduction in the consumption of energy and materials in construction, and good resource management. Indeed, Falk argues that 'the most convincing argument of all for conserving old buildings is the idea of the minimisation of waste. Old buildings represent past energy stored up in a usable form' (1993, p.163).

Conversion and re-use can be considered as recycling and they introduce less waste material and pollution into the environment than redevelopment. Also, the process of re-use uses less new materials and less energy in construction than new build. Significantly, 'embodied energy' has become a consideration as attitudes towards sustainability have changed. The concept is concerned with calculating the energy cost of building an existing structure and modifying it, compared to the energy costs of its demolition and replacement, a formula which often suggests that the former is a more energy efficient solution.

Waste production is another major consideration in the re-use versus redevelopment debate. It is currently estimated that 70 million tonnes of construction and demolition waste – which equates to 16% of the country's total – are produced each year in the UK. With growing environmental and economic pressures – such as the introduction of landfill tax – this amount will become of greater significance. Boyd and Jankovic argue that the costs of redevelopment will also become significantly higher if global and local environmental impacts of demolition have to be accounted. They argue that 'This may come as a government tax on such action or as legal restrictions on the procedures that can be used in demolition' (1992, p.107).

The majority of buildings becoming available for adaptive re-use to residential are in urban centres. As stated above, the benefits of increasing the number of people living in the city centre are long term and wide ranging, including the need and desire to reduce out-of-town shopping and long commuting times.

Many of the theories regarding residential intensification are contained within the 'compact city' concept. However, this is not without its critics. Indeed, Breheny (1995) has argued that the increase in urban densities required to effect more sustainable cities is unrealistic. Increased density has also been equated with city cramming and a deterioration in the quality of residential environments. However, whilst a shift towards a high-density compact city is possibly undesirable for whole urban areas, the conversion of existing buildings to residential use does not necessarily generate such problems. Adaptive re-use is one means of preventing the development of open spaces within urban areas whilst protecting the countryside. In addition, such development will help to realise other numerous direct and indirect benefits of increasing resident populations in our urban centres.

Conclusions and recommendations

Existing towns and cities can and should take a bigger share of new housing units than at present, making them more vibrant and more enjoyable places in which to live. The current sustainability debate promotes urban compaction and intensification, and as roads continue to become more congested, and public transport services eroded, many people will increasingly seek to live closer to facilities and their places of work. Additional residents in our city centres will encourage revitalisation, enhancing the stability, safety and vitality of the urban core, instead of leaving downtown areas abandoned in the evening with a mass exodus to the suburbs. The conversion of obsolete buildings into residential use can play an important role in the revitalisation of our city centres, help to meet the growing pressure for homes, and encourage the use of public transport. In addition, the provision of more residences in the city centre can help to relieve some of the pressure for development in the countryside.

The very notion of what constitutes a sustainable city will inevitably change over time. However, few would disagree with Elkin *et al.* who argue that:

> sustainable development must aim to produce a city that is 'user friendly' and resourceful, in terms not only of its form and energy efficiency, but also its function, as a place for living. (1991, p.12)

The opportunity offered by the supply of obsolete buildings in our towns and cities provides one means of meeting the goals of conserving resources and creating more livable settlements. To achieve these goals, the issue of the physical capacity of urban areas to accommodate household growth must be addressed. So too must the issue of reversing trends in decentralisation. Changes to the planning system can help in achieving this aim but much needs also to be done to reverse public opinions and market realities. This said, the late 1980s and the 1990s have seen increasing numbers of residents returning to central locations. This renaissance of city living has seen increasing numbers of active retired, childless couples, students and people with alternative lifestyles choosing city centre living. Cities are also attracting significant numbers of part-time residents, residing in urban centres close to their places of employment from Monday to Friday (Coupland, 1997). In addition, there is an increasing number of corporate lettings for companies to accommodate both employees and visitors. These may include people whose work requires them to move between different locations or whose family life is elsewhere. These groups all contribute significantly to the local economy through patronage of restaurants, and entertainment, retail and leisure facilities.

While repopulating the city centre will do much to revive urban areas, it cannot do it alone, and government policy must also focus on other policy areas to create places fit to accommodate household growth. The impacts of public policies on crime, education, transport, social exclusion, economic development and many other issues will all affect the livability of the city centre. The opportunities offered by obsolete buildings are too important to be left to the *ad hoc* whims of the market. Local authorities need to be more pro-active in encouraging conversions and must use all mechanisms at their disposal. Equally, parts of the city centre can be promoted and developed as residential quarters through marketing, feasibility studies, development briefs and 'talking up' development and helping to build confidence in the city centre as a potential residential area. In order to make urban housing financially attractive it is important to stimulate the market. In the medium term this market change is likely to happen, but there is a place for public subsidies in the short term to pump prime this process.

If the potential of obsolete buildings is to be seized through adaptive re-use, then there is a need for a more supportive environment for city centre living. This will necessitate investment in the public realm both in terms of environmental improvements, safety, and infrastructure. There is also a need for better information regarding demand and supply, funding routes, and the potential and/or constraints of adaptive re-use. To accommodate household growth it will be necessary to exploit every opportunity available. Despite their importance, converted buildings will only provide for a small proportion of a much greater move back to city centre housing. However, the arguments are not about absolutes but about the balance between different solutions. Nevertheless, in the short term, adaptive re-use has a particularly important role to play both in terms of meeting housing need and providing a sustainable use for existing resources. The chance to create a more sustainable city through adaptive re-use can be grasped through the co-ordination of a plethora of measures at both local and national level, together with initiatives related to development, transport, energy efficiency and resource conservation.

Katie Williams, Elizabeth Burton and Mike Jenks
Achieving Sustainable Urban Form:
Conclusions

The title *Achieving Sustainable Urban Form* is positive in its tone. It implies that urban form can theoretically be more sustainable than it is at present, and that such a form, or forms, are attainable. It suggests that some of the unsustainable development patterns of the past can be corrected, or avoided in the future. So, it seems fair to ask whether the contributors to the book have shared this optimism. In the Introduction two questions were posed. First, what is sustainable urban form? and second, how can it be achieved? Now it is possible to assess whether these questions have been answered.

What is sustainable urban form?
In Part 1 it was argued that 'A prerequisite to achieving sustainable urban form is knowing what it is. To realise the "sustainable city" there has to be a clear and common-held concept of what it will look like, how it will function, and how it will change over time'. The chapters which followed, in Parts 1 and 2, offered evidence of the sustainability of different forms. With a collection of chapters such as these, it was unlikely that there would be complete agreement on which forms are more, or less, sustainable, but some clear messages emerged. A summary of each of chapter's key findings is given in Table 1 below. It shows which urban forms each of the authors tested and what their findings were. Then, some key conclusions are drawn.

Authors	Urban form investigated	Conclusions
Guy and Marvin	multiple 'pathways' to numerous sustainable futures	There is a multiplicity of pathways towards different sustainable futures that co-exist within a single city. The pathways are competing, and contested within a locality.
Burton	compactness	Investigated the impact of compactness on social equity in the UK. Used 41 indicators of compactness and found that some are beneficial for social equity, such as high-density housing, a large range and high number of services and facilities, re-urbanisation, and development on derelict land, but some are not. Not only is the type of compactness important for social equity, so too is the way it comes about.
Williams	urban intensification	Tested the environmental, economic and quality of life impacts of urban intensification policies in England. Found some benefits were evident, such as a sustainable use of land, increased vitality and liveliness, and some economic benefits,

but some key policy aims were not met. The most important of these were that traffic had not been reduced and social benefits were not apparent. There were also major negative side effects such as bad neighbour effects, social tensions and reductions in environmental quality. Intensification was more beneficial in inner mixed-use areas than in residential suburbs.

Newton	alternative growth scenarios: **compact city** **edge city** **corridor city** **ultra city fringe** **city**	Tested the environmental sustainability impacts of future growth trends for Melbourne. Found that the compact city is most fuel efficient and has the lowest carbon dioxide emissions – savings of up to 43% in fuel are possible. More concentrated forms reduce pollutant emissions. Concentrated corridor, edge, fringe and compact 'zones' are beneficial for air quality. But compact city proposals are not good for exposure to particles because a high number of people are affected. Overall though, a trend to a more compact city, however defined, will lead to environmental improvements.
Buxton	**traditional neighbourhood design** (increased self-containment) and **urban villages**	Tested traditional neighbourhood design (TND) (which has 25 dwellings per hectare, a mix of housing types, local retail and employment opportunities, an inter-connected street pattern, good public transport services and 70% solar access to plots) against conventional metropolitan fringe development and development meeting the criteria of the residential design code for Victoria. Found that the TND had the potential to reduce carbon dioxide emissions by 42%, provide transport energy savings of 57%, save 26% in energy (by designing homes to make the most of solar energy), and reduce time and distances travelled. Also studied the effects of accommodating Melbourne's future growth in urban villages within the city and found that urban expansion could be reduced by one third, and savings of between 3% and 14% in energy and greenhouse gas emissions could be made over existing urban consolidation scenarios.
Masnavi	**density and mix of uses at the neighbourhood scale**	Tested the impacts of density and mix of uses on travel patterns, accessibility and social issues such as safety and perceptions of attractiveness of the area. Found that the compact, mixed-use area was better for accessibility to facilities, the low-density areas were better for environmental quality, and the single-use compact areas were best for social contacts, safety and security. Suggests that the compact city may be able to reduce the use of cars by up to 70% and reduce trips for non-work activities by 75%, but will not eliminate the need for the car for some uses.
Newton, Tucker and Ambrose	**apartments and detached houses**	Found that the life cycle energy usage of apartments is 10–30% less, in terms of energy per person, than for detached houses. The life cycle carbon dioxide emissions per person are 20–40% lower for apartments than for detached houses.
Alberti	**components of urban form which might affect ecosystems**	Urban form has a significant effect on ecosystems, but as yet it is not clear which forms are best. Patch structure (size, composition, persistence, and inter-connectivity) is the key element affecting animal and plant species survival. There are 'thresholds' in the disturbances which urban forms create for

		natural ecosystems, above which ecosystem processes break down. To support ecosystems, natural patches should be as large and interconnected as possible.
Scoffham and Marat-Mendes	**components of urban form which aid adaptability over time**	Found that space is the asset that allows change to occur incrementally and sustainably. The perimeter block, with adequate space, offers the best form for allowing change over time, but without disrupting the original urban plan or form.
Newman and Kenworthy	**density**	Investigated the relationship between density and car dependency in cities worldwide. Found that density is a major explanatory variable for the level of transport energy use. There are also cost savings for public transport associated with higher densities. Hence certain strategies will be beneficial, such as nodes and corridors of high density development, revitalising inner cities, focusing development around the existing rail system, discouraging further sprawl, and developing public transport in combination with developing new villages in the suburbs.
Simmonds and Coombe	**compact city**	Tested compact city scenarios against a trend scenario (continued decentralisation) for Bristol. Found that the compact city offers only fractional savings in total person kms, and that it does not reduce the number of trips made by car: it increases traffic in the central area, but reduces it in the rest of the built-up area. Found that proximity has only a weak influence on travel demand.
Reneland	**density and size of town**	Tested accessibility to various services and facilities in Swedish towns between 1980 and 1995. Found that higher densities facilitated better accessibility to facilities, and that for most services and facilities large towns provided better accessibility than smaller ones.
Van and Senior	**mix of uses**	Tested the effect of mixed use on travel behaviour. Found that a mix of uses encourages walking and cycling, and deters car use for light food shopping trips. But land use mix does not affect the mode of choice for bulk food shopping or commuting.
Titheridge, Hall and Banister	**intensification extensification decentralisation new towns**	Tested the sustainability of proposed new housing location strategies in terms of personal travel demand and associated energy consumption and emissions for Leicestershire and Kent. Found that different growth strategies had different effects depending on travel mode and purpose studied. Intensification performed best in terms of reducing trip length, and hence energy consumption and emissions. There were similar benefits associated with New Town strategies, but the findings are dominated by the effect of each strategy on future trends in journeys to work by car.
Headicar	regional housing location strategies: **developing housing in larger urban areas, restricting it in**	Tested regional housing strategies for their effects on travel demand in the Oxfordshire area. Found that urban size is not the only important factor when considering housing location: settlement location in relation to employment centres is also important. Concentration *per se* will not be effective, it has to be in the right location, i.e. in the vicinity of the largest urban

	villages and small towns, avoiding development of small new settlements	areas or in corridors where closely spaced settlements provide for employment concentrations similar to those of the largest urban area in aggregate. Hence, development could take the form of peripheral development of the principal city in a region, and/or smaller new settlements and expansions on transport corridors to link with nearby freestanding towns. New settlement proposals in relatively isolated locations should be resisted, and urban concentration should only be encouraged to take place in modest amounts in the most rural areas far from any employment centres.
Stead, Williams and Titheridge	components of urban form which might affect travel patterns	Tested urban form variables against socio-economic characteristics to explain differences in travel patterns. Found that socio-economic variables explain about half of the variation in travel distances whereas land use characteristics explain about a third of the variation. Some land use characteristics, such as mix of uses and density, are still important (for example, land use characteristics may account for up to 40% of variations in car ownership). The success of the compact city may result as much from the socio-economic characteristics of the inhabitants as the land use and form.

Table 1.
Conclusions on
Sustainable
Urban Forms

Compactness, centralisation, concentration and intensification

The relationship between urban compactness and travel patterns is central to the sustainable urban form debate. It has been commonly accepted that a degree of compactness, in any of several forms, reduces demand for car travel. Most of the authors who addressed this issue agreed, to varying extents, with the assumption that compaction leads to fewer car journeys. However, they also deconstructed the simple causal relationship between high-density development and reductions in travel demand and added more detailed information about specific savings for different compaction scenarios, journey types and modes. For example, Newton found distinct benefits in urban compaction in terms of fuel efficiency, but these benefits were not confined to the 'compact city' form, they were also achievable through compact zones throughout the city, such as in corridors or on the edge of the city. Likewise, Buxton found that substantial transport energy savings could be realised through traditional neighbourhood developments, built at higher densities than usual suburban developments, and supported by other environmentally beneficial measures. Newman and Kenworthy asserted the influence of density on reducing car dependence and, in an argument similar to Newton's, indicated certain areas where development should be located for maximum gains. Masnavi found that compactness had an influence on some trips (such as non-work), but less so on others (commuting).

These findings are in opposition to those in some of the other chapters. Simmonds and Coombe found that a strategy of compaction for the Bristol area would have only a minor effect on traffic. There are a number of reasons for this, including the slow pace of urban change, the small proportion of the population accommodated through a policy of compaction, and the fact that proximity to a desired facility is only a weak indicator of people's choice of travel mode. Headicar's findings on the effects of compaction on trips between settlements at the regional scale also cast doubts on the effectiveness of current housing location strategies which focus on urban compaction and concentration. His conclusion that concentration *per se* is not effective, but that the location of development, in relation to employment opportunities, is important, broadens the debate about compactness to incorporate inter-urban travel as well as travel patterns within a town or city.

Another key issue was the importance of behavioural and socio-economic criteria in explaining differences in travel patterns. Simmonds and Coombes' differentiation between the need and desire to travel is significant. If people's choice of mode of travel is not related to the proximity of the facility they are visiting, then compaction or mixed-use policies are unlikely to reduce car use. The findings, from Stead *et al.*'s research, that socio-economic characteristics may explain more of the differentiation in travel distances than land uses do, also reveals much about the potential of different policy options in reducing car travel.

The message from these chapters is complex. It seems that, on balance, compaction in various forms is likely to lead to some reductions in travel demand at the city and neighbourhood scales. Benefits can be realised by clustering development in certain locations, such as corridors served by public transport, and near public transport nodes. This said, the way that compaction strategies fit into the regional context is also important. Intra and inter urban travel patterns need to be considered if overall travel distances are to be reduced. Urban compaction should not take place in locations where there are few local employment opportunities, as commuting to nearby settlements will result. It is also important to be realistic about the magnitude of change possible through a policy of compaction. If only small population shifts are being accommodated then only minimal travel benefits can be expected. Likewise, the counter effects of other trends, such as rising car ownership rates or worsening public transport services, must also be taken into consideration. If these trends are outstripping potential savings brought about by changes in land uses then compaction alone is unlikely to bring the predicted benefits. More attention should also be paid to the relationship between proximity and mode of travel. Most authors assert that people will make short trips on foot or by bicycle, yet other research evidence counters this (Simmonds and Coombes). The nature of this relationship is central to the success of compaction policies.

It is important, though, that the compaction debate does not become overshadowed by the transport issue. Other key sustainability impacts are also influenced by compact forms. Alberti's chapter gives an important reminder that turning any natural land over to urban uses has negative impacts for natural species diversity. The potential impact of urban compaction on environmental quality is also important, as the analyses presented by Williams, Masnavi, and Guy and Marvin show. Compaction may need to be extremely carefully managed if high quality urban environments are to be achieved. Finally, social and economic impacts are also significant, although they have received far less attention than environmental aspects to date. Burton's work on the effects of urban compaction on social equity shows the importance of considering social impacts when considering different development scenarios.

Overall, the chapters suggest that there are both costs and benefits associated with urban compaction. The main benefits are likely to be related to land efficiency and travel, and the main costs to environmental quality and, perhaps, quality of life. A great deal more is known now then when the compact city was first suggested as a solution to problems of unsustainable cities. The importance of compaction, alongside centralisation and concentration have been studied, and the various ways in which compaction can come about (intensification, newly-built high-density development, traditional neighbourhood developments and so on) have been investigated. Yet there are still uncertainties, particularly in the areas of ecology, and social and economic impacts. More information is still required to enable a balanced assessment of the merits of urban compaction.

Mix of uses
Several of the chapters addressed the sustainability of mixed uses within a town, city or

neighbourhood. Overall, the effects were largely positive. Burton found that a mix of uses contributed to social equity. Buxton found that a mix of residential, employment and retail opportunities in a traditional neighbourhood development contributed to major reductions in time and distances travelled, and therefore in transport energy. Mixed uses were also found, by Masnavi, to improve accessibility to services and facilities. Van and Senior concurred with Masnavi and found that mixed uses deterred car use for some trips, such as light food shopping, and encouraged walking and cycling. However, they found they had little effect on car use for heavy food shopping and commuting.

The main problem with mixed uses is the effect on environmental quality, and therefore acceptability to urban residents. Masnavi's finding that environmental quality was lower in mixed-use areas indicates this. Likewise, Williams found that introducing a mix of uses into residential areas was seen to reduce environmental quality. However, improving the mix within an already diverse neighbourhood was welcomed by local residents. Therefore, the key to the acceptability of a range of uses may be the extent to which the area is already mixed.

The importance of acknowledging the complexity of urban systems

More than any other message, the chapters communicate the importance of recognising the complexity of urban systems. Time and again they show the importance of 'detail'. They demonstrate how previous assumptions made about relationships between urban form and sustainability have been discredited because they are too sweeping. In order to formulate a meaningful understanding of the ways in which urban form impacts on various issues, both the components of urban form and the issues under investigation have to be defined and tested. This does not suggest a reductionalist approach, or one that is segregated, but it does suggest the need for rigour and thoroughness of analysis, and for a sophisticated synthesis of research findings, before claims can be asserted with any degree of confidence or replicability.

A key illustration of this is given by Burton in her work on social equity and compactness. In previous research and policy, generalisations had been made about the benefits of more compact forms for social equity. Burton examined this relationship in detail by developing large sets of indicators of both compactness and equity. The findings, that different types of compactness have varying impacts on different components of equity, reveal that previous presumptions have been misleading and simplistic. The research presented by Newton and Buxton illustrates a similar point. Suppositions have been made in the past that urban compaction has certain environmental benefits. Newton found that for most of the environmental impacts he tested, the compact city did have beneficial effects, but there were important exceptions, such as exposure to particles, which is worse in a compact city because more people are exposed to the pollutants. Buxton's work reflected that sustainability benefits are more likely to accrue in compact areas, but only if supported by certain road configurations, levels of public transport and so on: densities alone were not sufficient. Likewise, Scoffham and Marat-Mendes picked out not just density, but also configuration in the form of perimeter blocks, as being significant for sustainability in terms of their adaptability. The richness of the findings on travel patterns is further evidence of the importance of detail. By concentrating on the purpose of the trip and mode of transport, Masnavi, Van and Senior, Titheridge *et al.* and Stead *et al.* all added depth to the information available on the relationship between urban forms and travel behaviour.

This new research does not weaken arguments about the relationship between urban form and sustainability: it strengthens them by sharpening our understanding of the interactions of the components of the urban system. It is a reminder of the dangers of taking causal relationships about forms and their consequences at face value. It is also a salutary warning for policy makers that some key sustainable development strategies may not achieve their aims, and may have unforeseen consequences which could jeopardise sustainability.

Commentary

Taken together, the chapters in Parts 1 and 2 go a considerable way towards answering the question 'what is sustainable urban form?' However, no definitive solution with universal benefits has emerged. So how can the facts that have been gathered be used? An acknowledgement of the multiplicity of potential sustainable urban forms, and their need to be adaptable over time, as discussed by Guy and Marvin, and Scoffham and Marat-Mendes respectively, is important in putting these findings into context. Guy and Marvin argued that there are multiple pathways to a sustainable future, and hence multiple forms which could facilitate it. These pathways may co-exist within a city. Hence it is the job of urban managers and policy makers to decide which pathways the city should take, and what the desired outcomes should be. This viewpoint sees sustainability as a process rather than an end state, and therefore suggests that changes in urban forms should be open to adaptation over time, as more information is gathered, and social, economic and environmental changes occur. This need for an adaptable urban form was the focus of Scoffham and Marat-Mendes' work. They emphasised the need for urban form to respond to demands from citizens for new uses and agendas. These chapters have shown that there are aspects of urban form that can be seen to be more sustainable than others; but that the context and scale of application are important. Hence, making decisions about the most sustainable form in any given circumstance, and seeing development through to completion, are critical process. The chapters in the next two Parts address how they can be achieved.

How can sustainable urban form be achieved?

The chapters in Parts 3 and 4 gave examples of approaches and strategies for achieving sustainable urban form, and examples of schemes and projects designed to meet the goal of sustainability. Some themes emerged from these chapters, and a brief summary of these helps to assess what has been learnt.

An emphasis on process rather than product and on objectives rather than standards

A key theme to emerge from Part 3 was a move away from prescribing one 'end product', in terms of urban form (Ravetz, Guy and Marvin, Raymond), towards an emphasis on the need to formulate and practise effective information gathering and decision making processes to ensure the right solution in any given location (Crilly and Mannis, Jenks, de Roo and Raymond). This trend was typified by Raymond's account of the development of a design guide for Kent, which disregards previous fixed standards in favour of a flexible set of objectives to be achieved through new development. The emphasis, by de Roo, on determining the right decision making process for a particular environmental problem also reflects this. He argues that rigid standards are not always appropriate, and that, for some environmental problems, a more discursive, locally-based method of problem solving is required. Howes, in line with these ideas, outlines principles for environmental improvements, backed up by strategies which may be useful in achieving these, as an alternative to quantitative guidelines.

A key element in these 'softer' processes is adaptability. The ability of methods which aid decision making about sustainable urban form to adapt as circumstances change over time was seen as essential. Jenks, Crilly and Mannis, Raymond, Ravetz and de Roo all stress the need for flexible and adaptive approaches which can act as decision supports, rather than prescriptive models. This adaptability enables decision makers to address the complexity of the urban system and place specificity, and to respond to change.

In addition to adaptability, many authors stress the need for inclusivity, through consensus-based decision making. Raymond's description of the processes involved in formulating new tools to deliver sustainable urban form in the local authority sector illustrates inclusive, transparent approaches which move from technical methods to more open, flexible tools. Crilly and Mannis advocate a bottom-up approach to deciding what sustainable urban form may be in a locality, and how best to develop it. Their research shows the importance of reflecting complexity in decision making, while still communicating the characteristics and implications of future development to the widest group of stakeholders. Jenks suggests using urban residents' opinions to assess the acceptability of urban intensification, and hence formally includes local perceptions in a decision support tool.

The importance of examples of sustainable developments

Another clear theme in Parts 3 and 4 was the importance of developing new ways of conceiving the future built environment. In particular, successful demonstrations projects, and adaptations of the existing built environment were seen as important ways of broadening perceptions about what can be achieved. Van Vliet described how innovative methods can change not only the built form itself, but also the institutional structures responsible for change. New methods can help break out of rigid ways of thinking and doing. His argument, that innovation is constrained by multiple barriers (attitudinal, behavioural and institutional) will have some resonance with practitioners in this field attempting new building types and forms. Van Vliet argues these barriers can be overcome by a process of 'social learning', aided by the achievement of successful projects.

A range of solutions

It is now clear that a range of options for future development are likely to be needed to match the requirements of different locations. As Ravetz stated, '… a portfolio of complimentary patterns and incremental processes is needed in a fast changing world'. The examples of design and built form solutions given in Part 4 open up possibilities about what future forms could be. Some of the solutions, such as urban villages and the re-use of buildings, are more established than others, but all have been carefully constructed to meet various interpretations of sustainable urban form. Most of the authors evaluate the solutions they describe, and several discuss constraints to achieving them. Nevertheless, the schemes all serve the purpose of demonstrating that advances in sustainability can and have been made, and that sustainable forms can offer environmental, social and economic benefits.

Although, at first glance, the schemes are very different some common traits are apparent. Most of the solutions promote compaction and mix of uses to achieve communities or neighbourhoods. Several discuss the importance of inclusive adaptive processes used to develop their schemes. Thompson-Fawcett's account of the urban villages movement illustrates a solution which incorporates high densities, a sense of place and well-connected transport routes, amongst other key features. Thus, the urban village has benefits over most new urban and suburban development. The 'Homes for Change' project at Hulme is an impressive example of community involvement in the design and planning process, with a successful outcome: a mixed use development where residents work and live. Hulme, in addition to the Kolding housing blocks (Van Vliet and Gade), Playa Vista (Kalamaros), the Sustainable Urban Matrix (Hasic) and the Sustainable City Implantation (Dumreicher *et al.*), provide alternative views of what future development could be. Similarly, Heath's analysis of the re-use of buildings for residential uses shows that demonstration projects have had an impact. Certain types of conversions, such as offices to houses, were previously thought unfeasible, yet are now very popular. These are all examples of competing pathways (Guy and Marvin) towards a sustainable future.

Conclusion

Overall, it appears that there are a variety of urban forms which are more sustainable than typical recent development patterns. In the main they are characterised by compactness (in various forms), mix of uses and interconnected street layouts, supported by strong public transport networks, environmental controls and high standards of urban management. Many of the sustainable forms described are more akin to traditional neighbourhoods than zoned, single-use forms. This said, there is room for a great deal of flexibility in the delivery of such forms, and different aspects of sustainability can be emphasised in different schemes. The development of a variety of solutions, derived from an agreed set of sustainability objectives seems a feasible strategy given the reality of urban development, where adaptation and manipulation of built form is continual, and hardly ever begins with a 'clean slate'. Hence a portfolio of solutions is appealing, but it must be treated with caution. It does not represent a free-reign in terms of development scenarios, but an approach to finding an appropriate solution given the existing characteristics of an area and the sustainability 'pathway' chosen for it, at local and strategic levels.

Devising such development scenarios and 'pathways' requires a sophisticated understanding of the impacts of different forms, and of their capacities to deliver future benefits. Hence, the findings on the importance of the complexity of urban systems are important. It is clear that urban form has a range of impacts on travel patterns, social conditions, environmental quality, ecology and so on. Balancing these impacts, or determining which should have priority in a given area is problematic. This is why the development of sophisticated and effective decision making processes is so important. Achieving a consensus about future built form patterns is rarely easy, but if decisions have come about through inclusive and adaptive processes developments are more likely to be supported by stakeholders.

Having said this, the importance of policies and strategies other than those associated with urban form should not be overlooked. Changes in form alone will not achieve sustainable cities. Supportive transport, environmental, economic and social policies are also required alongside shifts in attitudes and lifestyles. Sustainable urban forms will only be achievable if they are underpinned by a policy background which commits to global sustainability goals, but leaves room for local formation and implementation of solutions. Nevertheless, a significant contribution to sustainability can be made by putting urban infrastructure in place which offers urban residents the choice to live more resource-efficient lifestyles.

Perhaps the most optimistic message, however, comes from the numerous examples of sustainable forms. These are invaluable in changing opinions about what is achievable. They form part of a long tradition of trial and error in urban form and, consequently, some schemes will prove more successful than others. Yet each scheme contributes towards achieving sustainable urban form by revealing potential sustainable futures, and by testing the numerous processes through which they could be realised. A great deal still needs to be learnt about the complexity of different forms and their impacts, but the progress made in the short time since sustainability became a global aim should not be underestimated.

References

Introduction

Katie Williams, Elizabeth Burton and Mike Jenks
Achieving Sustainable Urban Form: *An Introduction*

Barton, H. (1990) Local global planning. *The Planner*, 26 October, p.12-15.

Breheny, M. (1992) *Sustainable Development and Urban Form*, Pion, London.

Breheny, M. and Rookwood, R. (1993) Planning the sustainable city region, in *Planning for a Sustainable Environment* (ed. A. Blowers), Earthscan, London.

DETR (Department of the Environment, Transport and the Regions) (1997) *Developing an Integrated Transport Strategy*, The Stationery Office, London.

ECOTEC (1993) *Reducing Transport Emissions through Planning*, HMSO, London.

Elkin, T., McLaren, D. and Hillman, M. (1991) *Reviving the City: Towards Sustainable Urban Development*, Friends of the Earth, London.

Farmer, J. (1996) *Green Shift: Towards a Green Sensibility in Architecture*, Architectural Press, Butterworth Heinemann, Oxford.

FOTE (Friends of the Earth) Europe (1995) *Towards Sustainable Europe*, Friends of Earth Europe, Brussels.

Haughton, G. and Hunter, C. (1994) *Sustainable Cities*, Jessica Kingsley, London.

Jenks, M., Burton, E. and Williams, K. (eds) (1996) *The Compact City: A Sustainable Urban Form?* E & FN Spon, an imprint of Chapman and Hall, London.

Leff, E. (1990) The global context of the greening of cities, in *Green Cities: Ecologically Sound Approaches to Urban Space* (ed. D. Gordon), Black Rose Books, Montreal.

Papanek, V. (1995) *The Green Imperative: Ecology and Ethics in Design and Architecture*, Thames and Hudson, London.

Potter, S. (1997) *Vital Travel Statistics: A Compendium of Data and Analysis about Travel Activity in Britain*, Open University, Milton Keynes.

Rudlin, D. and Falk, N. (1999) *Building the 21st Century Home: The Sustainable Urban Neighbourhood*, URBED, Architectural Press, Oxford.

Smith, M., Whitelegg, J. and Williams, N. (1998) *Greening the Built Environment*, Earthscan Publications Ltd, London.

Sustainable London Trust (1996) *Sustainable London*, Sustainable London Trust, London.

WCED (1997) World Commission on Environment and Development (1987) *The Brundtland Report, Our Common Future*. Oxford University Press, Oxford.

WHO (World Health Organisation) (1992) *Report of the Panel on Urbanization*, WHO Commission on Health and Environment, WHO, Geneva.

Part 1: Defining Sustainable Urban Form

Simon Guy and Simon Marvin
Models and Pathways: *The Diversity of Sustainable Urban Futures*

Breheny, M. (1996) Centrists, decentrists and compromisers: views on the future of urban form, in *The Compact City: A Sustainable Urban Form?* (eds M. Jenks, E. Burton and K. Williams), E & FN Spon, an imprint of Chapman and Hall, London.

Fulford, C. (1996) The compact city and the market: the case of residential development, in *The Compact City: A Sustainable Urban Form?* (eds M. Jenks, E. Burton and K. Williams), E & FN Spon, an imprint of Chapman and Hall, London.

Guy, S. (1998) Developing alternatives: energy, offices and the environment. *International Journal of Urban and Regional Research*, **22(2)**, pp.264-282.

Guy, S. and Marvin, S. (1996a) Disconnected policy, the shaping of local energy management. *Environment and Planning C*, **14(1)**, pp.145-158.

Guy, S. and Marvin, S. (1996b) Managing water stress: the logic of demand side infrastructure planning. *Journal of Environmental Planning and Management,* **39(1)**, pp.125-131.

Guy, S. and Marvin, S. (1998) Electricity in the marketplace: reconfiguring the consumption of essential resources. *Local Environment*, **3(3)**, pp.313-331.

Haughton, G. (1997) Developing sustainable urban development models. *Cities*, **14(4)**, pp.189-195.

Jenks, M., Burton, E. and Williams, K. (eds) (1996) *The Compact City: A Sustainable Urban Form?* E & FN Spon, an imprint of Chapman and Hall, London.

Marvin, S. and Guy, S. (1997) Infrastructure provision, development processes and the co-production of environmental value, *Urban Studies*, **34(12)**, pp.2023-2036.

Moss, T., Marvin, S. and Guy, S. (1998) *Technical Networks as Instruments of Sustainable Flow Management: A Comparative Analysis of Infrastructure Policy and Planning in European Urban Regions*, Final Report for EC Environment and Climate Programme Theme 4: Human Dimensions of Environmental Change.

Smyth, H. (1996) Running the gauntlet: a compact city within a doughnut of decay, in *The Compact City: A Sustainable Urban Form?* (eds M. Jenks, E. Burton and K. Williams), E & FN Spon, an imprint of Chapman and Hall, London.

Thomas, L. and Cousins, W. (1996) A new compact city form: concepts in practice, in *The Compact City: A Sustainable Urban Form?* (eds M. Jenks, E. Burton and K. Williams), E & FN Spon, an imprint of Chapman and Hall, London.

Elizabeth Burton
The Potential of the Compact City for Promoting Social Equity

Beer, A. (1994) Spatial inequality and locational disadvantage. *Urban Policy and Research*, **12(3)**, pp.181-199.

Blowers, A. (1992) Planning for a sustainable society. *Streetwise*, **10**, pp.3-10.

Bourne, L. (1992) Self-fulfilling prophecies? Decentralisation, inner city decline and the quality of urban life. *Journal of American Planning Association*, **58**, pp.509-513.

Bozeat, N., Barrett, G. and Jones, G. (1992) The potential contribution of planning to reducing travel demand, in *PTRC, 20th Summer Annual Meeting, Environmental Issues: Proceedings of Seminar B*, PTRC, London.

Breheny, M. (ed.) (1992) *Sustainable Development and Urban Form*, Pion, London.

Bromley, R. and Thomas, C. (1993) The retail revolution, the carless shopper and disadvantage. *Transactions of the Institute of British Geographers*, **18**, pp.222-236.

Brotchie, J. (1992) The changing structure for cities. *Urban Futures*, Special Issue 5, February, pp.13-23.

Burton, E. (1997) *The Compact City: Just or Just Compact?*, unpublished PhD thesis, Oxford Brookes University, Oxford.

Castells, M. and Hall, P. (1994) *Technopoles of the World: The Making of Twenty-First Century Industrial Complexes*, Routledge, London.

CEC (Commission of European Communities) (1990) *Green Paper on the Urban Environment*, EUR 12902, EEC, Brussels.

CIDA (Canadian International Development Agency) (1991) *A Strategy for Implementing Sustainable Development*, Policy Branch, Ottawa, Ontario, Canada.

Craig, J. (1985) *A 1981 Socio-Economic Classification of Local and Health Authorities of Great Britain*, OPCS Studies on Medical and Population Subjects no. 48, HMSO, London.

Des Rossiers, F. (1992) Urban sprawl and the central city.

Plan Canada, November, pp.14-18.

DoE (Department of the Environment) (1992) *The Effects of Major Out of Town Retail Development*, HMSO, London.

DoE and DoT (Department of the Environment and Department of Transport) (1994) *Planning Policy Guidance 13: Transport*, HMSO, London.

DoE and Welsh Office (1992) *Local Housing Statistics, England and Wales*, No. 103, October 1992, Government Statistical Service, London.

ECOTEC (1993) *Reducing Transport Emissions Through Planning*, HMSO, London.

Elkin, T., McLaren, D. and Hillman, M. (1991) *Reviving the City: Towards Sustainable Urban Development*, Friends of the Earth, London.

Forster, C. (1994) Spatial inequality and locational disadvantage. *Urban Policy and Research*, **12(3)**, pp.181-199.

Fox, J. (1993) Making a case for strategic urban containment. *Town and Country Planning*, **62(9)**, pp.242-245.

Freeman, H. (1992) The environment and mental health. *Streetwise*, **11**, pp.22-28.

Goodchild, B. (1994) Housing design, urban form and sustainable development. *Town Planning Review*, **65(2)**, pp.143-157.

Hamnett, C. (1991) The blind men and the elephant: the explanation of gentrification. *Transactions of the Institute of British Geographers*, **16**, pp.173-189.

Jacobs, J. (1961) *The Death and Life of Great American Cities*, Random House, New York.

Jenks, M., Burton, E. and Williams, K. (1996) *The Compact City: A Sustainable Urban Form?*, E & FN Spon, an imprint of Chapman and Hall, London.

Knight, C. (1996) Economic and social issues, in *The Compact City: A Sustainable Urban Form?* (eds M. Jenks, E. Burton, and K. Williams), E & FN Spon, an imprint of Chapman and Hall, London.

Laws, G. (1994) Oppression, Knowledge and the Built Environment. *Political Geography*, **13(1)**, pp.7-32.

McLaren, D. (1992) Compact or dispersed? Dilution is no solution. *Built Environment*, **18(4)**, pp.268-284.

Minnery, J. (1992) *Urban Form and Development Strategies: Equity, Environmental and Economic Implications: The National Housing Strategy*, Australian Government Publishing Service, Canberra.

Newman, P. (1992) The compact city – an Australian perspective. *Built Environment*, **18(4)**, pp.285-300.

OPCS (1993) *1991 Mortality Statistics: Area – England and Wales*, Series DH5, No.18, Microfiche, HMSO, London.

Petherick, A. (1991) Benefits of over-the-shop schemes for local authorities, in *Living Over the Shop*, Working Paper No. 3, University of York, York.

Porter, M. (1991) America's green strategy. *Scientific American*, **264(4)**, p.96.

Rees, J. (1988) Social polarisation in shopping patterns: an example from Swansea. *Planning Practice and Research*, **6**, pp.5-12.

Schwartz, J. (1994) PM10, ozone and hospital admissions of the elderly in Minneapolis-St Paul, Minnesota. *Archives of Environmental Health*, **49(5)**, pp.366-374.

Stretton, H. (1994) Transport and the structure of Australian cities. *Australian Planner*, **31(3)**, pp.131-136.

Stretton, H. (1996) Density, efficiency and equality in Australian cities, in *The Compact City: A Sustainable Urban Form?* (eds M. Jenks, E. Burton and K. Williams), E & FN Spon, an imprint of Chapman and Hall, London.

Town and Country Planning Association (1994) City or suburbia? (editorial). *Town and Country Planning*, **63(9)**, p.226.

Troy, P. (1996) Urban consolidation and the family, in *The Compact City: A Sustainable Urban Form?* (eds M. Jenks, E. Burton and K. Williams), E & FN Spon, an imprint of Chapman and Hall, London.

Valuation Office (1991) *Property Market Report: Autumn 1991*, Valuation Office, London.

Van Kempen, E. (1994) The dual city and the poor: social polarisation, social segregation and life chances. *Urban Studies*, **31(7)**, pp.995-1015.

Yiftachel, O. and Hedgcock, D. (1993) Urban social sustainability: the planning of an Australian city. *Cities*, **10(2)**, pp.139-157.

Katie Williams

Does Intensifying Cities Make them More Sustainable?

Banister, D. (1994) Reducing the need to travel through planning. *Town Planning Review*, **65(4)**, pp.349-354.

Bell, S. (1995) *Watch This Space: Urban Greenspace Policy Study,* Metropolitan Planning Officers Society, Oldham.

Breheny, M. (ed.) (1992) *Sustainable Development and Urban Form*, Pion, London.

Breheny, M. (1995) Compact cities and transport energy consumption. *Transactions of the Institute of British Geographers*, **20(1)**, pp.81-101.

Business Statistics Office of the CSO, The (1995) *VAT Registered Businesses 1994*, CSO, London.

CEC (Commission of the European Communities) (1990) *Green Paper on the Urban Environment.* EUR 12902 EN, CEC, Brussels.

Church, C. (1995) Sustainable cities. *International Report*, February, pp.13-14.

Crookston, M., Clarke, P. and Averley, J. (1996) The compact city and the quality of life, in *The Compact City: A Sustainable Urban Form?* (eds M. Jenks, E. Burton and K. Williams), E & FN Spon, London.

DoE (Department of the Environment) (1988a) *Planning Policy Guidance 12: Local Plans*, HMSO, London.

DoE (Department of the Environment) (1988b) *Planning Policy Guidance 2: Green Belts*, HMSO, London.

DoE (Department of the Environment) (1988c) *Planning Policy Guidance 4: Industrial and Commercial Development and Small Firms*, HMSO, London.

DoE (Department of the Environment) (1992a) *Planning Policy Guidance 3: Housing (revised)*, HMSO, London.

DoE (Department of the Environment) (1992b) *Evaluating the Effectiveness of Land Use Planning*, PIEDA Plc. in association with CUDEM, Leeds Polytechnic and D. Diamond, HMSO, London.

DoE (Department of the Environment) (1992c) *Planning Policy Guidance 12: Development Plans and Regional Guidance*, HMSO, London.

DoE (Department of the Environment) (1993a) *Planning Policy Guidance 6: Town Centres and Retail Development (revised)*, HMSO, London.

DoE (Department of the Environment) (1993b) *Alternative Development Patterns: New Settlements*, M. Breheny, T. Gent and D. Lock, University of Reading and David Lock Associates, HMSO, London.

DoE (Department of the Environment) (1994) *Planning Policy Guidance 4: Industrial and Commercial Development and Small Firms*, HMSO, London.

DoE (Department of the Environment) (1995) *Planning Policy Guidance 2: Green Belts (revised)*, HMSO, London.

DoE (Department of the Environment) (1996) *Planning Policy Guidance 6: Town Centres and Retail Development (revised)*, HMSO, London.

DoE and DoT (Department of the Environment and Department of Transport) (1994) *Planning Policy Guidance 13: Transport*, HMSO, London.

DETR (Department of the Environment, Transport and the Regions) (1998) *Planning for the Communities of the Future*, The Stationery Office, London.

DETR (Department of the Environment, Transport and the Regions) (1999) *Planning Policy Guidance 3: Housing* (public consultation draft), The Stationery Office, London.

DETR (Department of the Environment, Transport and the Regions) (forthcoming) *Urban Intensification: Impacts and Acceptability*, Oxford Brookes University and Entec UK, unpublished.

Dunstone, M. and Smith, J. (1994) Is urban consolidation economical? the Australian Capital Territory's North Watson case. *Urban Policy and Research*, **12(4)**, pp.222-241.

Evans, A. (1988) *No Room! No Room! The Costs of the British Town Planning System*, Institute of Economic Affairs, London.

Evans, A. (1990) *Rabbit Hutches on Postage Stamps: Economics, Planning and Development in the 1990s*, 12th Denman Lecture, Granta Editions, Cambridge.

Findlay, A., Rogerson, R. and Morris, A. (1988) In what sense 'indicators of quality of life'? *Built Environment*, **14(2)**, pp.96-106.

Handy, S. (1992) Regional versus local accessibility: neo-traditional development and its implications for non-work travel. *Built Environment*, **18(4)**, pp.253-267.

Healey, P. (1997) *Collaborative Planning: Shaping Places in Fragmented Societies*, Macmillan, Basingstoke.

Hillier Parker (1996) *Shopping Centres of Great Britain*, Hillier Parker Research, London.

HM Govt (1990) *This Common Inheritance: Britain's Environmental Strategy*, Cm 1200, HMSO, London.

HM Govt (1994) *Sustainable Development: The UK Strategy*, Cm 2426, HMSO, London.

HM Govt (1995) *Our Future Homes, Opportunity, Choice, Responsibility, the Governments' Policies for England and Wales*, Department of the Environment and Welsh Office, HMSO, London.

HM Govt (1996) *Household Growth: Where Shall we Live?* presented to parliament by the Secretary of State for the Environment by command of Her Majesty. Cm 3471, London.

Hubbard, P. (1994) Professional versus lay tastes in design control: an empirical investigation. *Planning Practice and Research*, **9(3)**, pp.271-287.

Jenks, M., Burton, E., and Williams, K. (eds) *(*1996) *The Compact City: A Sustainable Urban Form?* E & FN Spon, London.

Knight, C. (1996) Economic and social issues, in *The Compact City: A Sustainable Urban Form?* (eds M. Jenks, E. Burton, and K. Williams), E & FN Spon, an imprint of Chapman and Hall, London.

LBC (London Borough of Camden) (1992) *London Borough of Camden Unitary Development Plan, Consultation Draft* (supplemented by proposed amendments, 1996), London Borough of Camden, London.

LBC (London Borough of Camden) (1994) *Camden Residents' Survey*, London Borough of Camden, London.

LBH (London Borough of Harrow) (1994) *Harrow Unitary Development Plan*, London Borough of Harrow, London.

LBH (London Borough of Harrow) (1997) *Development monitoring in Harrow: An analysis of planning decisions from 1993-1996*, Department of Development Services, Planning and Transportation Division, London Borough of Harrow, London.

Llewelyn-Davies (1992) *Housing Capacity Study for London*, Llewelyn-Davies, London.

LPAC (London Planning Advisory Committee) (1994) *1994 Advice on Strategic Planning Guidance for London*, LPAC, London.

LPAC (London Planning Advisory Committee) (1995) *State of the Environment Report for London*, LPAC, London.

McLaren, D. (1992) Compact or dispersed? Dilution is no solution. *Built Environment*, **18(4)**, pp.268-285.

Nicholas, J. (1994) Reversing the Car Culture. *Town and Country Planning*, **63(5)**, pp.131-132.

OPCS (Office of Population Censuses and Surveys) (1993) *1991 Census – Great Britain Summary and Review: Local Authorities*, HMSO, London.

OPCS (Office of Population Censuses and Surveys) (1995) *London Facts and Figures*, OPCS, London.

Petrakos, G. C. (1992) Urban concentration and agglomeration economies: re-examining the relationship. *Urban Studies*, **29(8)**, pp.1219-1230.

Phoenix Group (1989) *Green Belts or Green Gardens?*, Marketforce Publications, London.

Reade, E. J. (1982) Section 52 and corporatism in planning. *Journal of Planning and Environmental Law*, January, pp.8-16.

Rogers, R. (1995) Looking forward to the compact city. *The Independent*, 20 Feb.

Rydin, Y (1992) Environmental dimensions of residential development and the implications for local planning practice. *Journal of Environmental Planning and Management*, **35(1)**, pp.43-61.

Smyth, H. (1996) Running the gauntlet: a compact city within a doughnut of decay, in *The Compact City: A Sustainable Urban Form?* (eds M. Jenks, E. Burton and K. Williams), E & FN Spon, London.

Stationery Office, The (1997) *Regional Trends 32*, Government Statistical Service, London.

Stretton, H. (1996) Density, efficient and equality in Australian cities, in *The Compact City: A Sustainable Urban Form?* (eds M. Jenks, E. Burton and K. Williams), E & FN Spon, London.

Troy, P. (1996) Urban consolidation and the family, in *The Compact City: A Sustainable Urban Form?* (eds M. Jenks, E. Burton and K. Williams), E & FN Spon, London.

Williams, K. (1998) *The Effectiveness of the UK Planning System in Delivering Sustainable Development via Urban Intensification*, unpublished PhD Thesis, Oxford Brookes University, Oxford.

Williams, K. (1999) Urban intensification policies in England: problems and contradictions. *Land Use Policy*, **16(3)**, pp.178-199.

Williams, K., Jenks, M. and Burton, E. (1999) How much is too much? urban intensification, social capacity and sustainable development. *Open House International*, **24(1)**, pp.17-26.

Wootten Jeffreys Consultants (1989) *Harrow: An Environmental Assessment of Residential Areas*, A Report for the London Borough of Harrow, London.

Peter Newton
Urban Form and Environmental Performance

Dieleman, F. (1997) Planning compact urban form: Randstad Holland 1965-95, *Environment and Planning A.* **29**, pp.1711-1715.

Ewing, R. (1997) Counterpoint: is Los Angeles-type sprawl desirable? *Journal of the American Planning Association*, **63(1)**, pp.107-126.

Gipps, P., Brotchie, J., Hensher, D., Newton, P. and O'Connor, K. (1997) *Journey to Work, Employment and the Changing Structure of Australian Cities*, Australian Housing and Urban Research Institute, Monograph 3, Melbourne.

Gordon, P. and Richardson, H. W. (1997) Are compact cities a desirable planning goal? *Journal of the American Planning Association*, **63**, pp.95-106.

Jenks, M., Burton, E. and Williams, K. (1996) *The Compact City: A Sustainable Urban Form?*, E & FN Spon, an imprint of Chapman and Hall, London.

Manins, P. (1995) Regional air pollution modelling for planners. *Terrestrial Atmospheric and Oceanic Sciences*, **6(3)**, pp.393-401.

Marquez, L. O. and Smith, N. (1997) A framework for linking urban form and air quality, paper presented at the *Pacific Regional Science Conference*, Wellington, December.

Minnery, J. R. (1992) *Urban Form and Development Strategies: Equity, Environmental and Economic Implications*, The National Housing Strategy Background Paper 7, AGPS, Canberra.

Mumford, L. (1968) *The Urban Prospect*, Secker and

Warburg, London.

Newton, P. W. (ed.) (1997) *Re-Shaping Cities for a More Sustainable Future: Exploring the Nexus between Urban Form, Air Quality and Greenhouse Gas Emissions*, Research Monograph 6, Australian Housing and Urban Research Institute, Melbourne.

Newton, P. W. and Wulff, M. G. (1998) Working at home: emerging trends and spatial implications, in *Essays in Honour of Christopher Maher* (ed. K. O'Connor), Monash University, Melbourne.

O'Connor, K. (1997) Continuing suburbanisation? *Urban Policy and Research*, **15(2)**, pp.139-144.

Pressman, N. (1985) Forces for spatial change, in *The Future of Urban Form* (eds J.F. Brotchie, P. Newton, P. Hall and P. Nijkamp), Croom Helm, London.

Trinidad, G. and Marquez, L. (1998) Interfacing GIS with models for urban planning and analysis. *Failure and Lessons Learned in IT Management*, **2**, pp.33-38.

Troy, P. N. (1996) *The Perils of Urban Consolidation*, The Federation Press, Sydney.

Michael Buxton

Energy, Transport and Urban Form in Australia

ABS (Australian Bureau of Statistics) (1994) *Yearbook Australia*, Australian Government Printing Office, Canberra.

Armstrong, G., Birrel, R., Buxton, M., Johnstone, P. and Stanley, J. (1995) *Green Cities*, Australian Urban and Regional Development Review Strategy, Paper no. 3, Canberra.

Banister, D. (1992) Energy use, transport and settlement patterns, in *Sustainable Development and Urban Form* (ed. M. Breheny), Pion, London.

Brindle, R. (1994) Lies, damn lies and automobile dependence, *Australasian Transport Research Forum: Proceedings*, **19**, pp.117-146, Transport Research Centre, University of Melbourne.

Brisbane City Council (1992) Urban renewal: inner north eastern suburbs, Brisbane, *Urban Futures*, **2(1)**, pp.9-17.

Brotchie, J. (1992) The changing structure of cities. *Urban Futures*, **5**, pp.13-26.

Brotchie, J., Anderson, M. and McNamara, C. (1993) *Changing Metropolitan Commuting Patterns*, CSIRO, Melbourne.

Brotchie, J., Gipps, P. and Newton, P. (1995) Urban land use, transport and the information economy: metropolitan employment, journey to work trends and their implications for transport. *Urban Futures*, **17**, pp.37-49.

Bureau of Transport and Communications Economics (BTCE) (1995) *Greenhouse Gas Emissions from Australian Transport: Long Term Projections*, Report no. 88, AGPS, Canberra.

Buxton, M. and Searle, R. (1997) *Environmental Innovations in Australian Cities*, Metropolitan Environmental Improvement Program, The World Bank, Washington DC.

Calthorpe, P. (1993) *The Next American Metropolis: Ecology, Community and the American Dream*, Princeton Architectural Press, New York.

Calthorpe and Associates (1992) *Transit Supportive Development Design Guidelines*, Calthorpe Associates, City of San Diego.

Cervero, R. (1986) *Suburban Gridlock*, Centre for Urban Policy Research, New Brunswick, New Jersey.

Cervero, R. (1989) *America's Suburban Centres: The Land Use-Transportation Link*, Unwin Hyman, Boston.

Cervero, R. (1997) *Transit Villages in the 21st Century*, McGraw Hill, New York.

CSIRO (Commonwealth Scientific and Industrial Research Organisation), ABS (Australian Bureau of Statistics), Department of Geography, Monash University, and Institute of Transport Studies, University of Sydney (1994) *Employment, Housing and the Journey to Work*, Department of Housing and Regional Development, Canberra.

Daly, M. (1998) Reshaping Sydney: the inner city revival. *Urban Policy and Research*, **16(1)**, pp.59-63.

Department of Housing and Regional Development (1995) *Better Cities*, Occasional Paper Series 2, Australian Government Publishing Service, Canberra.

Department of Infrastructure (1997) *Consolidating Our City: Redevelopment in Melbourne*, 2nd issue, Melbourne.

Department of Infrastructure (1998a) *From Doughnut City to Café Society*, Government of Victoria, Melbourne.

Department of Infrastructure (1998b) *Residential Land Bulletin: March Quarter*, Government of Victoria, Melbourne.

Department of Planning and Development (1993) *Metropolitan Population Targets*, Government of Victoria, Melbourne.

Duany, A. (1992) The second coming of the American small town. *Wilson Quarterly*, **16(1)**, pp.19-49.

ECOTEC (1993) *Reducing Transport Emissions through Planning*, HMSO, London.

Frank, L. and Pivo, G. (1994) Impacts of mixed use and density on utilization of three modes of travel: single-occupant vehicle, transit and walking. *Transportation Research Record*, **1466**, pp.44-52.

Garreau, J. (1991) *Edge City: Life on the New Frontier*, Doubleday, New York.

Holliday, S. and Norton, R. (1995) Sydney's future: quo vadis? *Urban Futures*, **17**, pp.13-19.

Katz, P. (1994) *The New Urbanism*, McGraw Hill, New York.

Kaufman, C. and Morris, W. (1995) Transit supportive urban design, in *Transit Supportive Development: Benefits and Possibilities*, Occasional Paper Series, Better Cities Program, Australian Government Printing Office, Canberra.

Kemp, D. (1994) *Employment, Work and Social Trends in Australia and their Implications for Urban Form*, Queensland Department of Business, Industry and Regional Development, Brisbane.

Kinhill Engineers (1995) *Smart Planning not Sprawl: The Costs and Benefits of Alternative Fringe Development*, Australian Urban and Regional Development Review Discussion Paper No. 5, Canberra.

Kirwan, R. (1992a) Urban form, energy and transport: a note

on the Newman–Kenworthy thesis. *Urban Policy and Research*, **10(1)**, pp.6-19.

Kirwan, R. (1992b) Urban consolidation. *Australian Planner*, **30(1)**, pp.13-20.

Maunsell, D. and Glazebrook and Associates (1994) *Urban Public Transport Futures*, Australian Urban and Regional Development Review Workshop Paper, Canberra.

McGlynn, G., Newman, P. and Kenworthy, J. (1991) *Towards Better Cities: Reorganization and Transport Energy Scenarios*, a report prepared for Australia's Commission for the Future, Melbourne.

McKenzie, F. (1996) *Beyond the Suburbs: Population Change in the Major Exurban Regions of Australia*, Australian Department of Immigration and Multicultural Affairs, AGPS, Canberra.

Mees, P. (1994) Continuity and change in 'Marvellous Melbourne'. *Urban Futures*, **3(4)/4(1)**, pp.1-17.

Mees, P. (1995) Dispersal or growth? The decentralisation debate revisited. *Urban Futures*, **18**, pp.35-41.

Minnery, J. and Barker, R. (1998) The more things change: Brisbane and South East Queensland. *Urban Policy and Research*, **16(2)**, pp.147-152.

Morris, B. (1993) The car user's perspective, in *Transport, the Environment and Sustainable Development* (eds D. Banister and K. Button), Spon, London.

Newman, P. and Kenworthy, J. (1989) *Cities and Automobile Dependence: An International Sourcebook*, Gower, Aldershot.

Newman, P. and Kenworthy, J. (1992) Transit oriented urban villages: design solutions for the '90s. *Urban Futures*, **2(1)**, pp.50-58.

NGGIC (National Greenhouse Gas Inventory Committee) (1996) *National Greenhouse Gas Inventory 1988 to 1994*, Canberra.

O'Connor, K. (1992) Economic activity in Australian cities: national and local trends and policy. *Urban Futures*, **5**, pp.87-95.

O'Connor, K. (1994) *Getting to Work: Thirty Years of Travel in Melbourne*, Graduate School of Government, Monash University, Melbourne.

O'Connor, K. (1998) Understanding metropolitan Melbourne– without being confused by coffee and doughnuts. *Urban Policy and Research*, **16(2)**, pp.139-145.

O'Connor, K. and Stimson, B. (1994) Economic change and the fortunes of Australian cities. *Urban Futures*, **4(2/3)**, pp.1-12.

O'Connor, K. and Stimson, B. (1996) Convergence and divergence of demographic and economic trends, in *Population Shift: Mobility and Change in Australia* (eds P. Newton and M. Bell), AGPS, Canberra.

OECD (Organisation for Economic Co-operation and Development) (1994) *Climate Change Policy Initiative Update Vol. 1*, OECD, Paris.

Owens, S. (1986) *Energy, Planning and Urban Form*, Pion, London.

Pears, A. (1995a) *Environmental Aspects of Urban Energy Supply and Consumption*, Background Paper to the Australian Urban and Regional Development Review,

Sustainable Solutions, Melbourne.

Pears, A. (1995b) *Non-Transport Energy Issues for Urban Villages: A Report for the Urban Villages Project*, Government of Victoria Urban Villages Project, Melbourne.

Pucher, J. (1990) Review of Newman and Kenworthy. *Transportation Research*, **24A(4)**, pp.315-6.

Reynolds, J. and Porter, L. (1998) Melbourne's inner city revival. *Urban Policy and Research*, **16(1)**, pp.63-68.

Royal Commission on Environmental Pollution (1994) *Eighteenth Report: Transport and the Environment*, HMSO, London.

Self, P. (1995) *The Australian Urban and Regional Development Review: What Can it Achieve?*, Urban Research Program Working Paper No.46, Australian National University, Canberra.

Spiller, Gibbons and Swan Pty Ltd. (1998) *The SGS Bulletin*, Urbecon, Sydney.

Stretton, H. (1996) Density, efficiency and equality in Australian Cities, in *The Compact City: A Sustainable Urban Form?* (eds M. Jenks, E. Burton and K. Williams), E & FN Spon, an imprint of Chapman and Hall, London.

Troy, P. (1992) The new feudalism. *Urban Futures*, **2(2)**, pp.36-44.

Troy, P. (1996) Urban consolidation and the family, in *The Compact City: A Sustainable Urban Form?* (eds M. Jenks, E. Burton and K. Williams), E & FN Spon, an imprint of Chapman and Hall, London.

Wettenhall, G. (1994) *Australian Cities and Regions: A National Approach*, Australian Urban and Regional Development Review, Canberra.

Wilkenfeld, G., Faichney, G., Dames and Moore Pty Ltd., and Woodlands and Wetlands Pty Ltd. (1995) *Australia's National Greenhouse Gas Inventory 1988 and 1990: Cross Sectoral Analysis of Emissions*, Department of the Environment, Sport and Territories, Canberra.

Mohammad-Reza Masnavi

The New Millennium and New Urban Paradigm: *The Compact City in Practice*

Breheny, M. (1992a) The compact city: an introduction. *Built Environment*, **18(4)**, pp.241-246.

Breheny, M. (ed.) (1992b) *Sustainable Development and Urban Form*, Pion, London.

CEC (Commission of European Communities) (1990) *Green Paper on the Urban Environment*, COM 90218, CEC, Brussels.

Crookson, M., Clarke, P. and Averley, J. (1996) The compact city and the quality of life, in *The Compact City: A Sustainable Urban Form?* (eds M. Jenks, E. Burton and K. Williams), E & FN Spon, an imprint of Chapman and Hall, London.

DoE (Department of Environment) (1994) *Quality in Town and Country*, HMSO, London.

Elkin, T., McLaren, D. and Hillman, M. (1991) *Reviving the City: Towards Sustainable Urban Development*, Friends of the Earth, London.

Gordon, P., Kumar, A. and Richardson, H. W. (1989) The influence of metropolitan spatial structure on commuting times. *Journal of Urban Economics*, **26**, pp.138-149.

Gordon, P., Richardson, H. W. and Jun, M. J. (1991) The commuting paradox: evidence from top twenty cities. *Journal of the American Planning Association*, **47(4)**, p.416.

Greene, J. and D'Oliviera, M. (1989) *Learning to Use Statistical Tests in Psychology: A Student's Guide*, Open University, Milton Keynes.

Handy, S. L. (1992) Regional versus local accessibility: neo-traditional development and its implications for non-work travel. *Built Environment*, **18(4)**, pp.253-267.

Hillman, M. (1996) In favour of the compact city, in *The Compact City: A Sustainable Urban Form?* (eds M. Jenks, E. Burton and K. Williams), E & FN Spon, an imprint of Chapman and Hall, London.

Jenks, M., Burton, E. and Williams, K. (eds) (1996) *The Compact City: A Sustainable Urban Form?*, E & FN Spon, an imprint of Chapman and Hall, London.

Masnavi, M. R. (1998a) Sustainable development, the compact city and the sprawl city, in *The Proceedings of the First International Conference on Buildings and the Environment*, in Asia, CIB, TG8 – Environmental Assessment Methods Intl. Council for Building Research Studies and Documentation, Singapore.

Masnavi, M. R. (1998b) Sustainability of the compact city: can it be a new paradigm for urban planning in the new millennium?, in *The 20th Century Urban Planning Experience, Proceedings of the 8th International Planning History Conference* (4th Australian Planning/Urban History), 15-18 July 1998, University of New South Wales, Sydney, Australia.

Masnavi, M. R. (1998c) *Urban Sustainability: Compact versus Dispersed in terms of Social Interaction and Patterns of Movement*, unpublished PhD thesis, the Mackintosh School of Architecture, Glasgow University, Glasgow.

Masnavi, M. R., Porteous C. and Lever, W. F. (1997) The relationship between urban form and the pattern of transportation: the case of West Scotland, in *Buildings and the Environment*, The Second International Conference, June 9-12 1997, Paris, France, published by Centre Scientifique et Technique du Batiment, Paris.

Masnavi, M. R. Porteous, C. and Lever, W. F. (1998) 'Quality of life' (QoL) and sustainable development: will the compact city improve the quality of life?, in *The Proceedings of the First International Conference on Quality of Life in Cities: Issues and Perspectives*, 4-8 March 1988, University of Singapore, Singapore.

Newman, P. W. and Kenworthy, J. R. (1992) Is there a role for physical planners? *Journal of the American Planning Association*, **58(3)**, pp.353-361.

Scoffham, E. and Vale, B. (1996) How compact is sustainable: how sustainable is compact?, in *The Compact City: A Sustainable Urban Form?* (eds M. Jenks, E. Burton and K. Williams), E & FN Spon, an imprint of Chapman and Hall, London.

Strathclyde Regional Council (1994) *Strathclyde Social Trends, No. 3*, Chief Executive's Department, Glasgow.

Strathclyde Regional Council (1995) *Strathclyde Social Trends, No. 4*, Chief Executive's Department, Glasgow.

Troy, P. N. (1996) Urban consolidation and the family, in *The Compact City: A Sustainable Urban Form?* (eds M. Jenks, E. Burton and K. Williams), E & FN Spon, an imprint of Chapman and Hall, London.

UK Government (1994) Sustainable Development: The UK Strategy, Cm 2426, HMSO, London.

Urban Villages Group (1992) *Urban Villages: A Concept for Creating Mixed-Use Urban Developments on a Sustainable Scale*, Urban Villages Group, London.

Peter Newton, Selwyn Tucker and Michael Ambrose
Housing Form, Energy Use and Greenhouse Gas Emissions

ABS (Australian Bureau of Statistics) (1995) *Catalogue No. 8731.0*, ABS, Canberra.

ABS (Australian Bureau of Statistics) (1996) *CData 1996* (CD-ROM), ABS, Canberra.

AGO (Australian Greenhouse Office) (1998) What is my household's greenhouse impact? Australian Greenhouse Office web page, http://www.greenhouse.gov.au/pubs/gwci/page22.html.

Berry, M. (1996) Housing demand and housing outcomes in Australia: past developments and future possibilities, in *Globalization and Housing Industry* (eds H. S. Chung and D. S. Lee), Korea Housing Institute, Nanam Publishing, Seoul, Korea.

Burke, T., Newton, P. and Wulff, M. (1990) Australia, in *International Handbook of Housing Policies and Practices* (ed. D. Van Vliet), Greenwood Press, New York.

Green Street Joint Venture (1991) *Attitudes to Housing in Australia: A Summary of the Findings*, Government Printer, Canberra.

Government of Victoria (1995) *The Good Design Guide for Medium Density Housing*, Government of Victoria, Melbourne.

King, R. (1981) *Melbourne Housing Study Interim Report*, MMBW (Melbourne Metropolitan Board of Works), Ministry of Housing Victoria and MBA (Master Builders Association), Victoria.

Leyshon, P. (1992) Housing attitudes and consumer behaviour. *Proceedings of the National Housing Conference: Housing for Better Urban Environments*, Canberra, June.

Maddocks, D. and PA Consulting Services Pty Ltd. (1978) *Exploring the Housing Attitudes of Future Home-Buyers in Four Australian Cities*, project for the Committee of Inquiry into Housing Costs, PA Consulting Services Pty Ltd., Melbourne.

NatHERS (1998) *Nationwide House Energy Rating Scheme Software for Windows*, Version s.2, CSIRO (Commonwealth Scientific and Industrial Research Organisation), Australia Division of Building, Construction and Engineering, Melbourne.

Troy, P. (1996) *The Perils of Urban Consolidation*, The Federation Press, Sydney.

Tucker, S. N. (1996) Minimising environmental impact of buildings by design: a case study. *Proceedings of CII*

Annual Conference, Sydney, 11-12 April.

Tucker, S. N. and Rahilly, M. (1993) *Predicting Housing Maintenance Costs*, Report AM1/93, National Public Works Council, Canberra.

Tucker, S. N., Ambrose, M. D. and Mackley, C. (1998) A 3D CAD model of embodied energy for assessment of sustainable construction. *Proceedings of CIB World Building Congress: Construction and the Environment*, Gavle, 7-12 June, pp.1,919-1,926.

Tucker, S. N., Salomonsson, G. D., Treloar, G. J., MacSporran, C. and Flood, J. (1993) *Environmental Impact of Energy Embodied in Building: Main Report*, DBCE DOC 93/39M, CSIRO (Commonwealth Scientific and Industrial Research Organisation) Australia Division of Building, Construction and Engineering, Highett.

Woodhead, W. D. (1994) The economics of higher density housing. *Urban Futures*, **3(4)/4(1)**, pp.43-49.

Wulff, M. G. (1992) *An Overview of Australian Locational Preference Studies: Choices and Constraints in the Housing Market*, National Housing Strategy, Canberra.

Marina Alberti
Urban Form and Ecosystem Dynamics: *Empirical Evidence and Practical Implications*

Alberti, M. (in press) Urban patterns and environmental performance: what do we know? *Journal of Planning Education and Research*.

Allan, J., Erickson, D. and Fay, J. (1997) The influence of catchment land use on stream integrity across multiple spatial scales. *Freshwater Biology*, **37**, pp.149-161.

Beissinger, S. and Osborne, D. (1982) Effects of urbanisation on avian community organization. *Condor*, **84**, pp.75-83.

Blair, R. and Launer, A. (1997) Butterfly diversity and human land use: species assemblages along an urban gradient. *Biological Conservation*, **80**, pp.113-125.

Blair, W. and Walsberg, G. (1996) Thermal effects of radiation and wind on a small bird and implications for microsite selection. *Ecology*, **77(7)**, p.2228(9).

Bolger, D., Alberts, A., Sauvajot, R., Potenza, P., McCalvin, C., Tran, D., Mazzoni, S. and Soulé, M. (1997) Response of rodents to habitat fragmentation in coastal Southern California. *Ecological Applications*, **7(2)**, pp.552-563.

Bolger, D., Alberts, A. and Soulé, M. (1991) Occurrence patterns of bird species in habitat fragments: sampling, extinction, and nested species subsets. *American-Naturalist*, **137(2)**, p.155(12).

Bolger, D., Scott, T. and Rotenberry, J. (1997) Breeding bird abundance in an urbanizing landscape in coastal Southern California. *Conservation Biology*, **11(2)**, pp.406-421.

Bond, R. R. (1957) Ecological distribution of breeding birds in the upland forests of Southern Wisconsin. *Ecological Monographs*, **27**, pp.351-384.

Bowers, M. and Breland, B. (1996) Foraging of gray squirrels on an urban-rural gradient: use of the GUD to assess anthropogenic impact. *Ecological Applications*, **6(4)**, pp.1135-1142.

Boyden, S., Millar, S., Newcombe, K. and O'Neill, B. (1981) *The Ecology of a City and its People: The Case of Hong Kong*, Australian National University Press, Canberra.

Breheny, M. (ed.) (1992) *Sustainable development and Urban Form*, Pion, London.

Brothers, T. and Spingarn, A. (1992) Forest fragmentation and alien plant invasion of central Indiana old-growth forests. *Conservation Biology*, **6**, pp.91-100.

Brittingham, M. and Temple, S. (1983) Have cowbirds caused forest songbirds to decline? *BioScience*, **33**, pp.31-35.

Chen, J., Franklin, J. and Spies, T. (1992) Vegetation responses to edge environments in old-growth Douglas-fir forests. *Ecological Applications*, **2**, pp.387-396.

Clergeau, P., Savard, J., Mennechez, G. and Falardeau, G. (1998) Bird abundance and diversity along an urban-rural gradient: a comparative study between two cities on different continents. *The Condor*, **100(3)**, pp.413-425.

Collinge, S. (1996) Ecological consequences of habitat fragmentation: implications for landscape architecture and planning. *Landscape and Urban Planning*, **36**, pp.50-77.

Dickman, C. (1987) Habitat fragmentation and invertebrate species richness in an urban environment. *Journal of Applied Ecology*, **24**, pp.337-351.

Douglas, I. (1983) *The Urban Environment*, Edward Arnold, Baltimore, MD.

Faeth, S. and Kane, T. (1978) Urban biogeography: city parks as islands for Diptera and Coleoptera. *Oecologia*, **32**, pp.127-133.

Fahrig, L. and Merriam, H. (1985) Habitat patch connectivity and population survival. *Ecology*, **66**, pp.1762-1768.

Fahrig, L. and Paloheimo, J. (1988) Effect of spatial arrangement of habitat patches on local population size. *Ecology*, **69(2)**, pp.468-475.

Forman, R. (1995) *Land Mosaics: The Ecology of Landscapes and Regions*, Cambridge University Press, Cambridge, England.

Forman, R. and Godron, M. (1981) Patches and structural components for a landscape ecology. *BioScience*, **31**, pp.733-40.

Forman, R. and Godron, M. (1986) *Landscape Ecology*, John Wiley and Sons, New York.

Frissel, C., Liss, W., Warren, C. and Hurley, M. (1986) A hierarchical framework for stream habitat classification: viewing streams in a watershed context. *Environmental Management*, **10(2)**, pp.199-214.

Germaine, S., Rosenstock, S., Schweinsburg, R. and Richardson, S. (1998) Relationships among breeding birds, habitat, and residential development in greater Tucson, Arizona. *Ecological Applications*, **8(3)**, pp.680-691.

Godron, M. and Forman, R. (1982) Landscape modification and changing ecological characteristics, in *Disturbance and Ecosystems: Components of Response* (eds H. Mooney and M. Gordon), Springer-Verlag, New York.

Gregory, S. V., Swanson, F. J., McKee, W. A. and Cummins, K. W. (1991) An ecosystem perspective of riparian zones. *BioScience*, **41**, pp.541-51.

Gustafson, E. (1998) Quantifying landscape spatial patterns: what is the state of art? *Ecosystems*, **1**, pp.143-156.

Harris, L. (1984) *The Fragmented Forest: Application of Island Biogeography Principles to Preservation of Biotic Diversity*, University of Chicago Press, Chicago.

Hawikins, C., Kershner, J., Bisson, P., Bryant, M., Decker, L., Gregory, S., McCullough, D., Overton, C., Reeves, G., Steedman, R. and Young, M. (1993) A hierarchical approach to classifying stream habitat features. *Fisheries*, **18(6)**, pp.3-10.

Howard, E. (1898) *Garden Cities of Tomorrow*, second edition, 1902, Sonnenschein, London.

Jenks, M., Burton, E. and Williams, K. (eds) (1996) *The Compact City: A Sustainable Urban Form?*, E & FN Spon, an imprint of Chapman and Hall, London.

Jo, H. K. and McPherson, G. (1995) Carbon storage and flux in urban residential greenspace. *Journal of Environmental Management*, **45(2)**, pp.109-25.

Karr, J. (1981) Assessment of biotic integrity using fish communities. *Fisheries*, **6(6)**, pp.21-27.

Karr, J. and Dudley, D. (1981) Ecological perspective on water quality goals. *Environmental Management*, **5**, pp.55-68.

Kaufman, M. and Marsh, W. (1997) Hydro-ecological implications of edge cities. *Landscape and Urban Planning*, **36**, pp.277-290.

Kerans, B. and Karr, J. (1994) A Benthic Index of Biotic Integrity (B-IBI) for rivers of the Tennessee Valley. *Ecological Applications*, **4**, pp.768-85.

Lammert, M. and Allan, D. (1999) Assessing biotic integrity of streams: effects of scale in measuring the influence of land use/cover and habitat structure on fish and microinvertebrates. *Environmental Management*, **23(2)**, pp.257-270.

Leopold, L. (1968) *Hydrology for Urban Planning*, Geological Survey Circular 554, US Governmental Printing Office, Washington DC.

Levenson, J. (1981) Woodlots as biogeographic islands in southern Wisconsin, in *Forest Island Dynamics in Man-Dominated Landscapes* (eds R. Burgess and D. Sharpe), Springer-Verlag, New York.

Levins, R. (1969) Some demographic and genetic consequences of environmental heterogeneity for biological control. *Bulletin of Entomological Society of America*, **15**, pp.237-240.

Lynch, K. (1961) The patterns of the metropolis. *Daedalus*, **90(1)**, pp.79-98.

Lynch, K. (1981) *Good City Form*, MIT Press, Cambridge, MA.

Lynch, J. and Whigham, D. (1984) Effects of forest fragmentation on breeding birds communities in Maryland, USA. *Biological Conservation*, **28**, pp.287-324.

MacArthur, R. and Wilson, E. (1967) *The Theory of Island Biogeography*, Princeton University Press, Princeton, New Jersey.

Marzluff, J., Gehlbach, F. and Manuwal, D. (1998) Urban environments: influences on avifauna and challenges for the avian conservationist, in *Avian Conservation: Research and Management* (eds J. Marzluff and R.

Sallabanks), Island Press, Washington.

Matthiae, P. and Stearns, F. (1981) Mammals in forest islands in southeastern Wisconsin, in *Forest Island Dynamics in Man-Dominated Landscapes* (eds R. Burgess and D. Sharpe), Springer-Verlag, New York.

McDonnell, M., Pickett, S., Groffman, P., Bohlen, P., Pouyat, R., Zipperer, W., Parmelee, R., Carreiro, M. and Medley, K. (1997) Ecosystem processes along an urban-to-rural gradient. *Urban Ecosystems*, **1**, pp.21-36.

McPherson, E. G., Nowak, D. J. *et al.* (1994) *Chicago's Urban Forest Ecosystem: Results of the Chicago Urban Forest Climate Project*, Northeastern Forest Experiment Station, Radnor, PA.

Moore, N. and Hooper, M. (1975) On the number of bird species in British woods. *Biological Conservation*, **8**, pp.239-250.

Murcia, C. (1995) Edge effects in fragmented forests: implications for conservation. *Trends Ecological Evolution*, **10**, pp.58-62.

Naiman, R. J. and Decamps, H. (eds) (1990) *The Ecology and Management of Aquatic Ecotones: Man and the Biosphere Series, Vol. 4*, UNESCO, Paris.

Newmark, W. (1987) A land-bridge island perspective on mammalian extinction in western North American parks. *Nature*, **325(6103)**, pp.430-32.

O'Neill, R., DeAngelis, D., Waide, D. and Allen, T. (1986) *A Hierarchical Concept of Ecosystems*, Princeton University Press, Princeton, NJ.

Owens, S. (1984) Energy demand and spatial structure, in *Energy Policy and Land Use Planning* (eds D. Cope, P. Hills and P. James), Pergamon Press, Oxford.

Owens, S. (1986) *Energy, Planning and Urban Form*, Pion, London.

Owens, S. amd Rickaby, P. (1992) Settlements and energy revisited. *Built Environment*, **18(4)**, pp.247-252.

Pickett, S. and Cadenasso, M. (1995) Landscape ecology: spatial heterogeneity in ecological systems. *Science*, **269**, pp.331-334.

Ranney, J., Bruner, M. and Levenson, J. (1981) The importance of edge in the structure and dynamics of forest islands, in *Forest Island Dynamics in Man-Dominated Landscapes* (eds R. Burgess and D. Sharpe), Springer-Verlag, New York.

Richard, C., Host, G. and Arthur, J. (1996) Identification of predominant environmental factors structuring stream macroinvertebrate communities within a large agricultural catchment. *Freshwater Biology*, **29**, pp.285-294.

Risser, P. G., Karr, J. R. and Forman, R. T. (1984) *Landscape Ecology: Directions and Approaches*, Special Publication No. 2, Illinois Natural History Survey, Champaign.

Robbins, C., Dawson, D. and Dowell, B. (1989) Habitat area requirements of breeding forest birds of the Middle Atlantic States. *Wildlife Monographs*, **103**, pp.1-34.

Rolando, A., Pulcher, G. and Giuso, A. (1997) Avian community structure along an urbanization gradient. *Italian Journal of Zoology*, **64**, pp.341-349.

Rosenberg, D. K., Noon, B. R. and Meslow, E. C. (1987) Biological corridors: form, function and efficacy. *BioScience*, **47(10)**, pp.677-88.

Ruszczyk, A. (1996) Spatial patterns in pupal mortality in urban palm caterpillars. *Oecologia*, **107**, pp.356-363.

Schlosser, I. (1991) Stream fish ecology: a landscape perspective. *BioScience* **41(10)**, pp.704-712.

Soulé, M., Bolger, D., Albert, A., Wright, J., Sorice, M. and Hill, S. (1988) Reconstructed dynamics of rapid extinsions of chaparral-requiring birds in urban habitat islands. *Conservation Biology*, **2(1)**, pp.75-92.

Tilghman, N. (1987) Characteristics of urban woodlands affecting breeding bird diversity and abundance. *Landscape and Urban Planning*, **14**, pp.481-495.

Turner, II B., Skole, D., Sanderson, S., Fischer, G., Fresco, L. and Leemans, R. (1995) *Land-Use and Land-Cover Change Science/Research Plan,* IGBP Report No. 35 and HDP Report No. 7; *The International Geosphere-Biosphere Programme: A Study of Global Change (IGBP) and The Human Dimensions of Global Environmental Change Programme (HDP)*, Stockholm and Geneva, Science/Research Plan, IGBP Report No. 35 and HDP Report No. 7.

Turner, M. (1989) Landscape ecology: the effect of pattern on process. *Annual Review Ecological Systems*, **20**, pp.171-197.

Turner, M. and Gardner, R. (eds) (1991) *Quantitative Methods in Landscape Ecology*, Ecological Studies, Springer, New York.

Vizyova, A. (1986) Urban woodlots as islands for land invertebrates: a preliminary attempt in estimating the barrier effect of urban structural units. *Ecology*, **5**, pp.407-419.

Wear, D., Turner, M. and Naiman, R. (1998) Land cover along an urban–rural gradient: implications for water quality. *Ecological Applications*, **8(3)**, pp.619-630.

Webb, N. and Hopkins, P. (1984) Invertebrate diversity on fragmented Calluna heathland. *Journal of Applied Ecology*, **4**, pp.569-580.

Whitcomb, R., Robbins, C., Lynch, J., Whitcomb, B., Klimkiewicz, K. and Bystrak, D. (1981) Effects of forest fragmentation on avifauna of the eastern deciduous forest, in *Forest Island Dynamics in Man-Dominated Landscapes* (eds R. Burgess and D. Sharpe), Springer-Verlag, New York.

White, R. and Whitney, J. (1992) Cities and the environment: an overview, in *Sustainable Cities: Urbainization and the Environment in International Perspective* (eds R. Stren, R. White and J. Whitney), Westview Press, Oxford.

Wolman, M. G. (1967) A cycle of sedimentation and erosion in urban river channels. *Geografiska Annaler, Series A: Physical Geography*, **49(2-4)**, pp.385-395.

Ernie Scoffman and Teresa Marat-Mendes
The 'Ground Rules' of Sustainable Urban Form

Abercrombie, P. (1944) *Greater London Plan*, London County Council, London.

Architectural Design (1971) Pollards Hill, Merton: Architectural Design Project Award 1968, **71(10)**, pp.613-18.

Architectural Design (1974) Milton Keynes Development Corporation, central Milton Keynes: central area housing, **74(8)**, pp.515-26, and **74(10)**, pp.660-5.

Architectural Design (1977) MacCormac and Jamieson, AD Profiles 8, British Architecture, **77(9/10)**, pp.691-3 and p.701.

Architects' Journal (1974) Eastfields, Acacia Avenue, Mitcham, housing study: DoE Housing Design Awards, **159**, pp.177-9.

Architectural Review (1971) Housing at Merton, **149(890)**, pp.204-6.

Barnett, W. and Winskell, C. (1977) *A Study in Conservation*, Oriel Press, Newcastle upon Tyne.

Beresford, M. W. (1967) *New Towns of the Middle Ages*, Lutterworth, London.

CML (Camera Municipal de Lisboa) (1987) *Planta de Lisboa, escala 1:2000*, CML, Lisbon.

Davey, P. (1980) Perimeter planning and its evolution. *Architectural Review*, **167(998)**, pp.207-20.

França, J. A. (1965) *Lisboa Pombalina e o Iluminismo*, Livros Horizonte, Lisbon.

GEO, CML (Gabinete de Estudos Olisiponenses, Camera Municipal de Lisboa) – CNIG (Centro Nacional de Informacao Geografica, Ministerio do Planeamento e da Administracao do Territorio) (1993) *Atlas de Lisboa: A Cidade no Espaco e no Tempo*, Contexto Editora.

Habraken, N. J. (1972) *Supports: An Alternative to Mass Housing*, Architectural Press, London (first published 1961, as *De Dragers en de Mensen*, Scheltema and Holkema, Amsterdam).

Howard, E. (1945) *Garden Cities of Tomorrow*, Faber, London (first published 1898, as *Tomorrow, a Peaceful Path to Real Reform*, Swan Sonnenschein, London).

MacCormac, R. (1978) Housing and the dilemma of style. *Architectural Review*, **163**, p.205.

March, L. (1967) Homes beyond the fringe. *Architects' Journal*, **146**, pp.156-8.

March, L. (1972) An examination of layouts. *Built Environment*, **1(6)**, p.378.

Martin, L. and March, L. (1966) *Land Use and Built Form*, Cambridge Research, April.

Martin, L. and March, L. (1972) *Urban Space and Structures*, Cambridge University Press, Cambridge.

Moholy-Nagy, S. (1968) *Matrix of Man*, Pall Mall Press, London.

Morris, A. E. J. (1979) *History of Urban Form*, George Godwin, London.

Mumford, L. (1945) Introductory essay, in *Garden Cities of Tomorrow* (ed. E. Howard), Faber, London.

Muthesius, S. (1982) *The English Terraced House*, Yale University Press, New Haven, USA.

Rasmussen, S. E. (1980) Open-plan city. *Architectural Review*, **168**, p.141.

Scott-Moncrieff, G. (1965) *Edinburgh*, Oliver and Boyd, Edinburgh and London.

Summerson, J. (1969) *Georgian London*, Penguin Books, London.

Tarragó, S. (1996) *Cerdà Ciudad y Territorio, una Visión de Futuro*, Fundació Catalana per la Recerca, Sociedad Editorial Electa España, Barcelona.

Turner, J. F. C. (1976) Principles for housing. *Architectural*

Design, **66**, p.101.

Unwin, R. (1912) *Nothing Gained by Overcrowding*, P. S. King, London.

Vernez-Moudon, A. (1986) *Built for Change; Neighbourhood Architecture in San Francisco*, MIT Press, Cambridge, Massachusetts, and London.

Youngson, A. J. (1966) *The Making of Classical Edinburgh*, Edinburgh University Press, Edinburgh.

Part 2: Urban Form and Transport: New Dimensions

Peter Newman and Jeff Kenworthy
Sustainable Urban Form: *The Big Picture*

Bachels, M., Newman, P. and Kenworthy, J. (1998) *Indicators of Urban Transport Efficiency in New Zealand's Main Cities: An International City Comparison of Transport, Land Use and Economic Indicators*, a Report for the Canterbury Regional Council, Christchurch City Council, Wellington Regional Council, Auckland City Council, Auckland Regional Council, Landcare Research, and the Energy Efficiency and Conservation Authority. Christchurch, October.

Beimborn, E. and Rabinowitz, H., with Gugliotta, P., Mrotek, C. and Yan, S. (1991) *Guidelines for Public Transport Sensitive Suburban Land Use Design*, US Department of Transportation Report, DOT-T-91-13, Washington DC.

Bernick, M. and Cervero, R. (1997) *Public Transport Villages in the 21st Century*, McGraw Hill, New York.

Brotchie, J., Batty, M., Blakely, E. and Hall, P. (1995) *Cities in Competition: Productive and Sustainable Cities for the 21st Century*, Cheshire, Melbourne.

Calthorpe Associates (1990) *Public Transport-Oriented Development Design Guidelines*, Calthorpe Associates, Sacramento County Planning and Community Development Department, November.

Calthorpe, P. (1993) *The Next American Metropolis: Ecology and Urban Form*, Princeton Architectural Press, New Jersey.

Campbell, C. J. (1991) *The Golden Century of Oil 1950-2050: The Depletion of a Resource*, Kluwer Academic Publishers, Dordrecht, The Netherlands.

Castells, M. (1989) *The Informational City: Information Technology, Economic Restructuring and the Urban Regional Process*, Blackwell, Oxford.

Castells, M. and Hall, P. (1994) *Technopoles of the World*, Routledge, London.

Center for Livable Communities (1996) *Participation Tools for Better Land Use Planning: Techniques and Case Studies*, Local Government Commission, Sacramento.

Cervero, R. (1986) Urban public transport in Canada: integration and innovation at its best. *Transportation Quarterly*, **40(3)**, pp.293-316.

Cervero. R. (1998) *The Public Transport Metropolis: A Global Inquiry*, Island Press, Washington DC.

Energy Victoria, Environment Protection Authority, Department of Infrastructure and Energy Research and Development Corporation (1996) *Urban Villages Project: Encouraging Sustainable Urban Form*, Summary Report, Government of Victoria, August.

Gehl, J. (1987) *Life Between Buildings*, Van Nostrand Reinhold, New York.

Gordon, P. and Richardson, H. W. (1989) Gasoline consumption and cities: a reply. *Journal of the American Planning Association*, **55(3)**, pp.342-345.

Hall, P. (1997) Reflections past and future in planning cities. *Australian Planner*, **34(2)**, pp.83-89.

Katz, P. (1994) *The New Urbanism: Toward an Architecture of Community*, McGraw Hill, New York.

Kenworthy, J. R. and Laube, F. B. with Newman, P., Barter, P., Raad, T., Poboon, C. and Guia, B. (Jr) (1999) *An International Sourcebook of Automobile Dependence in Cities 1960-1990*, University Press of Colorado, Boulder (in press).

Naisbett, J. (1994) *Global Paradox: The Bigger the World Economy, the More Powerful its Smaller Players*, Allen & Unwin, Sydney.

Newman, P. and Kenworthy, J. (1989) *Cities and Automobile Dependence: An International Sourcebook*, Gower, Aldershot.

Newman P. and Kenworthy J. (1999) *Sustainability and Cities: Overcoming Automobile Dependence*, Island Press, Washington DC.

Ohmae, K. (1990) *The Borderless World*, Fontana, London.

Rabinowitz, H., Beimborn, E., Mrotek, C., Yan, S. and Gugliotta, P. (1991) *The New Suburb*, US Department of Transportation, Report DOT-T-91-12, Washington DC.

Rainbow, R. and Tan, H. (1993) *Meeting the Demand for Mobility*, Selected Papers, Shell International, London.

Sassen, S. (1994) *Cities and the World Economy*, Pineforge Press, Thousand Oaks, California.

Troy, P. N. (1996) *The Perils of Urban Consolidation*, The Federation Press, Leichardt, Sydney.

Webber, M. (1963) Order in diversity: community without propinquity, in *Cities and Space: The Future Use of Urban Land* (ed. L. Wingo), John Hopkins Press, Baltimore.

Webber, M. (1964) The urban place and the non-place urban realm, in *Explorations into Urban Structure* (authors M. Webber, J. Dyckman, D. Foley, A. Guttenberg, W. Wheaton and C. Bauer Wurster), University of Pennsylvania Press, Philadelphia.

Webber, M. (1968) The post city age. *Daedulus*, **97(4)**, pp.1093-1099.

Willoughby, K. (1994) The 'local milieux' of knowledge based industries, in *Cities in Competition* (eds J. Brotchie, P. Newton, P. Hall, E. Blakeley and M. Battie), Cheshire, Melbourne.

Winger, A. R. (1997) Finally: a withering away of cities? *Futures*, **29(3)**, pp.251-256.

David Simmonds, and Denvil Coombe
The Transport Implications of Alternative Urban Forms

Barton, H. (1992) City transport: strategies for sustainability, in *Sustainable Development and Urban Form* (ed. M.

Breheny), Pion, London.

Brotchie, J. F. (1984) Technological change and urban form. *Environment and Planning A*, **16**, pp.583-596.

Brotchie, J. F. (1986) Technological change and urban development, in *Advances in Urban Systems Modelling* (eds B. Hutchinson and M. Batty), Elsevier, Amsterdam.

Coombe, D., Bates, J., Guest, P., Le Masurier, P. and MacLennan, C. (1997) Study of parking and traffic demand: 1. The research programme. *Traffic Engineering and Control*, **38(2)**, pp.62-67.

De la Barra, T. (1989) *Integrated Land Use and Transport Modelling: Decision Chains and Hierarchies*, Cambridge University Press, Cambridge.

DoE and DoT (Department of the Environment and Department of Transport) (1994) *Planning Policy Guidance 13: Transport*, HMSO, London.

ECOTEC/TPA (Transportation Planning Associates) (1993) *Reducing Transport Emissions through Planning*, Report to the Department of the Environment and Department of Transport, HMSO, London.

Farthing, S., Winter, J. and Coombes, T. (1996) Travel behaviour and local accessibility to services and facilities, in *The Compact City: A Sustainable Urban Form?* (eds M. Jenks, E. Burton and K. Williams), E & FN Spon, an imprint of Chapman and Hall, London.

Hunt, J. D. and Simmonds, D. C. (1993) Theory and application of an integrated land-use and transport modelling framework. *Environment and Planning B*, **20**, pp.221-244.

Jenks, M., Burton, E. and Williams, K. (eds) (1996) *The Compact City: A Sustainable Urban Form?*, E & FN Spon, an imprint of Chapman and Hall, London.

Mackett, R. L. (1990) The systematic application of the LILT model to Dortmund, Leeds and Tokyo. *Transport Reviews*, **10**, pp.323-338.

Mackett, R. L. (1991) LILT and MEPLAN: a comparative analysis of land-use and transport policies for Leeds. *Transport Reviews*, **11**, pp.131-154.

May, A., Timms, P., Rand, L. and Toffolo, S. (1997) OPTIMA – optimisation of policies for transport integration in metropolitan areas: a review of the results for nine European cities, *Proceedings of Seminar E, 25th European Transport Forum*, pp.161-172, PTRC, London.

MVA Consultancy, David Simmonds Consultancy and the Institute for Transport Studies, University of Leeds (1996) *Transport Effects of Urban Land-Use Change*, Report to the Department of Transport.

Paulley, N. J. and Webster, F. V. (1991) Overview of an international study to compare models and evaluate land-use and transport policies. *Transport Reviews*, **11**, pp.197-222.

Rickaby, P. A. (1987) Six settlement patterns compared. *Environment and Planning B*, **14**, pp.193-223.

Rickaby, P. A., Steadman, J. P. and Barrett, M. (1992) Patterns of land use in English towns: implications for energy use and carbon dioxide emissions, in *Sustainable Development and Urban Form* (ed. M. Breheny), Pion, London.

Roberts, M. and Simmonds, D. C. (1997) A strategic modelling approach for urban transport policy development. *Traffic Engineering and Control*, **38**, pp.377-384.

Shepherd, S. P., Emberger, G., Johansen, K. and Jarvi-Nykanen, T. (1997) OPTIMA – optimisation of policies for transport integration in metropolitan areas: a review of the method applied to nine European cities, *Proceedings of Seminar E, 25th European Transport Forum*, pp.149-160, PTRC, London.

Simmonds, D. C. and Coombe, D. (1997) Transport effects of urban land-use change. *Traffic Engineering and Control*, **38**, pp.660-665.

Still, B. G. (1992) *Reducing Transport Impacts via Land-Use Patterns*, unpublished MSc thesis, Department of Civil Engineering, University of Leeds, Leeds.

Webster, F. V., Bly, P. and Paulley, N. J. (1988) *Urban Land-Use and Transport Interaction: Policies and Models*, Report on Phase 1 of the International Study Group on Land-use/Transport Interaction, Avebury, Aldershot.

Wegener, M. (1995) *Reduction of CO_2 Emissions of Transport by Reorganisation of Urban Activities*, Paper presented to the World Conference on Transport Research, Sydney.

Mats Reneland
Accessibility in Swedish Towns

Boverket (1996) *Den Måttfulla Staden*, Boverket, Karlskrona.

Reneland, M. (1998a) *Begreppet Tillgänglighet*, STACTH 1998:4, Stads - och trafikplanering, Chalmers Tekniska Högskola, Göteborg.

Reneland, M. (1998b) *Kollektivtrafikens Effektivitet*, STACTH 1998:8, Stads - och trafikplanering, Chalmers Tekniska Högskola, Göteborg.

Reneland, M. (1998c) *Befolkningens Avstånd till Service*, STACTH 1998:5, Stads - och trafikplanering, Chalmers Tekniska Högskola, Göteborg.

Reneland, M. (1998d) *Elevers Avstånd till Närmaste Skola*, STACTH 1998:6, Stads - och trafikplanering, Chalmers Tekniska Högskola, Göteborg.

Reneland, M. (1998e) *Pensionärers Avstånd till Service*, STACTH 1998:7, Stads - och trafikplanering, Chalmers Tekniska Högskola, Göteborg.

Reneland, M. and Hagson, A. (1994) *Analys av Boendetäthet som Förutsättning för Kollektivtrafikens Servicenivå och Kostnad, Utveckling av en Modell med Exemplifiering från 51 Svenska Tätorter*, STACTH 1994:2, Stads - och trafikplanering, Chalmers Tekniska Högskola, Göteborg.

SCB (1984) *Folk - och bostadsräkningen 1980, Del 2:3 Tätorternas areal och Folkmängd Utveckling mellan 1975 och 1980*, Liberförlag, Stockholm.

SCB (1996), *Tätorter 1995*, Statistiska meddelanden Be-16-SM-9601, Statistiska Centralbyrån, Stockholm.

Statens Planverk (1972) *Bostadens grannskap - Råd och anvisningar för planering*, Rapport 24 remisshandling, Statens Planverk, Stockholm.

Statens Planverk (1982) *TRÅD - allmänna råd för planering av stadens trafiknät*, Statens Planverk, Stockholm.

Uyen-Phan Van and Martyn Senior
The Contribution of Mixed Land Uses to Sustainable Travel in Cities

Aitkin, M., Anderson, T., Francis, B. and Hinde, J. (1989) *Statistical Modelling in GLIM*, Clarendon Press, Oxford.

Aldous, T. (1992) *Urban Villages*, Urban Villages Group, London.

Banister, D. (1997) Reducing the need to travel. *Environment and Planning B*, **24**, pp.437-439.

Boarnet, M. G. and Sarmiento, S. (1998) Can land-use policy really affect travel behaviour? A study of the link between non-work travel and land-use characteristics. *Urban Studies*, **35(7)**, pp.1155-1169.

Breheny, M. (1995) Counterurbanisation and sustainable urban forms, in *Cities in Competition* (eds J. Brotchie, M. Batty, E. Blakely, P. Hall and P. Newton), Longman Australia, Melbourne.

Cervero, R. (1996) Mixed land uses and commuting: evidence from the American Housing Survey. *Transportation Research A*, **30(5)**, pp.361-377.

Cervero, R. and Kockelman, K. (1997) Travel demand and the 3Ds: density, diversity and design. *Transportation Research D*, **2(3)**, pp.199-219.

Crane, R. and Crepeau, R. (1998) Does neighbourhood design influence travel? A behavioural analysis of travel diary and GIS data. *Transportation Research D*, **3(4)**, pp.225-238.

DETR (Department of the Environment, Transport and the Regions) (1998) *A New Deal for Transport: Better for Everyone,* The Government's White Paper on the Future of Transport, Cm3950, The Stationery Office, London.

DoE (Department of the Environment) (1997) *Planning Policy Guidance 1: General Policy and Principles*, The Stationery Office, London.

DoE and DoT (Department of the Environment and Department of Transport) (1994) *Planning Policy Guidance 13: Transport*, The Stationery Office, London.

DoE and DoT (Department of the Environment and Department of Transport) (1995a) *PPG13: A Guide to Better Practice*, The Stationery Office, London.

DoE and DoT (Department of the Environment and Department of Transport) (1995b) *Implementation of PPG13: Interim Report*, Department of the Environment, London.

ECOTEC (1993) *Reducing Transport Emissions Through Planning*, HMSO, London.

Ewing, R., Haliyur, P. and Page, G. W. (1994) Getting around a traditional city, a suburban planned unit development, and everything in between. *Transportation Research Record*, **1466**, pp.53-62.

Frank, L. D. and Pivo, G. (1994) Impacts of mixed use and density on utilisation of three modes of travel: single occupant vehicle, transit and walking. *Transportation Research Record*, **1466**, pp.44-52.

Handy, S. L. (1992) Regional versus local accessibility: neo-traditional development and its implications for non-work travel. *Built Environment*, **18(4)**, pp.253-267.

Handy, S. L. (1996) Methodologies for exploring the link between urban form and travel behaviour.

Transportation Research D, **1(2)**, pp.151-165.

TEST (Transport and Environment Studies) (1991) *Changed Travel – Better World? A Study of Travel Patterns in Milton Keynes and Almere*, TEST, London.

Helena Titheridge, Simon Hall and David Banister
Assessing the Sustainability of Urban Development Policies

AGI (Association for Geographic Information) (1995) *Local Government GIS Survey*, AGI, London.

Ahlvik, P., Eggleston, S., Gorißen Hassel, D., Hickman, A., Joumard, R., Ntziachristos, L., Rijkeboer, R., Samaras, Z. and Zierock, K. (1997) *COPERT II: Computer Programme to Calculate Emissions from Road Transport: Methodology and Emission Factors*, Final Draft Report, European Environment Agency, Copenhagen.

Banister, D. (1992) Energy use, transport and settlement patterns, in *Sustainable Development and Urban Form* (ed. M. Breheny), Pion, London.

Banister, D. and Esteves, R. (1995) *Modelling the Effects of Changes in Public Transport on Fuel Consumption and Emissions*, Working Paper 14, The Bartlett School of Planning, University College, London.

Banister, D., Stead, D. and Watson, S. (1997) *Transport Energy Profiles in Selected Locations in Leicestershire*, UKCEED, Cambridge.

Blowers, A. (ed.) (1993) Planning for Sustainable Development, Town and Country Planning Association Report, Earthscan Publications, London.

Breheny, M., Gent, T. and Lock, D. (1993) *Alternative Settlement Patterns: New Settlements*, Report for the Department of the Environment, HMSO, London.

Commission of the European Communities (1992) *Towards Sustainability: A European Community Programme of Policy and Action in Relation to the Environment and Sustainable Development*, COM 92(23), CEC, Brussels.

Commission of the European Communities (1998) *The Common Transport Policy – Sustainable Mobility: Perspectives of the Future*, COM(1998)716, Final, CEC, Brussels.

DETR (Department of the Environment, Transport and the Regions) (1997) *National Travel Survey 1994/96*, The Stationery Office, London.

Fritsche, U. and Rausch, L. (1993) *Total Emission Model for Integrated Systems (TEMIS): User's Guide for TEMIS Version 2.0*, Oko Institut, Darmstadt/Freiburg.

Mensink, G. (1990) Creating self sufficient cities, in *Proceedings of the PTRC Annual Conference*, London, September.

Owens, S. (1987) The urban future: does energy really matter?, in *Energy and Urban Built Form* (eds D. Hawkes, J. Owers, P. Rickaby and P. Steadman), Butterworth, Sevenoaks.

Owens, S. (1991) *Energy Conscious Planning*, Report prepared for the Council for the Protection of Rural England, London.

Rickaby, P. (1987) Six settlement patterns compared. *Environment and Planning B*, **14**, pp.193-223.

Rickaby, P. (1991) Energy and urban development in an

archetypal English town. *Environment and Planning B*, **18**, pp.153-176.

Titheridge, H., Boyle, G. and Fleming, P. (1996) Development and validation of a computer model for assessing energy demand and supply patterns in the urban environment. *Energy and Environment*, **7(1)**, pp.29-40.

TPK (1996) *Micheldever Quantification of Travel Demand*, Tucker Parry Knowles Partnership, Newbury.

Peter Headicar

The Exploding City Region: *Should It, Can It, Be Reversed?*

Atkins, D., Champion, T., Coombes, M., Dorling, D. and Woodward, R. (1996) *Urban Trends in England: Latest Evidence from the 1991 Census*, HMSO, London.

Banister, D., Watson, S. and Wood, C. (1994) *The Relationship Between Energy Use in Transport and Urban Form*, Working Paper 10, Planning and Development Research Centre, University College, London.

Bibby, P. and Shepherd, J. (1995) *Urbanisation in England: Projections 1991-2016*, HMSO, London.

Breheny, M. (1992) The contradictions of the compact city, in *Sustainable Development and Urban Form* (ed. M. Breheny), Pion, London.

Breheny, M. (1995) Counterurbanisation and sustainable urban forms, in *Cities in Competition Productive and Sustainable Cities for the 21st Century* (eds J. Brotchie, M. Batty, E. Blakely, P. Hall and P. Newton), Longman Australia Pty Ltd., Melbourne.

Breheny, M. and Hall, P. (1996) *The People – Where Will They Go?*, Town and Country Planning Association, London.

Champion, T. and Dorling, D. (1994) Population change for Britain's functional regions 1951-91. *Population Trends*, **77**, p.14.

CEC (Commission of the European Communities) (1990) *Green Paper on the Urban Environment*, CEC, Brussels.

Curtis, C. and Headicar, P. (1994) *The Location of New Residential Development: Its Influence on Car-based Travel (1): Research Design and Methodology*, Working Paper no. 154, School of Planning, Oxford Brookes University, Oxford.

DETR (Department of the Environment, Transport and the Regions) (1997) *National Road Traffic Forecasts (Great Britain) 1997*, The Stationery Office, London.

DoE (Department of the Environment) (1995) *Planning Policy Guidance 2: Green Belts*, HMSO, London.

DoE and DoT (Department of the Environment and Department of Transport) (1994) *Planning Policy Guidance 13: Transport*, HMSO, London.

DoT (Department of Transport) (1996) *National Travel Survey 1993/95*, HMSO, London.

ECOTEC (1993) *Reducing Transport Emissions Through Planning*, HMSO, London.

Graham, D. (1998) *Sustainable Development Locations*, Vale of White Horse District Council, Abingdon.

Hall, P. and Ward, C. (1998) *Sociable Cities: The Legacy of Ebenezer Howard*, John Wiley, Chichester.

Headicar, P. (1997) *Potential Travel Patterns from Upper Heyford*, Report for Oxfordshire County Council, School of Planning, Oxford Brookes University, Oxford.

Headicar, P. and Curtis, C. (1998) The location of new residential development: its influence on car-based travel, in *Transport Policy and the Environment* (ed. D. Banister), E & FN Spon, London.

Higgitt, M. (1998) A *Comparison of Travel Behaviour Between Households on New and Established Residential Developments*, unpublished MSc dissertation, Oxford Brookes University, Oxford.

OPCS (Office of Population Censuses and Surveys) (1992) *1991 Census: Preliminary Report for England and Wales*, OPCS, London.

Owens, S. (1986) *Energy, Planning and Urban Form*, Pion, London.

Oxford Brookes University and WS Atkins Ltd. (1996) *The Land Use Effects of Planning Policy Guidance and Increasing Congestion*, Research Report to UK Department of Transport.

Potter, S. (1996) The passenger trip length 'surge'. *Transportation Planning Systems*, **3(1)**, p.7.

Potter, S. (1997) *Vital Transport Statistics*, Landor, London.

Rickaby, P. (1987) Six settlement patterns compared. *Environment and Planning B*, **14**, pp.193-223.

Webster, B. (1998) *Survey of New Housing Developments in West Oxfordshire*, West Oxfordshire District Council, Witney.

Dominic Stead, Jo Williams and Helena Titheridge

Land Use, Transport and People: *Identifying the Connections*

Balcombe, R. and York, I. (1993) *The Future of Residential Parking*, Transport Research Laboratory Report, Crowthorne.

Banister, D. (1992) Energy use, transport and settlement patterns, in *Sustainable Development and Urban Form* (ed. M. Breheny), Pion, London.

Banister, D. (1997) Reducing the need to travel. *Environment and Planning B*, **24(3)**, pp.437-449.

Banister, D., Watson, S. and Wood, C. (1997) Sustainable cities, transport, energy, and urban form. *Environment and Planning B*, **24(1)**, pp.125-143.

Breheny, M. (1995) Counterurbanisation and sustainable urban forms, in *Cities in Competition Productive and Sustainable Cities for the 21st Century* (eds J. Brotchie, M. Batty, E. Blakely, P. Hall and P. Newton), Longman Australia Pty Ltd., Melbourne.

Cervero, R. (1989) Jobs-housing balancing and regional mobility. *Journal of the American Planning Association*, **55(2)**, pp.136-150.

Cervero, R. (1994) Transit-based housing in California: evidence on ridership impacts. *Transport Policy*, **1(3)**, pp.174-183.

Cervero, R. (1996) Jobs-housing balancing revisited. *Journal of the American Planning Association*, **62(4)**, pp.492-511.

Curtis, C. (1995) Reducing the need to travel: strategic housing location and travel behaviour, in *Reducing the Need to Travel: Some Thoughts on PPG13* (eds J. Earp, P.

Headicar, D. Banister and C. Curtis), *Oxford Planning Monographs,* **1(2)**, pp.29-47.

Damm, D. (1981) Theory and empirical results: a comparison of recent activity-based research, in *Recent Advances in Travel Demand Analysis* (eds P. Jones and S. Carpenter), Gower, Aldershot.

DoE (Department of the Environment) (1994) *Policy Planning Guidance 13: Transport,* HMSO, London.

DETR (Department of the Environment, Transport and the Regions) (1997) *National Travel Survey 1994/96,* The Stationery Office, London.

ECOTEC (1993) *Reducing Transport Emissions Through Land Use Planning,* HMSO, London.

Ewing, R. (1995) Beyond density, mode choice, and single trips. *Transportation Quarterly,* **49(4)**, pp.15-24.

Ewing, R., DeAnna, M. and Li, S-C. (1996) Land use impacts on trip generation rates. *Transportation Research Record,* **1518**, pp.1-6.

Farthing, S., Winter, J. and Coombes, T. (1996) Travel behaviour and local accessibility to services and facilities, in *The Compact City: A Sustainable Urban Form?* (eds M. Jenks, E. Burton and K. Williams), E & FN Spon, an imprint of Chapman and Hall, London.

Flannelly, K. and McLeod, M. (1989) A multivariate analysis of socioeconomic and attitudinal factors predicting commuters' mode of transport. *Bulletin of the Psychonomic Society,* **27(1)**, pp.64-66.

Frank, L. and Pivo, G. (1994) Impacts of mixed use and density on utilization of three modes of travel: single-occupant vehicle, transit, and walking. *Transportation Research Record,* **1466**, pp.44-52.

Giuliano, G. and Small, K. (1993) Is the journey to work explained by urban structure? *Urban Studies,* **30(9)**, pp.1485-1500.

Goodwin, P. (ed.) (1995) *Car Dependence,* RAC Foundation for Motoring and the Environment, London.

Gordon, I. (1997) Densities, urban form and travel behaviour. *Town and Country Planning,* **66(9)**, pp.239-241.

Gordon, P., Kumar, A. and Richardson, H. (1989a) Congestion, changing metropolitan structure and city size in the United States. *International Regional Science Review,* **12(1)**, pp.45-56.

Gordon, P., Kumar, A. and Richardson, H. (1989b) Gender differences in metropolitan travel behaviour. *Regional Studies,* **23(6)**, pp.499-510.

Handy, S. (1992) Regional versus local accessibility: neotraditional development and its implications for non-work travel. *Built Environment,* **18(4)**, pp.253-267.

Hanson, S. (1982) The determinants of daily travel-activity patterns: relative location and sociodemographic factors. *Urban Geography,* **3(3)**, pp.179-202.

Headicar, P. and Curtis, C. (1994) Residential development and car-based travel: does location make a difference? *Proceedings of Seminar C: Environmental Issues, 22nd PTRC European Transport Forum,* Warwick, September, pp.117-130.

Hillman, M. and Whalley, A. (1983) *Energy and Personal Travel: Obstacles to Conservation,* Policy Studies Institute, London.

Kitamura, R., Mokhtarian, P. and Laidet, L. (1997) A micro-

analysis of land use and travel in five neighbourhoods in the San Francisco Bay area. *Transportation,* **24(2)**, pp.125-158.

Levinson, D. and Kumar, A. (1997) Density and the journey to work. *Growth and Change,* **28(2)**, pp.147-172.

McDougall, G. and Mank, R. (1982) Consumer energy conservation policy in Canada: behavioural and institutional obstacles. *Energy Policy,* **10(3)**, pp.212-224.

Mogridge, M. (1985) Transport, land use and energy interaction. *Urban Studies,* **22(6)**, pp.481-492.

Næss, P. (1993) Transportation energy in Swedish towns and regions. *Scandinavian Housing and Planning Research,* **10(4)**, pp.187-206.

Næss, P. and Sandberg, S. (1996) Workplace location, modal split and energy use for commuting trips. *Urban Studies,* **33(3)**, pp.557-580.

Næss, P., Røe, P. and Larsen, S. (1995) Travelling distances, modal split and transportation energy in thirty residential areas in Oslo. *Journal of Environmental Planning and Management,* **38(3)**, pp.349-370.

Newman, P. and Kenworthy, J. (1988) The transport energy trade-off: fuel efficient traffic versus fuel efficient cities. *Transportation Research,* **22A(3)**, pp.163-174.

Newman, P. and Kenworthy, J. (1989) *Cities and Automobile Dependence: An International Sourcebook,* Gower Technical, Aldershot.

Owens, S. (1986) *Energy Planning and Urban Form,* Pion, London.

Prevedouros, P. (1992) Associations of personality characteristics with transport behavior and residence location decisions. *Transportation Research A,* **26(5)**, pp.381-391.

Prevedouros, P. and Schofer, J. (1991) Trip characteristics and travel patterns of suburban residents. *Transportation Research Record,* **1328**, pp.49-57.

Spence, N. and Frost, M. (1995) Work travel responses to changing workplaces and changing residences, in *Cities in Competition: Productive and Sustainable Cities for the 21st Century* (eds J. Brotchie, M. Batty, E. Blakely, P. Hall and P. Newton), Longman Australia Pty Ltd., Melbourne.

Stead, D. (1999) *Planning for Less Travel: Identifying Land Use Characteristics Associated with more Sustainable Travel Patterns,* unpublished PhD thesis, Bartlett School of Planning, University College London, London.

Titheridge, H., Hall, S. and Hall, P. (1999) *Journey to Work Travel Patterns in the South East: A Final Report,* TRANSZ Working Paper 4, Bartlett School of Planning, University College London, London.

Valleley, M., Jones, P., Wofinden, D. and Flack, S. (1997) The role of parking standards in sustainable development, in *Proceedings of Seminar C: Policy, Planning and Sustainability, 25th PTRC European Transport Forum,* Uxbridge, September, pp.393-411.

Williams, J. (1997) *A Study of the Relationship between Settlement Size and Travel Patterns in the United Kingdom,* URBASSS Working Paper 2, Bartlett School of Planning, University College London, London.

Williams, J. and Banister, D. (1998) *A Review Document: Bartlett School of Planning,* URBASSS Working Paper

4, Bartlett School of Planning, University College London, London.

Williams, J. and Banister, D. (1999) *Local Provision and Population Threshold Analysis*, URBASSS Working Paper 5, Bartlett School of Planning, University College London, London.

Winter, J. and Farthing, S. (1997) Co-ordinating facility provision and new housing development: impacts on car and local facility use, in *Evaluating Local Environmental Policy* (ed. S. Farthing), Avebury, Aldershot.

Part 3: Approaches and Strategies for Achieving Sustainable Urban Form

David van Vliet
Development/Demonstration: *An Adaptive Strategy*

Aldous, T. (1992) *Urban Villages: A Concept for Creating Mixed Use Urban Developments on a Sustainable Scale*, Urban Village Forum, The Urban Villages Group, London.

Allen, R. E. (ed.) (1992) *The Concise Oxford Dictionary*, Clarendon Press, Oxford.

Argyris, C. and Schön, D. (1978) *Organizational Learning: A Theory of Action Perspective*, Addison-Wesley, Reading, Massachusetts.

Blowers, A. (1993) *Planning for a Sustainable Environment*, Earthscan, London.

CEC (Commission of the European Communities) (1993) *Towards Sustainability: A European Community Programme of Policy and Action in Relation to the Environment and Sustainable Development*, the EC's 5th Action Programme on the Environment, CEC, Brussels.

Daly, H. E. and Cobb, J. B. (1989) *For the Common Good*, Beacon Press, Boston.

Friedmann, J. (1976) *Innovation, Flexible Response: A Problem in the Theory of Meta-Planning*, Geographical Papers no.49, University of Reading, Reading.

Friedmann, J. (1987) *Planning in the Public Domain*, Princeton University Press, Princeton.

Funabashi, City of (1994) *Urban Environmental Plan of Ecocity*, Funabashi, Japan.

Goldsmith, E. (1992) *The Way: An Ecological Worldview*, Rider, London.

Gunderson, L. H., Holling, C. S. and Light, S. S. (eds) (1995) *Barriers and Bridges to the Renewal of Ecosystems and Institutions*, Columbia University Press, New York.

Holling, C. S. (1992) New science and new investments for a sustainable biosphere, in *Investing in Natural Capital: The Ecological Economics Approach to Sustainability* (eds A-M. Jansson, M. Hammer, C. Folke and R. Costanza), Island Press, Washington.

Holling, C. S. (1995) What barriers? What bridges? in *Barriers and Bridges to the Renewal of Ecosystems and Institutions* (eds L. H. Gunderson, C. S. Holling and S. S. Light), Columbia University Press, New York.

Jantzen, E. B. (1994) *New Directions in Planning Orientations – In a Time of Change*, unpublished monograph, Hørsholm.

Lee, K. N. (1993) *Compass and Gyroscope: Integrating Science and Politics for the Environment*, Island Press, Washington DC.

Milbrath, L. (1989) *Envisioning a Sustainable Society: Learning Our Way Out*, State University of New York, New York.

Moore, J. (1997) Inertia and resistance on the path to healthy communities, in *Eco-City Dimensions* (ed. M. Roseland), New Society Publishers, Gabriola Is.

Mumford, L. (1938) *The Culture of Cities*, Harcourt Brace, Jovanovich.

Munkstrup, N. and Sørensen, J. C. (1995) *Gode Eksempler på Byøkologi*, Byplanlaboratorium, København.

Novem (1995) *The Road to Ecolonia: Evaluation and Residents' Survey*, by Rutten communicatie-advies for Bouwfonds Woningbouw Hoevelaken and Novem Sittard, Netherlands.

NRCan. (Natural Resources Canada) (1994) *Innovative Housing 1993, Vol. 2 Proceedings: Planning and Design Innovations*, Minister of Supply and Services, Ottawa.

NRCan. (Natural Resources Canada) (1998) *Conference Proceedings – Green Building Challenge '98*, October, Vancouver.

OECD (Organisation for Economic Co-operation and Development) (1996) *Innovative Policies for Sustainable Urban Development*, OECD, Paris.

Osborne, D. and Plastrik, P. (1997) *Banishing Bureaucracy: The Five Strategies for Reinventing Government*, Addison Wesley Inc., New York.

Perks, W. T. and van Vliet, D. (1994) *Assessment of Built Projects for Sustainable Communities*, Canada Mortgage and Housing, Ottawa.

Senge, P. (1990) *The Fifth Discipline: The Art and Practice of the Learning Organization*, Currency Doubleday, Toronto.

van Vliet, D. (1999) *Sustainable Community Planning and Design, A Demonstration Project as Pathway: The case of Egebjerggård, Ballerup, Denmark*, unpublished doctoral dissertation, School of Community and Regional Planning, University of British Columbia, Vancouver.

Michael Crilly and Adam Mannis
Sustainable Urban Management Systems

Alger, C. (1990) The world relations of cities – closing the gap between social science paradigms and everyday human experience. *International Studies Quarterly*, **34**, pp.493-518.

Allen, J. (1996) Environment: where European statistics and geography became engaged. *Sigma*, Summer, pp.16-17.

Allen, P. M. (1997) Cities and regions as evolutionary, complex systems. *Geographical Systems*, **4**, pp.103-130.

Appleyard, D. (1981) *Livable Streets*, University of California Press, Berkeley.

Bentley, I., Alcock, A., Murrain, P., McGlynn, S. and Smith, G. (1985) *Responsive Environments: A Manual for Designers*, The Architectural Press, London.

Bogan, R. and Taylor, J. (1975) *Introduction to Qualitative*

Research Methods: A Phenomenological Approach to the Social Sciences, John Wiley & Sons, New York.

Burgess, R. G. and Bryman, A. (1994) *Analysing Qualitative Data*, Routledge, London.

Burrough, P. A. (1992) Development of intelligent geographical information systems. *International Journal of Geographical Information Systems*, **6(1)**, pp.1-11.

Clark, N., Perezfrejo, F. and Allen, P. (1995) *Evolutionary Dynamics and Sustainable Development – A Systems Approach*, Edward Elgar, Aldershot.

Clayton, A. M. H. and Radcliffe, N. J. (1996) *Sustainability – A Systems Approach*, Earthscan, London.

Crilly, M., Mannis, A. and Morrow, K. (1999) Indicators for change – taking a lead. *Local Environment*, June, forthcoming.

Denzin, N. K. (1972) The research act, in *Symbolic Interaction* (eds J. G. Manis and B. N. Meltzer), Allyn and Bacon, Boston.

DoE (Department of the Environment) (1987) *Handling Geographic Information:Report of the Committee of Enquiry Chaired by Lord Chorley*, HMSO, London.

DoE NI (Department of the Environment for Northern Ireland) (1996) *Belfast Urban Area Plan 2001 Reassessment of Development Land - Urban Design Technical Supplement*, HMSO, Belfast.

Downs, R. M. (1982) Cognitive dimensions of space and boundary in urban areas, in *Urban Patterns: Studies in Human Ecology* (ed. G. Theodorson), Pennsylvania State University Press, Pennsylvania.

Etzioni, A. (1967) Mixed scanning: a 'third' approach to decision-making. *Public Administration Review*, **27(5)**, pp.385-392.

Fedra, K. (1993) GIS and environmental modelling, in *Environmental Modelling with GIS* (eds M. L. Goodchild, B. O. Parks and L. T. Steyaert), Oxford University Press, New York.

Ferguson, F. (1975) *Architecture, Cities and the Systems Approach*, George Braziller, New York.

Finger, M. and Kilcoyne, J. (1995) Learning our way out: indicators of social environmental learning, in *A Sustainable World: Defining and Measuring Sustainable Development* (ed. T. C. Trzyna), International Centre for Environment and Public Policy, Sacramento, California.

Foote-Whyte, W. (1943) *Street Corner Society: The Social Structure of an Italian Slum*, University of Chicago Press, Chicago.

Frankenberg, R. (1966) *Communities in Britain: Social Life in Town and Country*, Penguin, Middlesex.

George, A. L. (1959) Quantitative and qualitative approaches to content analysis, in *Trends in Content Analysis* (ed. I. S. Pool), University of Illinois Press, Urbana.

Glaser, B. G. and Strauss, A. L. (1967) *The Discovery of Grounded Theory: Strategies for Qualitative Research*, Aldine, New York.

Goldsmith, E. (1978) Complexity and stability in the real world. *Ecologist Quarterly*, Winter, pp.305-316.

Golledge, G. (1978) Learning about urban environments, in *Making Sense of Time* (eds T. Carlstein, D. Parks and N. Thrift), Edward Arnold, London, pp.76-98.

Grossmann, W. D. and Watt, K. E. F. (1992) Viability and sustainability of civilizations, corporations, institutions and ecological systems. *Systems Research*, **9(1)**, pp.3-41.

Guise, R. (1995) Conservation and aesthetics, in *A Guide to Local Environmental Auditing* (eds H. Barton and N. Brunder) Earthscan, London.

Hester, R. (1987) Community design: making the grassroots whole. *Built Environment*, **13(1)**, pp.45-60.

Hester, R. (1985) Subconscious landscapes of the heart. *Places*, **2(3)**, pp.10-22.

Jones, P. (1996) A model for energy and environmental planning for sustainable cities. Conference paper presented to the second meeting of *The Sustainable Cities Network*, University of Newcastle upon Tyne, February 7.

Kaufman, J. L. and Jacobs, H. M. (1987) A public planning perspective on strategic planning. *Journal of the American Planning Association*, **53(1)**, pp.323-343.

Lancashire County Council (1997) *Lancashire's Green Audit 2*, Lancashire County Planning Department, Preston.

Lee, T.R. (1976) Cities in the mind, in *Social Areas in Cities: Spacial Perspectives on Problems and Policies* (eds D.T. Herbert and R.J. Johnson), John Wiley & Sons, London, pp.159-187.

Levett, R. (1997) Tools, techniques and processes for municipal environmental management. *Local Environment*, **2(2)**, pp.189-202.

LGMB (Local Government Management Board) (1996) *Creating Community Visions*, LGMB, London.

LGMB (Local Government Management Board) (1995) *Sustainability Indicators Research Project: Consultants' Report of the Pilot Phase*, LBMB, Luton.

Lynch, K. (1990) A process of community visual survey, in *City Sense and City Design: Writings and projects of Kevin Lynch* (eds T. Banerjee and M. Southworth), M.I.T. Press, Cambridge, Massachusetts.

Madanipour, A. (1996) *Design of Urban Space: An Inquiry into a Socio-Spatial Process*, John Wiley and Sons, Chichester.

Martin, D. (1996) *Geographic Information Systems – Socioeconomic Applications*, Routledge, London.

Nyerges, T. L. (1993) Understanding the scope of GIS: its relationship to environmental modelling, in *Environmental Modelling with GIS* (eds M. L. Goodchild, B. O. Parks and L. T. Steyaert), Oxford University Press, New York.

Okely, J. (1994) Thinking through fieldwork, in *Analysing Qualitative Data* (eds A. Brugman and R. G. Burgess), Routledge, London.

O'Regan, B. and Moles, R. (1997) Applying a systems perspective to environmental policy. *Journal of Environmental Planning and Management*, **40(4)**, pp.535-538.

Perkins, H. C. (1988) Bulldozers in the southern part of heaven: defending place against rapid growth part 1: local residents' interpretations of rapid urban growth in a free-standing service-class town, *Environment and Planning A*, **20**, pp.285-308.

Philip, L. J. (1998) Combining quantitative and qualitative

approaches to social research in human geography – an impossible mixture? *Environment and Planning A*, **30**, pp.261-276.

Porterfield, G. A. and Hall, K. B. (1995) *A Concise Guide to Community Planning*, McGraw-Hill, New York.

Rees, W.E. (1997) Is 'Sustainable City' an oxymoron? *Local Environment*, **2(3)**, pp.303-310.

Rowland, J. (1973) *Community Decay*, Penguin, Middlesex.

Smith, D. A. and Timberlake, M. (1995) Cities in global matrices: toward mapping the world-system's city system, in *World Cities in a World System* (eds P. Knox and P. J. Taylor), Cambridge University Press, Cambridge.

Spradley, J. P. (1980) *Participant Observation*, Rinehart and Winston, New York.

Stake, R. E. (1995) *The Art of Case Study Research*, Saga, Thousand Oaks, California.

Steadman, P. (1996) A land use, transport and energy model for a medium-sized city. Conference paper presented to the fourth meeting of *The Sustainable Cities Network*, Cardiff, November 13.

Stringer, P. (1999) Mapping urban morphology. *Landscape Design*, **277**, pp.39-40.

Taylor, G. (1996) GIS and the third dimension – and beyond? *Surveying World*, July/August, pp.18-20.

UNCED (United Nations Conference on Environment and Development) (1992) *Earth Summit: Agenda 21 – The United Nations Programme of Action from Rio*, United Nations, New York.

Walford, N. (1995) *Geographical Data Analysis*, John Wiley and Sons, Chichester.

Wallner, H. P., Narodoslawsky, M. and Moser, F. (1996) Islands of sustainability – a bottom-up approach towards sustainable development. *Environment and Planning A*, **28**, pp.1763-1778.

Wates, N. (1996) *Action Planning: How to Use Planning Weekends and Urban Design Teams to Improve your Environment*, The Prince of Wales Institute of Architecture, London.

Webster, C. (1990) Rule-based spatial search. *International Journal of Geographical Information Systems*, **4(3)**, pp.241-259.

Wood, D. (1992) *The Power of Maps*, Routledge, London.

Yoshikawa, S. (1997) Computer-assisted environmental design system: regional information visualizer. *International Planning Studies*, **2(2)**, pp. 211-228.

Joe Ravetz
Urban Form and the Sustainability of Urban Systems: *Theory and Practice in a Northern Conurbation*

AGMA (Association of Greater Manchester Authorities) (1995) *Strategic Guidance Monitoring Report*, AGMA, Wigan.

Alexander, C. (1986) *A Pattern Language*, Oxford University Press, Oxford.

Borja, J. and Castells, M. (1997) *The Local and the Global: Management of Cities in the Information Age*, Earthscan, London.

Bramley, G. and Watkins, C. (1996) *Circular Projections:* *Housing Need and Housing Supply in Context*, Campaign for the Protection of Rural England, London.

Breheny, M., Gent, T. and Lock, D. (1994) *Alternative Development Patterns: New Settlements*, HMSO, London.

Brotchie, J. Hall, P. and Newton, D. (eds) (1987) *The Spatial Impact of Technological Change*, Croom Helm, London.

Calthorpe, P. (1994) *The Next American Metropolis*, Princeton Architectural Press, New York.

Carley, M. and Spapens, P. (1997) *Sharing the World: Sustainable Living and Global Equity in the 21st Century*, Earthscan, London.

City of Manchester (1945) *City of Manchester Development Plan*, City of Manchester, Manchester.

Comedia and Demos (1999) *The Richness of Cities: Urban Policy in a New Landscape*, ECO Distribution, Leicester.

Dicken, P. (1998) *Global Shift: Transforming the World Economy*, Paul Chapman, London.

DoE (Department of Environment) (1995) *Projections of Households in England to 2016*, HMSO, London.

DETR (Department of the Environment, Transport and the Regions) (1998) *Planning for the Communities of the Future*, Stationery Office, London.

Ecotec (1993) *Reducing Transport Emissions Through Planning*, HMSO, London.

Entec (1997) *The Application of Environmental Capacity to Land Use Planning*, The Stationery Office, London.

Evans, R. and Herring, H. (1989) *Energy Use in the UK Domestic Sector to the Year 2010*, Department of Energy, HMSO, London.

Fothergill, S., Monk, S. and Perry, M. (1987) *Property and Industrial Development*, Hutchinson, London.

Garreau, J. (1991) *Edge City: Life on the New Frontier*, Doubleday, New York.

Geddes, P. (1915) *Cities in Evolution: An Introduction to the Town Planning Movement*, Benn, London.

GMR (Greater Manchester Research, Information and Planning Unit) (1995) *Greater Manchester: Facts and Trends*, AGMA, Oldham.

HBF (Housebuilders' Federation) (1996) *Families Matter*, HBF, London.

Hebbert, M. (1998) *London: More by Fortune than by Design*, John Wiley, London.

Hooper, A. (1994) Land availability and the suburban option. *Town and Country Planning*, **63(9)**, pp.239-242.

Howard, E. (1898) (reprinted in 1985) *Garden Cities of Tomorrow: A Peaceful Path to Real Reform*, Attic, Eastbourne.

Jacobs, J. (1965) *The Death and Life of Great American Cities*, Penguin, Harmondsworth.

Levett, R. (1998) *Monitoring, Measuring and Target Setting for Urban Capacity*, Town and Country Planning Association, London.

Max-Neef, M. (1992) Development and human needs, in *Real-Life Economics: Understanding Wealth Creation* (eds P. Ekins and M. Max-Neef), Routledge, London.

Mollison, W. (1991) *Permaculture: A Designer's Manual*, Tagari, NSW Australia.

Nicholas, R. and McWilliams, G. A. (1962) Planning the

city of the future, in *Manchester and its Region*, Manchester University Press, Manchester.

Nijkamp, P., Lasschuit, P. and Soeteman, F. (1992) Sustainable development in a regional system, in *Sustainable Development and Urban Form* (ed. M. Breheny), Pion, London.

NWRA (North West Regional Association) and Llewellyn-Davies (1997) *A Methodology for Estimating Urban Capacity at the Regional Scale*, NWRA, Wigan.

Rapaport, A. (1987) *Human Aspects of Urban Form: Towards a Man-Environment Approach to Urban Form and Design*, Pergamon, Oxford.

Ravetz, J. (1996) Towards the sustainable city-region. *Town and Country Planning*, **65(5)**, pp.152-155.

Ravetz, J. with the Town and Country Planning Association (1999) *City-Region 2020: Integrated Planning for Long Term Sustainable Development*, Earthscan, London.

Ravetz, J. (1998) Capacity problems – sustainability solutions. *Town and Country Planning*, **67(5)**, pp.173-175.

Rees, W. and Wackernagel, M. (1995) *Our Ecological Footprint: Reducing Human Impact on the Earth*, New Society Publishers, Gabriola Island, British Columbia.

Robson, B., Bradford, M., Deas, I., Hall, E., Harrison, E., Parkinson, M., Evans, R., Garside, P. and Harding, A. (1994) *Assessing the Impact of Urban Policy*, HMSO, London.

Rudlin, D. and Falk, N. (1999) *Building the 21st Century Home: The Sustainable Urban Neighbourhood*, Architectural Press, Oxford.

Rydin, Y. (1995) The greening of the housing market, in *Housing and the Environment: A New Agenda* (eds M. Bhatt, J. Brooke and M. Gibson), Chartered Institute of Housing, London.

Sachs, W. (1998) *Greening the North: A Post-Industrial Blueprint for Ecology and Equity*, Zed Books and Wuppertal Institute, London.

Solow, R. M. (1970) *Growth Theory: An Exposition*, Clarendon, Oxford.

TCPA (Town and Country Planning Association) (1996) *Where Will the People Go?*, TCPA, London.

TCPA (Town and Country Planning Association) (1998) *Urban Housing Capacity: What Can be Done?*, TCPA, London.

Urban Villages Forum (1998) *Making Places: A Guide to Good Practice in Undertaking Mixed-Use Development*, Urban Villages Forum and English Partnerships, London.

von Weizsacker, E., Lovins, A. and Lovins, L. H. (1997) *Factor Four: Doubling Wealth, Halving Resource Use*, Earthscan, London.

World Resources Institute (1997) *Resource Flows: The Material Basis of Industrial Economies*, WRI, Washington DC.

Gert de Roo

Compact Cities, Environmental Conflicts and Policy Strategies: *Complexity as a Criterion for Decision Making*

Amdam, R. (1994) *The Planning Community: An Example of a Voluntary Communal Planning Approach to Strategic Development in Small Communities in Norway*, Rapport 9404, Moreforsking Volda.

Amsterdam (Municipality) (1994a) *Amsterdam Open Stad*, Ontwerp Structuurplan 1994, Deel II, De toelichting, dienst Ruimtelijke Ordening, Amsterdam.

Amsterdam (Municipality) (1994b) *Bestemminsplan IJ-Oevers*, dienst Ruimtelijke Ordening, Amsterdam.

Amsterdam (Municipality) (1995) *Stedebouwkundig Programma van Eisen, Houthavens*, Gemeentelijke projektgroep Houthavensgebied, Amsterdam.

Anderson, N., Hanhardt, E. and Pasher, I. (1997) From measurement to measures: land use and environmental protection in Brooklyn, New York, in *Urban Environmental Planning* (eds D. Miller and G. de Roo), Ashgate, Aldershot.

Bartelds, H. and de Roo, G. (1995) *Dilemmas van de Compacte Stad: Uitdagingen van Beleid*, VUGA, The Hague.

Blanco, H. (1999) Lessons from an adaptation of the Dutch model for integrated environmental zoning (IEZ) in Brooklyn, NYC, in *Integrating City Planning and Environmental Improvement* (eds D. Miller and G. de Roo), Ashgate, Aldershot.

Blanken, W. (1997) *Ruimte Voor Milieu; Milieu/Ruimte-Conflicten in de Stad; Een Analyse*, Faculty of Spatial Sciences, Groningen.

Boei, P. J. (1993) Integrale milieuzonering op en rond het industrieterrein Arnhem-Noord, in *Kwaliteit Van Norm en Zone: Planologische Consequenties van (Integrale) Milieuzonering*, Geo Pers (ed. G. de Roo), Groningen.

Borst, H., de Roo, G., Voogd, H. and van der Werf, H. (1995) *Milieuzones in Beweging: Eisen, Wensen, Consequenties en Alternatieven*, Samsom H. D. Tjeenk Willink, Alphen aan den Rijn.

Brimblecome, P. and Nicholas, F. (1995) Urban air pollution and its consequences, in *Environmental Science for Environmental Management* (ed. T. O'Riordan), Longman Scientific and Technical, Harlow.

Cohen, M. D., March, J. G. and Olsen, J. P. (1972) A garbage can model of organizational choice. *Administrative Science Quarterly*, **17**, pp.1-25.

Dryzek, J. (1990) *Discursive Democracy: Politics, Policy and Political Science*, Cambridge University Press, Cambridge.

Friedmann, J. (1973) *Retracking America: A Theory of Transactive Planning*, Anchor Press/Doubleday, Garden City/New York.

Healey, P. (1992) Planning through debate: the communicative turn in planning theory. *Town Planning Review*, **63(2)**, pp.143-162.

Hough, M. (1989) *City Form and Natural Process: Towards a New Urban Vernacular*, Routledge, London.

Innes, J. E. (1995) Planning theory's emerging paradigm: communicative action and interactive practice. *Journal of Planning Education and Research*, **14(3)**, pp.183-189.

IPO, VNG and VROM (1997) *Bever Beleidsvernieuwing Bodemsanering: Verslag van het Bever-Proces* (eds S. Ouboter and W. Kooper), VROM, Den Haag.

Koekebakker, M. O. (1997) *Herstructureren van Bestaande*

Bedrijventerreinen, Kwaliteit op Locatie, **9**, VROM, The Hague, pp.3-9.

Kreileman, M, and de Roo, G. (1996) Aanspraken op vinex-uitleglocaties kunnen huizenbouw stevig frustreren: bestaande milieudruk op woningbouwlocaties gewogen. *ROM Magazine*, **12**, pp.20-22.

Kuijpers, C. B. F. and Aquarius, L. G. M. (1998) Meer ruimte voor kwaliteit: intensivering van het ruimtegebruik in stedelijk gebied. *Stedebouw en Ruimtelijke Ordening*, **1**, pp.28-32.

Marshall, A. (1924) *Principles of Economics*, Macmillan, London.

MIG (Modernisering Instrumentarium Geluidbeleid) (1998) *Nota MIG*, 3e concept, versie 29-01-1998/NM, DGM, Directie Geluid en Verkeer, Projectburo MIG, Den Haag.

Miller, D. and de Roo, G. (1996) Integrated environmental zoning: an innovative Dutch approach to measuring and managing environmental spillovers in urban regions. *Journal of the American Planning Association*, Summer, pp.373-380.

Miller, D. and de Roo, G. (1997) *Urban Environmental Planning*, Ashgate, Aldershot.

Mishan, E. J. (1972) *Cost-Benefit Analysis*, Unwin University Books, George Allen and Unwin Ltd., London.

Miura, M. (1997) *The Housing Pattern in the Residential Area in Japanese Cities and Wind Flow on Prevailing Wind Direction*, Shibaura Institute of Technology, Department of Architecture and Environmental Systems, Fukasaku, Omiya-Shi, Japan.

Nieuwenhof, R. Van den and Bakker, H. (1989) Zones rond industrieen om milieuverstoringen in te perken: planologische maatregelen op grond van milieunormen. *ROM*, **10**, pp.6-12.

O'Riordan, T. (ed.) (1995) *Environmental Science for Environmental Management*, Longman Scientific and Technical, Burny Mill, Harlow.

Osleeb, J., Kass, D., Blanco, H., Zoloth, S. R., Sivin, D. and Baimonte, A. (1997) *Baseline Aggregate Environmental Loadings (BEAL), Profile of Greenpoint-Williamsburg, Brooklyn, Draft Report*, Hunter College, New York City University, New York.

Peters, G. H. J. and Westerdiep, J. (1993) Milieu en ruimtelijke ordening hand in hand: casus Kop van Zuid, in *Kwaliteit van Norm en Zone* (ed. G. de Roo), Geo Pers, Groningen.

Pinch, S. (1985) *Cities and Services; The Geography of Collective Consumption*, Routledge and Kegan Paul, London.

Prigogine, I. and Stengers, I. (1990) *Orde uit Chaos: De Nieuwe Dialoog Tussen de Mens en de Natuur*, Uitgeverij Bert Bakker, Amsterdam.

Roo, G. de and Miller, D. (1997) Transitions in Dutch environmental planning: new solutions for integrating spatial and environmental policies. *Environment and Planning B: Planning and Design*, **24**, pp.427-436.

Rotterdam (Municipality) (1994) *Rapport Strategie Maas-Rijnhaven: Een Inventarisatie naar de Mogelijkheden van Woningbouw in Relatie met Milieu-Aspecten*,

Werkgroep Diverse Diensten, Rotterdam.

SCMO-TNO (1993) *Evaluatie van de Bedrijfstypen aan Zoneerbare Milieubelastingen, Bevolkingsaantallen Blootgesteld aan Niet-Verwaarloosbare Belastingen*, TNO, Delft.

Stuurgroep IMZS Drechtsteden (1991) *Rapportage Eerste Fase: Inventarisatie Milieubelasting*, The Hague.

Tan, T. G. and Waller, H. (1989) *Wetgeving als Mensenwerk; De Totstandkoming van de Wet Geluidhinder*, Samsom H.D. Tjeenk Willink, Alphen aan den Rijn.

Teisman, G. R. (1992) *Complexe Besluitvorming: Een Pluriceentrisch Perspektief op Besluit-Vorming Over Ruimtelijke Investeringen*, VUGA, Den Haag.

VM (Ministry of Health and Environmental Hygiene) (1972) *Urgentienota Milieyhygiene*, Second Chamber, 1971-1972, 11906, 2, The Hague.

Voerknecht, H. (1993) Saneren en bestemmen in een regionale aanpak, in *Kwaliteit van Norm en Zone; Planologische Consequenties van (integrale) Milieuzonering* (ed. G. de Roo), Geo Pers, Groningen.

VROM (Dutch Ministry of Housing, Spatial Planning and the Environment) (1990a) *Ministeriele Handreiking voor een Voorlopige Systematiek voor de Integrale Milieuzonering*, Integrale Milieuzonering Deel 6, Directie Geluid, DGM, The Hague.

VROM (Dutch Ministry of Housing, Spatial Planning and the Environment) (1990b) *Fourth Memorandum on Spatial Planning*, Deel d: Regeringsbeslissing, TK 20490, 9-10, Sdu, The Hague.

VROM (Dutch Ministry of Housing, Spatial Planning and the Environment) (1995) *Waar Vele Willen Zijn, is ook een Weg*, Stad and Milieu Rapportage, Directoraat Generaal Milieubeheer, Den Haag.

VROM (Dutch Ministry of Housing, Spatial Planning and the Environment) (1996) *Binnen Regels naar Kwaliteit, Stad and Milieu, Rapportage Deelproject*, VROM, The Hague.

VROM (Dutch Ministry of Housing, Spatial Planning and the Environment), V&W, LNV, EZ, BZ (1993) *Second Dutch National Environmental Policy Plan*, VROM, The Hague.

VROM (Dutch Ministry of Housing, Spatial Planning and the Environment), V&W, EZ, LNV, F, BZ (1998) *Third Dutch National Environmental Policy Plan*, VROM, The Hague.

Woltjer, J. (1997) De keerzijde van het draagvlak; ruimtelijke ordening niet altijd gebaat bij maatschappelijke discussie. *Stedebouw en Ruimtelijke Ordening*, **4**, pp.47-52.

Mike Jenks

The Acceptability of Urban Intensification

Batty, M. (1994) A chronicle of scientific planning: the Anglo-American modelling experience. *Journal of the American Planning Association*, Winter, pp.7-16.

Bertuglia, C. and Rabino, G. (1994) Performance indicators and evaluation in contemporary urban modelling, in *Modelling the City: Performance, Policy and Planning* (eds C. Bertuglia, G. Clarke and A. Wilson), Routledge,

London.

Brandon, P., Lombardi, P. and Bentivegna, V. (eds) (1997) *Evaluation of the Built Environment for Sustainability*, E & FN Spon, London.

Breheny, M. (ed.) (1992) *Sustainable Development and Urban Form*, Pion, London.

Breheny, M. (1997) Urban compaction: feasible and acceptable? *Cities*, **14(4)**, pp.209-217.

Breheny, M. and Ross, A. (1998) *Urban Housing Capacity: What Can be Done?*, Town and Country Planning Association, London.

Burton, E., Williams, K. and Jenks, M. (1996) The compact city and urban sustainability: conflicts and complexities, in *The Compact City: A Sustainable Urban Form?* (eds M. Jenks, E, Burton and K. Williams) E & FN Spon, London.

CPRE (Campaign for the Protection of Rural England) (1996) *Urban Footprints*, CPRE Publications London.

CEC (Commission of the European Communities) (1990) *Green Paper on the Urban Environment*, European Commission, Brussels.

DoE (Department of the Environment) (1994) *Housing Attitudes Survey*, Housing Research Report, B. Hedges and S. Clemens, Social and Community Planning Research, HMSO, London.

DETR (Department of the Environment, Transport and the Regions) (forthcoming) *Urban Intensification: Impacts and Acceptability*, Oxford Brookes University and Entec, E. Burton, K. Williams and M. Jenks, DETR, London.

DETR (Department of the Environment, Transport and the Regions) (1998) *Planning for the Communities of the Future*, Stationery Office, Norwich.

ECOTEC (1993) *Reducing Transport Emissions through Planning*, HMSO, London.

Elkin, T., McLaren, D. and Hillman, M. (1991) *Reviving the City: Towards Sustainable Urban Development*, Friends of the Earth, London.

Entec UK Ltd (1997) *The Application of Environmental Capacity to Land Use Planning*, DETR, London.

Essenius, E., Sim, M., Simon, N., Kist, P. and Gerhardt, W. (1998) *A Working Generic Economical Schematic UIMS for an ODBMS*, in Proceedings, UDB4, L'Aquila.

European Commission, Expert Group on the Urban Environment (1996) *European Sustainable Cities*, European Commission, Brussels.

Haughton, C. and Hunter, C. (1994) *Sustainable Cities*, Jessica Kingsley, London.

HM Govt (1996) *Household Growth: Where Shall We Live?* Cm 3471, The Stationery Office, London.

Jenks, M., Burton, E. and Williams, K. (forthcoming) Urban consolidation and the benefits of intensification, in *Strategies and Methods for Improving Environmental Quality in Compact Cities* (eds G. de Roo and D. Miller), Ashgate, Aldershot.

Jenks, M., Burton, E. and Williams, K. (eds) (1996a) *The Compact City: A Sustainable Urban Form?* E&FN Spon, London.

Jenks, M., Burton, E. and Williams, K. (1996b) A sustainable future through the compact city? Urban intensification in the United Kingdom. *Environments by Design*, **1(1)**, pp.5-21.

Jenks, M. and Gerhardt, W. (1998) Sustainable urban form: a dynamic, interactive and predictive decision support system, in proceedings, *International Conference on Systems Research, Informatics and Cybernetics*, Baden-Baden, Germany.

Jenks, M., Williams, K. and Burton, E. (1997) *Urban Consolidation and the Benefits of Intensification*. Paper to International Conference on Strategies and Methods for Improving Environmental Quality in Compact Cities, Groningen, Netherlands.

Levett, R. (1998) *Urban Housing Capacity and the Sustainable City: Monitoring, Measuring and Target Setting for Urban Capacity*, Town and Country Planning Association, London.

Sherlock, H. (1996) Repairing our much abused cities: the way to sustainable living, in *The Compact City: A Sustainable Urban Form?* (eds M. Jenks, E. Burton and K. Williams), E & FN Spon, London.

Sherlock, H. (1991) *Cities are Good for Us*, for Transport 2000, Paladin, London.

Timmermans, H. (ed.) (1997) *Decision Support Systems in Urban Planning*, E & FN Spon, London.

United Kingdom Round Table on Sustainable Development (1997) *Housing and Urban Capacity*, UK Round Table on Sustainable Development, Portland House, London.

Urban Task Force (1999) *Towards an Urban Renaissance*, E & FN Spon, London.

White, R. (1994) Strategic decisions for sustainable urban development in the Third World. *Third World Planning Review*, **16(2)**, pp.103-16.

Williams, K. (1997) *The Effectiveness of the UK Planning System in Delivering Sustainable Development via Urban Intensification*, unpublished Ph.D thesis, Oxford Brookes University, Oxford.

Williams, K. (1998) Can planners implement urban intensification policies? *Town and Country Planning*, **67(10)**, pp.340-342.

Williams, K., Burton, E. and Jenks, M. (1996) Achieving the compact city through intensification, in *The Compact City: A Sustainable Urban Form?* (eds M. Jenks, E. Burton and K. Williams) E & FN Spon, London.

Williams, K., Jenks, M. and Burton, E. (1999) How much is too much? urban intensification, social capacity and sustainable development. *Open House International*, **24(1)**, pp.17-25.

Wegener, M. (1994) Operational urban models: state of the art. *Journal of the American Planning Association*, Winter, pp.17-29.

Wood, G. and Rodriguez-Bachiller, A. (forthcoming) GIS in environmental impact assessment, in *Methods of Environmental Impact Assessment*, 2nd Edition (eds P. Morris and R. Therival), UCL Press, London.

WECD (World Commission on Environment and Development) (1987) *Our Common Future*, Oxford University Press, Oxford.

WRI (World Resources Institute) (1996) *The Urban Environment*, Oxford University Press, Oxford.

Hugh Howes

Sustainable Development Comes of Age: *The Thames Environment 21 Experience*

Environment Agency (The) (1998) *Thames Environment 21: The Environment Agency Strategy for Land-Use Planning in the Thames Region*, The Environment Agency, Reading.

DoE (Department of the Environment) (1995) *Projections of Households in England to 2016*, HMSO, London.

HM Government (1996) *Household Growth: Where Shall we Live?*, Paper presented to Parliament by the Secretary for the Environment by Command of Her Majesty, Cm3471, The Stationery Office, London.

Abigail Raymond

The Kent Design Initiative: *Towards a Sustainable Future*

Association of Police Officers Project and Design Group (1994) *Advice Note: Secured by Design*, HMSO, London.

BRE (Building Research Establishment) (1998) *BREEAM '98 for Offices: Environmental Assessments for New and Existing Offices*, BRE, London.

BRE (Building Research Establishment) (1995) *Environmental Standards: Homes for a Greener World*, J. Prior, BRE, London.

CEC (Council of the European Communities) (1992) *Directive 93/43/EEC*, CEC, Brussels.

Countryside Commission (1996a) *Village Design Statements*, Countryside Commission, London.

Countryside Commission (1996b) Countryside Design Summaries, Countryside Commission, London.

DETR (Department of the Environment, Transport and the Regions) (1998) *A New Deal for Transport: Better for Everyone*, Stationery Office, London.

DoE (Department of the Environment) (1997a) *Planning Policy Guidance 1: General Policy and Principles*, Stationery Office, London.

DoE (Department of the Environment) (1997b) *Planning Policy Guidance 7: The Countryside*, Stationery Office, London.

DoE (Department of the Environment) (1995) *Quality in Town and Country Urban Design Campaign*, HMSO, London.

DoE (Department of the Environment) (1994a) *Planning Policy Guidance 9: Nature Conservation*, HMSO, London.

DoE (Department of the Environment) (1994b) *Planning Policy Guidance 23: Planning and Pollution Control*, HMSO, London.

DoE (Department of the Environment) (1994c) *Quality in Town and Country: A Discussion Document*, HMSO, London.

DoE (Department of the Environment) (1994d) *Circular 5/94: Planning Out Crime*, HMSO, London.

DoE and DoT (Department of the Environment and Department of Transport) (1994) *Planning Policy Guidance 13: Transport*, HMSO, London.

Environment Agency (1998) *Saving Water: On the Right Track*, Environment Agency, London.

Essex County Council (1997) *Essex Design Guide*, Essex County Council and Essex Planning Officers Association, Essex County Council, Basildon.

Kent County Council (1995) *Kent Design Guide*, Kent County Council, Maidstone.

Leeds City Council (1996) *Sustainable Development Design Guide*, Leeds City Council, Leeds.

Lincolnshire County Council (1996) *Lincolnshire Design Guide*, Lincolnshire County Council, Lincoln.

Norfolk County Council (1998) *Norfolk Residential Design Guide*, Norfolk County Council, Norwich.

NRA (National Rivers Authority) (1995) *Saving Water: The NRA's Approach to Water Conservation and Demand Management*, NRA, Worthing.

Suffolk County Council (1993) *Suffolk Design Guide for Residential Areas*, Planning and Highways Authorities, Suffolk County Council, Ipswich.

Guiseppe Zanré

Review of the Wycombe District Local Plan: *Comparative Strategic Site Assessment – the Goals Achievement Matrix*

Barton H., Davies E. and Guise, R. (1995) *Sustainable Settlements: A Guide for Planners, Designers and Developers*, University of the West of England and Local Government Management Board, Luton.

BCC (Buckinghamshire County Council) (1996) *Buckinghamshire County Structure Plan 1991-2011*, BCC, Aylesbury.

BDP (Building Design Partnership) (1996) *A Review of Public Open Space Needs and Provision in Wycombe District*, Building Design Partnership, BDP, Bedford.

DoE (Department of the Environment) (1992) *Planning Policy Guidance 3: Housing*, HMSO, London.

Gillespies (1997) *Wycombe District Comparative Landscape Assessment of Strategic Sites*, Gillespies, Oxford.

Halcrow Fox (1998) *Comparative Strategic Site Assessments: Transport Surveys*, Halcrow Fox, London.

Fordham Research Services (1996) *Housing Needs Survey*, Fordham Research Services, London.

FRCA (The Farming and Rural Conservation Agency) (1998) *Wycombe District Local Plan: Agricultural Land Classification ALC Map and Summary Report*, FRCA, Reading.

WDC (Wycombe District Council) (1998) *Wycombe District Local Plan to 2011*, Planning Policy Unit, Planning, Transport and Development Directorate, Wycombe.

WDC (Wycombe District Council) (1995) *Wycombe District Local Plan*, Wycombe District Council, Wycombe.

WDC (Wycombe District Council) Planning Policy Unit (1998a) *Urban Capacity Study*, Planning, Transport and Development Directorate, Wycombe.

WDC (Wycombe District Council) Planning Policy Unit (1998b) *Comparative Strategic Site Assessment: Detailed Site Schedules*, Planning, Transport and Development Directorate, Wycombe.

WDC (Wycombe District Council) Planning Policy Unit (1997a) *Pre-Issues Report*, Planning Transport and Development Directorate, Wycombe.

WDC (Wycombe District Council) Planning Policy Unit (1997b) *Planning, Environment and Transportation Committee, 17 November 1997*, Planning, Transport and Development Directorate, Wycombe.

WDC (Wycombe District Council) Planning Policy Unit (1996) *Planning, Environment and Transportation Committee, 9 September 1996*, Planning, Transport and Development Directorate, Wycombe.

Part 4: Built Form and Design Solutions

Michelle Thompson-Fawsett
The Contribution of Urban Villages to Sustainable Development

Aldous, T. (1992) *Urban Villages*, Urban Villages Group, London.

Bressi, T. (1994) Planning the American dream, in *The New Urbanism: Towards an Architecture of Community* (ed. P. Katz), McGraw-Hill, New York.

Crown Street Regeneration Project (1994) *Phase 2 Development Brief*, Crown Regeneration Project, Glasgow.

Crown Street Regeneration Project (1995) *The Background, Crown Street Regeneration Project*, Glasgow.

EDAW (Eckbo, Dean, Austin and Williams) (1997) *Crown Street Regeneration Project Mid Term Review*, EDAW, Drew Mackie Associates, University of Strathclyde Department of Environmental Planning, Glasgow.

Langdon, P. (1994) *A Better Place to Live in: Reshaping the American Suburb*, Harper Perennial, New York.

Scully, V. (1994) The architecture of community, in *The New Urbanism: Toward an Architecture of Community* (ed. P. Katz), McGraw-Hill, New York.

Thompson-Fawcett, M. (1998) *Envisioning Urban Villages*, unpublished D.Phil thesis, University of Oxford, Oxford.

Heidi Dumreicher, Richard S. Levine, Ernest J. Yanarella and Taghi Radmard
Generating Models of Urban Sustainability: *Vienna's Westbahnhof Sustainable Hill Town*

Dumreicher. H. and Levine, R. S. (1995) *Stadthugel Westbahnhof: Ein Kostprobe*, Oikodrom, Vienna.

Dumreicher, H. and Levine, R. S. (1996) *Stadhugel Wien Westbahnhof: Zweiter Teil Die Dreidimensionale Stadt Strassen, Platze, Menschen, Arbeit*. Oikodrom, Vienna.

European Sustainable Cities and Towns Campaign (1994) *The Charter of European Cities and Towns Towards Sustainability* (Aalborg Charter), ICLEI , Toronto. (http://www.iclei.org/europe/echarter.htm)

Levine, R. S. (1982) The coupled pan space frame: a structural framework for solar conserving buildings. *Progress in Passive Solar Energy Systems: Proceedings*, American Solar Energy Society, 7th National Passive Solar Conference, Knoxville, Tennessee.

Levine, R. S. (1987) The future medieval city. *Spazio e Societa*, **10**, pp.18-24.

Levine, R. S. (1989) The sustainable city: a necessary utopia, in *Utopia e Modernita: Teorie e Prassi Utopiche Nell'eta Moderna e Postmoderna* (eds G. S. Del Buffa and A. O. Lewis), Gangemi editore, Rome.

Levine, R. S. (1994) *The Sustainable City: The Scientific Design Study and the Sustainable City Game*, unpublished.

Levine, R. S. (1996) The Sustainability Engine© and the city. *Stadtplaene*, **1**, pp.41-44.

Levine, R. S. and Radmard, T. (1990) Sustainable village implantations. *American Solar Energy Conference/15th National Passive Solar Conference*, Austin, Texas.

Levine, R. S. and Yanarella, E. J. (1994) Don't pick the low-lying fruit: sustainability from pathway to process. *19th National Passive Solar Conference*, American Solar Energy Society, San Jose, California.

Levine, R. S., Yanarella, E. J. and Dumreicher, H. (1998) Cities and regions: co-evolution towards sustainable development, in *Regions – Cornerstones for Sustainable Development* (eds I. Gabriel and M. Narodoslawsky), Osterreichisches Netwzwerk Umweltforschung, Graz.

Levine, R. S., Yanarella, E. J. and Radmard, T. (1991) The development of an interactive computer aided design model for generating the sustainable city. *International Solar Energy Society World Solar Congress*, Denver, Colorado.

Redclift, M. (1987) *Sustainable Development: Exploring the Contradictions*, Methuen, New York.

WCED (World Commission on Environment and Development) (1987) *Our Common Future*, Brundtland Commission, Oxford University Press, Oxford.

Yanarella, E. J. and Levine, R. S. (1992a) Does sustainable development lead to sustainability? *Futures*, **24**, pp.759-774.

Yanarella, E. J. and Levine, R. S. (1992b) The sustainable cities manifesto: pretext, text, and post-text. *Built Environment*, **18(4)**, pp.301-313.

Alexander E. Kalamaros
Sustainable Development in Southern California: *The Case of Playa Vista*

Hise, G. (1996) Homebuilding and industrial decentralization in Los Angeles: the roots of the post World War II urban region, in *Planning the Twentieth-Century American City* (eds M. C. Sies C. and Silver) The John Hopkins University Press, Baltimore.

Katz, P. (1994) *The New Urbanism: Toward an Architecture of Community*, McGraw-Hill, New York.

Myers, D. (1989) The ecology of quality of life and urban growth, in *Understanding Growth Management: Critical Issues and a Research Agenda* (eds D. J. Brower, D. R. Godschalk and D. R. Porter) ULI (the Urban Land Institute), Washington DC.

Playa Capital Company, LLC (1998) *Playa Vista Residential Sustainable Performance Guidelines* (Draft), unpublished report, Playa Capital Co., LLC, Los Angeles.

Ray, P. H. (1997) The emerging culture. *American Demographics Magazine*, February.

Peter G. Fauset
The Hulme Estate and the 'Homes for Change'
Development: *Britain's First Major Sustainable Housing
Project*

Engels, F. (1844) *The Conditions of the Working Class in
England*, reprinted by Panther Books (1969), London.
Fauset, P. G. (1994) The life and death of British urban public
housing, in *Visions of Urban Public Housing*, University
of Cincinnati, Cincinnati.
Hulme Regeneration Ltd (1994) *Rebuilding the City: A
Guide to Development in Hulme*, Hulme Regeneration
Ltd, Manchester
Manchester City Planning Department (1965) *A New
Community: The Redevelopment of Hulme*, Manchester
City Council, Manchester.
Newman, O. (1973) *Defensible Space: People and Design
in the Violent City*, Architectural Press, London.
Rudlin, D. and Falk, N. (1995) *21st Century Homes: Building
to Last*, Joseph Rowntree Foundation, York.

David van Vliet and Torben Gade
Sustainable Urban Renewal: *Kolding Denmark*

Fisker, O. (1995) *Green Ideas for Kolding*, debate, 31 May
(former Director of the Planning Department in
Kolding).
Madsen, L. (1998) *Tanker fra en Pyramide*, in Byøkogisk
Årbog, Dansk Center for Byøkologi, Arhus.

James Morgan and Roger Talbot
Sustainable Social Housing for No Extra Cost?

AGSD (The Secretary of State's Advisory Group on
Sustainable Development) (1997) *The Secretary of State
for Scotland's Advisory Group on Sustainable
Development 1997 Report*, Scottish Office, Edinburgh.
Aldous, T. (1992) *Urban Villages: A Concept for Creating
Mixed-Use Urban Developments on a Sustainable Scale*,
Urban Villages Group, London.
Brewerton, J. and Darton, D. (1997) *Designing Lifetime
Homes*, Joseph Rowntree Foundation, York.
Capra, F. (1996) *The Web of Life: A New Synthesis of Mind
and Matter*, Harper Collins, London.
DoE (Department of the Environment) (1994) *Sustainable
Development: The UK Strategy*, Cmnd 2426, HMSO,
London.
DoE (Department of the Environment) (1995) *Making Waste
Work: A Strategy for Sustainable Waste Management
in England and Wales*, HMSO, London.
DoE (Department of the Environment) (1997) *Housing
Quality Indicators: A Feasibility Study*, DoE, London.
DoE and DoT (Department of the Environment and
Department of Transport) (1994) *Planning Policy
Guidance 13: Transport*, HMSO, London.
DETR (Department of the Environment, Transport and the
Regions) (1998a) *Opportunities for Change:
Consultation Paper for a UK Strategy for Sustainable
Construction*, The Stationery Office, London.
DETR (Department of the Environment, Transport and the

Regions) (1998b) *Construction Research and
Innovation Business Plan: Promoting Innovation in the
Construction Industry*, The Stationery Office, London.
DETR (Department of the Environment, Transport and the
Regions) (1998c) *Rethinking Construction: The Report
of the Construction Task Force to the Deputy Prime
Minister on the Scope for Improving the Quality and
Efficiency of UK Construction (The Egan Report)*, The
Stationery Office, London.
Eco-Logica and Williams, N. (1996) *Life Cycle Analysis of
Housing: Scottish Homes Working Paper*, Scottish
Homes, Edinburgh.
Engineering Council (1994) *Guidelines on Environmental
Issues*, The Engineering Council, London.
Karn, V. and Sheridan, L. (1994) *New Homes in the 1990s*,
Joseph Rowntree Foundation, York.
Page, D. (1993) *Building for Communities: A Study of New
Housing Association Estates*, Joseph Rowntree
Foundation, York.
Rodger, A. (1997) *Sustainable Canberra*, Private
Communication, October 1997.
Rudlin, D. and Falk, N. (1995) *21st Century Homes: Building
to Last*, Joseph Rowntree Foundation, York.
Sangster, K. (1997) *Costing Lifetime Homes*, Joseph
Rowntree Foundation, York.
Scottish Homes (1995a) *Scottish Homes Guidance Note 95/
09: Barrier Free Housing*, Scottish Homes, Edinburgh.
Scottish Homes (1995b)*The Design of Barrier Free Housing*,
Scottish Homes, Edinburgh.
Scottish Homes (1996a) *The Physical Quality of Housing:
A Framework for Action*, Scottish Homes, Edinburgh.
Scottish Homes (1996b) *Glasgow City District Plan*, Scottish
Homes, Glasgow.
Scottish Homes (1998a) *Tackling Rural Housing: Scottish
Homes Policy Statement*, Scottish Homes, Edinburgh.
Scottish Homes (1998b) Housing Association Grant (HAG)
Competition, *Precis*, **75**, Scottish Homes, Edinburgh.
Scottish Office (1996) *National Planning Policy Guidance
3: Land for Housing*, HMSO, Edinburgh.
SEPA (Scottish Environment Protection Agency) (1997)
Draft National Waste Strategy for Scotland, SEPA,
Edinburgh.
US Green Building Council (1996) *Sustainable Building
Technical Manual: Green Building Practices for
Design, Construction and Operation*, Public
Technology Inc., The US Green Building Council and
the US Department of Energy, Washington D.C.
Wilcox, S. (1997) *Housing Finance Review 1997/98*, Joseph
Rowntree Foundation, York.

Tigran Hasic
A Sustainable Urban Matrix: *Achieving Sustainable Urban
Form in Residential Buildings*

Alexander, C., Davis, H., Martinez, J. and Corner, D. (1985)
The Production of Houses, Oxford University Press,
Oxford.
Alexander, C., Ishikawa, S. and Silverstein M. with
Jacobson, M., Fiksdahl-King, I. and Angel, S. (1977) *A
Pattern Language – Towns, Buildings, Construction*,

Oxford University Press, Oxford.

Anderson, J. R. (1982) Components of housing design – social and behavioural, in *Housing* (ed. J. Macsai), John Wiley and Sons, New York.

Calthorpe, P. (1993) *The Next American Metropolis – Ecology, Community and the American Dream*, Princeton Architectural Press, New York.

Cervero, R. and Bernick, R. (1996) *Transit Villages in the 21st Century*, McGraw Hill, New York.

Duany, A. and Plater-Zyberk, E. (1991) *Towns and Town-Making Principles*, Rizzoli, New York.

Edwards, B. (1996) *Towards Sustainable Architecture: European Directives and Building Design*, Butterworth Architecture, Oxford.

Hasic, T. (1997) *Locus Amoenus (A Pleasant Place) - Towards a New Sustainable Housing: Spatial and Social Aspects*, Royal Institute of Technology Press, Stockholm.

Katz, P. (1994) *The New Urbanism – Towards an Architecture of Community*, McGraw-Hill, New York.

Kelbaugh, (1997) *Common Place – Toward Neighbourhood and Regional Design*, University of Washington Press, Seattle.

Kunstler, J. H. (1996) *Home from Nowhere: Remaking Our Everyday World for the 21st Century*, Touchstone, New York.

Langdon, P. (1997) *A Better Place to Live: Reshaping the American Suburb*, University of Massachusetts Press, Amherst.

Norberg-Schulz, C. (1993) *The Concept of Dwelling – On the Way to Figurative Architecture*, Electa/Rizzoli, New York.

Roseland, M. (1998) *Toward Sustainable Communities – Resource for Citizens and their Governments*, New Society Publishers, Gabriola Island.

Tim Heath
Achieving Sustainable Urban Form through the Adaptive Re-use of Buildings for Residential Use

Barlow, J. and Gann, D. (1993) *Offices into Flats*, Joseph Rowntree Foundation, York.

Barlow, J. and Gann, D. (1996) Flexibility in building use: the technical feasibility of converting redundant offices into flats, *Construction Management and Economics*, **14**, pp.55-66.

Blowers, A. (ed.) (1993) *Planning for a Sustainable Environment*, Earthscan, London.

Boyd, D. and Jankovic, L. (1992) The limits of intelligent office refurbishment. *Property Management*, **11(2)**, pp.102-113.

Breheny, M. (ed.) (1992) *Sustainable Development and Urban Form*, Pion, London.

Breheny, M. (1995) Counter-urbanisation and sustainable urban forms, in *Cities in Competition: Productive and Sustainable Cities for the Twenty-First Century* (eds. J. Brotchie, M. Batty, E. Blakely, P. Hall and P. Newton), Longman, Melbourne.

CEC (Commission of the European Communities) (1990) *Green Paper on the Urban Environment*, Commission of the European Communities (EUR 12902 EN), Brussels.

Cooke, M. (1998) Building on a level playing field. *Urban Environment Today*, 5 February, p.8.

Coupland, A. (ed.) (1997) *Reclaiming the City: Mixed Use Development*, Chapman and Hall, London.

Davidson, I. (1995) Do we need cities any more? *Town Planning Review*, **66(1)**, pp.iii-vi.

DETR (Department of the Environment, Transport and the Regions) (1998) *A New Deal for Transport: Better for Everyone*, HMSO, London.

DoE (Department of the Environment) (1994a) *Planning Policy Guidance 15: Planning and the Historic Environment*, HMSO, London.

DoE (Department of the Environment) (1994b) *Sustainable Development: The UK Strategy*, HMSO, London.

DoE (Department of the Environment) (1995) *Our Future Homes: Opportunity, Choice and Responsibility – the Government's Housing Policies for England and Wales*, HMSO, London.

DoE (Department of the Environment) (1996a) *Household Growth: Where Shall We Live?*, HMSO, London.

DoE (Department of the Environment) (1996b) *Planning Policy Guidance 6: Town Centres and Retail Development*, HMSO, London.

DoE (Department of the Environment) (1997) *Evaluation of Flats over Shops*, HMSO, London.

DoE and DoT (Department of the Environment and Department of Transport) (1994) *Planning Policy Guidance 13: Transport*, HMSO, London.

Elkin, T., McLaren, D. and Hillman, M. (1991) *Reviving the City: Towards Sustainable Urban Development*, Policy Studies Institute/Friends of the Earth, London.

Falk, N. (1993) Regeneration and sustainable development, in *Urban Regeneration, Property Investment and Development* (eds J. Berry, S. McGreal, and B. Deddis), E & FN Spon, London.

Goodchild, B. (1998) Learning the lessons of housing over shops initiatives. *Journal of Urban Design*, **3(1)**, pp.73-92.

Gummer, J. (1996) Better use of urban areas is key to household growth, Press Conference to launch *Household Growth: Where shall we Live?*, DoE, HMSO, London.

Harrison, D. (1996) The civilising of our cities. *The Observer: Modern Living*, 10 November, p.12.

Haughton, G. and Hunter, C. (1994) *Sustainable Cities*, Jessica Kingsley Publishers, London.

HBF (House Builders Federation) (1998) *House Building in the 21st Century*, HBF, London.

Hirst, C. (1996) Flexible lifeline thrown to empty city offices. *Planning Week*, 3 October, p.8.

Jacobs, J. (1961) *The Death and Life of Great American Cities: The Failure of Town Planning*, Random House Inc., New York.

Kelly, R. (1998) Granny moves in on the action. *The Times Weekend*, 21 November, p.14.

Lichfield, N. (1988) *Economics in Urban Conservation*, Cambridge University Press, Cambridge.

LOTS (Living Over the Shop) (1994) *Living over the Shop*,

LOTS, York.

LPAC (London Planning Advisory Committee) (1998) *Dwellings In and Over Shops*, LPAC, London.

Petherick, A. and Fraser, R. (1992) *Living Over The Shop: A Handbook for Practitioners*, University of York, York.

Prescott, J. (1998) The Green Belt is safe with us. *The Times*, 26 January, p.20.

Ratcliffe, J. and Stubbs, M. (1996) *Urban Planning and Real Estate Development*, UCL Press, London.

Ravetz, A. (1995) The barriers to LOTS conversions. *Town and Country Planning*, **64(5/6)**, 136-137.

RICS (Royal Institute of Chartered Surveyors) (1998) *Back to the Centre: A New Lease of Life for Redundant Commercial Buildings?*, Research report by the University of Westminster, Grimley and London Residential Research, RICS, London.

Sherlock, H. (1991) *Cities Are Good For Us*, Paladin, London.

Smith, N. (1996) *The New Urban Frontier: Gentrification and the Revanchist City*, Routledge, London.

Tiesdell, S., Oc, T. and Heath, T. (1996) *Revitalising Historic Urban Quarters*, Butterworth-Heineman, Oxford.

URBED (1998) *Tomorrow: A Peaceful Path to Urban Reform*, Friends of the Earth and WISE, London.

Zukin, S. (1989) *Loft Living: Culture and Capital in Urban Change*, Rutgers University Press, New Jersey.

Index